Torture and Brutality in Medieval Literature

Negotiations of National Identity

Torture and Brutality in Medieval Literature

Negotiations of National Identity

Larissa Tracy

D. S. BREWER

© Larissa Tracy 2012

All Rights Reserved. Except as permitted under current legislation no part of this work may be photocopied, stored in a retrieval system, published, performed in public, adapted, broadcast, transmitted, recorded or reproduced in any form or by any means, without the prior permission of the copyright owner

The right of Larissa Tracy to be identified as the author of this work has been asserted in accordance with sections 77 and 78 of the Copyright, Designs and Patents Act 1988

First published 2012
D. S. Brewer, Cambridge
Paperback edition 2015

ISBN 978 1 84384 288 0 hardback
ISBN 978 1 84384 393 1 paperback

D. S. Brewer is an imprint of Boydell & Brewer Ltd
PO Box 9, Woodbridge, Suffolk IP12 3DF, UK
and of Boydell & Brewer Inc.
668 Mount Hope Ave, Rochester, NY 14620–2731, USA
website: www.boydellandbrewer.com

A CIP catalogue record for this book is available from the British Library

The publisher has no responsibility for the continued existence or accuracy of URLs for external or third-party internet websites referred to in this book, and does not guarantee that any content on such websites is, or will remain, accurate or appropriate

Contents

Acknowledgements	vii
Abbreviations	ix
Introduction	1
1. Rending the Flesh: The Orthodoxy of Torture in Hagiography	31
2. Resisting the Rod: Torture and the Anxieties of Continental Identity	70
3. The Matter of the North: Icelandic Sagas and Cultural Autonomy	108
4. The Matter of Britain: Defining English Identity in Opposition to Torture	132
5. Laughing at Pain: The Comic Uses of Torture and Brutality	191
6. Medieval Torture and Early-Modern Identity	243
Conclusion	292
Select Bibliography	299
Index	319

Acknowledgements

This project has had an extended evolution, and there are many people to whom I owe a debt of gratitude for their input, insight, assistance, and guidance. I would like to thank my current colleagues at Longwood University for their support and suggestions, and my former colleagues at American University, Georgetown University, George Mason University, and the University of Mary Washington (then Mary Washington College) for their suggestions and advice over the years.

In particular I extend my warmest gratitude and thanks to the following people who have helped me along the way and contributed in various ways to my research and education: Terry Barry, Betty Bennett, Julia Boffey, Rachael Bork, Niall Brady, John Bradley, Rhonda Brock-Servais, Jesse Byock, Christa Canitz, Melissa Castle, Mark Chambers, Margaret Connolly, Helen Cooney, Eugene Crook, Raymond Cormier, Angela Dadak, Carol Dover, Ian Doyle, Martha Driver, Warren Edminster, A.S.G. Edwards, Samantha Elliot, Melissa Elmes, Susanna Fein, Rachel Frier, Angie Gleason, Richard Hamer, Thomas D. Hanks, Aisling Hayden, J. Patrick Hornbeck, Steven Isaac, Renata Lana, Charles Larson, Katherine Lewis, Nicolas Lizop, Susan May, Rick McDonald, Sarah McNamer, Jeffrey Middents, Jo Ann Moran Cruz, Gerald Morgan, Samantha Mullaney, Eilleán Ní Cuilleanáin, Marianne Noble, Dan O'Sullivan, Edward Peters, J.D. Pheifer, Amanda Piesse, Sherry Reames, Roberta Rubenstein, Vida Russell, Catherine Sanock, Matthew Solomon, A.P. Smyth, Kristen Stazioski, Myra Sklarew, Penn Szittya, Kelley Wickham-Crowley, and Jocelyn Wogan-Browne.

Chapter Five is the product of a National Endowment for the Humanities Research seminar on Old French fabliaux directed by R. Howard Bloch at Yale University. I am grateful for his encouragement and the continued community of my fellow NEH seminarians: Peter G. Beidler, Sam Bloom, Holly Crocker, Ellen Friedrich, Susanne Hafner, Jean Jost, Mary Leech, Dan Murtaugh, Sheila Nayar, Kiril Petrov, Dorothy Schrader, Christian Sheridan, Nicole Sidhu and Judith Tshann. Chapter Six was inspired by a National Endowment for the Humanities Teaching Institute at the University of Maryland, hosted by the Center for Renaissance and Baroque Studies, directed by Adell Seef. I am grateful to my colleagues at that institute for their ideas, suggestions and input, specifically Thomas Herron and Susannah Brietz Monta.

For editing earlier versions of this manuscript, I wish to thank Jeff Massey. I am indebted to Alice Kirby for collating the references and for cross-checking my notes. I am extremely grateful to Derek Pearsall for reading the entire manuscript and offering his generous and encouraging criticism and to Martha Cook for copy-editing the final version.

I would like to thank Caroline Palmer for her continued direction and guidance, and for helping me make sense of it all. I owe an enormous debt of gratitude to David F. Johnson and John Scattergood. I would also like to thank my parents, Robert Tracy and Nina Zerkich, for their continued support. Rikk Mulligan has been my steadfast companion, proofreader, and sounding board from the inception of this project, and I could not have done it without him.

Finally, I would like to thank the manuscript departments at Trinity College, Dublin; the British Library, London; the Bodleian Library, Oxford; the Beinecke Library at Yale University; the Folger Library, Washington D.C.; and the Bibliothèque Nationale Française, Paris for their assistance in compiling this volume and granting me access to select manuscripts. I am indebted to Toshi Takamiya for his generous permission to study the fifteenth-century prayer roll that is part of his private collection, and for his insights on this text.

Sections of Chapter 5 first appeared as 'The Uses of Torture and Violence in the Fabliaux: When Comedy Crosses the Line', *Florilegium* 23.2 (2006): 143–68. Some material in Chapter 1 previously appeared in 'Torture Narrative: The Imposition of Medieval Method on Early Christian Texts', *Journal of the Early Book Society* 7 (New York: Pace University Press, 2004): 33–50. Chapter 1 also includes some material from my book *Women of the Gilte Legende: A Selection of Middle English Saints' Lives* (London: D.S. Brewer, 2003). I am grateful to the readers and editors of Boydell and Brewer, *Florilegium* and *JEBS* for their insightful and excellent comments, their suggestions regarding these articles in their first form, and for permission to reproduce revised versions here.

This project has been partly funded by a generous publishing grant from the Cook-Cole College of Arts and Sciences at Longwood University.

Abbreviations

Actes and Monuments	John Foxe, *Actes and Monuments of these Latter and Perillous Days, Touching Matters of the Church*. Ed. Rev. M. Hobart Seymour. New York: Worthington Co., 1850.
Agatha	*The Life of Saint Agatha* in *Gilte Legende*. Ed. Richard Hamer with the assistance of Vida Russell. Vol. 1, EETS, os 327. Oxford: Oxford University Press, 2006: 175–9; and *The South English Legendary, Corpus Christi College Cambridge MS 145 and British Museum MS Harley 2277*. Ed. Charlotte D'Evelyn and Anna J. Mill. Vol. 1, EETS, os 235. Oxford: Oxford University Press, 1956, reprinted 1967: 54–9.
Christina	*The Life of Saint Christina* in *Gilte Legende*. Ed. Richard Hamer with the assistance of Vida Russell. Vol. 1, EETS, os 327. Oxford: Oxford University Press, 2006: 483–6; and *The South English Legendary, Corpus Christi College Cambridge MS 145 and British Museum MS Harley 2277*. Ed. Charlotte D'Evelyn and Anna J. Mill. Vol. 1, EETS, os 235. Oxford: Oxford University Press, 1956, rpt. 1967: 315–27.
De Connebert	*De Connebert* (*Li prestre ki perdi les colles*), in *Nouveau Recueil Complet des Fabliaux*. Ed. Willem Noomen and Nico van den Boogaard. 10 vols. Assen: Van Gorcum, 1983–1998. Vol. 7, 1993.
EETS, os	Early English Text Society, Original Series
GiL	*Gilte Legende*. Ed. Richard Hamer with the assistance of Vida Russell. 2 vols, EETS, os 327, 328. Oxford: Oxford University Press, 2006–7.
Havelok	*Havelok the Dane* in *Middle English Romances*. Ed. Stephen H.A. Shepherd. New York: W.W. Norton and Company, 1995: 3–74.
Hrafnkels saga	*Hrafnkels saga freysgoða*, from Jón Jóhannesson, *Hrafnkels saga freysgoða*, Íslenzk Fornrít, 11, Reykjavik: Hið islenzka fornritafélag, 1950, in *An Introduction to Old Norse*. Ed. E.V. Gordon. Oxford: Oxford Clarendon Press, second edition, 1956.
Laurence	*The Life of Saint Laurence* in *The Early South-English Legendary or Lives of Saints, MS Laud 108 in the Bodleian Library*. Ed. Carl Horstmann. EETS, os 87. Oxford: Oxford University Press, 1887; reprinted 2000: 340–5.
Lawrence	*The Life of Saint Lawrence* in *Gilte Legende*. Ed. Richard

	Hamer and Vida Russell. Vol. 2, EETS, os 328. Oxford: Oxford University Press, 2007: 552–60.
LgA	Jacobus de Voragine, *Legenda aurea*, *The Golden Legend: Readings on the Saints*. Trans. William Granger Ryan, Vols 1 and 2. Princeton NJ: Princeton University Press, 1993.
Njals saga	*Brennu-Njals saga*. Ed. Einar Ól. Sveinsson. Íslenzk Fornrít, 12, Reykjavik: Hið islenzka fornritafélag, 1954; and *Njal's Saga*. Ed. and trans. Robert Cook. London: Penguin Books, 2001.
The Roland	*La Chanson de Roland, Oxford, Bodleian Library MS Digby 23*. Ed. Léon Gautier. Tours: Mame et fils, 1872; and *The Song of Roland*. Trans. Glyn Burgess. London: Penguin Books, 1990.
SEL	*The South English Legendary, Corpus Christi College Cambridge MS 145 and British Museum MS Harley 2277*. Ed. Charlotte D'Evelyn and Anna J. Mill. Vol. 1, EETS, os 235. Oxford: Oxford University Press, 1956, reprinted. 1967; and *The Early South-English Legendary or Lives of Saints, MS Laud 108 in the Bodleian Library*. Ed. Carl Horstmann. EETS, os 87. Oxford: Oxford University Press, 1887; reprinted 2000.
Walewein	Penninc and Pieter Vostaert, *Roman van Walewein*. Ed. and trans. David F. Johnson. New York: Garland, 1992.

The individual saints' lives are cited from both the *South English Legendary* and the *Gilte Legende*; the provenance of the reference is given in the text and accompanying footnote in each case. Translations and original text editions are also clearly marked in the text and in accompanying footnotes in each case.

Since this is a study grounded in linguistic analysis as well as literary motifs and conventions, original language text and translations have been provided for all of the literary works under discussion. All of the translations are from published editions, except where one does not exist. In those rare cases, I have provided my own translations. As is standard, Middle English texts have not been translated. In the interests of space, excerpts of primary texts used as supplementary support, like Urban II's speech at Clermont, Jean de Meun's *Romance of the Rose* and Peter Abelard's *Historia calamitatum*, have only been provided in translation, though the original text has been provided in footnotes when available. For the Norse names, I have followed the most recent and most common spelling conventions, using the Norse.

Introduction

> 'Under torture or the threat of torture, a man says not only what he has done but what he would have liked to do even if he didn't know it.'
> Brother William of Baskerville, *The Name of the Rose*, Umberto Eco.[1]

Torture – that most notorious aspect of medieval culture and society – has evolved into a dominant mythology, suggesting that the Middle Ages was a period during which sadistic torment was inflicted on citizens with impunity and without provocation. Figures like Bernard Gui, presented to the twentieth century as the evil inquisitor of Umberto Eco's *The Name of the Rose* employing his toys of torture with monstrous delight masked by righteous authority, have imprinted this evil institution on the modern mind. Popular museums of medieval torture displaying barbarous implements like the rack, the *strappado*, the gridiron, the wheel, and the Iron Maiden can be found in many modern European cities. This barbaric image of medieval torture re-emerged within recent discussions on American foreign policy and the introduction of torture legislation as a weapon in the 'War on Terror' during the administration of the former President, George W. Bush (2001–2008). The current debate over torture legislation in the United States, and President Barack Obama's reversal of several Bush administration policies regarding 'enhanced' interrogation, has again raised questions about the history and reality of torture in the Middle Ages, particularly its proliferation in some medieval literary genres and its relative absence from others. The body in pain and its representation in art, literature and historical record have created a modern impression of the Middle Ages as barbaric, bloodthirsty and consumed with cruel desire. Many people, non-academics and scholars alike, have formed their image of the medieval period based on a foundational belief that violence was a commonly-enjoyed spectacle, 'normative,'[2] and that torture was a pervasive part of medieval life.

This book offers a revisionist argument, challenging preconceived ideas about the prevalence of torture and judicial brutality in medieval society by arguing that representations of them in literature are not mimetic. Instead, medieval and early-modern literary depictions of torture and brutality represent satire,

---

[1] Umberto Eco, *The Name of the Rose*, trans. William Weaver (New York: Warner Books/Harcourt Brace Jovanovich, 1983), p. 469.
[2] Mark D. Meyerson, Daniel Thiery and Oren Falk, 'Introduction' in *'A Great Effusion of Blood'?: Interpreting Medieval Violence*, ed. Mark D. Meyerson, Daniel Thiery and Oren Falk (Toronto: University of Toronto Press, 2004), p. 6.

critique and dissent; they have didactic and political functions in opposing the status quo. Torture and brutality are intertextual literary motifs that negotiate cultural anxieties of national identity; by situating these practices outside their own boundaries in the realm of the barbarian 'Other', medieval and early-modern authors define themselves and their nations in opposition to them.

Torture and National Identity

A former Guantanamo Bay detainee, Binyam Mohamed, remarked upon his release and transfer back to Great Britain that he had been tortured in Morocco while detained, an experience he never expected to encounter in his 'darkest nightmare'. In a statement released through his lawyers, he said it was still difficult to believe 'that I was abducted, hauled from one country to the next, and tortured in *medieval* ways – all orchestrated by the United States government'.[3] Two days later, on 25 February 2009, President Obama stated 'without equivocation: The United States does not torture'. This assertion, made in Obama's first presidential address to the American people, signalled that his administration would no longer tolerate the policies of the previous administration (which were highly murky on the subject). Obama's statement was necessary to reinstate American national identity in both the minds of the American people and the larger global community as one grounded in justice and law, and one that has rejected interrogatory torture since the era of George Washington. As Brigadier General Patrick Finnegan wrote in a letter to the *New Yorker* (3 May 2010), 'for a country that professes to stand for the rule of law and individual rights, we look like the worst kind of hypocrite'.[4] America defines itself partly by its policy against torture – when that is undermined, the very identity of America is threatened. Other modern nations, particularly in Europe, are currently engaged in a similar debate regarding national identity and the use of torture. In that respect, western civilization has not changed much from the Middle Ages. As early as the twelfth century and throughout the thirteenth and fourteenth centuries European nations emerged seeking to define their national identities in opposition to those of their enemies, their neighbours or even their own past. The use of torture in judicial procedure, much like in modern society, formed part of that definition.

---

[3] 'Binyam Mohamed: His Full Statement', BBC News, 23 February 2009. My italics. http://newsvote.bbc.co.uk/mpapps/pagetools/print/news.bbc.com. Accessed 23 Feb. 2009. See also: 'Guantanamo Detainee Mohamed Sent to Britain', National Public Radio, 23 February 2009. www.npr.org/templates/story/story.php?/storyId101027892. Accessed 23 February 2009.

[4] Brigadier General Patrick Finnegan, 'Re: Counterfactual, A Letter in Response to Jane Mayer's Article (March 29, 2010)', *The New Yorker* (3 May 2010); online: http://www.newyorker.com/magazine/letters/2010/05/03/1005. Accessed 4 May 2010.

In *The Making of Europe*, Robert Bartlett outlines the cultural anxieties prevalent in early and late medieval Europe, including conquest, colonization, expansion, and uniformity of religious doctrine, language, law and legitimacy of rule. Medieval definitions of 'race' were almost entirely cultural rather than biological.[5] Implicit in the development of national identity are anxieties about cultural changes, legal and linguistic assimilation, and the codification of religious doctrine and canon law. Torture, painful measures applied specifically in the process of interrogation to obtain a confession, and judicial brutality, legal or extra-legal punishment that exceeds both legal and cultural custom, are facets of this development and both figure in conceptions of cultural identity – much as they do today.

The canonist Regino of Prum offered four categories for classifying ethnic variation: 'The various nations differ in descent, customs, language and law,'[6] and it is customs, language and law that emerge as the primary badges of ethnicity.[7] Language and vernacular literature had a significant role in defining nationality.[8] Bartlett writes: 'As the vernaculars emerge into literary and documentary record in the High Middle Ages, they reveal large tracts of Europe possessing a relatively high degree of linguistic and cultural homogeneity and dominated by more or less standard languages: examples are English in England, Languedoil north of the Loire, Languedoc south of it, Low German in north Germany, High German in south Germany.'[9] But in conquered and colonized peripheries, languages of completely different linguistic families were being spoken in the same settlement or street; and bilingualism was not unusual at many social levels throughout Europe.[10] As such, a 'growing strand of linguistic nationalism or politicized linguistic consciousness emerges in the later Middle Ages.'[11] Since ethnicity was constituted not only by custom and language, but also by law,[12] legal practices including interrogatory torture and judicial brutality became issues of national identity. The codification of canon law and its implications for secular and ecclesiastical authority are part of this cultural anxiety – to whom is allegiance owed? Who exacts what punishment? As people crossed boundaries and borders expanded, establishing a sense of national identity became fraught with these questions: How does a people define itself? Is it possible to maintain regional or national autonomy in the face of this expansion? Many medieval literary texts engage with these issues, negotiating the cultural anxieties implicit

---

[5] Robert Bartlett, *The Making of Europe: Conquest, Colonization and Cultural Change 950–1350* (Princeton NJ: Princeton University Press, 1993), p. 197.
[6] Regino of Prum, qtd. in Bartlett, *The Making of Europe*, p. 197.
[7] Bartlett, *The Making of Europe*, p. 197.
[8] Bartlett, *The Making of Europe*, p. 198.
[9] Bartlett, *The Making of Europe*, p. 198.
[10] Bartlett, *The Making of Europe*, p. 199.
[11] Bartlett, *The Making of Europe*, p. 201.
[12] Bartlett, *The Making of Europe*, p. 204.

in European expansion, establishing a firm distrust and rejection of torture and judicial brutality by casting it as a literary motif wielded by a barbarian Other, alien to their society.

In defining the Other, many emerging nations placed themselves against old enemies, such as England and France; for some communities, the Other appeared as the Church exercising authoritarian control over practice, belief and doctrine in the form of crusades or inquisitorial courts. Some smaller nations set themselves up against outside forces that manifested as larger empires stretching their boundaries and engaging in colonial endeavours: Iceland versus Norway, the Netherlands versus France. Still for some, the Other lurked within the unpleasant realities of society and of cultural inheritance to which authors responded by demonizing the unsavoury aspects of their own societies as in the Old French fabliaux, the tensions of the Anglo-Normans concerning the Frankish past in *La Chanson de Roland*, Anglo-Scandinavian inheritance versus an Anglo-Saxon past in *Havelok the Dane*, excising the 'Other within' and revising their past in favour of a more enlightened model. Bartlett finds three focal points for ethnic antagonism in high medieval 'peripheries' that can be applied to discussions of torture and judicial brutality in the larger context of medieval Europe: the Church, the princely court and the burgess community.[13] In regions where Christian peoples of different law and language intermingled, the Church became an arena of ethnic competition.[14] Princely courts, as culturally distinct institutions set apart from the surrounding society as centres of patronage by conspicuous consumption, cosmopolitanism and fashion, might 'easily inflame clerical, puritanical or backwoods critics'.[15] But as epicentres of political dynasticism, these courts routinely harboured foreign elements and were often the target for native tensions and suspicions about foreign-born monarchs, consorts or 'native-born rulers who favoured foreigners and fostered an ethnically distinct body of soldiers, administrator and courtiers'.[16] The burgess community, consisting of a largely urban, immigrant population, gave rise to a town-country dichotomy that 'came to be paralleled and reinforced by ethnic oppositions, for many urban settlements were inhabited predominantly or exclusively by immigrants'.[17] It is within this framework that medieval authors situate their own anxieties about cultural identity and legal practice surrounding the adoption of interrogatory torture and the persistence of judicial brutality.

The thirteenth century

> is an extraordinary period in medieval history that positions an epistemic break, and witnesses the rise of a new epistemic formation in medieval culture: a forma-

---

[13] Bartlett, *The Making of Europe*, p. 221.
[14] Bartlett, *The Making of Europe*, p. 221.
[15] Bartlett, *The Making of Europe*, p. 230.
[16] Bartlett, *The Making of Europe*, pp. 230, 232.
[17] Bartlett, *The Making of Europe*, p. 233.

tion in which institutions of control are innovatively expanded, intensified, and refined through instruments of inquisition, regulation, and discipline that continue through the later centuries of the Middle Ages.[18]

It is also the century in which 'inscriptions of medieval nationalism begin to call attention to themselves'.[19] And so, even as torture became more common in continental jurisprudence, particularly in France, other nations resisted its application and many medieval authors engaged in this resistance by presenting torture as a technique used by outside forces: the barbarian Other against which they sought to define themselves. According to St Thomas Aquinas (c. 1225–1274), a barbarian was one 'who did not live according to the rational rules of a civil society, of a *civitas*, and who did not speak a systematic language'.[20] Across Europe, poets and philosophers sought to define those boundaries of *civitas* and their place within them. This is particularly true in England, a cultural and linguistic melting pot where the matter of national identity was 'always complex and often controversial'.[21] Rupert T. Pickens asserts that in the twelfth century the Francophone elite in England laid claim to a French cultural identity, feeling themselves to be 'French', not out of patriotism or political allegiance, 'but in an awareness of a manner of speaking, a manner of thinking, and a manner of viewing the world that constitute a shared experience in common with others whom they consider to be like themselves'.[22] During the twelfth and thirteenth centuries, however, the Anglo-Normans were also becoming 'English', invading their Celtic neighbours, and attempting to assimilate the pre-Conquest past[23] – a trend that many English rejected in the course of the thirteenth century, seeking a non-Norman, non-French identity grounded in Anglo-Saxon heritage instead. Bartlett suggests that the 'Europeanization of Europe, [...] the spread of one particular culture through conquest and influence, had its core areas in one part of the continent, namely in France, Germany west of the Elbe and north Italy, regions which had a common history as part of Charlemagne's Frankish empire'.[24] In many instances, this battle of national identity focuses on the pivotal role of France and French influence on the European stage.

---

[18] Geraldine Heng, 'The Romance of England: *Richard Coer de Lyon*, Saracens, Jews, and the Politics of Race and Nation', in *The Postcolonial Middle Ages*, The New Middle Ages, ed. Jeffrey Jerome Cohen (New York: Palgrave, 2001) 135–71, p. 137.

[19] Heng, 'The Romance of England', p. 137.

[20] Arno Borst, *Medieval Worlds: Barbarians, Heretics, and Artists in the Middle Ages* (Chicago: The University of Chicago Press, 1996), p. 9.

[21] John Gillingham, *The English in the Twelfth Century: Imperialism, National Identity and Political Values* (Woodbridge: The Boydell Press, 2000), p. xv.

[22] Rupert T. Pickens, 'Implications of Being "French" in Twelfth-Century England', in *Chançon legiere a chanter*, ed. Karen Fresco and Wendy Pfeffer (Birmingham AL: Summa, 2007) 373–87, p. 384.

[23] Gillingham, *The English in the Twelfth Century*, p. xv.

[24] Bartlett, *The Making of Europe*, p. 267.

During the twelfth century, as concepts of national identity took shape, England, France and the Italian states 'witnessed a rapid transformation of legal structures', but this was not the case in the Netherlands and Germany, where a 'bewildering profusion of overlapping customary law jurisdictions prevailed'.[25] Hand-in-hand with state building went the consolidation of legal institutions. Mitchell B. Merback writes:

> New legal systems were developed first for the Church (canon law) and then for secular political orders – often in competition with the former. Thus canon law, royal law, feudal and manorial law, and eventually mercantile law and urban law all evolved their own courts, their own bodies of legislation, their own class of professional jurists, their own 'scientific' legal literature and curricula in the universities (schools of neo-Roman law were founded at Ravenna, Bologna and Pavia).[26]

The revival of torture took place during a period when, technically, 'torture had never ceased to be used in the laws of parts of Spain, notably Castile', but it was abolished in Aragon in 1325.[27] Torture is mentioned in the statutes of Vienna in the middle of the thirteenth century in the form of a prohibition, though regional legal codes had developed a fuller jurisprudence of torture by the fourteenth century.[28] In Germany, the wheel was a common implement of both torture and execution, though the frequency of its use is debatable.[29] As

---

[25] Mitchell B. Merback, *The Thief, the Cross and the Wheel: Pain and the Spectacle of Punishment in Medieval and Renaissance Europe* (London: Reaktion Books, 1999), p. 130; Julia Kristeva, *Powers of Horror: An Essay on Abjection*, trans. L. S. Roudiez (New York, 1982), p. 3; qtd. in Merback, *The Thief, the Cross and the Wheel*, p. 130.

[26] Merback, *The Thief, the Cross and the Wheel*, p. 130.

[27] Edward Peters, *Torture* (Philadelphia: University of Pennsylvania Press, 1985), p. 60. Peters specifically notes that torture had no place in English law after the Assize of Clarendon in 1166, but it was not a tenet of pre-Conquest Anglo-Saxon law which usually relied on the ordeal, punitive mutilation or monetary compensation. See: Katherine O'Brien O'Keefe, 'Body and Law in Late Anglo-Saxon England', *Anglo-Saxon England* 27 (1998): 209–32.

[28] Peters, *Torture*, pp. 59–60.

[29] Merback, *The Thief, the Cross and the Wheel*, p. 158. Merback suggests that the inquiry into the proliferation of the wheel as punishment will probably remain a matter of debate among historians for some time: 'while some go so far as to declare it practically a daily occurrence in parts of Europe, others give a more modest accounting. In the records published by Richard van Dülmen for the city of Nuremberg, we find that between 1503 and 1743 only 55 out of a total of 939 executions were performed with the wheel. However, the ratio of wheelings to total executions in those German cities for which records exist appears to have been much greater in the late Middle Ages than in the following centuries. Its heyday was most likely the second half of the fifteenth century through to about 1600, when execution rates overall began to decline in Germany and most of Europe.' (p. 158). However frequently it was used, some of the most gruesome accounts of torture and execution in late-medieval iconography depict the wheel, though a large proportion are German sources that date from the end of the fifteenth century. I am indebted to Stephen Ledebur for engaging in this debate with me.

Edward Peters writes, 'after the mid-thirteenth century, torture had a secure place in ecclesiastical inquisitorial procedure'.[30]

The earliest body of evidence for the application of new inquisitorial procedures, which may have included torture, dates from Paris in 1210.[31] In France an *ordonnance* of Louis IX in 1254 allowed it, but forbade the torture of 'honest people of good reputations, even if they are poor' on the basis of the testimony of a single witness, 'the formal "half-proof" of general Romano-Canonical procedure'.[32] By the fourteenth century in France, the king's procurator stepped into the place of the old accuser, 'or the more recent *fama*, judge, or *denunciatio*', and torture, part of the *extraordinary procedure*, was the routine procedure for serious crimes.[33] The most notorious accounts of torture come from the depositions and surviving trial documents of the Knights Templar, arrested in France on Friday, 13 October 1307, when royal instructions were given by Philip IV that prisoners 'were to be terrorised by threats and torture in advance of their official appearance before the inquisitors'.[34] Most were fed on bread and water and kept in shackles. The rack and *strappado* were the most common forms of torture employed against the Templars, but some had flames applied to the soles of their feet; others confessed upon seeing the implements of torture laid out before them.[35] However, English Templars were not interrogated under torture, as will be discussed in greater detail in Chapter 4. Trevor Dean argues that the first 'damnable' element of French procedure was its use of torture, but 'in France, too, inquisitorial procedure was seen as an erosion of privileges by both

---

[30] Peters, *Torture*, p. 65.

[31] J.M.M.H. Thijssen, 'Master Amalric and the Amalricians: Inquisitorial Procedure and the Suppression of Heresy at the University of Paris', *Speculum* 71.1 (Jan. 1996): 43–65: pp. 47–8, 59.

[32] Peters, *Torture*, p. 60.

[33] Peters, *Torture*, pp. 63–4.

[34] Malcolm Barber, *The Trial of the Templars* (Cambridge: Cambridge University Press, 1978, reprinted Canto Edition, 1993), p. 53. Peters draws parallels between the trial of the Templars and the graphic punishments depicted in Dante's *Inferno*: 'As sins came to be classified in various ways (including differing degrees of gravity), the kind of purgation required for them became more extensive, and the kind of punishment that purgation was designed to avert became both more severe and more graphic. [...] From *The Apocalypse of Paul* through the vision-literature of the Middle Ages down to Dante, a spiritual universe of judgment, fear, and torment grew up side by side with the terrestrial practices condemned by Tertullian, Lactantius, Augustine, and Nicholas I. [...] But simultaneously with the case of the Templars, as Dante's *Commedia*, especially the *Inferno* and *Purgatorio*, makes abundantly clear, the punishments in the afterworld become more graphic as well': Edward Peters, 'Destruction of the Flesh – Salvation of the Spirit: The Paradoxes of Torture in Medieval Christian Society', in *The Devil, Heresy and Witchcraft in the Middle Ages: Essays in Honor of Jeffrey B. Russell*, ed. Alberto Ferreiro (Leiden: Koninklijke Brill, 1998) 131–48, pp. 134, 146–7.

[35] Barber, *The Trial of the Templars*, p. 56.

towns and nobility'.[36] Contemporaries were very much aware of the danger in employing torture, specifically that it might pervert justice.[37] Torture was not part of English law. Torture was legal in France, the Italian city-states, the German principalities, Flanders and Spain – but these countries still produced literature that rejected its use and condemned those who resorted to it.[38] This study investigates the appearance of interrogatory torture or judicial brutality in literary texts from France, Flanders and Iceland and places particular emphasis on England. What many critics call 'torture' often technically is not according to medieval definitions, but rather constitutes judicial brutality – punitive measures that occur within the context of a judicial or extra-judicial proceeding. In the literature under discussion here, torture and judicial brutality function as cultural motifs that give voice to anxieties about the correct application of law and national identity.

Despite Benedict Anderson's assertion that nationalism is a product of modernity with seeds in the Enlightenment,[39] numerous medievalists have convincingly argued, based on medieval self-perceptions, that nationalism has its roots much deeper in the past. Guibert of Nogent (c. 1109) wrote of the French nation, despite the fractured nature of French territories and the persistent opposition to 'French' rule in the southern regions of Languedoc and Provence. Matthew Paris (c. 1200–1259) literally defined the English nation in his maps,[40] through which Thorlac Turville-Petre has thoroughly argued for the emergence of an English nation in the early thirteenth century.[41] John Gillingham examines twelfth-century English nationalism and its impact on imperial endeavours in Ireland and Scotland. As Geraldine Heng notes, medievalists agree that from at least the thirteenth century onward 'discourses of the nation are visible and can be read with ease in medieval England';[42] and there are traces of national discourse evident in vernacular literatures across Europe, regardless of whether they resembled modern 'nation states'. Heng writes: 'the medieval cartographer's projection of a geopolitical category – territorial space coincident with the

---

[36] Trevor Dean, *Crime in Medieval Europe* (London: Pearson Education, 2001), pp. 15, 9. See also: Lisa Silverman, *Tortured Subjects: Pain, Truth, and the Body in Early Modern France* (Chicago: University of Chicago Press, 2001).

[37] Dean, *Crime in Medieval Europe*, p. 16.

[38] I have not found any references to either torture or judicial brutality in German or Spanish texts, and despite some infrequent references in Boccaccio's *Decameron*, torture in Italian texts seems confined to Dante. This work does not claim to be an exhaustive study; other instances of torture in medieval literature may well exist and they require further analysis in a future study.

[39] Benedict Anderson, *Imagined Communities: Reflections on the Origin and Spread of Nationalism* (London: Verso, 1983, rpt. 1991).

[40] Heng, 'The Romance of England', p. 151.

[41] Thorlac Turville-Petre, *England the Nation: Language, Literature and National Identity, 1290–1340* (Oxford: Oxford University Press, 1996).

[42] Heng, 'The Romance of England', p. 151.

name of the nation, uniquely shaped and set off – is a powerfully performative moment, a moment that enacts and points to the performativity of nationalist discourse, and the power of such discourse to bring nations into being.[43] The discourse of torture and judicial brutality in these literary sources, concerned as it is with boundaries both legal and geographical, contributes to the sense of national identity. While they seem disparate and unconnected, these texts vocalize cultural anxieties of the thirteenth and fourteenth centuries – war, plague, the dichotomy of the body and soul, the religious upheavals of heresy trials, crusades, nationalism and the Schism – anxieties rooted in shared traditions and inheritances influenced by French literature and legal practice. As Jocelyn Wogan-Browne has noted, questions of language and linguistic influence, particularly between the French and English, are far less clear-cut than many critics suggest.[44] Literary responses to the perceived 'degenerate state of the law in the late Middle Ages' generally took one of three forms: 'predictably some writers turned to satire, while others chose to romanticize opposition to the law in the person of the outlaw; a third group reveal their unease in a nostalgia for the old folklaw and its ways.'[45] Much of the unease in these texts about the use of torture and judicial brutality is voiced in comparisons with other cultures and societies. For Flanders and Iceland, this unease is represented by adaptations or rejections of French literary forms, which for Iceland were facets of Norwegian colonial endeavours. In the case of England it is often reflected in a nostalgic retreat to the pre-Conquest era when the land was governed by Anglo-Saxon law untainted by Norman or French influence. Torture and judicial brutality are two of the 'categories of identity that define Englishness as a coherent term, despite significant changes in the political and ethnic makeup of the country'.[46] The form of the English nation in the thirteenth and fourteenth centuries is that of the *communitas regni* – an imagined political *community of the realm*, 'a medieval nation-as-kingdom, with the ruler at its apex – rather than a constitutionally

---

[43] Heng, 'The Romance of England', p. 151. Anthony Smith investigates the problem of defining the concept of national identity, positing that nationalism is an 'ideological movement for attaining and maintaining identity, unity and autonomy on behalf of a population deemed by some of its members to constitute an actual or potential "nation"'. Anthony D. Smith, 'National Identities: Modern and Medieval?', in *Concepts of National Identity in the Middle Ages*, ed. Simon Forde, Lesley Johnson and Alan V. Murray. Leeds Texts and Monographs, New Series 14 (Leeds: University of Leeds, 1995) 21–46, p. 25.

[44] Jocelyn Wogan-Browne, 'What's in a Name: the "French" of "England"', in *Language and Culture in Medieval Britain: The French of England c. 1100–c. 1500* (York: York Medieval Press, 2009) 1–13, p. 3.

[45] Richard Firth Green, 'Medieval Literature and Law', in *The Cambridge History of Medieval English Literature*, ed. David Wallace (Cambridge: Cambridge University Press, 1999) 407–31, p. 418.

[46] Catherine Sanok, *Her Life Historical: Exemplarity and Female Saints' Lives in Late Medieval England*. The Middle Ages Series (Philadelphia: University of Pennsylvania Press, 2007), p. xii.

driven modern nation-state, with state apparatuses'.[47] As such, the justice of law rested with the king and for English audiences a king who resorted to torture or brutal punishment undermined the entire inheritance of Anglo-Saxon 'gode olde law' by which the nation defined itself.

Torture was not a pervasive means of medieval judicial control, despite accounts of public brutality and secular punishment; it did exist but it had a very definite place within the framework of Romano-canonical law. As its use progressed, developed and was abused, governments looked for other ways of finding truth, but the application of torture increased with the divisions of the Reformation, gathering force and visibility until the Enlightenment decried it. It emerged again in scholarly debates and studies of the nineteenth century.[48] Today, in the face of tyranny and global atrocities, torture remains a part of modern society; we wrestle with its applicability, morality and effect on our identity even now. But the tendency – and fallacy – is to place torture in the past, as a specifically medieval aberration. Doing so implies a complicit audience, suggesting that medieval people revelled in the perceived commonality of brutality spurred on by the powerful spectacles of punishment perpetrated by Church and crown. But there is an undercurrent of dissent in these thirteenth- and fourteenth-century texts that suggests that medieval audiences, and authors, were appalled by the need for and existence of judicial torture or punitive brutality, especially when careful regulation was thwarted and the practice was abused. Examining torture and judicial brutality in medieval literature thus encourages us to rethink our interpretation of the period, and our interpretation of our own society and cultural norms – our own national identities. The literary historian Jody Enders writes:

> What is at stake [...] is the demystification of both the aesthetics of violence and the critical response to it. In the case of torture, the critical tendency to condemn, to overexplain, or to excuse might ultimately derive less from a true sensitivity to the Middle Ages than from a false notion of our own moral superiority. [...] It is difficult not to accept [Paige DuBois'] succinct refutation of Foucault's claim that 'we are now far away from the country of tortures, dotted with wheels, gibbets, gallows, pillories' (*Discipline and Punish*, 307). Eloquently debunking the myth of alienation, she offers a simple rejoinder: 'Tell it to the El Salvadorans.'[49]

In the aftermath of 11 September 2001 and the implementation of dubious interrogation techniques by American authorities, the rejoinder could just as easily be 'tell it to the Iraqis'. The perception of national identity is influenced by our own culture of violence (real and imaginary), and perhaps our continuation of this debate on medieval torture and brutality brings us closer to the very society from which we attempt to disassociate ourselves. The literature of the Middle Ages makes a similar disclaimer, that part of national self-definition involved rejecting

---

[47] Heng, 'The Romance of England', p. 153.
[48] Peters, *Torture*, pp. 104–5.
[49] Jody Enders, *The Medieval Theater of Cruelty: Rhetoric, Memory, Violence* (Ithaca NY: Cornell University Press, 1999), p. 23.

torture and brutality. Today we consider ourselves far away from the medieval country of tortures 'dotted with wheels, gibbets, and racks' that Michel Foucault envisions,[50] if such a landscape ever actually existed.

Modern Misconceptions of Medieval Torture

Perhaps it is easier to distance ourselves from the violence (and even torture) in the modern era if we can situate it firmly in the past and convince ourselves that we are not as violent as medieval society.[51] Enders, in her foundational study on torture, memory and spectacle on the medieval stage, suggests there is a critical tendency to 'view the Middle Ages as a distant, irrecuperable Other' that has actually 'masked certain affinities'.[52] For modern audiences inside academia and without, these 'affinities' include the persistence of torture as an interrogation technique in judicial proceedings, against a backdrop of seemingly pervasive cultural violence on a global scale despite societal condemnation of the practice. Popular historian Barbara W. Tuchman codified these assumptions in her 1978 study of the fourteenth century, arguing that

> Violence was official as well as individual. Torture was authorized by the Church and regularly used to uncover heresy by the Inquisition. The tortures and punishments of civil justice customarily cut off hands and ears, racked, burned, flayed, and pulled apart people's bodies. In everyday life passersby saw some criminal flogged with a knotted rope or chained upright in an iron collar. They passed corpses hanging on the gibbet and decapitated heads and quartered bodies impaled on stakes on the city walls. In every church they saw pictures of saints undergoing varieties of atrocious martyrdom – by arrows, spears, fire, cut-off breasts – usually dripping blood. The Crucifixion with its nails, spears, thorns, whips, and more dripping blood was inescapable. Blood and cruelty were ubiquitous in Christian

---

[50] Michel Foucault, *Discipline and Punish: The Birth of the Prison*, trans. Alan Sheridan (New York: Random House (Vintage), 1977/79), p. 307. It should be noted, however, that Foucault's groundbreaking work on the birth of the prison deals far more with developments from the seventeenth century and less with medieval punitive methods, and even then is more philosophy than history. Foucault's work has become a major theoretical framework through which many critics evaluate medieval violence; however, many of his suggestions ignore the historical context of the Middle Ages.

[51] As Paul Freedman and Gabrielle M. Spiegel write, 'Any attempt to argue the importance and relevance of medieval history in the United States, therefore, must first overcome its evident "otherness," its lack of connection to any visible, shared national or cultural "American" past.' 'Medievalisms Old and New: The Rediscovery of Alterity in North American Medieval Studies', *The American Historical Review* 103.3 (Jun. 1998): 677–704, p. 678. More specifically, noted American medievalists like Lee Patterson have argued that the Middle Ages 'has from the beginning served postmedieval Western historical consciousness as one of the primary sites of otherness by which it has constituted itself'. 'Critical Historicism and Medieval Studies', in *Literary Practice and Social Change in Britain, 1380–1530*. Ed. Lee Patterson (Berkeley CA, 1990), p. 2.

[52] Enders, *The Medieval Theater of Cruelty*, p. 21.

art, indeed essential to it, for Christ became Redeemer, and the saints sanctified, only through suffering violence at the hands of their fellow man.[53]

The image that Tuchman creates of a brutal and savage fourteenth-century Europe is perhaps the most enduring of all modern stereotypes of the Middle Ages, one that has formed the basis for both popular and academic discussions about medieval violence.[54] Some medievalists have facilitated this mythology by resting on the opinions of late nineteenth- and early twentieth-century scholars like Henry Charles Lea and Johan Huizinga who emphasized the pervasiveness of torture in medieval society. Huizinga suggests that a society that preserves and circulates literature depicting brutality or torture can only be barbaric and bloodthirsty.[55] In *The Waning of the Middle Ages*, first published in 1919, Huizinga titles the first chapter 'The Violent Tenor of Life' in which he discusses 'the high degree of irritability which distinguishes the Middle Ages from our own time' and the 'excitability of the medieval soul', describing a people that could not 'get their fill of seeing the tortures inflicted, on a high platform in the middle of the market-place, on the magistrates suspected of high treason'.[56] However, Lea was convinced that much of medieval European history had been written from the 'wrong perspective, that, to be understood, it had to be read in terms of its own culture, not from the point of view of nineteenth-century standards superimposed upon the past'.[57] Other scholars, such as Peters, have also attempted to dispel the mythology perpetuated by both American and European medievalists by constructing and examining the historical reality of torture in the Middle Ages and its persistence in modern global contexts.

---

[53] Barbara W. Tuchman, *A Distant Mirror: The Calamitous Fourteenth Century* (New York: Ballantine Books, 1978), p. 135. Tuchman provides further examples of torture and brutality in her discussion of Bernabó Visconti, who ruled jointly with his brother Galeazzo in Lombardy and established a regime in which murder, cruelty, avarice and savage despotism alternated with effective government, respect for learning and encouragement of the arts (p. 240). She provides a lurid description of the *Quaresima*, 'a forty-day program of torture attributed to Bernabó and his brother, supposedly issued as an edict on their accession' which she hopes was intended to frighten, 'rather than for actual use': 'With the *strappado*, the wheel, the rack, flaying, gouging of eyes, cutting off of facial features and limbs one by one, and a day of torture alternating with a day of rest, it was supposed to terminate in death for "traitors" and convicted enemies' (p. 241).

[54] Jean Jost, 'Why is Middle English Romance So Violent? The Literary and Aesthetic Purposes of Violence', in *Violence in Medieval Courtly Literature: A Casebook*, ed. Albrecht Classen (New York: Routledge, 2004) 241–67.

[55] Johan Huizinga, *The Waning of the Middle Ages*, trans. Federick Jan Hopman (London: Penguin Books, 1924; reprinted 1990), pp. 14, 19, 23.

[56] Huizinga, *Waning of the Middle Ages*, pp. 14, 19, 23.

[57] Edward Peters, *Inquisition* (Berkeley CA: University of California Press, 1989), p. 288. See: Henry Charles Lea, *Superstition and Force: Torture, Ordeal, and Trial by Combat in Medieval Law* (New York: Barnes and Noble Books, 1996).

In modern terms, medieval torture is associated with the rites and punishment of the 'Inquisition', an entity that has assumed a greater mythology than the practice of torture itself and is erroneously assumed to have tramped freely across medieval Europe subjecting innocent peasants and simple dissenters to various torments for no apparent reason, inventing charges of heresy for the slightest infraction. Norman F. Cantor vehemently refutes this image by arguing that 'contrary to the widespread belief in the nineteenth and early twentieth centuries, the inquisitors were, with few exceptions, not psychotic sadists who were insatiably seeking vengeance upon heretics through death penalties'.[58] Peters has also done much to dispel the mythology surrounding both the application of torture and the nature of the inquisitorial process, arguing that the 'myth itself was universalized in a series of great artistic works into an indictment, by a modern world, of an earlier Europe for its crushing of the human spirit'.[59] According to Henry Ansgar Kelly, the term 'inquisition' has been misunderstood and misused by historians, personified and 'endowed with a diabolical omniscience or made to stand for a central intelligence agency with headquarters at the papal curia'.[60] The spectre of the 'Inquisition' has, in part, created the modern misconception that torture and brutality were everyday occurrences, simply facets of life in a primitive, backward time.

In an effort to put distance between the violence of the modern world and civilized nations, many of whom perpetuate that violence, critics and commentators qualify excessive brutality and the use of torture as 'medieval', denying the modern resort to such measures. In 1984, the medieval scholar Fred C. Robinson vented his annoyance with the way 'ultramodern techniques for administering torture and waging war are frequently described as "medieval"', citing media examples from 1968 to 1982.[61] The US Defense Secretary Donald Rumsfeld asserted, upon the death of Jordanian terrorist Abu Musab al-Zarqawi on 8 June 2006, that Zarqawi 'personified the dark, sadistic and medieval vision of the future of beheadings and suicide bombings and indiscriminate killings'.[62] In an interview on 3 April 2008 on National Public Radio's *Diane Rehm Show*, Nile Gardiner, director of the Margaret Thatcher Center for Freedom at the Heritage Foundation, opined that the Taliban in Afghanistan is 'almost medieval

---

[58] Norman F. Cantor, *The Civilization of the Middle Ages* (New York: Harper Collins, 1963, reprint 1993), p. 425.
[59] Peters, *Inquisition*, p. 1.
[60] Henry Ansgar Kelly, 'Inquisition and the Prosecution of Heresy: Misconceptions and Abuses', *Church History* 58:4 (Dec. 1989): 439–51; p. 439.
[61] Fred C. Robinson, 'Medieval, the Middle Ages', *Speculum* 59:4 (Oct. 1984): 745–56; p. 753. Robinson further argues that the word 'medieval' often has pejorative connotations for modern audiences and that it has variously meant 'outmoded', 'hopelessly antiquated' or just simply 'bad' as well as signifying violence and torture (p. 752).
[62] William Branigin, 'Across the U.S., Zarqawi's Death Hailed as Victory', *The Washington Post* (8 June 2006), www.washingtonpost.com. Accessed 8 June 2006.

in its savagery'.[63] These comments typify modern assumptions about the medieval period embedded in the popular imagination. The current debate about the use of torture in the interrogation of 'terror' suspects has intensified since the attacks of 11 September 2001, and torture and all its medieval associations have been pushed into the popular spotlight. In 2008, the comedian Stephen Colbert in *The Colbert Report* lampooned the defence of torture by the then President George W. Bush and his administration as an interrogation technique in a Justice Department memo dated August 2002, and reminded his audience that President Bush said, '"The United States does not torture." [6 September 2006] So, by definition, anything you do is not torture, so I say, go medieval.'[64] During the US Democratic National Convention in August 2008, the Bush administration's resort to torture was criticized by both the Governor of New Mexico Bill Richardson and the former Vice President Al Gore in their speeches on the final night of the convention that led to Senator Barack Obama's nomination acceptance speech.[65] In January 2011, the British High Commissioner in Bangladesh, Stephen Evans, denied torture allegations, insisting that: 'Our security co-operation with other countries is consistent with our laws and our values'.[66] John H. Langbein, in the preface to his 2006 edition of *Torture and the Law of Proof*, clarifies the need for a discussion about medieval torture and current foreign policy: 'A book about how the Western legal tradition rid itself of its centuries-long dependence on tortured confessions is again in demand, because questions about the legality of torture have surfaced anew in contem-

---

[63] Nile Gardiner, director of the Margaret Thatcher Center for Freedom at the Heritage Foundation, interview, 'NATO Summit', *Diane Rehm Show*, hosted by Susan Page, 3 April 2008.

[64] Stephen Colbert, 'The Word', *The Colbert Report*, air date: Tuesday, 29 July 2008. There have been several articles on torture in the American media in recent years, many of which focus on the institution of torture as an interrogation method in detention centres in Iraq and Guantanamo Bay, Cuba. See the following articles from CNN.com: 'Video shows interrogation of teen at Guantanamo'; 'Ex-Pentagon official defends "harsh treatment"'; 'Ashcroft defends waterboarding before House panel'; 'Previously secret torture memo released', www.cnn.com/2008/POLITICS. Accessed 1 August 2008; Martha Nussbaum, 'Under Pressure: From the Laboratories of Stanford to the Cells of Abu Ghraib: How Imagination Can Halt Man's Cruelty to the Powerless', *Times Literary Supplement* (19 October 2007), pp. 3–5; Karen Olsson, 'The Torturers Among Us: How the U.S. Became a Haven for Human-Rights Abusers', *Mother Jones* (May/June 2003): 56–61; and Adam Zagorin and Michael Duffy, 'Detainee 063: Inside the Wire at Gitmo', *Time* (20 June 2005): 26–33.

The investigative television programme *Justice Files*, in a report titled 'Face to Face with Evil' (2005) describes the murder scene of a serial killer, Toby Travis, in St Louis, Missouri, as a 'torture chamber' where, according to the commentator, 'medieval cruelty was dished out with modern efficiency'.

[65] Bill Richardson and Al Gore, Democratic National Convention, 28 August 2008.

[66] 'UK Denies Bangladesh Torture Allegations', BBC News, South Asia (18 January 2011), http://www.bbc.co.uk/news/world-south-asia-12220454. Accessed 18 January 2011.

porary affairs'.[67] Medieval society is not so far removed from modern cultural concerns in vocalizing dissent through literary means where torture is categorized as the practice of barbarians and tyrants, tainting whoever resorts to its use.

My intention is to contribute to a new understanding of how medieval literature functioned as a mode of popular dissent against judicial torture and brutality, and how poets and their audiences envisioned themselves and their national identities in opposition to those cultures that employed torture and seemed to sanction excessive brutality. One of the most strident medieval voices against such violence, a voice that concretely fixed these deeds in the realm of the Other, was Pope Urban II. He defined torture as a practice of barbarians in his speech at Clermont in 1095, encouraging a crusade against these uncivilized hordes: 'an accursed race, a race utterly alienated from God [...] has invaded the lands of those Christians and has depopulated them by the sword, pillage and fire; it has led away a part of the captives into its own country, and a part of it has destroyed by cruel tortures'.[68] Modern American society attempts to disassociate itself from the atrocities of Abu Ghraib and Guantanamo Bay by defining those actions as 'medieval' – distancing itself from the accountability that comes with enacting such policies and engaging in brutality that is generally considered excessive. Carolyn Dinshaw skilfully deals with modern society's appropriation of the torture-laden adjective 'medieval' in her analysis of the phrase 'getting medieval', famously employed in the film *Pulp Fiction* (1994), that has since become an ironic association denoting torture's pervasive presence in the medieval world. Dinshaw dissects the resonance of the ominous phrase uttered by Ving Rhames in modern popular culture and its effect on modern perceptions of what is 'medieval'.[69] Most of these conversations assume a medieval legacy of torture and brutality based on a misconception of medieval belief, practice and acceptance of torture as a judicial norm – a misconception contradicted by literary evidence that is often minimized in historical studies or discussions on art and theatre. Historical realities, according to Derek Pearsall, cannot

---

[67] John H. Langbein, *Torture and the Law of Proof: Europe and England in the Ancien Régime* (Chicago: The University of Chicago Press, 1976, revised 2006), p. ix.
[68] Robert the Monk, *Historia Hierosolymitana*, trans. Dana C. Munro, in *Urban and the Crusaders* (Philadelphia: the Department of History of the University of Pennsylvania, 1895), pp. 5–8; reproduced and quoted in *Vengeance in Medieval Europe: A Reader*, ed. Daniel Lord Smail and Kelly Gibson, Readings in Medieval Civilizations and Cultures: XIII (Toronto: University of Toronto Press, 2009), pp. 185–7. Urban further accuses the Persians of evisceration: '"When they wish to torture people by a base death, they perforate their navels, and dragging forth the extremity of the intestines, bind it to a stake; then with flogging they lead the victim around until the viscera having gushed forth the victim falls prostrate upon the ground"' (p. 185). Cf. p. 125 n. 76.
[69] Carolyn Dinshaw, *Getting Medieval: Sexualities and Communities, Pre- and Postmodern* (Durham NC: Duke University Press, 1999), p. 184. She also analyses the particular effect of this construct in terms of sexuality and sexual discourse, and posits that medievalists, 'especially queer medievalists, instead of sinking lower beneath the pop-culture surface, might instead conceive of ourselves as specially equipped to view this movie' (p. 184).

simply be 'read off' of literary texts, they are 'mutated and mediated in all sorts of complex ways',[70] but literary texts do provide a sense of social consciousness, of cultural acceptance and rejection. Medieval society, like its modern descendants, also attempted to distance itself from the acknowledged practice of judicial brutality and voice opposition to the application of torture by attributing its use and acceptance to 'barbaric' peoples, pulling away from the cruelty of the Other.

The art historian Robert Mills argues that Huizinga (in 1919), 'envisaged the fifteenth century as an epoch of "barbaric" judicial cruelty'.[71] Even though hanging was one of the most common medieval forms of capital punishment, Mills points out that chroniclers often omit records of simple hangings, preferring to dwell on the rarer, but more spectacular forms of execution associated with traitors. Many of the punishments analysed here are examples of these methods – flaying and equine quartering – that figure as popular literary motifs.[72] This creates a disproportionate image of violence in medieval society, which contributes to a 'distorted picture of medieval penal practice' and suggests that 'pre-modern people were accustomed to witnessing extravagant, showy execution rituals with unremitting frequency'.[73] While this may have been the case in some towns and cities at particular times in medieval Europe, 'the overall picture painted by court records is that the majority of criminals unfortunate enough to be sentenced to death met more ignominious ends at the end of a rope'.[74] And while hanging is a horrible way to die and a horrible spectacle to watch, it is certainly a far cry from the daily public mutilation supposedly witnessed in Tuchman's view of the

---

[70] Derek Pearsall, personal correspondence, 7 November 2010.
[71] Robert Mills, *Suspended Animation: Pain, Pleasure, and Punishment in Medieval Culture* (London: Reaktion Books, 2005), p. 9.
[72] Mills analyses the late medieval iconography of flayed bodies in Gerard David's 1498 diptych *Judgment of Cambyses*, recounting the old Persian legend, recorded first by Herodotus in his *Historiae*, of a corrupt judge, Sisamnes, who was flayed as punishment for his crimes. A medieval version of this legend appears in the compilation *Gesta Romanorum*, translated into French and published in the late fifteenth century (*Suspended Animation*, p. 59). Mills questions whether paintings of the *Judgment of Cambyses* reflect actual penal practice, particularly because there is little evidence that flaying was practised on offenders anywhere during the Middle Ages, and that any records of the penalty actually being carried out are 'exceptional' (p. 65). Mills does, however, refer to occasional mentions of flaying in Anglo-Saxon law and rare historical instances of the practice, mainly in English and French contexts, such as the 'skinning of Hughes Gérard, Bishop of Cahors, indicted for an attempt to poison Pope John XXII of Avignon in 1317' (p. 65). It may be these exceptional cases to which the poet is alluding because of the impact of flaying on the imagination. Mills further writes that the significance of flaying for 'visual and literary expression' is all too apparent: 'like bodily executions more generally, skin removal had an imaginary and symbolic potency out of all proportion to its frequency in lived experience' (pp. 65–6). Mills does note, however, that flaying is 'persistently associated with various forms of treason' in literary sources (p. 66). Flaying will be discussed in more detail in Chapter 4.
[73] Mills, *Suspended Animation*, p. 26.
[74] Mills, *Suspended Animation*, p. 26.

medieval world. Some critics have argued that for medieval people, violence was 'normative social practice, a form of social discourse utilized not just by kings, knights, inquisitors, and mobs to oppress and abuse others, but by artisans and peasants, men and women of whatever religion, to lay claim to honour and integrity, and to establish and defend a place for themselves and their families in local society'.[75] But as John Bellamy points out, medieval people were not inherently violent, nor did they necessarily take any pleasure in the violence of their world; 'when medieval men were cruel there was usually a good reason for it. Rarely were they brutal out of sheer sadism.'[76] Some violence was expected and even desired within the boundaries of law and civil society, though 'violence is now seen not merely as characteristic of a safely medieval and barbaric past but as integral to the historical processes that have brought us to our present condition, as foundational to what we have become'.[77] However, violence in medieval secular literature is often a transgressive or subversive commentary on power and tyranny. Several excellent studies have been conducted concerning the legal aspects of torture,[78] the visual representations of violence and punishment,[79] and the evolution of cruelty in Western culture.[80] An analysis of torture and judicial brutality in medieval literary texts, as modes of dissent or signifiers of national identity, is significantly absent from recent criticism, yet torture is one of the most recognizable cultural signifiers — even now, we hear 'torture' and we think 'medieval', however erroneously. Where torture does occur in medieval literature, it is often treated as a mimetic representation of accepted practice, but these episodes are neither mimetic nor uniform in their portrayal. They voice an opposition to torture and authoritarian brutality as stridently as Urban's call to arms on the field of Clermont.

Despite a modern cultural desire to displace torture onto a medieval 'Other', torture has not faded into the murky realms of the past. As public debate continues on a global scale, it is important to look more deeply into that past and investigate modern assumptions of the medieval acceptance of torture and judicial brutality, an investigation in which literary texts are key. The modern imagination often reads this presence as an acceptance, if not an outright embrace, of violence, brutality and torture. But to record or to depict cruelty to convey a message is not necessarily to celebrate or even condone its use, any more than

---

[75] Meyerson, Thiery and Falk, 'Introduction', p. 6.
[76] John Bellamy, *Crime and Public Order in England in the Later Middle Ages* (London: Routledge and Kegan Paul, 1973), p. 66.
[77] Meyerson, Thiery and Falk, 'Introduction', p. 4.
[78] Langbein, *Torture and the Law of Proof*; and Peters, *Torture*.
[79] Merback, *The Thief, the Cross and the Wheel*; Mills, *Suspended Animation*; Enders, *The Medieval Theater of Cruelty*.
[80] Daniel Baraz, *Medieval Cruelty: Changing Perceptions, Late Antiquity to the Early Modern Period* (Ithaca NY: Cornell University Press, 2003); Ramsay MacMullen, *Changes in the Roman Empire: Essays in the Ordinary* (Princeton NJ: Princeton University Press, 1990).

violent films like *Natural Born Killers* or *Kill Bill* record a modern lust for blood or a delight in brutality.[81] Each audience responds differently to media, to what they read or see or hear. It is impossible and anachronistic to invent a general or typical 'medieval' response to torture. Audiences for these medieval texts range from the illiterate folk at an oral performance of fabliaux to the nobility of medieval courts with many a merchant and rising bourgeoisie in between. In some cases, as with *Arthur and Gorlagon* and *Havelok the Dane*, there is only one extant version, so reconstructing audience reception and response becomes more difficult. Literature is a compelling historical record, and the texts analysed here within their historical context show a diverse and surprising approach to judicial brutality, specifically to torture. By the thirteenth century the trappings of modern society were being established as 'kings, cities, and other sovereign entities were busily setting down legal codes and statutes aimed at regulating, even criminalizing, homicide and vengeance'.[82] The use of torture in judicial proceedings, both religious and secular, was being tried and tested as some communities, like England, rejected it. Many secular texts make torture the tool of barbarians and its application the practice of the unjust, contradicting modern misconceptions about medieval brutality as a self-inflicted and self-defining practice.

Defining Torture and Brutality

Torture was neither wholly accepted nor celebrated by medieval audiences or authors as a means of enacting justice. Medieval and early-modern literary sources – religious, secular and comic – decry the use of torture and judicial brutality as tools of unstable authority. Not every scenario under discussion here strictly qualifies as interrogatory torture, but each occurs within a legal context and functions as judicial brutality. There is a distinct difference – torture was allowed under law to extract a confession; judicial brutality operates in contravention of just legal practice, and while an authority may enact it, its excess is transgressive. Many of the recent studies carried out in the last ten years on violent and brutal acts are grounded in the earlier work of Michel Foucault and Elaine Scarry.[83]

---

[81] Though a number of modern critical studies have argued that modern films and media *are* mimetic and do record either a modern bloodlust, or at least desensitization to violence and brutality.

[82] Daniel Lord Smail and Kelly Gibson, eds., *Vengeance in Medieval Europe: A Reader*, Readings in Medieval Civilizations and Cultures: XIII (Toronto: University of Toronto Press, 2009), p. 317.

[83] Foucault, *Discipline and Punish*; Scarry discusses the role of torture in destabilizing authoritarian regimes and the illusion of power that the application of torture gives those regimes in the first chapter of her groundbreaking study on physical violence. Elaine Scarry, 'The Structure of Torture: The Conversion of Real Pain into the Fiction of Power', *The Body in Pain: The Making and Unmaking of the World* (Oxford: Oxford University Press, 1985) 27–59.

Foucault's work focuses on torture in its judicial context, but also on its punitive purpose:

> To be torture, punishment must obey three principal criteria: first, it must produce a certain degree of pain which may be measured exactly, or at least calculated, compared and hierarchised; death is a torture in so far as it is not simply a withdrawal of the right to live, but is the occasion and culmination of a calculated gradation of pain: from decapitation (which reduces all pain to a single gesture, performed in a single moment – the zero degree of torture), through hanging, the stake and the wheel (all of which prolong the agony), to quartering, which carries pain almost to infinity; death-torture is the art of maintaining life in pain, by subdividing it into a 'thousand deaths', by achieving before life ceases 'the most exquisite agonies'. Torture rests on a whole quantitative art of pain. But there is more to it: this production of pain is regulated. Torture correlates the type of corporal effect, the quality, intensity, duration of pain, with the gravity of the crime, the person of the criminal, the rank of his victims.[84]

Working from Foucault's definition of torture, Merback delineates modern responses to violent visuals from medieval ones, arguing that for medieval people 'the experience of *seeing and imagining* a body that was ravaged and bleeding from tortures inflicted upon it lay at the centre of a constellation of religious doctrines, beliefs and devotional practices'.[85] Torture is a common motif in medieval religious art and literature,[86] but it had a very specific definition within the context of law separate from sanctioned violence dictated by regular practice in which 'custom rather than law defined acceptable social practice, and violence was one means of safeguarding custom'.[87] Given the historical record, the existence of torture and its use is not in question, but 'it remains to be shown how far torture was a routine part of late medieval criminal trials. [...] The problem is that trial records often omit any mention of torture, even when its use alone can explain a sudden change in a suspect's readiness to talk'.[88] Literary episodes, since they are not strictly mimetic, do not provide an accurate record of practice, but do provide potential sources for reactions to torture and judicial brutality.

Torture was established as a form of judicial inquiry in the Roman Empire but was not a sanctioned part of western European jurisprudence until the

---

[84] Foucault, *Discipline and Punish*, pp. 33–4.
[85] Merback, *The Thief, the Cross and the Wheel*, p. 19.
[86] The violence inflicted on female virgin martyrs has been discussed at length. See: Joan Ferrante, *To the Glory of Her Sex: Women's Roles in the Composition of Medieval Texts* (Indianapolis: Indiana University Press, 1997); and Katherine J. Lewis, 'Model Girls? Virgin Martyrs and the Training of Young Medieval Women in Late Medieval England', in *Young Medieval Women*, ed. Lewis, Noël James Menuge and Kim M. Phillips (Stroud: Sutton, 1999) 25–46.
[87] Paul Fouracre, 'Attitudes towards Violence in Seventh- and Eighth-Century Francia', in *Violence and Society in the Early Medieval West*, ed. Guy Halsall (Woodbridge: The Boydell Press, 1998) 60–75, p. 71.
[88] Dean, *Crime in Medieval Europe*, p. 16.

twelfth century. During the early Middle Ages, most societies relied on various forms of the ordeal as judicial proof.[89] Interrogatory torture was introduced into the European tradition with the rediscovery of Roman law, as a means of eliciting a confession tied to rhetorical notions of truth inscribed upon the body.[90] Medieval hagiographers, historians and philosophers adapted Roman material to their own time, recording and embellishing atrocities in their narrative accounts as the techniques of barbarian pagan judges attempting to wring confessions and conversions from dissenting Christians. Many of the methods of torture described in these graphic accounts are anachronistic portrayals of medieval interrogation techniques rather than accurate historical renderings of early Christian martyrdom.[91]

In detailing the persecution of early Christians at the hands of emperors such as Diocletian and Nero, Lea makes allowances for medieval historians who described these 'frightful agonies':

> The indiscriminate cruelty to which the Christians were thus exposed without defence, at the hands of those inflamed against them by all evil passions, may, perhaps, have been exaggerated by the ecclesiastical historians, but that frightful excesses were perpetuated under sanction of law cannot be doubted by anyone who has traced, even in comparatively recent times and among Christian nations, the progress of political and religious persecution.[92]

The spectacles of Roman cruelty were horrific and savage, and the 'rediscovery' of Roman law in medieval jurisprudence was no less savage in its application, but not every instance of excessive brutality enacted by authorities qualifies as torture.[93] The Christianization of the Roman Empire after Constantine resulted

---

[89] Judicial ordeals, such as the hot water, hot iron and fire ordeals, are separate entities from judicial torture. The ordeal is a system of proofs intended to determine guilt or innocence. Confession or the extraction of 'truth' is not an issue, nor is it a form of punishment; the ordeal is evidence, a form of trial in and of itself. As Robert Bartlett explains, the existence of ninth-century material concerning ordeals demonstrates that it was possible, even in the Carolingian period, to be hostile to this form of evidence; objections were raised against the practice early in its history and it reveals the grounds for those objections. *Trial by Fire and Water: The Medieval Judicial Ordeal* (Oxford: Clarendon Press, 1986), p. 75.

[90] In the *Rhetoric*, Aristotle considers laws, the testimony of witnesses, contracts, oaths and evidence or testimony extracted from slaves under torture as inartificial proofs, proofs furnished at the outset of the judicial case and not 'constructed by the speaker's techne'. *Rhetoric*, trans. George A. Kennedy, *Aristotle on Rhetoric: A Theory of Civic Discourse* (New York and Oxford: Oxford University Press, 1991): 109–18, qtd. in Rita Copeland, 'The Pardoner's Body and the Disciplining of Rhetoric', in *Framing Medieval Bodies*, ed. Sarah Kay and Miri Rubin (Manchester and New York: Manchester University Press, 1994) 138–59, p. 157 n. 27.

[91] Larissa Tracy, 'Torture Narrative: The Imposition of Medieval Method on Early Christian Texts', *Journal of the Early Book Society*, vol. 7 (2004): 33–50.

[92] Lea, *Superstition and Force*, pp. 329–30.

[93] According to the *Oxford English Dictionary*, 'torture' was originally defined as '(a disorder

in the amelioration of some of the most horrific methods of torment and execution in the Roman legal process, but the Christian emperors also preserved the jurisprudence upon which they had originally been based.[94] Medieval canon lawyers and legal philosophers attempted to establish legal procedures that would provide reliable 'truth', and implemented torture as part of that process. Pope Innocent III is usually credited with the institution of the *inquisitio* as a criminal procedure in all ecclesiastical courts as a response to the 'shortcomings of the ancient accusatorial system'.[95] His decretals *Nichil est pene* (1199), *Licet Heli* (1199) and *Qualiter et quando* (1206) 'made explicit new judicial procedures that may already have been in practice for some time'.[96] When Roman law was revived and adopted by the universities of Italy and France during the late twelfth century, torture experienced a resurgence in the judicial process as it replaced the system of ordeals previously in place. What Bartlett considers the 'unanimity' of clerical opinion in the thirteenth century contrasts decisively with the 'hesitancy' of the twelfth century and secular authorities everywhere had to devise new methods to replace the ordeal; so 'the inquest and torture came into their own'.[97] However, torture was neither universally accepted nor condoned. Gratian, one of the greatest scholars of ecclesiastical law in the twelfth century, echoed centuries of ecclesiastical prohibition of torture in his *Concordia discordantium canonum*, or *Decretum* (c. 1140), writing that 'confession is not to be extorted by the instrumentality of torture'.[98]

Jean Dunbabin points out that it would probably be wrong to suggest that torture methods were unknown in western Europe before 'intellectuals rediscovered their late antique use'; but, more importantly, there is no evidence that these methods were systematically used by judges or gaolers before the revival

---

characterized by) contortion, distortion, or twisting', later as '(the infliction of) severe physical or mental suffering; anguish, agony, torment'. It is also defined as the 'infliction of severe bodily pain as punishment or as a means of interrogation or persuasion; a form or instance of this': *Oxford English Dictionary* (Oxford: Oxford University Press, 2002).

[94] Peters, 'Destruction of the Flesh', p. 135.

[95] Thijssen, 'Master Amalric and the Amalricians', p. 53.

[96] Thijssen, 'Master Amalric and the Amalricians', p. 53. Innocent III was also the first to put heresy on a par with treason (*crimen laesae majestatis*), focusing on 'clear juridical action involving the secular arm as well' (p. 60).

[97] Bartlett, *Trial by Fire and Water*, p. 101. Bartlett further notes that torture was part of a developing process of proofs in response to the demise of the ordeal: 'the extension of existing proofs into cases previously resolved by ordeal; the swift progress towards the trial jury in England and some other countries; and most important of all, the rise of torture to replace the ordeal' (p. 135).

[98] Peters, *Torture*, p. 49. According to Peters, 'the history of torture in western Europe may be traced from the Greeks, through the Romans, through the Middle Ages, down to the legal reforms of the eighteenth century and the abolition of torture in criminal legal procedure virtually throughout western Europe by the first quarter of the nineteenth century' (*Torture*, p. 5).

of studies of Roman law got under way.[99] In circumstances where torture was employed to extract a confession, its use was based on the assumption that the accused 'would not have been arrested unless there were good grounds for thinking him guilty, and that confession was worth obtaining by any possible means'.[100] Despite legal attempts to regulate the use of torture strictly there were abuses. By the second half of the thirteenth century, in some prisons torture by rack or by beating confessions out of prisoners had become part of judicial routine; and, in some cases, witnesses were subjected to torture to ensure that they provided complete accounts.[101] However, Dunbabin explains that the image of prisons in western Europe by 1300 should not 'automatically include a torture chamber or an official specially trained in the application of its techniques; where these existed, we should not assume that they were part of normal procedure'.[102]

Records mention torture by the early thirteenth century and it was widely used by the sixteenth century at the latest.[103] In 1252 Innocent IV licensed the use of torture to obtain evidence from suspects, and by 1256 inquisitors were allowed to absolve each other if they used the instruments of torture themselves, rather than relying on lay agents for the purpose; 'those who shrank from shedding blood learned how to use the thumbscrew and the rack'.[104] But in a medieval context torture has a very specific definition: it was a legal means of painfully extracting truth, specifically a confession, from a criminal who already had a 'so-called half proof' against him, which meant either one eyewitness, or 'circumstantial evidence of sufficient gravity, according to a fairly elaborate tariff of gravity worked out by later jurists'.[105] According to Langbein, this demanding law of proof was originally designed as a safeguard against judicial error or corruption, but the nascent national legal systems became dependent on its use and so the application of torture and coerced confessions could not be reconciled with the notion of judicial safeguard.[106] Langbein concludes that European criminal procedure failed at making these confessions reliable and abandoned the practice instead, 'reworking their law of proof and their criminal sanctions'.[107] Torture was a legal experiment rooted in the desire to prosecute criminals, not a

---

[99] Jean Dunbabin, *Captivity and Imprisonment in Medieval Europe 1000–1300*, Medieval Culture and Society Series (New York: Palgrave MacMillan, 2002), pp. 22–3.
[100] Dunbabin, *Captivity and Imprisonment*, p. 108.
[101] Dunbabin, *Captivity and Imprisonment*, p. 125.
[102] Dunbabin, *Captivity and Imprisonment*, p. 127.
[103] Robert Thurston, *Witch, Wicce, Mother Goose: The Rise and Fall of the Witch Hunts in Europe and North America* (London: Pearson Education, 2001), p. 134.
[104] Dunbabin, *Captivity and Imprisonment*, p. 153.
[105] Langbein, *Torture and the Law of Proof*, p. 5. Langbein explains further that in a case where a suspect is caught with the dagger and the loot, 'each of those indicia would be a quarter proof. Together they cumulate to a half proof, and he could therefore be dispatched to a session in the local torture chamber.' (p. 5). See also: Peters, *Torture*, p. 50.
[106] Langbein, *Torture and the Law of Proof*, p. x.
[107] Langbein, *Torture and the Law of Proof*, p. x.

culturally accepted brutality designed to persecute the innocent via the threat of physical harm. As Jeffrey Burton Russell notes, the application of torture in the struggle between orthodoxy and heresy is an indictment of both parties, placing both the dissenters and their opponents in the dock, but dissent still flourished and was one of the elements 'shaping medieval civilization'.[108]

The legal application of torture was founded in rhetorical discussions of discovery, not in 'purported medieval superstition or backwardness'.[109] Authorities often justified the use of torture within specific boundaries that delineated the structures of society; 'just' violence was to be carried out 'by someone in a right relationship with authority', but more than that, the authorities had to ensure that violence was undertaken only against certain people, 'the necessity for an agent of violence to act under authority inhibited the exercise of just violence against a social superior'.[110] Local magistrates and officers of the court applied torture but not necessarily as a regulated form of interrogation.[111] Peters writes that 'as police powers broadened, informal torture was used from the early thirteenth century on, but originally as a *methode policière*, and only much later assimilated into legal procedure. Citizens protested its use, at least against fellow citizens of good repute, but they approved it in the case of those generally of ill fame'.[112] In the twelfth century, Huguccio instituted the rule that ecclesiastical judges should employ only moderate forms of torture, which was interpreted in the fourteenth century by John Andrew as 'rods or switches or leather whips rather than the rack or claws and cords'.[113] The principles of due process, including the presumption of innocence, were an important part of late medieval continental law, and often it was thought better to leave a criminal unpunished than to condemn an innocent man, a precept borrowed from classical Roman law and 'recycled' by medieval Roman lawyers.[114] This adherence to due process contradicts the assumption that torture was employed indiscriminately as a standard means of interrogation or punishment, though torture was a standard 'canonistic doctrine that all ecclesiastical judges were able to employ'.[115] Despite the presence of torture in Roman law and its accepted application in many European regions, particularly southern France, some secular authorities resisted its implementation and only gave way in the face of papal pressure.

---

[108] Jeffrey Burton Russell, *Dissent and Reform in the Early Middle Ages* (Berkeley CA: University of California Press, 1965), pp. 2, 4.
[109] Thurston, *Witch, Wicce, Mother Goose*, p. 134.
[110] Philippa C. Maddern, *Violence and Social Order: East Anglia 1422–1442*, Oxford Historical Monograph Series (Oxford: Clarendon Press, 1992), pp. 84–5.
[111] Peters, *Torture*, p. 49.
[112] Peters, *Torture*, p. 49.
[113] Kelly, 'Inquisition and Prosecution of Heresy', p. 445.
[114] Dean, *Crime in Medieval Europe*, p. 5.
[115] Kelly, 'Inquisition and Prosecution of Heresy', p. 444.

There was a fear that brutality might interfere with the soul and for all their violence many of the eleventh- and twelfth-century nobility shared an 'anxiety over salvation' and 'experienced the apparent disjunction between the demands of a Christian life and the necessities of exercising authority in this world'.[116] Those anxieties did not recede in the thirteenth and fourteenth centuries as torture became more widespread and became a staple of popular devotional literature where the virtuous resist tyranny embodied by numerous tortures disguised as legal proceedings. There was legislation in place to prevent the wanton use of torture, but those restrictions were often laid aside, a trend that escalated in the fourteenth and fifteenth centuries.[117]

Eventually, restrictions were placed on the use of torture by 'papally appointed heresy inquisitors because of reported abuses',[118] including documented complaints from Florence in 1346 of prisoners dying from its misapplication.[119] These abuses appear to escalate later in the medieval period in conjunction with discussions of Roman law by academic lawyers and the growth of princely power in the fifteenth century which seem to go 'hand in hand in expanding the arbitrary power of judges against the fixed penalties of customary or statute law'.[120] This development is mirrored in the increase in torture and brutality in the public spectrum and popular literature. As power was wielded with more force, the public became jaded by the abuse of power, the corruption of the judicial process and the judicial excesses that resulted. The law was not corrupt, but many of those who worked for it were; they twisted the law, justice and punishment to their own ends, justifying their excess in the interests of a falsely constructed truth. Both religious and secular literature responds to those excesses by configuring the authorities who use torture as the cruellest, most brutal and most dishonourable figures. The use of torture and judicial brutality that transgresses the boundaries of custom and law taints those who employ it, often along the lines of national definitions. The systematic abuse of torture by authorities invested by the law to protect the populace contributes to the presence of torture as a literary motif protesting inappropriate application of force or vigilante justice. It may be that public complaint led to the eventual restriction of torture, and authorities responded to popular dissent about the corruption of power and judicial procedure voiced openly or through the dissemination of critical literary texts. Ignoring prohibitions against the abuse of torture explains its ignominious portrayal in medieval literature – the *vox populi* against tyrannical abuses that distort and corrupt law, a progress of cruelty that gathers momentum in the late Middle Ages and erupts in the political and religious turmoil of the early-modern period. The regulation of torture could not prevent

---

[116] Peters, 'Destruction of the Flesh', p. 136.
[117] Dean, *Crime in Medieval Europe*, pp. 15–16.
[118] Kelly, 'Inquisitions and Prosecutions of Heresy', p. 445.
[119] Dean, *Crime in Medieval Europe*, p. 16.
[120] Dean, *Crime in Medieval Europe*, p. 18.

its abuse. Its destabilizing effects are most frequently displayed in literature that openly dissents against its use (rather than mimicking it) and makes torture the tool of corrupt authorities *outside* the national boundaries.

The use of coercion in 'matters of ecclesiastical discipline' troubled many European thinkers,[121] but this image of institutional torture is often in the back of modern minds when it comes to discussions of medieval violence, law, culture and society. Enders notes, 'it has become somewhat ordinary these days to read in scholarly analysis of both medieval literature and the modern media that the ubiquity of violence dulls an audience's senses to violence'.[122] There are infrequent references to torture, but diverse forms of violence permeate medieval literary sources, from beheadings and flayings to equine quartering and general dismemberment. However, these episodes generally condemn the graphic displays of violence. In the thirteenth and fourteenth centuries torture and judicial brutality functioned as intertextual literary motifs, crossing genres and cultural boundaries as authors reshaped material and texts to appeal to the nationalist sensibilities of their audiences.

The Intertexuality of Torture and Brutality

In the immense body of secular literature written over the course of 700 years in widely diverse cultures, languages, and traditions, torture plays a minuscule part (except in hagiography), and in some genres is completely absent. The almost marginal references to torture criticize those who use it illegitimately or dishonourably in contravention of accepted public practice and law. This suggests that torture had a specific (but limited) place in medieval society delineated by strict boundaries and rules for application, that medieval audiences were no more desensitized to its use and abuse than modern audiences, and that when those boundaries were transgressed the *vox populi* often resisted. Societies sought to define themselves as nations that did not resort to torture, even if the reality was different, and authors urged their audiences to reject torture and its associations.

Torture and brutality figure as intertextual motifs – tying genres and cultures together in their shared repugnance for excesses in judicial interrogation and punishment, perhaps reflecting a larger European resistance to measures promoted by religious and political authorities. Intertextuality considers the 'writer as reader – as the shaping mind negotiating between the present text (or "intertext") and the texts that surround it in its literary culture'.[123] Michael Twomey notes that while intertextuality is a feature of any literature, it is 'partic-

---

[121] Peters, 'Destruction of the Flesh', p. 131.
[122] Enders, *The Medieval Theater of Cruelty*, p. 22.
[123] Michael W. Twomey, 'Morgain la Fée in *Sir Gawain and the Green Knight*: From Troy to Camelot', in *Text and Intertext in Medieval Arthurian Literature*, ed. Norris J. Lacy (New York: Garland, 1996) 91–115, p. 91.

ularly pronounced in a literary culture in which originality means reworking older texts, retelling tales that have always already been told'.[124] Most of the texts under discussion here are based on earlier versions, and many of them enhance the brutality and torture in the narrative, in some cases inventing it altogether. Medieval authors did not adhere to a concept of genre like those established in modern criticism,[125] nor was it necessary for them to come to terms with 'intertextuality' – but literary production in medieval Europe was intertextual, drawing from a shared base of narrative traditions, religious ideologies and proscriptions, and cultural ideals.

Secular literature of the Middle Ages is founded on a wealth of classical legends, epics and sagas, taking much of its style and subject matter from ancient works; in some instances torture is a product of source material rather than medieval invention. There are incidents of torture and excessive punitive brutality in classical literature; the eternal punishment of Prometheus, Sisiphus, and Tantalus in the depths of Tartarus may have provided a blue-print for later accounts of torture like that of Loki in Old Norse/Icelandic tradition who endures the dripping poison of the dragon Nidhogg on his head while chained to the World Tree, Yggdrasil, for instigating the murder of Baldur. They certainly influenced the presence of torture in Dante's conception of Hell. These are accounts of punishment, rather than interrogatory torture, and they deal mainly with gods and immortals for whom the sentence is intended to be eternal. As characters, these figures are separated from audiences by the veil of myth – their torment is a moral, not a reality, a literary motif rather than actual practice. Medieval romances, for the most part, do not contain graphic accounts of torture because the practice of inflicting sustained pain outside the legitimate violence of the battlefield or tournament is contrary to the ideals of chivalry and courtesy embodied in the Arthurian tradition and romance. It is the nature of romance to have a happy ending.[126] However, in certain circumstances, the antagonists threaten torture against the chivalrous or wield it in an exposition of their own tyranny in opposition to the ideal society where torture is unnecessary. The pattern of romances was emulated throughout western Europe, making it an apt forum for views on torture and brutality as in the *Roman van Walewein* and *Arthur and Gorlagon*. As Jeffrey Jerome Cohen explains, 'Since the romance authors were convinced that they could have a delimiting effect upon their audiences, it seems natural to speak of the genre as a culturally engaged practice connected in its genesis to containment, diffusion, and the construction of a

---

[124] Twomey, 'Morgain La Fée in *Sir Gawain and the Green Knight*', p. 91.
[125] Donald Maddox, 'Generic Intertextuality in Arthurian Literature: The Specular Encounter', in *Text and Intertext in Medieval Arthurian Literature*, ed. Norris J. Lacy (New York: Garland, 1996) 3–24, p. 3.
[126] Derek Brewer, 'Escape from the Mimetic Fallacy', in *Studies in Medieval English Romances*, ed. Derek Brewer (Cambridge: D.S. Brewer, 1988, rpt. 1991), p. 8.

proper ethic of masculinity'.[127] A certain amount of bravado and martial violence is to be expected of such a genre, and it was expected in its cultural context – but despite the proliferation of battles, individual combats, dismemberings and decapitations, judicial torture is significantly absent and excessive brutality taints even the most noble characters.

Seemingly disparate cultures – Flanders, Scandinavia, and England – synthesize literary traditions and situate torture as a practice of the Other. The texts in this study are connected by a transmission process that saw literary texts, genres, motifs and themes permeate most of medieval western Europe. Generic forms of intertextuality were widespread in Francophone Europe by the second half of the twelfth century; historiography in Latin, history or pseudohistory in Latin or French, romance in French – 'all proliferated at the time, were encouraged by some of the same patrons, read by the same readers, copied by the same scribes, produced by writers whose cultural baggage and formal training were the same, who had learned their trade by reading the same *auctores*'.[128] The medieval world of the late twelfth to the fourteenth centuries was fairly small – stories (written and oral) travelled with seafarers, merchants, diplomats and missionaries; the Church attempted to ensure a unity of doctrine, a uniformity of legal practice, and various societies either adopted or rejected it. As intertextual motifs, torture and brutality negotiate the cultural anxieties of evolving nations, and provide a means by which societies defined themselves through a shared literary inheritance.

Literary Accounts of Medieval Torture

This study challenges modern preconceptions of medieval brutality and the acceptance of torture as a viable means of extracting 'truth' by examining literary sources that interrogate social and judicial 'norms' and judge those who use excessive brutality or torture as tyrants. It also places the question of English national identity within the context of legal practice in opposition to the authorities on the Continent who employed torture as a means of obtaining a confession and investigates nationalist concerns in the literature of other European societies. Chapter 1 looks at the English saints' lives of the thirteenth-century *South English Legendary* (*SEL*) and the fifteenth-century Middle English translation of the Latin *Legenda aurea* (*LgA*), the *Gilte Legende* (*GiL*). In opposition to the use of torture against heretical sects in southern France, English hagiography provides models of resistance for heterodox sects persecuted by orthodox authorities. The

---

[127] Jeffrey Jerome Cohen, 'Decapitation and Coming of Age: Constructing Masculinity and the Monstrous', in *The Arthurian Yearbook III*, ed. Keith Busby (New York: Garland, 1993) 173–92, p. 180.

[128] Barbara N. Sargent-Baur, 'Veraces Historiae aut Fallaces Fabulae?', in *Text and Intertext in Medieval Arthurian Literature*, ed. Norris J. Lacy (New York: Garland, 1996) 25–39, p. 31.

LgA was produced in Italy in the late thirteenth century, but the *SEL* resituates the narrative of brutality in terms of an English consciousness, contextualizing that brutality as something alien to English society. The *SEL* violently establishes an English voice in hagiography – not necessarily because the English hagiographers were more violent but because they envisioned themselves as less violent than their continental contemporaries. The English native saints in particular represent a continuity of English resistance to violent and barbarous invasion embodied by the Danish raiders of the Anglo-Saxon past. The fifteenth-century *GiL* engages its vernacular audience at a time when heterodoxy was again on the rise, echoing its thirteenth-century predecessor and providing strident English voices for opposing religious tyranny. In the construction of audience, hagiographers placed their English subjects and Roman saints in an exalted and idealized position in opposition to a more violent and less civilized Other that could be read in terms of the Church authorities who used torture against heterodox sects and other political dissenters.

Chapters 2 and 3 examine the way in which other evolving cultures of the thirteenth and fourteenth centuries tried to establish their own cultural identities based on an institutional rejection of judicial torture. In Chapter 2, the Anglo-Norman *Chanson de Roland* provides a template for later works, especially in England, where excessively brutal judicial punishments are presented as contrary to law and good governance. The *Roland* also reveals anxieties of cultural inheritance between England's Norman rulers and their French heritage in light of an upswell of 'Englishness' at the end of the twelfth and beginning of the thirteenth century and may illuminate fears of the 'Other within'. While torture was sanctioned in France and Germany in the thirteenth and fourteenth centuries, Scandinavia and the Low Countries had no mechanism for using torture as a judicial tool. Flanders adopted French literary traditions but resisted the influence of Romano-canonical law as outside powers threatened Flemish autonomy. The Middle Dutch hero Walewein is a rejection of French romance models; the *Roman van Walewein* signals a cultural unease with torture, and the poets define their society in opposition to foreign legal influence. Chapter 3 focuses specifically on Icelandic texts and the stigma of inherited brutality that shaped Old Norse/Icelandic identity and literary endeavours. In the face of Norwegian imperialism, the Icelandic authors of *Hrafnkels saga* and *Brennu Njals saga* reject literary forms popular in Norway and establish nationalist Icelandic literature in which torture has no legal or moral place – resisting continental influences and emulating a shared Anglo-Saxon heritage.

Furthering the question of national identity and the abuse of power, Chapter 4 works off the foundation of violence in English vernacular hagiography and examines the English secular literary response to judicial torture, both in terms of an imagined historical continuity and in relation to the sense of English identity embedded in native religious texts. Part of this can be seen in the *SEL* manuscripts that contain native saints' lives and native English secular romances, like *Havelok the Dane*, which deviate greatly from earlier Anglo-Norman sources and clearly place torture and judicial brutality in opposition to civilized and correct English rule. *Havelok* specifically engages with cultural anxieties of the 'Other within', Anglo-Danish descendants integrated into English society whose lineage could potentially align them with Normans. *Arthur and Gorlagon* negotiates the Arthurian tradition and its French heritage by emphasizing the greater qualities of Arthur as an English king and locating both interrogatory torture and judicial brutality well outside of his realm. In this Anglo-Latin romance, the hegemonic powers attempt to assert their dominance through brutality and modes of torment that exceed historically prescribed forms of punishment, tainting the legitimacy of their rule and subverting the course of justice. Even though the text ends with a reaffirmation of that power, the structure itself has been destabilized and the foundations eroded. Poets like Geoffrey Chaucer include momentary references to torture in larger narratives about law and justice, as in the *Man of Law's Tale*, but reject excessive brutality and unsanctioned torture in texts like the *Prioress's Tale* where the audience response both within and outside of the poem is gauged by silence rather than acceptance and approbation.

In the comic milieu violence is often part of the humour, but parodies of institutional punishment and judicial torture interrogate the deeply destabilizing effect of wanton brutality in juridical and extra-juridical circumstances. Chapter 5 focuses on the comic uses of brutality, integrating the English rejection of torture and brutality in the *Miller's Tale* and the *Knight's Tale* with the cautionary narratives of the Old French fabliaux in which violence is a common element but still has boundaries. Stories like *Du prestre crucefié* (The Crucified Priest), *De Connebert* (*Li prestre ki perdi les colles*) (The Priest Who Lost his Balls), and *La Dame escoillee* (The Gelded Lady) engage in realistic forms of torture, designed to cause prolonged pain in a public demonstration of power and dominance. But that power is often illegitimate and destabilized in enacting public rituals of castration in spectacles of vigilante justice. This chapter addresses the possible motivations behind depicting such excessive forms of violence in the guise of a cleverly crafted tale, and juxtaposes the violently transgressive vengeance of cuckolded husbands and an arrogant son-in-law against the comedy of Chaucer's *Miller's Tale* and the sobriety of martial violence in the *Knight's Tale*.

Chapter 6 follows a supposed legacy of 'medieval' judicial practice into the early-modern period and challenges modern and early-modern assumptions of medieval brutality and torture. The early-modern perspective of the Middle Ages is that of a 'millennium of middleness, a space of empty waiting and virtual death until the reawakening of the West to its proper nature and purpose in the period of the Renaissance'.[129] However, these terms are not absolute – there is no definitive end date for the Middle Ages, nor a universally accepted beginning date for the early-modern period. There is considerable overlap. Situating torture within the context of sixteenth-century religious upheaval, English playwrights

---

[129] Freedman and Spiegel, 'Medievalisms Old and New', p. 678.

and authors responded loudly to the implementation of brutal interrogation techniques in investigations of heresy or political intrigue, rejecting this mode of interrogation as alien and Other. As the Reformation swept across Europe, conflicting religious ideologies sought to sanctify their martyrs with the language of medieval hagiography. John Foxe employs the methods of medieval hagiographers, but situates the narratives of his contemporary martyrs within the judicial framework of Elizabethan England, condemning torture but artfully negotiating the realities of recent history. Playwrights such as Christopher Marlowe and William Shakespeare and writers like Thomas Nashe attribute torture and brutality to diseased states, vocalizing opposition to its adoption in England. They include them as motifs in their popular narratives emphasizing barbaric Otherness in xenophobic displays of brutality and elevating the civilized society of England. The use of interrogatory torture in sixteenth-century England is a contradiction of England's medieval past, and rather than accepting responsibility for the genesis of English judicial torture, early-modern authors attempted to distance themselves culturally from that violence and create a narrative of inheritance rather than invention – a model followed by many modern audiences that ignores the long and troubled history of torture and its invention of truth within the rule of law.

1

Rending the Flesh:
The Orthodoxy of Torture in Hagiography[1]

> 'It revolts me to have recourse to measures the church has always criticized when they are employed by the secular arm. But there is a law that governs and directs even my personal feelings. Ask the abbot to provide a place where the instruments of torture can be installed.'
> Bernard Gui, *The Name of the Rose*, Umberto Eco (pp. 465–6)

One of the enduring literary motifs of medieval hagiography is the array of vicious tortures to which saints, particularly virgin martyrs, are subjected in their steadfast defiance of pagan authorities. In Christian terms, the tortured body of the saint is, for the hagiographer and his audience, 'a testimony to the power of God and the Church' and the failure of these horrific tortures 'functions as proof that steadfast spiritual faith can overcome physical suffering'.[2] The monstrous actions of the tormentors are juxtaposed against the righteous stance of the saints; and in their resistance to torture, which rarely has a permanent effect on them, their sanctity is assured.[3] Historically, medieval torture is most commonly associ-

---

[1] Select material in this chapter, specifically some of the discussion regarding *Christina* and *Agatha*, appears in a much earlier form in Larissa Tracy, *Women of the Gilte Legende: A Selection of Middle English Saints' Lives*, The Library of Medieval Women (Cambridge: D.S. Brewer, 2003).

[2] Beth Crachiolo, 'Female and Male Martyrs in the *South English Legendary*', in *'A Great Effusion of Blood'?: Interpreting Medieval Violence*, ed. Mark D. Meyerson, Daniel Thiery and Oren Falk (Toronto: University of Toronto Press, 2004) 147–63, p. 147.

[3] Torture is a common motif in religious literature, in part because of its renewed place in legal procedure. Jocelyn Wogan-Browne questions whether this connection can be 'causatively attributed to changes in juridical practice and the morphology of torture in contemporary interrogation or execution' and she points out that the represented torture in the *passio* 'is less juridical than rhetorical and epistemological' (pp. 106–7). *Saints' Lives and Women's Literary Culture c. 1150–1300: Virginity and its Authorisations* (Oxford: Oxford University Press, 2001). Wogan-Browne points to Thomas H. Bestul's suggestion in *Texts of the Passion: Latin Devotional Literature and Medieval Society* (Philadelphia: University of Pennsylvania Press, 1996) that the development of the Inquisition and its adoption of juridical torture may have led to the increase in represented torture, and repeats Caroline Walker Bynum's observation

ated with judicial proceedings against heretics during the period of inquisitorial courts from the late twelfth century onwards, notably the Albigensian Crusade (1209–1229) through to the inception of the notorious Spanish Inquisition in 1478. The form and frequency of torture in hagiography may have provided models of resistance and defiance for heterodox sects who saw themselves and their suffering at the hands of Church authorities reflected in the stories of early Christian saints, even though they rejected the adoration of those saints. In the case of native English saints' lives, particularly in the *South English Legendary* (*SEL*) and *Gilte Legende* (*GiL*), torture participates in a discourse of national identity; the enemies of England are portrayed as barbarically as possible, while the exemplarity of the saints is a model for emulation.

This chapter focuses on a selection of *vitae* that engage specifically in the discourse of torture and judicial brutality. Saints Christina and Laurence are two examples of vocal defiance and stoic opposition – both challenge the legitimacy of the authorities that torture them, providing (inadvertent) models of resistance for heterodox sects. Saint Agatha reflects anxieties about the gendered depiction of mutilation and torture. These three lives contain some of the most graphic examples of torture and judicial brutality in hagiography. Their *vitae* were translated and adapted in both the *SEL* and *GiL* and the episodes of torture and defiance are poignant examples of the English rejection of torture. These English narratives are more gruesome than their Latin analogues and sources, and even as the English hagiographers adapted the Latin texts, they encoded their own legal sensibilities into the figures of these saints.

The hagiographical tradition did not rely solely on the verbatim transmission of saints' lives, but also on the ability and desire of scribes to author their own revisions, interpreting and rewriting legends to appeal to their chosen audience, or to a wider more European audience rather than a particular geographic region. Hagiography is formulaic; there are patterns of abuse that saints *must* endure, miracles that *must* be performed and conversions that *must* occur. In these texts, torture functions as an intertexual motif, the brutality evolving from one adaptation to another, reflecting cultural anxieties about legal procedures that permitted interrogatory torture and engaging in a nationalist discourse in societies where the law prohibited it.[4] In these accounts, torture plays a prominent role in the saint's achievement of martyrdom. Gruesome punishments are conjured up by pagan judges and emperors who feel their temporal power slip-

---

in *Fragmentation and Redemption* (New York: Zone Books, 1992), that the church allowed certain forms of torture, and forbade the kind of dismemberment featured in hagiography (p. 107 n. 40). I agree with Bestul's argument, and the literature does seem to point to a definitive connection between the reintroduction of torture in legal process and the increasing brutality of religious literature, specifically thirteenth-century to fifteenth-century hagiography.

[4] Catherine Sanock, *Her Life Historical: Exemplarity and Female Saints' Lives in Late Medieval England*, The Middle Ages Series (Philadelphia: University of Pennsylvania Press, 2007), pp. 83–115.

ping away, and in the interests of reaffirming their diminishing authority in the face of a rising Christian population, they resort to torture to force a conversion or a confession of error. In the Latin *Legenda aurea* (*LgA*) the descriptions of these torments – applied one after the other in an attempt to break the body and spirit of the saint – are unembellished. There is no condemnation, no commentary – merely the fact of a saint enduring these torments without any sense of pain or discomfort, defying and often taunting the civil authority that attempts to exercise control through barbaric practice. The lack of graphic descriptions and the dispassionate delivery may signal acceptance of the canonical practice of torture, or of the hagiographic formulae, or it may indicate silent disapproval of the procedure by elevating the discourse of dissent. Caroline Walker Bynum writes that the intensely graphic imagery or idea of torment is necessary to reinforce the doctrine of resurrection, that in achieving grace there was no pain, rather an 'anesthesia of glory'.[5] A natural assumption would be that these violent passages were designed to evoke compassion for the saint's suffering, but the descriptions of 'grisly tortures are almost invariably accompanied by assurances that the saint feels nothing'.[6] As collections like the *LgA* were disseminated, adapted and translated into French and Middle English, the torture became more gruesome and more explicit but the descriptions never reach the level of brutality displayed in the examples in the *SEL*. However, the greatest impact of these depictions of torture is not its presence or its application, but its failure. Torture was historically employed against accused heretics with the intention of extracting a confession and a recantation of heresy, but in hagiography the saints resist torture and do not recant, urging defiance despite the threat of torture, and perhaps unintentionally provoking resistance among heretics and potentially encouraging the rejection of Church authority. Torture in religious narratives became a double-edged sword as the Church waged its war against heresy and violated its own principles regulating the use of torture in ecclesiastical court proceedings, plummeting into corruption and abuse that would invariably spark further dissent and could be inverted to provide a model for heterodox sects against orthodox authority.[7]

---

[5] Caroline Walker Bynum, *The Resurrection of the Body in Western Christianity, 200–1336* (New York: Columbia University Press, 1995), p. 45 n. 95.
[6] Karen Winstead, *Virgin Martyrs: Legends of Sainthood in Late Medieval England* (Ithaca NY: Cornell University Press, 1997), p. 73.
[7] Torture in religious texts is also linked to cultural anxieties about suffering and questions of eternal punishment. Some of the most terrifying aspects of medieval religious literature are the visual representations of Hell that prey on the imagination and the guilt of the audience, warning both readers and recipients to adopt better lifestyles to avoid the infamous pit. Many of these divine torments were extracted from prevailing legal practice of the time, and the methods concurrent with medieval interrogation became the tools of eternal punishment in devotional art and literature. Peters writes, 'the new imperial protectors of Christianity had taken up a number of offenses against the Church and the faith and incorporated them into imperial criminal law, and they incorporated some of them, like heresy, into the stiffest

Literacy was relatively widespread among the laity of medieval Europe, and saints' lives often figured in the personal devotions of accused heretics well into the fifteenth century.[8] The Middle English *SEL* (1270–1280) evolved independently of Jacobus de Voragine's thirteenth-century *LgA* (1255–1266). The *LgA*, of which some one thousand manuscripts survive, was translated into French (*Legende dorée*, 1380–1480)[9] and Middle English (the *GiL*, c. 1438)[10] and later printed by William Caxton as *The Golden Legend* (1483).[11] These collections circulated widely and popularized legends devoted to the tribulations

parts of that law, the *crimina publica*.' 'Destruction of the Flesh', p. 135. However, Dante's use of torture in his depiction of Hell in the *Inferno* is beyond the scope of this study.

[8] See *Heresy and Literacy, 1000–1530*, ed. Peter Biller and Anne Hudson (Cambridge: Cambridge University Press, 1994). The essays in this volume provide detailed and compelling evidence of literacy among the medieval laity, and its role and influence on the development of heresy.

[9] Geneviève Hasenohr records the popularity of the *LgA* and its French vernacular translation the *Legende dorée* in northern France, an area relatively untouched by heresy, in her article 'Religious Reading amongst the Laity in France in the Fifteenth Century', in *Heresy and Literacy, 1000–1530*, ed. Biller and Hudson, pp. 205–21.

[10] Many of the *Gilte Legende* manuscripts refer to a Latin exemplar from which the story was translated, or as British Library MS Harley 630 says, 'drawen into englissh bi worthi clerkes and doctours of Diuinite suengly after þe tenure of þe Latin' [drawn into English by worthy clerks and doctors of divinity faithfully after the fashion of the Latin]. One manuscript, Bodleian Library MS Douce 372, says that the *Gilte Legende* is the English version of the Latin *Legenda Aurea*, 'which was drawen out of Frensshe into Englisshe the yere of oure lorde, a MCCCC and xxxviij bi a synfulle wrecche' [Which was drawn out of French into English, the year of our Lord 1438 by a sinful wretch]. The *Gilte Legende* is a product of translation and compilation, depending on the scribe who copied it. Harley MS 630 clearly says the material was translated directly from the Latin, while the Douce manuscript says it was translated from Latin to French and then into Middle English. This leads to a certain amount of variance in the contents of each manuscript as well as the text. These conflicting reports have been the starting point of many debates on the date and authorship, or rather translatorship, of the *Gilte Legende* as a whole.

[11] The *Legenda aurea* has been translated and edited by both William Granger Ryan and Christopher Stace. See: Jacobus de Voragine, *The Golden Legend: Readings on the Saints*, trans. and ed. William Granger Ryan, 2 vols. (Princeton NJ: Princeton University Press, 1993); and *The Golden Legend*, ed. Christopher Stace with an introduction by Richard Hamer (London: Penguin Books, 1998). Richard Hamer edited the lives of three male saints from all the *Gilte Legende* manuscripts in 1978. Auvo Kurvinen completed an edition of the life of Saint Katherine from seven manuscripts in 1958 for her Oxford DPhil thesis, which has never been published. Richard Hamer and Vida Russell have produced the critical edition of the *Gilte Legende* for the Early English Text Society, the final volume of which is forthcoming. See: *Three Lives from the Gilte Legende Edited from MS BL Egerton 876*, ed. Richard Hamer (Heidelberg: Universitätsverlag Carl Winter, 1978); *Gilte Legende*, ed. Richard Hamer with the assistance of Vida Russell, Vol. 1, EETS, os 327 (Oxford: Oxford University Press, 2006); *Gilte Legende*, ed. Richard Hamer with the assistance of Vida Russell, Vol. 2, EETS, os 328 (Oxford: Oxford University Press, 2007); and *Supplementary Lives in Some Manuscripts of the Gilte Legende*, ed. Richard Hamer and Vida Russell, EETS, os 315 (Oxford: Oxford University Press, 2000).

of saints, providing a scintillating spectacle of violence and torture. The *SEL* was assembled in the south-west Midlands during the second half of the thirteenth century and was revised and supplemented around 1380–90. There are more than sixty extant *SEL* manuscripts, and its adaptation of Latin material is marked by a specific attention to native English saints' lives, making it one of the best-represented works in Middle English, next to *Prick of Conscience*, the *Canterbury Tales*, and *Piers Plowman*.[12] Together these native legends relate the history of the English church from a time 'when Christianity was first brought to England by St Augustine [of Kent] up to the thirteenth century when the *SEL* was composed'.[13] As Klaus Jankofsky notes, its 'singularity consists in the new tone and mood of compassion and warm human empathy for the lives and deaths of its protagonists and in the pedagogic care and pastoral concern for its intended original audience, which seems to have consisted at one time of unlettered listeners, probably women'.[14] The *SEL* engages with its contemporary English audience by providing extensive details of local place names, laws, death duties, the situation of the poor, the rights of the Church versus the state, historical conflicts, particularly between the Old English and the Danes, as well as accounts of Old English kingdoms.[15] In these highly localized accounts, the brutality of judicial torture, which is primarily a formulaic motif in the Latin *LgA*, takes on an additional, national agenda considering the English prohibition against it. The tormentors are even *more* barbarous, even *more* alien to the English audience. The 'national characteristics' of the *SEL* 'the embedding of

---

[12] Winstead, *Virgin Martyrs*, pp. 71–2. For further information on the South English Legendary, see: Manfred Görlach, *The South English Legendary, Gilte Legende and Golden Legend* (Braunschweig: University, Braunschweiger Anglistische Arbeiten 3, 1972), reiterated in *Studies in Middle English Saints' Legends* (Heidelberg: Universitätsverlag Carl Winter, 1998); and Oliver Pickering, 'The Temporale Narratives of the South English Legendary', *Anglia* 91 (1973): 425–5; *The South English Ministry and Passion: Ed. from St. John's College, Cambridge, MS B.6*, Middle English Texts (Heidelberg: Universitätsverlag Carl Winter, 1984); and 'The outspoken South English Legendary poet', in *Late Medieval Religious Texts and Their Transmission: Essays in Honor of A.I. Doyle*, York Manuscripts Conference, ed. A.J. Minnis (Cambridge: D.S. Brewer, 1994) 21–37.

[13] Renee Hamelinck, 'St Kenhelm and the Legends of the *South English Legendary*', in *Companion to Early Middle English Literature*, ed. N.H.G.E. Veldhoen and H. Aertsen (Amsterdam: VU University Press, 1995) 19–28, p. 19.

[14] Klaus P. Jankofsky, 'National Characteristics in the Portrayal of English Saints in the *South English Legendary*', in *Images of Sainthood in Medieval Europe*, ed. Renate Blumenfeld-Kosinski and Timea Szell (Ithaca NY: Cornell University Press, 1991) 81–93, p. 83. There has been significant debate about the nature of the *SEL* audience, and while it has been agreed that it was composed for a lay audience, there is no agreement on the nature of that audience. Winstead, *Virgin Martyrs*, p. 72.

[15] Jankofsky, 'National Characteristics', p. 84. Also see: Jill Frederick, 'The *South English Legendary*: Anglo-Saxon Saints and National Identity', in *Literary Appropriations of the Anglo-Saxons from the Thirteenth to the Twentieth Century*, ed. Donald Scragg and Carole Weinberg, Cambridge Studies in Anglo-Saxon England (Cambridge: Cambridge University Press, 2000) 57–73.

information indicative of the English people and their culture at a given time, rather than national character traits,'[16] has its parallels in the romance *Havelok the Dane* (discussed in more detail in Chapter 4) and clearly situates the use of interrogatory torture and judicial brutality as an English concern.

Some of these lives contain direct references to political issues significant to establishing English identity apart from earlier ancestors (English/Danish conflicts) or the French, as in the anti-Norman sentiments in *Saint Wulfstan* in the account of the Battle of Hastings.[17] William is described as the 'Bastard' who 'þouȝte to winne Enguelond: þoruȝ strencþe and tricherie' and 'destruyde and nam al þat he fond: and þat folk sore aferde' (*SEL* 20:64–8).[18] Anti-Danish sentiment is particularly vehement in the life of King Edmund; the Danes are vicious murderers who 'slowen to grounde/ And robbeden and barnden al to nouȝt: and destruyden al þat huy/ founde' (*SEL* 44:10–12).[19] Hinguar, one of the leaders, is said to have slain 'al þat he miȝt of-gon/ ȝong and old, wyf and mayde: he sparede neuere on./ children fram heore moder breste: he drov and let heom quelle/ And al-to-hewe before þe moderes þat reuþe it was to telle;/ þare-After he let þe moderes a-sle: sorewe þare was I-nouȝ!' (*SEL* 44:21–5). The *SEL* is full of political and cultural commentaries, so its condemnation of torture should not be surprising. Specifically, the native saints are not subjected to the same litany of tortures as the Latin saints; they usually depart from 'the hagiographic schema of multiple tortures typical of the "Latin" martyrs, with perhaps Saint Alban [...] and Edmund the King (841–69) the exception.'[20] Though Edmund is not systematically and repeatedly tortured, he is beaten, shot full of arrows like Saint Sebastian and beheaded. Wulfstan does not die a martyr, but succumbs to a fever. His sanctity comes from his defiance of William and the miracles he is said to perform: 'the deaths of the English saints are put into a more concrete, historical framework, often with reference to political struggles in which the

---

16 Jankofsky, 'National Characteristics', p. 85.
17 Jankofsky, 'National Characteristics', p. 85.
18 *Saint Wulfstan*, in *The Early South-English Legendary or Lives of Saints, MS Laud 108 in the Bodleian Library*, ed. Carl Horstmann, EETS, os 87 (Oxford: Oxford University Press, 1887; reprinted 2000) 70–7.
19 *Saint Edmund, King*, in *The Early South-English Legendary or Lives of Saints, MS Laud 108 in the Bodleian Library*, ed. Carl Horstmann, EETS, os 87 (Oxford: Oxford University Press, 1887; reprinted 2000) 296–9. It is important to point out that two surviving manuscripts of the *SEL* were bound with romances in the fourteenth century: Bodleian Library MS Laud 108 includes the *SEL*, *Havelok the Dane* and *King Horn*; and King's College, Cambridge, MS 13 contains the *SEL* and *William of Palerne*. Since the earliest extant *SEL* manuscript also contains *Havelok*, and its compilation has been placed in areas populated by those of Anglo-Danish descent, similar issues of identifying the 'Other within' may exist in the anti-Danish sentiment of the *SEL* native lives. The anti-Danish tenor of *Edmund* contrasts sharply with the 'heroic' image of Havelok in MS Laud 108. This issue will be discussed in more detail in Chapter 4.
20 Jankofsky, 'National Characteristics', p. 89.

saints took part or to social injustices and ills that they tried to redress.'[21] Besides providing didactic models of piety and sanctity, the *SEL* presents clear models for defiance and resistance, either against torture in the largely fictitious lives of canonical saints or against the injustices of invaders, foreign Others, and corrupt authority in the native English narratives. Native saints' lives develop an idea of Englishness that is 'not limited to and does not depend on dynasty: by turning to the saintly past of England before the Norman Conquest, it imagines an English Christian identity that bypasses the crisis in dynastic authority and lineage' of thirteenth- and later fifteenth-century England, creating an idea of Englishness independent of the legitimacy of the current monarch.[22] Despite the brutality of these lives (which is remarkable), it is a 'characteristic of the entire *SEL* that it attempts to provide didactic instruction that is both profitable and pleasant and that this endeavour shows signs of the same "delightful Englishness" that scholars appreciate in Chaucer'.[23] Like the works of Chaucer which respond in their own way to excesses in judicial violence, these texts highlight the alien nature of torture and brutality – it is the Danes, the Normans, or the pagan judges of old who perpetuate such violence, and it is up to the steadfast and pious to resist it, and even to resist the Church in Rome if necessary. Embedded deeply within that 'Englishness' is a cultural aversion to torture that persists through the *GiL*.

In addition to the *SEL*, the *LgA* provided the most complete and comprehensive model for hagiographical collections. Jacobus de Voragine, in turn, took his legends from a variety of sources, sometimes using the works of Church Fathers such as Saint Ambrose and Saint Jerome as his basis, other times constructing his narratives from fragmentary pieces in martyrologies and calendars of saints.[24] In hagiography, placing the use of torture in the past serves as a model for the present – a model of defiance by which English hagiographers defined themselves; 'late medieval writers and readers recognized what was at stake in representing or reading the present as a continuation of, or departure

---

[21] Jankofsky, 'National Characteristics', p. 89.
[22] Sanock, *Her Life Historical*, p. 84.
[23] Jankofsky, 'National Characteristics', p. 90.
[24] Richard Hamer, 'Introduction', in Jacobus de Voragine, *The Golden Legend*, ed. Christopher Stace (London: Penguin Books, 1998), p. x. Jacobus left a list of his major works, six in total, in his *Chronicle of Genoa*, probably written between 1295 and 1297. These works include the *Chronicle* itself, the *LgA*, a *Marialis*, and three volumes of sermons. The popular saints of the liturgical calendar comprise his collection, and he includes the most up-to-date lives of the most recent saints, including Elizabeth of Hungary who died in 1231. Due to the overriding desire for current material, many of the legends vary in style, length, and content; for example, in *Saint Elizabeth*, Jacobus may have turned to the most readily available material, the official documentation of her canonization, to write her legend. Hamer, 'Introduction', *The Golden Legend*, p. xii. Jacobus acknowledges his three main sources as the *Ecclesiastical History* of Eusebius, the *Tripartite History* of Cassiodorus, and the *Scholastic History* of Peter Comestor. Jacobus also says that he adds many things of his own, asserting his own role in shaping the legends and their material to his own purposes.

from, the past'.[25] The extraordinary brutality of the SEL Roman legends engages in a discourse of Englishness by locating torture and brutality not only outside the physical boundaries of England, but outside the temporal boundaries of the thirteenth century. This pattern is followed by the fifteenth-century GiL, which also includes a mix of native and Roman saints. The legends suggest that this kind of interrogatory and punitive torture belongs to the barbarian Other represented by the pagan Roman authorities and to an earlier, primitive time.

The majority of saints' legends may deal in fiction by modern definitions but to the medieval reader they were accepted as historical accounts, however fantastic.[26] The fact that many of these lives are highly formulaic fictional inventions should not detract from their powerful presence in the collections of hagiography; these saints are potent symbols of resistance to corrupt authority as historical figures defying tyranny by enduring torture.[27] In reality, withstanding such a litany of torments would be unthinkable, but hagiography provides models for how it *may* be done by those with enough spiritual fortitude. Audience response to these legends could not be homogeneous or uniform: some may have found them necessary for elevating the holiness of the saint; others may have revelled in the violence of these episodes out of a voyeuristic sadism; others still may have empathized with the saints, hoping to emulate them in their steadfastness and endurance. Audiences of hagiography ranged from the literate to illiterate, noble to merchant, cleric to courtier. Hagiography filled all these needs for emotive response but also vilified the very institution that encouraged their production.

The stories were extremely popular, 'retold with gusto', and in the retelling, 'horrors became more horrible, even as triumph over pain, decay and fragmentation became more impressive and more improbable'.[28] Beth Crachiolo argues that the martyrological narratives of the SEL function 'more as audience entertainment than as didactic models of the Christian life' because they lack 'doctrinal teachings', and that the torture and brutality are a major component of their 'entertain-

---

[25] Sanock, *Her Life Historical*, p. xv.

[26] Jane Tibbetts Schulenburg examines the validity of saints' lives as historical record in her article 'Saints' Lives as a Source for the History of Women, 500–1100', in *Medieval Women and the Sources of Medieval History*, ed. Joel T. Rosenthal (Athens GA: University of Georgia Press, 1990) 285–320, and in her study on female sanctity, *Forgetful of Their Sex: Female Sanctity and Society ca. 500–1100* (Chicago: University of Chicago Press, 1998).

[27] Their role as icons of saintly behaviour is important considering some of the strictures placed on women's behaviour in the Middle Ages, because it removes them from the traditional place as homemaker and childbearer. Many of these legends openly defy those roles, promoting a chosen life of religious contemplation instead. The legends also show that many of the disparities in rights and freedoms were based on class and not gender, for wealthy women were much more likely and able to leave their mark on literature and history than poor women who were more concerned with feeding their families than contributing to the lasting impression of medieval society.

[28] Bynum, *Fragmentation and Redemption*, p. 269.

ment function.'[29] Crachiolo's suggestion plays into many modern misconceptions about medieval torture and denies the very real aesthetic effect these narratives were designed to have. Vernacular hagiography is particularly important for understanding that the 'constitutive relationship between literary form and social institutions works in the other direction as well: narrative traditions themselves construct a relationship to social practices and particular communities through fictions of address and ideal response'.[30] While one of the distinguishing features of the *SEL* is its graphic description of torture, 'which by far exceeds what we find in both the *Legenda aurea* and in most contemporary vernacular legends',[31] the narratives can be read as a reaction against that torture rather than a celebration of it – a reaction grounded in a sense of English identity. For English audiences of the *SEL* and *GiL*, the torturers in these narratives are truly the Other because of the actual English legal prohibition against judicial torture; historically, those who employ torture are breaking English law (especially the spirit of it) and could expect popular dissent and perhaps even rebellion and so literary representations reflect historical transgression.

The *SEL* was compiled after the first major wave of heretical extermination on the Continent, and at a time when French interests controlled the papacy. At the end of the thirteenth century, there was a succession of French popes, Urban IV (1261–1264), Clement IV (1265–1268), the Blessed Innocent V (1276), and Martin IV (1281–1285) before the papacy relocated to Avignon during the tenure of Clement V (1305–1314). The Avignon papacy saw seven more French popes, and English audiences may have seen the barbarity of torture as a product of French papal control and a corrupting influence that should be resisted. The *GiL* circulated at a time when the countries of Europe fought among themselves and within their own borders. The Wars of the Roses (1450–1470) of the English nobility rumbled on and heterodox theologies that began in the fourteenth century instigated a new wave of religious persecution. Gender roles were challenged as women, such as Elizabeth Woodville, the wife of the Yorkist king Edward IV, and Margaret of Anjou, Henry VI's queen, exercised a great deal of power and influence. In this climate of struggle and change the *GiL* was translated, compiled and disseminated, a prescient reminder of the role of religion, faith and defiance in the face of tyranny and oppression.

The *SEL* and *GiL* circulated freely in the vernacular at a time when translating biblical texts was considered heresy; the exemplarity of these legends and the defiance of the saints may have inspired a certain amount of heterodoxy. Some of the most prolific heterodox sects like the Waldensians and the Cathars spread hastily-made vernacular translations of the New Testament and the Prophets, and gave their own words credibility by attributing them to '"the

---

[29] Crachiolo, 'Female and Male Martyrs', pp. 151, 148.
[30] Sanock, *Her Life Historical*, p. xi.
[31] Winstead, *Virgin Martyrs*, p. 73.

writings of such and such a saint or doctor'".[32] The Church was very effective in its brutal repression of the Albigensian heresy and other heterodox movements. But in promoting martyrdom literature and the veneration of early Christian saints who defied secular and religious authority, and who resisted conversion or reversion to paganism by withstanding savage tortures designed to extract a recantation of Christianity, the Church also inadvertently provided potential models of defiance to the very sects it was trying to eliminate. It is one of the paradoxes, like women preachers, with which the Church was confronted in its promotion of vernacular hagiography. If the early saints were to be venerated for facing down the corrupt authority of pagan judges, then thirteenth-, fourteenth-, and fifteenth-century dissenters could take their strength and their resistance from those orthodox exempla – particularly in England.

Vocal Defiance and Models of Resistance

The legends of these violent deaths are written as 'historical' accounts, but the hagiographic collections contain anachronistic details about the persecution of early Christian martyrs more reminiscent of the medieval period than second- and third-century Rome, evoking contemporary anxieties for audiences familiar with the potential abuses of the authorities. As Martha Easton notes in terms of the Huntington *LgA*, the criminal justice practices of the medieval period 'offer striking evidence that the martyrdom scenes, both textual and visual [...] would have had particular resonance for a contemporary viewer'.[33] She points out that in hagiography, public ceremonies of torture and execution were 'conceived as lavish spectacles of power, confirming an authoritative right to mete out punishment in public on a grand scale'[34]; however, in hagiography that power is portrayed as illegitimate and corrupt. The resort to torture is destabilizing and potentially dangerous – inciting audience response against authoritarian rule, which then resorts to more brutality to keep its illusory order. The addition of medieval torture motifs to earlier Christian narratives during the course of the Middle Ages reflects the introduction of torture in medieval jurisprudence, and perhaps serves as a response to increased abuses among ecclesiastical authori-

---

[32] Raymonde Foreville and Jean Rousset de Pina, *Du premier concile du Latran à l'avènement d'Innocent III* (Paris: Librairie Bloud & Gay, 1953) 342–3; Bernard Gui, *Manuel de l'Inquisiteur*, ed. G. Mollat (Paris: Champion, 1926), trans. Mary Martin McLaughlin, in James Bruce Ross and Mary Martin McLaughlin, *The Portable Medieval Reader* (New York: The Viking Press, 1949) 202–16; qtd. in Jeffrey Burton Russell, ed., *Religious Dissent in the Middle Ages* (New York: John Wiley and Sons, 1971), p. 42; p. 50.

[33] Martha Easton, 'Pain, Torture and Death in the Huntington Library *Legenda aurea*', in *Gender and Holiness: Men, Women and Saints in Late Medieval Europe*, ed. Samantha J.E. Riches and Sarah Salih, Routledge Studies in Medieval Religion and Culture (London and New York: Routledge, 2002) 49–64, p. 55.

[34] Easton, 'Pain, Torture and Death', p. 55.

ties whose grip on the religious populace was tenuous at times. Saint Christina, whose life appears in the *SEL* and the *GiL*, is one of the most forceful and vocal saints, defending her body and her religion against a traditional authority that attempts not only to force a religious recantation from her, but also to silence her completely. She challenges not only the authority of the pagan Roman prelates but also the paternal authority wielded by her father.[35] Her defiance rocks the very foundations of patriarchal authority structures (religious and secular), causing a great deal of turmoil within the narrative as various male authority figures struggle to silence this impetuous and seemingly indestructible young woman.

Saint Christina

Following the traditional pattern of youth and nobility, Christina is born in Tyro, Italy, to noble parents who lock her in a tower. She is sought after by many young suitors but her father insists on dedicating her to pagan religious service instead. While locked in her tower surrounded by gold and silver idols, Christina is taught by the Holy Spirit to dread these gods. She rebels against her duties, hiding the incense for the pagan rituals in a window alcove and refusing to participate in them, defying her father's commands and the religious expectations of her society. She is subjected to a litany of tortures: she is beaten, stripped, scourged, shackled by the neck in prison, hung up; her flesh is ripped off, she is cast into a furnace, healed, thrown into the sea with a stone around her neck, rescued by Jesus, scourged again, boiled in oil, cast into an oven for three days; snakes are thrown at her, her breasts are cut off, her tongue is cut out and she is stabbed in the side before she finally yields her spirit.

The *GiL* version of *Christina* follows the *LgA* very closely while the *SEL* expands a number of the scenes between Christina and her father and emphasizes the brutality of her torments. In both texts, Christina's response to the myriad of tortures inflicted upon her by her father and two other judges is vocally defiant, but rather than simply renouncing this violence against her, after being beaten she taunts the men for failing in their strength and urges them to pray to their gods to sustain them in punishing her: 'And thanne saide Cristen to her fader: "O thou withe oute worshipp or shame and abhominable to God, seest thou not hou þei faylen? Praie thi goddes that [they] yeue hem vertu and strength."' (*GiL* 28–30).[36] Infused with divine strength, Christina is endowed with religious authority to denounce her father and resist any of his actions against her. He turns from father figure to civil authority, and what was paternal prodding and punishment now becomes a matter for public trial.

---

[35] The implications of gender and torture will be discussed in more depth later in this chapter.

[36] All quotations of the *GiL Christina* are from Richard Hamer and Vida Russell's edition: *Gilte Legende*, Vol. 1, EETS, os 327 (Oxford: Oxford University Press, 2006) 483–6. Line numbers are given in parenthesis.

In the English vernacular, these scenes of torture would have been particularly striking to an audience for whom torture was a legal anathema and justice rested with a jury system. Mirroring the legal precedent of both Roman law and medieval jurisprudence, hagiographic torture is only threatened in the public venue of the court once the accused have proven unrelenting in their opposition to authority and in their refusal to recant or confess. Christina's father, now acting as the civil judge, orders her to perform her religious devotions or face being disowned as well as tortured: "'Sacrafice to oure goddes or elles thou shalt suffre diuerse tormentes and thou shalt no more be called my doughter." And Cristin ansuered hym and saide, "Now hast thou do me a gret grace sithe I shall no more be called the deuelys doughter, for he that is born of the deuel is the deuel, and thou art fader of the same Sathanase.'" (*GiL* 40–5). She decries him as an agent of Satan, and essentially challenges him to try and wrest back that authority and control. At this point, the torture begins in earnest; her father orders her flesh to be torn with hooks and 'all her membres tore from other' (*GiL* 46–7). Without displaying any pain, or even pausing at the brutal treatment of her body, 'Þis maide gripte pece and oþer [and] fram hure body rende/ And caste hure uader aȝen þe teþ [and] almest him ablende (*SEL* 157–8).[37] She cries 'þou vnwreste uode/ And fret al rau þi nowe fleiss and þin owe blode/ For þou nere neure uol monnes fleiss to drawe/ þer þou miȝt of þin owene inou bo[þ]e frete [and] gnawe' (*SEL* 159–62). In the *GiL*, Christina 'toke an handefull of her flesshe and threw it to her fader and saide, "Holde, thou tyraunt, and ete the flesshe that þou hast gote"' (*GiL* 48–9). She renounces him now, not only as her father but as a representative of the civil authority that allows judges to torture young women who refuse to be controlled. Her father's attempts at re-establishing the social power structure have failed and he resorts to more and more brutal torments in his unsuccessful efforts to subdue her and force her to submit. He orders her broken on a wheel under which is placed oil and fire, but a great flame leaps out and kills 1500 of the men witnessing the brutality against her – by participating in the spectacle as a receptive audience the onlookers are a party to the injustice done to Christina; unlike the audience of the contemporary legend *Agatha*, no one rebels or tries to stop it so they are all consumed by flames. In the *SEL* version of *Christina*, female witnesses to Elius' torture of Christina chastise him for being so brutal to a woman: "'Iustice" hi seide "þou art an vnwreste man/ Þat þou so ssenfolliche defoulest a womman/ In ssennesse of alle oþere boþe nou and er/ Alas þat eny womman so luþer mon ber'" (*SEL* 243–6). They criticize his wickedness, potentially representing the cultural witnesses of England and voicing the hagiographer's concerns about judicial torture.

A litany of torments and trials follow: Christina is thrown into the sea with a

---

[37] *Saint Christina, The South English Legendary Corpus Christi College Cambridge MS 145 and British Museum MS Harley 2277*, ed. Charlotte D'Evelyn and Anna J. Mill, Vol. 2, EETS, os 235 (Oxford: Oxford University Press, 1956, rpt. 1967) 315–27. Line numbers are given in parenthesis.

millstone around her neck, returned to land by divine intervention, thrown into a huge iron cauldron filled with burning oil, pitch and tar, where she simply feels as though 'she shulde be rocked in a cradell as a childe' (GiL 72–3). Her head is shaved and she is led naked to the temple of Apollo where she destroys the idol, and charms snakes sent against her to rebound on her tormentors and kill them instead. When all their attempts to break her or kill her fail, the judge Julianus turns his wrath back on her body:

> And thanne Iulian comaunded that she shulde haue her brestes cutte of, and oute of hem come melke in stede of blood. And aftre that, he made her tungge [to] be cutte of, but she lost neuer her speche therfor but she toke the pece of her tungge that was cutte of and threwe it in the iugez visage and smote oute bothe hys eyen therwithe. (GiL 90–5)

Christina is subjected to torments that target her gender, but rather than simply emphasizing the brutal mutilation of a young female body, they heighten the barbarism of the judges who successively increase the severity of their tortures each time they fail without recognizing the futility of such violence, and who are demonic in their frenzied attempts to harm her.

Like most virgin martyr narratives *Saint Christina* is very brief, but full of forceful, aggressive dialogue between Saint Christina and her various tormentors as she withstands one torture after another. She endures far more ordeals than many of her fellow martyrs, like Lucy and Agnes, and does so with eloquence and dignity. For a female saint, whose role as a woman is traditionally one of silence, her speech elevates her above the societal constraints of her gender but also voices opposition to the cruelty of pagan authority manifested in the repeated attempts to make her suffer.[38] In this narrative, the tyrant is demonized for his brutality and indicted for resorting to torture; it is an eloquent rejection of religious tyranny and provides potentially damning evidence against using torture in the judicial process and (perhaps unwittingly) provides a model for further defiance against the Christian Church whose torture methods resemble those used against the martyr.

Christina's speech is authoritative enough to overthrow pagan gods, drive out serpents – the symbols of Satan and the fall – and raise the dead (GiL 89) without supplicating Christ.[39] Her prayers are never mentioned; she demonstrates her own ability and authority to carry out God's will through her speech.[40] The judge Julianus commands that her tongue be cut out because it appears to be the root of her power but, significantly, that does not stop her from speaking

---

[38] Larissa Tracy, 'Silence and Speech in the Female Lives of the *Gilte Legende* and Their Influence on the Lives of Ordinary Medieval Women', in *Women of the Gilte Legende: A Selection of Middle English Saints' Lives*, ed. Larissa Tracy, The Library of Medieval Women (Cambridge: D.S. Brewer, 2003) 101–27, p. 111.
[39] Tracy, 'Silence and Speech', p. 111.
[40] Tracy, 'Silence and Speech', p. 111.

or from blinding him with the severed organ. In the *SEL*, it is Julianus who throws the severed tongue, not Christina, as he rants about 'hure speech' (329):

> He þo3te for heure holy word do a feble wreche
> He let kerue of hure tonge faste bi þe more
> And 3ute spake þis holy maide noþe later þereuore
> Ferst he nom hure holi tonge wiþ wel stordi mod
> And þis Iustice harde þreu as heo biuore him stod
> Þis tonge sprong al abrod al þis men iseie
> And þis Iustice harde smot [and] hutte out eiþer-ei3e. (*SEL* 330–6)

What she says is not mentioned, but when Julianus hurls the tongue, 'the narrative returns explicitly to sight, as the tongue blinds the tormentor and turns *him* into a spectacle'.[41] Those additional scenes are absent from the *GiL*; Christina is given complete agency in her speech; and in the absence of the female witnesses, Christina is the sole voice raised in opposition to her torture. Christina does not succumb meekly to the blows of the executioner but must be grievously tortured and shot with arrows (or stabbed, depending on the version) in order to finally receive her crown of martyrdom – and even when she is being boiled, her voice triumphs as she sings with the angels for five days. In her unwavering devotion and relentless defiance, Christina becomes a shield for Christianity, a steadfast line of defence in the face of pagan persecution, like all virgin martyrs of her time whose lives were recorded as hagiography.[42] But the brutality of her narrative also indicts corrupt authorities, religious and secular, which abandon justice and jurisprudence by giving free reign to violence. Her power manifests in her words and her resistance to torture. By continuing to speak and affirm her faith, Christina undermines the religious authority that initially questions her and in their repeated and desperate attempts to exercise control over her through violence, the judges forgo any semblance of questioning. What had been an interrogative process seemingly within the boundaries of law becomes a frenzy of brutality. In the text, the law has subverted itself through its excessive and unjust application of torture and the authorities end up destroying only themselves.

Like their female counterparts, some of the male martyrs were venerated by heretical sects for their steadfast refusal to give in to illegitimate authority. The *Passau Anonymous* complains that Waldensians used Laurence as an exemplar for the lay administration of the Eucharist;[43] and in Caesarius of Heisterbach's account of the burning of heretics in Cologne, the heretical leader Arnold places his hand on the heads of his dying disciples and invokes St Laurence, a comparison Caesarius rejects: '"Stand fast in your faith, for this day you shall be with

---

[41] Crachiolo, 'Female and Male Martyrs', p. 161.
[42] Kathleen Coyne Kelly, *Performing Virginity and Testing Chastity in the Middle Ages* (London: Routledge, 2000), p. 13.
[43] The Passau Anonymous: *On the Origins of Heresy and the Sect of the Waldensians*, in *Heresy and Authority in Medieval Europe: Documents in Translation*, ed. Edward Peters (Philadelphia: University of Pennsylvania Press, 1980) 150–63, p. 159.

Laurence," and yet they were very far from the faith of Laurence'.[44] Laurence is one of a few male saints tortured in a similar manner to the female virgin martyrs; he resists through equally vocal defiance, and in the same way, the narrative of his death provides subversive material to opponents of church authority.

Saint Laurence

In his legend, Laurence is subjected to torture by the provost Valerian under the Emperor Decius; however, it is the Emperor Valerian (AD 253–60) who ordered the persecution of Sixtus and his deacons in AD 258.[45] As Jocelyn Wogan-Browne and Glyn Burgess note, Valerian's edict specified immediate execution of these men if caught, so 'much of the narrative of Laurence's imprisonment and torture is apocryphal'.[46] The episodes of torture are necessary to emphasize the strength and steadfast resistance of Laurence, just as they are with Agatha and Christina, because when saintly bodies remain intact and unharmed, or are triumphantly reconstituted after torture, 'they function as powerful signs of integrity an wholeness, of triumph over dismemberment and death'.[47] For his refusal to yield the material wealth of the Church to the authorities, distributing it instead among the poor, he is beaten severely and repeatedly with various implements and finally roasted to death on a gridiron.

In the SEL and GiL, Laurence's life (like *Christina*) reads very much like the trial transcript of an accused heretic. He is brought before the emperor and his provost, he is questioned, he refuses to yield the answers they want (one of the inquisitors even converts in an effort to gain the earthly treasure), but finally Laurence is threatened with and subjected to torture when all other questioning fails. He curses them for their brutality: "'þov wrechche," seide þis holie man: "mi wille hath euere i-beo/ For-to come to þis murie solas: þat ich here nouþe i-seo./ Wel mo tormenz þane here beoth: to þe beoth i-mad al-ȝare/ In þe pine of helle: ȝwane ich schal to þe Ioye of heue ne fare"' (SEL 108–11).[48] As in the

---

[44] Caesarius of Heisterbach, *Dialogue on Miracles: At the Stake*, in *Heresy and Authority in Medieval Europe: Documents in Translation*, ed. Peters, 193–4, p. 193.

[45] The legend of Saint Laurence is usually told in conjunction with that of Saint Sixtus and the other deacons who accompanied him to Rome. A native of Spain, Laurence is known to be a historical figure but the version of his life that forms the basis for the legend in the LgA and GiL is largely apocryphal. It was a popular legend, as Laurence was a popular saint, and there are extant versions outside of the major hagiographical collections, including an Anglo-Norman text that was commissioned by a woman. *Virgin Lives and Holy Deaths: Two Exemplary Biographies for Anglo-Norman Women*, trans. Jocelyn Wogan-Browne and Glyn S. Burgess (London: J.M. Dent, Everyman, 1996).

[46] Wogan-Browne and Burgess, 'Introduction', in *Virgin Lives and Holy Deaths*, p. xxxvi.

[47] Wogan-Browne and Burgess, *Virgin Lives and Holy Deaths*, p. xiii.

[48] All SEL quotations from *Saint Laurence* are from *The Early South-English Lengendary or Lives of Saints, MS Laud 108 in the Bodleian Library*, ed. Carl Horstmann, EETS, os 87 (Oxford: Oxford University Press, 1887; reprinted 2000) 340–5. Line numbers are given in parenthesis.

female saints' lives, the description of these torments is cold and dispassionate as Decius commands that 'he shulde be bete with scourges and that alle maner turmentes were brought before hym' (*GiL* 133–4).[49] Even though Laurence's body is not an object of sexual desire he is stripped naked like some of his female counterparts and beaten 'withe yerdes and withe staues, and peces of brenninge iren were sette faste to hys sydes' (*GiL* 141–2). This is a continuous process but Laurence remains constant. The *GiL* version downplays his suffering, unlike the *SEL* which makes it explicit, and Laurence pleads with God to release him and receive his spirit. A heavenly voice replies for all to hear, '"Many turmentes be dewe to the yet" (*GiL* 152), signalling that the saint is not allowed to give up, but must continue to endure (which pleases him), and so he adopts a rather jocular attitude for the rest of the process.

In the face of repeated tortures, Laurence is not as vocal as the virgin martyrs, though his final words are defiant and he resists the desires of the corrupt emperor and his minions. When he is stretched out on the gridiron, placed over burning coals and turned with fire forks, there is no divine intervention, nor do the flames reach out into the crowd burning the witnesses for their complicity. The *SEL* describes the process in detail, but also makes the point that he *suffers*,[50] whereas most female martyrs feel nothing:

> Þe tormentores stoden al-a-boute: and bleowen þat fuyr wel faste;
> with Irene pikes huy pulten him: and schouen In faste a-boue.
> Louerd, muche was þe pyne: þat he soffrede for þi loue!
> Þat fuyr bi-neoþe rostede him: al quic mid flesch and blode,
> And þe Irene pikes in is flesch: ful bitterliche huy wode. (*SEL* 157–61)

This is Laurence's desired martyrdom, and he meets it gladly relishing his suffering: '"Vnderstonde, thou cursed wreche, and see how the coles yeue me refresshinge, and to the euerlasting turment, and oure Lorde knowithe that I haue be accused and haue not renyed hym, and whanne I haue be examyned I haue confessed Ihesu Crist, and I rosted, yelde thankingges to oure Lorde Ihesu Crist'" (*GiL* 184–9). The emphasis in this scene is on Laurence's ability to stand up to interrogation and endure torture without recanting his true belief. He has been accused, he has stood firm, and the only confession he gives is his Christian testimony. The brutal form of execution mirrors the earlier torments of female saints and depicts the Roman authorities as unjust and cruel.[51] The

---

[49] All *GiL* quotations from *Lawrence* are taken from Richard Hamer and Vida Russell's edition: *Gilte Legende*, Vol. 2 EETS, os 328 (Oxford: Oxford University Press, 2007) 552–60. Line numbers are given in parenthesis.
[50] As Winstead notes, 'Despite their graphic representation of torture and dismemberment, however, late medieval artists rarely suggest that the saints suffer. In this respect, the iconography of martyrdom differs from the iconography of the Passion which was so profoundly concerned with Christ's agony.' *Virgin Martyrs*, p. 88.
[51] There is some levity in his final words to Decius when he taunts him to finish his cooking:

rest of *Laurence* involves miracles performed at his tomb with his intervention or by his relics, so the actual scenes of torture are circumscribed compared with the accounts in *Christina*. But the emotive impact is the same: the pious saint endures torture at the hands of a corrupt authority that employs it not out of a sense of justice or law, but to serve its own foul ends, abusing its power. The torture methods applied would be recognizable to a medieval audience as the tools of the papal inquisitors who were known to have crossed a few boundaries of their own. Thus, like his female counterparts, Laurence provides a potential model for resistance against inquisitorial authority and denounces any power that would resort to torture as a means of control.

The image of demonically-inspired torturers relentless in their desire to force a confession through any and every means provides a sinister model of corrupt authorities against which the pious and faithful should rebel, but that may mean resisting the orthodox authority of the Church. Even though secular authorities were often called in to administer punishment or extract confessions when the clerical prohibition against drawing blood interfered with the interrogatory process, clergy would employ torture and then absolve themselves, justifying the practice as vital to the proceedings.[52] The significant aspect of torture in medieval Christian texts is its application by pagan authorities against Christian saints. Torture becomes one of the defining factors separating pagan and apostate tyranny from Christian authority – only pagans would employ such barbaric means against innocents. Torture enhances pagan brutality and intensifies the sanctity of the martyr's sacrifice, but it is a dangerous precedent, for in employing torture in its judicial procedures the Church allies itself with its doctrinal enemies. Hagiographical accounts of saints who vocally oppose their pagan persecutors, welcoming torture and death, bear an eerie resemblance to medieval trial transcripts where condemned heretics denounce Church authorities, embracing martyrdom like their early Christian predecessors.

Peter Waldo, or Valdes (c. 1140–c. 1218), founder of the Waldensian sect, denied the Communion of the saints but believed 'every just man had the power of preaching the Gospel, absolving of sin and presiding over the Lord's Supper'.[53] The Waldensians lived the actions of the saints, even though they rejected the Communion because they, like many saints, believed the common man could carry and transmit the word of God. Bernard Gui complained in his fourteenth-century *Practica officii inquisitionis* or *Manual for Inquisitors* (1322/3) that the 'erring followers and sacrilegious masters of this sect' claim they are not subject to the papal authorities, and declare that 'the Roman Church has persecuted

---

"'Thou cursed, thou hast rosted that one syde, turne that other and ete it'" (*GiL* f. 182r: 189–90). His defiance in the face of his imminent death echoes Christina's sentiments when she throws her mutilated flesh at her father, daring him to eat what he has begotten.
[52] Dunbabin, *Captivity and Imprisonment*, p. 153.
[53] Russell, *Religious Dissent in the Middle Ages*, p. 42.

and condemned them unjustly and undeservedly'.[54] In withstanding their own persecution the Waldensians, and later the Cathars, emulated the steadfastness of saints proclaiming that they were following God's commands to the apostles; according to Gui, they boldly declared themselves to be the imitators and successors of the apostles, 'by a false profession of poverty and the feigned image of sanctity'.[55] David of Augsburg, writing on the Waldensians of Bavaria in 1270, complained that members of this sect picked out the words of Church Fathers and short passages from their books 'in order to prove their illusions and to resist us'.[56] These heretics, according to David, dressed up their 'sacrilegious doctrine with fair passages from the saints; but they pass over in silence those passages of saints which seem to contradict them, and by which their error is refuted'.[57] They taught each other 'to repeat' the Gospels, the sayings of the apostles and other saints 'by heart, in the vulgar tongue, so that they may know how to teach others and lead the faithful astray'.[58]

The *Passau Anonymous*, a tract detailing the heresy of the Waldensians, confirms that they rejected belief in the saints, their legends and passions, and yet their defiance of temporal authority mirrors the language of these narratives: 'They condemn judges and princes and claim that malefactors are not condemned. Their occasion for this is that princes and judges are tyrants ... and that justice is venal in the tribunals of laity and clergy alike.'[59] The use of torture against accused heretics reinforced a connection to earlier saints and encouraged further resistance. Until the end of the thirteenth century, 'investigations, including those against heresy, were on the whole restrained by judicial precedent and rules. But Boniface VIII's *Liber Sextus* (1298) overturned some of the earlier restraints.'[60] As these restraints and safeguards against abuse were relaxed, torture was used more frequently in the interests of expediting proceedings and hastening a 'favourable' outcome: 'Confession by a suspect (under any circumstance, including threat of torture), was legally acceptable in lieu of formal charge'.[61] Ordinarily in judicial proceedings a confession or the testimony of at least two eyewitnesses was needed for a conviction, but eyewitnesses were often unobtainable and the accused was pressured to confess under torture or threat

---

[54] Gui, *Manuel de l'Inquisiteur*, qtd. in Russell, *Religious Dissent in the Middle Ages*, p. 44. See also: Russell, *Dissent and Order*, p. 71.

[55] Gui, *Manuel de l'Inquisiteur*, qtd. in Russell, *Religious Dissent in the Middle Ages*, p. 43.

[56] David of Augsburg, *On the Waldensians of Bavaria, 1270*, in *Heresy and Authority in Medieval Europe: Documents in Translation*, ed. Peters, 149–50, p. 150.

[57] David of Augsburg, *On the Waldensians of Bavaria, 1270*, p. 150.

[58] David of Augsburg, *On the Waldensians of Bavaria, 1270*, p. 150.

[59] *The Passau Anonymous*, *Heresy and Authority in Medieval Europe*, p. 163.

[60] Jeffrey Burton Russell, *Dissent and Order in the Middle Ages: The Search for Legitimate Authority*, Twayne Studies in Intellectual and Cultural History (New York: Twayne, 1992), p. 71.

[61] Russell, *Dissent and Order*, p. 71.

of torture.[62] Though the original reasons for this were grounded in the interests of the general public and the salvation of the confessed heretic, these practices inevitably led to abuses where the authorities would force a confession in order to confiscate the property of the accused.[63] In turn, these abuses may have led to more widespread but subtle dissent within the body of institutionally sanctioned religious literature. Where the pagan judges were condemned for their fraudulent trials and their recourse to torture in literature, so too could the populace condemn civil and ecclesiastical authorities that subverted the law for financial gain. The fiscal advantage to confiscating property 'presented a powerful impetus to loosen procedure, especially in a time of growing government with its attendant bureaucracy and need for revenue'.[64]

The reliance on torture as a means of eliciting confessions and harsher punishments for convicted heretics was not a drastic change in the law, rather a change in practice, 'which became more permissive to the prosecution and less fair to the defendant'.[65] Daniel Baraz notes that Nicolaus Eymeric's manual for inquisitors 'does not refer to torture as problematic or as related to cruelty' and that torture, in a legal sense was not considered cruel, suggesting perhaps that torture was accepted as part of the discovery of truth and therefore necessary, and that legal violence is 'never perceived as cruel from within the system'.[66] However, cruelty manifested in the application of torture could also be subversive. Baraz convincingly argues that 'the actions of inquisitors, when viewed apart from the justifying ideological context, could seem cruel as well as dangerously similar to the actions of ancient persecutors'.[67] In this climate, the potential for civil and religious authorities to subvert legal practice to their own ends by employing torture may well have met with opposition among the populace (both literate and illiterate), and that opposition may well have found an outlet in the very literature that was intended to promote and reinforce orthodox doctrine.

The inquisitors' guides were not a wholesale licence to torture either. The thirteenth-century *Tractatus de tormentis*, attributed to Guido Suzzara, places specific limits on torture, urging the avoidance of *excessive* torture, and outlining the judge's liability if he fails to observe this limit.[68] According to the publisher's foreword of a modern English translation of Bernard Gui's manual, in seventeen years of service (1307–24) Gui seems to have pronounced 536 judgments which show him to be 'more interested in penitence than punishment: he sentenced

---

[62] Russell, *Dissent and Order*, p. 71.
[63] Russell, *Dissent and Order*, p. 71.
[64] Russell, *Dissent and Order*, p. 71.
[65] Russell, *Dissent and Order*, p. 71.
[66] Baraz, *Medieval Cruelty*, p. 27.
[67] Baraz, *Medieval Cruelty*, p. 176.
[68] Baraz, *Medieval Cruelty*, p. 27.

45 to death (three by burning)'.[69] Nonetheless, his advice and instructions 'carry chilling echoes of other totalitarian regimes – true penitence can be proved, forgiveness won, by turning in the names, *all* the names, of other offenders'.[70] However, James Givens points out that Languedocian inquisitors, including Gui, saw imprisonment rather than torture as an integral component of interrogation strategies, and he further notes that the inquisitors in Languedoc rarely used torture to extract confessions.[71] There was resistance to the implementation of these judicial proceedings especially where there were abuses; opponents of the inquisitors 'not infrequently produced petitions and complaints directed to popes and kings'.[72] There is a clear contradiction in the prevalence of torture in hagiography; rather than mimicking actual practice or reinforcing a status quo, the saints' lives *defy* it by exaggerating it, challenging medieval authorities (as much as the narrative antagonists) to do their worst, even satirizing torture in the farcical portrayal of judges who go mad at the ineffectualness of their efforts.[73]

The relationship between torture and orthodoxy and the application of

---

[69] Publisher's foreword, *The Inquisitor's Guide: A Medieval Manual on Heretics*, Bernard Gui, trans. and ed. Janet Shirley (Welwyn Garden City, UK: Ravenhall Books, 2006), p. 13.

[70] Janet Shirley, 'Introduction', *The Inquisitor's Guide: A Medieval Manual on Heretics*, Bernard Gui, p. 13.

[71] James B. Givens, *Inquisition and Medieval Society: Power, Discipline, and Resistance in Languedoc* (Ithaca NY: Cornell University Press, 1997), pp. 53–4.

[72] Givens, *Inquisition and Medieval Society*, p. 2. Givens also provides examples of corrupt inquisitors, such as Menet de Robécourt (1320–1340s), who overstepped the boundaries of law and against whom the populace responded (p. 145).

[73] As incidents of torture in judicial proceedings increased so did the public fascination with and demand for religious literature of other kinds. Passion narratives describing the Crucifixion in brutally graphic language emphasizing the suffering and torture of Christ's body during the entire process of his journey and on the cross circulated widely from the thirteenth century onwards. Thomas H. Bestul has provided a comprehensive and detailed discussion on torture in Passion narratives in his work, and his chapter titled 'The Passion of the Christ and the Institution of Torture' effectively discusses the implications of graphic vernacular Passion narratives, their impact on popular audience and individual devotion. Bestul also notes that many of these accounts were embellished by their authors beyond the scope of the gospels, and argues that these 'narratives elaborations reveal late medieval attitudes toward the Passion which moved the weight of representation toward Christ's suffering in human form' (pp. 146–7). In his discussion of these spectacularized narratives, Bestul describes a clear evolution in the graphic imagery pointing out that the extreme representations of brutality and violence do not 'appear fully formed' but develop over time (p. 149). Many of his points are further supported by the graphic accounts of torture in hagiography under discussion here. In these narratives, the Roman authorities who persecute Christ are demonized by the torture they inflict, and their methods are portrayed as barbaric and hateful, and the audience – of all classes – was meant to see them as such. *Texts of the Passion: Latin Devotional Literature and Medieval Society* (Philadelphia: University of Pennsylvania Press, 1996). See also: Manuele Gragnolati, 'From Decay to Splendor: Body and Pain in Bonvesin da la Riva's *Book of the Three Scriptures*', in *Last Things: Death and the Apocalypse in the Middle Ages*, ed. Caroline Walker Bynum and Paul Freedman (Philadelphia: University of Pennsylvania Press, 2000) 83–97; Dyan Elliott, *Fallen Bodies: Pollution, Sexuality, and Demonology in the Middle*

torture in ferreting out heterodoxy has always been a troubled one. As Jeffrey Burton Russell points out, 'even in the Middle Ages there was at no time a clear division between heresy and orthodoxy, for definitions varied according to time, place, and individual attitudes.'[74] Severe punishment for heresy was rare before the thirteenth century,[75] but inquisitorial torture has been indelibly imbedded in the minds of modern audiences through popular culture. The question of torture and its effect on discovering 'truth' through the body emerges with the question of bodily suffering and the connection between body and soul in the thirteenth century, the central question of which was the relationship between pain and suffering and the body-soul union.[76] Church instability and the need to preserve the Christian community led to an increased use of torture; and as those power structures were threatened by heterodoxy and by societies seeking to define themselves not only as Christians but in nationalist terms dictated by secular concerns and authority, the proliferation of torture in hagiography may have backfired. The Church and its inquisitors looked more and more like the pagan judges of legend. As Peter Brown suggests, 'Now the martyr is the judge; and the gods of paganism, the demons who had stood behind his persecutors, are the culprits under interrogation.'[77] The 'heavy judicial overtones' associated with rituals of saints go back to late antiquity.[78] For the charged heretic of the Middle Ages the judicial scene would be much the same; even if he or she rejected the

---

Ages (Philadelphia: University of Pennsylvania Press, 1999); and Bynum, *Fragmentation and Redemption*.

[74] Russell, *Religious Dissent in the Middle Ages*, p. 3.

[75] Russell, *Religious Dissent in the Middle Ages*, p. 10.

[76] Donald Mowbray, *Pain and Suffering in Medieval Theology: Academic Debates at the University of Paris in the Thirteenth Century* (Woodbridge: The Boydell Press, 2009), p. 16. Bynum attributes the increasing fascination with brutality and dismemberment to a shift in ethos despite cultural fears about fragmentation, permitting division of the body that was practised on an increasing scale in the thirteenth century. The evolution of surgical procedure at the same time is part of this development; the first examples of autopsy to determine the cause of death in legal cases appear in the thirteenth century, and 'the first official dissections were carried out in medical schools in the years around 1300, for purposes of teaching as well as diagnosis'. The clinical approach to the body as an entity that can be dissected or disarticulated mirrors the callous application of torture in judicial proceedings which relies on seeing the body as an entity unconnected from the consciousness, or as a means of controlling the conscious response. It is this innovative interest in anatomical dissection that may have provided medieval inquisitors with a further justification for applying torture. Bynum draws a connection between the rise of surgical procedure, the revival of torture as a judicial practice, the significant increase in the use of mutilation and dismemberment to punish capital crimes, and the dissemination of saints' relics based on miraculous hagiographical accounts. There were limits placed on methods of torture; 'so highly charged was bodily partition that torturers were forbidden to effect it; they were permitted to squeeze and twist and stretch in excruciating ways, but not to sever or divide'. *Fragmentation and Redemption*, pp. 270–2.

[77] Peter Brown, *The Cult of the Saints: Its Rise and Function in Latin Christianity* (Chicago: University of Chicago Press, 1981), p. 109.

[78] Brown, *The Cult of the Saints*, p. 108.

veneration of saints, the image of their trials and sufferings (or lack thereof) at the hands of tyrannous authority was deeply embedded in the medieval psyche. It was a natural inversion for the 'heretic' to place himself in the role of martyr as it had been enacted in orthodox texts for centuries.

The SEL was produced during the height of heretical development, while competing discourses on millenarianism, Fraticelli, poverty, reform and mysticism raged on the Continent. In the thirteenth century, and then in the fifteenth, the vernacular hagiographies set potentially dangerous precedents in a number of spheres, not only in provoking vocal dissent and resistance to authority, or in the emphasis on and inclusion of native saints in greater numbers, reflecting a growing national consciousness,[79] but also in encouraging a preaching role for women. As Alcuin Blamires has noted, these precedents 'became well known to the laity through the dissemination of hagiography',[80] and they reveal 'persistent and acute paradoxes which must sometimes have embarrassed those holding the orthodox position and which heterodox groups could naturally exploit.'[81] Saints' lives were 'emphatically relevant' in promoting 'subversive notions about women preaching'[82] and in a similar manner they provided laudatory examples of lay people persisting in giving religious instruction and defying temporal authority in the face of brutal interrogation and punishment. Crachiolo makes a very valid point that there is a vast difference between *torture* and *representations* of torture, and that previous scholars writing about torture and pain (Peters, Scarry, and Foucault) have done so from the historical perspective of real world torture, whereas in hagiography torture is 'of an imaginary and rhetorical nature.'[83] But for medieval audiences there was no gap between history and hagiography, and like many literary texts, these narratives were often assumed to be based on fact despite their formulaic nature. Despite the rhetorical aspects of torture in hagiography many of the torture methods employed against these early Christians in literature were medieval inventions (rather than Roman) and certainly did reflect *real* practice, a reality that would have been troubling to many audiences as the influence of canon law spread, and with it the use of torture in inquisitorial procedure.[84]

---

[79] Sanock, *Her Life Historical*, p. 85.

[80] Alcuin Blamires, 'Women and Preaching in Medieval Orthodoxy, Heresy, and Saints' Lives', *Viator: Medieval and Renaissance Studies* 26 (1995): 135–52, p. 136.

[81] Blamires, 'Women and Preaching in Medieval Orthodoxy, Heresy, and Saints' Lives', p. 136.

[82] Blamires, 'Women and Preaching in Medieval Orthodoxy, Heresy, and Saints' Lives', p. 142.

[83] Crachiolo, 'Female and Male Martyrs', p. 153.

[84] This is particularly evident in the accounts describing the trial of the Knights Templar, and the response of critics to their torture. Peters, paraphrasing Barber, records Pierre de Bologna's eloquent argument that the 'methods of assault on the Order by Philip the Fair and others deprived the knights of "freedom of mind, which is what every good man ought to have," since once a man is deprived of his free will through imprisonment, confiscation of

As the Church attempted to maintain its authority and control of Christian thought in medieval Europe, it relied on practices and methods that would prove unreliable and fallible. The power of the Church was deemed legitimate because it allegedly derived from God, and it exercised this authority against all dissent, against all those who challenged any prevailing religious views.[85] Russell writes that there was a constant and constructive tension in medieval Christianity between dissent and order, and that *authority* is a fluid concept 'because ideas about what channels God uses to express his will for the Christian community shift'.[86] As the foundations of Christian theology were being tested by various religious sects seeking to define Christian belief for themselves, the boundaries of Church authority were also being tested within the spheres of civil governance. According to Russell, as the prosecution of heresies by the civil authorities increased rapidly through the thirteenth century, 'the tension between dissent and orthodoxy increased. The means of repression begun at Verona in 1184 and formalized at the Fourth Lateran Council in 1215 were extended.'[87] This increase in prosecutions led to slips in legal proceedings despite codified measures to protect defendants; defendants were always entitled to legal counsel, but it was often hard to find because lawyers were unwilling to place themselves in jeopardy and were afraid of 'persecution as "helpers" themselves'.[88] So the door was opened to abuse and tyranny, which hagiographers (in an appeal to the general populace) may have resisted through literary modes – texts where torture and judicial brutality are demonized and attributed to corrupt authorities or regimes, especially as the civil authorities increased the prosecution of heresies themselves or initiated them for their own political or financial interests.

Gender and Torture in Hagiography

The gendered nature of hagiographical torture has concerned many readers and critics since the Middle Ages because, despite the rare accounts of select male saints like Laurence and Bartholomew, the majority of saints who are subjected to heinous torments are women, usually *very* young women. One of the most prominent medieval voices against authoritarian control, Christine de Pizan (1365–c. 1434), uses the torture narratives of young female saints, centrally Saint Christina, to defy the patriarchal suppression of women. In the *Book of the City of Ladies* (c. 1405), she addresses a fundamental trend among Church fathers and medieval male authors of vilifying women in their texts – high-

---

his property, the exercise of power against him, and torture, he is deprived of all good things: "knowledge, memory, and understanding"'. 'Destruction of the Flesh', p. 147.
[85] Russell, *Dissent and Order*, p. 1.
[86] Russell, *Dissent and Order*, p. 1.
[87] Russell, *Dissent and Order*, p. 70.
[88] Russell, *Dissent and Order*, p. 70.

lighting their faults and their role in the fall of man.[89] She reproduces examples of brutally tortured women not merely as a means of elevating their sanctity above social gender constraints but as models of resistance against corrupt patriarchal authority, including these women 'because of their constancy during martyrdom'.[90] She commends them for their bravery and their opposition to the standard expectations of women, using them as examples of 'good' women who do not fit the stereotype perpetuated in the 'masculine myth' espoused by patristic writers like Saint Augustine.[91] Her work is a response to Augustine and her incorporation of female saints as vehicles for faith and defiance, and for potential resistance to male authority, is a clear reversal of examples – turning the Church's models against them and undermining the structure of authority they were meant to reinforce. At the end of her life, Christine would break an eleven-year silence to venerate another woman persecuted, tortured and then executed for defying male secular and ecclesiastical authorities, Joan of Arc, in her *Ditié de Jehanne d'Arc* (1429).[92] The lives and savage deaths of these women would have resonated with thirteenth- and fourteenth-century audiences, particularly in the French court where Christine was based, for whom dissent, especially in religious heterodoxy, could mean being subjected to interrogatory torture or execution.

Giving female figures a voice in texts that were intended for devotional contemplation, if not emulation, could have striking and unintended consequences. As Henrietta Leyser points out, the Church could not control the hagiographic discourse[93] and audience reception could manipulate what was meant to promote Church orthodoxy into heterodox models of dissent and resistance. Blamires notes that the greatest impact was exerted by the legends of virgin martyrs who were highest on the scale of female sanctity.[94] These legends were strikingly popular throughout the medieval period, however, because 'the incon-

---

[89] Christine de Pizan, *The Book of the City of Ladies*, trans. Earl Jeffrey Richards (New York: Persea Books, 1998) pp. 232–4, 241. Christine discusses a number of female saints: Dorothy, III.9.2–4; Christina, III.10.1; and Marina, III.12.1.

[90] Christine de Pizan, *The Book of the City of Ladies*, pp. 232–4, 241.

[91] Natalie Zemon Davis, 'Foreword', *The Book of the City of Ladies*, Christine de Pizan, p. xxxiii. For a discussion of Christina's speech and Christine de Pizan's answer to the antifeminist clerics, see Kevin Brownlee's article 'Martyrdom and the Female Voice: Saint Christine in the *Cite des Dames*', in *Images of Sainthood in Medieval Europe*, ed. Renate Blumenfeld-Kosinski and Timea K. Szell (Ithaca NY: Cornell University Press, 1991) 115–35 and Maureen Quilligan, *The Allegory of Female Authority: Christine de Pisan's Cite de Dames* (Ithaca NY: Cornell University Press, 1991).

[92] Richards, 'Introduction', *The Book of the City of Ladies*, p. xxviii.

[93] Henrietta Leyser, *Medieval Women: A Social History of Women in England 450–1500* (London: Phoenix Grant, 1995), p. 223. She writes: '[The Virgin] Mary of the Gospels is given only few words; those anxious to reinforce the Pauline message that women were to be silent in church found this a reassuring precedent. But for many late medieval men and women, the Virgin they knew stepped out of vernacular drama, not Latin Gospels.'

[94] Alcuin Blamires, *Woman Defamed and Woman Defended: An Anthology of Medieval Texts* (Oxford: Clarendon Press, 1992), p. 13.

sistencies and ambiguities [...] allowed the virgin martyr legend, more than any other hagiographical genre, to mean different things to different people.'[95] Uncomfortably for modern audiences (and many critics) the young female virgin saints are most frequently abused and tortured in a manner specific to their gender: their breasts are cut off, their tongues are ripped out (which for women represents the prohibition on female speech often expounded by Church authorities, derived from Pauline doctrine), they are threatened with brutal rape, or in rare and extremely shocking instances, their genitalia are mutilated. It is important to note that in most virgin martyr legends the women are protected from rape or sexualized torture, except for mastectomies, because they must remain intact as a virgin – genital mutilation borders on sexual violation and could threaten their purity. The version of Saint Margaret's life in the *SEL* is a notable exception because her womb is ripped out and her 'deorne limes hi totere' (*SEL* 1: 296).[96] The saint's body is imagined 'in the throes of extreme sexualized violence – her breasts, too, are removed – while she simultaneously remains inviolate and sexually pure', conveying an 'essential and ubiquitous hagiographic paradox: the juxtaposition of violence and virginal impermeability'.[97] Some critics have seen this as a deliberate attempt on the part of hagiographers to either objectify the bodies of female saints in particular or to titillate themselves in reproducing images of disarticulated and mutilated bodies. Crachiolo suggests that the audience of the *SEL* were entertained specifically by the use of torture and that the stories of violence and torture 'were at a least assumed to appeal to a popular audience'.[98] But torture is a standard motif for saints and the purer the virgin, the more innocent the body, the greater the effect of ripping it to shreds.[99] Without the

---

[95] Winstead, *Virgin Martyrs*, p. 5.

[96] *Saint Margaret, The South English Legendary Corpus Christi College Cambridge MS 145 and British Museum MS Harley 2277*, ed. Charlotte D'Evelyn and Anna J. Mill, Vol. 1, EETS, os 235 (Oxford: Oxford University Press, 1956, rpt. 1967), p. 126. Crachiolo contends that the nakedness of the female body is part of the virgin martyr legend, that 'women martyrs are routinely deprived of their clothes just before they are tortured', which functions as a facet of the torture and humiliation to which these women are subjected (p. 158). However, in most instances when the judges attempt to strip the martyr they are unsuccessful; either the clothes cling fast, their hair grows to cover their bodies, or the woman is shrouded in divine light which blinds the pagan witnesses or strikes them down. The purity of the virgin martyr must remain intact, her virginity *and* her modesty. Many artistic renderings of these legends depict the martyrs in various states of undress that lends to the visual aspects of the torture, but it is rarely a component of the narrative legends except in the *South English Legendary*. For further information on visual aspects of torture in medieval art, see: Mills, *Suspended Animation*. Karen Winstead has also edited and translated a selection of virgin martyr legends from various English collections. See: Karen Winstead, *Chaste Passions: Medieval English Virgin Martyr Legends* (Ithaca NY: Cornell University Press, 2000).

[97] Mills, *Suspended Animation*, p. 117.

[98] Crachiolo, 'Female and Male Martyrs', pp. 149, 153, 161.

[99] There have been several valuable studies on female saints and the male gaze, as well as the construction of female saints by male authors. In addition to both Winstead and

apparent objectification of the victim of torture, there can be no response to the brutality of the torture. Torture objectifies both the saints and the tormentor; the saint is sanctified, the tormentor is demonized and the use of torture resonates with the audience as a tool of the barbarian Other.

By giving female martyrs a voice equal to their male counterparts, hagiographers presented medieval women with vocal, defiant role models that allowed them to reconsider their own position in society, the same way that accused heretics, male or female, may have found exempla for their own defiance. Winstead writes that virgin martyr legends did not 'simply embody tensions about changing gender roles and relation' but that they often show the disintegration of other traditional power relations, such as lordship and patriarchal structure of authority.[100] This disintegration is further exemplified in the resort to torture and the cultural anxieties rooted within it. Mills argues that female saints' lives produce their own disruptive effects in the context of torture, because while male martyrs might be 'divested of certain signifiers of earthly masculinity' during their torture, 'the battles that female virgin martyrs undergo to protect their chastity potentially associate them with privileges that, in late medieval culture, were normally gendered male: speaking eloquently, for instance, or thumping demonic entities with hammers'.[101] In these texts, speech is inextricably linked to the application of torture in a discovery of 'truth' – the more vehement the saint's protestations of faith, the more brutally she will be tortured. Consistent vocal resistance met with equally consistent but increasingly horrific torments as the exclusively masculine pagan authority attempts to wring from her flesh a rejection of her Christian beliefs. The female virgin martyr stands above traditionally proscribed gender roles and defends Christian doctrine, at the same time testing the boundaries of civil authority and destabilizing the basis of its power and legitimacy.

Saint Agatha

Like many contemporary early Christian saints, Saint Agatha of Catania is a highborn, beautiful maiden. She is a devout Christian pursued by the libidinous

---

Wogan-Browne's excellent books, see: Anne Clark Bartlett, *Male Authors, Female Readers: Representations and Subjectivity in Middle English Devotional Literature* (Ithaca NY: Cornell University Press, 1995); Catherine M. Mooney, ed., *Gendered Voices: Medieval Saints and Their Interpreters* (Philadelphia: University of Pennsylvania Press, 1999); Sarah Salih, *Versions of Virginity in Late Medieval England* (Cambridge: D.S. Brewer, 2001).

[100] Winstead, *Virgin Martyrs*, p. 109.

[101] Mills, *Suspended Animation*, p. 173. Mills sees male saints as being 'visually de-phallicized' by being decapitated, disembowelled and flayed; and female saints such as Barbara and Agatha as purportedly 'de-sexed' by having their breasts removed (p. 173). However phallocentric the image of disembowelment or decapitation may seem to modern critics, medieval audiences would not necessarily have read the torture of male saints as sexualized in any way, except in the rare cases of castration; and female genital mutilation was equally rare, the sexualization of torture for female saints being generally enacted in the mastectomies. But in either case, the saints' transcendence of physical abuse elevates them from the corporeal world and debases their persecutors.

tyrant Quintianus, a base-born consular official in Sicily who wishes to subject her to his sexual desires, steal her wealth and force her to sacrifice to his gods. Agatha's legend appears in the *LgA*, the *SEL*, and the *GiL* with some variation among the three versions; however, the basic story follows the pattern of most virgin martyr legends. The *GiL*, as the latest vernacular version of these *vitae*, reflects the endurance of these legends into the later medieval period, as questions of reformation and orthodoxy were gathering steam. Agatha's *vita* is very short and she suffers far fewer torments than Christina, but in her case the nature of the torture centres specifically around her female gender. She is threatened with defilement and prostitution, her breasts are ripped off, she is to be burned but is saved by an earthquake that destroys the hall, only to ask for death and receive it. Aphrodisia and her nine daughters are given a month to bring Agatha to lechery and force her to submit to Quintianus. Agatha defies them, assuring the prostitutes that she cannot be defiled despite their threats of pain because of the strength of her faith: "'My thought and myn entencion is sadder thanne any stone,[102] for it is founded in Ihesu Crist. Your wordes bene wynde, youre behestes bene reyne and youre dredfull manasses bene but iapes, fore whateuer thei do thei mowe not make the foundement of myn hous to falle.'" (*GiL* 16–20).[103] Her strength and her refusal to capitulate move Aphrodisia to tell Quintianus that she will not submit; enraged, Quintianus summons Agatha for interrogation.

In proceedings that echo many of the medieval heresy trials, Quintianus questions Agatha about her social status and why she debases herself as a slave to Christ when she is a highborn woman. Even in the Roman setting of the tale, this process of interrogatory torture is transgressive because Roman law prohibited the torture of citizens, especially those of noble birth. For medieval audiences, lay and clerical, this resort to torture represents the most insidious aspect of judicial proceedings and undermines the authority of those who employ it. When her answers do not please him, Quintianus resorts to threats: "'sacrifice to oure goddes or ellis receiue diuerse tormentis'" (*GiL* 36). Agatha rejects his threats and insults him by wishing that his wife be like his goddess Venus and that he be like his god Jupiter, lascivious and corrupt. Further enraged, he commands that she be 'bete withe bofettis aboute her hede' (*GiL* 39), telling her that she should not 'jangle' with her presumptuous mouth by insulting a judge. She makes a very valid and cogent argument in response, telling him that if he truly venerates his gods then he should not be insulted to be compared to them, and if he reviles them so much then he must feel as she does. Exasperated, Quintianus repeats

---

[102] Prov. 27:3., or more likely Matt. 16:18, 'And I say to thee: That thou art Peter; and upon this rock I will build my church, and the gates of hell shall not prevail against it.'
[103] All quotations of the *GiL Agatha* are from Richard Hamer and Vida Russell's edition: *Gilte Legende*, Vol. 1, EETS, os 327 (Oxford: Oxford University Press, 2006) 175–9. Line numbers are given in parenthesis.

his threat and Agnes responds with further defiance, pointing out that no matter what he does to her it will have no effect:

> Agas ansuered, 'If thou behight me wilde bestes and whan thei here the name of God her cruelte will assuage; and yef thou deliuer me to fere the aungeles of heuene wil ministre a suete dewe; yef thou make me receyue woundes or tormentis, I haue the holy goste witheinne me bi whom I despise all these thingges.' (GiL 48–53)

This process continues as Agatha is consigned to prison, brought out and questioned again, and then subjected to torture. Her body heals sufficiently each time so that she maintains her virginal aspect and her feminine beauty is preserved. Quintianus orders her to be crucified upside down, in the same manner as St Peter, aligning her with one of the most venerated male martyrs and endowing her with spiritual authority unusual in holy women. In the GiL the actual torment is not described, only the threat of it and her defiant response welcoming whatever else he may devise. Agatha condemns the men who beat her as butchers, explaining that enduring these torments is required for martyrdom, and while she never specifically says she feel no pain, the sparse prose lacks any emotional markers other than her defiance, anger and eventual triumph.

The LgA version records the same response from Agatha almost verbatim; however, rather than being subjected to hanging on a cross, the LgA calls for her to be 'stretched on the rack and tortured'[104] without any more specificity. Jacobus depicts tools of torture immediately recognizable to his thirteenth-century clerical audience – tools that had been employed vigorously in the persecution of heresy in recent memory. In the SEL version there is no mention of crucifixion either; the author focuses on the next torment, one that is actually carried out in graphic detail. In the SEL Agatha, Quintianus orders hooks and whips and tells his men 'to hure breste binde/ And let þerwiþ is tormentors hure bresten of wynde' (SEL 59–60).[105] The GiL account is less graphic and more concise, focusing more on her angry verbal response without any indications of pain or suffering:

> Quincyen comaunded that her brestes shulde be drawe of, and whanne thei hadde be longe drawen thei were cutte of. Thanne Agas saide to hym: 'O thou cruel and wicked tyraunt, art thou not ashamed and confused that thou hast made cutte of a woman that [thou] thiselff soukedest in thi moder? I haue withinne my soule hole brestes wherwith I norishe al my wittes, the whiche I haue fro my yougthe sacred to oure Lorde.' (GiL 67–73)

---

[104] Translations from the LgA are from Jacobus de Voragine, *The Golden Legend: Readings on the Saints*, trans. William Granger Ryan, Vols. 1 and 2 (Princeton NJ: Princeton University Press, 1993).

[105] Quotations from the SEL version of *Agatha* are from *The South English Legendary Corpus Christi College Cambridge MS 145 and British Museum MS Harley 2277*, ed. Charlotte D'Evelyn and Anna J. Mill, Vol. 1, EETS, os 235 (Oxford: Oxford University Press, 1956, rpt. 1967) 54–9. Line numbers are given in parenthesis.

In this instance, Agatha is tortured and then thrown into prison where an old man visits her and applies an ointment to her wounds, healing and fully restoring her breasts and her physical femininity. Often the torn breasts express milk rather than blood (as in the *SEL Christina*), tying their sacrifice not only to the sacrifice of the virgin body, but also to the sacrifice of their potential motherhood. Agatha's denouncement of Quintianus focuses sharply on the maternal and life-giving function of the breasts he has removed: he has cut off the same part with which his mother nourished him. She taunts him with the knowledge that in her soul she is complete, that she has dedicated her body to Christ and that will sustain her. The restorative power of her faith manifested in the figure of the old man and his salve mitigates the punitive aspect of her mutilation and nullifies any power the tyrant may have sought to gain over both her female body and her Christian soul. The torture turns against the torturer because it has no lasting effect, and the tyrant will be increasingly demonized in his every attempt to brutalize her. By the fifteenth century, the potential for being subjected to interrogatory torture had not faded, in fact by the end of the century as England became embroiled in civil war, the long-standing prohibition against torture by which English jurisprudence defined itself was threatened. Both political and religious dissenters faced the possibility of torture as Europe hurtled towards the upheaval of the Reformation in which female martyrs, like Anne Askew (discussed in Chapter 6), played a prominent role. Perhaps the fifteenth-century English adaptor of the *GiL* felt that dwelling on the specific forms of torture called too much attention to contemporary Church practice at a time when the English monarchy under the Lancastrian rule of Henry IV and his grandson Henry VI had become more orthodox and conservative, whereas the earlier *SEL* author enhanced and embellished the accounts of torture, making the uncomfortable allusions more pronounced.

Though the *Life of Saint Agatha* is fraught with scenes of actualized torture, much of which is focused specifically on her gender, Agatha alleviates any sexual dimension to her mutilation when she denies shame in the presence of the old man, saying: "'Wherfore schold y be a[sham]id sithe þou arte of grete age and y al torente with turment þat no man may take delite in me?'" (*GiL* 87–8). The mutilation of her body, while centred on her sexual 'parts' is not sexually charged, and she is clear that she should not be an object of desire in her state but an object of compassion and celebration in her courage. She refuses aid from the old man, pronouncing her Christian devotion, which signifies her endurance. The old man reveals himself as an apostle (St Peter), heals her immediately for her faith, and effects his cure. The application of torture rebounds on the persecuting authority and taints him with that brutality. Torture is the weapon of unstable regimes and the rhetoric of its application potentially destabilizes the intended propaganda of the narrative, calling the entire system into question.

The constant abuse and torture of Agatha produces an unintended civil response in the text – rebellion – a profound warning of the consequences of using torture, especially in a judicial capacity. Quintianus brings her before him again and interrogates her about her miraculous recovery. Displeased with her answers, he orders her to be rolled naked over potshards and hot coals on the floor. But 'as þay were aboute to ordeygne þerfore' (GiL 115), an earthquake rocks the city, destroys the palace and crushes two of Quintianus' officials. The people rise against him protesting the injustice of his harsh treatment of Agatha, claiming that this has brought the natural disaster upon them: "'We suffre þis vengaunce for þe turmente that þou doist to Agas withoute reson'" (GiL 118–19). Faced with the possibility of a civil rebellion and afraid of another earthquake, Quintianus throws her back into prison. The use of torture by the authorities turns the people against them when it threatens the safety and stability of the realm. Agatha does not die an agonizing death, nor is she actually subjected to any of Quintianus' threatened tortures except the violent mastectomy, and for her ability to endure that torment without suffering or complaint she is healed. Her death (which she prays for) is her release and her reward, but the torture has left an indelible mark on the audience within the text and without: abuse of power manifested in the application of torture (in interrogation or as punishment) should be defied, by popular uprising if necessary. The ability of a young woman to stand up to the secular authorities, withstand torture, and defy repeated attempts to do her further harm serves not only as Christian religious propaganda, but also as a model of resistance that may have had unintended consequences in its dissemination across medieval Europe. The more saints like Agatha and Christina could withstand, the more they were venerated, and the more their legends were translated and transmitted, reaching wider lay audiences. By the fifteenth century many had grown suspicious of consolidated Church power and attempts to regulate belief and so, combined with other important religious texts like John Lydgate's long poem (c. 1439) *Saint Alban and Saint Amphabel* (based on the version in the GiL)[106] and accounts of the Passion, the torture episodes in the GiL resonated. Combined with the vocal defence of faith and the female body, torture becomes a tool not of those who wield it but those who endure it.

The texts imply that these women would probably not have been tortured had they consented to the sexual demands made upon them. Their religion plays a secondary role to the preservation of their chastity. The purity of their bodies becomes a manifestation of the purity of their faith and the application of torture is assigned to lustful pagans and associated with demonized judges in direct opposition to the 'truth' that torture in medieval jurisprudence was meant to extract. But in most cases there is no *actual* defilement and only a threat of sexualized torture. The othering occurs when the threat is made, because only barbaric and corrupt authorities would even *think* of employing such measures, particularly for their own sexual gain. There is a lively critical debate regarding

---

[106] Larissa Tracy, 'British Library MS Harley 630: John Lydgate and St Albans', *Journal of the Early Book Society*, vol. 3 (2000): 36–58.

the sexualization of torture and its specific use against young virgins.[107] Warner discusses the specific torture of female saints based on their gender and surmises that it is related to the power of virginity, which was used by the Church Fathers to redeem women, who were tainted by the Fall; therefore 'the defense of virginal state was worth all the savagery to which saints like Catherine of Alexandria (d.c. 310) submitted'.[108] The female body was a mystery to male ecclesiastics, and this led to a muted fear of women's bodies:

> An oft-noted feature of medieval women's religious experience is its bodily expression. Medieval texts regularly describe holy women, much more than holy men, as fasting, swooning, swelling, bleeding, or otherwise manifesting their interior spiritual dispositions through concrete physical signs. Women, as scholars agree, are embodied physicality in a way that men, more often identified with mind and spirit, are not.[109]

Easton notes that in the Huntington *LgA*, Laurence is depicted on his gridiron, naked but modestly covering his genitalia. She writes, '[e]ven though male and female martyrs may in some instances renegotiate the body and transcend the binary system of gender, ultimately it is through their bodies that they attain salvation and holiness'.[110] Gender is a factor in the way saints are tortured and displayed, and so 'martyrs escape the confines of gender only to have them reinscribed in the images of their bodies'.[111] While Laurence is not persecuted by lascivious judges and provosts, he is persecuted by authorities with a lust for wealth. Considering the number of women who were charged as heretics or involved in heterodox movements like Lollardy which seemed to give them more agency and independence, these narratives would have a particular resonance with female audiences who could read them as examples of defiance, spiritual constancy or both. Catherine Sanock argues that vernacular legends construct a feminine audience, one that contributed to the increasing visibility of women's participation in Middle English literary culture.[112]

Even though judicial torture is not limited to female saints, the formulaic accounts of these young, beautiful virgins provide some of the most shockingly

---

[107] For contributions to this debate on the sexualization of torture in hagiography, see: Katherine J. Lewis's article '"Lete me suffer": Reading the Torture of St. Margaret of Antioch in Late Medieval England', in *Medieval Women: Texts and Contexts in Late Medieval Britain: Essays for Felicity Riddy*, ed. Jocelyn Wogan-Browne, et al. (Turnhout, Belgium: Brepols, 2000) 69–82; and Sarah Salih, 'Performing Virginity: Sex and Violence in the Katherine Group', in *Constructions of Widowhood and Virginity in the Middle Ages*, ed. Cindy L. Carlson and Angela Jane Weisl (New York: St. Martin's Press, 1999) 95–112.

[108] Marina Warner, *Alone of All Her Sex: The Myth and Cult of the Virgin Mary* (New York: Vintage Books, 1976), p. 69.

[109] Catherine Mooney, *Gendered Voices: Medieval Saints and Their Interpreters* (Philadelphia: University of Pennsylvania Press, 1999), p. 13.

[110] Easton, 'Pain, Torture and Death', p. 60.

[111] Easton, 'Pain, Torture and Death', p. 60.

[112] Sanock, *Her Life Historical*, p. ix.

graphic episodes of medieval torture. As Samantha J.E. Riches and Sarah Salih explain, gender affects sanctity and sanctity affects gender: 'Sainthood often works by breaking with normal social values, and gendered identity may be amongst these: constructing one's gender identity differently may be a marker of holiness'.[113] Crachiolo argues that female saints' lives are more brutal because the spectacle of the suffering female body is an object of entertainment in these narratives, and that while men are the models of steadfastness and action, women are models of steadfastness and *reaction*, and 'are therefore objects to be acted upon'.[114] Male holiness 'can be a kind of default position, due to male dominance of the Church, but it may also demand a radical break from the secular norms of masculinity'.[115] As such, the majority of male saints live pious lives and/ or suffer horrible death, but are not subjected to the same kind of potentially degrading scrutiny as female martyrs. It is a specific trope of female martyr-legends that they be hideously tortured in a visual spectacle that displays them before a complicit audience. The primary focus for the audience of hagiography is the steadfastness of the saint, male or female, in the face of pagan tyranny and sadistic torments, and in order for those saints to be elevated beyond their role on earth, they must undergo the most heinous torture and *survive* until they are formally and intentionally executed. As Riches notes, one factor that tends to separate male martyrs from female martyrs is that 'the narratives of male martyrs generally concentrate on one specific torture, such as St Erasmus with his windlass and St Sebastian with his arrows' while female martyrs are subjected to a number of different torments.[116] In fact, most male saints, with a few notable exceptions such as George[117] and Laurence, are not actually tortured or interrogated but are simply executed in a particularly gruesome manner – a horrific and slow end, and a pure exercise in judicial brutality rather than a systematic and repetitive cycle of torments and ordeals.

Saint Bartholomew is most notable not only for the pious and dedicated life he led but for his heinous and brutal death by flaying, and in iconography he is often depicted holding his skin in his hands. Though flaying is not technically torture and was rarely practised as a method of capital punishment in the medi-

---

[113] Samantha J.E. Riches and Sarah Salih, 'Introduction' in *Gender and Holiness: Men, Women and Saints in Late Medieval Europe*, ed. Samantha J. E. Riches and Sarah Salih. Routledge Studies in Medieval Religion and Culture (London and New York: Routledge, 2002) 1–8, p. 5.
[114] Crachilolo, 'Female and Male Martyrs', p. 161.
[115] Riches and Salih, 'Introduction', p. 5.
[116] Samantha J.E. Riches, 'St George as a Male Virgin Martyr', in *Gender and Holiness*, ed. Riches and Salih, 65–85, p. 71.
[117] In her article 'St George as a Male Virgin Martyr', Riches provides an eloquent and detailed discussion of various narratives of St George and the variety of tortures to which he was subjected – including dismemberment, boiling and sawing in half – arguing that St George was a 'borrower *par excellence*' and his story appropriates many of the torture methods found in female hagiography in an effort to focus on his status as a virgin.

eval period, the flayed body is a graphic canvas on which the punitive excesses of the secular authority may be written.[118] In most literary instances, like that in *Havelok the Dane* (discussed in Chapter 4), the resort to flaying is just as reprehensible in its brutality as the reliance on torture. Flaying is generally reserved as a punishment for traitors and the application of such a horrific torment to such a saintly man subverts the civil authority. As a male saint, however, Bartholomew's body is not subjected to the prolonged abuse or to the same scrutiny as his female contemporaries. There is no mention of his genitalia; nothing that is done to him marks him as 'male'; he is not tortured according to his gender – his masculine body is not the central focus of his sanctity. For most male saints, their torment is the form of their execution and the end of the torment is the release of death, but women saints endure, taunt, argue, and vilify their persecutors, urging them on to greater acts of brutality, not because they enjoy it but because their power lies in undermining the power of corrupt authority by not suffering and so resisting the effect of the torture.[119] Like many of the female virgin martyrs, there is an element of ironic humour to the lives of Laurence and Bartholomew, though Crachiolo sees this as a trait exclusive to the male saints. She writes that making a joke of the torture of 'male martyrs' means that neither the audience nor the men upon whom torture is perpetrated need take it seriously, nor does the audience need to focus on the horrific sight of the tortured body'.[120] However, there is also a certain amusing irony to the image of Christina singing away in a furnace with angels, or to her father striking himself on the forehead because he just *cannot* get her to suffer. Humour serves a similar purpose in all hagiography because the saints are the clever ones; they subvert the tyrants and the corrupt justices through language, debate, and endurance.

The virgin martyrs are the most physical as well as vocal female saints *because* their bodies are the focus of their faith and sanctity. Kelly asserts that virginity was defined by the Church as a political means of controlling women and its enemies: 'Chrysostom thus politicizes virginity, using it as a weapon against the perceived enemies of the Church. *De Virginitate* is a formative document in an emerging policy that makes the Christian Church the only institution with the power to define, recognize, and reward virginity.'[121] She also suggests the saints represent the Church that, like the virgins, had resisted violation at the hands

---

[118] Mills analyses various images of flaying in his study of medieval art, including depictions of Saint Bartholomew's execution and his stoic response to the removal of his skin. He explains medieval notions of skin as memory, and writes that 'to flay someone alive would be to tear away the bodily surface onto which transitory memories and identities could be inscribed – only to fashion an etched parchment in its place (the dead skin), from which "timeless" moral lessons could be read'. *Suspended Animation*, p. 68.

[119] Crachiolo acknowledges the role of torture in the dynamics of power, though her primary point is that the women saints, unlike the men, really have no agency in these narratives. 'Female and Male Martyrs', p. 148.

[120] Crachiolo, 'Female and Male Martyrs', p. 155.

[121] Kelly, *Performing Virginity*, p. 4.

of pagan persecutors.[122] The use of torture by non-Christian authorities represents the brutality of the pagan Other in contrast to the righteous endurance of the Church. The authors of hagiography used the definition proscribed by the Church to make their female role models, particularly the virgins, beyond reproach. However, if the clerics were intent on controlling women by providing these examples, then allowing them to voice their opposition so vehemently works against them because their speech provides an instrument of defiance, not submission.[123] While the narratives of saints like Agnes and Lucy focus on the inability of pagan persecutors to violate them sexually, preserving their faith through the preservation of their virginity,[124] the narratives that catalogue the numerous torture methods used against women like Agatha and Christina are far more powerful in providing models of defiance and endurance. It is in martyrdom where the application of torture plays the most crucial role, casting the saint in opposition to authority that should be defied, that *must* be defied, against all threats of pain or punishment. And since the medieval Church was the primary authority applying torture in judicial proceedings against accused heretics, this was a very dangerous sentiment indeed. While there was little chance of throngs of women, or certain classes of men for that matter, storming castles or cathedrals with manuscripts of hagiography clutched to their breasts, providing readable and secularized accounts of open defiance and heroes proclaiming religious doctrine open for individual interpretation had a potentially destabilizing effect on Church authority and may have suggested or promoted certain unorthodox ideologies.

The majority of the female audience for whom the legends were intended could not ascribe to the ideal of virgin martyrdom, but they could take strength

---

[122] Kelly, *Performing Virginity*, p. 41. Also see: Kathleen Coyne Kelly, 'Useful Virgins in Medieval Hagiography', in *Constructions of Widowhood and Virginity in the Middle Ages*, ed. Cindy Carlson and Angela Jane Weisl (New York: St. Martin's Press, 1999) 135–64.

[123] Tracy, *Women of the Gilte Legende*, p. 12. Many of these virgins were also venerated through their torture and torment as brides of Christ, refusing to wed a mortal man because of their marital commitment to God. Their legends are punctuated by textual examples of this union: visions of marriage beds and references to their heavenly spouse. But the virgins are not the only example of saints wedded to their Saviour. Saint Theodora, a holy transvestite and repentant sinner, and Saint Elizabeth, the medieval nun who forsakes her children for her heavenly husband, join Saint Dorothy and other martyred virgins at the wedding feasts of Christ. This is the supreme expression of a saint's love for her God; she becomes wedded to him, relinquishing her family, her status and her body to serve him.

[124] In their individual narratives, virgin saints like Agnes and Lucy challenge their tormentors to do their worst, urging them to apply the most gruesome methods of torture possible against them, not from a masochistic desire to feel pain nor from any sense of sexual voyeurism on the part of the hagiographer, but because in order for the full potential of this martyrdom to be realized the martyrs must endure with defiance and dignity the torments used against them. However, despite their taunts and exhortations to torture neither of these virgins is actually tortured. They are threatened with sexual defilement, which is never actually realized, and any attempt to cause them harm, in this case to burn them in a bonfire, fails, and the saints must be finally dispatched by steel.

from the descriptions of the theological debates and the refusal of these virgins to submit to their male persecutors. Hagiographical legends could have a significant impact on the everyday lives of women because they illustrate the importance of sanctity and provide positive, assertive examples not tainted by the didactic intentions of some patristic writers like Thomas Aquinas and Jerome, who often criticized their female exempla. The legends are rarely definitive about anything: 'rather, contradictory messages coexist, ready to be exploited to different ends'.[125] Medieval women could interpret the legends according to their own position and find a voice in them, a voice of dissent, satire and even overt political condemnation. Danielle Régnier-Bohler points out that women spoke in public as well as private, exercising their 'linguistic powers in a variety of ways, rich, subtle, and vehement; they spoke and they wrote'.[126] Within heretical movements, the equality of women and their vocality was often an issue, and women were tortured during interrogations as severely as men, and were also burned at the stake for their convictions. The female audience for the hagiographical collections consisted mainly of monastic or noble women, both classes being in positions of influence and self-reliance. Belonging to a religious community or to the nobility gave women a greater amount of autonomy. These independent and noble women were perhaps inspired by the legends intended for their edification 'recited in their monastic choirs [...] read to nuns in chapter and in the refectory during their meals, as well as in their workrooms while they occupied themselves with various manual tasks such as weaving, sewing and embroidery'.[127] The legends of women saints were part of the everyday lives of many medieval women, both in the cloister and out. Writing about Anglo-Saxon saints' lives, Leslie Donovan explains that hagiography was an educational tool:

> [T]he lives of women saints were a means by which the medieval church sought to shape popular understanding of women's roles within Christian culture. The facts of women's lives encoded in these texts provide evidence for understanding the history of women in Christianity, medieval religious thought, and medieval popular culture, as well as the development of women's spirituality.[128]

Many prominent and powerful women during the early Middle Ages were active as patrons of monasteries and churches as well as authors, and their commissions for works of hagiography reflect their influence on the social and political climate of that period. Theresa Coletti writes that hagiography participated in cultural shifts and power dynamics. She says, 'New understandings of the

---

125 Winstead, *Virgin Martyrs*, p. 5.
126 Danielle Régnier-Bohler, 'Literary and Mystical Voices', in *A History of Women in the West, vol. II: Silences of the Middle Ages*, ed. Christiane Klapisch-Zuber, trans. Arthur Goldhammer (Cambridge MA: Belknap Press of Harvard University Press, 1992) 427–82, p. 429.
127 Tibbetts Schulenburg, 'Saints' Lives as a Source for the History of Women', p. 288.
128 Leslie Donovan, *Women Saints' Lives in Old English Prose* (Cambridge: D.S. Brewer, 1999), pp. 11–12.

role of the saints in the Middle Ages, however, have stressed the ways in which hagiographic narrative and cultic practice, far from simply representing a stable, transhistorical realm of Christian values, participated in crucial ways in the production of social and political power'.[129] The very texts meant to reinforce orthodox Christian doctrine could destabilize it and produce heresy, or at least encourage male and female heretics to dissent against corrupt authority in the fashion of their saintly models. The hagiographical trend shifted later in the medieval period when female saints such as Elizabeth of Hungary (one of the last saints included in the *LgA*) were venerated not for being outspoken but instead for being humble and silent. The Church attempted to circumscribe the public roles for women, but even as social strictures became tighter, the production of hagiographies increased as did the graphic portrayals of torture. These attempts were further thwarted by the rise of heterodox sects like the Lollards in the fourteenth century who promoted women as equals and repeated the rhetoric of martyrdom, urging their adherents to withstand persecution like earlier Christian saints and prevail in the face of Church tyranny.

Saint Christina's speech instructing her father on Christian theology, for which he threatens her with the first round of torments, has several parallels to the tenets of the Lollards, specifically in allowing women to instruct others in theological questions. Christina says to him: "'Thou hast wisely spoken that art vncunynge. [For] I offre to God the fader, to God the sone, to God the holy goste, thre persones and one God." Ande thanne her fader saide, "Yef thou worship thre goddes, why worshipest thou not other as wel?" To whom she saide, "For these .iij. that I worshipp is one Godhede.'" (*GiL* 17–22). Her defiance of her father does not merely manifest itself in petulant rebellion; Christina is given the knowledge and authority to instruct her father on the nature of the Trinity, authority that traditionally rests with priests. The power of her speech is emphasized by this act and by her role as a preacher. She preaches to her father the notion of the Trinity after he, who is 'unkunnynge' or without the ability to understand, questions the existence of one God. She instructs her father many times, overturning the traditional patriarchal and familial relationship, condemning his worship and him as a product of the devil, and delighting in the fact that he disowns her for not performing a sacrifice.[130] As a woman,

---

[129] Theresa Coletti, 'Paupertas est donum Dei: Hagiography, Lay Religion, and the Economics of Salvation in the Digby *Mary Magdalene*', *Speculum* 76, no. 2 (2001): 337–78, p. 339.

[130] The legends of the early Christian saints, including those who were much quieter than their virgin contemporaries, continued to circulate and gain popularity, even though their message seemed contradictory. Monique Alexandre explains that while justifying a reinforcement of the traditional subordination of women, many of these texts opened up a realm of freedom. 'Early Christian Women', in *A History of Women in the West, vol. I: From Ancient Goddesses to Christian Saints*, ed. Pauline Schmitt Pantel (Cambridge MA: Harvard University Press, 1992) 409–44, p. 410. Many of these 'silent' saints were venerated because their defiance took a much more feasible form, like Elizabeth of Hungary who defies the conven-

Christina would have been denied spiritual authority, but her defiance of torture and her status as a martyr elevates her beyond the medieval gender constraints and endows her with agency that would have been uncomfortable for many male clerics. Gendering hagiography provided not only potential models for heterodox sects in defiance of the Church, but also provided vocal exempla within orthodox tradition for women constrained by social and religious doctrine and tradition.

The shocking images conjured up with the descriptions of painful torture serve as an indictment of the brutality of the past and a criticism of the time in which they were written when torture was a tool employed by churchmen invested with the inquisitorial powers. It should be no great surprise that the hagiographers who wrote to edify the human spirit also wrote in defiance of tyranny that existed in their own time. In describing the medieval methods of torture employed by the ecclesiastical authorities, including the papal inquisitors, authors and scribes of vernacular hagiography, appealed directly to the fears and sensibilities of their audience and continued to provide successive generations with a record of the medieval period reflected in their narratives. They also provide a literary record of dissent and rebellion against abusive authority, one that was often mirrored in the historical persecution of heretics and their renunciation of papal power, and may have also ignited a few fires of heterodox religious fervour contrary to the Church's intentions. The presence of torture in hagiography also plays into the anxieties of cultural identity and reinforces a sense of justice and civilized law in societies that reject its use. The *SEL* establishes a sense of English national identity in its inclusion of native saints and in the intensified brutality of its adaptation of continental, Latin *vitae*.

In hagiography, the consequences of vocal defiance – torture, dismemberment and death – may have been meant as a spiritual guide while being a physical deterrent from actually engaging in it; however, it is impossible to gauge the extent of this kind of influence. Crachiolo contends that the gruesome episodes in these legends, regardless of the vocal defiance of their subjects, normalized torture as an event with little or no real world consequence. She suggests that 'they are not warnings against transgression but safe, entertaining episodes of the larger narrative of church history'.[131] This assumes that medieval audiences found torture amusing or entertaining and would have related more to the alien judges applying the torture than to the saint enduring it. This is particularly problematic in the English context of the *SEL* because of the legal process in place and because of the French associations with torture in the aftermath of the Albigensian Crusade. Mills argues that these spectacular punishments, specifi-

---

tions of her social position and family to adopt a contemplative life but does so without great speeches or vocal displays. She is not subjected to either torture or martyrdom because it would have been untenable – for a thirteenth-century noble woman to be tortured or punished for orthodox devotion would have provoked anger rather than piety.

[131] Crachiolo, 'Female and Male Martyrs', p. 153.

cally in artistic renderings, do not reflect 'realism', because that would assume that medieval viewers witnessed comparable scenes in real life. He also posits that the representation of these bodies depicts sufferings graphically and realistically, but aestheticized suffering displaced imaginatively to 'a space beyond the image' to facilitate an identification with the subject.[132] In reference to the fifteenth-century German altarpiece, the *Martyrdom of St Barbara*, attributed to Master Francke, Mills suggests that the impact of the torture may not rest in the specific methods employed since, he says, 'the torments of St. Barbara were unreal and unthinkable in penal practice (there is little evidence that mastectomy or burning with brands were penalties regularly imposed on women in late medieval Europe)'.[133] He acknowledges that there may be parallels 'with judicial reality of a different sort' pointing to the sense of expectation and suspense that conditions depictions of martyrdom and secular hanging iconography.[134] However, there is physical evidence from the late Middle Ages of breast rippers, flesh hooks and branding irons, whether there are prolific records of their being used or not. The narratives of female martyrs may well have reflected a judicial reality in the Middle Ages, but as Gail Ashton notes, the 'focus of virgin martyrology is an exemplary death rather than an exemplary life', so the reality of practice becomes incidental.[135]

In these texts, judicial torture employed in a corrupt legal proceeding in the quest for knowledge vindicates the saint and enhances the strength of their conviction. In these cases the torture illuminates the tyranny of the pagan judges, the Romans, or the Pharisees – those who use brutality in a futile attempt to reinforce their elusive power, but in the end provide the graphic and bloody evidence needed to reinforce the message of faith requisite for the medieval Church. Torture teaches – the more the saints withstand, the greater their sacrifice and their veneration; the power of faith is demonstrated in the powerlessness of torture and an inverted judicial process. In these narratives torture is a symptom of corrupt power and its use inverts the perceived power of the pagan authorities while potentially destabilizing the orthodox authority that sanctioned the collections in the first place. These narratives also come dangerously close to rejecting medieval Church authority for its application of torture against heretics because, as Scarry points out, 'the physical pain is so incontestably real that it seems to confer its quality of "incontestable reality" on that power that has brought it into being. It is, of course, precisely because the reality of that power is so highly

---

[132] Mills, *Suspended Animation*, p. 121.
[133] Mills, *Suspended Animation*, p. 121.
[134] Mills, *Suspended Animation*, p. 121.
[135] Gail Ashton, *The Generation of Identity in Late Medieval Hagiography: Speaking the Saint* (London: Routledge, 2000), p. 33. For further studies on the authorization of female virginity, specifically in Anglo-Norman texts, and the representation of virgins in hagiography, see Jocelyn Wogan-Browne, *Saints' Lives and Women's Literary Culture: Virginity and its Authorisations* (Oxford: Oxford University Press, 2001).

contestable, the regime so unstable, that torture is being used.'[136] Torture figures most prominently in the *vitae* of female saints who defy their tormentors and endure a myriad of brutal punishments, challenging the notion of female frailty and setting an example of piety as well as defiance. In a cyclic process of dialogue and torment, these narratives echo the trials of medieval heretics, and in their continued resistance of pagan authority, the female saints are models of dissent and vocal defiance. The specific pain inflicted upon them as women emphasizes their bodies as a means of achieving divinity; their voluntary exit from the world and the truth of Christian faith is inscribed on their bodies. At the same time the reliance on torture demonizes the pagan persecutors and testifies to their inherent barbarism and cruelty, which is necessary to the elevation of the saint who, in her own time, would have been considered a criminal. Medieval hagiographers invented material more recognizable to their audiences; they were not merely copyists,[137] they manipulated details to suit their own purpose – a warning against wielding power through violence, a rebellion against secular or religious tyranny, or a passionate and emotional response to the suffering and constancy of a saint whose veneration is foundational for the Catholic belief system. Mills writes that 'dominant power structures in medieval society were partly sustained through the deployment of representations of punishment and pain: these images possessed a strong ideological remit.'[138] The 'truth' inscribed on the bodies of these saints destabilizes all authority that attempts to contain and control the application of torture, disguised as a mode of discovery.

---

[136] Scarry, *The Body in Pain*, p. 27.
[137] Sheila Delany, 'Introduction', *Legends of Holy Women: A Translation of Osbern Bokenham's Legends of Holy Women* (Notre Dame, IN: University of Notre Dame Press, 1992), p. xxxi.
[138] Mills, *Suspended Animation*, p. 16.

2

Resisting the Rod: Torture and the Anxieties of Continental Identity

> 'An inquisitor never tortures. The custody of the defendant's body is always entrusted to the secular arm.'
> Brother William of Baskerville, *The Name of the Rose*,
> Umberto Eco (p. 451)

As nations sought to define themselves through legal and literary means, the spectre of torture encouraged by secular and ecclesiastical institutions loomed large and was cast as a weapon of tyranny. As Caroline Smith points out, the thirteenth century was 'a vital one in the formation of France and its literary culture'.[1] This formation is evident in the implicit resistance in literary sources to the legal application of torture, the perception of which is rooted in the proliferation of inquisitorial tribunals, particularly in Languedoc, in the twelfth and thirteenth centuries.[2] James Given explains that the work of inquisitors in Languedoc is 'persuasive testimony to the power medieval rulers could generate through the careful and determined applications of [torture] techniques', but the same techniques employed by inquisitors for 'seeking out, isolating, breaking down, and condemning heretics or imagined heretics were not effective in generating active support for their work'.[3] In an attempt to quell heretical uprisings and stamp out individual sects, Pope Gregory IX codified the existing legislation concerning heresy in 1231, creating the Inquisition as an institution. It was not a single autonomous body but individual tribunals that were never unified; 'indeed, virtually no provision was made to assure mutual cooperation between them'.[4] Despite the lack of cohesive definition and coordination, all medieval inquisitorial tribunals possessed an extraordinary jurisdiction, and a large number

---

[1] Caroline Smith, 'Introduction', in *Joinville and Villehardouin: Chronicles of the Crusades*, ed. and trans. Caroline Smith (London: Penguin Books, 2008), p. xx.
[2] James Given, 'The Inquisitors of Languedoc and the Medieval Technology of Power', *The American Historical Review* 94.2 (April 1989): 336–59, pp. 336–7.
[3] Given, 'The Inquisitors of Languedoc', p. 359.
[4] Given, 'The Inquisitors of Languedoc', p. 339.

of these bodies operated throughout southern France.[5] As a consequence, the application of torture seemed to radiate out of France to the rest of Europe and into regions like the German principalities. French influence was felt almost everywhere in medieval Europe as the universities of Paris (like the university of Bologna) developed and refined canon law and argued about its application.[6]

French literary traditions (particularly Arthuriana) permeated the cultural fabric of medieval Europe lending their beauty, grace and subject matter, as well as some cultural *mores*, to indigenous literary works. This chapter will investigate the use of torture and judicial brutality within the *Chanson de Roland* and its Norman context as a manifestation of the 'Other within', and literary sources from the Low Countries in terms of continental literary and legal influence. The *Roland* negotiates the difficulties of Anglo-Norman and Frankish tradition; the Middle Dutch *Roman van Walewein* transforms the French tradition for Flemish interests. These texts deal with different forms of torture or judicial brutality; however, each instance reveals cultural anxieties about justice and law embedded within individual societies. The abuse and horrific execution of Ganelon in the *Roland* questions the efficacy of Frankish, and by inheritance, Anglo-Norman justice. *Walewein* does not engage with real acts of torture but its threatened use against the noble protagonist highlights the barbarity of societies where torture is an acceptable practice. Each one embodies a struggle for national identity and self-definition within the sphere of European influence as England and France contended for primacy.

The authority wielded by the kings of France, in both geographical and qualitative terms, grew substantially in the thirteenth century as the Capetians used 'political manoeuvring, military might and judicious marriage alliances to secure meaningful recognition of their supremacy over regions close to their power base in the north as well as territories further south'.[7] The French model was tested, revised and developed during the thirteenth and fourteenth centuries as France embarked on violent crusading endeavours. The thirteenth century certainly provided an excess of violence in crusades against the 'Muslims in Spain, Africa,

---

[5] Given, 'The Inquisitors of Languedoc', p. 339.

[6] These regions were the origin of Roman law which then spread through the rest of Europe: 'The inquisitory process and the criminal jurisprudence that it generated developed earliest in northern Italy, parts of southern France, and, within the wide circle of its jurisdiction, the courts of the Church'. The writings of university-based jurists circulated even more widely so 'in a number of places that did not formally recognize Roman law and which indeed preserved older kinds of procedure and older or laxer means of proof, there was nevertheless the influence of and familiarity with the Romano-Canonical system' (Peters, *Torture*, pp. 69–70). Peters points out that as the twelfth century went on 'Roman law began to influence all the laws of Europe, not merely those in France and Italy. [...] The doctrines regarding torture in Roman law were there when Europeans needed them, but they did not force themselves upon legal reformers, nor was anyone obliged to begin torturing defendants simply because Roman law contained a number of provisions for doing so' (*Torture*, p. 47).

[7] Smith, 'Introduction', *Joinville and Villehardouin*, p. xxii.

the Holy Land and Apulia, the Mongols, non-Christian peoples in the Baltic, heretics in Languedoc, Germany, Italy and the Balkans, Orthodox Christians in Greece and the Hohenstaufen rulers and their supporters in Italy and Germany'.[8] As France defined itself in part as a military state with its crusades, England defined itself as a distinctly separate state, deeply grounded in its Anglo-Saxon heritage in opposition to its more recent Norman influence and any connection to the French throne. The desire for an ordered society like that of Arthur's court in the Middle Dutch *Walewein* or even that advocated in the Old Norse/Icelandic *Hrafnkels saga* is understandable in the thirteenth and fourteenth centuries. After the death of Richard I in 1199 soon after the Third Crusade the power structure of England was destabilized as John (finally) legally took power, and then had to contend with French designs on his throne and the loss of lands in France. At the same time that John and Philip of France were engaged in their wars, the Church was mounting a crusade to Jerusalem that would end in the (forbidden) sack of Constantinople by the Franks in 1204. Innocent III sent letters both reprimanding and begging the kings of England and France to put aside their differences and come to the cause, chastising them as 'they harass one another in turn with inexorable hatred, while one strives to take vengeance on the other in return for his injuries, not one is moved by the injury done to the Crucified One. They pay no attention to the fact that our enemies now insult us.'[9] Shortly thereafter, beset by instability in Rome, the Church engaged in another crusade, this one centred in southern France against the Albigensian heretics, a crusade marked by systematic violence and brutality as well as the prolific use of judicial torture.

While Pope Innocent III voiced his strenuous disapproval of the French sack of Constantinople, authors like Geoffrey Villehardouin and John of Joinville recounted the deeds of their countrymen with little condemnation. The French revelled in their martial achievements, despite their brutality, and in this climate literature flourished; poets adapted and interpolated native and foreign material to fit their particular cultures and societies. Their knightly peers would have listened to the *chansons de geste*, the tales of knightly quests for 'spiritual fulfillment or the affection of their beloved' in romances, or to songs whose lyrics touched on the 'dilemmas or desires' of men and women of high standing.[10] But the brutality of the crusades and the reports of torture in inquisitorial

---

[8] Christoph T. Maier, *Crusade Propaganda and Ideology: Model Sermons for the Preaching of the Cross* (Cambridge: Cambridge University Press, 2000), p. 3. There has been a great deal written about English versus French identity in the thirteenth century, which seems to be the nexus of forming national identity. Heng, 'The Romance of England'. See also: Geraldine Heng, *Empire of Magic: Medieval Romance and the Politics of Cultural Fantasy* (New York: Columbia University Press, 2003).

[9] Innocent III, Register 1:336, 15 August 1198, in *Contemporary Sources for the Fourth Crusade*, ed. Alfred J. Andrea, with contributions by Brett E. Whalen, revised edition (Leiden and Boston MA: Koninklijke Brill, 2000), pp. 11–12.

[10] Smith, 'Introduction', *Joinville and Villehardouin*, p. xxii.

courts created an unflattering portrait of the French despite the chivalric ideals of the romance tradition and the idealistic portrayal of 'heroic' deeds. The dual tendencies in knighthood, towards violence and piety, were troubling to medieval people.[11] Torture enacted outside the realm of judicial process takes on an aura of outlawed brutality, and even in the hands of the authorities that might generally try to regulate its use, torture was a tool of oppression and corruption. According to Enders, the European Middle Ages inherited a 'classical rhetorical legacy that characterized torture as a hermeneutic legal quest for truth, a mode of proof, a form of punishment enacted by the stronger on the weaker, and a genre of spectacle or entertainment'.[12] It is within the context of a struggle for national identity in both France and England – in opposition to each other – and elsewhere on the European continent that the application of torture and judicial brutality and their depiction in secular literature play a prominent role.

French literary production had a profound effect on other continental literatures – its presence and influence were felt as far afield as the Scandinavian courts of Norway and its possession (after 1262), Iceland. Even French authors were troubled by the use of torture, and like their European contemporaries, they condemn the practice in certain texts. French poets and the *jongleurs* that crafted the Old French fabliaux engaged in a discourse of dissent as canon law expanded the use of torture in judicial procedures and the practice became more widespread. Continental cultures seeking models of literary resistance to the use of interrogatory torture and judicial brutality need look no further than the late twelfth-century French romances of Chrétien de Troyes, who openly condemns those who resort to torture in *Cligés*. The doctors who interrogate the catatonic Fenice through the application of various tortures are set upon, battered and defenestrated by the outraged ladies of the court.[13] Chrétien's outraged response to torture in his romance may reflect an early unease about the introduction of torture into French law in the late twelfth century.[14] The silence of other French authors on torture may be born of a fear of openly criticizing what was a fairly widespread practice among the French authorities in the thirteenth and fourteenth centuries. The same might be said of authors writing in the German vernaculars who rarely mention torture or judicial brutality as a literary motif despite its presence throughout the German principalities and the Holy Roman Empire.[15] Other societies may have felt more confident in condemning practices

---

[11] Smith, 'Introduction', *Joinville and Villehardouin*, p. xxi.
[12] Enders, *The Medieval Theater of Cruelty*, p. 3.
[13] Chrétien de Troyes, *Cligés*, in *Arthurian Romances*, trans. William W. Kibler (London: Penguin Books, 1991), p. 195–7.
[14] Torture, while ominously present in French legal and ecclesiastic judicial procedure, is largely absent from French literature, though its presence in French drama and performance has been thoroughly and adroitly examined by Enders.
[15] Even though torture was mentioned in thirteenth-century German statutes in the form of a prohibition, by the fourteenth century 'local regional codes had developed a fuller

alien to their cultures. The absence of torture in French literature, particularly courtly narratives and romance, may suggest an aversion to the subject, a desire of poets and authors to create a world – far from their own – of chivalry and honour where such measures are unnecessary, where brutality of this kind is alien and alterior and therefore excluded.

French literature was extremely popular and many medieval societies sought to emulate the French romance or fabliaux traditions. As Jeffrey Jerome Cohen writes, 'romance literature was promulgated in part to propagate the ideals of its chivalric code, which while mainly a literary and historical fantasy, were also intended as a system of social control'.[16] One of the special features of romance is idealization, used in Old French and Anglo-Norman romances to 'glorify an exclusive, feudal elite', whereas in Middle English romance it is turned toward the glorification of a society that perceives itself, accurately or not, 'as more centralized and integrated'.[17] Julie Nelson Couch writes that Middle English romances 'typically promote the proper fulfillment of roles within boundaries of family, social class, kingdom, and church, and these institutions are represented as entities that intertwine to form ideal society'.[18] *Havelok the Dane* and other Middle English romances 'never presume to duplicate an idealization of aristocratic culture' and anxiety is incorporated into the very structure of heroic identity.[19] Romance authors exclude torture from their tales, preferring more chivalric modes of violence, and implying that torture was not an appropriate mode of social control. Far from being a mimetic device whereby poets and authors reflect common judicial practice in their own worlds, torture or brutal punishment (such as flaying or equine quartering as in the *Roland*) appear primarily as condemnations of abusive authority. A desire for cultural definition that does not rely on or condone torture as a method of judicial investigation is embedded in this resistance. The resort to torture or its rejection becomes a factor in fashioning national identity. Episodes of torture become a forum for voicing cultural anxieties about absorbing *too much* from neighbouring nations, and for expressing fears about the loss of autonomy. Middle Dutch traditions may have been framed as responses to French legal and literary influence, perhaps condemning Church authorities that advocated and implemented torture in interrogations. In casting the use of torture outside their own society, these Flemish authors struggle with their own cultural identity and their debt to other Continental influences. It is

---

jurisprudence of torture, as did the regional laws of central and eastern Europe, generally under the influence of revived Roman law', Peters, *Torture*, p. 60. See also: *Torture*, p. 70.

[16] Jeffrey Jerome Cohen, 'Decapitation and Coming of Age: Constructing Masculinity and the Monstrous', *The Arthurian Yearbook III*, ed. Keith Busby (New York: Garland, 1993) 173–92, p. 180.

[17] Julie Nelson Couch, 'The Vulnerable Hero: *Havelok* and the Revision of Romance', *The Chaucer Review* 42, No. 3 (2008): 330–52, p. 331.

[18] Couch, 'The Vulnerable Hero', p. 332.

[19] Couch, 'The Vulnerable Hero', p. 332.

within this framework that cultural resistance to torture can be read, particularly in the case of a text like the *Roland* where the dissolution of the narrative begins with a judicial proceeding, one that is rife with personal vengeance and seems utterly devoid of justice.

The rejection of torture in these texts suggests an audience aversion to unrepentant violence and excessive brutality despite a modern critical tendency to read these episodes as desensitizing. Jean Jost argues that violence 'is a natural human shortcoming imperfectly kept in check by those who temporarily or permanently lack self-discipline, rationality, or perspective. Violent people, in life and literature, forget their social function, and operate as egocentric individuals, as if their claims alone were operative.'[20] Jost further suggests that the danger of vicarious violence (like actual violence) is that it 'breeds further violence, requires more of the same to evoke an equally exciting "thrill", as the person becomes inured to its power',[21] implying that literature is violent because society is violent. This would mean that episodes of torture are mimetic, mere representations of social norms or cultural expectations, but the fear of torture and brutality instigates their rejection, not emulation. Richard Kaeuper argues that while the violence of the medieval world would astound a modern time-traveller, there is a good evidence that many medieval people 'saw this violence as a problem distorting the more ordered society they were creating: they say so repeatedly in their writings; they instituted a peace movement in the late tenth century; during the following centuries they strengthened judicial institutions in the search for peace.'[22] Unchecked judicial brutality and the application of torture threaten ordered society in these texts and reveal the instability inherent in their use.

Chanson de Roland

In the *Gesta Dei per Francos* (1106–1109) Guibert of Nogent expounds on the actions of the Frankish participants in the First Crusade (1095–1099), emphasizing the particular piety of his countrymen:

> I say truly, and everyone should believe it, that God reserved this nation for such a great task. For we know certainly that, from the time that they received the sign of faith that blessed Remigius brought to them until the present time, they succumbed to none of the diseases of false faith from which other nations have remained uncontaminated either with great difficulty or not at all.[23]

---

[20] Jean Jost, 'Why is Middle English Romance So Violent? The Literary and Aesthetic Purposes of Violence', in *Violence in Medieval Courtly Literature: A Casebook*, ed. Albrecht Classen (New York: Routledge, 2004) 241–67, pp. 246–7.
[21] Jost, 'Why is Middle English Romance So Violent?', p. 242.
[22] Richard Kaeuper, 'The Societal Role of Chivalry in Romance: Northwestern Europe', *The Cambridge Companion to Medieval Romance*, ed. Roberta L. Krueger (Cambridge: Cambridge University Press, 2000) 97–114, p. 99.
[23] Guibert of Nogent, *The Deeds of God through the Franks: Gesta Dei per Francos*, trans. Robert Levine (Woodbridge: The Boydell Press, 1997), p. 41.

The 'nation' to which Guibert is referring is that of the Franks, which will more fully take shape as France in the thirteenth century.[24] But even as early as 1106, Guibert spoke of his 'nation' above all others, as an example to the rest of Europe: 'Because it has carried the yoke since the days of its youth, it will sit in isolation, a nation noble, wise, war-like, generous, brilliant above all kinds of nations. Every nation borrows the name as an honorific title; do we not see the Bretons, the English, the Ligurians call men "Frank" if they behave well?'.[25] This laudatory image of France is, in part, based on the cultural inheritance of Charlemagne's empire – an empire grounded in ideals of order and justice before the reintroduction of Roman law. The institution of torture as a method of interrogation and 'discovery' could be seen as a betrayal of those earlier Carolingian ideals. As France adopted the methods of inquisitorial courts and relied on torture as both an ecclesiastical and secular tool of interrogation, this earlier image of the Frankish kingdom as a model of governance, piety and justice fostered cultural resistance among other evolving nations of Europe in the thirteenth and fourteenth centuries, particularly England. The Frankish self-image was perpetuated by the Anglo-Normans who saw themselves as courteous and chivalrous with the 'responsibilities that this role necessitates in a civilized society, such as the conversion of barbarians'.[26]

The consequences of violence and the good of the societal order are juxtaposed in the execution of the traitor Ganelon in the *Chanson de Roland*. The epic, extant in its earliest form in the twelfth-century Oxford, Bodleian MS Digby 23 and in other versions in at least five different manuscripts,[27] repre-

[24] Smith writes that it is worth noting that the terms 'France' and 'French' did not refer to clearly defined geographical, political or linguistic units in the central Middle Ages. 'Introduction', *Joinville and Villehardouin*, p. xxi.

[25] Guibert of Nogent, *The Deeds of God through the Franks*, p. 41.

[26] Wendy Hoofnagle, 'Creating Kings in Post-Conquest England: The Fate of Charlemagne in Anglo-Norman Society' (PhD Dissertation: University of Connecticut, 2008), unpublished, pp. 76–7. I am grateful to Hoofnagle for sharing her insights on the *Chanson de Roland* and for providing me with a copy of her excellent dissertation.

[27] Oxford, Bodleian Library, MS Digby 23 dates from the twelfth century, approximately 1130–1170. The composition of the poem has been dated as early as 1060 and as late as the second half of the twelfth century, but Glyn Burgess points out that the most frequently accepted date is around the very end of the eleventh century, circa 1098–1100. There are two versions in the Library of St Mark in Venice: Venice IV from the fourteenth century, and Venice VII from the late thirteenth century. There are also versions in the municipal libraries of Châteauroux (late thirteenth century) and Lyon (fourteenth century), in the Bibliothèque Nationale, Paris (late thirteenth century), in Trinity College, Cambridge (fifteenth century) and some fragmentary French texts. Glyn Burgess, 'Introduction', *The Song of Roland* (London: Penguin Books, 1990), pp. 7–8. Only the Oxford and Lyon manuscripts give such prominence to the trial. Emanuel J. Mickel, *Ganelon, Treason, and the 'Chanson de Roland'* (University Park PA: The Pennsylvania State University Press, 1989), p. 10. Based on comparative palaeography, Malcom Parkes (among others) dates the Oxford Digby 23 manuscript specifically between 1119 and 1149: 'The Date of the Oxford Manuscript of *La Chanson de Roland* (Oxford, Bodleian Library, MS. Digby 23)', *Medioevo Romanzo* X.2

sents an Anglo-Norman rendering of the tale recalling the national hero of continental France and of the 'expatriate Normans'.[28] In what has often been hailed as a poem of French nationalism, or at least nationalist heroism,[29] the Anglo-Norman poet of the *Roland* highlights the flaws of Frankish society, illuminating the chinks in the armour of the French heroic ideal that influenced numerous literary traditions throughout the Middle Ages. The interweaving of French and English interests troubles the categorization of the *Roland*. The trial of Ganelon for treason, an apparent addition of the Anglo-Norman poet,[30] highlights the brutality of the Frankish system (despite earlier chronicle accounts of Charlemagne's reign which emphasize its justice and mercy)[31] and presents an image of the great Charlemagne as a complex and contradictory figure driven to brutal punishment as revenge for his nephew's death. Patrick Geary points out that it would be 'hopelessly naïve to believe that Carolingian justice functioned without judicial torture or without corporal punishments, ranging from beheadings to mutilation to death in a variety of excruciating manners'.[32] However, contemporary authors like Theodulf of Orléans criticized the cruelty of judges and documented extremes in judicial punishment in his two poems *Paraenesis*

(1985), p. 175. Hoofnagle cites Andrew Taylor, asserting that internal evidence places it within 'the milieu of a pro-Angevin court of increasing importance to Insular politics makes it a potential candidate for understanding Anglo-Norman society and culture, much like *Beowulf* is studied for insight into the Anglo-Saxon society for which it was written even as its subject matter may not be strictly "English"': 'Creating Kings in Post-Conquest England', p. 90. See Andrew Taylor's discussion of the manuscript in its social and cultural context in *Textual Situations: Three Medieval Manuscripts and Their Readers* (Philadelphia: University of Pennsylvania Press, 2002), pp. 26–70. Dating the poem to the second half of the twelfth century more securely aligns the *Roland* with English ideas of national identity.

[28] Diane Speed, 'The Construction of the Nation in Medieval English Romance', in *Readings in Medieval English Romance*, ed. Carol M. Meale (Cambridge: D.S. Brewer, 1994) 135–57, p. 146.

[29] For a thorough discussion on the appropriation of the *Roland* as a French nationalist poem in the modern period, and potentially in the Middle Ages, see: Taylor, *Textual Situations*.

[30] The depiction of the trial in the Oxford *Roland* is quite different from the Châteauroux MS, and it is missing entirely in the *Carmen de proditione Guenonis*, 'one of the poems proposed as an intermediary between the legends and the poem in Digby 23': Mary Jane Schenck, 'If There Wasn't "a" Song of Roland, Was There a "Trial" of Ganelon?', *Oliphant* 22.3 (1998): 143–57, p. 146; Mickel, *Ganelon, Treason*, pp. 156–7.

[31] *Einhard and Notker the Stammerer: Two Lives of Charlemagne*, trans. with an introduction and notes by David Ganz (London: Penguin Books, 2008). Paul R. Hyams presents compelling evidence of the irregularities of Carolingian justice depicted in the *Roland* and argues that 'Ganelon's trial invites the historian to speculate on the power balance within vassal communities and the political ability with which lords were able to manage courts in their own interest quite as much as in that of some abstract justice': 'Henry II and Ganelon', *Syracuse Scholar* 4 (1983): 22–35, p. 30.

[32] Patrick Geary, 'Judicial Violence and Torture in the Carolingian Empire', in *Law and the Illicit in Medieval Europe*, ed. Ruth Mazo Karras, Joel Kaye, and E. Ann Matter (Philadelphia: University of Pennsylvania Press, 2008) 79–88, p. 81.

ad judices (*Address to Judges*) and *Comparison of Ancient and Modern Laws*.[33] Despite its focus on the valorous deeds of Charlemagne, his nephew Roland, and the thousands who die valiantly in battle, the *Roland* presents a vengeful and brutal portrait of the Franks that was reinforced by the disastrous Fourth Crusade (1204) and the Albigensian Crusade (1209–1229).[34] The application of torture before Ganelon's trial and his subsequent execution by equine quartering creates a template of Frankish brutality embodied by the 'Other within', interrogated by a poet with a shared heritage who may have seen contradictions in this judicial spectacle. The *Roland* engages with cultural anxieties of law, legitimacy and language – negotiating between the valorous Frankish past and the Angevin or Anglo-Norman present, torn between split identities.

However, extant as it is within the same manuscripts as a number of English romances, the Roland legend can be seen as a nationalist endeavour but not necessarily for France. Diane Speed writes,

> In such company, the various ultranational settings constructed as the homeland could all perhaps be read as the one nation which is a shared experience for writer and audience in the early English romance tradition. The subsequent broadening of that tradition, which sees the identity of the hero's homeland as less of an issue in itself, as apart from any suggestiveness in relation to particular adventures involved, accords with the critical stance that a nation which has actually emerged no longer needs to provide such an obviously nationalistic indication.[35]

The *Roland* was exceptionally popular among the Normans during their conquest of Anglo-Saxon England; the 'song' was believed to have been sung at Hastings by a member of Duke William's household, an event recorded in numerous accounts including Wace's *Roman de Rou*.[36] The early Normans were obsessed with the Continent, as Wendy Hoofnagle has pointed out, and 'a study of the influence of Carolingian practices on the Norman dukes, therefore, would elucidate much of William [I]'s approach to kingship in England, and that of his successors'.[37] It is perhaps this Carolingian influence in Anglo-Norman law to

---

[33] Geary, 'Judicial Violence and Torture', p. 83.

[34] Joseph R. Strayer, *The Albigensian Crusades* (Ann Arbor MI: The University of Michigan Press, 1971, rpt. 1992), p. i.

[35] Speed, 'The Construction of the Nation', p. 146.

[36] Andrew Taylor, 'Was There a Song of Roland?', *Speculum* 76.1 (Jan. 2001): 28–65, pp. 28–9. Pickens asserts that at 'the capital moment in Norman history, the traditions of literature and culture transcend the realities of geography and politics to display the commonly shared experience of "being French". So fundamental and so pervasive is this cultural fact in the Norman view depicted by Wace [in *Roman de Rou*] that such "realities" as the essentially Germanic character of Charlemagne and his court, not to mention that of the Normans themselves, can be ignored or forgotten.' Pickens further argues that the anti-French sentiment in the *Rou* is directed at French kings based in the Ile-de-France; in the *Roland*, 'France' is specifically the Carolingian Empire. 'Implications of Being "French"', pp. 379, 380, 381.

[37] Hoofnagle, 'Creating Kings in Post-Conquest England', p. 16.

which the *Roland*-poet is referring, urging Henry II (r. 1154–1189) not to follow Frankish traditions too closely, to heed his barons and not to govern through personal vengeance. Andrew Taylor provides a thorough and erudite examination of Oxford MS Digby 23, positing that the copyist was engaged in 'cultural negotiation, modifying a traditional script to meet new demands'.[38] The manuscript could have been copied on either side of the Channel,[39] as either a French endeavour or an English one. However, Taylor argues that the conjunction of worldly clerics and sophisticated barony particular to England 'insured that there were households where *Roland* might have found an audience', and the text may have been read aloud at gatherings of knights and squires.[40]

Even in the context of Anglo-Norman authorship, the content of the *Roland* is decidedly French – part of the legend of Charlemagne that supported the Capetians, against which Arthurian legend may have been set in an attempt to bolster the Angevin house.[41] In light of that, it may have been in the interests of the English monarchy (or its Anglo-Norman poet) to portray Charlemagne in a less than flattering light – to diminish or demonize the cultural inheritance of the French and reinforce a separate Anglo-Norman identity.[42] The events of the poem situate it in the south of France on the border with Spain (in Angevin territory) and at the time the poem was written ethnic divisions between those possessions and the ones in the north had become very pronounced. Robert of Torigni, a Norman Benedictine monk, established two themes in his work 'that were to have a substantial impact on the northern view of Aquitaine: traitors in Poitou, heretics in Gascony',[43] a view that may have influenced a developing desire in the twelfth and thirteenth centuries to define English identity

---

[38] Taylor, *Textual Situations*, p. 38. Taylor supports the twelfth-century date of the text but points out that there are thirteenth-century glosses throughout the manuscript, though few of them are in the *Roland*. He also suggests a connection between the Digby manuscript and the School of Chartres, arguing that some of the glossators may have studied there.

[39] Taylor, *Textual Situations*, p. 43.

[40] Taylor, 'Was There a Song of Roland?', p. 45; *Textual Situations*, pp. 38, 43.

[41] Jonna Kjær, 'Franco-Scandinavian Literary Transmission in the Middle Ages: Two Old Norse Translations of Chrétien de Troyes – *Ívens saga* and *Erex saga*', in *The Arthurian Yearbook II*, ed. Keith Busby (New York: Garland, 1992): 113–34, p. 117.

[42] However, Pickens argues that the 'sense of "being French" in England after the Conquest was particularly acute among the primarily and then also the secondarily Francophone elite because of the heightened awareness of cultural difference in an island with multiple sharply-defined cultural frontiers – between Francophone England and surrounding Celtic lands, on the one hand, and, on the other, between the French-speaking elite and the English-speaking underclass.' 'Implications of Being "French"', p. 384. The text is fraught with questions of identity and may mark the beginning of attempts to establish a sense of autonomy from the continental inheritance.

[43] John Gillingham, 'Events and Opinions: Norman and English Views of Aquitaine, c. 1152–c. 1204', in *The World of Eleanor of Aquitaine: Literature and Society in Southern France between the Eleventh and Thirteenth Centuries*, ed. Marcus Bull and Catherine Léglu (Woodbridge: The Boydell Press, 2005) 57–81, p. 57.

in opposition to that of France and its provinces. By the 1190s, the conventional opinion in England was that Aquitaine was ungovernable, *terra indomita*, a 'turbulent, disorderly and lawless land inhabited by a *gens indomita*' until taken in hand by Richard I.[44] This lawlessness is reflected in the *Roland* where the justice and stability of the French tradition is called into question with the brutal punishment of Charlemagne's brother-in-law Ganelon. The *Roland* represents the epitome of Anglo-Norman colonial influences, but also casts aspersions on the nature of French cultural inheritance. The potential dating of the Oxford *Roland* to the early thirteenth century[45] makes its criticism of Frankish brutality even more plausible, for what interest would an English poet at that time have in glorifying the French, or their legends?

Though this division in cultural identities was far more pronounced in the fourteenth century as France and England vied for supremacy, contemporary responses to the events of the thirteenth century suggest revulsion at both the martial brutality of the Fourth Crusade and the use and abuse of torture in the Albigensian Crusade. There was resistance to the latter and its leader Simon de Montfort: 'The hostilities between the crusaders and subsequently the French crown and the counts of Toulouse were concluded in the Treaty of Paris in 1229, but resistance persisted in areas of Languedoc into the 1240s'.[46] The events of the Fourth Crusade were recorded in a number of contemporary eye-witness accounts, letters, papal registers, and later adapted retellings and historical chronicles. Dishonour, betrayal, personal interests and petty disputes marked this crusade and distinctions were made between specific ethnic groups. Villehardouin, a participant in the Fourth Crusade, records the deeds of the Franks and Venetians in the *Conquest of Constantinople* and makes specific note of the English and Danish men who defended the walls of the city against the Frankish onslaught in the first siege in July–August 1203.[47] These men were members of the Varangian guard, an elite mercenary force employed by the Byzantine emperors since the ninth century, originally made up primarily of Scandinavians; but following the Norman Conquest displaced Englishmen were added to their ranks.[48] They represent both national and individual resistance to the

---

[44] Gillingham, 'Events and Opinions', p. 59.
[45] Mickel draws several compelling legal parallels between the trial of Ganelon and judicial procedure of the twelfth and thirteenth centuries, noting the number of times law codes of the twelfth or thirteenth century in both France and England are specifically relevant to Ganelon's trial, with the caveat that the law codes record custom and therefore 'always represent the law of a period somewhat earlier' (*Ganelon, Treason*, p. 155). Taylor points out that there are thirteenth-century marginal glosses in the Oxford manuscript, suggesting that it was still actively being read well into that century (p. 38).
[46] Elaine Graham-Leigh, *The Southern French Nobility and the Albigensian Crusade* (Woodbridge: The Boydell Press, 2005), pp. 1, 3.
[47] Geoffrey Villehardouin, *Conquest of Constantinople*, in *Joinville and Villehardouin*, ed. Smith, p. 45.
[48] *Joinville and Villehardouin*, ed. Smith, p. 355, n. 5.

Frankish endeavour. The Franks were disorganized and ill equipped even though many fought bravely. But news of their brutality and the atrocities committed in the sack of Constantinople spread quickly. The registers of Innocent III record the Pope's disgust and anger at the reports, and his fear that the actions of the crusaders would keep the Eastern Church from returning to the Roman fold:

> For how will the Greek Church, afflicted to some degree by persecutions, return to ecclesiastical unity and devotion to the Apostolic See, a church which has seen in the Latins nothing except an example of affliction and the works of Hell, so that now it rightly detests them more than dogs? For they, who were believed to be seeking things not for themselves but for Jesus Christ, showed no mercy for reasons of religion, age, or sex, staining with the blood of Christians swords that they should have used on pagans.[49]

Innocent's language is reminiscent of Urban II's polemic against the Saracens in his speech at Clermont in 1095, but this time it is the Franks who perpetuate the atrocities, a similarity that perhaps would not have been lost on the Anglo-Norman noble audience.

While the search for historical resonances and attempts to situate the poem in the context of medieval law have yielded valid and engaging suggestions about the poem's historicity, the *Roland* is still a fictional narrative where Charlemagne is 200 years old and Roland can symbolically and artfully arrange the dead before succumbing to his wounds himself. R. Howard Bloch points out that the battlefield violence in the *Roland* is an idealistic portrayal of martial endeavours, that the confrontations with 'their neat rows of opposing armies and successive single combats, do not reflect an historically accurate image of twelfth-century battlefield tactics. They do, nonetheless, set the standard of literary idealization by which subsequent engagements can be judged.'[50] The literary historian Albrecht Classen also situates *Roland* in a culture of violence. He writes that these literary and historical documents provide distinct examples of 'violent behavior, of the consequences of passionate love, and of the results of hatred and aggression. [...] Roland [...] could easily be viewed with considerable suspicion, as the "heroic action" tends to trigger more destructive behavior than constructive performance.'[51] There is a profusion of battlefield violence in the *Roland* marked by foolishly valorous deaths but, off the battlefield, the trial and execution of Ganelon is the most problematic part of the poem for its apparent approval of torture and brutality. Ganelon's execution sets a judicial precedent alien to its Anglo-Norman audience and problematic for its French subject.

---

[49] Innocent III, Reg. 8:127 (128), 12 July 1205, *Contemporary Sources for the Fourth Crusade*, p. 166.
[50] R. Howard Bloch, *Medieval French Literature and Law* (Berkeley CA: University of California Press, 1977), p. 80.
[51] *Violence in Medieval Courtly Literature: A Casebook*, ed. Albrecht Classen (New York: Routledge, 2004), p. 2.

Ganelon betrays his stepson (Charlemagne's nephew) Roland to the Saracens, who attack the rear guard and slaughter 20,000 of Charlemagne's soldiers, most notably the Twelve Peers. Roland, who refuses to blow his horn (Oliphant) until the last possible moment, dies not specifically from a battle wound but from the pressure of blowing the horn. But Ganelon is portrayed as the quintessential traitor, and as such is brutalized by the lower members of Charlemagne's entourage as the rest of his army rides too late to Roland's aid: 'Li Reis fait prendre le cunte Guenelun/ Si l'cumandat as cous de sa maisun' [The king has Count Ganelon seized/ And he handed him over to his household cooks] (lines 1816–17).[52] Charlemagne then gives the Master cook orders to guard Ganelon well, '"Bien le me guarde, si cume tel felun!"' ['as befits a criminal'] (line 1819) because he betrayed the king's household. The cook takes his injunction to heart and treats him as a criminal, assigning a hundred scullions to assault him:

> Icil li peilent la barbe e les gernuns,
> Cascun le fiert quartre colps de sun puign;
> Bien le batirent à fuz e à bastuns,
> E si li metent el' col un caeignun,
> Si l'encaeinent altresi cume un urs.
> Sur un sumier l'unt mis à deshonur;
> Tant le guarderent que l'rendent à Carlun.   (lines 1823–9)

> [They pluck out his beard and his moustache/ And each gives him four blows with his fist./ They beat him soundly with sticks and staves;/ They put an iron collar round his neck/ And place him in fetters like a bear./ To his shame they set him upon a pack-horse,/ Guarding him until they deliver him to Charles.]

Ganelon suffers an ignominious punishment fitting for a traitor while under arrest, but without any recourse to law or judicial procedure. This incident mimics interrogatory torture but their abuse of him is not designed to elicit a confession. It only serves as a brutal prelude to an eventual trial for treason with a predetermined verdict. Mary Jane Schenck asks whether there was a trial of Ganelon at all.[53] Emanuel J. Mickel cautions that critics 'must be careful to distinguish, however, between punishment meted out for convicted felons and a legal procedure of torture even prior to the trial'.[54] Léon Gautier refers to Ganelon's death as torture and considers it the first stage of medieval judicial procedure and a factor in establishing the Germanic nature of the trial.[55] According

---

[52] All textual citations are from *La Chanson de Roland*, edited with a facing-page modern French translation by Léon Gautier (Tours: Mame et fils, 1872). English quotations of the *Roland* are from Glyn Burgess's translation, *The Song of Roland* (London: Penguin Books, 1990).
[53] Schenck, 'If There Wasn't "a" Song of Roland', p. 155.
[54] Mickel, *Ganelon, Treason*, p. 39.
[55] Léon Gautier, 'Idée politique dans les chansons de geste' and his edition of *La Chanson de Roland* (Tours: Mame et fils, 1872), qtd. and trans. in Mickel, *Ganelon, Treason*, p. 38. Mickel outlines the various arguments about the presence of torture in Germanic law, and

to Mickel, Ruggero Ruggieri 'speculates rather implausibly that Ganelon is also tortured for about three days: one day while Charlemagne gains vengeance on Marsile, a second when he defeats Baligant, and a third as he returns to Aix and tells Alda of Roland's death', an idea that he argues is far-fetched.[56] Ruggieri also points out that 'the torture was certainly not an attempt to extract confession, inasmuch as the trial itself would confirm Ganelon's guilt or innocence'.[57] Despite the growing influence of Roman and canon law in the twelfth century, custom is the principal law for Anglo-Norman or Frankish *bellatores* and there is little recourse to torture in that process.[58] In its savagery, Ganelon's treatment contradicts both the laws of the era in which the poem is set and when it was composed.[59]

After the king returns from Spain and the field of battle, Ganelon once again becomes the focus of the narrative as the poet recounts his punishment and his trial by combat. Ganelon is in the citadel, in iron chains, where the servants have tied him to a post:

> Les mains li lient à curreies de cerf,
> Très bien le batent à fuz e à jamelz,
> N'ad deservit que altre bien i ait.
> A grant dulur iloec atent sun plait.   (lines 3738–41)
>
> [They bind his hands with thongs of deer-hide/ And beat him thoroughly with sticks and staves./ He has not deserved a different fate;/ In great anguish he awaits his trial there.]

Again, this reflects the process of interrogatory torture, but no confession is sought and the beatings serve no purpose other than simple brutality masked as justice. Stephen D. White aptly points out that in literary texts, accusations of treason are a 'particularly shameful way of attacking an enemy and gaining power

---

points out that M. Pfeffer in his 'Die Formalitäten des gottesgerichtlichen Zweikampfs in der altfranzösischen Epik', *Zeitschrift für romanische Philologie* 9 (1885) and Ruggieri 'both rejected the idea that torture was a formal part of trial procedure' (p. 39). Pfeffer did not find any instances of formal torture in the numerous accounts of combat he studied in medieval French literature, and he suggests that the torture of Ganelon 'was merely an outbreak of anger against his believed treachery' (qtd. in Mickel, *Ganelon, Treason*, p. 39).

[56] Mickel, *Ganelon, Treason*, p. 39.
[57] Ruggero Ruggieri, *Il processo di Gano nella Chanson de Roland* (Florence: Sansini, 1936), qtd. in Mickel, *Ganelon, Treason*, p. 39.
[58] Schenck, 'If There Wasn't "a" Song of Roland', p. 152.
[59] Hyams notes that 'twelfth-century law was quite central in the social life of the classes that mattered in twelfth-century society [...] Angevin England shared a common intellectual world with the rest of French-speaking Europe. Knightly mores and custom defined the social or legal limits of acceptable behavior all over northern Europe. [...] Differences of detail between the cross-Channel customs were hardly greater than those between continental areas within the western regions of France – Normandy, Brittany, and Poitou.' 'Henry II and Ganelon', p. 25.

at court and the defendant ultimately wins aquittal'.[60] There will not really be much of a trial; Charlemagne is clearly out for revenge and has already decided Ganelon's guilt. The poet echoes Ganelon's treachery and emphasizes the justice of this punishment; however, Charlemagne is still portrayed as an emotional and rash king who condemns anyone who opposes him. While this may be perfectly legitimate in terms of kingship and authority, Charlemagne seems to have an uneasy relationship with his barons.[61]

Historically speaking, it would have been appropriate for Charlemagne to be lenient in this case especially because of his familial connection to Ganelon. When faced with traitors including his own son Pepin, Charlemagne chose to treat the offenders with great clemency, or to enact swift and merciful justice by hanging or the sword.[62] In his *Life of Charlemagne* (c. 826–7), Einhard records the emperor's response to the treachery of his son Pepin and his fellow plotters: 'All the perpetrators were sent into exile, some blinded and others unharmed, but only three conspirators lost their lives; since they had drawn their swords to avoid arrest and had killed some people, they were slain because there was no other way to subdue them'.[63] Einhard notes that this conspiracy was probably caused by the cruelty of Queen Fastrada and Charlemagne's consent to it, going 'far beyond his usual kindness and gentleness'.[64] There is no question that Einhard is biased in favour of his subject, but there is a tone of rebuke in his account for allowing cruelty to flourish. Notker Balbulus (the Stammerer), in his *Deeds of Charlemagne* (c. 884–7), comments on Charlemagne's mercy and his practice of consulting his barons before passing sentence. In the case of two guards who fell asleep drunk when they are supposed to be guarding the king's tent on the field of battle, he called together all the great men of his kingdom 'and asked them what punishment seemed fitting for those who betrayed the head of the Franks into the hands of the enemy'.[65] The barons recommended

---

[60] Stephen D. White, 'The Ambiguity of Treason in Anglo-Norman-French Law, c. 1150–1250', in *Law and the Illicit in Medieval Europe*, ed. Ruth Mazo Karras, Joel Kaye and E. Ann Matter (Philadelphia: University of Pennsylvania Press, 2008) 89–102, p. 92.

[61] According to Hyams, barons, though manipulable, 'could not often be bludgeoned into unpopular decisions, for each feared that he might suffer in his turn under any harsh new custom whose creation he had negligently permitted' (p. 26). But in this case, Charlemagne asserts his sovereignty through Thierry's victory in the duel and the barons respond with a swift verdict that 'recognizes a new reality; it is as much a political as a legal act'. 'Henry II and Ganelon', p. 30.

[62] Mickel, *Ganelon, Treason*, pp. 137–8.

[63] Einhard, *The Life of Charlemagne*, in *Einhard and Notker the Stammerer: Two Lives of Charlemagne*, ed. David Ganz (London: Penguin Books, 2008) 17–44, p. 33. Einhard's account of Roland's death in battle makes no mention of Ganelon, nor of any treachery other than that of the Basques (p. 25).

[64] Einhard, *The Life of Charlemagne*, p. 33.

[65] Notker Balbulus, *The Second Book of the Deeds of Charles*, in *Einhard and Notker the Stammerer: Two Lives of Charlemagne*, ed. David Ganz (London: Penguin Books, 2008) 86–116, p. 88. Notker records a similar response to Pepin's treachery as Einhard (pp. 101–2).

death, but Charlemagne 'merely upbraided them with the harshest words and let them go unharmed.'[66] Again, Notker is biased. He wrote his work for the Emperor Charles the Fat, and it was in his best interest to emphasize Charlemagne's better qualities, but this image is consistent in Frankish chronicles, whereas it is sharply contradicted in the *Roland*. Comparing Ganelon's execution with that of the Merovingian Queen Brunhild (killed by being tied to a horse's tail and dragged), Mickel writes:

> This case is often cited to proclaim the idea that dragging and hanging, such a frequent punishment for treason later, was the unspoken traditional punishment throughout the Middle Ages. It is difficult to defend such an evaluation. [...] Whether the punishment of Brunhild represents a charge of treason is uncertain, but it is interesting to note that there are *no similar punishments* in any of the other cases of alleged treason in the Carolingian period.[67]

The execution of Ganelon is either 'anomalous in its cruelty',[68] a poetic invention to emphasize the heinous nature of Ganelon's crime, or the excessive violence of tyrannous rule. In late twelfth-century England, the latter would have particular resonance with Anglo-Norman courtly or clerical audiences subjected to the absence of Richard I and subsequent tyranny of John, when treason took on a whole new dimension.

While Ganelon's actions cannot be condoned, neither is Roland a sympathetic figure – his exaggerated sense of misplaced chivalry leads to the death of all his men, and there is a hint of earlier treachery against Ganelon. White notes that 'twelfth- and early thirteenth-century literary texts produced for the Francophone nobility of England and France almost always characterized appeals of treason pejoratively, by demonstrating in one of two ways that the defendant was accused of treason unjustly.'[69] Ganelon attempts to justify his case by pointing out Roland's flaws before the king: "'Rollanz m' forsfist en or e en aveir,/ Pur que jo quis sa mort e sun destreit;/ Mais traïsun nule n'en i otrei" ['Roland wronged me in respect of gold and wealth;/ For which reason I sought his death and his woe./ But I admit no treason in this act.'] (lines 3758–60). There is a suggestion that Ganelon is only responsible for betraying Roland, and that Roland is responsible for betraying his own men because he does not blow Oliphant early enough, preferring instead to fight a glorious fight (though futile and doomed) which ultimately results in the decimation of the entire rear guard. Ganelon reminds the audience of his feud with Roland and essentially lays the blame at Roland's feet for sending him on a suicide mission to King Marsile, which

---

[66] Notker Balbulus, *The Second Book of the Deeds of Charles*, p. 88.
[67] Mickel, *Ganelon, Treason*, pp. 137–8. My emphasis.
[68] Peter Haidu, *The Subject of Violence: The Song of Roland and the Birth of the State* (Bloomington: Indiana University Press, 1993), p. 169.
[69] White, 'The Ambiguity of Treason', p. 92. Hyams follows a similar path, outlining the process and problems with Ganelon's trial.

Ganelon escapes through his own wit and cunning: "'Jo desfiai Rollant le puig-neür/ E Olivier e tuz lur cumpaignun;/ Carles l'oït e si noble barun./ Vengiez m'en sui, mais n'i ad traïsun'" ['I challenged Roland the warrior/ And Oliver and all his companions;/ Charles heard it and his noble barons./ I avenged myself, but there is no treason in it'] (lines 3775–8). But his argument falls on deaf ears, and though the council convenes there is a palpable sense that this is all merely for show.

Ganelon gathers his kinsmen, most notably Pinabel who is acknowledged as 'bien set parler e dreite raisun rendre' [a skilled talker and good spokesman] (line 3784) in the sense of the Old Norse/Icelandic lawspeakers.[70] Pinabel pleads for Ganelon, suggesting that at least his own family sees the validity of his defence. In fact, the Bavarians, Saxons, Poitevins, Normans, Franks, Germans and Teutons, as well as those from the Auvergne, 'i sunt li plus curteis' [the most skilled at law] (lines 3793–6), agree to a peaceful settlement and argue that it is best to abandon the trial, beseeching the king to absolve Ganelon and "'Pois, si li servet par amur e par feid" ['Let him then serve him in love and faith'] (line 3801). The accord is unanimous, except for Thierry, the brother of Lord Geoffrey. When the barons all return this verdict to Charlemagne, he rejects it out of hand and declares them all traitors. Bloch writes that the battles in the *Roland* are clearly linked to a 'transcendent contest between good and evil', so that 'all physical combats between mortal opponents reflect a superhuman struggle'.[71] But the lines of good and evil are not necessarily clear as Thierry steps forward, the only one willing to condemn Ganelon and support the king. Bloch further writes that in summoning his barons, Charlemagne follows the process of law because the 'barons are, in this respect, a repository of collective truth, the customs of the community as expressed by the judge. Their attendance validates the entire proceeding, and no legal action can officially be admitted without them.'[72] But the process of law has collapsed.

Despite the consideration and moderation of his barons, Charlemagne will have revenge. According to Paul R. Hyams, 'inherent in vengeance is its own view of justice, which sometimes coincides with that of official law, or at other times presents an alternative that challenges the "official" view'.[73] Contradictory to the historical evidence of his mercy and clemency, by furthering this conflict Charlemagne is portrayed as a tyrant who exacts bloody vengeance despite a popular desire for a peaceful solution. Thierry is the only one willing to stand up for the king's vengeance, but he does not completely absolve Roland:

---

[70] Schenck suggests that Pinabel may be educated in the law, not in the model of the Danelaw 'law-speaker', 'but an educated member of the warrior class, aware of new methods of arguing cases and used to being a justice in ducal courts.' 'If There Wasn't "a" Song of Roland', p. 152.
[71] Bloch, *Medieval French Literature and Law*, p. 19.
[72] Bloch, *Medieval French Literature and Law*, p. 49.
[73] Paul R. Hyams, *Rancor and Reconciliation in Medieval England* (Ithaca NY and London: Cornell University Press, 2003), p. 39.

'Que que Rollanz Guenelun forsfesist,
Vostre servise l'en doüst bien guarir.
Guenes est fels d'iço qu'il le traïst,
Vers vus s'en est parjurez e malmis:
Pur ço le juz jo à pendre e à murir
E sun cors metre el' camp pur les mastins
Si cume fel ki felunie fist.' (lines 3827–31)

['Whatever Roland may have done to Ganelon,/ The act of serving you should have protected him./ Ganelon is a traitor in that he betrayed him;/ He committed perjury against you and wronged you./ For this I judge that he be hanged and put to death']

Thierry transfers the crime from one against Roland to one against the king, semantically reapportioning Ganelon's guilt so that he can be convicted as a traitor. But he only advocates the customary sentence of death by hanging, not the brutal execution that follows, and he does give Ganelon's kinsmen the opportunity to defy his charge via trial by combat.[74] Schenck points out that, contrary to the impression given in literary texts, 'the judicial battle was the court of last resort', and was often not fought because a means of compromise was typically found before or during the contest itself.[75] The Carolingian capitularies specifically condemn personal vengeance in favour of settling disputes through the payment and acceptance of *wergeld*. The capitulary of Charlemagne from AD 779, 'Sanctuary and enforcing the payment of *wergeld*', urges settlement: 'Anyone unwilling to accept the price [*wergeld*] paid to buy off vengeance should be sent to us so that we may send him where he can do the least damage.'[76]

William I of England based much of his style of kingship on Charlemagne, and however he may have 'envisioned a continuation of English custom in his reign as he claimed in his early writs, the reality remained that he initially shaped several aspects of the governance of his duchy and later his kingdom in a Carolingian royal mould as did his predecessors, which would ultimately have an impact on the Norman pursuit of *imperium* throughout Britain'.[77] If this is the case, then Anglo-Norman audiences would have recognized the parallels between Charlemagne and the Angevin kings descended from William, and the poet's depiction of Charlemagne's disregard for his own laws would have been troubling. This is

---

[74] Mickel acknowledges that this is the customary sentence: death by hanging. *Ganelon,Treason*, p. 74.

[75] Schenck, 'If There Wasn't "a" Song of Roland', p. 153.

[76] Charlemagne, 'Sanctuary and enforcing the payment of *wergeld*', doc. 15a, trans. Kelly Gibson, in *Vengeance in Medieval Europe: A Reader*, ed. Daniel Lord Smail and Kelly Gibson. Readings in Medieval Civilizations and Cultures: XIII (Toronto: University of Toronto Press, 2009), p. 69. Original document in *Monumenta Germaniae Historica: Capitularia* Vol. 1, ed. A. Boretius (Hanover: Hahn, 1883), pp. 48. Doc. 15c, 'Compelling peace', implemented by Charlemagne in 805, exhorts those involved in feuds to make peace, even if they are unwilling, and those who are unwilling should be compelled to make peace in his presence (p. 70).

[77] Hoofnagle, 'Creating Kings in Post-Conquest England', p. 16.

a text of extremes, where legal customs are presented and discarded in favour of uncustomary violence and judicial brutality that borders on torture. White argues that any 'debate about whether the defendant's alleged treason was truly treason is resolved by his condemnation and execution as a traitor'.[78] But the trial cannot be read in the 'conventional way as a legally compelling argument for royalist or statist ideology that legitimated a broad view of treason as opposed to an archaic ideology of early feudalism or lineage solidarity that might once have justified Ganelon's treason as legitimate violence'.[79] Pinabel appeals once more to the king, indicting him for continuing on the path of revenge and ignoring the order of law and the verdict of his barons: "'Sire, vostre est li plaiz;/ Kar cumandez que tel noise n'i ait'" ['Lord, this trial is yours;/ Order that this confusion should cease'] (lines 3841-2). In opposition to actual customary practice in France, where the best case is made through legal speeches and there is an attempt to mitigate feuds through compromise and adjudication, Charlemagne demands trial by combat and hostages.[80] He leaves justice in the hands of God insisting that the victor will be the truth. Charlemagne's insistence on following through with a trial by combat and the subsequent punishment of Ganelon (in direct contravention of his barons' verdict and custom) taint his rule and cast him as a despot more interested in exacting vengeance than perpetuating justice. This image of Charlemagne creates a gulf in cultural identity between the Normans and the French, and taps into the anxieties of an audience caught in a mesh of cultural inheritance struggling against the 'Other within'. It may also signal a desire on the part of a Norman audience to separate themselves from that shared cultural inheritance and forge a new national identity grounded in English law rather than French.

Pinabel asks Thierry to surrender and offers himself as Thierry's vassal if Ganelon can be reconciled to the king. His fair and chivalrous plea is rejected, though Thierry does offer Pinabel reconciliation with the king, insisting that "'De Guenelun justise iert faite tel'" ['Justice will be done to Ganelon'] (line 3904). This is not justice. The system of law has been undermined, and the brutality of Ganelon's execution is an abuse of power that costs not only Ganelon his life, but Pinabel as well. The Franks proclaim Pinabel's death a miracle, divine approbation of Ganelon's execution. Charlemagne proceeds to sit in judgment, not just on Ganelon, but on all his kinsmen who protested his innocence and whom

---

[78] White, 'The Ambiguity of Treason', p. 98.

[79] White, 'The Ambiguity of Treason', p. 98.

[80] Despite the legal parallels between the Franks and the Old Norse/Icelandic tradition, Hoofnagle argues that 'Scandinavian influences did not linger long among the early Normans, of whom many families were quick to assimilate into Frankish society', citing fading connections with the Scandinavian North through the tenth century observed in the decrease in the amount of Norman money in Scandinavian coin hoards. 'Creating Kings in Post-Conquest England', p. 8.

Charlemagne denounces as traitors for that support. Bloch writes that this is fitting because the crimes of one man reflected on the whole family:

> The clan or *comitatus* was responsible for the infractions of its own members as well as for avenging wrong inflicted upon it from without. Pecuniary reparation or compensation was paid by the whole group when one of their number was at fault; and it was divided appropriately when they had been wronged. Ganelon's thirty relatives rise to his defense at the end of the *Roland* and are condemned as a unit after his conviction.[81]

However, Hyams argues that to 'understand it as a guarantee of the truth of Ganelon's plea, with the consequence that they must share his punishment, seems harsh by twelfth-century standards.'[82]

The Franks decree that they should all die and in a sweeping display of power, Charlemagne sentences them all to hang: 'Trente en i ad d'icels ki sunt pendut./ Ki traïst hume, sei ocit e altrui' [There are thirty of them who were hanged./ A traitor kills himself and his fellows] (lines 3958–9). While Charlemagne can be seen as only following the wishes of his people, that interpretation raises questions because if his people had not cried out for blood, they faced being condemned as traitors as surely as Ganelon's kin. Mickel argues that this is the poet's condemnation of traitors and their families: 'In rendering a sentence of hanging, the poet is not merely exercising poetic license or exaggeration in meting out such severe punishment; he is passing his own judgment that Ganelon's kin had become accomplices in the act of treason and therefore must suffer the supreme penalty.'[83] This is one possibility, but the members of Ganelon's family defended him in good faith. As Hyams notes, 'in normal circumstances there would be no likelihood of the death penalty for them', but these are not normal circumstances.[84] It may be that the poet is not condemning those who stand beside their family members, but rather condemning the kings who subvert the law to exact personal vengeance. According to White, the arguments that were made or could have been made in Ganelon's defence were virtually identical to the ones endorsed in other literary trials contemporary with the Oxford *Roland* and there was 'nothing archaic' about them.[85] Charlemagne establishes his capacity for unilateral violence in this episode, which is further evidenced by the cowed return of the Bavarians, Germans, Poitevins, Bretons and Normans who acquiesce to the unnecessarily brutal execution of Ganelon. The poet proclaims that 'sur tuz les altres l'unt otriet li Franc/ Que Guenes moerget par merveillus ahan' [above all others the Franks agreed/ that Ganelon should die in terrible agony]

---

[81] Bloch, *Medieval French Literature and Law*, p. 69.
[82] Hyams, 'Henry II and Ganelon', p. 30.
[83] Mickel, *Ganelon, Treason*, p. 129.
[84] Hyams, 'Henry II and Ganelon', p. 30. He also points out that in the twelfth century capital punishment was rare, especially for vassals (p. 30 n. 16).
[85] White, 'The Ambiguity of Treason', p. 98.

(lines 3962–3), suggesting that the Franks are more bloodthirsty than any of their Germanic counterparts, or that they feel Roland's loss more profoundly. In much the same way, the *Havelok*-poet suggests the Danes are more apt to violent punishment than the English, which has similar implications for the establishment of national identity.

In a scene echoed in the brutality of Chaucer's *Prioress's Tale*,[86] Ganelon is ripped apart by horses, a mode of execution that is far more likely to be a literary device than an actual form of punishment. The poet devotes one stanza to the death of Ganelon, compared with the forty-four it takes to describe Roland's death, yet it is the final action of the poem, the final event of this narrative, so it carries exceptional narrative weight:

> Quatre destriers funt amener avant,
> Pois, si li lient e les piez e les mains.
> Li cheval sunt orgoillus e curant;
> Quatre serjant les acoeillent devant
> Devers une ewe ki est en mi un camp.
> Guenes est turnez à perditiun grant;
> Trestuit si nerf mult li sunt estendant
> E tuit li membre de sun cors derumpant;
> Sur l'herbe verte en espant li clers sancs.
> Guenes est morz cume fel recreant.
> Ki traïst altre, nen est dreiz qu'il s'en vant. (lines 3964–74)

> [They have four war-horses brought forward;/ Then they bind him by his hands and feet./ The horses are mettlesome and swift;/ Four servants goad them on/ Towards a stream which flows through a field./ Ganelon was given over to total perdition./ All his ligaments are stretched taut/ And he is torn limb from limb;/ His clear blood spills on the green grass./ Ganelon died a traitor's death./ A man who betrays another has no right to boast of it.]

Although the poet explains this death as fitting for a traitor, there are residual traces of injustice that cling to the scene and to Charlemagne, which may be an indictment not of the past itself but of reliving the past and glorifying it. It may also signal a break with French heritage and an assertion of a separate Norman identity. The heinous treatment of Ganelon may well be deserved; as Mickel writes, 'the guilt of Ganelon is more perfidious even than murder and treason. There is something even blasphemous and unspeakable in Ganelon's murderous attack upon a member of his own family.'[87] But if so, then some of that taint lies on Roland who volunteered his stepfather for a mission that would almost certainly lead to his death. While Charlemagne acts as king and uncle in his vengeful execution of Ganelon, he also acts against ties of marriage and a member of his own family since Ganelon is married to his sister. White suggests

---

[86] There is some debate about the nature of the punishment meted out to the Jews, which will be discussed at length in Chapter 4.
[87] Mickel, *Ganelon, Treason*, p. 85.

that the poet 'legitimated the outcome by means of an idiosyncratic rhetorical strategy of inverting and subverting the script followed in other literary treason trials'.[88] Perhaps the subversion does not legitimate such measures, but rather condemns them as illegitimate. White further suggests that the Oxford *Roland*-poet 'can justify the outcome of Ganelon's trial only by rhetorical means and not by force of a compelling legal argument'.[89] He argues that the trial is best read, 'not as a powerful statement of a newly ascendant legal ideology, but as a brilliantly idiosyncratic exercise in the cultural politics of treason at a time when other poets represented prosecutions for betraying kings with deep suspicion if not outright disfavor'.[90] This is plausible, but the poet's rhetorical use of brutality – excessive and unjust – suggests that his goal is not to justify the trial but to condemn it. As Hyams notes, sharp lines ought not be drawn between law and culture in this period.[91] The poet may be warning his own audience, not against the actions of Ganelon, but against the actions of kings who waste the lives of their men in senseless combat, who violate the marital bonds of family, who exercise vengeance rather than justice and subvert customary law.

The nature of Ganelon's treachery has been the subject of much debate, as has the historical accuracy and validity of his harsh punishment and eventual execution by equine quartering. The execution seems to be primarily a literary motif, a spectacular way to dispatch a villainous traitor. Several scholars have argued that while quartering by horses is not the standard mode of execution for treason in the twelfth century, Ganelon's abusive treatment before the trial, the trial itself, the failure of trial by combat and his death are perfectly in keeping with accepted legal practice at the time when the Oxford version of the *Roland* was written. Mickel notes that his punishment has 'all the markings of the twelfth and thirteenth century'.[92] Robert Francis Cook, who places *Roland* in the eleventh century, argues that the

> complications of the trial stem not from any ambiguity in what Ganelon has done or uncertainty about the guilt he bears, but from a renewed emphasis on the threat to feudal principles that human weakness and perversity can pose. The fair trial that Charles intends to give Ganelon comes perilously close to being a miscarriage of justice, thanks to the threatening intervention of Pinabel in favor of the guilty man, undertaken on grounds that have nothing to do with the issues at hand.[93]

Cook acknowledges that the trial comes 'perilously close to being a miscarriage of justice', but he contends that what is done to Ganelon is wholly justified and in

---

[88] White, 'The Ambiguity of Treason', pp. 98–9.
[89] White, 'The Ambiguity of Treason', p. 101.
[90] White, 'The Ambiguity of Treason', p. 101.
[91] Hyams, 'Henry II and Ganelon', p. 25.
[92] Mickel, *Ganelon, Treason*, p. 155.
[93] Robert Francis Cook, *The Sense of the Song of Roland* (Ithaca NY: Cornell University Press, 1987), p. 113.

no way excessive. Peter Haidu insists that any condemnation of violence in the *Roland* is anachronistic, arguing that 'the rough, injurious, or unjust use of force did not invariably bear coded, moral disapproval, however much individuals may have suffered from it.'[94] Haidu also asserts that the *Roland* celebrates violence and desperately negotiates its 'aporias.'[95] However, Ruggieri among others has argued that Ganelon is more of a tragic hero than Roland. He may have been the central figure in an earlier Germanic version of the poem[96] and his consuming desire for vengeance, rooted in the Germanic tradition, overwhelms his loyalty to Charlemagne and causes his downfall. Schenck suggests that the *Roland* is the product of propaganda, and the 'supposed trial – full of inconsistencies and time warps – seems there just to serve as a prelude to Ganelon's specular, spectacular dismembering, which is part of the propaganda for the monarchy and for holy war.'[97] At issue here is not Ganelon's guilt as a traitor but the nature of his punishment – the 'specular, spectacular dismembering' – the appropriateness of its brutality and how an Anglo-Norman audience concerned with questions of conflicted national identity might have responded. His death may have served as propaganda for the French monarchy, but the Anglo-Norman version casts aspersions on the Capetian notion of justice in opposition to developing English legal customs. In that case, an English audience (even one descended from Norman stock) may have been repulsed by this tyrannical display of brutality, especially at the hands of a king noted in contemporary chronicles for his sense of justice and mercy. In his comprehensive discussion of legal precedent in the context of the *Roland*, Mickel aptly points out that the treatment of traitors escalated in severity in the late twelfth and thirteenth centuries. In the thirteenth century, the long-held view in France that the king is sovereign (*rex in regno suo princeps est*) begins to have a telling effect on the perspective of treason, though the last Capetian kings did not prosecute treason vigorously and the harsh treatment of prisoners in England began much earlier.[98] But there is a pronounced increase in the punishment of traitors in France including the implementation of dragging, hanging, beheading, quartering, and mutilating during the Hundred Years War (1337–1453).[99] Mickel writes, 'that the popular imagination condemned treason in the strongest terms can be seen in the literature of the period where, as [W.R.J.] Barron notes, flaying was also thought to be a traditional way of

---

[94] Haidu, *The Subject of Violence*, p. 3.
[95] Haidu, *The Subject of Violence*, p. 1.
[96] Ruggieri, *Il processo di Gano nella Chanson de Roland*, qtd. in Mickel, *Ganelon, Treason*, p. 13.
[97] Schenck, 'If There Wasn't "a" Song of Roland', p. 155. Schenck also asks if 'we have tried too hard as editors and readers to find the historical reality of an archetypal "Frankish, feudal trial" where, in fact, there are merely fragments of various legal procedures fused in the service of a literary, if not hagiographic, spectacle' (p. 145).
[98] Mickel, *Ganelon, Treason*, pp. 145–6.
[99] Mickel, *Ganelon, Treason*, pp. 145–6.

punishing traitors'.[100] This may explain the excessive form of execution in both *Roland* and *Havelok*, but Barron concedes that the punishment was not common in reality, for it is not found in chronicles or the law'.[101] Barron further argues that it was always an *exceptional* penalty 'prescribed by ancient usage rather than written code',[102] but Mickel rejects this and quite correctly points out that such 'an assumption comes from our natural inclination to ascribe harsher penalties to an earlier, less enlightened age'.[103]

There are plenty of harsh and brutal executions in the records, many of which Gregory of Tours (c. 539–594) enumerates in his *History of the Franks*[104] and some of which involve being dragged behind a horse and then hanged, like William Fitz Osbert's execution for rebellion in 1196.[105] That is not to say that equine quartering *never* happened, but that it is far more likely to be a literary exaggeration on the part of the poet (or the poem's original author) to highlight the primitive excesses of an earlier age. Accepting the late eleventh- to mid twelfth-century date of the Oxford *Roland*, Schenck writes that the 'gravity of Ganelon's actions and his severe punishment are "primitive" but justified by the increasing danger of treason to the Capetians' drive to centralize that power',[106] which suggests the audience was Capetian, not Angevin. With such instability on both sides, treason would have been a grave and pressing concern, but contradicting customary law was not the way to deter it. The ferocity of Charlemagne's response and the disregard for the initial verdict of his barons undermines the justification for Ganelon's execution and creates a series of cracks in the underlying power structure. The thirteenth-century Middle English *Roland and Vernagu* unique to the Auchinleck Manuscript, which portrays Charlemagne as king of France, Denmark and England, as well as Gascony, Bayonne and Picardy, does not include any reference to Ganelon or to any treachery against Roland, so that poet did not feel the need to preserve such a violent event in his glorification

---

[100] Mickel, *Ganelon, Treason*, p. 147.
[101] W.R.J. Barron, 'The Penalties for Treason in Medieval Life and Literature', *Journal of Medieval History* 7 (1981): 187–202; p. 197, qtd in Mickel, *Ganelon, Treason*, p. 147 n. 303.
[102] Barron, 'The Penalties for Treason', p. 197.
[103] Mickel, *Ganelon, Treason*, p. 147 n. 303.
[104] Gregory of Tours, *The History of the Franks*, trans. and ed. Lewis Thorpe (London: Penguin Books, 1974). Among the various histories that Gregory recounts, many involve torture or mutilation as a punitive measure or as a form of execution or vengeance, such as 'Cautinus buries Anastasius alive' (IV.12:204–5); 'The evil behaviour of Duke Rauching' (V.3:257); 'Leudast is tortured to death' (VI.32:363); 'The conspiracy of Septimima' (IX.38:525); 'An attempt to assassinate Childebert II' (X.18–19:576). Gregory records the events of history but also of his own time, and there is a weariness of violence and bloodshed in the texts, not unlike the battle-weariness at the end of the *Roland*.
[105] Mickel, *Ganelon, Treason*, p. 147.
[106] Schenck, 'If There Wasn't "a" Song of Roland', p. 145.

of Roland.[107] It is also possible that the literary presence of this specific form of punishment influenced its increased use in subsequent centuries as later authorities looked to literary analogues in the treatment of traitors and emulated what they assumed was accepted custom. Mickel provides a number of examples of traitors being hanged, drawn and quartered (some by horses) in the thirteenth century, specifically the Welsh chieftain Rhys ap Meredith who was dragged and hanged in 1292, and Thomas de Turbeville who was torn asunder by horses in 1295.[108] He also makes note of the 1240 execution of four Jews in Norwich in the same manner – which may have in turn influenced Chaucer's suggested use of this form of punishment in the *Prioress's Tale*. Mickel writes that there are many more examples of such punishment from the thirteenth and fourteenth centuries, but more significantly they are not as common either in the poem's eighth-century setting or the twelfth century of the Oxford version.[109] The legal proceedings and the proscribed punishment may feel like justice in some sense, but the poet is clear to identify it as revenge, for which there is only fleeting satisfaction.

Defining Ganelon's execution as torture, Haidu argues that the brutality of this scene is shocking to modern audiences because of the 'combination of the graphic detail with which the torture is wrecked upon the body of the condemned man and the fact that this torture is publically enacted'.[110] In order for the power of the king to be realized it must be seen and felt by all audiences even if that power is corrupt. Haidu quite correctly points out that the audience for this scene includes the modern reader as well as the Bavarians, the Germans, the Poitevins, the Bretons, the Normans and the French; but it also includes the textual audience of the late twelfth- and early thirteenth-century Anglo-Normans who might have seen this episode as a gruesome act carried out contrary to law and tradition against a defendant denied a fair trial. At a time when the English judicial system and its reliance on jury trials was being threatened by John in his attempts to consolidate his power, this image of a king flouting the will of his barons and contravening the precedents of judicial tradition would have been particularly relevant. Considering the possibility of a later date for the Oxford manuscript (or its continued popularity), the poem responds

---

[107] *Roland and Vernagu*, The Auchinleck Manuscript (ff. 262va stub-267vb), National Library of Scotland online: http://www.nls.uk/auchinleck/mss/roland.html. Accessed 12 February 2010.

[108] Mickel, *Ganelon, Treason*, p. 147.

[109] Mickel, *Ganelon, Treason*, p. 147. Schenck reminds us that there are only a few pre-Carolingian law books, a handful of Carolingian legal decisions, and 'then virtually no books written on the customary law that governed the lives of the warrior class until the end of the twelfth century at the earliest.' 'If There Wasn't "a" Song of Roland', p. 146. Considering that legal texts were probably sparse at the time, literary texts were important sources of tradition and custom, and it may have been difficult to filter fiction from fact, evidenced by the biases of Einhard and Notker.

[110] Haidu, *The Subject of Violence*, p. 171.

directly to the issues of royal corruption and national identity that led to the signing of the *Magna Carta* on the field of Runnymede in 1215. Haidu calls the scene of Ganelon's execution one of gross inhumanity, 'spectacularly displayed to as broad a public as possible'; but he also says that the 'detailed ecphrasis, repugnant to what we take as basic human decency, is broadly flaunted to the horror of a fascinated gaze'.[111] As Foucault and Haidu both note, public execution is not about justice so much as it is about the reactivation of power.[112] But Charlemagne's power as king is publicly diminished in his wilful waste of honourable men. These gruesome spectacles seem more desperate in their attempts to retain power than they seem triumphant in its reactivation. Haidu implies that the medieval gaze was transfixed and amazed by such brutality, not repulsed by it, and that the torture of Ganelon is the 'final transformation of the text'.[113] He writes: 'Upon the body of the victim is inscribed the ultimate (in)justice done Ganelon, who had the system of relevant justice switched on him mid-course. [...] His execution is the ritual which ushers in the transformation of the feudal system of justice and the politics of power dispersion of which "feudalism" is the name'.[114] He further argues that it is the necessary means of transformation into monarchical dominance;[115] however, there is a residual feeling of injustice that lingers after the execution of Ganelon which casts doubt on the general acclaim with which this kind of violent scene may have been received and potentially destabilizes that same monarchical dominance.

Charlemagne is portrayed as a despondent, broken man at the end of the epic when he is charged (yet again) with conducting another seemingly senseless slaughter. The last two stanzas dwell on the repercussions of Ganelon's death and the futility of a continuing cycle of violence. The first describes the nature of Ganelon's execution specifically as vengeance, 'Quant l'Emperere ad faite sa venjance' [When the emperor has completed his vengeance] (line 3975). The second begins by switching tack and referring to it as justice, but notes that it is spurred by anger: 'Quant l'Emperere ad faite sa justise/ E esclargiée est la sue grant ire' [When the emperor has completed his justice/ And appeased his great anger] (lines 3988–9). The final lines linger on the image of an old and tired king who weeps at the prospect of fighting another war: '"Deus!" dist li Reis, "si penuse est ma vie!"/ Pluret des oilz, sa barbe blanch tiret' ['God', said the king, 'how wearisome my life is!'/ He weeps and tugs at his white beard'] (lines 4000–1). Gabriel calls upon him again to render his service to God, which Mickel interprets as a 'battle fought in the eternal present between the Christian Franks and their foes',[116] but which Charlemagne does not seem to want to fight. The

---

[111] Haidu, *The Subject of Violence*, p. 171.
[112] Foucault, *Discipline and Punish*, p. 172.
[113] Haidu, *The Subject of Violence*, p. 172.
[114] Haidu, *The Subject of Violence*, p. 172.
[115] Haidu, *The Subject of Violence*, p. 172.
[116] Mickel, *Ganelon, Treason*, p. 165.

king's power seems faded and dissolute, despite the powerful scene of Ganelon's execution. Charlemagne as a king is deflated and his legacy seems tarnished by his lack of mercy and the 'grant ire' that drives his brutal vengeance. This episode is a resounding critique of judicial brutality from which many later literary texts will take their lead, and which influences interpretations of medieval torture as public spectacle.

Roman van Walewein

Penninc and Pieter Vostaert's thirteenth-century Middle Dutch *Roman van Walewein* (c. 1250)[117] engages in the discourse of the Other by locating the acceptance of torture in far away Endi (India), in much the same way that Chaucer's Prioress sets her tale in 'Asye'. Only in distant countries would such brutality, especially against a knight, be tolerated or even considered. Walewein, in his quest for a flying chessboard, finds himself in a number of precarious positions and in varying degrees of danger. Following the chessboard at the behest of King Arthur, Walewein fights four young dragons and their mother, and is healed by a magical bed in the castle of the shape-shifting King of Wonder, who grants him the chessboard and sends him off on another errand to fetch for him King Amoraen's miraculous Sword with Two Rings. On his journey, Walewein (ever the courteous knight) lends his horse to a desolate young man, and on foot defeats a band of robbers who had been exacting 'indie felle toolne indie usaede' [the Evil Custom, the unjust toll] (line 1486)[118] from passersby. Finally achieving the sword, Walewein is asked by King Amoraen to acquire the fair Ysabele, the daughter of King Assentijn, in exchange. Following the tradition of Tristan and Isolde, Walwein fetches the princess in Endi but falls in love with her himself (a literary difficulty that will be dealt with through King Amoraen's convenient death). It is in Endi, and in his subsequent adventures in returning to Arthur's court, that this Arthurian romance takes a sinister turn when Walewein is threatened with torture on more than one occasion. But in the course of this narrative the torture is never enacted – the threat of its use is only a ruse to help Walewein escape captivity and further the action of the romance.

Walewein rejects torture and situates its use outside the bounds of civilized society, aligning Flemish culture with those where torture was prohibited. Its

---

[117] The romance of *Walewein* is preserved in two manuscripts: The 'Leiden Manuscript' (MS Leiden, Bibliotheek der Rijkuniversiteit, Letterkunde 195, ff. 121–182) which dates to 1350, is localized in western Flanders, and is the only complete surviving text of the romance; and the 'Ghent Manuscript' (MS Ghent, Bibliotheek der Rijkuniversiteit, 1619), a fragment dated to the second half of the fourteenth century, of Flemish provenance. David F. Johnson, 'Introduction', in Penninc and Pieter Vostaert, *Roman van Walewein*, ed. and trans. David F. Johnson (New York: Garland, 1992), p. xli.

[118] All Middle Dutch quotations and modern English translations are taken from: Penninc and Pieter Vostaert, *Roman van Walewein*, ed. and trans. David F. Johnson (New York: Garland, 1992). The Dutch text does not use internal quotations for dialogue, so they are only included in the English translations.

alterity locates the torturer in the realm of the Other. The *Walewein*-poets take a French literary genre and turn it to their own cultural ends using it to criticize practices that threaten to infiltrate Flanders through French cultural and legal expansion. The Flemish audience would have been aware of torture's pervasive presence closer to home and the encroaching effect of French influence. The rise of vernacular prose histories (and, arguably, indigenous romance) was a 'traumatic response to a crisis of aristocratic power in Flanders, in the face of an ever more aggressive French monarchy, the challenge to noble status and power from burgeoning mercantile wealth, and the impoverishing effects of rapid economic change'.[119] Flanders was in danger of being subsumed by France and undermined from within, anxieties captured in the othering of torture in *Walewein*. However, it seems that even in the distant country of Endi those in power are not so monstrous after all; they can be swayed into abandoning their barbaric and uncivilized practices by the justice and gentility of Arthur's best knight. Torture is simply not a technique of civilized or courteous men, and so in *Walewein* its presence indicates a deep-seated corruption in the societies that use it, and the adaptation of the French Arthurian tradition into a native Flemish text brings this disparity into sharper focus. As Matthew James Driscoll writes, 'Arthur and his knights were by this time quite clearly a mirror for the courts of Western Europe, and the *roman courtois* everywhere forwarded the interests of the monarchy'.[120] These interests involved the appearance of justice and benevolence as much as chivalry, and *Walewein* instructs monarchs in proper practice by distancing European courts from the alien Other. The popular Arthurian tradition provides a model of kingship, chivalry and courtliness to which the barbarian Other can aspire, and also aligns the values of thirteenth-century Flemish society with civilized values that do not include judicial torture.

In many respects, *Walewein* includes motifs outside the traditional romance canon; it is an original Arthurian romance that takes elements from other Continental sources but whose plot and narrative motifs are unique. *Walewein* was most likely written for a courtly audience in Flanders,[121] but its origins are controversial: 'some scholars have found it inconceivable that this important

---

[119] Daniel Power, 'The Stripping of a Queen: Eleanor of Aquitaine in Thirteenth-Century Norman Tradition', in *The World of Eleanor of Aquitaine: Literature and Society in Southern France between the Eleventh and Thirteenth Centuries*, ed. Marcus Bull and Catherine Léglu (Woodbridge: The Boydell Press, 2005) 115–35, p. 121.

[120] Matthew James Driscoll, 'The Cloak of Fidelity: *Skikkjurímur*, A Late-Medieval Icelandic Version of *La Mantel Mautaillié*', in *The Arthurian Yearbook I*, ed. Keith Busby (New York: Garland, 1991) 107–33, p. 111.

[121] Johnson, 'Introduction', *Roman van Walewein*, pp. xvi, xvii, xx. Johnson provides a comprehensive discussion on the possible provenance of *Walewein*, citing studies that place it at a Flemish court, possibly that of the Count of Flanders or the Duke of Brabant, possibly in Ghent where Arthurian romances were particularly popular, but he cautions against assuming too quickly that the audience was a *Flemish* court because noted poets of the Low Countries composed their works for nobles from the county of Holland and Thuringen as

romance could be indigenous and have consequently posited for it, despite a paucity (if not an absence) of evidence, a lost French source'.[122] But as Bart Besamusca notes, Middle Dutch Arthurian literature does not consist of translations and adaptations alone – from the middle of the thirteenth century onward, the *matière de Bretagne* inspired several poets to write indigenous romances.[123] Penninc informs his audience that despite the great respect with which French literature was held in the Low Countries, his story is not a translation but an indigenous romance,[124] and in doing so he clearly separates his text and the actions of the story from French influence. The Flemish poets adapt and transform their material, most significantly in the figure of their protagonist whom they present without a trace of irony. Unlike French manifestations of Gawain, Walewein 'makes his appearance as the ideal courtly knight, who does not lack a single virtue'.[125] The authors capitalize on an unfamiliar conception of Gawain/Walewein, manipulating reader response, rehandling and sometimes renewing 'numerous themes and motifs already familiar to readers of Arthurian romance'.[126] The *Walewein*-poets present their hero as the ideal knight and lover, in contrast with the Old French tradition that generally vilifies Gawain. This portrayal fits perfectly in the Arthurian literary development outside France, and is perhaps grounded in the oral tradition of the *matière de Bretagne* circulating in Flanders as early as the beginning of the twelfth century.[127]

Walewein's adventures take him on a journey into an 'Other' world, not the supernatural realm of Celtic Arthurian tradition, but three distinct places that highlight the civility of Arthur's court in their strange and foreign customs. As J.D. Janssens writes, there is an opposition between Arthur's court 'symbolic of a society characterized by order, peace, harmony, security and joy – and the outside world' where chivalry and courtliness do not exist.[128] For Penninc, says Ad Putter, the 'ultimate in extraordinariness is to turn the analogy into reality,

---

well. He concludes thus 'the court at which Penninc and Vostaert found their patronage and audience must for the time being remain a mystery' (p. xx).

122 Norris J. Lacy, 'Preface', *Medieval Arthurian Literature: A Guide to Recent Research*, ed. Norris J. Lacy (New York: Garland, 1996) vii–xii, p. ix.

123 Bart Besamusca, 'The Low Countries', in *Medieval Arthurian Literature: A Guide to Recent Research*, ed. Norris J. Lacy (New York: Garland, 1996) 211–29, p. 213.

124 Besamusca, 'The Low Countries', p. 211.

125 Bart Besamusca, 'Gauvain as Lover in the Middle Dutch Verse Romance *Walewein*', in *Arthurian Yearbook II* (New York: Garland, 1992) 3–12, p. 4.

126 Norris J. Lacy, 'Convention and Innovation in the Middle Dutch *Roman van Walewein*', in *Arthurian Literature XVII: Originality and Tradition in the Middle Dutch* Roman van Walwein, ed. Bart Besamusca and Erik Kooper (Cambridge: D.S. Brewer, 1999) 47–62, p. 50.

127 Besamusca, 'Gauvain as Lover', pp. 9, 10–11.

128 J.D. Janssens, *Koning Artur in de Nederlanden* (Utrecht: HES Uitgevers, 1985), qtd in Johnson, 'Introduction', *Roman van Walewein*, p. xxvii.

to make the romance world truly Other'.¹²⁹ As Matthias Meyer suggests, the imprisonment in Endi is obviously the crowning adventure,¹³⁰ and it is in this realm that the barbarity of judicial torture exists, not in the civilized world of Arthur. This is particularly striking given the development of the papal inquisition in southern and central Europe in the thirteenth century, though torture does not seem to have been a prominent feature of inquisitorial courts in the Netherlands and those courts were never fully established in Scandinavia.¹³¹ But the mere existence of such uncourtly realms, like Endi and later the duke's camp, threatens the stability of Arthur's court, so Walewein must prevail in his quest and rehabilitate the foreign despots.

In the land of Endi, Walewein is treated harshly from the very start when he is refused basic hospitality, and though he seeks no quarrel (lines 6297–8) he is forced to confront the guards with arms and battle his way into the castle. He leaves behind him a field of slaughter awash with blood and severed limbs, which the poet catalogues as costly lost securities: 'Sulc enen voet sulc ene hant/ Sulc sinen aerm sulc sijn die/ Sulc sijn been beneden den knie' [this one a foot, that one a hand;/ this one his arms, that one his thighs;/ this one his legs below the knee,/ and that one the head from his shoulders] (lines 6519–23). But this kind of violence is apparently acceptable in the face of barbaric inhospitality.¹³² If only

---

129 Ad Putter, 'Walewein in the Otherworld and the Land of Prester John', in *Arthurian Literature XVII: Originality and Tradition in the Middle Dutch Roman van Walwein*, ed. Bart Besamusca and Erik Kooper (Cambridge: D.S. Brewer, 1999) 79–99, p. 92. Putter argues that Penninc is working from contemporary accounts of India in his description and that he casts Assentijn's castle as positively 'paradisal' (p. 97); however, he does not consider the brutality that seems so common despite the idyllic setting.

130 Matthias Meyer, 'It's Hard To Be Me, or Walewein/Gawan as Hero', in *Arthurian Literature XVII: Originality and Tradition in the Middle Dutch Roman van Walwein*, ed. Bart Besamusca and Erik Kooper (Cambridge: D.S. Brewer, 1999) 63–78, p. 68.

131 Johnny G.G. Jakobsen, 'Dominicans as Inquisitors in the North', the English summary of chapter 12 in 'Prædikebrødrene samfundsrolle i middelalderens Danmark' (PhD Dissertation: University of Southern Denmark, 2008), unpublished, pp. 2, 4. I am grateful to Jakobsen for sharing his research with me and for providing me with copies of his chapter and his conference paper, 'Everybody Expects the Dominican Inquisition', delivered at the International Medieval Congress, Leeds, 2009. In his extensive research on Dominican inquisitors, Jakobsen says that 'from neither Flanders, present-day Netherlands, Northern Germany nor Poland do I recall any references at all to inquisitors' us[ing] torture. This is certainly not to say that torture was never used, at least in the most severe cases and where a rapid confession was important, I would expect that torture was indeed used. But the problem for today's historian in this matter is that the whole thing probably was of very secondary importance to the inquisitors themselves and their reports.' Personal correspondence, 5 August 2009.

132 Norbert Voorwinden finds the fight scenes of *Walewein* particularly violent and descriptive in his comparison of the text with the German analogues Wolfram von Eschenbach's *Parzival* and Heinrich von dem Türlin's *Diu Crône*. He argues that the poets may have been acquainted with the Old French *chansons de geste*, 'but their story is not situated in the ideal chivalric world as it is depicted in the romances of German authors […] or in those of their great French predecessor Chrétien de Troyes.' Fight Descriptions in the *Roman van Walewein*

the knights at the gate had welcomed the weary Walewein rather than threatening his life, he would not have had to resort to such measures. The 'Endians' lack of hospitality and their failure to behave like chivalric knights defines this land as a place of barbaric customs, evidenced by the frequent threats of torment and pain the knights ineffectually hurl at Walewein. In this land, torture is used not as a judicial means of extracting truth but as a punishment, thus signifying the subversion of law and the corruption of the Other society. To a thirteenth-century Flemish audience that kind of judicial corruption was all too close. As Johnny Jakobsen notes, 'several regions in late medieval Northern Europe occasionally had the "pleasure" of rather aggressive and vigilant inquisitors'.[133] Inquisitorial procedure was the standard form of criminal procedure throughout most of Europe, and though it was not completely adopted in England or the Scandinavian kingdoms, it 'strongly influenced local legal theory and practice'.[134] By the first half of the thirteenth century canon lawyers had approved the use of torture in civil law procedure, and some of the earliest records of its use involve the officers of the count of Flanders around 1260.[135] However, Peters notes that certain 'qualifications' of the laws in Flanders itself suggest 'further attitudes toward it'; specifically, in Ghent in 1297 'the count and his officers were forbidden to torture a citizen of the town without the approval of the town council'.[136] But in the growing, crowded cities of thirteenth-century Flanders, 'the enforcement of a centralized criminal law often fell to the lot of legal officers who had much to do before a case came to trial'; magistrates needed confessions, and as Peters points out, they found that 'torture was often able to extract them'.[137] This must have been a disturbing trend to those who witnessed this shift in judicial procedure, and that discomfort is registered in *Walewein*. Felicity Riddy writes,

> perhaps the self-confident ambition of this thirteenth-century Flemish romance, in which the hero's prowess earns him the right to a kingdom, picks up some of the drive to achievement that must have powered the social and economic transformation of Flanders and the struggles among the oligarchies of the Flemish towns, in the twelfth and thirteenth centuries. Read this way, Walewein is not an exemplar of courtly conduct but a way of writing social energy. He is the consciousness of the upwardly mobile as well as of the nobility.[138]

and in Two Middle High German Romances. A Comparison', in *Arthurian Literature XVII: Originality and Tradition in the Middle Dutch Roman van Walwein*, ed. Bart Besamusca and Erik Kooper (Cambridge: D.S. Brewer, 1999) 169–87, p. 187.

[133] Jakobsen, 'Dominicans as Inquisitors in the North', p. 2.
[134] Peters, *Inquisition*, p. 52.
[135] Peters, *Torture*, p. 49.
[136] Peters, *Torture*, p. 49.
[137] Peters, *Torture*, pp. 49–50.
[138] Felicity Riddy, 'Giving and Receiving: Exchange in the *Roman van Walewein* and *Sir Gawain and the Green Knight*', in *Arthurian Literature XVII: Originality and Tradition in the Middle Dutch Roman van Walwein*, ed. Bart Besamusca and Erik Kooper (Cambridge: D.S. Brewer, 1999) 101–14, p. 111.

As such, placing the presence of torture outside the borders of Flanders in Endi is in the interests of both the nobility whose power was eroded by such measures and a rising merchant class testing the boundaries of social mobility.

When Walewein is finally overwhelmed and captured, Princess Ysabele asks to have the knight delivered to her rather than killed. Yet as she says, under her hand, 'maer sine smerte en*de* sijn verdriet/ Dat wert groot bi miere trouwe' ['his torment and his misery/ will be great, by my faith'] (lines 7443–5). The king wants to exact revenge for the injuries inflicted by Walewein, but Ysabele attempts to forestall his anger and intended execution by threatening worse punishment and torture. Much like a saint facing martyrdom, Walewein welcomes this torment and execution if the princess kills him herself (lines 7698–7701). Neither her guards nor her father question her ability to inflict pain upon Walewein, though she does say that she wishes to be left in private with him:

> Van desen ridder ghewroke*n* gerne
> Die mine*n* vader pijnde te deerne
> Wedert mi quaet es ofte goet
> Ic moet emmer mine*n* moet
> Over hem coelen maer mi ware
> Leet wist yemen hopenbare
> Dat ic die bem ene joncfrouwe
> Enen ridder soude doen sulke*n* rouwe
> Keert ghi heren want ens niet
> Wel betamelijc dat ghi siet
> Want is sal hem groten toren
> Doen is segt ju wel te voren.   (lines 7822–34)

['I would eagerly be avenged upon this knight/ who has injured my father so severely./ Whether it is good for me or not,/ I must needs cool my anger/ on him, but it would grieve me/ if it were to become known publicly/ that I, a damsel,/ should have caused a knight such suffering./ Go now, my lords, for it is not/ seemly that you see it;/ for I shall inflict great torment/ upon him, this I say to you in advance.']

Ysabele has no intention of actually punishing Walewein, and yet her society obviously believes that not only is she capable, but that her actions are appropriate. The application of torture is a societal norm in Endi. Walewein must not only escape, but later instruct their king in justice, convincing him as he has succeeded in 'civilizing' Ysabele. The poets essentially argue that no society can be considered civilized and employ torture as part of its judicial or punitive process – a message most likely aimed at the upper levels of society who were most responsible for the introduction of torture to Flemish law, or who allowed the practice to infiltrate Flemish society.

Although she has been swayed and converted by her immediate love of Walewein, and his love for her, Ysabele has a propensity for cruelty and unnecessary violence. The poets stray from their narrative to explain how Ysabele ordered the craftsman who constructed her secret passageway 'stappans werpe*n* in die

riviere/ Daer hi verdranc en*de* sijns daer nare/ Nemmermeer ne wart niemare'
[to be thrown into the river/ where he drowned and was thereafter/ never seen
again] (lines 7921–4) to preserve its secrets. According to Janssens, Ysabele
'progresses from a deceitful and even cruel woman' to a 'loving, courtly lady
under the influence of Walewein's exploits'.[139] Ysabele is much like the dreaded
Modthryth of *Beowulf* who has men tortured and slain for looking at her, but
is finally tamed by the noble King Offa. In *Beowulf*, Modthryth in her cruelty is
compared to the good, noble, and just Queen Hygd, but her conversion indicates
that justice is possible and should prevail in civilized societies. The same can be
said for Ysabele and her father's kingdom. Just as Ysabele will be transformed
by her love for Walewein and reject the brutality that seems to proliferate in
her father's kingdom, so too will her father King Assentijn eventually realize
the uncivil nature of his rule and embrace the fairness and justice of Arthur's
court. This has interesting implications considering the Anglo-French tradition
of Arthuriana. Though drawing from French sources, Arthur is undisputedly an
English king, in which case perhaps it is the English court rather than the French
that is being held up for emulation:

> Thus in spite of the growing accommodation with torture on the part of canon
> lawyers in the thirteenth century (and canon law ran in England as surely as it
> ran elsewhere), and in spite of the discussion of torture in the *Liber Pauperum* of
> Vacarius, a scholar of Roman law at Oxford in the 1140s, the reforms of Henry II
> gave a procedure to the law of England that eliminated the use of torture in the
> very centuries in which continental legal reforms were drawing closer and closer
> to it.[140]

Penninc and Vostaert may not have only been interested in emulating the fictional
court of Arthur but the real court of England with which the Flemish had close
ties. Despite the presence of sizeable Flemish communities in England, Anglo-
Flemish literary relations in the later Middle Ages 'have not been subjected to
much scrutiny'.[141] However Anglo-Flemish contacts in the fourteenth century
(the date of the surviving *Walewein* manuscripts) extended from the nobility
to artisans: Edward III married Philippa of Hainault and took the title of king
of France at Ghent in 1340 during the Hundred Years War.[142] Riddy writes
that the 'vagaries of the war between England and France produced a pattern of
shifting Flemish allegiances between then and the end of the century, but trade
between the regions was always important, particularly for the English cloth

---

[139] Janssens, *Koning Artur in de Nederlanden*, qtd. in Johnson, 'Introduction', *Roman van Walewein*, p. xxix.
[140] Peters, *Torture*, p. 59.
[141] Riddy, 'Giving and Receiving', p. 102.
[142] Riddy, 'Giving and Receiving', p. 102. Riddy makes several compelling comparisons between *SGGK* and *Walewein*, suggesting that perhaps the *Gawain*-poet was familiar with the earlier Middle Dutch text.

industry'.¹⁴³ But like the Normans, the Flemish in England and on the Continent had to contend with cultural stereotypes and a past that depicted Flemings as nothing more than mercenaries.

There were so many Flemings involved in the Norman Conquest that William I singled them out with the Normans and the English in his writs of protection.¹⁴⁴ Flemings spread throughout Europe, so the tie between the French, English and Flemish was fraught with cultural anxieties about national identity. Centrally located between England, France and Germany, Flanders witnessed the early growth of a 'centralized feudal principality, had the most important cluster of commercial and manufacturing towns north of the Alps and probably attained a higher population density than any region of comparable size outside Italy'.¹⁴⁵ It was also pulled between cultural influences. Bartlett argues that even after the crises of the fourteenth century Flanders had sufficient vitality to produce a distinctive culture of its own, which is misleadingly called 'Burgundian'.¹⁴⁶ But this distinct culture emerges earlier and is evident in the cultural distinctions drawn in *Walewein*. Walewein is a Flemish hero exalted against the French tradition¹⁴⁷ who represents a cultural desire for civility and *courtois* evident in the French romance tradition but without the judicial baggage that accompanies the use of torture. Romance is not the only genre that Middle Dutch authors adapted from French sources. Geert H.M. Claassens writes that Charlemagne 'led both a historical and literary life throughout all of Europe. The original Middle Dutch *Karel ende Elegast* bears witness to this, as do translations and adaptations of the Old French *Renout de Montauban* and the *Geste des Loherains*.'¹⁴⁸ Just as the Anglo-Norman poet of the *Roland* may have reworked the French national narrative of Charlemagne as a potential critique of perceived Frankish brutality in his own time struggling with associations of the 'Other within', the *Walewein*-poets engage in a pointed criticism of torture through a French milieu transformed in their own national interests. Like the *Roland*, the presence of torture in *Walewein* highlights the cultural guilt associated with it, for only barbarians would resort to such methods and think them effective, and as such it challenges the cultural inheritance from the realm of Charlemagne.

King Assentijn initially revels in the thought of his daughter torturing Walewein, occupying himself 'ghelosede dicken en*de* vele/ Hoe dane doot hi dade bederven/ En*de* met diversen tormente*n* dade sterven' [constantly in imagining/ by what form of death he would have him perish, and/ under which numerous torments he would have him killed] (lines 7962–4). As a king, Assentijn is the

---

143 Riddy, 'Giving and Receiving', p. 102.
144 Bartlett, *The Making of Europe*, pp. 113–14.
145 Bartlett, *The Making of Europe*, p. 113.
146 Bartlett, *The Making of Europe*, p. 113.
147 Riddy, 'Giving and Receiving', p. 102.
148 Geert H.M. Claassens, 'Foreword', *Roman van Walewein*, p. xii.

distorted mirror image of Arthur; he is not just, his bravery is tarnished by his cruelty and he would prefer to have his daughter torture Walewein to death rather than act as a judge and carry out justice. This court thrives on unseemly violence and unchivalric practices which also appear to pervade their daily affairs. The jealous knight who betrays Ysabele and Walewein swears that he is telling the truth, offering to have it proven by being 'legghen eest niet waer' ['broken on the wheel if it is not true!'] (line 8021).[149] After witnessing her affair with Walewein, Assentijn proclaims that his daughter will 'sterven met groten sere' ['die under great torment!'] (line 8062). He slanders her before all his men and then attempts to surprise them in her chamber. After a fierce battle, Walewein is brought down, bound and seriously maltreated. King Assentijn also orders his daughter imprisoned (lines 8269–72).

The poets spend several lines describing the possible tortures to which both Walewein and Ysabele may be subjected, focusing on the cruelty of Assentijn and the injustice of employing torture as a means of punishment because he has 'ontliven soude met groten tormente' [threatened to kill them both/ under great torments] (line 8319). But it is not a grim catalogue of torments designed to appeal to the more bloodthirsty reader; rather, it is a rehearsal of Assentijn's capacity for cruelty, even against his own family. One lover wonders whether 'dene mict dat mense sal delven/ Levende oft bernen in een vier/ Dander mict nu werdic hier/ Verhangen of up een rat gheleit' [they would be buried/ alive or burned in a fire;/ the other thought, 'Now I shall be/ hanged here or laid on the wheel'] (lines 8326–29). But the torments are never carried out; the lovers are freed by the ghost of the Red Knight whom Walewein had slain for beating a woman, another correction of violent injustice. Such a system of barbarity – a barbarity emphasized by the use of torture – cannot hold. In the end, as David Johnson writes, 'Walewein's exploit in Endi brings about its rehabilitation and integration into courtly society, symbolized by King Assentijn's visit to Arthur's court in the final scene of the romance.'[150] From this point on, the audience assumes that Endi will change its barbaric, 'foreign', ways and no longer employ torture. But the reality of judicial torture was not that far from the poets' native borders, a proximity that may have been disquieting to the *Walewein*-poets, who recognized the potential for violent corruption in their own society and through this romance urge that justice prevail rather than tyranny.

Part of justice, of course (as the *Roland*) is the implementation of fair judicial procedure – which is absent from Endi and other outlying lands. The poets explicitly mock corrupt judicial proceedings later in the tale. Ysabele and Walewein are captured by a duke who decides to put Walewein to death 'mach doen sterven cortelike' [in the most merciless and degrading manner] (line 9060) for slaying his son in a lawful joust. When the body is brought forward, the

---

[149] Cf. Merback, *The Thief, the Cross and the Wheel*, p. 158.
[150] Johnson, 'Introduction', *Roman van Walewein*, p. xxix.

wounds bleed profusely in front of Walewein, who honourably admits his role in Ysemgrijm's death and relates the circumstances of their encounter (lines 8826–48). But the duke rejects the justice of his son's death and demands a public trial for Walewein and the execution of Ysabele. The duke heeds the advice of his knights who ask that Ysemgrijm's brother be sent for so he can 'den ridder helpen trahinen/ Die ju heeft brocht in deser pinen' ['help you torture/ the knight who has brought this misery upon you'] (lines 9083–4). The prisoners are clapped in irons and thrown into the dungeon to await their fate while water pours into their cell from the sea. Their gaoler baits them, gloating: 'dat men Waleweine up een rat/ Vlechten soude ende siere amie/ Gheven soude sonder andre vrie/ Stalknechten ende vulen garsoene/ Haren wille mede te doene' [Walewein would be broken on/ the wheel, and that his lover/ would be given without more ado/ to the stableboys and filthy servants/ to do with as they pleased] (lines 9140–44). He strikes Walewein who protests that shackled prisoners should not be beaten and tries to defend himself. He rushes the guard, fails because of the shackles, and Ysabele weeps at his pain. There they remain, weeping for each other's pain and contemplating death when the gaoler returns the next day with scant rations. The gaoler hits the knight again and Walewein protests their treatment, arguing against the abuse of prisoners who cannot defend themselves, particularly if they are noble: 'Dune souds ghenen prisonier' ['You should not treat any prisoner/ in this way'] (lines 9190–91). The beatings continue until Walewein breaks his chains in a miraculous feat of strength at the sight of Ysabele's blood. The valiant hero and his damsel escape after Walewein avenges their injuries on the cruel and pitiless gaoler (lines 9221–34). This society is even more unjust than that of King Assentijn, and the judicial proceedings are a sham that only *seems* to enact justice. The trial is never held because Walewein escapes, but the poets suggest that *had* there been a trial it would only be for show. Any torture inflicted upon Walewein would be gratuitous because he already confessed and he made no attempt to hide his actions in the first place. Like the *Roland*, the judicial proceedings enact a spectacle of punishment that questions the foundations of law. Calling for a trial implies justice, it implies legitimacy and fairness, but in both cases those trials and the punishment carried out *before* them are charades. They contravene cultural expectations of correct law and reveal a flawed and corrupt system.

Ultimately, compared with Walewein, everyone else must be seen as less noble and less honourable, so the desire of these 'monsters' to use torture for revenge makes sense. But in dressing the thirst for vengeance in the guise of a legal and public trail, the poets criticize the abuse of jurisprudence that existed within their own world. Here the threat of 'torture' is punitive, not interrogative, in direct contravention of medieval laws governing its acceptable use. But the very existence of torture in accepted legal practice makes its abuse possible. In this poem, torture is the supreme injustice threatened against the virtuous hero. There are problems with Walewein's character; he seems motivated by self-interest and the desire for material gain and Arthur emerges as the true representative of the courtly norm;[151] however, Walewein acts honourably and chivalrously throughout his dealings in Endi. His treatment is the worst kind of dishonour. His gaolers and judges are rash, cruel, corrupt and monstrous, and their use of torture reflects their flaws. Virtuous society is embodied by its justice, according to Janssens, its courtesy 'in language and attitude, correct methods of fighting, splendid meals and magnificent, luxurious artefacts, courtly table manners, kindness, the use of the sword in service of the needy – all these were presented as components of refined society'.[152] This poem exhorts society to behave properly, to follow its own ideals rather than participating in the same modes of violence enacted by Other, monstrous societies. In this context, the Arthurian court with its roots in English tradition is held up as a bastion of justice and civility compared with the Other courts where Walewein travels. In writing an indigenous romance grounded in Arthurian literary convention, the *Walewein*-poets firmly reject the application of torture – rejecting not only a literary tradition that avoids it, but also rejecting legal institutions that enabled its abuse.

A monstrously bloodthirsty medieval audience (if modern critics and politicians are to be believed) would have revelled in these taut descriptions of torment and brutality. But these are the actions of unchivalrous barbarians in a far distant land unrelated to the world of Arthur and his knights. Civilized society does not abuse its power; it does not unjustly try people for murder in self-defence and inflict pain for no other purpose than sadistic fulfilment; it does not abuse prisoners, or resort to torture. Penninc and Vostaert appeal to their noble and merchant-class audience and essentially urge a rejection of torture and judicial tyranny. Whether the poets were heeded is a matter for some debate, but their text and the genre to which it belonged were so popular that as early as the late eleventh and early twelfth centuries the Flemish nobility were bestowing upon their children Flemish variations of Arthurian chivalric names.[153] *Walewein* weighs and measures the consequences of violence against the good of society and the need to maintain order and security. In this discourse of torture and brutality, *Walewein* creates a specific Flemish identity within the romance genre and clearly casts the use of judicial torture as a practice of the Other.

Intertextuality brought cultures closer together, but the differences of law and legal procedures drove these cultures to define themselves in opposition to those who resorted to torture. *La Chanson de Roland* addresses the anxieties of inheritance and the tensions of the 'Other within' in its portrayal of the French heroic

---

151 Johnson, 'Introduction', *Roman van Walewein*, p. xxx.
152 J.D. Janssens, 'The "Roman van Walewein," and Episodic Arthurian Romance', in *Medieval Dutch Literature and its European Context*, ed. Erik Kooper (Cambridge: Cambridge University Press, 1994) 113–28, p. 125. See: W. Prevenier, 'Court and City Culture in the Low Counties from 1100 to 1530' in the same volume, pp. 11–29.
153 Johnson, 'Introduction', *Roman van Walewein*, p. xvii.

tradition and the iconic hero Charlemagne as vengeful and excessively brutal, wanton in his disregard for justice. There is no real judicial inquiry, no interrogation of the presumed guilty party; it is an episode of literary brutality that decries the excessive use of force in judicial proceedings and urges a balance between justice and revenge. In many ways, as Mickel and others have pointed out, the *Roland* does echo the older traditions of Germanic society where the family bonds and the perpetuation of blood feuds were pervasive. But even in the Germanic tradition and in the system of retributive violence there was a system of law that prohibited or at least discouraged torture as means of legal process or punishment. As a text steeped in traditions of national identity – one that was ostensibly French despite its Anglo-Norman composition or one that spoke to the conflicted identity of the English in opposition to the French as they attempted to define themselves – the *Roland* reflects tensions in the endurance of the Charlemagne legend in the light of developing continental legal and literary trends. As national identities emerged and the application of torture was codified or rejected, literary sources grounded in shared intertexual traditions like the *Roland* recorded varying responses to its use. The *Roland* speaks to audiences caught between the warring factions of France and England, or caught up in the martial endeavours of France in the late twelfth and early thirteenth century, while other continental romances incorporated torture in limited episodes designed to situate such practices well outside their own societies as alien or Other. In the Low Countries this influence was widely felt in the adaptation of French Arthurian romance and its integration into the indigenous literary tradition. At the same time the process of canon law and its inquisitorial reliance on torture also threatened to take hold in Flanders. Speaking to the Flemish nobility and the rising burgess community, Penninc and Vostaert in the *Roman van Walewein* hold up two opposing courts to their audience: that of the barbarian Other where torture is used wantonly and with impunity, and that of the Arthurian court defined by its civility and justice.

3

The Matter of the North: Icelandic Sagas and Cultural Autonomy

> In which justice is meted out, and there is the embarrassing impression that everyone is wrong   *The Name of the Rose*, Umberto Eco (p. 445)

While continental societies struggled to establish their place in the shadow of the growing powers of France and England and continuing dynastic disputes, Scandinavia was engaged in a similar discourse on identity. Icelandic saga authors attempted to define themselves in opposition to both Norwegian encroachment and a Viking past notable for savage atrocities. There was an 'extraordinary explosion of Icelandic literature in the twelfth, thirteenth and fourteenth centuries' when three distinct saga genres were composed, connecting the culture of Iceland to its own heritage and to the shared traditions with medieval western Europe.[1] The legendary sagas (*fornaldarsögur*), chivalric or 'knights' sagas (*riddarasögur*), and Icelandic family sagas (*Íslendingasaga*) situate Iceland and its heroes within a complex literary culture of identity. *Riddarasögur* arise 'from the traffic in translations of foreign literature', while *fornaldarsögur* 'adapt a tradition, indigenous and intimately linked to the image that Icelanders of the twelfth and thirteenth centuries formed of their own past, to a new form: fictional prose narrative'.[2] The *Íslendingasaga* is tied to 'the past of its authors and audience, but to a much more recent past'.[3] Anxieties about the earlier and more recent past are articulated in saga accounts of excessive judicial brutality that contravene acceptable modes of social governance. The Old Norse/Icelandic sagas resist the influence of outside forces in favour of native sentiment and genre. This chapter focuses on singular episodes of judicial brutality in the sagas that surpass the generally violent tenor of Scandinavian literature. Hamstringing and eviscera-

---

[1] Torfi H. Tulinius, *The Matter of the North: The Rise of Literary Fiction in Thirteenth-Century Iceland*, trans. Randi C. Eldevik, The Viking Collection: Studies in Northern Civilization, Vol. 13 (Odense: Odense University Press, 2002), p. 11.
[2] Tulinius, *The Matter of the North*, p. 11.
[3] Tulinius, *The Matter of the North*, p. 11.

tion figure in the family sagas *Hrafnkels saga* and *Brennu-Njals saga* respectively as moments of extraordinary and excessive brutality alien to Icelandic society.

In records of an earlier barbarian past, there are accounts of Viking raiders torturing prisoners for information about hidden monastic treasure during their forays into Britain,[4] but the majority of these reports are from the perspective of those the Vikings terrorized – the records of monks who eulogize the suffering of their fallen comrades with the rhetoric of hagiography. Alfred P. Smyth argues that these accounts point to a savagery among the Vikings, but it is not recorded in the bulk of Old Norse/Icelandic literature, especially the family sagas which contain a significant amount of standard societal violence. Iceland of the twelfth and thirteenth centuries (when these sagas were recorded) was a different, more ordered place than Britain and even France of the ninth and tenth centuries. Smyth writes:

> From Francia, we have an account of the torture of four monks at St-Bertin of whom only one survived. We are reminded of Blathmac's suffering in the account by Abbo of Fleury (*c.* 986) of the slaying of King Edmund of East Anglia by the Danes in November 869: 'His ribs were laid bare by numberless gashes, as if he had been put to the torture of the rack, or had been torn by savage claws.' Frank argued that Abbo's reference to 'rack' (*eculeus*) and 'claw' (*ungula*) as instrument of torture used on the unfortunate Edmund was nothing more than part of a stock motif and vocabulary drawn from late antique and early medieval writers and hagiographers. But if that were so it is curious that Abbo first attributed a form of death to Edmund which is borrowed from the Life of St Sebastian and then felt it necessary to add in a different form of torture and death altogether.[5]

Frankish and British ecclesiastics bent on demonizing their attackers to galvanize military support from their secular lords applied standard hagiographic motifs to their martyrs the same way Church hagiographers did for countless other saints. However, it is equally likely that the Viking raiders were bloodthirsty, greedy and murderous. Smyth writes, 'Revisionists who hold that allusions to Norse brutality and to human sacrifice in Old Icelandic literature belong to the realm of literary motif in a heroic genre, argue in the face of evidence from Icelandic sources themselves as well as from much earlier accounts of Norse behaviour in the written records of their victims and their enemies.'[6] Smyth makes further reference to the debate about 'blood-eagling' rituals in the ninth century and other forms of ritual slaying;[7] however, these instances are generally

---

[4] Alfred P. Smyth, 'The Effect of Scandinavian Raiders on the English and Irish Churches: A Preliminary Reassessment', in *Britain and Ireland 900–1300: Insular Responses to Medieval European Change*, ed. Brendan Smith (Cambridge: Cambridge University Press, 1999) 1–38, p. 16.
[5] Smyth, 'The Effect of Scandinavian Raiders', pp. 17–18.
[6] Smyth, 'The Effect of Scandinavian Raiders', p. 18.
[7] Smyth, 'The Effect of Scandinavian Raiders', p. 18.

absent from the sagas.[8] Ironically, by the thirteenth century it is in France – the former Francia that had been subjected to the bloody violence and torture of earlier Viking raiders – where torture is employed most frequently as part of the legal process of interrogation, while the practice was unknown in Scandinavia. At this point, Scandinavian societies, particularly Iceland, chafed against continental influence, some of which stemmed from earlier Viking interaction (often at the point of a sword) with the Frankish people.[9] Some of the Vikings who travelled south and formed the Varangian guard of Constantinople faced Franks at the siege of the Fourth Crusade in 1204. English nobles were also motivated to join the Varangian guard to escape the rule of William I after 1066 (their presence is recorded at the siege of Constantinople on the losing side), and many Scandinavians felt similar antipathy to the Norman conqueror. Snorri Sturluson mentions a poet named Þorkell whose seething anger at William for killing his English lord, Waltheof, is expressed in the poem *Valþjófsflokkr*. In it he accuses William of deceiving him in a state of truce,[10] an anger that many felt towards the Normans and later the French. Residual animosity between the continental powers and Scandinavians persisted as individual Nordic societies defined themselves and their own literary traditions.

Continental romances flourished in thirteenth-century Norway and the conventions of the genre were also introduced into other Scandinavian coun-

---

[8] While 'blood-eagling', referred to in Skaldic poetry and a few other sources is a brutal performative mutilation where the victory is inscribed on the body of the defeated, it appears to be largely post-mortem – the image of an eagle being carved upon the foe's back or the ribs being broken through the back of the corpse – and so while gruesomely dramatic it does not constitute torture. As a display of martial power this ritual serves a similar purpose as torture masked as judicial interrogation, used by those who seek to gain authority or reaffirm unstable authority structures. Both *Knútsdrápa* and *Orkneyinga saga* record this ritual, as Smyth points out. The battlefield episode in *Orkneyinga saga* is particularly brutal: 'Einar carved the bloody-eagle on [Halfdan's] back by laying his sword in the hollow at the backbone and hacking all the ribs from the backbone down to the loins, and drawing out the lungs; and he gave him to Odin as an offering for his victory.' A.P. Smyth, *Scandinavian Kings in the British Isles 850–880* (Oxford: Oxford University Press, 1977), p. 191; Smyth, 'The Effect of Scandinavian Raiders', p. 18. Smyth participates in the debate about the reality and frequency of blood-eagling, sparked by Roberta Frank's interpretation of the ritual in *Knútsdrápa*, and conducted in the pages of various academic journals. Roberta Frank, 'Viking Atrocity and Skaldic Verse: The Rite of the Blood-eagle', *EHR* 99 (1984): 341–3; p. 337; Bjarni Einarsson, 'De Normannorum Atrocitate, or on the Execution of Royalty by the Aquiline Method', *Saga-Book* 22.1 (1986): 79–82; Roberta Frank, 'The Blood-eagle Again', *Saga-Book* 22.5 (1988): 288; Roberta Frank, 'Ornithology and Interpretation of Skaldic Verse', *Saga-Book* 23.2 (1990): 81–3; Bjarni Einarsson, 'The Blood-eagle Once More: Two Notes', *Saga-Book* 23.2 (1990): 80–1. Smyth summarizes this debate and clarifies his position in 'The Effect of Scandinavian Raiders', pp. 18–19.

[9] Judith Jesch, *Ships and Men in the Late Viking Age: The Vocabulary of Runic Inscriptions and Skaldic Verse* (Woodbridge: The Boydell Press, 2001), p. 80.

[10] Magnús Fjalldal, *Anglo-Saxon England in Icelandic Medieval Texts* (Toronto: University of Toronto Press, 2005), p. 30.

tries – perhaps in an effort to dispel the historical stereotypes of earlier Viking communities perpetuated in chronicles.[11] The profusion of Arthurian texts commissioned by King Hákon of Norway is a testament to the desire to reinvent the Norse in the image of courtly society. King Hákon Hákonarson (r. 1217–1263) commissioned more than forty *riddarasögur*, translations of French Arthurian texts such as *Möttuls saga* and *Tristrams saga*, because French was then fashionable.[12] According to Matthew James Driscoll, it is generally accepted that Hákon wanted to introduce into Norway customs and conventions found in the courts of continental Europe, and the translation of chivalric literature was part of this policy.[13] One of the most popular subjects throughout Europe in the later Middle Ages, the *matière de Bretagne*, was quite well represented in Old Norse literature – 'better represented than, for example, in England'.[14] But Jonna Kjær argues that England seems to have played a role in the transmission of French texts in the Nordic countries.[15] Henry Goddard Leach remarked on this in 1921, arguing that Hákon intended these translations for profit and pleasure, 'to instruct those who surrounded him, in the ideals and customs, accoutrement and ceremonials of chivalry'.[16] At the same time, Hákon brought Iceland under Norse rule. But Hákon's imperial enterprise in Iceland was unpopular, and by preserving earlier literary traditions rather than adapting romance, saga authors may have been distancing themselves from Norwegian influence. Torfi H. Tulinius points out that in Iceland, narratives 'about ancient Scandinavian heroes would have played a role comparable to that of the medieval French works of fiction that exploited the three "matters" of Rome, France, and of Britain'.[17] These texts deal with 'problems and concerns endemic to thirteenth-century Iceland, a society undergoing massive change'.[18]

Unlike *Walewein*, the influx of Arthurian material in Norway was chiefly

---

[11] Eric J. Fehr inspired further research into this question with his conference paper, 'Rape, Pillage, and Burn: The Christian Demonization of Vikings', delivered at the fourth annual Meeting in the Middle undergraduate research conference in medieval studies, hosted by Longwood University, March 2010.

[12] Driscoll, 'The Cloak of Fidelity', pp. 110–11; also Kjær, 'Franco-Scandinavian Literary Transmission', p. 113. Marianne E. Kalinke points out, however, that the Arthurian *riddarasögur* are preserved solely in Icelandic manuscripts. Kalinke, 'Scandinavia', in *Medieval Arthurian Literature: A Guide to Recent Research*, ed. Norris J. Lacy (New York: Garland, 1996) 83–107.

[13] Driscoll, 'The Cloak of Fidelity', p. 110.

[14] Driscoll, 'The Cloak of Fidelity', p. 109.

[15] Kjær, 'Franco-Scandinavian Literary Transmission', p. 114.

[16] Henry Goddard Leach, *Angevin Britain and Scandinavia*. Harvard Studies in Comparative Literature, Vol. VI (Cambridge MA: Harvard University Press, 1921) p. 153; qtd. in Kalinke, 'Scandinavia', p. 153.

[17] Tulinius, *The Matter of the North*, p. 12.

[18] Tulinius, *The Matter of the North*, p. 12.

a literature of translation rather than indigenous adaptations,[19] but Marianne Kalinke notes that while the Norwegian court provided the primary impetus for the transmission of Arthurian matter to Scandinavia, there is at least one Icelandic exception.[20] Contrary to what occurred in the German-language realm,

> the translated Arthurian romances did not generate an indigenous sub-genre – that is, Arthurian romance – in Scandinavia. Rather the primary impact of Arthurian literature in the North may be seen in the introduction of new themes in such short narrative forms as ballads and folktales and in the transmission of certain motifs [...] that reappeared in indigenous Icelandic romance and even in some sagas of the Icelanders.[21]

Critics like Kalinke understand 'the discrepancies between the extant Icelandic texts and their ultimate French sources as the work of one or more Icelandic redactors'.[22] She explains that the 'divergences tell us more about the reception of the romances and the scribal practices and attitudes in Iceland than about translational methodology and ideology in Norway'.[23] The legendary sagas were 'very useful to the social class in power at this time in Iceland'.[24] As Tulinius argues, 'the Icelandic ruling class wished to imitate the aristocratic customs that flourished elsewhere in Europe'.[25] Specifically, this class was 'impelled by the desire to integrate itself with medieval Christendom while proving, to itself as well as to others, the nobility of its lineage, and while adopting aristocratic continental modes of life and thought.'[26] Tulinius finds it both 'possible and legitimate' to draw parallels between twelfth- and thirteenth-century French literature and Icelandic literature.[27] But while the legendary saga authors exploited the 'Matter of the North' in the same way as 'French and Anglo-Norman authors did the three "Matters" of Rome, France and Britain',[28] the authors of the family sagas did not; they were more concerned with the preservation of Icelandic cultural identity as an autonomous entity.

Indigenous Icelandic literature largely diverges from this influence, perhaps in response to Norwegian imperial endeavours that sought to acculturate Iceland according to Norwegian societal values. The Icelandic family sagas paint a picture of Norse chieftains as fiercely independent men 'for whom personal honor was of primary importance'.[29] While this picture may have been idealized, Hákon's

---

[19] Kalinke, 'Scandinavia', p. 84.
[20] Kalinke, 'Scandinavia', p. 85.
[21] Kalinke, 'Scandinavia', p. 86.
[22] Kalinke, 'Scandinavia', p. 88.
[23] Kalinke, 'Scandinavia', p. 88.
[24] Tulinius, *The Matter of the North*, p. 45.
[25] Tulinius, *The Matter of the North*, p. 45.
[26] Tulinius, *The Matter of the North*, p. 45.
[27] Tulinius, *The Matter of the North*, p. 46.
[28] Tulinius, *The Matter of the North*, p. 46.
[29] Driscoll, 'The Cloak of Fidelity', p. 111. See also: Jesse L. Byock, *Medieval Iceland: Society,*

interest in Arthurian texts like *Möttuls saga* may have been in impressing upon his men that the honour of the *king* was paramount, and that individual honour was expendable if necessary when the king's honour was at stake, thus denying the viability of 'Germanic individualism'.[30] As a consequence, the Icelandic family sagas are far less interested in the fantasy world of the Arthurian court and far more engaged with historical identity, which relies heavily on legal traditions independent of those which developed in the rest of Europe.[31] Kjær suggests that in their adaptations of romance material, legendary saga-authors have done the romances a service, 'for if the French audience was occasionally able to laugh in self-criticism when listening to them, the situation could not be the same for a Nordic audience which would have found the French courtly heroes simply ridiculous'.[32] But there are naturally reciprocal influences between the translated texts and the indigenous literature[33] that strips away the trappings of European *courtois* influence and grounds itself in a more recognizable, specifically Icelandic past, one in which torture plays no acceptable part. As in other medieval societies, Icelandic authors attempted to situate torture as a practice of the Other – if not actually outside their own social boundaries, then far enough in the past to be disavowed. The Icelandic sagas, whose societies were certainly influenced by continental trends, describe torture as a means to an end. In these texts, what is often referred to as torture strictly speaking is not, but is instead brutality in the guise of judicial punishment masked as justice.

The literature of northern Europe during the medieval period stands out against the romances of continental tradition for its stark realism. According to Vésteinn Ólason, with its

> strong human perspective, this is clearly a far different conceptual world from that found in the bulk of other medieval European literature, which tends to build upon either timeless, escapist fantasy or a divinely decreed order. […] While much European narrative literature of the Middle Ages makes lavish use of exaggeration and often tried to achieve effects through the sheer weight of clustered synonyms, the sagas are characterized by a careful choice of words and subtle understatement.[34]

Sagas, and Power (Berkeley CA: University of California Press, 1988). The date of the Icelandic family sagas is difficult to pinpoint since many of the events date to the pre-Christian period of the ninth and tenth centuries, but they survive in largely medieval manuscripts from the thirteenth century, and their existence in this period of Norwegian political domination suggests that the saga authors, or later scribes, were intent on preserving a distinct sense of Icelandic identity separate from that which evolved in Norway during the Middle Ages.

[30] Driscoll, 'The Cloak of Fidelity', p. 111.
[31] Jesse Byock fully addresses the evolution and development of Iceland's legal traditions, and its relationship with the rest of Europe, in *Medieval Iceland*, p. 3.
[32] Kjær, 'Franco-Scandinavian Literary Transmission', p. 117.
[33] Kjær, 'Franco-Scandinavian Literary Transmission', p. 131.
[34] Vésteinn Ólason, 'Introduction', in *Gisli Sursson's Saga and The Saga of the People of Eyri*, ed. and trans. Martin S. Regal and Judy Quinn (London: Penguin Books, 2003), p. xi.

The family sagas, in their reliance on 'historical' events may be a response to the fanciful world of chivalry and romance popular in the *riddarasögur* but alien to Icelandic society, just as their aversion to torture – or in the literary episodes discussed here, judicial brutality in the form of mutilation – may be a response to inquisitorial methods evolving on the Continent. Iceland's geographical location did not divorce it from shared literary traditions nor imbue its populace with a particular bloodthirstiness.

The family sagas differentiate between older cultural assumptions about bloodthirsty Vikings and Icelandic society under Norwegian rule struggling to maintain its independent identity under colonial control. Jesse Byock writes that Iceland retained much of its traditional law, culture and social structure throughout the transition leading to Norwegian rule, and part of that was the production of sagas.[35] From the late twelfth through to the early fourteenth century, saga writing became a national passion in Iceland, and as 'new and often foreign elements became important to the society they too were incorporated into this creative form of narration, thus enriching the oral saga, as it was transformed into a written genre.'[36] The image of the barbarous Viking Other proliferated in the medieval European psyche, particularly in England and France, and so the Norse past worked against the Icelanders. The saga authors attempted to distance themselves from 'their' past, focusing more on the progress of the people, their history and their peaceful transition to Christianity. Icelanders had a 'curious love-hate' relationship with the notion of kingship and royal courts, but through associations with Anglo-Saxon traditions they also compared their country, ruled by consensual order rather than royal hierarchy, with Norway with a very clear agenda: 'to contrast tyrannical, scheming, and murderous Norwegian kings to idyllic, generous, and friendly monarchs on the English throne.'[37] Just as *Walewein* appears to adopt the English aspects of Arthurian tradition rather than the French, the Icelandic saga authors look to England and its sense of Anglo-Saxon law and justice rather than Norway or other continental powers.

The same Germanic tradition of retributive violence in the *Roland* (and many Anglo-Saxon texts like *Beowulf*) is exhibited in the corpus of the family sagas. Despite the common image of ruthless Scandinavian raiders, sagas are governed as much by a strict adherence to legal procedure as they are by violence. All forms of violence are subject to the laws of the Althing – even self-defence demanded punishment, but that punishment rarely involved physical harm, which makes the select accounts of excessive brutality (beyond killing or maiming during a fight) even more insidious. Most of the family sagas like *Hrafnkels saga freysgoða* and *Brennu-Njals saga* exist in thirteenth- and fourteenth-century manuscripts.[38] Even if they represent an earlier tradition or reflect earlier events, their preserva-

---

[35] Byock, *Medieval Iceland*, p. 48.
[36] Byock, *Medieval Iceland*, pp. 48–9.
[37] Fjalldal, *Anglo-Saxon England*, p. 101.
[38] Though many of the sagas are notoriously difficult to date. Cf. note 29.

tion and transmission in the medieval period is a testament to their continued influence and importance in Icelandic society. As much as *Walewein* may respond to the growing force of inquisitorial courts in the Low Countries, the sagas reinforce older traditions and a unique legal system that has no place for judicial torture; it 'appears not to have been part of any Scandinavian laws until the sixteenth century, when it was introduced under the influence of new and more ambitious and influential criminal legal codes from Germany'.[39] According to William Ian Miller, the family sagas show only about three instances of torture, but other forms of violence occur much more frequently such as 'handhewing, and leghewing, and occasional geldings'.[40] These instances of mutilation are always in the heat of combat, in the process of fulfilling blood vengeance, not as a punitive judicial measure.

Even though blood vengeance is carried out regularly in sagas, its acceptance is not unconditional.[41] Herman Pálsson writes that the sagas are not merely catalogues of vendettas and murder, and even those that record incidents of torture like *Hrafnkels saga* owe much to the humanistic tradition of the Middle Ages: 'They are concerned with human emotions and sufferings and in them human dignity is taken for granted, irrespective of social position and wealth'.[42] The torture of Hrafnkel and his men, in fact, appears to be an aberration with a seemingly 'un-Icelandic flavor' which may indicate foreign subject matter introduced through oral or written accounts.[43] Murder and manslaughter were clearly defined, and anything beyond the standard taking of a life was a breach

---

[39] Peters, *Torture*, p. 60.

[40] William Ian Miller, *Bloodtaking and Peacemaking: Feud, Law, and Society in Saga Iceland* (Chicago: University of Chicago Press, 1990), p. 196; Andersson and Miller point out that torture certainly did happen, however infrequently. Theodore M. Andersson and William Ian Miller, *Law and Literature in Medieval Iceland: Ljósvetninga saga and Valla-Ljóts saga* (Stanford CA: Stanford University Press, 1989), pp. 44–5. Miller writes, 'The uneven distribution of these incidents between two types of saga seems to suggest the existence of a norm against it, but clearly not strong enough to prevent its frequent breach. [...] Explicit statements of the norm do not deal with mutilation per se but with the appropriateness of mutilating particular classes of people.' *Bloodtaking and Peacemaking*, p. 196.

[41] Ólason, 'Introduction', *Gisli Surssons's Saga*, p. xvi.

[42] Hermann Pálsson, 'Introduction', *Hrafnkel's Saga and Other Icelandic Stories*, trans. Hermann Pálsson (New York: Penguin Books, 1971), p. 19.

[43] Sigurður Nordal, *Hrafnkels Saga Freysgoða*, trans. R. George Thomas (Cardiff: University of Wales Press, 1958) p. 29, qtd. in Erik Wahlgren, 'Fact and Fancy in the Vinland Sagas', in *Old Norse Literature and Mythology: A Symposium*, ed. Edgar C. Polomé (Austin TX: University of Texas Press, 1969) 19–80, p. 60 n. 70. In a discussion of a torture episode in *Groenlendinga* (Saga of the Greenlanders), Wahlgren writes that a strangely 'alien impression' is conveyed by Leifr's 'torture' of Freydís' followers into a full confession: 'This suspectedly Christian and Continental sophistication is reminiscent of a fictional feature in the much later *Hrafnkels Saga Freysgoða*' (p. 60), adding that 'the two centuries by which GS may precede *Hrafnkatla* argue an importance for the oral tale, if our view is sustained that the Freydís incident is chiefly fiction' (p. 60 n. 70).

in this system. Ólason writes that 'Law' was a complex concept in the Icelandic commonwealth; 'it designated a corpus of originally unwritten but memorized rules or "articles", and also the community that accepted these rules and even the geographical area in which they were considered to be valid.'[44] Traditional law can be defined as an informal bundle of laws and 'legitimate, though not legally codified, customs which explain the real behavior of a society', stressing the maintenance of order and preservation of institutions.[45] Legal tradition was deeply embedded in the social fabric of Icelandic society and its threads are evident in the literary motifs of violence. Judicial torture, of the kind practised by inquisitorial courts is a foreign practice – one that could endanger Icelandic autonomous identity if allowed to spread through imperial endeavours – so saga authors are careful to condemn any excessive brutality.

In the family sagas, the idea of 'torture' appears as extra-juridical punishment for a heinous crime, as in the evisceration of Broðir in *Brennu-Njals saga*, or as a form of inappropriate humiliation, like the mutilation of Hrafnkel in *Hrafnkels saga* or Vǫlundr in the Eddic poem *Vǫlundarkviða*. These scenes are brutal; however, they may reflect literary motif rather than actual practice. Evisceration may never have been used in actual practice in the North, but developed instead as a literary convention (as in southern hagiography) to emphasize either the sacrifice of the hero or the evil nature of the criminal.[46] Extreme forms of torture-as-punishment – evisceration and hamstringing – provoke an extreme response against such tactics which do not figure in even the most violent sagas. *Grettis saga* has an example of every kind of violence and injustice, and yet none of its actors resort to torture. Despite the retributive killings, the ambushes, the injustice of the earl's rulings in Norway, Grettir, a man of little patience and even less tolerance, only employs traditional violence. Even in his outlawry, Grettir does not cross the boundary transgressed by figures like Sámr in *Hrafnkels saga* or the Irish who execute Broðir in *Njals saga*.

Hrafnkels saga and *Brennu-Njals saga* contain specific instances of public mutilation carried out as part of a judicial process, partly as punishment and partly as means of constraining an enemy in a barbaric display of abuse of power. But the rejection of these methods and the criminality associated with their use construct specifically Icelandic modes for justice in the light of pervasive continental legal developments. The sagas distance themselves from the terrifying images of the past, the savage raids and historical accounts of torture and brutality that came to be associated in the minds of many medieval Europeans with the Vikings – whatever their Scandinavian origin. Instead, the family sagas emphasize Icelandic national identity inherent in the rule of law and the disas-

---

[44] Ólason, 'Introduction', *Gisli Surssons Saga*, p. xxiii.
[45] William Pencak, *The Conflict of Law and Justice in the Icelandic Sagas* (Amsterdam: Rodopi, 1995), p. 6.
[46] John Frankis, 'From Saint's Life to Saga: The Fatal Walk of Alfred Ætheling, Saint Amphibalus and the Viking Broðir', *Saga-Book* 25: 2 (1999): 121–37.

trous and destabilizing effect of breaking those laws. Each text employs brutality as the tool of a barbarian Other, though in *Hrafnkels saga* Sámr only becomes the Other – an outlaw – because he resorts to torture, suggestive of the 'Other within' and of the potential for monstrous action that lurks within us all. In both *Njals saga* and *Vǫlundarkviða* the foreign Other, the Irish and Niðuðr, resort to brutality that would have been alien to thirteenth-century Icelandic society, and in these acts further define Icelandic identity as lawful and just.

Hrafnkels saga freysgoða

Produced in the 'Golden Age' of saga writing in the thirteenth century but set in the first half of the tenth century, *Hrafnkels saga freysgoða* presents few laudable or even sympathetic characters.[47] The story revolves around a blood feud sparked by the unnecessary (legally if not morally justified) killing of a young man (Einar) who defies the central authority, Hrafnkel. He rides Hrafnkel's favourite horse despite warnings against it and the threat of death if he disobeys. The rest of the saga details the legal proceedings, legal failings and continued retributive violence well known in Old Norse/Icelandic literature while also tracing the fall of a powerful man, his humiliation and subsequent reinstatement and revenge. In *Hrafnkels saga*, Sámr, who has taken up the mantle of the blood feud against Hrafnkel, tortures him as a physical and visual measure of his power; but had he real power within the society it would not have been necessary. Pálsson writes that the saga owes much to medieval humanism and is 'a far cry from the heroic poetry in the *Edda* with its idealized ethos and its strong emphasis on aristocratic background, fatalism, personal honour and physical courage, to the stark realism with which the Icelandic farmers and farmhands are described in our stories'.[48] The nostalgic anti-heroism of *Hrafnkels saga* which emphasizes the real struggle and violence of Icelandic life does not sanction the actions of Sámr and his men in mutilating and publicly humiliating Hrafnkel. Byock argues that Sámr shows compassion in letting Hrafnkel live considering his reputation and his prowess,[49] but because he relies on torturing rather than killing Hrafnkel, Sámr leaves the door open to his own potential destruction. When the tables are turned, Hrafnkel will show more compassion and restraint than Sámr.

---

[47] E.V. Gordon, *An Introduction to Old Norse*, 'Introduction', *Hrafnkels saga freysgoða* (Oxford: Oxford Clarendon Press, 2nd edition, 1956), pp. 58–9; Hermann Pálsson, 'Introduction', *Hrafnkel's Saga*, p. 7. Pálsson's translation of *Hrafnkels saga* is based on a defective paper manuscript dating from the early seventeenth century, AM 551c, 4to, preserved in the Arnamagnæan Library in Copenhagen. Pálsson explains that he filled the gaps from an eighteenth-century copy of that manuscript, AM 451, 4to, made when the original was in better condition, and replaced doubtful readings with passages from other seventeenth-century manuscripts: AM 156, fol.; AM 158, fol.; and AM 443, 4to. Except for a single vellum leaf, the text survives only in the later paper versions (p. 32).

[48] Pálsson, 'Introduction', *Hrafnkel's Saga*, p. 19.

[49] Jesse Byock, *Feud in the Icelandic Saga* (Berkeley CA: University of California Press, 1982; rpt. in paperback, 1993), p. 203.

Sámr's actions in the course of the feud culminate in a dishonourable scene in which he relies on deceit rather than open combat. Sámr ambushes Hrafnkel in bed and drags him with all the able-bodied men outside, herding the women and children into one room. Hrafnkel addresses Sámr's intentions and warns him that resorting to insult and humiliation will bring him dishonour:

> Af því ok heim á skálavegginn var skotit vaðasi einum. Þeir leiða Hrafnkel þar til ok hans menn. Hann bauð mǫrg boð fyrir sik ok sina menn. En er þat tjáði eigi, þá bað hann mǫnnum sínum lífs, – 'því at þeirhafa ekki til sakar gǫrt við yðr, en þat er mer engi ósœmð, þótt þér drepið mik. Mun ek ekki undan því mælask. Undan hrakningum mælumk ek. Er yðr engi sœmð í því. (5:561–67)[50]
>
> [In the home meadow there stood a storehouse and between it and the wall of the farmhouse was a beam for drying clothes. They led Hrafnkel up to the beam. He kept pleading for himself and his men, and when he realised that his efforts were in vain, he asked the lives of his men to be spared.
> 'They've done you no harm,' he said, 'but you can kill me without any discredit to yourselves. I'm not going to plead for my life, but I ask you not to torture me, for that would bring you no credit.'] (p. 57)[51]

Sámr's men ignore Hrafnkel's words and taunt him. Thorkel says this is just retribution for the lack of mercy that Hrafnkel has shown his opponents; however, Hrafnkel never resorts to torture or mutilation, and treats him own men and supporters very well. His actions, though reprehensible on many levels, are perfectly within the law. In his extensive research on Icelandic feuds and sagas, Byock details the legal proceedings for litigating personal feuds or family disputes, which hinged on the 'institutionalized concept that the government bore no responsibility for punishing an individual for breaking the law'.[52] Criminal acts were treated as private matters unless the participants brought the matter before the assembly at the Althing, and penalties 'could be restitutions or fines paid in the form of damages to the successful party'.[53] As Miller explains, bloodshed was one thing, torture quite another. In a body of literature that has more than its share of 'axings in the back, killings encompassed by treachery and trickery, narrated without accompanying moralizations [...] [t]he extent to which torture and maiming was expected or legitimate is hard to determine'.[54] There are no provisions for applying torture in judicial inquiry here. Pencak

---

[50] All textual citations for *Hrafnkels saga freysgoða* are taken from *An Introduction to Old Norse*, ed. E.V. Gordon (Oxford: Oxford Clarendon Press, 2nd edition, 1956). Gordon has reproduced the entire text of *Hrafnkels saga* from Jón Jóhannesson, *Hrafnkels saga freysgoða*, Íslenzk Fornrít, 11 (Reykjavik: Hið islenzka fornritafélag, 1950). While *hrakningum* (insult or humiliation) does not literally mean 'torture', Pálsson translates the sense of the word from what happens next.
[51] All translations are taken from *Hrafnkel's Saga and Other Icelandic Stories*, trans. Hermann Pálsson (New York: Penguin Books, 1971).
[52] Jesse Byock, *Viking Age Iceland* (London: Penguin Books, 2001), p. 184.
[53] Byock, *Viking Age Iceland*, p. 184.
[54] Miller, *Bloodtaking and Peacemaking*, p. 196.

argues that the true purpose of Icelandic law is a puzzle – whether law should exact strict personal justice or justice be tempered in the interest of keeping the peace and improving the community conditions.[55] *Hrafnkels saga* comes down on the side of community welfare, urging compromise and reconciliation rather than a continuance of brutal retribution.

Sámr mutilates Hrafnkel and his men but grants him his life in exchange for a grant of self-judgment.

> Þá taka þeir Hrafnkel ok hans menn ok bundu hendr þeira á bak aptr. Eptir þat brutu þeir upp utibúrit ok toku reip ofan ór krokum, taka síðan knifa sína ok stinga raufar á hásinum þeira ok draga þar í reipin ok kasta þeim svá upp yfir ásinn ok binda þá svá átta saman. (5:571–575)
>
> [Then they drew their knives, cut through the prisoners' heels behind the tendon, pulled the rope through the holes, strung the eight men together and hung them from the clothes' beam.] (pp. 57–8)

This is a form of humiliation that leaves Hrafnkel visibly vulnerable before his men and his household. His torture is a catalyst for the action of the saga; it is the pivot upon which the plot turns, but both the saga author and the society within the saga condemn it as illegitimate. Sámr has already publicly humiliated Hrafnkel at the assembly at the Law Rock by stripping him of everything, so this act of torture is unnecessary and excessive, and Hrafnkel specifically refers to the mutilation as an insult, *hrakningum*. Sámr's decision is foolish but it is also brutal and cruel. As Pálsson writes, 'Hrafnkel's opponents have no scruples in resorting to violence and unlawful acts themselves: they deny him the right to defend himself before the judges and use force to keep him out of court when his case is being heard. And their torture of him is not only a gross offence against human dignity but also a criminal act.'[56] In letting Hrafnkel live, Sámr leaves himself vulnerable to the possibility of his vengeance, which Hrafnkel exacts in a particularly cruel manner mirroring the humiliation to which he was subjected, but without resorting to mutilation.

When it comes to exacting vengeance upon Sámr, Hrafnkel reminds him of this act, yet does not repeat it. After biding his time, gathering his resources and his forces once again, Hrafnkel captures Sámr in bed, just as Sámr caught him, and makes him an offer:

> '[…] at ek á nu vald á lífi þínu. Skal ek nú eigivera þér verri drengr en þú vart mer. Mun ek bjóða þer tvá kosti: at vera drepinn – hinn er annarr, at ek skal einnskera ok skapa okkar í milli.' (9:831-4)
>
> ['Your life is in my hands. I'll be just as generous to you as you were to me, and give you the same choice; to live or to be killed. If you choose to live, the terms will be solely up to me.'] (p. 68)

---

[55] Pencak, *The Conflict of Law*, p. 11.
[56] Pálsson, 'Introduction', *Hrafnkel's Saga*, p. 15.

Sámr accepts his life, acknowledging that either option would be harsh. Hrafnkel lays out the terms: exile from Adalbol and reestablishment at a more distant farm in Leikskalar with only the goods he brought to Adalbol when he displaced Hrafnkel, who will resume his chieftaincy and his authority over the district, taking back the estate Sámr deprived him of and retaking all his goods. He denies Sámr compensation for the death of his brother Eyvind, 'fyrir því at þú mæltir herfiliga eptir inn fyrra frænda þínn' (9:844–5) ['because of the cruel revenge you took for the killing of your other kinsmen'] (p. 68) and limits the blood price for his cousin Einar (whose death began the feud) to what he has already received while enjoying Hrafnkel's power and position. Hrafnkel acknowledges that the lives that have been taken have been amply repaid and that there is no need for the feud to continue:

> 'En eigi þykki mer meira vert dráp Eyvindar ok manna hans en meizl við mik ok minna manna. Þú gerðir mik sveitarrækan, en ek læt mer líka, at þú sitir á Leikskálum, ok mun þat duga, ef þu ofsar þér eigi til vansa.' (9:848–51)
>
> ['I don't believe the killing of Eyvind was any worse than the torture I was made to suffer, nor was the death of his companions any worse than the maiming of my men. You had me outlawed from my own district, but I'll allow you to live at Leikskalar as long as you don't let your pride be your downfall.'] (p. 69)

Sámr accepts those terms, though his brothers reproach him for it later and for not killing Hrafnkel when he had the chance. But he lives out his days on his farm, 'fekk hann aldri uppreist móti Hrafnkeli, meðan hann lifði' (10:889–90) [without ever, for the rest of his life, being able to avenge himself on Hrafnkel] (p. 70).

While Hrafnkel is not a sympathetic character, neither is Sámr, and when Sámr crosses the boundary of acceptable violence and resorts to torture, he leaves himself open to criticism and retaliation. Even though he had the legal right to kill Hrafnkel, Sámr is now outside the law and has forfeited any right to legal restitution. After his ordeal Hrafnkel exacts vengeance, but also shows mercy even while remaining mindful of the earlier torture inflicted on him and his men. The author never overtly condemns Sámr for this act. However, its vivid description points not to a sense of grim pleasure, but to a deep dissatisfaction with those who contravene the law and destabilize the community, especially because Hrafnkel is reinstated at the end and both men live out their days and die in their beds. In this instance, the pseudo-judicial mutilation of Hrafnkel and his men probably reflects neither historical 'fact' nor actual practice, but does signal a distaste for excessive brutality in power struggles and urges restraint within the boundaries of accepted legal tradition. This episode also suggests that Icelandic law as an institution functions because there is a deep abiding interest in justice in that society – an interest that may be undermined by imperial interference.

The use of hamstringing in *Hrafnkels saga* may have its roots, not in historical social practice or even in continental tradition, but in pre-Christian mythology and heroic Eddic poetry preserved in Iceland despite the Christian conversion in AD 1000, specifically the *Vǫlundarkviða* (*Lay of Volund*) found in the *Elder Edda*, the oldest extant manuscript of which, the *Codex Regius*, was compiled in Iceland no earlier than 1270.[57] The preservation of the Eddic poetry in Iceland in the thirteenth century signals a desire to retain cultural autonomy and a sense of national identity despite a process of imperial control and influence. This mythical association suggests that the mutilation of Hrafnkel is a literary motif, a response to or rejection of an earlier tradition, or an instance of brutality inspired by poetic convention like equine quartering in the *Roland* or flaying in *Havelok*. The poem has cultural associations with ancient Germanic traditions but also with Anglo-Saxon England.

The subject of the *Vǫlundarkviða* is Vǫlundr, or Weland, one of the most recognizable figures in Norse legend and mythology who appears in tales as far afield as *Beowulf* and *Deor*. He is the elvish smith loved and abandoned by a valkyrie or *alvitr*, imprisoned and hamstrung by a wicked, tyrannical king interested only in accumulating wealth. Vǫlundr exacts vengeance by murdering the king's sons and raping his daughter before flying away, mocking the king in his escape. In *Vǫlundarkviða*, King Niðuðr captures Vǫlundr, steals his sword and the valkyrie's ring, and is goaded by his wife into mutilating the smith. She argues that it is necessary to prevent his revenge, when in fact it provokes it:

> 'Amon ero a/go
> ormi þeim enom frána,
> tenn hanom teygiaz,
> er hanom er teþ sverþ
> oc hann Ba/dvildar
> bá/g vm þeccir;
> sníþit er hann
> sina magni
> oc setiþ hann siþan
> i Sevarstavd!'
> Sva var gort, at scornar váro sinar i knessfotom, oc settr i holm einn, er þar var fyr lande, er het Sevarstaþr. Þar smiþaði hann konvngi allzkyns gorsimar. Engi maþr þorþi at fara til hans nema konvngr einn. (stanza 17: 1–13)[58]

> ['He [Völund] shows his teeth when he looks at the sword,/or watches Bodvild wearing the ring;/venomous snakes have eyes like Volund's./ Cut his hamstrings so he can't escape;/ set him on an island in the sea!' So it was done. They hamstrung Volund and set him on an island called Saeverstad, not far

---

[57] Despite the Christianization of Iceland, these poems were preserved; but the poems in the *Codex Regius* vary in antiquity and are not entirely whole; they are, according to Patricia Terry, 'marred by gaps and discrepancies'. Patricia Terry, 'Introduction', *Poems of the Elder Edda: Revised Edition*, trans. Patricia Terry (Philadelphia: University of Pennsylvania Press, 1969, revised edition 1990), p. xvi.

[58] *Vǫlundarkviða*, in *Sæmundar Edda*, ed. Sophus Bugge (1867), online http://etext.old.no/Bugge/volundar.html. Accessed 15 November 2010.

from the shore. There he wrought all kinds of treasures for Nidud. No one dared visit him except the king alone.][59]

Winifred P. Lehmann calls Vǫlundr's tale a ballad of revenge about a man outside a social group and mistreated by it, who is both treated like and regarded as an outlaw.[60] He may figure as the Other in this text, but it is Niðuðr and his family who behave more barbarically and are othered by their abuse of Vǫlundr. By subjecting this proud, supernatural foe to a humiliating punishment and forcing him to ply his trade as a servant, King Niðuðr crosses the boundaries of acceptable violence in Norse tradition, instigating the gruesome death of his sons and the violation and impregnation of his daughter Bǫðvildr. John McKinnell argues that sympathy for Vǫlundr is 'considerably modified' because of the brutality of his vengeance and the fact that he exacts it from the other members of Niðuðr's family.[61] However, Niðuðr and his entire family participate in the torment of Vǫlundr even if they do not wield the knife. McKinnell acknowledges their brutality and suggests, 'it is grimly appropriate that the tyrant whose motivation was greed for precious objects should receive the payment he deserves in such objects, made from the skulls of his sons'.[62] It is the death of the two boys that most offends McKinnell; however, blood feuds were family affairs and despite a tacit aversion to killing children, vengeance was often taken on collateral relatives.

In terms of justice, for their participation in Vǫlundr's captivity and abuse, the children represent the corruption of Niðuðr's rule and of his line that will most likely flourish and continue with them as they grow into adulthood and so Vǫlundr stops that line and that corruption by killing them.[63] McKinnell writes, 'Of course, their deaths are required for the completion of Vǫlundr's revenge, but it is a dubious justice which demands casual sacrifice of the innocent in this way, or which insists on the corporate responsibility of a whole family'.[64] Charlemagne uses a similar excuse for executing Ganelon's relatives in the *Roland*, but that occurs within the context of a trial not a simple blood feud, making it more problematic. Pointing to the scant reference to Vǫlundr's revenge in the Anglo-

---

[59] *The Lay of Volund*, trans. Patricia Terry, *Poems of the Elder Edda* (Philadelphia: University of Pennsylvania Press, 1969, revised edition 1990).

[60] Winifred P. Lehmann, 'Germanic Legal Terminology and Situation in the *Edda*', in *Old Norse Literature and Mythology: A Symposium*, ed. Edgar C. Polomé (Austin TX: University of Texas Press, 1969) 227–43, p. 232.

[61] John McKinnell, 'The Context of Vǫlundarkviða', in *The Poetic Edda: Essays on Old Norse Mythology*, ed. Paul Acker and Carolyne Larrington (New York and London: Routledge, 2002) 195–212, p. 206.

[62] McKinnell, 'The Context of Vǫlundarkviða', p. 208.

[63] There are several corresponding examples in the heroic sagas and poetry of killing children as part of a blood feud, or in the extermination of a corrupt line, as in *Vǫlsungasaga*, but even in those cases, no one resorts to torture. See: *Saga of the Volsungs: The Norse Epic of Sigurd the Dragon Slayer*, trans. Jesse Byock (Berkeley CA: University of California Press, 1990).

[64] McKinnell, 'The Context of Vǫlundarkviða', p. 209.

Saxon poem *Deor* and Alfred's *Boethius*, *Metrum* 10, McKinnell argues that the Anglo-Saxons seem to have 'some doubts' about the justice of his revenge, and that his brutal actions are an archaic motif. He writes, 'The poet of *Vǫlundarkviða* is enough of an artist to be more even-handed, and allows us our own view, but the tide of opinion was perhaps already running against such primitive "justice", and Vǫlundr's days as a hero were numbered'.[65] However, Vǫlundr's vengeance is not primitive considering the punishment meted out to him and the greed of Niðuðr and his line; it is appropriate, even if it is distasteful to modern audiences. It also suggests an appropriate Icelandic response, within the parameters of Icelandic law, to usurping kings who use brutality to reinforce their illegitimate power. Icelandic legal tradition allowed killing but it did not sanction premeditated mutilation as a means of control. As a king, Niðuðr exhibits a savagery unworthy of his status and that of his victim. It is the extreme suggestion of Niðuðr's queen, 'observant, ruthless and vindictive',[66] and Niðuðr's willingness to subject his prisoner to hamstringing that justifies Vǫlundr's equally extreme response. In his artistry, the poet crafts a tale that not only condemns the brutal injustice and tyranny of kings like Niðuðr, but also enumerates the consequences of such actions when the victim is in a position to retaliate. The author of *Hrafnkels saga* removes these actions from the realm of myth and legend, and situates them in the stark reality of family blood feuds, condemning the practice as it was condemned in the earlier poetry. Both texts deal with anxieties of cultural identity by establishing a model for specifically Icelandic justice and legitimate punishment when justice is corrupted, condemning the excessive punitive measures that vitiate justice and threaten social structures indigenous to Iceland that represent its cultural autonomy and national identity.

Brennu–Njalsaga

Few of the family sagas are as engaged with familial violence, blood feuds, and battle as the thirteenth-century saga of the burning of the honoured and wise Njal and his family, *Brennu–Njalsaga*.[67] The saga follows two families in the years before, during and after the Christian conversion in AD 1000, and encompasses dozens of characters who travel as far as Dublin, Rome and Constantinople in an exhibition of the breadth of Scandinavian influence across the medieval world. The saga is intimately engaged with the question of Icelandic sovereignty and national identity. There are many instances of brutality in *Njals saga* that would qualify for a discussion of violence in medieval literature,

---

[65] McKinnell, 'The Context of *Vǫlundarkviða*', p. 210.
[66] McKinnell, 'The Context of *Vǫlundarkviða*', p. 205.
[67] *Brennu–Njalsaga* survives in twenty-four manuscripts of varying length and completion, but the original manuscript has not survived. The earliest extant manuscript dates from c. 1300, about twenty years after the first version was written down. While *Njals saga* is not purely historical, it is based on historical people and events and incorporates material drawn from oral traditions and occasional written records. *Njal's Saga*, ed. and trans. Magnus Magnusson and Hermann Pálsson (London: Penguin Books, 1960).

particularly the Old Norse/Icelandic sagas, but none of them actually amounts to torture. However, an episode peripheral to the main plot of the killing of Gunnar, the burning of Njal, and the retribution that follows, comes very close. The evisceration of Broðir for the murder of Brian Boruma (Boru) at the battle of Clontarf in 1014[68] is one instance in this complex and nuanced saga where judicial punishment is meted out to an apostate and traitor in a heinous and brutal fashion. His execution (without trial) in the immediate aftermath of the murder is reminiscent of hagiographic accounts of torture; but it is carried out by the Irish who, while allies of the Christian Vikings, are still seen as outsiders. Because the Irish Church did not adopt 'Roman laws', native reformers thought they could not be 'God's people'.[69] As Bartlett points out, they were 'pagans in fact' regardless of their Christian creed and rituals, 'because their social order was deviant from the continental western European model'.[70] More importantly, because by the twelfth century their economy and social structure 'looked odd' to men of England, France and Italy, although the Irish were Christian, 'they could be described in terms and treated as though they were not'.[71]

This particular punishment involves not only drawing out the intestines from an abdominal incision, but tying the end of them to a stake in the ground or to a tree and compelling the victim with spears and swords to walk around the stake until he is tied to it with his own entrails and left to die, slowly.[72] This is an unusual form of punishment and rarely figures in medieval secular literature, but it is 'widely associated in patristic and medieval Christian Latin literature with the punishment of heretics, apostates, and traitors'.[73] Its presence here also

---

[68] According to Magnusson and Pálsson, the Brian episode of *Njals saga* (chapters 154–7) is based 'on a lost *Brian's Saga* of the late twelfth century or a lost *Earl Sigurd's Saga*. The Battle of Clontarf was fought just outside Dublin on Good Friday in 1014 (23 April). There are several Irish accounts of the battle, particularly the contemporary Annals of Ulster and the twelfth-century "War of the Gaedhil with the Gaill" (*Cogadh Gaedhel re Gallaibh*). The battle was fought between Brian Boruma, the ageing champion who had been High-King of Ireland since 1002; and on the other hand a Norse-Irish alliance led by Sigtrygg Silk-Beard (king of Dublin) and Maelmordha, king of Leinster, the brother of Brian's divorced wife Gormflaith (Kormlod). Brian's sons were Murchad (Margad), Donnchad (Dungad) and Tadc (Tadk), and his grandson was Toirhelbach (Kerthjalfad): only Murchad of Brian's sons took part in the battle. In the broadest outlines, the Irish sources and *Njal's Saga* agree' (Magnusson and Pálsson, p. 341, translator's note).
[69] Bartlett, *The Making of Europe*, p. 22.
[70] Bartlett, *The Making of Europe*, pp. 22–3.
[71] Bartlett, *The Making of Europe*, p. 23.
[72] Evisceration in this form appears in both *Brennu-Njals saga* and the *Life of St Alban and St Amphibal* which circulated in collections from the thirteenth century to the fifteenth and was transformed by John Lydgate in his long poem of the same name, c. 1439. Saint Erasmus is also eviscerated, but his entrails are drawn out and wound around a windlass while he lies on the ground.
[73] Thomas D. Hill, 'The Evisceration of Broðir in *Brennu-Njals Saga*', *Traditio* 37 (1981): 437–44, p. 443. Hill also provides information on evisceration as a tradition in Icelandic

speaks to the influence of continental and English texts on Icelandic narratives – as the characters travel the known medieval world, so do their stories; motifs, themes and social *mores* are adapted to each successive audience and society. John Frankis makes a convincing argument that evisceration, as depicted in this text and in the hagiographical accounts of Amphibalus and Alfred Ætheling, is a fictional exaggeration devised for literary purposes and should not be read as a signifier of actual practice. Frankis writes that it would be inappropriate to unquestioningly assume that 'the account has any historical validity or that it represents in any simple way actual reality'.[74] But it is the perceived reality and its implications for cultural identity that matter most. By making the Irish the agents of Broðir's evisceration, the saga author separates this kind of practice from his own people and locates it firmly (as hagiographers did) in the hands of a barbarian Other. This episode figures in a complex and conflicted discourse of Scandinavian and Irish identity. The Battle of Clontarf, fought between the 'most successful of Viking towns [Dublin]' against the 'most powerful Irish king', was 'perhaps the inevitable result of a century of military, economic and political struggles'.[75] The evisceration of Broðir represents a particularly nasty form of punishment meted out to an apostate mercenary who violates the code of battle by ambushing King Brian, who had sworn not to fight on Good Friday and was unarmed, protected only by a shield wall of retainers. At the same time this punishment implicates the Irish who eviscerate him as barbaric and unjust, unfettered by the constraints of law.

Thomas Hill explains that Broðir's execution is a means of punishing the murderer of a king where 'a particularly evil man was killed in a particularly cruel way'.[76] Broðir deserves this ignominious and gruesome death for ambushing

---

literature and Germanic law: 'For a convenient treatment in English of the theme of evisceration in Icelandic literature and Germanic law, see: Anthony Faulkes, ed. *Two Icelandic Stories: Hreiðrs þáttr, Orms þáttr* (Viking Society for Northern Research, Text Series 4, London, 1968) 100–101'.

[74] Frankis, 'From Saint's Life to Saga', p. 121.

[75] Mary A. Valante, *The Vikings in Ireland: Settlement, Trade and Urbanization* (Dublin: Four Courts Press, 2008), p. 101.

[76] Hill, 'The Evisceration of Broðir', p. 438. The hagiographic accounts of evisceration differ greatly from those found in the secular saga. One of the more common narratives is the evisceration of a fictitious saint, Amphibalus, who was 'accidentally' invented by Geoffrey of Monmouth from a mistranslation of the Latin word for cloak, *amphibali*, as a proper name. Frankis, 'From Saint's Life to Saga', pp. 121–37. See also: Larissa Tracy, 'British Library MS Harley 630: John Lydgate and St Albans', *Journal of the Early Book Society*, vol. 3 (2000): 36–58. This motif appears as early as 1095 in Pope Urban II's sermon launching the First Crusade, in which he describes the 'infidel': 'When they wish to torture people by a base death, they perforate their navels, and dragging forth the extremity of the intestines, bind it to a stake; then with flogging they lead the victim around until the viscera having gushed forth the victim falls prostrate upon the ground. Others they bind to a post and pierce with arrows.' Robert the Monk, *Historia Hierosolymitana*, in *Vengeance in Medieval Europe: A Reader*, Readings in Medieval Civilizations and Cultures: XIII, ed. Daniel Lord Smail

Brian. He is a mercenary, a Christian deacon who reverted to paganism, who uses sorcery to try to predict the outcome of the Battle of Clontarf, and finally decides to fight on Good Friday despite the portents of flying weapons, ravens and boiling blood that rain down upon his ships. In asking his sworn brother Ospak the meaning of the omens (after Ospak warns against fighting Brian), Broðir is told that he must attack no earlier than Good Friday or all his men will be killed. But if he attacks on Good Friday, Brian will have victory but lose his life. After prophesying Brian's death, Ospak sails to Ireland where he tells King Brian everything he learns, receives baptism from him and commits himself to his protection. There is a conflict of loyalties acted out in terms of Christian and pagan. Ospak, a Viking, betrays his sworn brother to the Irish high king, and converts. Broðir's execution may be justified but the method is excessive, and one which Brian himself would probably not have sanctioned. The saga-author has already lauded Brian as a good and wise king who follows the law, 'Hann var allra konunga bezt at sér' (154:440–1) [He was the best of all kings] (p. 296),[77] so his death at the hands of an apostate deacon is even more insidious: 'Brjánn konungr gaf upp útlǫgum sínum þrysvar ina sǫmu sǫk; en ef þeir misgerðu optar, þá lét hann dœma þá at lǫgum, ok má af þvílíku marka, hvílíkr konungr hann var' (154:442) [King Brian pardoned outlaws three times for the same crime, but if they did it again he let them be dealt with according to law, and from this it can be seen what sort of king he was] (p. 297). During the battle, Broðir sees Brian's men pursuing the fleeing Norsemen, leaving a small number in the shield wall to protect him:

> Hljóp hann þá ór skóginum ok rauf alla skjaldborgina ok hjó til konungsins. Sveinninn Taðkr brá upp við hendinni, ok tók af hǫndina ok hǫfuðit af konunginum, en blóð konungsins kom á handarstúf sveininum, ok greri þegar fyrir stúfinn. Broðir kallað þá hátt: <<Kunni þat maðr manni at segja, at Bróðir felldi Brján>>
> (157: 452–3)
>
> [He ran out of the woods and cut his way through the shield wall and swung at the king. The boy Tadk brought his arm up against it, but the blow cut off the arm and the king's head too, and the king's blood fell on over the stump of the boy's arm, and the stump healed at once. Then Brodir called loudly, 'Let word go from man to man – Brodir killed Brian!'] (p. 303)

Broðir's attack on Brian is neither brave nor honourable, and in killing the unarmed king he also maims his young son, who is miraculously healed by Brian's sanctity. After killing the king in such a manner, Broðir takes the time

and Kelly Gibson (Toronto: University of Toronto Press, 2009), p. 185. Cf. p. 15 n.68. See also: Margaret Cormack, 'Barbarian Atrocities and Hagiographic Motifs: A Postscript to Some Recent Articles', *Saga-Book* 25.3 (2000): 316–17. Of course, it is not surprising that Urban would attribute such heinous deeds to the enemy he hoped to defeat, and whose demonization was necessary to further galvanize his troops.

[77] All Norse quotations are from *Brennu-Njáls Saga*, ed. Einar Ól. Sveinsson, Íslenzk Fornrit 12 (Reykjavik: Hið islenzka fornritafélag, 1954); all English translations are from *Njal's Saga*, ed. and trans. Robert Cook (London: Penguin Books, 2001).

to boast making his deed as public as possible, which will have consequences in the public manner of his own execution. The king's brother, Ulf Hreda, and his grandson, Kerthjalfad, turn back and surround Broðir and his men, cover their weapons with tree branches and capture Broðir: 'Var þá Broðir hǫndum tekinn. Úlfr hræða reist á honum kviðinn ok leiddi hann um eik ok rakti svá ór honum þarmana; dó hann eigi fyrr en allir váru ór honum raktir. Menn Bróður váru ok allir drepnir' (157:433) [Brodir was then taken prisoner. Ulf Hraeda cut open his belly and led him around an oak tree and in this way pulled out his intestines. Brodir did not die until they were all pulled out of him. All of Brodir's men were killed too] (p. 303).

Brian's death follows hagiographic tradition more than it follows motifs in the family sagas, which firmly aligns Broðir with Roman persecutors of Christian saints; however, the Irish resort to a punishment that also aligns them with the same demonized Romans. Hill argues that the episode is not merely 'one more instance of the barbarism of viking warfare,' and points to a more meaningful interpretation of this as a hagiographic eulogy for King Brian and a clear indictment of Broðir's treachery rather than 'simply titillating his audience with ancient barbaric horrors'.[78] The evisceration of Broðir corresponds with the miraculous restoration of Brian's severed head to his body, 'hǫfuðit konungsins var gróit við bolinn' (157:453) [the king's head had grown back on the trunk] (p. 303),[79] signifying the sanctity of King Brian and the corruption of his murderer, but raising questions about the brutality of Brian's men and playing into anxieties of identity between the Irish and Norse, who often had a troubled alliance.[80] Similarly, in the hagiographic account of *Alban and Amphibal* evisceration is used to contrast the beheading of Alban (the proto-martyr of Britain), a knight sanctified by his conversion and self-sacrifice, to the evisceration of his teacher. Amphibalus is singled out for this particular form of execution because he is responsible for turning Alban against the Romans; and in welcoming and withstanding this torture, he proves his own sanctity in opposition to the barbarism of the Roman authority. Amphibalus is left bound while those converted by the sight of him tied to the stake with his own entrails (seemingly unharmed) are slaughtered. Then he is stoned and finally killed with an arrow.[81] As a hagiographical narrative, the evisceration of Amphibalus serves a didactic purpose like the narratives discussed in Chapter 1, emphasizing the sanctity of the man responsible for converting Alban and demonizing the unstable authority that must resort to brutality to reinforce its tenuous power. Amphibal is tried and executed for his role in turning Alban to Christianity; but there is no inter-

---

[78] Hill, 'The Evisceration of Broðir', p. 438; p. 444.
[79] Hill, 'The Evisceration of Broðir', p. 439.
[80] Valante discusses the intricacies of political relations between the Irish and the Vikings in depth, specifically in the context of the Battle of Clontarf. *The Vikings in Ireland*, pp. 101–17.
[81] This is the standard version of the *Life of St Alban and St Amphibal*, and is found in the *Gilte Legende*. This synopsis is from British Library MS Harley 630.

rogation, merely punishment and the hagiographer (as in most hagiographies) condemns the Romans as savage and alien. In the same way, the evisceration of Broðir is a judicial punishment, and as with the Romans who inflict this punishment on Amphibalus, the Irish are demonized by their brutal action, no matter how justified it may be. To a thirteenth-century Icelandic audience looking back to the savage and unruly age of the tenth and eleventh centuries, these practices are primitive and uncivilized, perpetuated by the alien Irish Other and non-Christian Vikings.

Broðir is captured after his assassination of Brian and the punishment is swift and complete without any recourse to law. On a battlefield, laws were often suspended in the interests of victory, and the Irish could be forgiven for not taking Broðir before a secular authority. But in presenting the Irish as capable of the same kind of punishment meted out by pagan persecutors of hagiographic tradition, the author taints them, drawing a clear line between the civilized Christian society of medieval Iceland and the wilds of the western borders with Ireland.[82] There is a distinction between pagan and Christian, Viking and Irish, though the concerns of national identity are troubled by the diversity of the Scandinavian population in Ireland. They were not merely an amorphous mass of 'foreigners' – 'that was not how the Vikings saw themselves nor was it how the Irish dealt with them.'[83] There were Danes, Norwegians and Icelanders, all of whom contended with issues of allegiance. Between AD 980 and 1014, the Scandinavians were fully integrated into the Irish political scene; but the battle of Clontarf was fought 'as the men of Dublin [Vikings] worked to maintain their position against the growing power of the Irish high kings.'[84] Despite Irish/Viking assimilation in Ireland, to the Icelandic audience the Irish are still a foreign Other and Broðir represents the worst of their society; he gives the Vikings a bad name. It is not simply a portrayal of good Christian versus bad pagan; the shared Scandinavian heritage is problematic. Broðir is disinherited by the Icelandic saga-author and subjected to a well-deserved death but the method of execution aligns the Irish with the Roman torturers of hagiography.

Robert Cook argues that excessive violence permeates *Njals saga*. He writes that much blood is shed in the saga, 'but much of it is shamefully shed – not exactly what seekers after Viking adventure want to read. [...] Rather than violent action, it is spiritual qualities that occupy the centre of interest in this saga – intelligence, wisdom, decisiveness, purposefulness, a shrewd business sense, the ability to give and follow advice, decency, a sense of honour.'[85] Violence, however, plays an equally central role and provides the backdrop for the nobler

---

[82] It should also be noted that Brian had Scandinavian mercenaries on his side, 'and that the allies of Dublin came from abroad, not from within Ireland'. Valante, *The Vikings in Ireland*, p. 115.
[83] Valante, *The Vikings in Ireland*, p. 101.
[84] Valante, *The Vikings in Ireland*, p. 102.
[85] Robert Cook, 'Introduction', in *Njal's Saga*, ed. and trans. Cook, p. xv.

qualities to which Cook refers, but that violence has boundaries and is limited to the battlefield and the blood feud. In attributing this method of execution to the Irish, the Icelanders escape its associations and the nobler qualities of the characters remain intact. Hill concludes that there is some aversion to the method of Broðir's execution and that 'though the saga author expresses the horror of Broðir's death succinctly and without overt authorial comment, one specific detail – that Broðir did not die until all his intestines were drawn out – emphasises the grotesque cruelty of his death.'[86] He reserves direct comment, which could either be taken as an approbation of the punishment, or as a silent reminder that even justified actions carried out through excessive brutality are invalidated. Implicit in this episode are the anxieties of cultural identity; the saga author makes these cultural divisions clear in the savagery of the Irish despite the shared religious belief and the assimilation of Scandinavians into Irish culture and politics. Perhaps the saga author is warning against the corrupting influence of political and cultural assimilation, a process whereby the Icelanders may lose themselves and their distinct identity.

The use of torture and brutality in the Old Norse/Icelandic sagas reflects the cultural anxieties of people trying to preserve their own sense of autonomy in a shrinking European sphere. Saga authors distance themselves from the continental influences of judicial torture by eschewing it altogether and locating instances of extra-judicial brutality in the outlaws and outlying Others – the Irish. As Iceland struggled to maintain an autonomous national identity in the face of Norwegian imperialism, family-saga authors rejected the genre of continental romances in favour of national sagas centred on the founding families and heroic deeds of its own people. While it is tempting to read violent realism in the accounts of Old Norse/Icelandic literature, texts like *Brennu–Njals saga* and *Hrafnkels saga* suggest an uneasy relationship with certain kinds of punishment and an effort to distance Icelandic society from treacherous acts of brutality and torture. The mutilation visited on Vǫlundr is a popular motif repeated in most versions of the tale; like the mutilation of Hrafnkel and his men it is a shameful act that justifies Vǫlundr's revenge. However, despite the prevalence of Vǫlundr's legend, hamstringing does not occur frequently in other Norse literature. The exchange of violence may not differ greatly from the legal action and counter-action in the sagas,[87] but Niðuðr does far more than merely imprison Vǫlundr and force him to produce *gorsimar*. The author of *Hrafnkels saga* may well be making a literary comparison between the tyrant king of legend, who uses mutilation as a means of controlling and containing a more powerful supernatural foe and enslaving him to his will, and Sámr, who takes on the more prominent and powerful Hrafnkel, seeking to subdue him through physical mutilation and humiliation.

---

[86] Hill, 'The Evisceration of Broðir', p. 438.
[87] Lehmann, 'Germanic Legal Terminology', p. 234.

Broðir's execution, recorded in less gruesome terms in other sources about the Battle of Clontarf, is necessary to highlight the dramatic nature of his betrayal, not only the betrayal in ambushing Brian, who would not fight on Good Friday, but in turning his back on Christianity. Broðir's death is juxtaposed against the execution of Christian saints and heretics, which Frankis calls 'a simplistic dichotomy of good and evil' where Brian is a saint and Broðir 'wholly evil'.[88] But the saga is not so absolute. For all its grim commentary on treachery and betrayal, the Battle of Clontarf is peripheral to the saga: it occurs as an epilogue to the burning of Njal and his family and the cycle of vengeance that follows, and further exemplifies the complexities of blood feud. Relating this 'history' is a means of establishing Iceland's legal past in the face of colonizing pressure to adopt both Norwegian rule and continental influences. As Cook points out, more than any other family saga, *Njals saga* is about law, and the legal details reflect the author's time (the thirteenth century) rather than the saga age (circa AD 1000) when the story takes place; yet the irony of the saga is that 'law, even the elaborate law code of medieval Iceland, is incapable of controlling violence'.[89]

Produced during a period when medieval law was being codified and widely enforced by inquisitorial courts on the Continent, *Njals saga* raises significant questions of *correct* legal practice and the abuse of power. According to the saga author, this failure of law persists in Ireland as well and even though the Christian Irish are fighting on the 'correct' side, their response to Broðir's crime is excessive. But no matter how brutal the fictional account of the Battle of Clontarf and Broðir's much deserved punishment, Frankis further argues that this method 'owes less to realism than to gruesome fantasy'.[90] Smyth points out that there was realism in saga violence, but that is not the primary issue; instead 'the significant question is not whether the Vikings were more violent and brutal than others, which seems unlikely, but rather what effect their violence had, directed as it was to somewhat different ends than that of their Christian contemporaries.'[91] These episodes of torture and brutality may well be residual traces of pre-Christian Norse society when Vikings were 'uninhibited by Christian taboos against abuse of the human person';[92] however, the violence of these acts is presented in contravention of accepted practice. It is neither laudable nor acceptable, and it may well reflect an attempt by later, Christian Icelandic authors to distance themselves from a more barbaric past – or a future without its characteristic Icelandic identity.

In these texts, the brutality of the past is rejected in the interests of stabilizing the present and validating an independent Icelandic identity, one that does not resort to torture or excessive punishment, despite outside influences. Instances

---

[88] Frankis, 'From Saint's Life to Saga', p. 121.
[89] Cook, 'Introduction', in *Njal's Saga*, ed. and trans. Cook, pp. xxiii–xxv.
[90] Frankis, 'From Saint's Life to Saga', p. 122.
[91] Smyth, 'The Effect of Scandinavian Raiders', p. 24.
[92] Smyth, 'The Effect of Scandinavian Raiders', p. 24.

of torture and brutality are situated outside Icelandic borders in Ireland where definitions of national identity had become clouded. Like the romances *Walewein* and the *Roland* in Chapter 2, the sagas were popular among all strata of Icelandic society. The message of national identity bound by order, justice and law would have been appealing to the more democratic Icelanders, who relied on the strength of their laws and traditions to maintain society. Unspoken in the Icelandic sagas is a recognition that not all great powers and courts resort to torture, and in the thirteenth century that power was represented by England which, grounded in many of the same legal principles as the Scandinavian world, faced its own anxieties of national identity bound up with questions of torture and justice.

4

The Matter of Britain: Defining English Identity in Opposition to Torture

> 'There is only one thing that arouses animals more than pleasure, and that is pain. Under torture you are as if under the dominion of those grasses that produce visions. [...] Under torture you say not only what the inquisitor wants, but also what you imagine might please him, because a bond (this, truly, diabolical) is established between you and him.' Brother William of Baskerville, *The Name of the Rose*, Umberto Eco (p. 63)

As continental legal practice developed sophisticated mechanisms for extracting confessions or facilitating 'discovery', and as Scandinavian outposts like Iceland resisted that corrupting influence in sagas, often by allying themselves with the good rule of Anglo-Saxon kings,[1] few medieval societies had such an uneasy relationship with torture as England. Balanced on the edge of the medieval world, England could resist the cultural and legal developments on the Continent. But by the thirteenth century, it was in danger of succumbing to political pressures as Angevin kings pressed their claims in France and the two cultures seemed destined to meld into one. Matthew Paris (c. 1200–1259) complained in his *Chronica Majora* that the presence of so many outsiders was causing problems in England. Coming over at the invitation of the king, they had taken over all the best positions, growing fat on the country's wealth and 'trampling native-

---

[1] Fjalldal, *Anglo-Saxon England in Icelandic Medieval Texts*, pp. ix, 26, 28, 29. Fjalldal cites Henry G. Leach who argues that the 'distinguishing trait of Icelandic scholarship during the Middle Ages was its cosmopolitan interest in the history of other nations' (p. ix). Fjalldal finds a touch of envy for England in the histories of Norwegian kings, and that regardless of the limited direct contact between England and Iceland before and after the Conquest, Icelanders fantasized about the role of the the Norse in shaping Anglo-Saxon society (pp. 26, 28). He suggests that the desire among thirteenth-century saga authors to credit the Norse with a role in founding key English cities may come from a long history of interaction and power struggles between Scandinavians and the English, or perhaps wishful thinking (p. 29). See also: Henry Goddard Leach, *Angevin Britain and Scandinavia*.

born Englishmen under their heels'.[2] The pope gave preference to non-English speakers, placing them in key offices in the English church, and outside influence was felt throughout the country. Norman-French had become the prestige vernacular in England, and for some, French remained the preferred vernacular of courtly literature until the fourteenth century, but the use of English increased for various purposes during the thirteenth century.[3] That is not to say that one language stamped out another, or that variations of the two did not co-exist, just as there were different Francophone dialects on the Continent. According to Wogan-Browne, it is not a matter of 'conceptualizing two separate vernacular languages and traditions, the English of England and the French of England'.[4] She writes, 'The idea of a culture as a monoglot entity proceeding in organic linearity through time and within the territories of a modern nation state cannot adequately represent medieval textual production and linguistic and cultural contacts.'[5] It is these nuances in linguistic development and their effect on literary production that contribute to anxieties of identity – how do a people define themselves if they have no claim to a specific language or culture? Diane Speed points out that after 1204 members of the Anglo-Norman ruling class had few options but to focus their interests in England once their Norman possessions (except Calais) were lost and the need for a shared vernacular with continental associates diminished.[6] She writes, 'they seem in any case to have been in the process of taking on an insular identity distinct from that of their continental ancestors'.[7] English poets endeavoured to forge their own cultural identity apart from continental influences, and one factor in this distinct identity is the approach to torture in English literary texts. During the thirteenth and fourteenth centuries, torture most frequently appears in secular literature at the same time that national concerns appear in early romances, and the notion of a specific English identity comes to the fore.[8] As Roman law was reintroduced into medieval jurisprudence late in the twelfth century, and Norman influence developed into 'English' culture,[9] literature became a vehicle for social change

---

[2] Thorlac Turville-Petre, *England the Nation: Language, Literature and National Identity, 1290–1340* (Oxford: Oxford University Press, 1996), p. 1; *Matthaei Parisiensis: Chronica Majora*, ed. Henry Richards Luard (7 vols; Rolls Series 1872–87) iii, 390, and cf. v. 184, qtd. in Turville-Petre, *England the Nation*, p. 1.

[3] Speed, 'The Construction of the Nation', pp. 139–40.

[4] Wogan-Browne, 'What's in a Name', p. 5. Several essays in Wogan-Browne's collection, *Language and Culture in Medieval Britain*, address questions of identity and language and reveal a nuanced tradition of adaptation and translation well into the fifteenth century that reflects certain anxieties about cultural inheritance.

[5] Wogan-Browne, 'What's in a Name', p. 5.

[6] Speed, 'The Construction of the Nation', p. 140.

[7] Speed, 'The Construction of the Nation', p. 140.

[8] Speed, 'The Construction of the Nation', p. 136.

[9] John Gillingham provides convincing evidence that Anglo-Norman kings, specifically Henry II, saw themselves as 'English', an idea founded on the military triumphs of the

often voicing public opinion on specific practices or abuses, or attempting to sway popular thought about newer judicial proceedings. Romances in particular operate 'as one medium through which communal concern regarding legal innovations could be articulated'.[10] Torture appears more frequently in English literary texts than in continental ones, usually in the form of a critique where its use is relegated to barbarian lands and corrupt authorities, or represents the systematic breakdown of civil structures. Torture may be used more freely as a literary motif in English texts specifically because torture was not part of English law. English authors could more vocally condemn its use, claim national autonomy from such practices and take pride that England's traditions were grounded in a more just Anglo-Saxon past.

This chapter focuses on the fraught relationship between English literary texts, often more violent than their sources, and the legal prohibition against interrogatory torture in English law. *Havelok the Dane* engages with the 'Other within' by negotiating cultural anxieties about Norman and Danish inheritance in its episodes of judicial brutality. Like *Walewein*, the Anglo-Latin *Arthur and Gorlagon* sets the Arthurian court up as a model of chivalric courtesy in opposition to the courts of the barbarian Other (including a werewolf) where interrogatory torture and judicial brutality are employed with impunity. Geoffrey Chaucer voices a societal distaste for judicial brutality in the *Prioress's Tale* and interrogates the justice of using torture in the tales of the Second Nun and Man of Law. Though both *Havelok* and *Arthur and Gorlagon* occur in unique manuscripts, they speak to noble audiences about the dangers inherent in resorting to torture and judicial brutality, dangers echoed in Chaucer's popular tales, that threaten the perception of English national identity as grounded in 'gode olde law'.

The late thirteenth- or early fourteenth-century metrical chronicle of Robert of Gloucester reminds his audience in Normanized England that their country has an 'English past which predates recent Norman-usurped history, and which is, into the bargain, a past enshrining values of good, and Godly, governance which has, unhappily for the people, been corrupted'.[11] Robert's anxieties about

---

Norman past (p. 130). *The English in the Twelfth Century: Imperialism, National Identity and Political Values* (Woodbridge: The Boydell Press, 2000). Pickens, in contrast, argues that the Francophone elite saw themselves as "French" in the twelfth century. 'Implications of Being "French"', p. 384. Cf. p. 5. However, the tide shifted in the thirteenth century as Norman and English ideas of identity stratified.

10 Robert Allen Rouse, 'English Identity and the Law in *Havelok the Dane*, *Horn Childe and Maiden Rimnild* and *Beues of Hamtoun*', in *Cultural Encounters in the Romance of Medieval England*, ed. Corinne Saunders, Studies in Medieval Romance (Cambridge: D.S. Brewer, 2005) 69–83, p. 71.

11 Sarah Mitchell, 'Kings, Constitution and Crisis: "Robert of Gloucester" and the Anglo-Saxon Remedy', in *Literary Appropriations of the Anglo-Saxons from the Thirteenth to the Twentieth Century*, ed. Donald Scragg and Carole Weinberg, Cambridge Studies in Anglo-Saxon England (Cambridge: Cambridge University Press, 2000) 39–56, p. 43. Mitchell explains that the 'Robert of Gloucester' chronicle is extant in two recensions containing the

foreigners, much like those of Matthew Paris, are directed against the people whom he describes as the French, 'particularly because of the preferment given to them over the English' by the royal family.[12] The Anglo-Norman Angevins, represented by the notorious King John (1199–1216), his son Henry III (1216–1272), his grandson Edward I (1272–1307) and great-grandson Edward II (1307–1327), found themselves in a difficult position as questions of national identity based on cultural inheritance and right to rule came to the fore. Hyams notes that local and national enmities 'interact in civil strife'; in the thirteenth century 'men often chose their loyalties in national conflicts on grounds of local loyalties, to fight with friends and against enemies'.[13] Robert of Gloucester's chronicle narrates contemporary disturbances like the barons' rebellion, the battle of Evesham (1265),[14] and further woes that were to be expected under Henry's reign if it did not return to the 'gode olde law' of the Anglo-Saxon past.[15] As Carole Weinberg notes in her analysis of Laȝamon,

> kings who rule firmly and peacefully are commended even though these same kings may be subjected to disapproving comments concerning other less favorable attributes. Contextualizing King John within this view of king and country leaves him falling short of good kingship, and an early-thirteenth century audience might be less concerned with the cultural affinities of King John than with the dangers facing England caused by a king who had antagonized his barons to the point of rebellion and was, at his death, 'struggling not to lose his kingdom to an invading foreign prince'.[16]

King John, forced by his barons to relinquish a certain amount of royal control at Runnymede in 1215 after losing most of England's French possessions in 1204, was caught between his Norman lineage and a growing sense of separate Englishness. This reached a climax in the fourteenth century as Edward III

---

same material until 1135, at which point they divide, the first (longer) recension goes up to 1271; the second recension provides a lengthy account of Stephen's reign and ends with a brief account of the accession of Edward I in 1272. The chronicle can be dated to the late thirteenth/early fourteenth century, the earliest surviving manuscript of which is London, British Library, Cotton Caligula A.xi, dated on palaeographical grounds to 1300–1330 (p. 39 n. 3).

[12] Mitchell, 'Kings, Constitution and Crisis', pp. 43–4.

[13] Hyams, *Rancor and Reconciliation*, p. 252.

[14] Which marked the defeat of Simon de Montfort, earl of Leicester, an Anglo-French noble (and son of the crusader Simon de Montfort who was killed at the siege of Toulouse in 1218 during the Albigensian Crusade) who opposed Henry III.

[15] Mitchell, 'Kings, Constitution and Crisis', p. 41. Systematic of this breakdown, in an act of particular brutality, after his defeat Simon de Montfort's head and testicles were sent as a gift to Lady Wigmore and the parts of his body were scattered throughout England. Kaeuper, 'The Societal Role of Chivalry in Romance', p. 101; Mickel, *Ganelon, Treason*, p. 147.

[16] Carole Weinberg, 'Victor and Victim: A View of the Anglo-Saxon Past in Laȝamon's *Brut*', in *Literary Appropriations of the Anglo-Saxons from the Thirteenth to the Twentieth Century*, ed. Donald Scragg and Carole Weinberg, Cambridge Studies in Anglo-Saxon England (Cambridge: Cambridge University Press, 2000) 22–38, p. 37.

(John's great-great-grandson) attempted to assert his claims not only to French land, but to the French throne.[17] Edward III's assertion of his rights in France, 'the pretext that inaugurates the so-called Anglo-French war of a hundred years', was merely the culmination of 'a long process of nationalist self-assertion at the expense of England's territorial enemies'.[18] Robert Allen Rouse explains that the continental wars brought into focus the differences between the English and their continental neighbours, who may have appeared as an attractively simple Other, producing a sense of English identity in opposition to those continental enemies.[19] Each of the texts addressed in this chapter engages in a discourse about the anxieties of good kingship and national identity established in large part by the recourse to good and just laws and a rejection of torture as a part of that law. *Havelok the Dane*, *Arthur and Gorlagon* and *The Prioress's Tale* all participate in conversations of kingship and mediate the disparities between societies where interrogatory torture or judicial brutality is acceptable and those where they are not. These poets exhort their audiences, as Robert of Gloucester does in his attempts to assert a 'claim for Englishness',[20] to hold their monarchy to three standards: 'first, a desire for English freedom and autonomy; second, English traditional law as a guarantor of that freedom and autonomy; and third, the harmony of the spiritual and worldly, within the life and governance of the nation'.[21] In these narratives, torture is a symptom of corrupt governance and disregard for law in opposition to the basic elements of English identity.

Like its Scandinavian analogues, English medieval literature reflects the legal prohibition against torture by demonizing its application and making its use a trait of violent outsiders – often Danish or French – who represent potentially corrupting influences. England in the thirteenth century included Anglo-Scandinavians of Danish descent, those of Anglo-Saxon ancestry, Anglo-Normans who comprised the ruling class torn between French and English identities (while also claiming descent from the Danes of Normandy), as well as the

---

[17] John even adopted the Anglo-Saxon Saint Wulfstan as his patron and, breaking from the family tradition of his father Henry II, his mother and older brother Richard I, all buried at Fontevraud Abbey near Chinon, had himself buried between Wulfstan and Saint Oswald in Worcester. Weinberg, 'Victor and Victim', pp. 36–7. His son, Henry III, though he decreed that his heart should be buried at Fontevraud, was an ardent adherent of Saint Edward the Confessor and invested thousands of pounds in giving the Anglo-Saxon king-saint a suitable home at Westminster Abbey in London. Henry III was the first English king since the Conquest to give his children Anglo-Saxon names, and his case shows 'how the Normanization of English nomenclature was modified by a contrary movement as the immigrant French dynasts and aristocrats adopted the cults of the native saints'. Bartlett, *The Making of Europe*, p. 273.

[18] Heng, 'The Romance of England', pp. 151–2.

[19] Robert Allen Rouse, *The Idea of Anglo-Saxon England in Middle English Romance*, Studies in Medieval Romance (Cambridge: D.S. Brewer, 2005), p. 84.

[20] Mitchell, 'Kings, Constitution and Crisis', p. 43.

[21] Mitchell, 'Kings, Constitution and Crisis', p. 43.

Welsh, Scots and Cornish. As Speed explains, 'A chronological consideration of the broad field of medieval English literature in relation to the discourse shows why the creative literature of the latter part of the thirteenth century, as England ceased to function as a colony in the control of an alien aristocracy, may specifically be said to mark the clear emergence of English literature as the text of the nation'.[22] Thorlac Turville-Petre explains that the 'establishment and exploration of a sense of national identity is a major preoccupation of English writers of the late thirteenth and early fourteenth centuries: Who are the English; where do they come from; what constitutes the English nation?'[23] Adapted for audiences struggling with a shared past of Scandinavian and then French settlement, Middle English literature attempts to find a sense of English identity by creating brutal narratives from French sources,[24] adding to their narrative threads a violence nonexistent in their originals and embedding in them a disapproval of torture and brutality. English authors sought to distance themselves from the potential influence of continental jurisprudence and the application of torture. Langbein points out that neither 'the European law of proof, nor the system of judicial torture to which the European law of proof gave rise, was applied in England'.[25] Medieval England was graced not simply with 'a single, monolithic form of law, but several distinct types of law, sometimes competing, occasionally overlapping, invariably invoking different traditions, jurisdictions and modes of operation'.[26] The jury system, distinctive of English judicial procedure, spared England from the European law of torture.[27] John Bellamy points out that during the later Middle Ages as a whole, 'crimes involving deliberate cruelty against the victims were relatively few', and those who sought to emulate methods of maintaining public order by using torture 'had little in English common law to copy from. Only when the accused stood mute in court, refusing to plead, was a form of torture used, and mutilation was generally a punishment associated only with borough custom.'[28] Excessive brutality was not a hallmark of medieval English law, and any abuse of authority that resulted in the application of torture or the implementation of brutal punishments outside the law or without recourse to

---

[22] Speed, 'The Construction of the Nation', p. 139.

[23] Thorlac Turville-Petre, 'Havelok and the History of the Nation', in *Readings in Medieval English Romance*, ed. Carol M. Meale (Cambridge: D.S. Brewer, 1994) 121–34, p. 121.

[24] Donna Crawford examines episodes of heightened violence in her article '"Gronyng with grisly wounde": Injury in Five Middle English Breton Lays', in *Readings in Medieval English Romance*, ed. Carol M. Meale (Cambridge: D.S. Brewer, 1994): 35–52.

[25] Langbein, *Torture and the Law of Proof*, p. x.

[26] Anthony Musson, *Medieval Law in Context: The Growth of Legal Consciousness from Magna Carta to the Peasants' Revolt* (Manchester: Manchester University Press, 2001), pp. 2, 9.

[27] Langbein, *Torture and the Law of Proof*, pp. x, xi. Torture was only 'officially' legal in England between 1540 and 1640, and its use subsided early in the seventeenth century.

[28] Bellamy, *Crime and Public Order*, p. 67.

legitimate legal procedure would have met with resistance and potentially rebellion. Kings and commoners alike rejected torture.

Despite the troubles of his forebears, his own difficulties against the Scots and his own unhappy nobles, Edward II's refusal to employ 'enhanced' interrogation techniques against the English Knights Templar in 1307 is a striking example of English resistance to the use of torture, which has its parallels in thirteenth- and fourteenth-century English literary texts. Edward II defied his soon-to-be father-in-law (Philip IV), arguing that he wasn't prepared to believe the accusations against the Templars.[29] Even after receiving the bull *Pastoralis praeeminentiae* from Pope Clement V, authorizing the seizure of the Templars in the name of the papacy, Edward took his time arresting the English members.[30] He would not allow papal inquisitors to interrogate English knights under the threat of torture because English common law, 'based on custom and precedent, rather than Roman law, as was used in France and canon (Church) law',[31] forbade it. The inquisitors who were sent to England to examine the imprisoned knights met with resistance and were unable to facilitate mass confessions on the same

---

[29] Helen J. Nicholson, *The Knights Templar on Trial: The Trial of the Templars in the British Isles 1308–1311* (Stroud: The History Press, 2009), p. 24. There was even French dissent against the torture of the Templars contemporary to their arrest and interrogation. In the first months of 1308, when the French Templars had been suffering indescribable pains for about three months, a defence of the Templars was released. This *Lamentacio*, extant in a unique manuscript of English origin, Cambridge, Corpus Christi College MS 450, offers a reasoned defence of the Order combined with 'savage partisanship'. It is a piece of outspoken propaganda, and C.R. Cheney argues that its author 'writes as a Frenchmen' whose respect for Philip IV, 'whom he represents as misguided', may simply be discretion. Cheney writes: 'By the time that this *Lamentacio* was written confessions had been extracted by torture, and many of the prisoners had already died under their harsh treatment' (p. 69). Cheney further argues that the letter's most impressive feature, 'visible through all the rancour and rhetoric, is the reasoned condemnation of a procedure which was designed not to elicit the truth but to convict the suspect' (p. 70). The fact the letter is preserved in an English manuscript, an 'anthology of politico-ecclesiastical records which may reflect the interests of an English clerk in the service of the king or of some prelate in the reign of Edward II' (p. 71) indicates that the torture of the Templars was a serious issue for both English and French clerics. C.R. Cheney, 'The Downfall of the Templars and a Letter in their Defence', in *Medieval Miscellany presented to Eugene Vinaver by Pupils, Colleagues and Friends*, ed. F. Whitehead, A.H. Diverres and F.E. Sutcliffe (Manchester: Manchester University Press, 1965), 65–79.

[30] Malcolm Barber, *The Trial of the Templars* (Cambridge: Cambridge University Press, 1978, rpt. 1998), p. 195.

[31] Nicholson, *The Knights Templar on Trial*, p. 99. The inquisitors could not find anyone in England willing to torture the Templars because it violated the king's jurisdiction. The thirteenth-century *Mirror of Justices* contends that heresy was *lese majesty*, 'damage to the king's majesty, and so a matter for the king's courts, not the Church courts', and English common law and the king's courts did not use torture as a method of interrogation (p. 99). The author of the *Mirror of Justices* further notes that the 'convicted traitor should suffer torture and death as the king wishes and that notorious cases need not even receive proper trial in due form' (Mickel, *Ganelon, Treason*, p. 146).

scale as in France, where the Inquisition had been accepted and was used as a tool of the monarchy.[32] In England, previous generations viewed the inquisitorial process with suspicion, relying instead on a jury system composed of their local peers: 'the Norman and Angevin kings had developed a sophisticated and uniform legal machinery applying to all free men of the land, which left no room for an Inquisition which was sometimes seen as an agent of foreign popes'.[33] As a consequence, the papal inquisition never functioned in England. When the pope's inquisitors arrived to interrogate the Templars, there was no mechanism or tradition upon which to draw, 'for English law relied upon the opinion of local jurors and did not employ torture'.[34] So while torture was being applied as part of the inquisitorial process in Paris, and French Templars were subjected to the rack, the *strappado*, threats of torture and imprisonment,[35] the English Knights Templar were secure in the knowledge that their laws prohibited such treatment and resisted confessing to the charges against them.

When Edward II was finally pressured into allowing the inquisitors to apply torture during their investigations, he offered an ambiguous statement that permitted them to 'act and to proceed against the Templars as related to their office, although nothing should be done against our crown or the state of our kingdom'.[36] This is the earliest and perhaps only official use of English torture 'proper' before the reign of Edward IV.[37] In this instance, the use of torture was permitted, contrary to English custom and law, and (at least temporarily) the authority of the pope supplanted the authority of the king. But it seems that even with permission, torture was not being applied systematically, and the inquisitors complained in a letter to the archbishop of Canterbury, dated 16 June 1310, that they 'could find no one to carry out tortures properly, and that the procedure ought to be by ecclesiastical law as in France'.[38] They suggested the process be transferred across the Channel to the county of Ponthieu, which, 'although part of the lands of the English king, did not suffer from the disadvantage of English law'.[39] Faced with a change of venue and the potential loss of control over the proceedings, Edward II stepped up his efforts to comply with the papal demands for torture, but there was still an effort to prevent severe bodily harm. It was decided that knights who did not confess should be 'put to

---

[32] Barber, *The Trial of the Templars*, p. 197.
[33] Barber, *The Trial of the Templars*, p. 197.
[34] Barber, *The Trial of the Templars*, p. 197.
[35] Barber, *The Trial of the Templars*, pp. 54–8.
[36] *Councils and Synods with Other Documents Relating to the English Church*, 11, A.D. 1205–1313, pt. 2, 1265–1313, ed. F.M. Powicke and C.R. Cheney (Oxford: Oxford University Press, 1964), pp. 1267–9; qtd. in Barber, *The Trial of the Templars*, p. 197.
[37] Bellamy, *Crime and Public Order*, p. 139.
[38] Barber, *The Trial of the Templars*, p. 198.
[39] Barber, *The Trial of the Templars*, p. 198.

the question', but in such a way 'that these questions should be made without mutilation or permanent injury to any members and without violent effusion of blood'.[40] But it appears that even with those conditions, the English king refused to bow fully to continental pressures. By December 1310, Clement V was still trying to persuade Edward II to allow the trial to relocate to Ponthieu, suggesting that torture was still not being used systematically.[41] Despite the demands of the papal inquisitors, it seems that torture was not properly applied, if at all, until the summer of 1311 – nearly two years after the proceedings began in England.[42] Malcolm Barber concludes that 'the proceedings in the British Isles show the general failure at making the charges stick, except with the aid of torture'.[43] It is also clear that the English people, as well as the civil authorities (including the king), were reluctant to employ torture and saw it as antithetical to their system of justice and an intrusion of continental law – an attempt to undermine English autonomy under papal authority.

Havelok the Dane

Havelok the Dane, composed between 1295 and 1310 but set in the earlier Anglo-Saxon period, reflects a developing sense of national identity and English justice in its portrayal of the hero and the punishment meted out to the usurping tyrants who interfere in the lives and happiness of Havelok and Goldeboru. Godard murders Havelok's sisters, orders his death and takes over the Danish throne. Havelok is saved, raised by good people, and taken to England where he meets the dispossessed Goldeboru, the daughter and heir of Æthelwold. She is forced to marry Havelok by the nasty Godrich, who thinks he is simply a kitchen boy. Goldeboru recognizes his worth through divine revelation (light shines from his mouth while he sleeps) and they set out to take back their respective thrones. Havelok defeats Godard in battle, then has him tried, flayed and hanged. Returning to England, they defeat Godrich, and Goldeboru (as the English queen) merely sentences him to death by burning. Correct rule is reinstated and the romance ends on a high note.

Havelok is based on the exile-and-return tales in the Anglo-Norman romances of the late twelfth to early thirteenth centuries,[44] specifically Gaimar's *Haveloc*

---

[40] *Councils and Synods*, 11, pt. 2, p. 1290; qtd. in Barber, *The Trial of the Templars*, p. 199.
[41] Barber, *The Trial of the Templars*, p. 199.
[42] Barber, *The Trial of the Templars*, p. 203.
[43] Barber, *The Trial of the Templars*, p. 204.
[44] Rosalind Field, 'The King Over the Water: Exile-and-Return Revisited', in *Cultural Encounters in the Romance of Medieval England*, ed. Corinne Saunders, Studies in Medieval Romance (Cambridge: D.S. Brewer, 2005) 41–53, p. 43.

episode (1135–40)[45] and the *Lai d'Haveloc* (1190–1220).[46] The Middle English poem 'adapts and expands its source material in order to create a portrait of the growth and education of the ideal king', producing a romance 'which is a mirror of thirteenth-century political life and a portrait of the ideal king delineated from the point of view of the lower classes'.[47] But as a romance unhesitatingly accepted as a history in the early fourteenth century,[48] *Havelok* also engages in a discourse of national identity and shared ancestry with the Danes and Normans embodied in the use of torture and brutality. Turville-Petre notes the persistence of Anglo-Norman romances such as *Havelok* and *King Horn* in the English tradition from the mid-thirteenth century on, explaining that the continued transcription of Anglo-Norman versions into the fourteenth century 'shows that some of the descendants of their original audiences continued to enjoy French, yet others now preferred English and were finding French something of a struggle'.[49] But the translation of these texts may also indicate a shift in national and linguistic associations as English poets sought to establish themselves and their language in the literary canon. Because of the wars between England and France, the French were a 'useful cultural Other against which the English could define themselves'; however, Rouse contends that there is little in the Matter of England romances that 'supports the use of the French (or other continentals) as a national Other for the English'.[50] Even though Havelok's father, the Danish King Birkabein, is held up with King Æthelwold as a just and law-abiding ruler,[51] in *Havelok* the cultural Other are the Danes, which would have had uncomfortable associations for their Anglo-Scandinavian descendants. The location of the tale in north Lincolnshire, where a stable population of partly Scandinavian origin and an economy based on the local industries of farming and fishing 'fostered a strong sense of a separate cultural heritage which could not fit comfortably into the

---

[45] Gillingham argues that Gaimar's work is an exercise in English nationalism, though from the Norman perspective, and that his sections on the Anglo-Saxon history of England are the basis for the prose *Brut*. *The English in the Twelfth Century*, pp. 113–22. It has also been suggested that the *Lai d'Haveloc* was composed in the northeast Midlands, 'where the Danes had once ruled and dominated linguistically'. *Four Romances of England: King Horn, Havelok the Dane, Bevis of Hampton, Athelston*, ed. Ronald B. Herzman, Graham Drake, and Eve Salisbury. TEAMS Middle English Texts Series (Kalamazoo MI: University of Western Michigan, 1999), p. 78.
[46] Speed, 'The Construction of the Nation', p. 150. Turville-Petre also gives a thorough account of the earlier versions of the Havelok story and its transmission in *England the Nation*, pp. 143–55.
[47] David Staines, '*Havelok the Dane*: A Thirteenth-Century Handbook for Princes', *Speculum* 51:4 (Oct. 1976): 602–23, p. 602.
[48] Turville-Petre, '*Havelok* and the History of the Nation', p. 121.
[49] Thorlac Turville-Petre, *Reading Middle English Literature* (Oxford: Blackwell, 2007), p. 12.
[50] Rouse, *The Idea of Anglo-Saxon English in Middle English Romance*, pp. 84–5.
[51] Herzman, Drake, and Salisbury, *Four Romances of England*, p. 75.

overarching national myth,[52] forces a confrontation between a sense of national identity and the anxieties of earlier Danish myths – myths not unlike those confronted by Icelandic authors attempting to establish their own identity apart from Norway as discussed in Chapter 3.

In the light of the brutality of the Danes in the poem, these descendants become the 'Other within', but the poet was not necessarily targeting those Danes who integrated into English culture and society. Rosalind Field argues (after G.A. Loud) that the Normans saw themselves as part of the Trojan diaspora, tracing their descent, via the Danes and Dacians, from the Trojans.[53] John Niles suggests that Geoffrey of Monmouth's *Historia* portrays the Norman Conquest as a restoration of the land to its rightful owners, the British and by extension the Normans, 'after the misrule of the usurping English'.[54] From this perspective, not only the Britons but also the Normans can claim to be returning to their lands, not conquering them.[55] At a time when national identities were shifting, questions of ownership, kingship, correct rule and justice were troubled. The deprivation of identity in *Havelok* and its sources can be tied to anxieties of national identity in the English of Danish heritage or Normans trying not to be French. As in continental and Scandinavian literary sources, where torture or judicial brutality does appear in medieval English works it implies abuse or corruption, often painting those who resort to it or revel in it with an unsavoury brush of tyranny.

Just as Icelandic texts held the earlier Anglo-Saxon courts up for emulation, *Havelok* turns to the Anglo-Saxon past as a model of 'gode olde law'. And like Robert of Gloucester's chronicle, *Havelok* proposes a return to these laws, rejecting the contemporary corruption of the Anglo-Norman rule many saw as a plague on thirteenth-century England. *Havelok* was produced at about the same time as the *South English Legendary* and appears in one of the earliest *SEL* manuscripts, Bodleian Laud MS Misc. 108.[56] The evidence of surviving verse romances

---

[52] Turville-Petre, *England the Nation*, p. 143.
[53] G. A. Loud, 'The Gens Normannorum – myth or reality?' in *Proceedings of the Battle Conference 1981, Anglo-Norman Studies IV*, ed. R. Allen Brown (Woodbridge: Boydell Press, 1982) 104–16, p. 113; Field, 'The King Over the Water', p. 49.
[54] John D. Niles, 'The Wasteland of Loegria: Geoffrey of Monmouth's Reinvention of the Anglo-Saxon Past', in *Reinventing the Middle Ages and the Renaissance*, ed. William F. Gentrup, Arizona Studies in the Middle Ages and the Renaissance, 1 (Turnhout: Brepols, 1998) 1–18, p. 12, qtd. in Field, 'The King Over the Water', p. 50.
[55] Field, 'The King Over the Water', p. 50.
[56] Of the *SEL* manuscripts, only two also contain Middle English Romances, Bodelian MS Laud Misc. 108 and King's College Cambridge MS 13. In both manuscripts the *SEL* sections are fragmentary, but the lives they do contain are largely the *vitae* of Anglo-Saxon saints. MS Laud Misc. 108 is the earliest surviving *SEL* manuscript and the King's College manuscript dates to about 70 years later, but there is codicological evidence that the two manuscripts, each of which is in two distinct parts, were either in the same place at the same time and decorated by the same rubricator, or passed through the same scriptorium. This research is ongoing, but the marginal decorations, which are consistent throughout both manuscripts, appear to

in English, including *Havelok*, suggests that the new literary form became a socio-cultural institution fairly quickly.[57] Speed notes the substantial intertextuality amongst the various romances which frequently involved the recurrent use of generic conventions with sometimes-apparent borrowing from one work to another.[58] Like the *South English Legendary*, *Havelok* 'reflects the historical trends and tendencies that began to manifest themselves in the thirteenth and fourteenth centuries, the need to consolidate the boundaries of England as well as the growing sense of English nationalism that appears to have been developing concurrently with the re-emergence of the English language as the dominant tongue'.[59] The baronial concerns of Anglo-Norman romances were replaced by the nationalistic tone of the Middle English adaptations, appealing to what 'had by the later Middle Ages become a varied and heterogeneous audience'.[60] While the 'integration of divided loyalties is the driving force behind *Havelok*', constructing a revised national story in which the Lincolnshire community plays a central part,[61] Havelok's brutality in Denmark still marks him as a Danish outsider. The *Havelok*-poet draws clear boundaries of inclusion, divorcing the Anglo-Scandinavian population of Lincolnshire from the barbaric Danish past and establishing England's civilizing effect on the invading population. Because, as Turville-Petre writes, 'however much the nation exploits and otherwise ignores the region, the desire to belong is overwhelming'.[62] The physical manifestations of *Havelok*'s Lincoln provide authenticating evidence but also demonstrate that

---

be very similar and suggest that the two manuscripts may have been decorated the same way because the rubricator recognized the distinctly English aspects of the Laud manuscript and the King's manuscript and may have intended to put them together. See: Kimberly K. Bell and Julie Nelson Couch, eds., *The Texts and Contexts of Oxford, Bodleian Library, MS Laud Misc. 108: The Shaping of English Vernacular Narrative*, Medieval and Renaissance Authors and Texts 6 (Leiden: Koninklijke Brill, 2011). Kimberly K. Bell, 'Resituating Romance: The Dialectics of Sanctity in MS Laud Misc. 108's *Havelok the Dane* and Royal *Vitae*', *Parergon* 25.1 (2008): 27–51.

[57] Speed, 'The Construction of the Nation', p. 144.

[58] Speed, 'The Construction of the Nation', p. 144. Grouping of romances according to the national 'matter' to which they pertain can be traced to the *chansons de geste*, and modern scholars regularly add to the traditional matters of France, Britain, and Rome a matter of England, most of whose constituent texts create myths of origin for the emergent nation. The English-language romances of the matter of England are concerned with the traditional heroes Horn, Havelok, Bevis of Hampton, and Guy of Warwick (plus his son Reinbrun), for all of whom earlier Anglo-Norman accounts are known (p. 145).

[59] Jill Frederick, 'The *South English Legendary*: Anglo-Saxon Saints and National Identity', in *Literary Appropriations of the Anglo-Saxons from the Thirteenth to the Twentieth Century*, ed. Donald Scragg and Carole Weinberg, Cambridge Studies in Anglo-Saxon England (Cambridge: Cambridge University Press, 2000) 57–73, pp. 72–3.

[60] Rouse, 'English Identity and the Law', p. 72.

[61] Turville-Petre, *England the Nation*, p. 143.

[62] Turville-Petre, *England the Nation*, p. 143.

'past actions have their consequences in present conditions'.[63] For this poet, 'the present grows out of the past; but it is the past, not a confused medley of past and present'.[64] The institutional invocations of torture and brutality must be left in the past and on the Continent.

Havelok captures the essences of chivalric violence, the intricacies of English jurisprudence, the clarity of royal justice and the effects of good rule free from corruption or abuse in its unique additions. The excessively violent executions in the Middle English version are a deviation from the Anglo-Norman sources. English adaptations often create additional scenes and scenarios that specifically enhance the brutality of the narrative, it is a fairly consistent trend in Middle English romances, and *Havelok* provides some of the best examples.[65] In *Havelok*, Godrich and Godard are traitors and corrupt rulers who betray the trust placed in them to protect and secure their charges. Godrich is Goldeboru's wicked foster father, and Godard is a treacherous usurper who shamelessly murders Havelok's sisters, slitting their throats, threatening their younger brother and handing him over to be drowned. Considering the depth of their treachery and the abuse of power they represent, as well as their need to rule by force and fear, their trials should be a reinstitution of law and correct rule. Havelok conducts the proceedings according to Danish legal tradition, and his adherence to the *vox populi* sets him in opposition to the corruption of Godard and Godrich, but the brutality he exhibits is questionable.

When Godard is trapped on the battlefield, the poet foreshadows his fate with an air of disdain: 'But Godard one (that he flowe/ So the thef men dos henge,/ Or hund men shole in dike slenge)' (lines 2433–5).[66] He will be flayed, as a thief is hanged or a dead dog is thrown into a ditch. His death will be ignominious, a fitting end for an evil tyrant. But he will be judged first, a legal proceeding which he has denied his own people, and which emphasizes the return to law at his defeat. Nevertheless, his final punishment is brutal in its dispassionate delivery and, like the Irish in *Njals saga* who eviscerate Broðir, Havelok is tainted by this brutality.

Bound hand and foot, Godard is led before Havelok in the humiliating position of riding backwards on a mare: 'And keste him on a scabbed mere;/ Hise nese went unto the crice' (lines 2449–50). This form of ridicule is fitting for a criminal who not only deprived Havelok of his birthright, but also murdered

---

[63] Turville-Petre, *England the Nation*, p. 147.
[64] Turville-Petre, *England the Nation*, p. 149.
[65] Other notable examples are *William of Palerne* and *Sir Launfal*. Neither text includes episodes of torture, but the poems exhibit a good bit more violence than their sources. *Sir Launfal*, Thomas Chestre's fifteenth-century adaptation of texts ranging from the late twelfth-century *Lanval* and early fourteenth-century *Sir Landeval*, adds numerous scenes for the sake of violence.
[66] All textual citations are from *Havelok the Dane*, *Middle English Romances*, ed. Stephen H.A. Shepherd (New York: W.W. Norton and Company, 1995) 3–74.

his sisters and attempted to have him drowned, an event recounted throughout the poem to remind the audience of Godard's crimes and his betrayal. To judge Godard, Havelok, acting as a just ruler who follows the dictates of law, asks Ubbe to call together all his earls and barons, burghers and knights for a public trial that includes a jury of people across social strata: 'He setten hem dun bi the wawe,/ Riche and povere, heye and lowe,/ The helde men and ek the grom,/ And made ther the rithe dom' (lines 2470–3). Their sentence is particularly brutal and bloody, but this does not necessarily signal an approbation of this kind of public spectacle.

Unlike the trial of Ganelon in the *Roland*, this punishment is carried out with full consent of the nobility, which may signify the bloodthirsty inheritance of the Anglo-Danish from which these descendants must separate themselves in a new, more uniformly English national identity. Rouse writes: 'The concern for law in the romances, manifested through the romance hero's judicial crises, represents the legal anxieties of the community. These anxieties can be seen to be representative of the changing interests of the romance audience.'[67] This is clearly evident in *Arthur and Gorlagon*, but Havelok's punishment of Godard is not presented as a judicial crisis; he calls together a parliament, which passes judgment and calls for the brutal sentence that is then carried out with almost no commentary. Godard's final punishment is excessive and an air of revenge clings to it:

> 'We deme that he be al quic flawen,
> And sithen to the galwes drawen
> At this foule mere tayl,
> Thoru is fet a ful strong nayl,
> And thore ben henged wit two feteres;
> And thare be written thise leteres:
> 'This is the swike that wende wel
> The King have reft the lond, il del,
> And hise sistres, with a knif,
> Bothe refte here lif.'
> This writ shal henge bi him thare.
> The dom is demd; seye we na more.' (lines 2476–87)

Once the judgment is pronounced, Havelok, 'that stille sat so the ston' (line 2475), says nothing and the sentence is carried out without any further discussion; however, Godard is at least allowed to confess and be shriven. In this instance, gruesome punishment is meted out with full approval of legal proceeding. Despite the detail and the gory nature of Godard's treatment, the poet's description does not celebrate this violence but indicts such brutality. There is no sense that Havelok enjoys or revels in Godard's punishment. However, he does deny mercy when Godard cries out for it, and his demeanour suggests satisfaction at the fulfilment of personal and state revenge similar to Charlemagne's in the

---

[67] Rouse, 'English Identity and the Law', p. 72.

Roland. The poet paints a graphic picture of this punishment as Godard is flayed beginning at his toes and begins to roar in his pain and beg for mercy:

> Sket cam a ladde with a knif
> And bigan rith at the to
> For-to ritte and for-to flo;
> And he bigan for-to rore
> So it were grim or gore,
> That men mithe thethen a mile
> Here him rore – that fule file!
> The ladde ne let nowith forthi,
> They he criede, 'Merci! Merci!'
> That he ne flow everil del,
> With knif mad of grunden stel.   (lines 2493–2503)

His unheeded pleas for mercy evoke sympathy; even though he is a tyrant and deserves harsh punishment, this goes too far. He is bound once again upon the pathetic mare facing her tail to be taken to the gallows, 'Nouth bi the gate, but over the falwes' (line 2509) – a rough and uncomfortable ride. At the gallows he is hanged and the poet unceremoniously proclaims his death, 'Thanne he was ded, that Sathanas' (line 2512), but not before he chastises any who would feel sympathy for Godard or protest the means of his execution: 'Datheit hwo recke; he was fals!' (line 2511).

The poet's interjection seems unnecessary at this point because the case against Godard is so overwhelming and the trial so seemingly fair and just. The public execution of traitors sent a strong signal of justice in action, and the 'gathering of crowds of ordinary people to watch and cheer at the gruesome fate of traitors was itself redolent both of the attitude of awe, respect and fear which the Crown wished to inculcate and the way in which the public at large could be attracted by or drawn into such events'.[68] The fact that the poet does interject suggests that some sympathy may lie with Godard due to the brutality of his punishment and that no matter what his crimes, the final form of his execution will appear excessive to some and have residual effects on the idea of justice – if not in England, then for other societies that resort to such measures.

The poet condemns the usurpation of inherited right, but more strenuously condemns the abuse of power that follows and the need to rule through fear. However, the poet makes a distinction between Godard and Godrich, allowing 'direct comparisons between the treatment of the two traitors [...] and of the processes by which they are judged and punished', engaging in a deliberate discourse of law and national identity.[69] While the English Godrich disinherits Goldeboru and violates his oath to her father, overturning the justice and peace of Æthelwold's reign as a consequence, he does not resort to infanticide. He does not murder, so he is not subjected to the same brutal punishment – flaying – as

---

[68] Musson, *Medieval Law in Context*, p. 19.
[69] Rouse, 'English Identity and the Law', p. 75.

the Dane Godard, though he is burned at the stake (a punishment most often reserved for heretics). Even so, it is hard to imagine that former subjects and supporters, however cowed and oppressed, would condemn a traitor, even one as villainous as Godard, to the torturous penalty of being publicly flayed alive. Rouse sums up the interpretative debate that has waged over these episodes: 'Some scholars have seen the pragmatic violence of the execution as an indicator of the intended audience of the poem, positioning it squarely within the realm of the tavern and the inn. Others have viewed the violence differently, seeing it as an indication of an unrealistic narrative mode – the "naive fantasy world" of the poem'.[70] This suggests that audiences of commoners rather than nobles would have enjoyed the spectacle of brutality more, especially since the victim of the brutality (unsympathetic as he may be) is a royal usurper. But a tavern audience of lower or merchant classes may have been far more aware of the implications of that brutality: torture and brutality as weapons of unstable rule, most often used against the common classes. Even though flaying appears in English texts, it was not an English practice, but it was practised on the Continent: 'In France they might be flayed alive or hanged and quartered, first being dragged, as they were in England, to execution at the horse's tail'.[71] But while flaying is associated with treason in both French and English *literature*, it was not a common punishment in *reality*. Barron says, 'It was apparently always an exceptional penalty, prescribed by ancient usage rather than written code, and reserved for punishment of crimes for which society felt a particular abhorrence'.[72] As in *Saint Bartholomew* and *Havelok*, such depictions draw attention only to the 'representational status of flaying in medieval culture', not to its actual practice.[73] Mills highlights the medieval cultural associations surrounding the removal of skin, specifically the place of flaying within medieval penal imagery, 'the network of visual and textual significations that transform the violated bodies of executed criminals into discourse and fantasy'.[74] The violence may seem fantastic, but the greater question involves *who* is being violent, not what kind of violence is used.[75] Because of the nature of Godard's crime, flaying might very well seem in order, but Mickel goes further, rejecting its use and arguing 'that there is no substantiation for considering flaying to have been an "ancient usage"'.[76] It may be this kind of association that the poet wishes to avoid, placing such a barbarous punishment both in the past and outside England's borders. This is Havelok's first

---

[70] Rouse, 'English Identity and the Law', p. 75.
[71] J.G. Bellamy, *The Law of Treason in England in the Later Middle Ages* (Cambridge: Cambridge University Press, 1970), p. 13. See also: W.R.J. Barron, 'The Penalties for Treason in Medieval Life and Literature', *Journal of Medieval History* 7 (1981): 187–202.
[72] Barron, 'The Penalties for Treason', p. 197.
[73] Mills, *Suspended Animation*, p. 66.
[74] Mills, *Suspended Animation*, p. 65.
[75] Mills, *Suspended Animation*, pp. 65–6.
[76] Mickel, *Ganelon, Treason*, p. 147 n. 303.

official act as king, followed by his redistribution of the lands and goods that Godard stole from him as a child, and it begins his reign with a sense of judicial restoration tainted by the excessive and bloodthirsty nature of the justice. This taint will cling to Havelok as he and the Danes embark for England to restore Goldeboru to her stolen throne.

Resorting to torture is a desperate measure and suggests civil instability; it corrupts those who employ it as well, no matter how noble their intentions. The Anglo-Norman material is adapted to make the 'romance genre the vehicle for the depiction of an ideal king; more importantly, at the same time he made this depiction the vehicle for a critical overview of the contemporary political situation and the desires and complaints of the lower classes'.[77] Part of this complaint may well have been a fear of torture or excessive violence at the hands of the aristocracy or the monarchy. The concept of the *rex pacificus* was an important ideal in both romances and popular ideals of governance, and in literature it was used as a model both to criticize and to advise contemporary rulers.[78] While Havelok seems to embody this ideal, his 'justice' is potentially destabilizing, and while he achieves peace it is with excessive force. What David Staines calls the 'deliberate intention underlying the poet's reworking of the tale'[79] applies to the repeated scenes of graphic violence, the repeated rehearsal of Godard's crimes and the injustices perpetrated against the two protagonists. In depicting the development of Havelok as an ideal king, the poet makes a profound distinction between the Danes and the English, portraying the English – embodied by the displaced Queen Goldeboru – as more just, more tolerant and more merciful than their Danish brethren.

In dealing with Godrich, whose crimes are many but not as violent as Godard's, Havelok leaves the judgment to Goldeboru, the rightful queen of England, who enacts swift and just punishment without resorting to bloodshed or the public spectacle of flaying. Judith Weiss points out that Godrich is not nearly as villainous as Godard so his punishment is confined to humiliation and burning.[80] The scenes are parallel, but the difference in their judicial culmination is striking. Godrich is led to his punishment, also facing the back end of a mare, humiliated for his presumption and betrayal and then quickly burned as a traitor. The potential for a more violent end is there, but in exercising her rights as queen Goldeboru specially orders her men not to beat Godrich: 'And bad she sholde don him gete,/ And that non ne sholde him bete/ Ne shame do, for he was knith,/ Til knithes haveden demd him rith' (lines 2762–65). As a knight,

---

[77] Staines, 'Havelok the Dane', p. 607.
[78] Rouse, 'English Identity and the Law', p. 72. Rouse further notes that by the time the Matter of England romances were written in Middle English, the concerns regarding English law were likely to be varied indeed (p. 72).
[79] Staines, 'Havelok the Dane', p. 607.
[80] Judith Weiss, 'Structure and Characterisation in *Havelok the Dane*', *Speculum* 44:2 (April 1969): 247–57, p. 248.

Godrich must be judged by his peers, and it is by exercising justice according to law that the English people 'heye and lawe' (line 2767) recognize Goldeboru as England's rightful heir. Horrific as it is, Godrich's end is far less gruesome than Godard's; and Goldeboru can begin her rule with mercy and justice that *are* signifiers of the Anglo-Saxon past, untainted by Norman Conquest.

Havelok, as king of Denmark, and Goldeboru, as queen of England, represent the differences in their natural sensibilities and culture, and even though the end of the poem emphasizes the integration of the Danes into the fabric of English identity as part of the English 'national stock',[81] there are residual anxieties of national heritage in the discussion of justice. *Havelok* is an acknowledged celebration of national identity that shows a 'patriotic attitude' reflecting the 'emergence of English nationalism in the thirteenth century',[82] but part of that national pride lies in the temperance of English justice. Rouse argues that the *Havelok*-poet's construction of England as a realm characterized by the rule of lawful peace invites cultural comparison with Denmark.[83] But the particularly brutal mode of Godard's death indicates legal difference, real or imagined, between the two countries.[84] The Danes enact brutal and vengeful punishment whereas the English exercise restraint and do not torture (despite even the heinous nature of Godrich's crimes). The poet may be advising his sovereign on the proper use of English justice or he may be gently rebuking the king and nobility, reminding them that English justice does not resort to torture or vengeful punishment. The discussion of Æthelwold's reign where 'all estates [...] are subjected to and protected by his laws [...] [h]arks back to a utopian age of the universal application of law, a far cry from the reality of the legal segregation of the clerical and secular courts'.[85] Æthelwold is not only held up as a foil for the evil deeds of the two traitors and a model for Havelok and Goldeboru, but also as a reminder of England's judicial traditions and the justice of earlier reigns before the Norman Plantagenet line was in place. There is a boundary to the justice served in *Havelok*. Godard's treachery is heinous but flaying and then hanging does not fit the crime; thus, this form of punishment represents the potential for brutality in the punishers as well as the cruelty of the punished. The means of his execution are so extreme that Havelok cannot escape marginal association with the Romans who employed violent and excessive means of torture and punishment to establish their own rule.[86] The punishment of traitors was fairly

---

[81] Turville-Petre, *England the Nation*, p. 154.
[82] Weiss, 'Structure and Characterisation', p. 251.
[83] Rouse, 'English Identity and the Law', p. 75.
[84] Rouse, 'English Identity and the Law', p. 75.
[85] Rouse, 'English Identity and the Law', p. 74.
[86] Bell has examined the hagiographical motifs of *Havelok* and makes a compelling argument that *Havelok* should be read as hagiography. She writes that when considered in the context of its unique manuscript, the secular nature of the romance 'gives way to elements that align it with the fundamental spirituality of the manuscript's overwhelming number of hagiographic

consistent in literature – flaying, dragging by horse and hanging – as evidenced in the *Chanson de Roland*, *Havelok*, and Chaucer's *Prioress's Tale*, but there should be no satisfaction in these executions. The worst punishment for treachery is a necessary evil, but it is not done lightly nor with any sense of sadistic pleasure. In these texts there are no roaring, cheering crowds: all is done in performative silence. Goldeboru, as England's queen, will avoid any association with the traitors who usurped her and her husband's throne and will proceed according to the customs of her people.

As in the *Roland* and *Walewein*, *Havelok* engages in a narrative of law through the depiction of a trial – but the use of brutality intrudes on the sense of justice. The traitors are condemned for their crimes by popular acclaim, and in the case of Godrich, by a jury of common Englishmen in a particularly English display of law. *Havelok*'s association with Anglo-Saxon England includes a 'great emphasis on legal practices and social institutions'.[87] So the precise historical location places the narrative in a time with real law and real justice – where the use of torture is automatically outside the realm of justice. Those who use it actively contravene the law and act as tyrants. Turville-Petre writes that the poem is 'structured around a pattern of stability, conflict, and return to stability, as Havelok and Goldebrow [sic] restore the peace and just rule that Godrich and Godard have upset'.[88] This return to justice is the pivot point of the tale and in order for their reign to be considered the most just it is set in opposition to the most unjust – rulers who use brutality to wield power. For thirteenth-century English audiences aware of the brutality at Constantinople in 1204, of the atrocities in southern France during the Albigensian Crusade, as well as the dynastic struggles within their own country, this image would have had particular resonance. But the recourse to brutal punishment by Havelok, however justified, leaves the audience in an uncomfortable position, especially those descended from the Danes who did settle in England. Here is a king who has correctly and rightfully overthrown a usurper and murderer, but in enacting justice he exacts vengeance in a brutal and violent way. Anthony Musson notes that re-establishing rule after the deposition of a usurper did not necessarily take the form of physical violence. He writes,

> The public exhibition of rebellious or deposed leaders, where they were ritually humiliated, their ambitions parodied and their treasonous behaviour signified to the masses attending, was intended to underline royal supremacy and instill by

texts', the *SEL* fragment. Bell, 'Resituating Romance', p. 28. In a similar vein, Julie Nelson Couch argues that reading the 'responsive role of the *Havelok* audience as possessing a meditative aspect aligns the poem with the manuscript's devotional concerns and practices. Ultimately, *Havelok* directs an audience's affective receptivity toward an investment in rightful secular power.' Julie Nelson Couch, 'Defiant Devotion in MS Laud Misc. 108: The Narrator of *Havelok the Dane* and Affective Piety', *Parergon* 25.1 (2008): 53–79, p. 53.

[87] Turville-Petre, *England the Nation*, pp. 143–4, 145.
[88] Turville-Petre, *England the Nation*, p. 144.

visual means the authority of the law. This was achieved not only literally through physical punishment, but symbolically through a shared culture of iconography and ritual.[89]

The punishment of traitors was nothing new to thirteenth- and fourteenth-century England, and those executions were ostensibly public affairs, but the poet omits any sense of public approbation and emphasizes the sobering effect of this spectacle. In subjecting Godard to more gruesome torments there is a clear delineation between Havelok as a *Dane* and Goldeboru as an *English* ruler, potentially drawing on English fears of foreign invasion in portraying the Danish process as more prone to violence or acknowledging cultural anxieties concerning the chronicle accounts of Danish raiders, but firmly locating them in the *past* – emphasizing the synthesis of Danish and English justice at the end and alleviating any association of the contemporary Anglo-Scandinavian audience with their ancestors.

The fear of foreign invasion did not entirely dissipate after 1066; the French Prince Louis (later Louis VIII) nearly gained the English throne with an expeditionary force supported by English barons in 1217. Even as Godrich rallies his nobles to fend off Havelok when he lands in England, he uses the rhetoric of foreign invasion to galvanize support, playing on fears of Danish invaders – an image that would resonate with any English audience – and lies about Havelok's intentions:

> 'Lokes hware here at Grimesbi
> Hise uten-laddes here comen,
> And haves nu the priorie numen.
> Al that ever mithen he finde,
> He brenne kirkes, and prestes binde;
> He strangleth monkes and nunnes bathe.
> Wat wile ye, frend, her-offe rathe?
> Yif he regne thus-gate longe,
> He moun us all over-gange –
> He moun us all quic henge, or slo,
> Or thral maken and do ful wo,
> Or elles reve us ure lives,
> And ure children and ure wives.' (lines 2579–91)

Godrich plays on the fears of the populace to bolster his forces and drive them to the fight, and even though Havelok does not perpetuate any cruelty on the English people, the English themselves have no difficultly believing that the Danish forces are capable of such violation. The allusion to the standard image of Viking pillagers is made in order to reject it because it is Godrich who is the traitor and he relies on cultural fears to resist the Danish invaders by reanimating the spectres of the past.[90] His accusations are patently untrue, as Turville-Petre

---

[89] Musson, *Medieval Law in Context*, pp. 231–2.
[90] Turville-Petre, *England the Nation*, p. 153.

notes, but Havelok's resort to flaying associates him with the traditional portraits of Danes in the chronicles rather than with merciful, just and heroic English kings. More immediately to the thirteenth-century audience, this action associates Havelok with accounts of atrocities in the inquisitorial courts on the Continent. The execution of Godard sets a precedent for employing brutality as a form of jurisprudence. So while the poet does not condemn torture or brutal forms of execution outright, he does acknowledge that there are others who might, and who might see Havelok's justice tainted by his denial of mercy to Godard. While the poem may end with 'a vision of harmony throughout society, as people not only of different ranks but also of different ethnic origins witness the coronation in London' where 'Danish and English, rich and poor, are finally integrated into one nation of England',[91] there is still a residual indictment against the application of torture that tarnishes this portrait of unity. If this is the shared past of the English people then torture too must be part of that past. But the poet attempts to distance his contemporary audience from that savagery by making the English less brutal than their Danish counterparts, emphasizing the ethnic differences and situating the events firmly in distant history while making prescient observations about his own society.

The *Havelok*-poet addresses the Anglo-Danish descendants of Vikings, but as Rouse points out, that acculturation is by no means unidirectional. While *Havelok* 'integrates the Danes into England, England simultaneously has a cultural, and legal, impact upon Havelok and Denmark'.[92] The poem suggests that English influence can have a civilizing effect – England's laws can be emulated in other European contexts, as in *Walewein* or the Icelandic sagas. As Rouse writes, 'situating the narrative in the Anglo-Saxon past, the text makes use of the popular post-Conquest view of the Anglo-Saxon period as a Golden Age of law and order. This Golden Age is envisaged as being specifically English, and is explicitly linked to the rule of a rightful king who rules within the bounds of the law of the realm.'[93] For a thirteenth-century audience, whether Anglo-Danish or English, noble or within the environs of tavern or inn, this would mean correct English law untainted by the draconian measures of the inquisitorial courts – untainted by the use of torture. The English had a long tradition of maintaining their own laws, and *Havelok* interrogates the uses of law, punishment and torture as a quality of national identity.

The choice of punishment for Godard may represent an incomplete process of acculturation of Denmark, a 'legal vacuum, ready to be colonized by English legal process through the body of its Anglicized king, Havelok'.[94] However, Havelok is not the best vehicle for the justice inherent in Anglo-Saxon tradition despite the divine revelation of his noble heritage. He still ordains brutality

[91] Turville-Petre, '*Havelok* and the History of the Nation', p. 134.
[92] Rouse, 'English Identity and the Law', p. 77.
[93] Rouse, 'English Identity and the Law', p. 77.
[94] Rouse, 'English Identity and the Law', p. 76.

despite the trappings of legal proceeding and his actions seem somewhat vindictive even though the Danish people sanction them. This could be an indictment of Danish law, or of the relative lawlessness of Denmark in the past. But Denmark of the thirteenth century emulated English law more than the laws of its past or its contemporary neighbours – it resisted the influence of inquisitorial courts and the use of torture as much as England. England had been greatly influenced by Danish custom during the period of the Danelaw (ninth and tenth centuries), particularly in Yorkshire, Lincolnshire, Leicestershire and Northamptonshire, where 'relatively peaceful coexistence between originally English and more recently acculturated Anglicized Scandinavian settlers created conditions favorable to cultural interchange and the adaptation of Danelaw customs to English usage'.[95] During that time, those who lived under the Danelaw, of both English and Danish ancestry, enjoyed particular 'legal and political freedoms and – perhaps as a result – economic success unknown elsewhere in England during this period'.[96] The residual effects of English and Danish legal synthesis resound within *Havelok*. The Anglo-Danish descendants of *Havelok*'s audience may have been equally content to accept that their forebears were 'civilized' by their settlement in England, just as Denmark in the poem appears to be civilized by Havelok's return. In fact, the *Havelok*-poet may imply that contemporary Denmark has been shaped by this Anglo-Saxon influence.

The poem's audience is one of mixed ancestry, and so the poet addresses the Anglo-Danish descendants troubled by the cultural inheritance of earlier Viking raiders: 'The chronicles tell only of pagan bands raping and pillaging; *Havelok* presents a revisionist view of the Vikings, bringing justice, peace, and social integration'.[97] These warriors were defined by the English chroniclers emphasizing the Saxon origins of the English nation, as an alien race who 'conquered the English and have unjustly imposed their yoke on a proud people ever since'.[98] Havelok's brutal punishment of his enemy has some resonance with that cultural stereotype and reinforces anxieties of assimilation with the Anglo-Danish population. In this construction of ethnic identity, only those of Saxon blood are, and indeed ever can be, English; 'those descended from the Danes will forever remain an alien and unintegrated people', a view that is not motivated by contemporary realities.[99] It was exceptionally difficult to take pride in an ancestry steeped in savage violence:

---

[95] Jonathan Evans, 'Danes: Contributions to English Culture', in *J.R.R. Tolkien Encyclopedia: Scholarship and Critical Assessment*, ed. Michael D.C. Drout (New York: Routledge, 2001), 113–14, pp. 113–14.
[96] Evans, 'Danes: Contributions to English Culture', p. 114.
[97] Turville-Petre, *England the Nation*, p. 152.
[98] Turville-Petre, 'Havelok and the History of the Nation', p. 132; Turville-Petre, *England the Nation*, p. 149.
[99] Turville-Petre, *England the Nation*, p. 149.

The story of England as offered by the chronicles presents the Vikings as invaders, Cnut and his sons as foreign kings ruling as a consequence of English treachery, and the Danes as arrogant aliens imposing themselves on a resentful native population. With this history it is impossible to be a loyal Englishman and at the same time to have pride in one's Danish ancestry.[100]

Havelok instils this pride but also emphasizes the supremacy of the English system of justice by which Havelok will temper his rule. Situating the events of the poem in the Anglo-Saxon past allows the poet to alleviate the concerns of his present audience. It also allows a more subtle association of Havelok's Danes of the past with the Normans of the present, suggesting that the Anglo-Danish who settled centuries earlier were far more integrated into English society than the Normans who only arrived in 1066.

The poem has been described as a warning to princes, specifically to Edward I, about the dangers of misrule and the corruption of power, emerging as a missive to the thirteenth-century English monarchy 'of the needs and demands of the lower classes'.[101] But more than that, *Havelok* urges restraint in employing royal prerogative and exercising royal justice. It also highlights the barbarity of torture and brutality by setting its use outside the realm of England. The deliberate judicial vengeance in the Middle English poem is a later addition; the torture and barbarity of the traitor's punishment is absent from the earlier twelfth-century version that only includes standard scenes of military violence, hand-to-hand combat and battlefield slaughter. Many scholars, including Staines, envision Havelok as a pure hero who represents the reestablishment of just rule, discussing the torture and execution of both Godard and Godrich as part of that justice: 'The portrait of Havelok becomes an analogue to depictions of the proper ruler in political and legal treatises, in political songs, and in the chronicles'.[102] For Edward I and his heirs, descended as they were from the Normans, *Havelok* provides a means of integrating into and adapting the Anglo-Saxon past – Robert of Gloucester's remedy to the woes of England. Through Goldeboru a royal genealogy is traced via the Saxon female line that 'bypasses the Norman invasion, and represents the imagined political community as newly remade from the shards of an older past nostalgically retrievable in an array of linguistic and narrative artifacts, from weapons, to lineages, to toasts',[103] to a legal prohibition on interrogatory torture. However, the warning embedded in *Havelok* may not simply apply to the betrayal of trust exhibited by the two traitors, but may also be an indictment of just rulers who sometimes take their own vengeance too far in the name of the law and walk the very fine line of power and corruption. The development of the Havelok story encodes a history of the English nation,[104]

---

100 Turville-Petre, *England the Nation*, p. 151.
101 Staines, 'Havelok the Dane', p. 602.
102 Staines, 'Havelok the Dane', p. 613.
103 Heng, 'The Romance of England', p. 156.
104 Speed, 'The Construction of the Nation', p. 150.

but however just Havelok's actions are in restoring himself and his wife to their respective thrones, the use of brutal punishments and torture illuminates the complications of identity and embodies cultural anxiety about English heritage and the societal capacity for excessive violence. As Turville-Petre writes, more than any other 'so-called' romance, '*Havelok* communicates a sense of society, a diversity of people together involved in the actions of just kings and faithless lords'.[105] But it also engages in a vigorous censure of tyranny and abuse at the hands of rightful rulers, and interrogates the limits of law, even in the hands of lawful kings.

Arthur and Gorlagon

The question of correct governance and the application of torture to extract a confession in judicial proceedings has an unusual prominence in the body of werewolf narratives circulating in England beginning with the late twelfth-century Anglo-Norman *Bisclavret* of Marie de France. Often coupled with the motif of a faithful husband transformed into a wolf with human consciousness by an adulterous woman who extracts a confession of his metamorphic capability through guile and verbal persuasion, torture is the retributive response to her treachery and is used to elicit the truth of her actions and the husband's true form. Following the pattern established in sources such as *Bisclavret*,[106] the fourteenth-century Latin romance *Arthur and Gorlagon*[107] includes scenes where

[105] Turville-Petre, '*Havelok* and the History of the Nation', p. 133.
[106] George Lyman Kittredge discusses potential sources and analogues for *Arthur and Gorlagon*, as well as other werewolf narratives, in his edition of the text in '*Arthur and Gorlagon*', *Harvard Studies and Notes in Philology and Literature* 8 (1903), 149–273, reprinted as an individual text by Haskell House (New York) in 1966. For an updated discussion of Kittredge's findings, and the possible Irish analogues to these tales, see: John Carey, 'Werewolves in Medieval Ireland', *Cambrian Medieval Celtic Studies* 44 (Winter 2002): 37–72. Charlotte F. Otten includes Frank A. Milne's translation of *Arthur and Gorlagon*, in *Folk-Lore* 15 (1904): 40–67, in her collection of lycanthropic materials: *A Lycanthropy Reader: Werewolves in Western Culture*, ed. Charlotte F. Otten (Syracuse NY: Syracuse University Press, 1986): 234–55. Mildred Leake Day presents a thorough discussion of *Arthur and Gorlagon* in her introduction to her edition and translation of the text in *Latin Arthurian Literature* (Cambridge: D.S. Brewer, 2005). Jeff Massey addresses the questions of transformation and comedy in these tales in his paper '"There, wolf ... there, castle": Comedy, Romance, and the Self-Deconstructing Medieval Monster', delivered at the annual meeting of the International Medieval Congress at the University of Western Michigan, Kalamazoo, 2007. I am indebted to Jeff Massey for providing copies of this material to me. I am also grateful to him for bringing the torture episodes of *Arthur and Gorlagon* to my attention, and for providing me with a copy of his conference paper.
[107] *Arthur and Gorlagon* survives in one manuscript, Bodleian Library Rawlinson MS B 149 dating from the end of the fourteenth century to the beginning of the fifteenth century. Kittredge suggests that this version is a later redaction of a much earlier text, dating from the twelfth century.

torture is applied as a means of judicial interrogation prescribed by inquisitorial procedure: a just authority (the king) questions a treacherous and disloyal subject (the wife) and a usurper who ruled as a tyrant; when neither party confesses to their crime, the secular authority applies torture until a confession is extracted. In these two texts the werewolf is not the only alien Other; so are those who contravene civilization and society by committing treachery, thus forcing the just monarch to resort to cruel methods to uncover their perfidy. In both *Bisclavret* and *Arthur and Gorlagon*, the torture episodes are sparse and warrant only a few lines; however, they lead to the final resolutions of their narratives and the restoration of the werewolves to their human forms, suggesting that torture was acceptable in certain circumstances when employed in the process of justice. But as in *Havelok* the use of torture is a double-edged sword and there are risks involved for the maintenance of just rule. Neither poet dwells on the torture, nor describes its effects in gruesome detail; it is the option of last resort for these kings, who would much rather exercise justice without recourse to unnecessary violence. However, in the context of the werewolf narrative, which has its antecedents in Norman, Norse and Celtic mythology and folklore, the use of torture is bound up in questions of national identity as surely as in *Havelok*. While the monstrous aspect of these tales is tied to the lycanthropic transformation of the protagonist, each narrative engages in a certain amount of brutality that troubles the definition of these courts as places of justice and correct rule. As in many medieval tales of the supernatural or Otherworld, the magical inhabitants exist to highlight the flaws of the mortal world – to shine a light in the darker corners of castle and court and reveal the chinks in courtly armour. For thirteenth- and fourteenth-century audiences, these courtly failings had become far too frequent and far too obvious to ignore. The early part of the fourteenth century was marked by the overthrow and gruesome murder of Edward II in 1327, and the end of the fourteenth century (the date of the Rawlinson manuscript) was similarly marred by the deposition and suspicious death of Richard II (1399/1400). As Keith Busby has noted, the French influence on Middle English (or even Anglo-Latin) literature is 'almost incalculable, as it is both pervasive and persistent and assumes many forms'.[108] Just as Middle Dutch authors transformed French forms and texts into indigenous literature in their vernacular, so did English authors rework and adapt French material, as seen in *Havelok*. As Busby notes, English poets tailor French texts to 'fit the tastes and requirements of a new and different audience'.[109] The noble and rising-merchant-class audience of late thirteenth- and fourteenth-century England was one facing a crisis of identity represented by a growing desire to form distinctly English literary models that harkened back to a pre-Conquest past, but which also elevated and reinstated

---

[108] Keith Busby, '*Dame Sirith* and *De Clerico et Puella*', in *Companion to Early Middle English Literature*, ed. N.H.G.E. Veldhoen and H. Aertsen, 2nd edition (Amsterdam: VU University Press, 1995), 67–78, p. 67.
[109] Busby, '*Dame Sirith* and *De Clerico et Puella*', p. 67.

the English (or at least British) origins of the Arthurian tradition. Even though it is written in Latin, *Arthur and Gorlagon* takes the werewolf story, grounded in Norman, French and Scandinavian traditions, and weaves it into an Arthurian story that questions the ability of kings to learn from the mistakes of others and still govern justly in times of crisis.

The critique of the court in werewolf narratives is nothing new in the thirteenth and fourteenth centuries. Marie de France, writing (perhaps) in the court of her (perhaps) half-brother Henry II, clearly instructs the Angevin court in the dangers of adultery, deception and treachery that lurk within. In *Bisclavret*, Marie de France clarifies that this will not be a characteristic werewolf story of a savage beast in the Norman tradition, but instead a different story:

> Garualf, c[eo] est beste salvage:
> Tant cum il est en cele rage,
> Hummes devure, grant mal fait,
> Es granz forez converse e vait.
> Cest afere les ore ester;
> Del Bisclavret [vus] voil cunter. (lines 9–14)[110]
>
> [A werewolf is a savage beast;/ while his fury is on him/ he eats men, does much harm,/ goes deep into the forest to live./ But that's enough of this for now:/ I want to tell you about the Bisclavret.][111]

She proceeds to tell the story of a man (a werewolf) who spends three days of the week in that form. Suspecting him of infidelity, the wife pressures him to reveal his whereabouts on these days; the more he resists, the more she pressures him. R. Howard Bloch writes that this is a tale about the 'irresistibility of the question' and her curiosity despite knowing that the answer will cause her harm.[112] As such it is also about the dangers of discovery – dangers inherent to any inquisitorial process where the subject is unwilling to reveal his or her secrets. The husband finally bows to his wife's interrogation and confesses; rather than satisfying the wife's curiosity about his fidelity, he gives her a reason to betray him and become unfaithful 'as if her desire (for the knight) from the beginning were to discover her husband's secret so that she might more fully live a secret of her own'.[113] She steals his clothes, the means by which he reverses his transformation, and moves on with her life and her new husband, the knight whose attentions she had previously spurned. The wolf remains in the woods until he is found by a benevolent and generous king who, moved by his docile nature, takes him home as a pet. The wolf lives in the castle peacefully until he

---

[110] Marie de France, *Bisclavret*, ed. Alfred Ewert (Oxford: Basil Blackwell, 1963).
[111] Translations of *Bisclavret* are taken from *The Lais of Marie de France*, trans. Robert Hanning and Joan Ferrante (Grand Rapids MI: Baker Books, 1978, seventh printing 2002).
[112] R. Howard Bloch, *The Anonymous Marie de France* (Chicago: The University of Chicago Press, 2003), p. 79.
[113] Bloch, *The Anonymous Marie de France*, p. 81.

sees the knight who usurped his marital rights and mauls him severely. Everyone wonders what injury the knight could have done Bisclavret for him to behave so violently, but the matter rests until the wolf, unable to hold back, attacks his duplicitous wife and bites off her nose. He is surrounded by men who threaten to tear him apart, but one of the king's companions, a wise old man, intervenes and reasons with the king that Bisclavret has never harmed anyone, and so must have a reason for doing so now. He recommends that the king '"Fetes li dire s'el le seit!" ['Make her tell what she knows!'] (line 258). The king follows his advice, and 'De l'autre part la dame ad prise/ E en mut grant destresce mise./ Tant par destresce e par poür/ Tut li cunta de sun seignur' [took the wife and subjected her to torture;/ out of fear and pain/ she told all about her husband] (lines 263–6). Upon her confession, Bisclavret's clothes are retrieved, the wolf regains his human form and the treacherous woman is exiled, bearing noseless children as a reminder of her betrayal.

The application of torture in this episode is very brief and acts as a means to an end, culminating in the restoration of Bisclavret and the exile of his wife. At the end of the twelfth century when Roman legal tradition, including torture as an interrogation method, was just beginning to emerge in medieval European jurisprudence, the use of force in interrogating a prisoner would not necessarily have seemed inappropriate. Marie is careful not to give details about the kind of force to which the wife is subjected, only that 'tant par destresce e par poür' [for pain and fear] (line 264) she confesses. This tale is about the re-establishment of justice as much as it is about re-establishing the knight to his human form and in *Bisclavret*, like *Arthur and Gorlagon*, torture, or the threat of torture, brings about the resolution. There is no overt suggestion that the king should have done otherwise, and this trope continues in later versions of the werewolf tale, where additional scenes of violence and punishment complement the description of the torture.[114] However, at a time when torture was a relatively new instrument of inquisitorial courts and was prohibited by law in England, its application here may have sat poorly with an English (or Anglo-Norman) courtly audience, perhaps even with Marie herself. Henry II was profoundly interested in maintaining good law and order, and retained the older traditions of Anglo-Saxon law to further this end.[115] The events of the lais are firmly located in Brittany, and while that is the convention of the Breton lai it also draws a geographical boundary between the events of the poem and the English audience. Marie de

---

[114] In the fourteenth-century Middle English *William of Palerne*, a translation and adaptation of the twelfth-century French verse romance *Guillaume de Palerne*, torture in the form of execution by burning, is threatened as a punishment for the evil Spanish queen if she will not restore her stepson to his original state. Faced with the prospect of hot coals, she relents and agrees to reverse her magic and return him to human form. She is not interrogated like the treacherous wives in *Bisclavret* and *Arthur and Gorlagon*, and though she is punished, the threat of physical violence never needs to be carried out.
[115] Peters, *Torture*, p. 59.

France was writing in Henry II's English court, but that court was composed primarily of Anglo-Norman nobles. And yet the question of Anglo-Saxon legal precedent was a pressing issue among nobility and the ruling house that found itself challenged within (as abroad) on a regular basis. Many nobles saw themselves as 'English' or rather as 'new' English replacing the Saxons. The twelfth-century chronicler Henry of Huntingdon felt the Normans were 'the legitimate heirs of the kingdom, much less a scourge than the Danes had been, and had been sent by God to punish the English for their sins'.[116] As Gillingham notes, 'the devastating experience of 1066 had meant that the correspondence between a kingdom and a people, a community of tradition, custom, law and descent [...] no longer applied in England'.[117] But there is considerable evidence that the sense of an English nation survived the Norman Conquest in the minds of creative writers,[118] and that this consciousness included defining the 'foreignness' of other ethnic groups, especially the French. In the thirteenth century writers like Robert of Gloucester complain about the influx of Normans in 1066 and after, and the fact that in his time the heirs of these Normans are still in control of lands belonging to native English.[119] Even in the late twelfth century when Marie is writing, those ethnic divisions had begun partly as Anglo-Normans sought to distance themselves from the Franks or the southern French of Aquitaine which, by 1190, was deemed ungovernable.[120] France itself was fairly unstable; 'power was a fragile commodity everywhere in France, even in the supposedly strongest principalities such as Normandy, Anjou and Flanders. If the kings of France had troubles with their counts and castellans, so too did "every territorial prince".'[121] In this context it is understandable that Marie would present an ideal court where the king is governed by loyalty and reason, and where law punishes treachery and adultery. But the resort to torture casts a pall on this otherwise noble court and suggests that perhaps tyranny is never far away. It is possible that Marie, conscious of her French lineage, elevates French law – which by the end of the twelfth century allowed torture, but she passes over it fairly quickly and neither revels in its application nor comments on its justice.

Arthur and Gorlagon bears a striking similarity to some aspects of *Bisclavret*, but it is a longer prose narrative framed within an Arthurian quest, a genre that was often used as a vehicle for cultural commentary. The author of the late fourteenth-century alliterative *Morte Arthure* seems to criticize Edward III's

---

[116] Gillingham, *The English in the Twelfth Century*, p. 128.
[117] Gillingham, *The English in the Twelfth Century*, p. 128.
[118] Donald Scragg and Carole Weinberg, 'Introduction', in *Literary Appropriations of the Anglo-Saxons from the Thirteenth to the Twentieth Century*, ed. Scragg and Weinberg, Cambridge Studies in Anglo-Saxon England (Cambridge: Cambridge University Press, 2000), 1–21, p. 5.
[119] Mitchell, 'Kings, Constitution and Crisis', p. 44.
[120] Gillingham, 'Events and Opinions', p. 59.
[121] Gillingham, 'Events and Opinions', p. 60.

warlike policies by portraying Arthur as a 'bloodthirsty and ambitious tyrant, whose war against the Roman Emperor Lucius only brought misery on both sides of the Channel, just as many in the author's own time wanted a respite from the Hundred Years War between England and France'.[122] *Arthur and Gorlagon* is a romance and as such bears many brutal markers of that genre, though Jeff Massey has made a compelling argument that it was also meant to be performed as dinner theatre.[123] In her discussion of *Richard Coer de Lyon* (*RCL*), begun in the thirteenth century, Geraldine Heng examines how popular romance 'organizes the emergence of the medieval nation, by manipulating racializing discourses through the circuit of an aggressive, cannibalistic joke'.[124] There are several similarities between the 'cannibalistic joke' of *RCL*, which involves an ill Richard I unwittingly dining on a young fat Saracen who has been killed, opened up, flayed, boiled with saffron and served up in lieu of pork,[125] and the somewhat cannibalistic (at least bloodthirsty) werewolf narrative and its final reveal of an embalmed severed head on a platter at a feast. In *RCL*, restored by his meal of Saracen, Richard returns from a skirmish and demands to dine on the head of the same swine. At this point, the cook returns on his knees with the 'black, grinning head of the dead (and eaten) Saracen, in a scene that triumphantly stages the horror of the head, its racial difference, and its inhuman, devilish nature'.[126] While *Arthur and Gorlagon* does not present such a barbarous scene (Richard is pleased to find the Saracen so tasty), it does engage in the discourse of brutality and the implications for national identity. In a foreign court, the English King Arthur has been presented with this tale of treachery, brutality and torture, and finally with the severed head of one of the guilty parties itself as a lesson, but what kind of lesson is what makes the depiction of brutality problematic. Heng notes that the scene with the Saracen head is attached to Richard to 'announce and embellish, not to condemn his legend'.[127] In other Arthurian texts, Arthur is much like Richard, 'the ideal symbol to figure a magnitude of cultural drives pulsing through the long centuries of [*RCL*]'s formation: aggressive territo-

---

[122] John Aberth, *A Knight at the Movies: Medieval History on Film* (New York: Routledge, 2003), p. 5.

[123] Jeff Massey, 'The Werewolf at the Head Table: Metatheatric "subtlety" in *Arthur and Gorlagon*', in *Heads Will Roll: Decapitation in the Medieval and Early Modern Imagination*, ed. Larissa Tracy and Jeff Massey, Medieval and Renaissance Authors and Texts (Leiden: Koninklijke Brill, forthcoming).

[124] Heng, 'The Romance of England', p. 135.

[125] Heng, 'The Romance of England', p. 136.

[126] Heng, 'The Romance of England', p. 136. Siobhain Bly Calkin makes several compelling comparisons between the portrayal of Saracens and the quest for English identity in the romances of the Auchinleck Manuscript. See: *Saracens and the Making of English Identity: The Auchinleck Manuscript*, Studies in Medieval History and Culture (New York: Routledge, 2005).

[127] Heng, 'The Romance of England', p. 136.

rial ambitions, the consumption and discipline of alien communities, and the nascent, overarching impulse toward the formation of the medieval nation'.[128] But in *Arthur and Gorlagon*, King Arthur seems singularly out of his depth, mystified and befuddled by the entire exercise; and the image of the great king is somewhat diminished. Perhaps this portrayal of Arthur, the legendary King of England, reflects native tensions in fourteenth-century England rife with war (at home and with France), undermined by papal pressure to subvert English law in favour of papal interests with the trial of the Templars, and destabilized by questions of dynastic succession and popular uprising when men, base and noble, looked to their king for knowledge, justice and law and found him wanting.[129]

Despite the fact that *Arthur and Gorlagon* is a Latin text, and its audience most likely chivalric, whose class culture, Heng argues, 'constitutes chivalry as an international formation whose loyalties exceed the merely local or national',[130] its concerns, particularly in the episodes of torture and brutality, engage with a nationalist discourse and the anxieties of English identity. The one extant version of the text dates from the end of the fourteenth to the beginning of the fifteenth century when England's laws and justice were being tested while Richard II exercised his claim to the French throne and tried to hold on to his own, and where questions of torture and brutality were particularly relevant as power structures shifted and toppled. *Arthur and Gorlagon* is fraught with questions of kingly behaviour and cultural boundaries. Arthur, having kissed his queen *cunctis intuentibus* [in the sight of all],[131] responds to her embarrassment by sending himself, Kay and Gawain on a quest to discover the true nature of women and what they want, reminiscent of Chaucer's contemporary *Wife of Bath's Tale*. Within his quest to find what is perhaps an intangible answer, three brothers lead him on a wild-wolf chase; kings invite him in and then send him on to the next one when they cannot answer his question. It is the final king, Gorlagon, who offers to tell him a story about the nature of women. This story has two parts, and therefore two sets of punishment and retribution. Throughout, the author stresses his hero's humanity emphasizing the disparity 'between his lupine form and his inner reality'[132] – but there is still a savagery in the mode of vengeance and in the repeated recourse to interrogatory torture.

Rather than transforming through a voluntary act (as in *Bisclavret*), the king in *Arthur and Gorlagon* can only be transformed by magic and he does not

---

[128] Heng, 'The Romance of England', p. 137.
[129] Both Siân Echard and Jeff Massey suggest that *Arthur and Gorlagon* was composed on the Welsh border, which opens other possibilities for anxieties of national identity. Siân Echard, *Arthurian Narrative in the Latin Tradition* (Cambridge: Cambridge University Press, 2005); Massey, 'The Werewolf at the Head Table'.
[130] Heng, 'The Romance of England', p. 139.
[131] Massey, 'There, wolf'.
[132] Leslie A. Sconduto, *Metamorphoses of the Werewolf: A Literary Study from Antiquity through the Renaissance* (Jefferson NC: McFarland, 2008), p. 85.

actively seek that transformation. In his garden grows a sapling tied to a curse placed upon him at some point in his life. If anyone cuts the sapling, strikes him on the head and says, '"Sis lupus, et habeas sensum lupi!" statim lupus fieret et sensum lupi haberet' ['be a wolf and have the understanding of a wolf,' immediately he would become a wolf and have the senses of a wolf] (214: 8–9).[133] The king tends the sapling religiously, piquing the curiosity of his suspicious and already mentally unfaithful wife, who assumes that he is going to the garden to meet a mistress. Looking for a way to challenge her husband so she can be with her young pagan prince, who is clearly identified as the pagan Other and is more alien than the wolf, she questions him when he returns late from a hunting trip. Manipulating her husband into revealing his secret, the wife plots to transform him.

Taking advantage of his absence the following day, she cuts the sapling and lies in wait with the branch concealed in her flowing sleeve. She throws her arms around him, as if to kiss him, but instead hits him on the head with the sapling, uttering the curse incorrectly: '"Sis lupus, sis lupus" uociferans; "habeasque sensum lupi" uolens adicere, "sensum hominis" adiunxit "habeas". Nec mora fit ut ipsa dixerat, canibusque ab ea incitatis eum insequentibus ad siluas concitus fugit, sed humanus sensus ei ex integro remansit' ['Be a wolf! Be a wolf!' she cried out. She intended to say, 'and have the mind of wolf,' but instead repeated, 'have the mind of a man'. Without a moment's delay, he became as she had spoken, and when she set the dogs on him, he fled into hiding in the forest, but his human sense of self remained intact] (216: 20–3). Stripped of his human form, but not his human mind, the wolf flees to the woods where he integrates into the wild. He mates with a she-wolf, produces two cubs, and waits for a chance to avenge himself on his human wife. His society has been held up as savage and barbaric and so he turns to the natural world. The wolf is essentially outlawed, and as in Old Norse/Icelandic and English tradition is neither party to nor bound by the laws of society. The outlaw narratives of the fourteenth century were a clear literary and oral response to the abuses of law and miscarriages of justice rampant in England. John Aberth writes that 'political poems, such as the *Song of the Venality of the Judges* and the *Outlaw's Song of Trailbaston*, both dating to the early fourteenth century, harp on the abuses of the current legal system and, in the case of the *Outlaw's Song*, look for relief to the greenwood of "Belregard," where "there is no deceit there, nor any bad law"'.[134] Similarly, *Arthur and Gorlagon* condemns bad law, and juxtaposes the human and the wolf worlds. The wolf acts as an outlaw, unrepentant in his savagery when he takes his revenge.[135] Taking vengeance is a human trait that highlights the brutality of

---

[133] All textual citations and translations are from *Narratio de Arthuro rege Britanniae et rege Gorlagon lycanthropo*, in *Latin Arthurian Literature*, ed. and trans. Mildred Leake Day (Cambridge: D.S. Brewer, 2005), 208–35. Page and line numbers are given in parenthesis.
[134] Aberth, *A Knight at the Movies*, p. 157.
[135] In the Old Norse/Icelandic *Saga of the Volsungs*, Sigemund and Sinfjotli stumble across

humanity rather than that of the beast since he has retained his human mind. He attacks his former wife's two children by her new husband and tears out their vitals. The wolves return a second time and disembowel the wife's two brothers. The wolf-king's new lupine family is captured and the cubs hanged, but the wolf escapes, ravaging the neighbouring countryside in his sorrow.

Presenting himself as a humble pet, the wolf finally finds refuge with a third king who also has an adulterous wife (a staple trope of these narratives). Here the plot diverges into another story of betrayal, witnessed by the wolf. After he mauls her lover (the seneschal) in front of her and she has to explain his wounds, the wife accuses the wolf of killing her child whom she has hidden. The king is skeptical of her story and the wolf reveals the child's hiding place. For a court audience this succession of betrayals and adultery may have struck a nerve, and while some may have been able to laugh at the discomfort of their peers, the portrait of this world is unflattering, violent and merciless. To avoid any association of this world with his own, the poet locates it not only in a foreign land, but in the mythical Arthurian past; but perhaps his point is that fourteenth-century England is not that far removed from this kind of treachery and brutality.

At this moment the inquisitorial process comes into sharper focus as the king – who has already established his wife's guilt – carries out an interrogation. There is no need to extract a confession through torture, but the king proceeds with the judicial farce, and the trappings of justice and law fade behind a scene of merciless vengeance. With full knowledge of their duplicity the king questions the injured seneschal, who admits nothing and tells the same lie. The king does not attempt to extract a confession, but instead confronts him with what he knows to be the truth, urging him to confess or be consigned to the flames:

'Insistente rege tum minis tum blandiciis, dapifer commissum confitetur, facinus ut sibi indulgeret suppliciter exorans. Rex autem nimio succensus furore, dapifero carcerali mancipato custodie, illico tocius sui regni principes coadunauit a quibus super tanto scelere iudicium exigit. Sentencia datur dapifer uiuus excoriatur, et laqueo suspenditur. Regina menbratim ab equis distracta ignium globis traditur.'
(226: 25–30)

['When the king pressed the seneschal, sometimes with threats, sometimes with blandishments, the man confessed to the crime he had committed, pleading that he might be forgiven. The king, now, blazing in fury, ordered the seneschal to be kept in prison, and he immediately called together the lords of the realm, by whom judgment would be rendered concerning so great a crime. Sentence was given: the seneschal was to be flayed alive and hanged; the Queen, torn limb from limb by wild horses and given over to be burned.']

---

magical wolfskins and, after killing their owners, they take wolf form in the woods and nearly kill one another. Once they remove the skins, they destroy them, but there is a lingering sense that they were wolfish without the skins and the magic merely enhanced their original traits. *Saga of the Volsungs: The Norse Epic of Sigurd the Dragon Slayer*, trans. Jesse Byock (Berkeley CA: University of California Press, 1990), pp. 44–7.

Torture is never actually applied in this scene, though the implication is in the king's threat that he uses as a tool of intimidation, not interrogation. The seneschal pleads for mercy and the king could be criticized for not granting it; however, he transfers the responsibility to the lords of his land, a jury of peers, who will bear the weight of the judgment. Similarly to the trial of Ganelon in the *Roland* and Godard in *Havelok*, the peers are implicated in the judgment and punishment. These trials do not occur in England, but the tales are crafted for a predominantly English audience. The use of a jury is foundational to English law, and so the brutality of the sentence diminishes the sense of justice and undermines the process. As noted earlier in reference to *Havelok*, the king was *rex infra et supra legem*,[136] but *Arthur and Gorlagon* explores the consequences when kings operate outside the law or when the law gives no justice, a poignant concern for fourteenth-century England when 'distinctive legal status was one way of recognizing or constituting separate ethnicity'.[137] The sentence the jury delivers corresponds with other literary executions for treason, like that in the *Roland*, *Havelok*, and the *Prioress's Tale*. As with Godard in *Havelok*, the faithless seneschal is 'excoriatur, et laqueo suspenditur' [flayed alive and hanged] (226: 29), while, much like Ganelon, the queen suffers being 'menbratim ab equis distracta ignium globis traditur' [torn limb from limb by wild horses and given over to be burned] (226:30). Flaying is a symbolic and largely literary punishment, as discussed earlier. There is also little early evidence that equine dismemberment was an actual form of execution for treason as discussed in the context of Ganelon's execution in Chapter 2, but by the fourteenth century it had become more common in actual practice, perhaps because of the high incidence of it in literary texts; a case of life imitating art.[138] And yet it is savage here, blurring the boundaries between wolves and humans. Despite the gruesome nature of the lovers' punishment; however, the author does not linger on its description. The wife and seneschal are executed, and the story moves on without acclaim or approbation. Gorlagon relates these events dispassionately during a feast without further commentary suggesting that he has no concerns about the nature of justice meted out; he shows no mercy, no compassion, raising questions about his fitness as king and the legitimacy of the model he presents to Arthur.

Once the wolf leads the king back to his own lands, the audience is confronted with the tyranny under which the people have lived in this land since the queen supplanted her lupine husband and installed her pagan prince in his place: 'Omnes uero nobiles et ignobiles prouincie illius, regis qui lupo successerat importabilem gemebant tirannidem, suumque dominum fraude et dolo sue coniugis transmutatum utpote benignum et mansuetum una uoce conquerebantur' [Indeed, all the men of the province, nobles or commoners, were groaning under the intolerable

---

[136] Rouse, 'English Identity and the Law', p. 72.
[137] Bartlett, *The Making of Europe*, p. 78.
[138] Cf. discussions of equine quartering in Chapter 2 and later in this chapter in reference to the *Prioress's Tale*.

tyranny of the man who had succeeded the wolf. With one voice they lamented their lord, who by the craft and subtlety of his wife had been changed into a wolf, remembering what a kind and gentle master he had been] (230:9–12). The correct and just rule of the king-turned-wolf is juxtaposed against the misrule of his wife's lover who has usurped his place. In this instance, the lover is not only a traitor but a foreigner and a pagan as well, the insidious Other against whom brutality seemingly is more acceptable. And yet by applying torture to interrogate the wolf's wife, the king who helps him aligns himself with that Other. Like the usurpers in *Havelok*, these traitors will be dealt with as soon as their guilt is formally established; but, like Havelok, the king will be somewhat tainted by the brutality of that justice as he restores the wolf to his throne. The wolf-king is not entirely blameless; his wife took a foreign love and supplanted him for a reason, and his actions as a wolf hint at what those may be. He is willing to slaughter children to achieve his vengeance. It is significant that the king acting on behalf of the wolf does not simply kill these traitors, which would not only kill the secret of restoring the wolf to his human form but would tar this king with the same brush of tyranny as the usurpers. The king questions the wolf's queen in front of the assembled council of the kingdom, a public interrogation in front of a jury of peers. He does not resort to torture immediately, but threatens it to loosen her tongue:

> 'O,' ait, 'perfidissima et nequissima feminarum! Que te demencia tuo domino tantam fraudem machinari compulit? Sed nolo diucius tecum uerba disserere, que digna nullius censeris colloquio, rem quam a te inquisiero mihi cicius notifica, aut certe fame et siti inexquisitisque te faciam interire tormentis, nisi illam' ait 'uirgam qua eum transformasti quo lateat manifestes. Forte uero quam perdidit humanam formam recuperari poterit.' (230: 23–9)
>
> ['O most perfidious and wicked of women, what madness induced you to plot such villainy against your lord? But I wish to bandy words no longer with one who has been judged untrustworthy of testimony. So answer the question I put to you at once. I will certainly order your death from starvation and thirst and extreme torture, unless you show me where the sapling lies hidden with which you transformed your husband into a wolf. By some chance it may be able to restore the human form he has lost.']

The king establishes the queen's position as untrustworthy, diminishing her legal and moral standing in front of the court, but also making it clear that if she does not answer correctly she will be subjected to torture. The queen is not moved to confess. She swears ignorance and claims that it is well known that the sapling was broken up and burned. The king recognizes her lie, and 'Uerumtamen fateri nolentem rex illam tradidit tortoribus, cotidie torquendam, cotidie suppliciis exanimandam, nichil cibi uel potus ei prorsus indulgens' [So as she would not confess, the King handed her over to the inquisitors to be tortured constantly, exhausted with torments, and allowed neither food nor drink] (230:31–3). In this realm, the king keeps inquisitors on hand and they work for him. The method of torture is not explained; *torquendam* suggests that she was twisted on the rack, or the *strappado*, but the mere fact of the torture is enough. The author, while not criticizing the use of torture to extract the necessary information, does not glorify it or indulge in the sadistic pleasure of detailed torment. However, the use of torture is effective: 'Tandem penarum coacta angustiis uirgam protulit regique porrexit' [At last, compelled by the severity of her punishment, she produced the sapling and handed it to the King] (230:33–4).

Torture serves a distinct purpose in this text, reinforcing the legal application of pain in judicial inquiries: the queen is a traitor, an adulteress and a usurper; when questioned under just the threat of torture she lies, so it becomes necessary to carry out the threat. But there is no lingering sense that the author revels in the necessity for such brutal measures. There are no gruesome details, no lasting image of her body being broken or damaged (though the audience can assume the queen must have been a sorry sight when she finally gave in); the torture is merely described as an interrogatory necessity, one that the queen brings upon herself. Unlike hagiography, the torturers are not actively portrayed as demonized Others. However, the use of torture aligns this society with the barbarian Other – its practices are alien to the English audience and suggest an underlying brutality foreign to English concepts of justice. Torture is also alien to the Arthurian setting in which martial violence is expected but excessive brutality is often condemned. The process also has an eerie resonance with inquisitorial procedure familiar to a noble audience in the aftermath of the persecution of the Templars. Once the queen does confess, the author moves on to the restoration of the wolf to human form, the joy of the two men at the generosity and consideration of the other, the restoration of the wolf-king to his throne, and the reaffirming loyalty oaths of his nobles. Similar to Goldeboru's tempered justice in *Havelok*, the restored wolf-king judges the two usurpers, condemning the pagan lover to death and divorcing the queen, sparing her life though she is portrayed as unworthy of such clemency. However, the application of judicial torture and the sentence of gruesome punishment are not so simple. The justice is swift, but is it just? For an English audience of the fourteenth century the wanton cruelty of the kings, even within the legal structure of rule, would seem excessive. These narratives construct an image of English law as being specific to England, separating England and the English from the rest of the romance world.[139] Torture was still illegal in England, though it (or the threat of it) was most likely used as a weapon in the conflicts of the time. While certainly not all audiences would be troubled by the violence in the text, they may have been sorely troubled about what it said about them and their society. For the noble audience of *Arthur and Gorlagon*, even one that may have enjoyed this tale as a spectacle at a feast, the implications are clear: kings and courts are full of violence, treachery, adultery and lawlessness – even just kings resort to brutality to maintain law and order. Mildred Leake Day writes that the artistic achievement of *Arthur and*

---

[139] Rouse, 'English Identity and the Law', p. 82.

Gorlagon is entertainment for a court, a 'dinner show' in Latin, that would appeal to an audience with a variety of native languages but fluent in courtly Latin.[140] The atrocities of the Hundred Years War were well known particularly to the nobility, many of whom had probably perpetuated some of that slaughter. The poet situates the violence of his text in a foreign land, carried out by foreign kings (and wolves), and suggests in Arthur's bewilderment that these actions are very un-English. It can be read either as an indictment of an English court that had become desensitized to violence or as a reminder to knights and ladies that animalistic brutality lurks beneath the surface of the courtly façade and it is important to remember what chivalry really means.

There is an even darker twist to the tale when Arthur inquires, for the first time in the narrative, about the grief-stricken woman sitting across the table from him and his storyteller cradling a severed head on a platter, kissing it each time the king kisses his wife. Gorlagon answers that he is the wolf of the tale and this woman is his faithless wife, condemned to shower the embalmed head of her lover with affection each time he caresses his new wife. Gorlagon justifies this seemingly cruel punishment, '"Sciui quippe quod nulla sibi grauior foret punicio quam in conspectu omnium tant sceleris iugis representacio"' ['For I knew that no punishment would be more severe than the constant display of her great crime in the sight of all'] (234:7–8). Her public humiliation compounds her disgrace and the pain she suffered under torture but it is presented as justice. Day contends that this scene with a severed head in a dish, considering the emphasis on eating throughout the tale, is the punchline of perhaps the funniest tale of Arthurian literature.[141] This would then be the same kind of cannibalistic joke as in *RCL*. The humour derives from the deflation of Arthur rather than the exposition of torture and brutality because he is bandied around from court to court and then is told a long tale about betrayal and adultery in response to his quest for the nature and desires of women. Arthur is impulsive and childish, but Day also acknowledges that part of the humour is his delayed reaction to the gruesome sight at the table. She writes, 'in the final scene with the lady and the head, not only is Arthur appalled but so are the listeners. They have been tricked by the storyteller to see the whole fantastic tale through King Arthur's eyes.'[142] Audience reception is the key to the humour, and like any audience it is impossible to assume a homogenous response, but Day suggests that if the audience had eaten well and drunk deeply, the repulsive final moment would be hilarious, even for courtiers 'who were the last to get the joke'.[143] Fourteenth-century nobility, steeped in warfare and bloodshed, may have found it funny, just

---

[140] Mildred Leake Day, 'Introduction', *Latin Arthurian Literature*, p. 46. See also: Echard, *Arthurian Narrative in the Latin Tradition*, and 'Latin Arthurian Literature', in *A History of Arthurian Scholarship*, ed. Norris J. Lacy (Cambridge: D.S. Brewer, 2006), 62–76.

[141] Day, 'Introduction', *Latin Arthurian Literature*, p. 46.

[142] Day, 'Introduction', *Latin Arthurian Literature*, p. 46.

[143] Day, 'Introduction', *Latin Arthurian Literature*, p. 46.

as in *RCL*. This incongruous introduction at the end of the tale does strike a humorous chord in its absurdity, but it also seems unnecessarily cruel. Massey draws a parallel between this graphic scene and the initial episode that started the quest, Arthur's public kiss: 'one begins a knight's conventional quest, the other ends a monster's didactic tale of vengeance. The latter forces the reader to re-evaluate the former, to recall the conventional romantic opening gambit as just that – a convention.'[144] In a similar vein, the torture in this tale is also a convention, a widespread folkloric and literary tradition of combining the quest motif with the treacherous queen's punishment,[145] but one that raises serious questions about its application in the real world and undermines the justice of kings and courts that resort to it.

The inclusion of torture in these werewolf tales is not a celebration or approbation of the existence of torture in medieval society and culture; it is a narrative technique that reinforces the guilt and dishonour of the treacherous queens, and suggests an underlying brutality in affairs of law and governance. By using King Arthur, the poet draws a parallel between England and the rest of Europe, suggesting that England, like Arthur, is susceptible to outside influences. Rouse writes that, 'endowed with a legal heritage of demonstrated provenance and virtue, law becomes a powerful element in the creation of an English Identity, standing as a point of differentiation for the Anglo-Saxon [or Arthurian] England of the romances and, vicariously, for the post-Conquest England of their audiences'.[146] The humour of *Arthur and Gorlagon* lies with the individual sensibilities of the audience; the author records no response other than Arthur's willingness to finally dismount and eat after his lengthy fast. Gorlagon warns Arthur at the start of his tale to listen well, but also says that he will be but little wiser for having heard it. There is no suggestion at the end that anyone has learned anything, except that women can be treacherous and unfaithful and that Gorlagon has a penchant for vindictiveness; for that is what his final punishment of his first wife is – vindictive and excessive. No one responds, no one comments; Arthur eats and departs and an external audience mindful of Guinevere's future infidelity and the collapse of the Round Table might assume he learned nothing.[147] But the enduring image, the one that determines an audience's response and potential laughter, is the gruesome spectacle of the grieving woman at a feast weeping over a decapitated head. Like the *Prioress's Tale*, where the Canterbury pilgrims remain conspicuously silent at the end, the silence in *Arthur and Gorlagon* is deafening. Despite the claim of justice in the tale, the taste of betrayal, torture and brutality lingers and the idea of just kingship is questioned.

---

[144] Massey, 'There, wolf'.
[145] Day, 'Introduction', *Latin Arthurian Literature*, p. 44.
[146] Rouse, 'English Identity and the Law', p. 82.
[147] Massey examines Guinevere as the 'third bad queen' missing from the Celtic triad pattern of the story: 'The Werewolf at the Head Table'.

Chaucer: *The Prioress's Tale*

Writing in English when fashion still turned to French, Geoffrey Chaucer shaped the English narrative, adapting, translating and appropriating material from numerous sources. Chaucer was also actively engaged in the political intrigue of the late fourteenth century at a fairly high level,[148] though John Scattergood cautions that for scholars interested in the social and political aspects of Chaucer's work, 'the evidence is uneven and difficult to apply'.[149] Chaucer concerns himself seriously with general issues including the role of the ruler, treating these matters indirectly, 'in an essentially narrative matrix, and often, humorously'.[150] Perhaps more than any other author, Chaucer's commitment to England and English identity is evident not only in his literary works but also in his civil service. He was a soldier, diplomat, tax collector, author, translator, and humanist (perhaps with Lollard tendencies or sympathies),[151] but above all he was an Englishman at a time when that term was crystallizing into a definitive sense of nationalism. The Hundred Years War was in full swing, Richard II vied for his own throne against the Lords Appellant, and segments of the population rose even in revolt in 1381.[152] English power struggled against French as France sought to control the Church and the papacy was split in two in the Great Schism (1378–1417). It was a tumultuous time marked by intrigue, uprisings, murder, war and violence. Chaucer deals with many forms of torment and violence in his tales: from the emotional suffering inflicted on Griselda, to the massacre of the Sultan of Syria and his followers by his mother and the forced exile of Custance in the *Man of Law's Tale*, to the heinous murder of the child in the *Prioress's Tale* and the subsequent execution of the Jews. But the literal and physical torture inflicted during an inquisitorial process is largely absent. Where it does occur, its use (masked by judicial necessity) taints those who apply it, especially when it is in

---

[148] John Scattergood, 'Social and Political Issues in Chaucer: An Approach to *Lak of Stedfastnesse*', in *Reading the Past: Essays on Medieval and Renaissance Literature*, Medieval Studies (Dublin: Four Courts Press, 1996), 192–214, p. 192. See also: Rory McTurk, *Chaucer and the Norse and Celtic Worlds* (Aldershot: Ashgate, 2005). McTurk makes a compelling argument not only for Chaucer's political activities, but also that his work was shaped by his travels in Ireland during the course of his political career.

[149] Scattergood, 'Social and Political Issues in Chaucer', p. 192.

[150] Scattergood, 'Social and Political Issues in Chaucer', p. 192.

[151] See: Frances McCormack, *Chaucer and the Culture of Dissent: The Lollard Context and Subtext of the* Parson's Tale (Dublin: Four Courts Press, 2007); Alastair Minnis, *Fallible Authors: Chaucer's Pardoner and Wife of Bath* (Philadelphia: University of Pennsylvania Press, 2008).

[152] Eve Salisbury examines the poignant effect the 1381 Peasants' Revolt had on both London society and its literary elite, specifically Chaucer's contemporary and colleague, John Gower. 'Violence and the Sacred City: London, Gower, and the Rising of 1381', in *'A Great Effusion of Blood'?: Interpreting Medieval Violence*, ed. Mark D. Meyerson, Daniel Thiery and Oren Falk (Toronto: University of Toronto Press, 2004), 79–97.

contravention of English law.[153] There are references to interrogatory torture in the *Man of Law's Tale*, *The Nun's Priest's Tale*, and *The Second Nun's Tale*; and a pretence of justice gives way to torture and cruel punishment in the *Prioress's Tale*. Chaucer's *Man of Law's Tale* is told by a narrator supposedly steeped in the traditions of the English judicial system and the contemporary trend to associate it with the ancient traditions of the Anglo-Saxons in the interests of promoting English national identity pre-Conquest, free from the ties to France with whom England was at war. But this tale includes only a brief, almost negligible reference to interrogatory torture. There is a faint reference to judicial torture in the *Nun's Priest's Tale*, which in many ways responds to the mob violence of the *Prioress's Tale*. The violence of the *Prioress's Tale* is also juxtaposed against the application of justice in the *Man of Law's Tale*. Maura Nolan notes that there is a tension, which Chaucer recognized, between the 'concrete and the abstract in legal discourse, finding it both appropriable and threatening, both useful and dangerous'.[154]

In the *Man of Law's Tale*, Alla is a just king who investigates the alleged crime rather than automatically executing Custance after she has been accused of murder, 'a trouthe for to lere' (line 630).[155] The use of Alla, or Ælle – one of the best known Anglo-Saxon kings in both Anglo-Saxon and post-Conquest English tradition[156] – situates this tale firmly in the Anglo-Saxon past, much like *Havelok the Dane*. But unlike *Havelok*, here it is the Anglo-Saxon king who employs torture as a method of interrogation, undermining the perception of Anglo-Saxon England as a time of justice and 'gode olde law'. Frankis writes that Chaucer's use of the Constance story 'does not on the face of it tell us very much about fourteenth-century views of Anglo-Saxon England', but it was central to his source, the Anglo-Norman chronicle by the early fourteenth-century Dominican friar Nicholas Trevet.[157] According to Frankis, the location of the *Man of*

---

[153] In *The Riverside Chaucer*, Larry Benson notes twenty-seven occurrences in all of Chaucer's works for *tormente*, *turmente* or some variant, such as *tormenten* or *turmented*, or the noun *tormentour*. But not all of these occurrences refer to torture in the judicial or interrogative sense, and many do not refer to the infliction of physical pain at all. Benson defines *tormente*, *turmente* as the verb 'torment, torture' in *Troilus* and the *Knight's Tale*, but in these texts it refers to the mental suffering of the character, not literal torture. *The Riverside Chaucer*, ed. Larry Benson (Boston MA: Houghton Mifflin, 1987), p. 1299.

[154] Maura Nolan, '"Acquiteth yow now": Textual Contradiction and Legal Discourse in the Man of Law's Introduction', in *The Letter of the Law: Legal Practice and Literary Production in Medieval England*, ed. Emily Steiner and Candace Barrington (Ithaca NY: Cornell University Press, 2002), 136–53, p. 137.

[155] All textual quotations from the *Canterbury Tales* are taken from *The Riverside Chaucer*, ed. Benson.

[156] John Frankis, 'King Ælle and the Conversion of the English: The Development of a Legend from Bede to Chaucer', in *Literary Appropriations of the Anglo-Saxons from the Thirteenth to the Twentieth Century*, ed. Donald Scragg and Carole Weinberg, Cambridge Studies in Anglo-Saxon England (Cambridge: Cambridge University Press, 2000), 74–92, p. 80.

[157] Frankis, 'King Ælle and the Conversion of the English', p. 76.

Law's Tale in England still had some vestigial significance but Chaucer does not overtly or implicitly expound on any clear view of Anglo-Saxon England; he 'plays down national references and gives greater prominence to the religious element', an emphasis at the expense of particular national consideration that 'may well have given Chaucer's version a wider appeal in his own day and for some time afterwards'.[158] Perhaps Chaucer's interest in including the brief torture reference is merely faithfulness to his source, or perhaps it was meant to stand out as contradictory to an Anglo-Saxon justice. That Ælle has torture used, even for admirable ends, suggests that England of the fourteenth century must no longer look to its synthesized past where boundaries between Anglo-Saxon and Norman have become blurred, and must instead forge a new, separate identity.

When the guilt of the knight who actually murders Hermengyld and implicates Custance is proclaimed by divine intervention, signalled by his eyes bursting out of his face (line 671), 'this false knyght was slayn for his untrouthe/ By juggement of Alla hastifly' (lines 687–8). There is a trial and a legal process, unlike in the *Prioress's Tale*, and there is no mention of torture being applied to interrogate the suspect. However, torture will be applied later against a messenger after the discovery of the deceptive exchange of letters that results in Custance's exile, but it is peripheral and mentioned in passing as a means of eliciting information about the plot to dispossess Custance. Alla has proceeded from fair, just and law-abiding to resorting to torture in desperation. Like Marie de France in *Bisclavret*, Chaucer does not dwell on the torture but merely says: 'This messager tormented was til he/ Moste biknowe and tellen, plat and pleyn' (lines 885–6). It is a means to an end carried out by proper authorities, but it is contrary to English law and makes their decision to use it problematic. Chaucer says nothing about the methods employed in 'tormenting' the messenger, only that it leads to answers: 'And thus, by wit and sotil enquerynge,/ Ymagined was by whom this harm gan sprynge' (lines 888–9). The use of 'sotil' suggests deceptive, shadowy means, implying that, while understandable in the context of the tale, the use of torture taints the reputation of an otherwise admirable king. With the information in hand, Alla ferrets out the plot and 'out of drede,/ his mooder slow – that may men pleynly rede – / For that she traitour was to hire ligeance' (lines 893–5), an action he later repents by taking a pilgrimage to Rome, which allows him to be briefly reunited with Custance. His repentance implies that he recognizes his transgressions of both law and morality. Torture is an instrument of unstable power; its presence is a part of actual medieval judicial procedure that Alla regrets having to use as much as he repents the deaths that result from the information it produces. Chaucer omits any specific details of the torture, and Alla's subsequent pilgrimage and repentance suggest that Chaucer does not approve of the brutality enacted by kings, even when it is for a good end. As a soldier and servant of the crown, Chaucer would have been intimately familiar

---

[158] Frankis, 'King Ælle and the Conversion of the English', p. 92.

with royal prerogative and its consequences, and perhaps he is urging his king, embroiled in his own wars and intrigues, to consider the lesson of Alla's repentance as a model for kingly behaviour.

In times of war it might be tempting to take a page from the other side and resort to such measures, but Chaucer makes torture an unpleasant thorn in the judicial side. The hysterical Chaunticleer, a well known character of French fable, refers to torture in a tale he tells about ferreting out murder. Torture appears briefly in the *Nun's Priest's Tale* as part of Chaunticleer's exposition on the power of dreams. Relating a tale taken from Cicero or Valerius Maximus,[159] Chaunticleer gives the example of a man who dreams of his fellow pilgrim's murder, ignoring the portent only to discover his companion's body in a dung cart as the apparition foretold. Echoing the Prioress's account of the child in the cesspit, Chaunticleer says the man began to cry, 'Vengeance and justice of this felonye:/ "My felawe mordred is this same nyght,/ And in this carte he lith gapyng upright./ I crye out on the ministres"' (lines 3040–3). He appeals to the magistrates to ferret out the culprits and bring them to justice. Chaunticleer praises the justice of God for revealing the deed and explains the swift civil actions of the magistrates:

> 'Mordre wol out; that se we day by day.
> Mordre is so wlatsom and abhomynable
> To God, that is so just and resonable,
> That he ne wol nat suffre it heled be,
> Though it abyde a yeer, or two, or thre.
> Mordre wol out, this my conclusioun.
> And right anon, ministres of that toun
> Han hent the carter and so soore hym pyned,
> And eek the hostiler so soore engyned,
> That they biknewe hire wikkednesse anon,
> And were anhanged by the nekke-bon.' (3052–62)

This reference to torture, 'so soore hym pyned' and 'so soore engyned', does not have a direct bearing on the tale – except in the context of Chaunticleer's preoccupation with the possibility of his own murder. Richard West contends that the Nun's Priest repeats and endorses the Prioress's 'savage thoughts on crime and punishment',[160] which in turn suggests that Chaucer does as well. But the presence of torture is problematic in an English context; what Chaunticleer lauds is what he (a highly-strung rooster) sees as the correct application of justice through legitimate authority, not the mob violence and mass slaughter of the

---

[159] Susan H. Cavanaugh, notes to the *Nun's Priest's Tale*, in *The Riverside Chaucer*, ed. Benson, p. 938.
[160] Richard West, *Chaucer 1340–1400: The Life and Times of the First English Poet* (New York: Carroll and Graf, 2000), p. 72.

Prioress's Tale.[161] However, Chaunticleer's tale, adapted from French sources, speaks more to the resort to torture in a climate of paranoia and murder. Chaunticleer, though correct in his paranoia, is a parody – he and his wife are caricatures of those in the populace who accept most things at face value and ask few questions. Hagiography assumes a similar simplicity and Chaucer's adaptation of even that genre challenges conventional assumptions. A medieval audience of almost any century would expect the tale of a female martyr, like the *Second Nun's Tale*, to engage in the discourse of brutality so common to the genre – a discourse that relies on graphic accounts of torture for its spiritual message. But Chaucer rejects that traditional assumption and mitigates the violence of the tale, emphasizing sanctity not brutality, perhaps as a message to the Church that, by the end of the fourteenth century, had spent far more time engaging in the latter at the expense of the former.

In the retelling of the *Life of Saint Cecilia* as the *Second Nun's Tale*, Cecilia's torture is tempered by the poet and reduced to a literary convention following the hagiographic model rather than any sadistic repetition of brutal torments. In the *Second Nun's Tale*, Chaucer employs the demonstration of power and subjugation coupled with the use of judicial torture that is a standard motif of medieval hagiography (explored in Chapter 1), translating and adapting the legend from the thirteenth-century *Legenda aurea* (*LgA*) and combining multiple versions.[162] Rather than choosing one of the more gruesome and graphic accounts of female martyrdom, Chaucer selected a tale in which torture is secondary to the triumph of the virgin over her earthly judge and the joy of Christian conversion. He does not focus on nor highlight the more gruesome details of her torment and martyrdom to which he dedicates only twenty-two lines, though Almacius orders that she be burned 'right in a bath of flambes rede' (line 514). Chaucer reproduces the legend of Saint Cecilia, not from a desire to disgust or shock his audience, but as a means of tapping into the popular genre of female hagiography which emphasizes not the pain of torture nor even the effects of the torments, but the absence of suffering and the steadfast devotion in the face of non-Christian tyranny and brutality.[163] As Helen Cooper explains, it is about 'the rational case for Christianity – Cecilia's explanation of the Trinity, her confounding of Almachius – though this case is made as a back-up to an

---

[161] The *Nun's Priest's Tale* also lists Ganelon in a catalogue of traitors used to describe Renard the fox (line 3227).

[162] Winstead, *Virgin Martyrs*, p. 85. Winstead notes that in writing this tale, 'Chaucer combined Jacobus de Voragine's version of the Cecilia legend with an anonymous abridgement from a Franciscan breviary to produce an even more animated encounter between Cecilia and Almachius than Jacobus had supplied' (p. 85).

[163] Helen Cooper argues that the narrative, 'not least the account of Cecilia's martyrdom, is altogether sparer: She feels "no wo", the flaming bath [...] but even the "torment" of her three day survival with her neck half-cut is curiously painless – the emphasis to the last falls on her preaching, not her suffering.' *Oxford Guides to Chaucer: The Canterbury Tales* (Oxford: Oxford University Press, 1989, rpt. 1996), p. 367.

impulse towards conversion initiated by the miraculous, as represented by the angel, the garlands, and the failure of the attempts to kill her'.[164]

According to the conventions of the genre, the *Second Nun's Tale* should have the clearest and most pronounced account of torture in the *Canterbury Tales*, but this tale is not about torture – it plays only a minor role perhaps providing a sample of his society's tastes and cultural *mores*. Winstead argues that Chaucer's inclusion of a female martyr legend signals the widespread popularity of the genre, that 'lay people themselves formed an enthusiastic audience for such tales'.[165] But Chaucer omits gruesome accounts of torture, even though they populated his sources, and focuses his narratives instead on the spiritual questions of morality and justice, questions that concerned every Englishman at a time when the Church itself was under threat and papal rule was divided in schism.

As in the *SEL* and *GiL*, the *Second Nun's Tale* draws a clear distinction between the barbarian pagan judges who employ torture and the judicial procedures of Chaucer's own time and nation that did not, demonizing the torturer and advocating resistance. The Second Nun's restraint is in strong contrast to the Prioress's vehemence, suggesting a certain sadistic delight in ignorant clerics who are willing to employ brutal methods as long as they have the desired outcome.[166] This portrayal plays upon the cultural anxieties of ecclesiastical corruption and potential brutality evident in a fourteenth-century England that was forced to take sides in the Schism.[167] Whereas the Prioress aims at a pathos that could be called sentimental, the Second Nun 'effaces the affective and the psychological in favor of an impassive triumphalism and doctrinal pedagogy that transcends human suffering'.[168] Chaucer's tale does not engage in the brutal spectacle of sacrifice common to hagiography, and instead rejects the more violent of these tales as his exemplar. As Lee Patterson writes, the Second Nun and her tale are none-too-subtle reminders to the Prioress to uphold the dignity of her office.[169] The Second Nun correctly focuses on matters of the soul while the Prioress

---

[164] Cooper, *Oxford Guides to Chaucer*, pp. 361–2.

[165] Winstead, *Virgin Martyrs*, p. 85.

[166] Sister Mary Hostia, 'The Prioress and Her Companion', *College English* 14.6 (Mar. 1953): 351–2, p. 352. Sister Mary Hostia also points out that in her devotion to the Virgin Mary, and then in her bigotry against the Jews, the Prioress forgets that Mary was a 'Jewess of the royal house of David' (p. 352). She writes that the Second Nun is more objective in her tale because she does not interject any personal opinion of the Roman persecutors (p. 352).

[167] Samantha Diaz argues that despite the absence of overt references to the Great Schism in *The Canterbury Tales*, Chaucer allegorizes the Schism in the conflict between Arcite and Palamon in the Knight's Tale. 'Papacy in Paganism: The Great Schism of Palamon and Arcite', MA Thesis, Longwood University (2009), unpublished.

[168] Lee Patterson, '"The Living Witnesses of Our Redemption": Martyrdom and Imitation in Chaucer's *Prioress's Tale*', *Journal of Medieval and Early Modern Studies* 31:3 (Fall 2001): 507–60, p. 512.

[169] Patterson, '"The Living Witnesses of Our Redemption"', p. 512.

engages with the discourse of the body and its potential corruption. The Second Nun may represent Chaucerian, or at least Ricardian, sympathies with Rome's claim to the papacy,[170] while the Prioress, with all her French pretensions, may represent the English view of the Avignon Papacy or Babylonian Captivity.

The tale told by the lively Prioress is the most problematic despite the references to torture in the *Nun's Priest Tale*, the violence of the *Man of Law's Tale* and the explicit use of torture in the *Second Nun's Tale*.[171] She tells of a virtuous boy brutally murdered in a Jewish ghetto in a far away part of 'Asye' for singing a religious hymn in praise of the Virgin Mary, and the summary execution of those held responsible. But the problems do not arise from the murder of the boy, whose throat is cut savagely before he is tossed into a privy, but from the anti-Judaic[172] treatment of the murderers who 'with torment and with shameful deeth echon' (line 628) are dragged behind horses (or quartered), and then hanged without trial or inquiry.[173] The word 'torment' in this context means torture, but in a punitive sense rather than an interrogative one, an explicit contravention of law. The execution of the Jews is similar to the execution of Ganelon in the *Roland* or the adulterous wife in *Arthur and Gorlagon*. It is judicial brutality enacted by legal authority, but unlike the trials of Ganelon and of the wife which operate within the legal tradition of the text (however flawed), there is no formal trial, no process of law, just summary execution carried out by the civil authority at the first suspicion of a crime and the discovery of a body. As Sheila Delany

---

[170] Walter Ullman, *The Origins of the Great Schism: A Study of Fourteenth-Century Ecclesiastical History* (Hamden CT: Archon Books, 1972), pp. 102, 105, 109.

[171] Greg Wilsbacher, 'Lumiansky's Paradox: Ethics, Aesthetics and Chaucer's "Prioress's Tale"', *College Literature* 32.4 (Fall 2005): 1–28, p. 2.

[172] In using the term anti-Judaic rather than anti-Semitic, I am referring specifically to medieval attitudes, as Michael Calabrese does in his article 'Performing the Prioress: "Conscience" and Responsibility in Studies of Chaucer's Prioress's Tale', *Texas Studies in Literature and Language* 44:1 (Spring 2002): 66–91, p. 85. Calabrese points out that the term anti-Semitic 'no longer conveys this historical specificity' and he only uses 'anti-Semitic', when discussing scholarship that was written before this distinction was made and the 'potentially anachronistic projection of modern attitudes back into time' (p. 85 n. 11). I will follow his lead.

[173] Being dragged to the gallows and hanged was the prescribed punishment for traitors in medieval Europe, though rarely in some places, such as France, the traitor might also be flayed. According to J.G. Bellamy, in general the punishment of traitors, like the scope of high treason, was similar all over Europe at this time. J.G. Bellamy, *The Law of Treason in England in the Later Middle Ages*, Cambridge Studies in English Legal History (Cambridge: Cambridge University Press, 1970, rpt. 2004), p. 13. Roger Dahood also focuses on the punishment of the Jews in his article 'The Punishment of the Jews, Hugh of Lincoln, and the Question of Satire in Chaucer's *Prioress's Tale*', *Viator* 36 (2005): 465–91. Dahood also chronicles other English accounts of child-murder in his article 'English Historical Narratives of Jewish Child-Murder, Chaucer's *Prioress's Tale*, and the Date of Chaucer's Unknown Source', *Studies in the Age of Chaucer* 31 (2009): 125–40. There is a critical debate about whether the Jews were equine quartered and then hanged or simply dragged behind horses to be hanged, but either way the scene involves the punitive torture of the Jews and a summary execution without recourse to a trial which amounts to judicial brutality. Cf. p. 180 n. 190.

says, the Jews are 'condemned, tortured, and executed on circumstantial evidence supported by a miracle'.[174] Greg Wilsbacher argues that they are tried, convicted and punished within the space of a stanza, 'in part because the goal of a unified Christian community requires their immediate disappearance'.[175] Miri Rubin recounts multiple instances of Christian mob violence against Jews in the fourteenth and fifteenth centuries where crowds, incensed by tales of host desecration, did not stop long to think, acting on a simple set of 'signs and prompts, almost like an animal lacking reason'.[176] In these instances, the Jews were often thrown into the fire, 'not at the ordered stake of secular punishment, but fires lit by townspeople or groups of people who assembled for the task of revenge',[177] or tortured in punitive spectacles. It may be these displays of mob rule to which Chaucer is responding in the *Prioress's Tale*, just as he does in the *Nun's Priest's Tale* in his singular reference to the Peasants' Revolt of 1381. The Christians in the tale act *en masse* calling for the provost, but the absence of legal proceedings would have sat poorly with an English audience used to a sophisticated system of law that required a trial by jury. Chaucer condemns this barely legal prelude to a lynching and his audience (noble, burgess, and clerical) would have also seen the uncomfortable effects of mob violence as a spectacle all too familiar in the late fourteenth century.

In the tale, of which there are numerous analogues, the seven-year-old child who lives in a 'greet citee' in 'Asye' (line 488) is being raised in a society where the different religious communities coexist, where the civil authorities have given the Jews licence to live because they are financially necessary: 'Amonges Cristene folk a Jewerye,/ Sustened by a lord of that contree/ For foule usure and lucre of vileynye,/ Hateful to Crist and to his compaignye' (lines 489–92). Cooper argues that setting the tale in 'Asye' removes any need for adhering to European legal procedures, that it 'allows the law to inflict a particularly horrific punishment; God's enemies come to a miserable end on this earth, the murdered child has his end not in the cesspit but in the procession before the Lamb. The Jews, like the Saracen mother-in-law of the *Man of Law's Tale*, are cast by definition as enemies of God'.[178] Delany refutes this and offers a more compelling connection between the setting and the question of justice, further noting that there is no

---

[174] Sheila Delany, 'Chaucer's Prioress, the Jews, and the Muslims', *Medieval Encounters* 5.2 (1999): 198–213. p. 205. Many of these arguments are also made in Sheila Delany, 'Asia in the Prioress's Tale', in *Chaucer and the Jews: Sources, Contexts, Meanings*, ed. Sheila Delany (London: Routledge, 2002) 43–68.

[175] Wilsbacher, 'Lumiansky's Paradox', p. 13.

[176] Miri Rubin, *Gentile Tales: The Narrative Assault on Late Medieval Jews* (Philadelphia: University of Pennsylvania Press, 2004), p. 88. West examines the accusations against Jews for spreading the plague, followed by massacres at Narbonne and Carcassone in 1348, and other atrocities across continental Europe that were condemned by Pope Clement VI (*Chaucer 1340–1400*, pp. 63–4).

[177] Rubin, *Gentile Tales*, p. 89.

[178] Cooper, *Oxford Guides to Chaucer*, p. 293.

confession, the actual murderer is never apprehended, and those punished are punished only for knowing about the murder, not for carrying it out.[179] If the tale is meant to take place in Islamic territory, as Delany suggests, then Islamic law 'would normally have required a rigorous court proceeding, in which the Jews would probably have won'.[180] Louise O. Fradenburg questions the reality of justice in the tale,[181] and the absence of law is a major point either way. Whether Chaucer's audience was familiar with Islamic or Judaic law or not, they knew that English custom required a trial and a verdict, and that summary execution was neither valid nor just. The authorities who employ torture and carry out the brutal punishment are the alien Other, as in *Walewein*, *Havelok* and the *Roland*. Authorities that resort to such brutality only undermine their rule and destabilize the power structure. Chaucer advocates an adherence to law and justice particular to England and absent outside its borders.

Woven into the traditional anti-Jewish invective is the medieval reality of simony and money lending. As Cooper notes, the Christians are not ideal; the Christian lord of the city is corrupted by the same money-lust as other members of the Canterbury pilgrimage, nor does Chaucer put the story into the mouth of the one of the ideal characters like the Parson.[182] But the Jews are not alien – not to the fictional setting of the tale nor to the well-travelled Chaucer – even if their presence would have seemed alien in fourteenth-century England.[183] The alien Other are the Christian authorities who flout the legal process familiar to an English audience and engage in unnecessary wholesale brutality.[184] The Prioress does not necessarily understand why the Jews have to be there, since to her they are such nasty people, but she does understand that their presence is required. Her emphasis is on the ignorant but well intentioned child who is willing to face punishment for neglecting his correct studies in order to memorize the *Alma*

---

[179] Delany, 'Chaucer's Prioress', p. 205.

[180] Delany, 'Chaucer's Prioress', p. 205.

[181] Louise O. Fradenburg, 'Criticism, Anti-Semitism, and the *Prioress's Tale*', *Exemplaria* 1 (1989): 69–115, p. 76. Fradenburg also points to historical accounts of Christian on Christian violence in her examination of justice in the tale, and suggests that the tale 'projects both the disorder of violence *and* the violence of order onto the Jews' because the 'tale fears change' and 'the incapacity for change' (p. 105).

[182] Cooper, *Oxford Guides to Chaucer*, p. 294.

[183] The Jews were officially expelled from England by Edward I in 1290. As Sylvia Tomasch explains, despite the Expulsion the perpetuation of the 'virtual Jew' remained an essential part of English devotion and national identity, and between 1290 and 1656 the English 'came to see their country defined in part by the fact that the Jews were banished from it'. 'Postcolonial Chaucer and the Virtual Jew', in *The Postcolonial Middle Ages*, The New Middle Ages, ed. Jeffrey Jerome Cohen (New York: Palgrave, 2001), 243–60, p. 244.

[184] Wilsbacher argues that within the fictional space of the tale, what he calls 'the anti-Semitic stage', the violence 'becomes a unifying principle for the Christian community through which it purges the aliens in its midst', but he does acknowledge that this unification is spurious, 'a scapegoating façade that masks its own internal discord by symbolically sealing that discord away beneath the weight of a marble slab.' 'Lumiansky's Paradox', pp. 12–13.

redemptoris mater. The *clergeon* 'does not understand the Latin, and fails in his attempts to have it explained to him'.[185] In fact, the emphasis on educating children suggests that this may be part of Chaucer's point: children learn what their elders teach them and if they are educated by the ignorant they will be ignorant themselves and perpetuate the atrocities of history. Peggy Knapp notes that nuns were often responsible for teaching younger children 'the little learning they themselves were possessed of', and if they had limited knowledge themselves, they were in danger of passing on that ignorance.[186] All these children 'ycomen of Cristen blood,/ That lerned in that scole yeer by yere/ Swich manere doctrine as men used there,/ This is to seyn, to syngen and to rede,/ As smale children doon in hire childhede' (lines 497–501) are blank slates upon which the tolerance or the bigotry of their elders will be inscribed.

The Prioress points out that the school is at the far end of the street, presumably requiring dozens of Christian children to walk through the Jewish ghetto every day, which they do unmolested until the devil supposedly convinces the Jews that this particular child must be exterminated:

> Our firste foo, the serpent Sathanas,
> That hath in Jues herte his waspes nest,
> Up swal, and seide, 'O Hebrayk peple, allas!
> Is this to yow a thyng that is honest,
> That swich a boy shal walken as hym lest
> In youre despit, and synge of swich sentence,
> Which is agayn youre lawes reverence?' (lines 558–64)

Satan appeals to the Jews' adherence to religious law in his efforts to turn them to murder, which is a striking contrast to the absence of civil law at the end of the tale when the Jews are punished before the child has miraculously spoken and revealed the truth of his death. The Prioress describes the murder in detail as the hired 'homycide' (line 567) grabs him, holds him fast and 'kitte his throte, and in a pit hym caste' (line 571). If there is any doubt about which kind of pit, the Prioress elaborates: 'I seye that in a wardrobe they hym threwe/ Where as thise Jewes purgen hire entraille' (lines 572–3). Any audience shocked by the brutality of the murder would be further disgusted by the image of the child's body being thrown into a privy among the excrement and waste. However, Daniel Pigg claims the murder of the boy only furthers what he sees as the comedy of the tale 'because rather than destroying the boy and his song, the murderers have

---

[185] Stephen Spector, 'Empathy and Enmity in the Prioress's Tale', in *Geoffrey Chaucer's The Canterbury Tales: A Casebook*, ed. Lee Patterson (Oxford: Oxford University Press, 2007) 183–209, reprinted from *The Olde Daunce: Love, Friendship, Sex, and Marriage in the Medieval World*, ed. Robert R. Edwards and Stephen Spector (Albany NY: State University of New York Press, 1991) 211–28, p. 186.

[186] Peggy Knapp, *Chaucer and the Social Contest* (London: Routledge, 1990), p. 49. Knapp also points out that it is not unlikely that the story the Prioress tells was customarily told to children.

set forward the action of the divine in continuing the song so that others may hear'.[187] He also notes that it is unclear whether others are converted by the singing,[188] which would have been expected in a miracle tale. In traditional saints' lives or miracles of the Virgin, the evildoers realise their error and are converted. If the tale followed its traditional conclusion, evident in other extant versions, that is what *should* happen but it does not. No one is converted, no one is given the opportunity to convert because the Jews are tortured and executed before they can fully witness the extent of the miracle. The Prioress explains that the widowed mother, desperate in her search for her son, goes to the ghetto and confronts the Jews who lie and say that they have not seen the child. With their lie, 'Jhesu of his grace/ Yaf in hir thoght inwith a litel space/ That in that place after hir sone she cryde,/ Where he was casten in a pit bisyde' (lines 603–6) and the child's voice rings out from the cesspit 'with throte ykorven' (line 611) with a resounding chorus of *Alma redemptoris*. The actions of the crowd are immediate. They send for the provost, he comes without tarrying and 'after that the Jewes leet he bynde' (line 620). There is no inquisition into the guilt of the accused, no threat of torture only its application, no questions asked at all. Any pretence of law has been shattered and all the legal structures circumvented. Their guilt is assumed and proclaimed with the arrival of the civil authority. The child's singing body is carried to the abbey and placed on the bier, where his mother, this 'newe Rachel' (line 627), weeps inconsolate.

With the punishment of the Jews, no one particular person is singled out; they are all condemned to death for their assumed part in hiring the murderer or their supposed knowledge of it:

> With torment and with shameful deeth echon,
> This provost dooth thise Jewes for to sterve
> That of this mordre wiste, and that anon.
> He holde no swich cursednesse observe.
> 'Yvele shal have that yvele wol deserve';
> Therfore with wilde hors he dide hem drawe,
> And after that he heng hem by the lawe.   (lines 628–34) [189]

The Jews are subjected to torture ('torment') based on an assumption of guilt – not in the interest of 'discovery' – and then executed. Many critics have argued that *drawe* means torn apart by wild horses (equine quartering) as per Ganelon

---

[187] Daniel F. Pigg, 'The Semiotics of Comedy in Chaucer's Religious Tales', in *Chaucer's Humor: Critical Essays*, ed. Jean E. Jost (New York: Garland, 1994) 321–48, p. 339.

[188] Pigg, 'The Semiotics of Comedy', p. 339.

[189] The Burton annal which records the death of Hugh of Lincoln and the subsequent punishment of the Jews, is triumphal and reports with evident relish many details of Copin/Jopin's torment. Compared with the Burton annals, which may have been one of Chaucer's sources for this material, the Prioress's tale is restrained and matter-of-fact, focusing on the 'justice of the punishment', keeping the description spare. Dahood, 'The Punishment of the Jews', p. 482.

in the *Roland*. But Roger Dahood effectively explains that it means being dragged by horses to the place of execution.[190] This may not *seem* as brutal as being torn asunder by horses like Ganelon. Criminals were often dragged to the gallows. But as it is, equine dragging, 'though its harshness is perhaps not quite so evident to the modern imagination as the harshness of equine quartering, is harsh indeed'.[191] However, the real brutality is the injustice of a mass execution without recourse to law, despite the Prioress's assertion that 'he heng hem by the lawe' (634). They have not been tried; they have been rounded up and lynched after being tortured. It is still a humiliating and unnecessarily excessive punishment for an entire group of people who had nothing to do with the crime. Dahood suggests that this only seems excessive 'at first blush' because the crime is murder, not treason, but he concludes that the Jews executed for the murder of Hugh of Lincoln in 1255 suffered the same fate and that Chaucer saw 'nothing offensive in it'.[192] Even though it is clear that Hugh was not murdered by Jews,[193] ninety-one were rounded up and held in the Tower of London for their part in the alleged blood ritual after a certain Copin (or Jopin) admitted, under threat of torture, to murdering the boy.[194] Copin was then executed, despite being promised protection if he confessed. Of those imprisoned, eighteen were hanged, their property confiscated by Henry III, and the rest pardoned and set free. There is some question as to whether anything would have been done at all had the royal authorities not intervened; since there is no evidence of prior secular action, 'one may wonder sadly whether the miscarriage of justice would have occurred had Henry III not passed through Lincoln that autumn with John de Lexinton'.[195]

---

[190] Dahood discusses the nature of this punishment at length, reviewing each of the possibilities for defining *drawe*, concluding that it means dragging along the ground rather than equine dismemberment or quartering. 'The Punishment of the Jews', pp. 466–9. He writes that the definition allows three interpretations of the Prioress's word: 'wild horses dragged the Jews without a vehicle, dragged them in a cart, or dragged them on a sledge. If the Prioress meant drawing the Jews on a cart or sledge, the point might be only to ensure before hanging the kind of public humiliation [...] Lancelot risks for Guinevere's sake in Chrétien's and later Malory's *Knight of the Cart*' (pp. 469–70). This interpretation is logical because in order for them to be hanged, there must be an intact body — they are drawn to the place of execution by horses and then hanged. However, Mickel explains that the treatment of Jews suspected of crimes was often synonymous with the punishment of traitors. He gives the example of four Jews accused of circumcising a youth 'and other atrocities' who were torn asunder by horses and later hanged, and says that religious offences often seemed to be regarded as similar to cases of treason (*Ganelon, Treason*, p. 147 n. 300).

[191] Dahood, 'The Punishment of the Jews', p. 470.

[192] Dahood, 'The Punishment of the Jews', pp. 472, 473.

[193] Florence Ridley, notes to the *Prioress's Prologue and Tale*, in *The Riverside Chaucer*, ed. Benson, pp. 913–16.

[194] Gavin I. Langmuir, 'The Knight's Tale of Young Hugh of Lincoln', *Speculum* 47:3 (July 1972): 459–82, p. 477. Also see: Florence H. Ridley, 'A Tale Told Too Often', *Western Folklore* 26:3 (July 1967): 153–6; and Dahood, 'The Punishment of the Jews', pp. 465–91.

[195] Langmuir, 'The Knight's Tale of Young Hugh of Lincoln', p. 477.

Dahood argues that Chaucer's connections to Lincoln and his loyalty to John of Gaunt, a direct descendant of Henry III, 'inclines against the likelihood of Chaucer's detachment from the prevailing anti-semitism [sic] of his time'.[196]

The gruesome details of this punishment are present in the Burton annals that record the events surrounding the murder of Hugh of Lincoln and his omission of those details suggests that Chaucer refused to fully participate in glorifying the wrongful execution of a group of people and the perpetuation of the mythology surrounding the blood libel and ritual murder.[197] If Chaucer was not offended by the mass execution of the Jews because they were Jews (as Dahood contends), then he may have been offended by the contravention of law alien to an English sense of justice. This is a climate that abhors social abuse, and even though torture was institutionally illegal, brutality was not uncommon; 'the perversion of justice by the very men expected to uphold the law – the judges, sheriffs, and juries who were taking bribes or extorting money for their own profit – was of particular concern to the political community of late medieval England'.[198]

The sentence is swift, absolute, and carried out according to thirteenth- and fourteenth- century standards of executing traitors. But whom did the Jews betray? Dahood argues that historically Henry III (Edward III's ancestor) may have felt a sense of betrayal over the murder of Hugh of Lincoln at the hands of Jews because they were under his protection, and he may well have felt personally responsible for their conduct, which might explain his drastic and erroneous response.[199] According to the Prioress and those who agree with the sentiments of her tale, the Jews' treachery stretches all the way back to the Crucifixion. In focusing her ending on unparalleled brutality, the Prioress taps into centuries of anti-Judaic sentiment. However, by giving the Prioress this tale, Chaucer critiques the hypocrisy of corrupt clergy who do not practise the tolerance and forgiveness they preach. He highlights the dangers of permitting ignorance to flourish among the upper levels of religious orders where it breeds bigotry and hatred, leading to social unrest and violence if unchecked. Interestingly enough, the comment of the provost that "'Yvele shal have that yvele wol deserve'" (line 632) is reminiscent of the motto of the Order of the Garter: 'Honi soi qui mal y pense', and perhaps makes reference to Henry III's part (more than a century

---

[196] Dahood, 'The Punishment of the Jews', pp. 483, 490.

[197] Richard J. Schoeck points out that the papacy repeatedly denounced the blood libel and other accusations against Jews, a well known fact in the fourteenth century, and that as charges of ritual murder became more frequent at the end of the thirteenth and during the fourteenth century, 'the popes had proclaimed the Truth and set up an ideal against which these excesses and tortures and false charges should have been seen for what they were'. 'Chaucer's Prioress: Mercy and a Tender Heart', in *The Bridge: A Yearbook of Judaeo-Christian Studies II*, ed. John M. Oesterreicher (New York: Pantheon Books, 1956), qtd. in West, *Chaucer 1340–1400*, p. 72.

[198] Aberth, *A Knight at the Movies*, p. 156.

[199] Dahood, 'The Punishment of the Jews', p. 475.

before) in the execution of the Jews of Lincoln (potentially for financial gain) after the death of Hugh of Lincoln. But while the execution of the Jews is suspect, and the anti-Judaic sentiment in the tale deplorable to a modern audience if not fully to a contemporary one, the punishment constitutes civil judicial brutality that would have been problematic for an English audience. Regard for the law has been subverted either by sectarian hatred or financial concerns. Chaucer may not be satirizing the Prioress as an individual, but he is satirizing the mindset that created her and that she perpetuates in her own ignorance.

Many critics have debated the nature of the Prioress and her tale, arguing over the potential interpretations of her character and the implications of her choice of narrative for Chaucer as well as his audience. George Lyman Kittredge lauds the Prioress, explaining that the tale was written expressly for her 'and exquisitely attuned to her character'.[200] Hers is the 'loveliest and most touching of all Marian stories', and she is the most 'sympathetically conceived and most delicately portrayed' of all the pilgrims, according to Kittredge.[201] But most recent scholars agree that it is through the Prioress, a woman esteemed in her position, elegant and fastidious, that Chaucer tells one of the most violent and bigoted stories in the *Canterbury Tales*. Many of these critics focus on the anti-Judaism of the text, and have debated the historical validity of assuming that Chaucer was more progressive than his contemporaries. Florence H. Ridley argues that tolerance for minority groups was not an attitude that Chaucer shared with modern audiences. She writes that 'in view of the religious intolerance of the poet's own time and place this should surprise no one; it would have been most unlikely for a fourteenth-century English poet to satirize a nun and a legend of the virgin in order to attack anti-Semitism'.[202] But there is evidence to suggest that Chaucer did not share the common view. Stephen Spector correctly challenges the 'assertion that Chaucer himself necessarily participated in a universal intolerance

---

[200] George Lyman Kittredge, *Chaucer and His Poetry* (Cambridge MA: Harvard University Press, 1920), p. 16.

[201] Kittredge, *Chaucer and His Poetry*, pp. 181, 175.

[202] Florence H. Ridley, *The Prioress and the Critics* (Berkeley CA: University of California Press, 1965), p. 1. Ridley is among a host of critics who have written on this issue. They are too many to cite in full, but important contributions in the debate include: D.S. Brewer, *Chaucer* (London: Longmans, 1953, rpt. 1961); Schoeck, 'Chaucer's Prioress'; also in *Chaucer Criticism Volume I: The Canterbury Tales*, ed. Richard J. Schoeck and Jerome Taylor (Notre Dame IN: Notre Dame University Press, 1960, rpt. 1965) 245–58; E.T. Donaldson, *Chaucer's Poetry* (New York: John Wiley and Sons, 1958, rpt. 1975); Paull F. Baum, *Chaucer: A Critical Appreciation* (Durham NC: Duke University Press, 1958); Raymond Preston, 'Chaucer, His Prioress, the Jews, and Professor Robinson', *Notes and Queries* CCVI (January 1961): 7–8; D.W. Robertson Jr, *A Preface to Chaucer* (Princeton NJ: Princeton University Press, 1962); Alan T. Gaylord, 'The Unconquered Tale of the Prioress', *Papers of the Michigan Academy of Science, Arts, and Letters* 47 (1962): 613–66; Ian Robinson, *Chaucer and the English Tradition* (Cambridge: Cambridge University Press, 1972); and Albert B. Friedman, 'The Prioress's Tale and Chaucer's Anti-Semitism', *Chaucer Review* 9 (1974–1975): 118–29.

toward Jews'.[203] In 1366, Chaucer was sent to Navarre, granted safe conduct by Charles II ('the Bad') where he travelled perhaps as a pilgrim, perhaps as a government agent working for Edward the Black Prince in support of Pedro the Cruel during the War of the Two Peters in 1367, referred to in the *Monk's Tale* (VII.2375).[204] While travelling through Europe, particularly the edges of the Iberian peninsula, Chaucer may have come into contact with a number of Jewish people, scholars, traders and fellow travellers, and may have witnessed first hand some of the communities that coexisted with those of Christians and Muslims. Delany cites similar evidence of Chaucer's travel and his interaction with both Muslim and Jewish communities, offering one interpretation that the 'obvious excess of [the Prioress's] tale would suggest ironically that neither Jews nor Muslims are the devil's spawn, that both may be rational or virtuous individuals even if not enlightened by Christian grace'.[205] In accordance with this, Chaucer may have chosen to document this coexistence by satirizing the ignorant bigotry of the Prioress without conflicting with the ideologies of his contemporaries.

At a time when England had to pick a pope (siding with Rome rather than France) and the stability and infallibility of the Church was in serious doubt, Chaucer's attitude toward Church brutality – or incitements to violence – may have been shared by many of his contemporaries. Chaucer alludes to Jews frequently and explicitly in the *Canterbury Tales*; ranging from the 'faintly positive to the explicitly negative', presenting Jews as 'proto-Christian prophets, wandering exiles, blasphemers and torturers, and anti-Christian murderers – all familiar depictions in his time'.[206] This suggests a far more ambivalent attitude on Chaucer's part or perhaps implies that, rather like his English audience, the Jews defy easy categorization and that the Prioress does not speak for everyone. Knapp writes that the Prioress 'maintains aristocratic standards of personal conduct and sensibility',[207] a woman who 'speaks the language of mainstream ideology, reinforcing rather than challenging dominant religious and social beliefs'.[208] As such, she becomes a figure of parody. She may speak for the aristocratic status quo, but then that status quo is seriously unstable. If she is a voice for orthodoxy, then orthodoxy is steeped in the blood of others and needs

---

[203] Spector, 'Empathy and Enmity', p. 184. Spector adroitly summarizes the body of scholarly work on the Prioress and her character and points out that 'the joining of contraries in paradox is thus as crucial to the Prioress's prayer as the joining of the contradictions in irony is to her General Prologue portrait'. Wilsbacher also provides a comprehensive history of criticism on the Prioress and argues that no previous study directly contends with the ethical dynamics revealed by reproducing the tale, and he assumes its inherent anti-Semitism in modern terms. 'Lumiansky's Paradox', p. 8.

[204] David Nirenberg, *Communities of Violence: Persecution of Minorities in the Middle Ages* (Princeton NJ: Princeton University Press, 1996), p. xviii.

[205] Delany, 'Chaucer's Prioress', p. 213.

[206] Tomasch, 'Postcolonial Chaucer and the Virtual Jew', p. 243.

[207] Knapp, *Chaucer and the Social Contest*, p. 45.

[208] Knapp, *Chaucer and the Social Contest*, p. 49.

to be challenged. The violence that the Prioress advocates, removed as it is from England by its location in Asye, was a familiar image to a fourteenth-century audience that had seen countless thousands die in the name of religion. By the end of the fourteenth century the Church had waged several crusades, (some of them against other Christians), had employed violence, brutality and torture in inquisitorial proceedings that condemned hundreds to the stake, and was at that time grappling with divisive factions within itself that threatened to tear Christendom apart.

The violence against the Jews in the *Prioress's Tale* can be analysed in the context of the Easter riots or Holy Week riots of the Crown of Aragon – from at least the thirteenth century, marking 'a transition from tolerance to intolerance'.[209] The tale of a child who memorizes his song without understanding its meaning or the implications of its repetition in the Jewish ghetto recalls the medieval association of children with memory, and the participation of 'tonsured children' in the symbolic, ritualistic Holy Week riots.[210] These riots were part of religious practice and followed the performance of Passion plays that are also noted for their brutality and vivid depictions of torture, but David Nirenberg argues that these forms of violence can be viewed as 'ritualized agnostic events reenacting and encapsulating the foundational history of Jewish-Christian relations'.[211] The brutality in these public performances, and in the story told by the Prioress, serves a ritualistic and formulaic role in Christian practice; it is senseless, barbaric violence, but in many cases it is only emblematic, not actualized. In her view of the world, in its absolutism, the Prioress is child-like and fulfils the mimetic role of the young boy who is killed; she has learned the story by rote, as well as the prejudices, and repeats them like a child seeking approbation without truly understanding the implications or contradictions in her tale. To her, the Jews are the natural enemy because the bulk of religious literature of her time says they are. She is symbolic of that blind acceptance and static repetition manifested in the ritualized but mainly ineffectual violence of the Easter riots, which Chaucer may have witnessed in Navarre or Italy. Just as the riots re-enacted the culpability of the Passion, so too does the Marian story of the Prioress. These tales of sacrifice and violence serve the same purpose – a reminder of Judeo-Christian religious history – but not one that advocates actual violence, torture or extermination of the Jews,[212] hence Chaucer's ability to satirize the Prioress for her ignorant anti-Judaism without necessarily embracing or advocating for the Jews. His view, from his travels, may have been more pragmatic, more closely aligned with the coexistence that manifested as tacit tolerance in specific provinces of

---

[209] Nirenberg, *Communities of Violence*, p. 200.
[210] Nirenberg, *Communities of Violence*, p. 225.
[211] Nirenberg, *Communities of Violence*, pp. 214–15.
[212] Nirenberg, *Communities of Violence*, p. 218.

the Iberian peninsula in the fourteenth century.[213] Chaucer's audience would have recognized the formula of the tale and expected the outcome; however, the other pilgrims' response of silence belies any sense of acceptance or approval at repeating such a brutal formula, no matter how traditional or fantastic.

The tale is situated between the riotously funny and bawdy fabliau told by the Shipman, and the hesitating and self-deprecating 'doggerel' told by Chaucer himself. When the Prioress finishes, 'Whan seyd was al this miracle, every man/ As sobre was that wonder was to se' (lines 691–2), Chaucer, staring at the ground, has to be coaxed from his silence by the host who urges him: '"Thou lookest as thou woldest fynde an hare,/ For evere upon the ground I se thee stare./ Approche neer, and looke up murily"' (lines 696–8). While it can be argued that Chaucer and the company are sitting silent in contemplation of the great miracle of the 'greyne' on the child's tongue, it is also possible that they have been stunned into silence by what Deanne Williams calls the Prioress's *faux pas*, rather than tacit agreement with 'her grim religious bigotry'.[214] Williams attributes this *faux pas* to the Prioress's pretensions toward Frenchness. She writes: 'Although the Prioress attempts to mobilize a modicum of Christian unity through an appeal to anti-Semitic sentiment, she is unsuccessful largely as a result of her efforts to cement this unity through shared esteem for French'.[215] But this implies agency on the part of the Prioress, and deliberate knowledge that what she is saying carries greater implications than just a simple tale. It also implies a general esteem for the French, the traditional enemies of the English despite the shared Anglo-Norman past, particularly in the fourteenth century when the Hundred Years War for control of the French throne was at its height.

The Prioress is aristocratic and refined but limited in her worldview as many in her position of enclosure might have been. She is 'ful symple and coy' (line 119) suggesting a sweet nature uninterested in learning anything more than

---

[213] In his appendix, Spector points to evidence of both persecution and tolerance, emphasizing the numerous documented accounts of personal respect and friendship between Jews and Christians often overlooked in favour of the more brutal and prejudicial episodes of this shared past. 'Empathy and Enmity', p. 198.

[214] Williams, *The French Fetish*, p. 48.

[215] Williams, *The French Fetish*, p. 48. Williams' textual analysis begins with Chaucer, focusing primarily on the Prioress, who she believes embodies Chaucer's French aspirations and those of his rude countrymen, who may try very hard to be and speak French, but who are doomed by their own inadequacy. She highlights the sexuality of the Prioress, implying that she is a lesbian and an object of sexual desire who misreads her audience with her anti-Semitic tale, whose appeal to prejudice 'falls on deaf ears as a result of her willed complicity with a class privilege defined by French' (p. 48). Williams initiates an interesting discussion on the proliferation of French in England with contemporary evidence of an English resistance to using and learning it, but she does not address the potential satire of Chaucer's work and the possibility that his portrait of the Prioress and her tale are elements of a greater criticism of religious hypocrisy, nor does she concede that the prevalence of French in the English lexicon could be a product of natural synthesis and assimilation. I similarly analysed Williams' work in a review for *Sixteenth Century Journal* 37:4 (Winter 2006).

what her life presents to her. She does her duties, pays her devotions, 'soong the service dyvyne,/ Entuned in hir nose ful semely' (lines 122–3) and speaks a local variety of French, 'ful faire and fetisly' (line 124) for 'Frenssh of Parys was to hire unknowe' (line 126). Williams argues that

> where the Prioress of the *General Prologue* misreads the codes of French court culture, in the *Prioress's Tale* she misreads her audience, and receives a 'sobre' reaction from them because they are not 'all French here'. The *Prioress's Tale* unsettles the Canterbury pilgrims because the Prioress assumes that her audience shares her feelings about French, and hence about class identity; feelings which in reality the pilgrims find both insulting and divisive.[216]

This implies that the violence of the tale should be read as 'French' and the resistance to it should be read as English. The literary violence of French texts rarely reaches such brutal conclusions as equine quartering. It is a motif of English adaptations of French romances, as with the *Roland*, and it is embedded in the earlier Anglo-Norman tradition represented by the werewolf narratives upon which *Arthur and Gorlagon* is based, all of which condemn excessive violence, torture and brutality and situate those aspects of society in the realm of the barbarian Other. Williams aptly points out that Chaucer diverges and divorces himself from French culture, though she contends that this is a fetish and that he aspires to be French.[217] There is no question that Chaucer was at least *inspired* by the French literary tradition. Chaucer was certainly familiar with the *Roland* and the trial and execution of Ganelon, whom he names in four other works.[218] But perhaps, rather than signifying his desire to assimilate French ideas and identity, this episode is Chaucer's subtle response to the unparalleled brutality at the end of the *Roland*. As that epic ends on a disquieting note of reproach and remorse with Charlemagne weeping over the prospect of more violence, the Prioress is greeted, not with acclaim, but silence. It is possible that Chaucer as a diplomat in France may have witnessed some of the judicial atrocities of the inquisitorial courts for which he registers his disapproval in the *Prioress's Tale*. The use of torture as a literary motif in societies where torture was either infrequent or illegal – and where French influence was keenly felt – is a rejection of inquisitorial authority and method, echoed in Chaucer's portrayal of the Prioress. The *Prioress's Tale* would not necessarily sit any better with a native French audience than it would with a fourteenth-century English one, but it does engage in the anxieties of English national identity evident in English adaptations of French texts. The violence in her tale is highly gratuitous and does not fit the model of similar tales where, traditionally, the story ends with the conversion or repentance of the Jews, or their exile rather than brutal execution.

---

[216] Williams, *The French Fetish*, pp. 48–9.
[217] Williams, *The French Fetish*, p. 48.
[218] Dahood, 'The Punishment of the Jews', pp. 467–8.

In her affectations, the Prioress embodies the image of France against which many thirteenth- and fourteenth-century English texts sought to define themselves. The Prioress is one who wholeheartedly embraces everything French even if she does not understand the implications, and regardless of the consequence. As a religious figure, the Prioress may represent the willingness of some to blindly adhere to canon law even when it called for torture and brutality, and the dangers of following a path of violence in religious jurisprudence in contradiction of English common law. There is no hint of malice or even hatred in this portrait, even if it is a satirical portrayal of a nun whose priorities are misplaced and whose mind is far more occupied with worldly things than her eternal soul. Ridley argues that it is her simplicity that Chaucer satirizes, not her religious prejudice.[219] Eileen Power says that she is a product of her time and that Chaucer wrote what he saw, images which have been passed down to modern audiences in the bishops' registers.[220] If so, then Chaucer is also commenting on the infiltration of French ideas and practices into English religious houses – an influence that, at least in the case of the Prioress, can be seen as corruptive.

The Prioress may be trying to sway the other pilgrims but does not succeed in appealing to the Miller or the Reeve, who would respond to her pretensions with 'a hearty expression of working-class rage'; nor to the Knight or the Squire, 'who would wish to keep their status and privilege to themselves'; nor to the Man of Law or the Clerk, 'for whom the Prioress represents their worst nightmare'.[221] Williams argues that any dissent would be based on class distinctions, but it may be that while the Prioress wants to be French, the other members of the pilgrimage do not and their silence is rooted in issues of English cultural identity as well as class. None of the pilgrims respond with rage or disdain – they do not respond at all. Wilsbacher suggests that this is because they are all of one accord, and because no one objects, 'no one is left out in the open; no one is *othered*'.[222] But in their collective silence, the *Prioress* is left out in the open – she is excluded from the jollity of the proceedings by their silence and their refusal to praise her tale or even respond as they do to the other tales. She becomes the monstrous Other who delights in repeating horrific tales of violence. Child murder, even in the guise of divine sacrifice, should incense every member of the audience except the most callous, as it did when Hugh of Lincoln was killed.[223]

---

[219] Ridley, *The Prioress and the Critics*, p. 35.
[220] Eileen Power, 'Chaucer's Prioress in Real Life', in *Readings on the Canterbury Tales*, ed. Don Nardo (San Diego: Greenhaven Press, 1997) 136–47, excerpted from *Medieval People* (London: Methuen, 1924).
[221] Williams, *The French Fetish*, p. 48.
[222] Wilsbacher, 'Lumiansky's Paradox', p. 14.
[223] Heng writes that the expulsion of the Jews from England can be viewed as a social as well as an economic phenomenon. In economic terms, the expulsion has been read as the 'culminating logic of a long process of systematic exactions that depleted the Jews' financial resources, with profit accruing to the crown also from the expulsion. In social terms, the eviction is legible as part of a processional logic of national consolidation that occurred in

If the *Prioress's Tale* truly dealt with the pure and senseless sacrifice of an innocent by evil outsiders, then the Miller and the Reeve, at least, could be expected to respond with approbation to the punishment of the Jews as just vengeance, but they do not. The audience is 'as sobre was that wonder was to se' (line 692) but not because they felt their class lines redrawn by the pretensions of the Prioress, nor because their only recourse is 'laughter or tears',[224] but because of the incongruent violence that seems incompatible with the devotional moral of the tale. The Prioress becomes the 'Other within' because she *should* be one of them. She *should* represent the cultural piety and religious sensibilities of the English Church, but she does not. If the pilgrims supported her conclusion, there would have at least been a token comment like that at the end of the equally controversial *Man of Law's Tale* where the Host proclaims, standing in his stirrups: '"Goode men, herkeneth everych on!/ This was a thrifty tale for the nones!"' (lines 1164–5). As violent as some of the other tales may be, this tale crosses all these boundaries and touches on a point of historical embarrassment for an English audience. Ridley points out that the tale has 'little connection with English life of the time' because the Jews had been banished in 1290,[225] and Dahood suggests that even if Chaucer had been critical of the Prioress's anti-Jewish sentiment, 'he would have known that on such audiences satire would be lost and would probably not have attempted it'.[226] But by inserting the reference to Hugh at the end of her tale, the Prioress picks at old wounds and raises the spectre of anti-Judaism, one that certainly had not dissipated from England with the expulsion of the Jews. When the seemingly upright and dainty Prioress erupts into a bloodthirsty moment of anti-Judaic venom, it is embarrassing to witnesses who watch in stunned horror as the speaker self-destructs. The Prioress tells her tale with reverence for her little *clergeon*, not anger, but the anti-Jewish rhetoric leaves its mark, as does the unparalleled brutality of their punishment. Her conclusion evokes silence and then disavowal as her companions distance themselves as much as possible from her narrative and her outburst, and the host turns to Chaucer himself to get things back on track.

This Prioress, beautiful and vain, sentimental and a bit silly, is 'so charitable and so pitous/ She wolde wepe, if that she saugh a mous/ Kaught in a trappe, if it were deed or bledde' (lines 143–5) and yet she tells a tale which culminates in what Cooper refers to as 'unparalleled' violence.[227] Dahood suggests that Chaucer *favoured* this particularly violent version 'over gentler analogues or

---

thirteenth-century England, a logic that renders the inassimilable aliens who are too intimately interwoven into the life of the Christian communal body to be useful through the very process of their excision from that body.' 'The Romance of England', p. 149.
[224] Kittredge, *Chaucer and His Poetry*, p. 181.
[225] Ridley, notes to the *Prioress's Prologue and Tale* in *The Riverside Chaucer*, pp. 913–14.
[226] Dahood, 'The Punishment of the Jews', p. 488.
[227] Cooper, *Oxford Guides to the Canterbury Tales*, p. 289.

inserted the drawing and hanging into a less vengeful source narrative.'[228] It is this possibility, and the contradictions of the Prioress that have caused numerous scholars over the years such difficulty because if the Prioress is taken at face value, if her portrait in *The General Prologue* is read literally, then she becomes Chaucer's messenger for a virulent anti-Judaism, not uncharacteristic for fourteenth-century England but in terms that would have been very uncharacteristic for an English audience with expectations of justice.[229] But if the Prioress is a satirical figure, part of Chaucer's indictment of religious hypocrisy and frivolity, then her tale with its beautiful moments of Marian devotion seems sadly abused. It is fair to argue that she is a combination of all those things, that she is part of Chaucer's satire of religious corruption but that she does not embody wilful hypocrisy, she just knows no better. As a product of fourteenth-century convents in which academic education had fallen off and there was far less emphasis on learning and knowledge than on the worldly pursuits of maintaining status and a household, and making the convent profitable,[230] the Prioress is a figure of ignorance who tells a tale she has heard but not really thought about. And that ignorant acceptance of judicial brutality has stark implications for Chaucer's audience. Patterson explores the mimetic parallels between teller and tale, establishing the *clergeon*'s song 'as a model of linguistic innocence, a privileged speech that the Prioress seeks to imitate.'[231] Like the little *clergeon* in the tale, she repeats the story without understanding its meaning, its implications, or even that its views are anachronistic and out-dated. She is the perfect portrait of religious ignorance, not a hateful woman, but one who unknowingly and blindly spreads hatred. Her tale need not be an indictment of anti-Judaism on a doctrinal level to abhor the treatment of the Jews. Through the contradictions of her character and her tale, Chaucer condemns the mentality of mob violence by adapting a standard story and adding the gruesome and unnecessarily brutal punishment at the end. The Prioress's ignorance and her delight in judicial violence in the context of her French pretensions reflect cultural anxieties about the infiltration and corruption of the English judicial system. The silence with which her tale is greeted is an English rejection of torture and brutality as a statement of English identity: 'we do not torture – nor tolerate those who do'.

---

[228] Dahood, 'The Punishment of the Jews', p. 472.
[229] Ridley (*The Prioress and Critics*) and Albert Friedman ('The Prioress's Tale') refute assertions about the reputed tolerance of the Church, and Derek Brewer (*Chaucer*) writes that her cruelty is manifest only from a point of view impossible to the Middle Ages. Spector contends that the 'assumption of an inescapable and constant medieval hatred of Jews in which Chaucer necessarily shared in drastically oversimplified'. 'Empathy and Enmity', p. 189.
[230] Power, 'Chaucer's Prioress', p. 143. Power writes that by Chaucer's time 'monks and nuns had grown more lazy, and did little work with their hands and still less with their heads, particularly in nunneries, where the early tradition of learning had died out and where many nuns could hardly understand the Latin in which their services were written' (p. 143).
[231] Patterson, '"The Living Witness of Our Redemption"', p. 508.

Despite its absence from medieval English legal proceedings, and a general resistance to its application, torture appears in more English medieval secular texts than those found either on the Continent or in the corpus of Old Norse/ Icelandic literature. Where torture appears in English medieval literature, like other European traditions, it is generally a condemnation of its use as a method employed by tyrants. Torture and excessive brutality are markers of the cultural Other, and their rejection is part of the discourses of the nation. This has particular resonance for the audience of Anglo-Danish descent addressed in *Havelok*, whose ancestry figured into the complexities of cultural inheritance and identity. Indeed, a nascent sense of 'English' identity among Anglo-Normans is evident in the chronicle histories from as early as the mid-twelfth century; in the work of Matthew Paris 'the great nationalist historian', the early thirteenth-century struggles between England and France 'assume the proportions of a contest between nations'.[232] The absence of torture is a trait of this identity, and authors who situate its use outside of England define their nation in opposition to those where it is legal. For noble audiences, *Havelok* and *Arthur and Gorlagon* speak to the justice of kingship and a royal rejection of torture and brutality exemplified by Edward II's refusal to torture the Templars. There is a clear connection between the literary examples in continental narratives and those in England, none of which fully embraces torture as a just and correct means of achieving justice. Its appearance as a motif suggests not a celebration of excessive violence or brutality; rather it is a fictional device aimed at elevating the judicial presence within a tale and highlighting the barbarity and brutality of others, either within English society or without. Chaucer's *Canterbury Tales* provide individual examples of atrocities and audience response, interrogating the reception of narratives of torture and brutality in fourteenth-century England, and injecting serious tones in often comical situations or comical situations with otherwise serious characters. Like the Middle English romances that adapt Anglo-Norman and French sources, making them more brutal in order to clarify the perceived differences in their societies, Chaucer also builds on the foundation of French comic literature and Old French fabliaux in his investigations of how far violence can go before the humour is lost.

---

[232] Heng, 'The Romance of England', p. 151; John Gillingham, 'Foundations of a Disunited Kingdom', in *Uniting the Kingdom? The Making of British History*, ed. Alexander Grant and Keith J. Stringer (New York: Routledge, 1995) 48–64, p. 54. Heng also notes that it is Matthew Paris who 'renders England as a territorially distinct and bounded political and symbolic entity in his detailed maps of England, which produce the nation as a mappable collectivity with a known geography, occupying a distinctive, separate space of its own' (p. 151).

5

Laughing at Pain:
The Comic Uses of Torture and Brutality

> 'Comedy is born from the Komai – that is, from the peasant villages – as a joyous celebration after a meal or a feast. Comedy does not tell of famous and powerful men, but of base and ridiculous creatures, though not wicked; and it does not end with the death of the protagonist. It achieves the effect of the ridiculous by showing the defects and vices of ordinary men.'
> Brother William of Baskerville, *The Name of the Rose*, Umberto Eco (p. 574)

Medieval comedy is often the refuge for gratuitous violence where pain is inflicted without any consequences, where an audience can laugh at the discomfort or dysfunction of a person or an institution without the implications of suffering. Medieval folk humour developed outside the official sphere of high ideology and literature, and 'in this unofficial existence medieval comedy was marked by exceptional radicalism, freedom, and ruthlessness.'[1] Since laughter was often frowned upon in official and religious spheres, exceptional privilege of licence and lawlessness was bestowed outside these arenas: 'in the marketplace, on feast days, in festive recreational literature. And medieval laughter knew how to use these privileges widely.'[2] However these privileges may have extended to ruthless displays of violence, there were boundaries to that violence and limits to the ultimate brutality of a joke in order for it to retain its humour. The representations of brutality in these texts are not mimetic; they are exaggerations of vigilante violence and brutality that satirize the excessive measures employed and question their validity. In medieval comic literature violence has often been accepted as part of the formula, but if that violence goes too far and enters the realm of overly realistic brutality manifested in bloody scenes of torture and unmitigated harm, then whatever humour may have been present is replaced by revulsion and

---

[1] Mikhail Bakhtin, *Rabelais and His World*, trans. Hélène Iswolsky (Bloomington IN: Indiana University Press, 1984), p. 71.
[2] Bakhtin, *Rabelais and His World*, pp. 71–2.

aversion. This does not mean that *some* violence was not funny, but it is violence without consequence, without realistic depictions of wounds, violence that never leaves a permanent physical mark. Once the picture of brutality is painted in vivid colours that an audience can imagine, what was funny becomes dangerous, potentially subversive.

Placing torture and judicial brutality (specifically castration) within the milieu of comic fabliaux, this chapter investigates the anxieties of identity and the 'Other within' embedded in three fabliaux: *Du prestre crucefié, De Connebert (Li prestre ki perdi les colles),* and *La Dame escoillee,* and analyses the persistence of this genre into English. Geoffrey Chaucer's Middle English adaptations of the fabliau form mitigate the violence of the French analogues, transforming the genre in terms of English sensibilities and cultural identity. The *Miller's Tale* and the *Knight's Tale* engage in a discourse of emulation and parody in which the Miller questions the Knight's portrayal of martial violence and presents potentially destabilizing vigilante brutality as a joke with no real consequences, underlining English discomfort with clerical abuses and the use of torture.

Satire and parody are common motifs of medieval comic literature, as common people get one over on their 'betters' and social structures are subverted and inverted as a means of either comic relief or social commentary. All facets of medieval society are lampooned in comedy, either in carnivalesque performances that mock liturgical ritual or plays that cast the demons of Hell as buffoons and blunderers rather than sinister agents of evil. But among the medieval literary genres, the body of Old French fabliaux – approximately 160 tales written between the end of the twelfth century and the middle of the thirteenth, adapted into English by Chaucer in the fourteenth century – capture the mood of medieval humour like nothing else. The fabliaux in their parody of society, particularly in France, capture the essence of anxiety over cultural identity – the fabliaux world is immediately recognizable. As part of the parody, torture is not an instrument of the alien Other as it is in other literary genres, but a tool of the corrupt Self – figures within the society who undermine it and the sense of cultural identity with their brutality.

The survival of these fabliaux in various manuscripts, some in several versions, attests to their widespread popularity among a variety of audiences; and the 160 extant are perhaps only a fraction of those that were circulating both orally and in written form during the Middle Ages.[3] Chaucer is one of the few English poets to adapt the French fabliaux into English at a time when England was very much concerned with its own identity, distinct and separate from France. As Thomas D. Cooke notes, among the twenty-one completed stories of Chaucer's seminal work *The Canterbury Tales* (c. 1387–1400), six are fabliaux.[4] His 'enthusiasm for the fabliaux is even more unusual since there is scant evidence

---

[3] Thomas D. Cooke, *The Old French and Chaucerian Fabliaux: A Study of Their Comic Climax* (Columbia MO and London: University of Missouri Press, 1978), p. 11.

[4] Cooke, *The Old French and Chaucerian Fabliaux*, p. 170.

that other English writers took much interest in them'.[5] Chaucer shapes what is obviously a French genre into an English one, transforming his fabliaux into commentaries on his own society and the anxieties of English identity. In these varied and diverse texts women dupe their husbands, priests engage in fornication, peasants wish for extra genitalia, knights are endowed with the capacity to make female parts talk, and dismembered and disembodied parts take on an independent existence. While there are no overt scenes of judicial torture in the corpus of the fabliaux, both the law and its stipulated punishments become the target of parody and social structures that rely on brutality to maintain control are deconstructed. In much the same way that Peter Abelard turned the injustice of his castration to his advantage in the *Historia calamitatum* to reshape his own intellectual identity, the fabliaux use excessive brutality, even in the form of castration, to their advantage.

Originating as oral tales and public tavern pieces, these texts are universal and timeless; they 'gained esteem and were deemed artistically worthy of being put down on parchment in the thirteenth century, a time of literary, social, and economic revival, and a time when they satisfied the need of one class to laugh at another one or at itself'.[6] The Old French fabliaux also participate in the new discourse about the body and its suffering that emerges in the early thirteenth century with the 'discovery' of Aristotelian texts which understood human beings as a 'composite of soul and body, spiritual and corporeal'.[7] In his extensive and important work on the fabliaux, Norris Lacy has classified these tales as conservative rather than subversive, but he acknowledges that it is uncertain whether that conservatism is both reflective and corrective.[8] He suggests that this indicates a desire to employ humour, 'one of the oldest of weapons', as a means of defending the status quo in a world where the established order was being upset and challenged.[9] If this is the case, then certain fabliau that insist on gratuitous violence to uphold the status quo, and rely on brutal imagery to make their point, lose their humour and are decidedly unfunny. Lacy writes that by its nature, 'laughter is an instrument of prevention, correction, or retribution, but not of subversion. It is a method of deflating pretensions and deriding those who themselves attempt to subvert an assumed natural order. It is the tool of a very conservative ideology.'[10] This is true in many cases in the fabliaux, but there are instances when the 'natural' order is lampooned for its corruption and the audience is forced to think about the justice of this order. Rather than

---

[5] Cooke, *The Old French and Chaucerian Fabliaux*, p. 170.
[6] Raymond Eichmann and John DuVal, 'Introduction', *The French Fabliau: B.N. Ms. 837*, ed. and trans. Raymond Eichmann and John DuVal, Vol. 1 (New York: Garland, 1984), p. xxii.
[7] Mowbray, *Pain and Suffering in Medieval Theology*, p. 14.
[8] Norris J. Lacy, *Reading Fabliaux* (New York: Garland, 1993), p. 45.
[9] Lacy, *Reading Fabliaux*, p. 45.
[10] Lacy, *Reading Fabliaux*, p. 45.

being the sole voice of dissent among medieval literary traditions, fabliaux echo the discomfort of other genres like the romances when it comes to torture and excessive punishment.

The comedy of the fabliaux allows some flexibility in presenting this satire and dissent, but the underlying lesson is consistent: those who employ brutality or resort to torture align themselves with tyrants and despots; torture is the refuge of unstable authority. Lacy argues that there is a strict and traditional social morality 'that opts for, or at least longs for, a neat and orderly arrangement of social relationships, sexual roles, and class distinctions'.[11] Both the French and Chaucerian fabliaux contradict the maintenance of order and stability, particularly Chaucer's Miller and his 'parodic fabliau' that are 'insistently and volubly iconoclastic in their attempts to "quite" the refined nobility and transcendent assurance of the sober knight and his courtly epic'.[12] Several fabliaux challenge notions of vengeance and justice in the accepted social order and subvert even the expectations of the genre itself by presenting realistic violence in graphic terms that cannot be reconciled with a humorous milieu. These episodes interrogate the 'Other within' – those who function within a society and a shared cultural identity, but who transgress societal norms and act in ways beyond social or literary sanction. This is not to say that some people did not find these episodes of violence funny; it is unlikely that a medieval audience would have been any more homogenous than a modern one, and in some cases what is humour to some is revolting to others. But particular forms of violence in these fabliaux, such as castration, cross boundaries of socially and legally acceptable punishment, and in using stigmatized violence in these tales, the tellers often criticize its application and those who cross the line.

Fabliaux are the essence of Bahktin's carnivalesque and violence is often a part of that humour which was directed at mixed audiences of peasantry, bourgeoisie, and nobility. Thomas J. Farrell explains that two of the genre's chief topoi are sexual triumph and physical battery, which are not realistic depictions of the 'fabric of life so much as powerful metaphors for private vengeance or domination'.[13] These metaphors provide a language of dissent within the fabliaux where authoritarian brutality and its social implications can be fully scrutinized and parodied. Cooke counters this assertion and argues that the fabliaux are famed for their realism, the exact nature and function of which is not fully understood, and that while the overall style is realistic, 'there are almost no fabliaux that portray completely realistic actions, for they range on a spectrum that moves

---

[11] Lacy, *Reading Fabliaux*, p. 45.

[12] Glenn Burger, 'Erotic Discipline … or "Tee Hee, I Like My Boys To Be Girls": Inventing with the Body in Chaucer's *Miller's Tale*', *Becoming Male in the Middle Ages*, ed. Jeffrey Jerome Cohen and Bonnie Wheeler, The New Middle Ages, Vol. 4 (New York: Garland, 2000) 245–60, p. 245.

[13] Thomas J. Farrell, 'Privacy and the Boundaries of Fabliau in *The Miller's Tale*', *ELH* 56.4 (Winter, 1989): 773–95, p. 773.

from the wild or far-fetched through the bizarre and incredible all the way to the impossible or supernatural'.[14] The 'reality' of torture in these tales is one of censure, not example – the potential for excessive brutality is realistic enough to both medieval and modern audiences, but the actions speak against themselves rather than reinforcing a perceived acceptance of this brutality as a consequence of medieval life. It is the most realistic action, the graphic depiction of castration that strikes the deepest cord in these tales, particularly for thirteenth- and fourteenth-century audiences familiar with the infamous story of Peter Abelard (1079–1142), Heloise (c. 1101–1164) and Fulbert's unsanctioned punishment of Abelard's transgressions where the castration 'is presented as a violation of an overpowered victim, not as just punishment for Abelard's own act of perceived violation'.[15] These performances of brutality, outside the realm of judicial sanction, create a vivid picture of corrupt authority; rather than celebrating its use through a sense of dislocation and fantasy, these tales play on very real medieval (and modern) anxieties of cultural identity and the brutality within a society. The violence is not located in the realm of the Other but within the confines of recognizable social communities in France and, for Chaucer, in England. The brutality in these tales questions the social assumption of civilization and the integrity of societies where violence proceeds unchecked.

Despite the tendency of the fabliaux to revel in the pain and discomfort of others, torture rarely plays a part in the comic discourse and has been mitigated over time as the stories are translated and transmitted. Not all fabliau violence manifests in irreparable damage, despite the proliferation of dislocated and dismembered body parts. R. Howard Bloch explains that dismemberment is not necessarily thematized as castration, since detached sexual organs are an integral part of the representation of the body in fabliaux and are more the rule than the exception.[16] He writes that both 'actual castration and the motif of the detached member are limit cases of a more general fetishization of body parts within the fabliaux'.[17] These migrating body parts and the emphasis on bodily function and interactions are part of the comedy, since comedy is, at its essence, 'rooted in the defective'.[18] Violence done to the body is a necessary component of humour, for like the humour of the medieval tale, 'the effectiveness of the joke seems always to imply an ill-tailoring of "verbal expression", a violence done to

---

[14] Thomas D. Cooke, 'Pornography and the Comic Spirit', in *Humor of the Fabliaux; A Collection of Critical Essays*, ed. Thomas D. Cooke and Benjamin L. Honeycutt (Columbia MO: University of Missouri Press, 1974) 137–62, p. 160.
[15] Martin Irvine, 'Abelard and (Re)writing the Male Body: Castration, Idenitity, and Remasculinization', in *Becoming Male in the Middle Ages*, ed. Jeffrey Jerome Cohen and Bonnie Wheeler, The New Middle Ages, Vol. 4 (New York: Garland, 2000) 87–106, p. 96.
[16] R. Howard Bloch, *Scandal of the Fabliaux* (Chicago: University of Chicago Press, 1986), p. 63.
[17] Bloch, *Scandal of the Fabliaux*, p. 63.
[18] Bloch, *Scandal of the Fabliaux*, p. 111.

words'.[19] Within the context of the later Middle Ages, the emergence of fabliaux focused on bodily humour reflects the 'era of heightened anxiety about the body and its sexuality. Discourse about the body, the marks or signs of sexual and gender identity, the soul/body dichotomy, and the correspondence between the material or physical conditions of the body and the mind and soul proliferated.'[20] As part of this discourse, torture emerged as one of the most problematic issues. The 'discovery' of truth extracted from the body through the application of pain emerged as a prominent legal and theological question in the twelfth century, and subsequent centuries continued to struggle with the legitimacy of causing pain in the interests of knowledge, justice or, in the fabliaux, comedy. The twelfth century was a 'time marked by strides toward and resistance to institutionalization and standardization in the intellectual, political, economic, and social *milieux*'.[21] But by the thirteenth century, the nature of the discussion about the body and its suffering was very different from that in the previous century due to the re-emergence or 'discovery' of Aristotelian texts.[22] Part of this changing discourse on the body involved the use of torture as it was introduced as an experiment along with the 'rediscovery' of Roman law, and the boundaries of authority were frequently tested as sanctioned modes of violence were abused.

While the corpus of Old French fabliaux abounds with episodes of comic violence, some of which can be classified as excessive brutality dressed up as mock judicial torture, Chaucer's fabliaux engage far less in this discourse of violence. In fact of the six fabliaux in the *Canterbury Tales* only one of them, the *Miller's Tale*, actually involves punitive physical damage. That Chaucer chose to shape the first section of his overall work based on a comic genre, and chose to reuse the form throughout the body of the *Canterbury Tales*, indicates that Chaucer saw these tales as worthy vehicles for both his narrative style and his satire. As Jean Jost points out, the Chaucerian canon is known for its humorous spirit.[23] However, Chaucer seems to shy away from the prolific violence of his French models, emphasizing instead the sexual play, the duplicity, the cunning and the final triumph that is often considered just. Only the *Miller's Tale* approaches the boundary of comic violence, but it skirts the edges without ever crossing over – comedy cannot have consequence and still remain funny. Glenn Burger argues that for all its 'carnivalesque bawdy, the tale ends with a vision of chas-

---

[19] Bloch, *Scandal of the Fabliaux*, p. 112. For a thorough analysis of the structure of logic and humour in the fabliaux, see: Roy J. Pearcy, *Logic and Humour in the Fabliaux: An Essay in Applied Narratology*, Gallica, Vol. 7 (Cambridge: D.S. Brewer, 2007).
[20] Irvine, 'Abelard and (Re)writing the Male Body', p. 87.
[21] Bonnie Wheeler, 'Origenary Fantasies: Abelard's Castration and Confession', in *Becoming Male in the Middle Ages*, ed. Jeffrey Jerome Cohen and Wheeler, The New Middle Ages, Vol. 4 (New York: Garland, 2000) 107–28, pp. 107–8.
[22] Mowbray, *Pain and Suffering in Medieval Theology*, p. 13.
[23] Jean E. Jost, ed., 'Introduction', *Chaucer's Humor: Critical Essays* (New York: Garland, 1994), p. xviii.

tened masculinity and restored social control that in many ways reproduces the *moralitas* of *The Knight's Tale*, albeit in starker colours and bolder strokes'.[24] But the tale ends without any reinstitution of social control, nor with any detailed exposition of justice or consequence – it simply ends and allows the audience, both inside the pilgrimage and out, to draw its own conclusions. The restoration of social control, as in many literary genres that present torture as a motif, is an illusion – there is no 'real' justice, and the implication is that Absolon will probably not face any greater sanction than the ill-placed kiss he already planted. He may behave 'like a proper man',[25] but he does not behave like a proper priest; his masculinity may have been asserted, but at the expense of justice. Absolon functions as the 'Other within' – the cruel potential of corrupt Church authority in England mitigated by comedy and farce. Despite the graphic nature of Nicholas's scalding and the vindictive manner of its delivery, Chaucer does not engage in the same graphic brutality of earlier French fabliaux, perhaps because the laws of England were far more stringent on enacting personal vengeance than those of France.[26] But any discussion of the *Miller's Tale*, particularly in its criticism of personal vengeance and excessive brutality, must include a discussion of how the *Miller's Tale* responds to the corresponding tropes in the *Knight's Tale* – which has a certain comic tone of its own in the two-dimensional portraits, farcical battles and exaggerated violence. Torture in the fabliaux interrogates social boundaries of retribution and just punishment, especially when it is applied in contravention of legal practice. But whether torture is part of the comedy or crosses the boundaries of humour can only be determined by audience response. With the fabliaux, a number of critics have condemned what seems to be an unabashed delight in violence, but there are limits to the suspension of disbelief in fabliaux comedy and some lines just cannot be crossed.

Old French Fabliaux[27]

Comic violence is a device used in the Old French fabliaux to mete out just punishments, to castigate transgression and to amuse a widely mixed audience

---

[24] Burger, 'Erotic Discipline', p. 246.
[25] Burger, 'Erotic Discipline', p. 246.
[26] Smail and Gibson, *Vengeance in Medieval Europe*, p. 317.
[27] This section also appears as 'The Uses of Torture and Violence in the Fabliaux: When Comedy Crosses the Line', *Florilegium* 23.2 (2006): 143–68, revised and reprinted with permission of *Florilegium*. I am grateful to *Florilegium*'s readers and editor for their insightful and excellent comments and suggestions regarding this article in its first form, and for permission to reproduce a revised version here.
 I am indebted to Holly A. Crocker and Raymond J. Cormier for their tireless support and invaluable suggestions regarding this section, and to R. Howard Bloch for inspiring it through his National Endowment for the Humanities summer seminar 'Old French Fabliaux and the Medieval Sense of the Comic' at Yale University, 2003.

for whom violence was all too common. Despite the farcical nature of most violence in the genre, some plots cross the line separating violence and torture from acceptable narrative motifs in medieval culture. It is in these thirteenth-century tales that a modern audience sees realistic medieval fears of power and dominance embedded in a society where justice is replaced by tyranny and violence is no longer merely a question of fun and amusement. *Du prestre crucefié*, *De Connebert* (*Li prestre ki perdi les colles*), and *La Dame escoillee* [28] depict realistic forms of torture, whose purpose is to cause prolonged pain in a public demonstration of power and dominance that parodies legal practice. *Du prestre crucefié* tells of a priest who poses as a figure on a crucifix to avoid detection by a suspicious husband and is emasculated both physically and psychologically, *De Connebert* narrates the consequences of cuckolding a blacksmith bent on revenge, and *La Dame escoillee* deals with a shrewish mother-in-law whose sharp tongue provokes a staged scene of pseudo-castration enacted with realistic violence. In each case, the 'torturer' is a member of the victim's community, reflecting anxieties about the potential for brutality within a limited social sphere. While medieval culture is often thought to have had a high tolerance for cruelty in daily life, these stories fuse violence and punishment in a formal manner that exceeds the usual limits of humorous spectacle. By depicting such excessive forms of violence in the guise of a cleverly crafted tale, each of these three fabliaux evokes horror and condemns the excessive brutality that stretches the limits of comic violence.

Generally, the humour of the fabliaux does not lie in violence itself but in its relative ineffectiveness: the lover still gets away, the husband is still duped, and the wife still manages to carry on as she wishes. However, in contrast to the notion of violence as levity illustrated in most fabliaux through farcical beatings and slapstick fights, these three tales present vivid scenes of sexual mutilation performed in public and motivated by a struggle for power. As Martin Irvine points out, 'narratives of emasculating mutilation abound in accounts of the crusades, local wars, and revenge in the twelfth- and thirteenth-centuries', reflecting social anxieties about this practice and its effect on the construction of French masculinity.[29] The fabliaux present this violence in a comic milieu; however, in these episodes of castration, the violence is premeditated and calculated, a deliberate act carried out as a public display of power. Irvine notes the existence of similar 'revenge narratives where men are castrated by other men offended by discovered sexual intercourse, usually consensual, with a kinswoman'.[30] He further notes that

---

[28] The Old French texts of all three fabliaux are available in *Nouveau Recueil Complet des Fabliaux*, ed. Willem Noomen and Nico van den Boogaard, 10 vols. (Assen: Van Gorcum, 1983–1998): *Du prestre crucefié*, 4:91–106; *Connebert*, 7:215–37; and *La Dame escoillee*, 8:1–125. The Old French text of *Du prestre crucefié* and its English translation are in *The French Fabliau*, ed. and trans. Eichmann and DuVal, 2:62–7.
[29] Irvine, 'Abelard and (Re)writing the Male Body', p. 88.
[30] Irvine, 'Abelard and (Re)writing the Male Body', p. 88.

castration was 'a recognized punishment for adultery in some regions, though the courts sought to control the application of the penalty'.[31] All the perpetrators in these scenes subvert the traditional judicial process by taking the law into their own hands, inflicting punishment on victims they have illegitimately tried and judged guilty. According to Bloch, 'The literary performance stood as a sporting version of trial – a ceremonial demonstration of the principles by which the community defined itself, at once the code and the inventory of its most basic values'.[32] The castration episodes in these three fabliaux parody the judicial process, mocking the law and authority, but the excessive punishment falls outside the boundaries of even carnivalesque humour and cries out for censure. Earlier scholars, like Joseph Bédier and Per Nykrog,[33] do not discuss the issue of castration, and while many scholars like Lacy and Bloch address violence as part of their larger discussion of the fabliaux, few analyse the specific cultural implications of brutality in these tales or compare these violent episodes to similar instances in other medieval literary texts. The castration episodes are often glossed over as anomalies or presented in the context of a theoretical and thus metaphorical interpretation, or are addressed as literal representations of the cruel delight of medieval poets, as the 'narrator's practice', according to Lacy, 'of savoring an unsavory subject'.[34]

If the poet actually enjoyed recounting scenes of unmitigated violence, as some critics suggest, there are greater implications for the presence of torture in secular literature. Rather than condemning the abuse of power, these three fabliaux are often regarded as a testament to it. Raymond Cormier writes that 'numerous brutal and bloody episodes in mid-twelfth-century French romance reveal an unrepentant and unreformed taste for violence, aggression, and revenge' and that the violent elements of medieval French romance 'very broadly speaking, reflect a certain reality – perhaps by trickle down – into poetry and letters' of the worst aspects of militaristic knighthood.[35] While military violence is commonly portrayed in medieval literature, peacetime civilian violence is far less frequently

---

[31] Irvine, 'Abelard and (Re)writing the Male Body', p. 88. According to Irvine, canon law also prescribed castration for a Christian European found guilty of adultery with a Saracen woman, and that other castration narratives 'indicate that genital mutilation was often used against clerics and monks for sexual crimes' (p. 88), but evidence in the French customary laws suggests it was not a widespread practice.

[32] Bloch, *Medieval French Literature and Law*, p. 3.

[33] See: Joseph Bédier, *Les Fabliaux: études de littérature populaire et d'histoire littéraire du moyen age*, 6th edn (Paris: Champion, 1964); and Per Nykrog, *Les Fabliaux: Étude d'histoire littéraire et de stylistique médiévale* (Copenhagen: Ejnar Munksgaard, 1957). Both authors address the violence of individual fabliaux, but their primary interest is the history, classification, and intended audience of the fabliau as a genre. Thus, the violence is discussed throughout each work as a means of categorizing and contextualizing the genre.

[34] Lacy, *Reading Fabliaux*, p. 60.

[35] Cormier, 'Brutality and Violence', pp. 67–8.

depicted, as discussed in previous chapters. In the castration scenes, the perpetrators subvert the process by which their grievances could be addressed and instead take the law into their own hands, wielding it with savagery and brutality. They flout the law and its system of proofs; rather than enacting justice, they exact revenge with punishments largely forbidden in the legal proceedings of the age. The legal and social systems are destabilized and undermined from within, a potential consequence of increasing the presence of torture – still relatively sparse – in French judicial procedure. As F.R.P. Akehurst points out: 'In a period such as the thirteenth century in France when the torture of witnesses was not systematic and may not have been practiced at all, perhaps only a supernatural fear could force witnesses or accused persons to tell the truth when it was to their probable detriment'.[36] In these three fabliaux the 'judge' does not use supernatural fear to force his victim into submission or to extract a confession; instead, he uses realistic fears of torture and dismemberment to wield power and subvert justice, crossing the boundaries of both legal procedure and humorous farce.

On the other hand, the fabliau author may cross these boundaries deliberately: possibly to emphasize the cruelty inherent in a domineering patriarchal society, potentially to condemn the abuse of power endemic to the upper levels of the feudal system, or in some cases to do both, as with the 'gelding' of the mother-in-law in *La Dame escoillee*. If the tales are to be taken at face value, then the torture must be too, and modern audiences would have to confront a sadistic medieval delight in violence and bloodshed unsupported by most secular literature of the time. In contrast to a critical position like that of Norris Lacy, who argues the fabliaux are literal renderings, it is my contention that the tales are subversive because they contain fragments of dissent and ironic humour. From this perspective, graphic portrayals of human cruelty form a much more complex portrait of medieval sensibilities. Certain fabliaux give modern readers a glimpse of a society plagued by secular abuse and tyranny, displaying excesses in condemnation rather than celebration of violence.

Within the corpus of fabliaux, slapstick violence abounds – beatings that leave no more than a momentary mark, draw no blood, and seem to do no harm at all. Women and men are flogged, trounced, dragged through the mud, beaten with sticks, stones, pots and pans; clothes are ripped and heads are bashed, yet none of this seems out of place in a genre that for the most part contravenes traditional expectations by imposing new ones. This kind of violence is reminiscent of the rhetorical violence enacted in medieval drama, in which, Enders writes,

---

[36] F.R.P. Akehurst, 'Name, Reputation, and Notoriety in French Customary Law', in *Fama: The Politics of Talk and Reputation in Medieval Europe*, ed. Thelma Fenster and Daniel Lord Smail (Ithaca NY: Cornell University Press, 2003), p. 91. See also: F.R.P. Akehurst, 'Customary Law in Old French Fabliaux', in *The Old French Fabliaux: Essays on Comedy and Context*, ed. Kristen L. Burr, John F. Moran, and Norris J. Lacy (Jefferson NC: McFarland and Co., 2007) 42–54.

'such comic beatings also recall the ambiguous relationship of rhetoric itself to pain and its pleasures.'[37] This ambiguity leads to the question of what is funny and what is excessive in the performance of pain represented in literary genres like the fabliau, and whether the violence enacted should be taken seriously or as subversive. Medieval cultural constructions of torture and the characteristics that distinguish it from other acts of violence represented in the genre provide good indicators in determining the subversive intent of this subset of fabliaux.

As discussed throughout this work, medieval torture was associated with the notion of truth, whether in its revelation, the extraction, or invention.[38] Peters argues that the term 'torture' should be applied only to judicial proceedings: 'judicial torture is the only kind of torture, whether administered by an official judiciary or by other instruments of the state. [...] The juxtaposition of familiar terms from one area of meaning to another for dramatic effect is a device of rhetoric, not historical or social analysis.'[39] However, in her study of the rhetoric of violence Enders observes that historians have increasingly focused on the relationship between torture and truth, but have devoted far less attention to 'the role of dramatic theory and spectacle in the rhetorical discovery, interpretation, enactment, and even theatricalization of torture'.[40] Torture attempts to enact authority dramatically; it is a deliberate practice performed publicly as an exercise of judicial domination, condoned by the authorities who believe in the illusion of power that torture creates.[41] Authorities pronounce this unstable power publicly, through the public application and display of torture and its effects,[42] but in Old French fabliaux that authority is illegitimately disseminated among the people who take vengeance rather than enacting justice, and the torture they inflict is tainted by the public abuse of power.[43]

In the fabliaux there are two public spheres: the characters who act as witnesses to the torture in the narrative and the audience to whom the jongleur is telling the tale. In contrast, Farrell argues that the 'privacy of the fabliaux also makes them inherently unjust, since medieval justice is never private or secret.'[44] However, this performance transforms what should be private into a public spectacle in

---

[37] Enders, *The Medieval Theater of Cruelty*, p. 179.
[38] Enders, *The Medieval Theater of Cruelty*, p. 3.
[39] Peters, *Torture*, p. 7.
[40] Enders, *The Medieval Theater of Cruelty*, p. 3.
[41] Scarry, *The Body in Pain*, p. 27.
[42] Peters, *Torture*, p. 3.
[43] In a similar manner, the circumstances and effects of Abelard's castration were debated in a very public forum, his letters to Heloise, her responses, the written attacks of his critics and the defence of his proponents. This kind of violence is public and the effect is to publicly destabilize authoritarian legal structures. As Irvine points out, the identity that was created within this discourse 'continues in the writings of Abelard's enemies right up to the time of his betrayal and condemnation at the Council of Sens (1140)' (p. 94).
[44] Farrell, 'Privacy and the Boundaries', p. 775.

order to highlight the injustice of the punishment. In *Du prestre crucefié* and *De Connebert* the public authority is supplanted by the outraged husbands, and in *La Dame escoillee* the count serves as his own authority. The brutality is not 'torture' in the judicial sense, but it serves the same public purpose. One man acts as judge and witness against his adversary – the accuser sets up a mock process in which he condemns the accused and exacts punishment. While the brutality is not enacted under the strict guidance of the law, these scenes adopt a quasi-judicial narrative, a 'trial' is held, the accused is found guilty in a public forum and summarily punished in front of a jury of his peers composed of his neighbours. Ulpian defines torture as an algorithm of judicial discovery: 'By "torture" we should understand torment and corporeal suffering and pain employed to extract the truth'.[45] This definition can be used to explore the truths extracted in these three brutal fabliaux – the truth of fear, domination and power, and the truth of crime and justice. In these narratives the 'truth' is less connected to the guilt of the victim than to the brutality of the abuser who attempts to establish himself as the law, to mimic the law, but who misunderstands and misinterprets its role. These 'truths' are also tied to anxieties of cultural identity and the means by which a society defines itself based on the actions of its members – some of whom transgress those boundaries. According to Margaret E. Owens, 'Dismemberment tends to expose the social and political inscription of the human body and hence of the subject'.[46] In the case of these three fabliaux, dismemberment in the form of castration inscribes on the body of these victims a visceral fear of aggression, retribution and emasculation, and raises the question of the notion of acceptable violence in a humorous milieu. Perhaps the torture of each victim was meant to elicit a confession of guilt, of adultery, or of contrariness – a confession that might justify the tormentor's actions – but no confession is made despite the savage methods. The castration in these tales is rhetorical torture; the violence may be extra-judicial but it serves a judicial purpose. It is torture, but the 'truth' extracted is questionable and illegitimate. In the fabliaux, incidents of torture rely on the public spectacle of the tale provided by the presence of an audience, in the text and outside it, as well as the dramatic effect of the narrative and the climax of this punishment.

These three fabliaux use the spectacle of violence in ways that vitiate humour; as in *Arthur and Gorlagon*, the joke becomes secondary and the emphasis is on the fact that such brutality is excessive, thus directly criticizing this degree of violence. The investigation into adultery, or in *La Dame escoillee* into pride and contrariness, leads to torture and punishment. In *Du prestre crucefié* and *De Connebert*, the husbands have suspicions about their wives' fidelity, and, in

---

[45] '"Quaestionem" intellegere debemus tormenta et corporis dolorem ad eruendam veritatem.' Justinian, *Digest*, 47.10.15.41. qtd. in Enders, *The Medieval Theater of Cruelty*, p. 26.
[46] Margaret E. Owens, *Stages of Dismemberment: The Fragmented Body in Late Medieval and Early Modern Drama* (Newark NJ: University of Delaware Press, 2005), p. 20.

order to confirm them, they develop elaborate schemes that will end in the 'justified' punishment of the philandering priests. All three tales are concerned with the establishment of male power and masculine domination, and are staged for dramatic effect to set up the expectations of the jongleur's audience. The formulaic structure relies on these recognizable motifs – the wayward wife, the pretense of a journey, the early return, the workshop as a stage, and the shrewish mother-in-law. The same set-up usually leads to a different result when the tale is sympathetic to the wife, who then outwits her suspicious husband. These three fabliaux provide an antidote for such tales. Every detail is carefully enhanced for the 'discovery' of the perceived crime in front of local witnesses. The comedy is presented in the form of the fabliau itself, the expectation developed by the formulaic nature of the genre. As Anne Elizabeth Cobby observes, 'We are led to varying expectations, but the means are essentially the same: our past experience of fabliaux [...] is recalled by the use of characteristic formulae, and particular reactions are prepared in line with the author's intentions'.[47] The brutal enactment of torture jars the audience from a comfortable, generic setting into the painful reality of retribution. This may be the poet's condemnation of vigilantism and of those who cross the boundaries of prescribed legal procedure by subverting the communal sense of justice. According to Peters, 'the ideal of a justice within reach of human determination came to be widely accepted' with the creation of uniform legal procedures,[48] but this justice is elusive when husbands ignore the uniform procedures for dealing with adulterers and attempt to exact their own vigilante justice. This subset of fabliaux deviates from the expectations of humour with the introduction of violent punishments: the husband (or son-in-law) punishes the wife who thought to outwit him, and the priest pays a heavy price for his presumption and transgressions. The farce is drowned in the display of unmitigated violence uncommon and unexpected in a genre largely designed to provoke laughter.

Many scholars have argued that the fabliaux are inherently misogynistic, and while Lacy demands that the fabliaux be judged individually,[49] he agrees that they indulge in brutal humour at the expense of hapless others: ignorant peasants, jealous and stupid husbands, lascivious priests, libidinous and insatiable women, and an occasional fallen philosopher. Lacy argues that 'It would be easy – but erroneous – to equate this irreverent spirit with subversion. Instead, the

---

[47] Ann Elizabeth Cobby, *Ambivalent Conventions: Formula and Parody in Old French* (Amsterdam and Atlanta GA: Rodopi B.V., 1995), p. 29.
[48] Peters, *Torture*, p. 43.
[49] Lacy warns that sweeping generalizations about the genre as a whole diminish the individual tales: 'Specifically, scholars have most often responded to the need to say something applicable to the entire genre, something concerning fabliau publics, for example, or fabliau parody, or women in the fabliaux. The results, unfortunately, tend to lose sight of the individual fabliau in a forest of generalizations about the fabliaux'. *Reading Fabliaux*, p. ix.

fabliaux as a group are profoundly conservative, even reactionary, compositions, using humor to preserve and enforce a status quo considered to be natural or even divinely instituted.'[50] If the fabliaux, as a whole or individually, support the status quo and are a reaction to subversion, then the implication of these three specific fabliaux is that brutality is justified, acceptable and legitimate, and that humour is derived from the feeling that the 'victim' got what he or she deserved. There would have to be an agreement that certain kinds of brutality are allowed, even laughable. According to Farrell, the main purpose of the fabliaux is to provide 'powerful metaphors for private vengeance or domination', where violence 'almost inevitably privileges individual vindictiveness (or whim) over social order'.[51] However, the context of these three fabliaux refutes the legitimacy of this violence – the torture and punishment meted out is condemned as excessive through the detailed language of pain. In other fabliaux, by contrast, there is a clear sense that no one is permanently injured, and that the bumps and bruises will heal without scars.

But the images of torture presented in these three fabliaux are too real, too vivid, to be humorous or rational. And while 'the entire medieval parody is based on the grotesque concept of the body',[52] these three scenes go beyond the grotesque of the carnival. The torture brings down the curtain of fantasy and destroys the comfort created by the suspension of disbelief. It is possible to categorize these scenes as farcical depictions of excessive cruelty that are humorous in their exaggeration, but the images are disturbing in that they are far from ridiculous or ludicrous. As Enders aptly points out, 'the potential assignment of "certain comic effects" to disfigured, bloodied bodies might eventually have fallen under the rubric of the "silly spectacles." [...] But there is nothing silly about staining the mind's dramatis personae with blood to enhance their evocative value.'[53] However, many scholars have debated whether a medieval audience would have been affected by scenes of gratuitous cruelty or if it would have embraced such spectacles as a natural part of life. Humour is subjective, but this portrayal of violence is excessive in a humorous milieu, no matter how accustomed an audience might be to violence in everyday life. Rather than satiating a gruesome sense of sadism, the authors of these three fabliaux may have used torture as a means of expressing fears inherent in their own society, provoking a response of disgust and repugnance at the actions of the 'Other within'. As Enders writes, 'If an urban legend "truly represents" real fears, then so too would a medieval allegation of real violence.'[54]

---

[50] Lacy, *Reading Fabliaux*, pp. 37–8.
[51] Farrell, 'Privacy and the Boundaries', p. 773.
[52] Bakhtin, *Rabelais and His World*, p. 27.
[53] Enders, *The Medieval Theater of Cruelty*, p. 69.
[54] Enders, *The Medieval Theater of Cruelty*, p. 209.

Du prestre crucefié

The shortest of the torture narratives addressed, *Du prestre crucefié*, begins as a formulaic tale of a wronged husband, his wife, and her lover. As in many other fabliaux, the husband (a crucifix carver) pretends to leave so that he can secretly return and witness his wife's transgression dramatizing what Irvine calls 'social anxieties about middle-class adultery with clergy'.[55] Seeing his wife and the priest sharing an intimate dinner, the woodcarver announces his return. The priest attempts to escape discovery by stripping and hiding naked in the husband's workshop, masquerading as one of the artist's life-size crucifix figures. Fully aware of the deception, the husband announces his intention to trim the excess off his 'statue' and castrates the priest. The wounded priest flees into the crowd of villagers who beat him, throw him in a ditch, and then return him to the husband, who exacts a ransom. The moral of the story is given as a remonstration against promiscuous clerics:

> Cest example nous moustre bien
> que nus prestres por nule rien
> ne devroit autrui fame amer,
> n'entor li venir ne aler,
> quiconques fust en calengage,
> que il n'i lest ou coille ou gage.　　(lines 93–8)[56]
>
> [This tale shows us well / That no priest for any reason whatsoever / Ought to love another man's wife,/ Or come or go around her;/ Nor should anyone get involved in a quarrel,/ Lest he leave either balls or forfeit.]

Farrell argues that the symmetry of this tale is so exact that it suggests poetic justice to modern readers, but that the fabliau treats 'whatever kind of justice the tale contains as inessential, and emphasises instead gleeful savagery and insistent vengeance'.[57] The moral suggests that the wife's punishment is a justified reaction to her infidelity; but the castration of the priest oversteps the boundaries of comic violence, and the poet presents the priest as a sympathetic character (with echoes of Abelard's castration), calling into question the husband's right to exact vengeance. Unlike other fabliaux in which the priest is caught with his trousers down, this priest *removes* his clothes to escape detection, an act which not only makes him more vulnerable but also strips him of plausible deniability, because naked he cannot deny a charge of adultery. He strips himself of his clerical identity before the husband strips him of his masculine one.

---

[55] Irvine, 'Abelard and (Re)writing the Male Body', p. 89. Irvine suggests that the dramatic climax is when the husband 'surprises his wife in bed with the priest', but they have not actually gone to bed, which further enhances the excessive reaction of the husband – he does not actually get 'proof' in the judicial sense.
[56] Old French quotations from *Du Prestre crucefié*, together with their English translations, are taken from *The French Fabliau*, ed. and trans. Eichmann and DuVal, 2:62–7.
[57] Farrell, 'Privacy and the Boundaries', pp. 777–8.

By all appearances, the meeting between priest and wife looks innocent: 'Par un pertuis les a veüz, / assis estoient au mengier' [Through a peekhole he saw them,/ Seated for a meal] (lines 28–9). However, the poet declares their guilt in a rhetorical move that suggests a need to situate the violence that is yet to come: 'Et sa fame seur toute rien/ avoit enamé un provoire' [But his wife had fallen / Desperately in love with a priest] (lines 8–9). But the husband steps out of line as the formulaic fabliau husband and the audience can sympathize with the disrobed priest, appalled by the gruesome public staging of what might otherwise appear to be a closed episode of 'domestic correction'. Both the wife and her lover are terrified by the husband before he does anything – this cruel act manifests the abuse of power and fear, physical fear rather than just the fear of public disgrace or loss of reputation. The husband seems to enjoy wielding this power; he takes perverse pleasure in his cruelty that need never have gone so far.[58] The potential comedy of this tale is diminished by the vivid description of the brutal act itself, especially paired with the paralysing fear that grips the priest and renders him immobile and thus incapable of escape until after the fact:

> Et ice vous di je por voir
> que vit et coilles li trencha,
> que onques rien[s] ne li lessa
> que il n'ait tout outre trenchié.   (lines 70–3)
>
> [And I tell you this in truth:/ That he cut off the prick and balls,/ So that he didn't leave a thing / That he didn't completely cut away.]

This castration moves beyond a figurative or linguistic removal of the testicles meant to evoke laughter at the disintegration of the husband's position and power. Rather it is a graphic account of the husband's attempt to assert power in a public display of cruelty. Castrating the priest in front of his wife, whom he has already cowed into submission, before letting him run for his life into a second arena of punishment cumulatively undermines the husband's claim to legitimate authority, especially since it also implicates the tale's external audience.

In this tale, as with all the episodes of torture in these three fabliaux, the audience is the public for whom the spectacle is intended, a witness necessary to the act of cruelty in order to re-establish a social order that has been inverted. Other characters in these three tales also act as witnesses, and in some cases participate in the punishment, adding to the public dimension of the torture. In this, it could be said that the poet rebels against his genre, placing the husband back in the position of patriarchal dominance and reaffirming the conventional social and gender roles expected in medieval society. Yet if this were the case, the husband would be far more sympathetic; he would be the *victim* of a crime rather than the perpetrator of another. He would not be the barbarian Other. This tale could be read more subversively as a rebellion against the Church and

---

[58] Cobby, *Ambivalent Conventions*, p. 30.

its excesses, a literary attempt to put priests into their prescribed place, that of sexless eunuch. It is possible that some audiences responded to the brutality in this tale as just retribution for the representative of a social sector that wielded its own power cruelly and with impunity, as Abelard suggests in his own admission of guilt, but in a homosocial society this kind of punishment was taboo. The *Costuma d'Agen* lists public humiliation for both the wife and her lover as the appropriate punishment. According to this thirteenth-century statute, the two offenders, having been caught and witnessed in the sexual act by a judge appointed after the initial accusation and two council members, would be bound together naked and led through the town preceded by trumpeters. The audience of assembled villagers could then gawk and even beat the two with clubs.[59]

---

[59] Agen, France, Archives départementales de Lot-et-Garonne, MS 42, fol. 42v., trans. and qtd. in Akehurst, 'Good Name, Reputation, and Notoriety', p. 89. While there seem to be no references to castration in French customary law, according to a collection of judicial precedents from thirteenth-century Spain, punishing the offending wife was acceptable, but the lover was protected by the law: 'A knight of Ciudad Rodrigo castrated another knight whom he caught sleeping with his wife. The relatives of the other man complained to the king [...]. The decision of the court was that the husband ought to hang, because [...] if the husband wanted to kill anyone, he could kill his wife with no penalties; [...] but since [he] had not killed his wife, he had taken the law into his own hands [and] had also dishonored his victim.' *Libro de los fueros de Castiella*, ed. Sanchez, 58–59, titulo 116. It is not a law, but a judicial decision called a *fazana*, which established a legal precedent. See: Theresa M. Vann, 'Private Murders and Public Retribution: Castilian Foral Law and the Blood Feud', in *Proceedings of the Tenth International Congress of Medieval Canon Law*, ed. Kenneth Pennington, Stanley Chodorow, and Keith H. Kendall, *Monumenta Iuris Canonici*, Vol. 11. (Vatican City: Biblioteca Apostolica Vaticana, 2001), p. 812. I am grateful to Theresa Vann and N.E. Dubin for this reference.

Mickel records a statute in the eleventh-century *Willelmi Articuli Retractati*, paragraph 17, that 'forbids anyone to be killed or hanged for any offense. The text prescribes that those who should be punished ought rather to have their eyes put out, their feet or hands cut off, or suffer castration.' (Mickel, *Ganelon, Treason*, p. 135). Mickel further notes that resorting to mutilation rather than death was not meant to be 'more humane' but rather was meant as greater deterrent against those who would commit treason, because the trunk of the offender remains alive as a sign of treachery and wickedness, and as a warning to others. (Mickel, *Ganelon, Treason*, p. 135 n. 266). In 1096, castration in conjunction with blinding was ordered for William of Eu, King William Rufus's kinsman, when he was defeated in single combat by Geoffrey Bainard after being accused of treason (Mickel, *Ganelon, Treason*, p. 142). James A. Brundage explains that castration was a punishment prescribed for homosexuality in certain municipal laws that were 'far more bloodthirsty' than religious statutes, specifically thirteenth-century Portuguese practice adapted from the *Fuero real* of Alfonso the Wise that followed castration three days later with hanging by the legs until death. James A. Brundage, *Law, Sex, and Christian Society in Medieval Europe* (Chicago: University Chicago Press, 1987), p. 473. Convicted rapists could also be castrated, according to some statutes like the Bologna *Statuti* (1288): 'Secular tribunals offered a choice of penalties, ranging from the death penalty through mutilation (castration was an obvious favorite, although by the end of the thirteenth century it had begun to fade out of fashion), exile, forfeiture of property, fines, compensation for the victim or her family, imprisonment, and, of course, flogging (but without the limits

The castration of Abelard for his sexual liaison with Heloise exemplifies this taboo. Abelard may have engaged in fornication, but nothing justified the vigilante justice meted out by Heloise's uncle. Fulbert's servants who carried out their master's revenge were subjected to the same punishment plus blinding.[60] Irvine contends that the cruelty of punishments like Abelard's castration 'was not unusual for the time; there are other accounts of judicial castration, sometimes combined with blinding'.[61] Its limited presence in judicial tradition does not automatically support its societal acceptance, however. The cultural anxieties about bodily mutilation inherent in torture, and in this case castration, suggest that public opinion was not uniform on the application of these cruelties, and the representation of these acts and their analogues in fabliaux are not merely mimetic displays of contemporary practice, but rather a systematic condemnation of sustaining them. While many of Abelard's critics revelled in his punishment (contrary to law as it may have been), others decried its brutality, and Abelard was remembered by later authors like Jean de Meun as a victim of vigilante brutality.[62] Jean's continuation of the *Romance of the Rose* (c. 1275) 'both extends twelfth-century discourse on sexuality and charts the popular reception of Abelard in the thirteenth century'.[63] Jean complains bitterly in Abelard's defence, and condemns the entire practice of castration:

> Anyone who castrates (*escoille*) a worthy man does him very great shame and injury. [...] It is a great sin to castrate a man. Anyone who castrates a man robs him not just of his testicles (*la coille*), nor of his sweetheart whom he holds very dear and whose fair face he will never see, nor of his wife, for these are the least; he robs him especially of the boldness in human ways that should exist in valiant men.[64]

Fulco, prior of Deuil, parodies Abelard's consolation epistle in a letter of 1118 (addressing it to him directly) in which he turns the public response to Abelard's castration into a 'mock-heroic satire with close affinities to fabliau'.[65] But the

---

imposed by canon law)' (Brundage, *Law, Sex*, p. 471). Bellamy also notes a diminishing trend in old Norman punishments of mutilation by the middle of the thirteenth century; he argues that while there are references to castration and blinding in connection with both rape and felonious wounding, 'in practice, like lip removal, they had probably ceased by the turn of the century' (Bellamy, *Crime and Public Order*, p. 181).

[60] Abelard, *Historia calamitatum*, in *The Letters of Abelard and Heloise*, ed. Betty Radice (London: Penguin Books, 1974), p. 75.

[61] Irvine, 'Abelard and (Re)writing the Male Body', p. 89.

[62] Irvine, 'Abelard and (Re)writing the Male Body', p. 90.

[63] Irvine, 'Abelard and (Re)writing the Male Body', p. 90.

[64] Jean de Meun, *Roman de la Rose*, trans. Charles Dahlberg, *The Romance of the Rose* (Princeton: Princeton University Press, 1971); lines 20007–44; pp. 329–30; qtd. in Irvine, 'Abelard and (Re)writing the Male Body', p. 90.

[65] Irvine, 'Abelard and (Re)writing the Male Body', p. 92.

fabliaux as a genre often engage in a carnivalesque parody of authority, inverting it as these three fabliaux invert the law.

In two of these fabliaux, where the victim of the castration is a priest, Abelard and his castration at the hands of Fulbert's servants for the perceived repudiation of his marital obligations to Heloise (Fulbert's niece)[66] may have provided the real and historical model for these texts and later poets. There is a fabliau-like triangulation in the story of Abelard, Heloise and her uncle Fulbert, though it is an ironic twist that it is the husband/priest who is castrated by representatives of the offended uncle. Bonnie Wheeler notes that Fulbert forms the third slot in this 'typical triangulation of desire – and had the insulted Fulbert later achieved his goal of un-manning Abelard, the organ that might more effectively have been excised was Abelard's tongue'.[67] As Irvine writes,

> Abelard's narratives of emasculation and strategies for remasculinization are part of a large field of discourse and genres that situate representations of bodily mutilation and castration in a network of social values and anxieties, and the cultural meaning of the events narrated in Abelard's letters must be sought in the larger social system of values and identities within which they were produced.[68]

France's adoption of torture as part of the reinstitution of Roman law forms part of this social system, and the cultural anxieties about its use and abuse permeated notions of French identity – a practice of the Other wielded by the Self. Abelard engages in that discourse of cultural anxieties by detailing these unfortunate events himself in his *Historia calamitatum*, 'a skilled, dense, complex, and aggressive confession of a life and of a life's work designed to engage the sympathies of the reader – and not just the reader's sympathy'.[69] Abelard manipulates the audience perception of brutality by refocusing the castration narrative, accepting some of the blame for his actions but centring the true blame for acting outside the law firmly upon Fulbert's men, though not Fulbert himself. Ironically, Abelard belonged and contributed to the very institution that advocated the use of torture as an instrument of discovery and perpetuated its use. Wheeler notes that his narrative is 'notoriously evasive'; he claims that castration was appropriate for his punishment, 'yet he finds it acceptable for his castrators to be punished. If justice required that the servants who castrated him be punished, why was it not necessary that Fulbert, who propelled the castration plot, be punished equally?'[70] Instead, Abelard centres his sorrow, not on the loss of his testicles but on the harm to his reputation and position as a scholar. He writes,

---

[66] Yves Ferroul, 'Abelard's Blissful Castration', in *Becoming Male in the Middle Ages*, ed. Jeffrey Jerome Cohen and Bonnie Wheeler, The New Middle Ages, Vol. 4 (New York: Garland, 2000) 129–49, p. 129.
[67] Wheeler, 'Origenary Fantasies', p. 114.
[68] Irvine, 'Abelard and (Re)writing the Male Body', p. 88.
[69] Wheeler, 'Origenary Fantasies', p. 109.
[70] Wheeler, 'Origenary Fantasies', p. 112.

I fell into thinking how great had been my renown and in how easy and base a way this had been brought low and utterly destroyed; how by a just judgment of God I had been afflicted in that part of my body by which I had sinned; how just was the betrayal by which he [Fulbert] whom I had first betrayed paid me back; how my rivals would extol such as fair retribution [...].[71]

But there is no question that the men who carried out the punishment had done so illegally and illicitly as conspirators who, by bribing his attendant, 'wrought vengeance upon me in a most cruel and most shameful manner and one which the world with great astonishment abhorred, namely, they cut off the parts of my body by which I had committed the deed which they deplored'.[72] As Wheeler points out, in this passage Abelard represents himself as a victim, condemning the acts as 'most cruel' and 'most shameful', soliciting sympathy; but he 'interrupts the narrative flow to pair and bracket the crime committed against him with the subsequent punishment of the perpetrators – their crime inexorably leads to their punishment'.[73] Abelard may have left himself open to such punishment, but Fulbert's men had no legal right to attack him in his sleep, and the only legal justice is the retributive violence enacted against them. Irvine contends that Fulbert would have assumed the rights of ownership over Heloise's body, as her uncle and guardian, and thus 'the castration of Abelard would have been an act of power over Abelard for violating the traffic laws' which dealt with the orderly traffic in women, 'where specific configurations of patriarchal culture are maintained by men controlling other men's access to women by strict adherence to class and rank', for which castration was often used as a punishment.[74] But while it may have been customary (after a fashion), Fulbert's order was illegitimate. Implicit in these fabliaux is not only the physical brutality but the enduring humiliation that follows – as it was with Abelard, whose castration narrative is 'cloistered within the humiliation narrative, which maintains Abelard's primary focus on his reputation and his renown'.[75] Abelard resigns himself to this justice, while at the same time denouncing its brutality and excess in his simple acknowl-

---

[71] 'Occurrebat animo quanta modo gloria pollebam, quam facili et turpi casu hec humiliata, immo penitus esset extincta, quam justo Dei judicio in illa corporis mei portione plecterer in qua deliqueram; quam justa proditione is quem antea prodideram vicem mihi retulisset; quanta laude mei emuli tam manifestam equitatem efferent [...]'. Peter Abelard, *Historia calamitatum*, ed. Jacques Monfrin (Paris: Vrin, 1962), p. 80 lines 600–6; English translation in *The Story of Abelard's Adversities*, trans. J.T. Muckle (Toronto: Pontifical Institute of Mediaeval Studies, 1964), p. 39.

[72] 'crudelissima et pudentissima ultione punierunt, et quam summa ammiratione mundus excepit, eis videlicet corporis mei partibus amputates quibus id quod plangebant commiseram.' Abelard, *Historia calamitatum*, ed. Monfrin, p. 79, lines 581–91; Muckle, p. 38.

[73] Wheeler, 'Origenary Fantasies', p. 110.

[74] Irvine, 'Abelard and (Re)writing the Male Body', pp. 96–7.

[75] Wheeler, 'Origenary Fantasies', p. 111.

edgement of his own guilt. We understand and relate to the frailty of man and are horrified at the events that unfolded.

The resonance of Abelard's castration and its implications for medieval audiences cannot be underestimated. Jean de Meun translated the letters of Abelard and Heloise as well as continuing the *Roman de la Rose*, in which he 'reveals a fascination with castration and dismemberment' and inserting various exempla dealing with the castration of Saturn, Origen, as well as Abelard;[76] and Christine de Pizan, writing in the late fourteenth century, attacks Abelard's suppression of Heloise while still condemning his punishment and its cruelty. The effect of such a brutal action enacted on such a prominent figure had serious implications for medieval ideas of justice, law and torture. Abelard's very public castration – public in the sense that it was part of the public discourse in his lifetime and in subsequent centuries – may have actually triggered the response against such brutality in the Old French fabliaux. As much as the fabliaux parody and comment on social ills from adultery to Church corruption, it makes sense to find a poetic and parodic response to such a widely known event. In *De Connebert* and *Du prestre crucefié* the victim of excessive and tortuous punishment – extrajudicial punishment – is a priest whose suffering parallels Abelard's at the hands of Fulbert. But unlike Abelard, the priests in these fabliaux are not given a voice to air their grievances, and any avenue to recourse seems closed to them. Abelard had his pulpit, his power (however contested and controversial) in the university, but these priests have no redress. The Church does not step in on their behalf, perhaps because of their adultery; or perhaps the poet, even in condemning the cruelty of the villagers' actions points out that philandering priests leave themselves vulnerable to such punishment, however unjust, and cannot count on Church or court for justice. Or perhaps it is a quiet condemnation of the Church's own application of torture in its judicial milieu. The secular judge may in fact relish the priest's predicament, and so does not answer his grievance, but that would also imply that the husband's action is somehow sanctioned.

De Connebert supports the evidence of this historical episode, where a cuckolded husband discusses revenge with his fellow cuckolds, all of who are terrified at the thought of religious retribution:

> 'Chastoiez vo fame, la fole,
> Qui tot vos destruit et afole:
> N'irons oan por li a Rome,
> Ainz remandron comme prodome!'   (lines 61–4)[77]
>
> ['Castigate your wives, the fool, / who destroy and cripple you, / For we won't go to Rome for that;/ thus we will remain wise men!']

---

[76] Irvine, 'Abelard and (Re)writing the Male Body', p. 90.
[77] Old French quotations from *Connebert* and *La Dame escoillee* are taken from *Nouveau Recueil Complet des Fabliaux*, ed. Noomen and van den Boogaard: *Connebert*, 7:215–37, and *La Dame escoillee*, 8:1–125. Translations of these two poems are my own, but I am grateful to Dr Ellen Friedrich for her expertise and assistance in verifying them. Any errors are mine.

The law would have also protected priests, and the wrath of the Church would have been a very real consequence for anyone who presumed to take justice into his own hands. The *Etablissements de Saint Louis* (1:89) are clear about the boundaries of secular jurisdiction.[78] The suggestion is that violence against a priest is synonymous with violence against the Church, a crime of heresy and treason, but even in these cases the perpetrator would not be punished with castration because it appears to have been forbidden. French customary law does not mention castration, but 'the customs deal with the interesting exceptions rather than the mainstream law. Everybody knew about the laws or customs that governed common or everyday situations, so it was not necessary to write them down.'[79] It is possible that a husband could punish his wife and perhaps her lover without legal sanction, but most evidence suggests that castration would have been taking an otherwise justified punishment too far, whether it was prohibited in writing or not.

De Connebert

Gautier le Leu's *De Connebert* diverges from the expectations set up by the introduction of the tale, and the warning issued by the other men of the village. A blacksmith finds that his wife is having an affair with the parish priest and seeks the counsel of his fellow villagers, discovering that the priest has made cuckolds and fools of them all. He devises a plan to punish the offending priest, but rather than resorting to murder which would anger Rome, the blacksmith chooses castration. The husband creates the illusion that he is hard at work in his forge while the priest scuttles into bed with the wife. When the blacksmith catches the lovers in the act, he drags the naked priest publicly through the village to the empty forge. There the wronged husband nails the priest's scrotum to the workbench, hands him a straight razor, and sets the shop on fire, telling the priest to choose between his life and his testicles. The priest deliberates, cuts himself free, and then runs away. A doctor heals him in time, after which the priest attempts

---

[78] *The Customs of Touraine and Anjou* 1:89 in *The Etablissements de Saint Louis*, pp. 58–9. This statute, 'On jurisdiction over clerks, and on handing over crusaders to Holy Church', sets the boundaries of secular jurisdiction: 'If the king or the count, or a baron or some vassal who has the administration of justice in his lands arrests a clerk, or a crusader, or some man of religion, even though he were a layman, he should be handed over to Holy Church, whatever crime he had committed. And if a clerk <commits an offense for which he should be hanged or killed, and he> does not have a tonsure, the secular authority should deal with him.<And if he has a tonsure and a clerk's habit and can read, no admission and no answer he makes can be to his detriment; for [the secular judge] is not the judge having jurisdiction over him [*ordinaire*]; and an admission before a judge who is not his proper judge is invalid, according to written law in the *Decretals*, De Judiciis, c. At si clerici and c. Cum non ab homine>'. *Decre. Greg. IX* 2.1.4, 10, cited by Akehurst, *The Etablissements de Saint Louis: Thirteenth-Century Law Texts from Tours, Orléans, and Paris*, trans. F.R.P. Akehurst (Philadelphia: University of Pennsylvania Press, 1996), p. 59 n.118.

[79] Akehurst, ed., *The Etablissements de Saint Louis*, p. xxxvi.

to seek retribution in an unsympathetic court that denies him compensation, to which he is entitled according to French customary law outlined in the *Etablissements de Saint Louis*, 2:24.[80] In the final stanza, Gautier describes hungry dogs fighting over and devouring the priest's now-roasted testicles.

On the surface, the actions of the husband may seem justified and the punishment warranted. But the intricate discussion of the husband's plan and of the way he carries it out transfers sympathy from the wronged husband to the lecherous priest. Charles Muscatine writes, 'in the fabliaux of the talented Gautier le Leu there is occasionally a perfervid excessiveness that suggests a temperament most congenial to the mood of confrontation. The sadism of his *Connebert* is remarkably insistent, as if to conjure up by its own violence a vision of the moral system it outrages.'[81] Even as Muscatine suggests that the use of torture is vindicated, he also acknowledges the shift in representation such excessive violence precipitates: the husband is depicted as cold, calculating and exceedingly unsympathetic.

From the beginning, the tale works to sway the audience's sympathy by announcing the outcome: an adulterous priest will be publicly castrated for what seems to be a private crime. Muscatine argues that this announcement creates irony at the expense of the priest 'that the audience is expected to enjoy more than it would a surprise at the plot's climax'.[82] The prelude serves as a disclaimer that this tale is not for the faint-hearted, but it does not diminish its effect. The poet evokes sympathy for this priest who is portrayed as the victim:

> D'un autre preste la matiere,
> Qui n'ot mie la coille antiere,
> Qant il s'an parti de celui
> Qui li ot fait honte et enui.   (lines 3–6)

> [About another priest martyr / who didn't have a bit of [his] balls / when he departed from him / who made him shamed and anxious.]

The nature of his castration is made worse by the unavoidable need for self-mutilation:

> Convint meïsmes a tranchier
> A un mout boen rasor d'acier,
> Mais il lo fist mout a enviz,
> Car mout en enpira ses viz!   (lines 17–20)

> [It suited him to cut himself/ with a very sharp razor of steel,/ but he did it very much against his will,/ for much did he worsen his prick!]

---

[80] *Customs of the Orléans District* 2:24, *The Etablissements de Saint Louis*, p. 144. This statute is entitled 'On fines in the court of high justice for spilling blood or causing bruises'.
[81] Charles Muscatine, *The Old French Fabliaux* (New Haven CT: Yale University Press, 1986), p. 160.
[82] Muscatine, *The Old French Fabliaux*, p. 52.

Despite the fact that he engages in lively sex with another man's wife, the priest appears as the foolish innocent who allows himself to be caught. He becomes the victim rather than the duper or arch-villain who carries out the deception and the misdeed.[83] When confronted by his peers with the possibility of Church retaliation, the husband suggests that cuckolds who do nothing should be burned at the stake. Since the priest has emasculated his friends, he says he will return the favour to avoid being 'unmanned' himself. Fearing the figurative castration of reputation, he will retaliate with physical castration, seeking vengeance, not justice.

This tale resonates with the story of Abelard who was forced to perform a second, figurative, emasculation by burning his own book, the fruit of his intellect, in public at the Council of Soissons in 1121.[84] As Wheeler notes, after his castration, Abelard 'locates his "torture" (but not sin, not guilt) in the burning of his books and the loss of his good name'.[85] Abelard's life and career are inextricably intertwined with a perception of injustice, contravention of law and corrupt authority, so his castration falls within those parameters and reflects a judicial failure to preserve justice. The stark reality of this tale is conveyed not only through the language of punishment, but also through the description of the blacksmith's shop stripped of its economic purpose and transformed quite literally into a torture chamber. As Muscatine concludes, the audience is left with 'an impression of dense physical reality through the use of details that accumulate in the course of the narrative'.[86] Muscatine calls *De Connebert* the product of a 'fableor with the oddest mind',[87] suggesting that the tale is merely a sick joke but a joke nonetheless like that at the end of *Arthur and Gorlagon*; however, the violence strips away laughter as the priest escapes and finds a place to recuperate. The poet is clear about the impact of his ordeal: 'fu esgenez' [he was tortured] (line 276). There is little room for humour in this tale which, according to Charles Livingston, 'exhale une brutalité et une haine qui atteignent à leur maximum dans les derniers vers (303 et s.) et qui en font le plus violent des fabliaux' [exudes a brutality and a hatred which attain their zenith in the last lines [303 etc.] and makes this the most violent of the fabliaux].[88] A sense of comedy is restored somewhat when the priest tries to prosecute his attackers and is told there is no compensation for adulterers, but the foul taste of violence still

---

[83] Mary Jane Stearns Schenck, *The Fabliaux: Tales of Wit and Deception* (Philadelphia: John Benjamins, 1987), p. 77.
[84] Irvine, 'Abelard and (Re)writing the Male Body', p. 97.
[85] Wheeler, 'Origenary Fantasies', p. 116.
[86] Muscatine, *The Old French Fabliaux*, p. 62.
[87] Muscatine, *The Old French Fabliaux*, p. 126.
[88] *Le Jongleur Gautier le Leu: Étude sur les Fabliaux*, ed. Charles H. Livingston (Cambridge MA: Harvard University Press, 1951), p. 219. My translation. Livingston also points out that this kind of violence is rare in this satirical genre: 'C'est l'un des rares poèmes de ce genre où l'intention satirique soit évidente'. *Le jongleur Gautier le Leu*, p. 219.

lingers with the feeling of injustice and excessive vengeance. Embedded in the priest's attempt to receive justice and its denial are cultural anxieties about the breakdown of law and order from within, as well as tensions between vigilante justice and sanctioned punishment.

La Dame escoillee

De Connebert has been labelled the most brutal of the fabliaux, and Muscatine suggests its violence is approached only by 'the antifeminist *La Dame escoillee*, which culminates in the pretended extraction of testicles from the wounded buttocks of a contrary mother-in-law'.[89] *La Dame escoillee* begins in courtly fashion: a woman is wooed by a man who loves her and then marries her, but his desire to accommodate her wishes is so irksome that she sets out to contradict him in everything. He adapts, presenting the opposite of his desires so that he can get what he wants. Their roles are reversed, she is not only contrary, but she has assumed the masculine role of dominance. When a count comes to woo their daughter based on her reputation for beauty, the husband pretends to forbid the match so that his wife will agree. The count is appalled by this social shift and sets examples for his new wife by killing the disobedient dogs and horse given to them as wedding gifts. She challenges his authority once, ordering the cook to use garlic sauce on their food. He responds by mutilating the cook, cutting off a hand and an ear and plucking out one of his eyes; and then he beats his wife so severely that it takes her three months to recover. When her parents come to visit, the count accuses his mother-in-law of having testicles and stages a pseudo-castration scene in which he slices open her buttocks and pretends to remove bull's testicles. She relents and lapses into submission when he threatens to cauterize the wounds to prevent the testicles from growing back. He then presents his father-in-law with the testicular 'evidence' and a newly malleable wife. Their daughter, recovered from her first 'lesson', is cowed into submission by the fear of being subjected to the same punishment.

Many scholars, including Lacy, argue that this is a text 'in which a condemnation of women is premise as well as conclusion' and which 'has achieved some notoriety as one of the most misogynistic texts belonging to a misogynistic genre'.[90] While he does not agree that all fabliaux are misogynist, Lacy argues

---

[89] Muscatine, *The Old French Fabliaux*, p. 127.
[90] Lacy, *Reading Fabliaux*, p. 60. Peter G. Beidler, in the introduction to an *ANQ* issue that showcased N.E. Dubin's translation of *La Dame escoillee* and eight new views on the text produced by graduate students in his medieval comedy seminar, writes that nothing is known of the author of *La Dame escoillee* except that 'he had a twisted sense of humor, and that he had an arrogant and exaggerated need to hold submissive wives up as good women and to ridicule husbands who foolishly allow themselves to be managed by their wives.' 'Introduction', '*The Gelded Lady*, an Old French Fabliau: New Views and a New Translation', *ANQ* 17.4 (Fall 2004): 3–37, p. 3. Beidler also notes the popularity of the tales, evident in the existence of six manuscript versions. Sharon Collingwood points out that only one of these six versions,

that 'readers are likely to find in this work an unadorned hatred of women and to attribute that view to the author'.[91] While on the surface this text appears to be a condemnation of women, the violence inflicted by the count on his wife, his cook, his dogs, his horse and his mother-in-law evokes more sympathy for his victims, obstinate though they may be. Sharon Collingwood writes that there is an extra effort made here to emphasize the arbitrary nature of the count's punishment, tarnishing his honour and perhaps placing him as the target of the fabliau's joke.[92] Even if somewhat deserved, his actions are excessive and cross the boundary of acceptable punishment. His transgression is a manifestation of social anxieties about the boundaries of feudal power and questions the legitimacy of justice enacted arbitrarily by a single authority. Despite the concern for 'rightful male dominance' strongly evident in the poem, Collingwood writes, 'there also seems to be censure of unthinking brute power'.[93] Many critics suggest that the violence in this tale is a product of misogyny, but if the poem is read as a parody, then the son-in-law's actions and the anti-feminist moral must also be parodies. Misogyny and the poet's presumed anti-feminism have informed the interpretation and sympathetic placement in tales like *La Dame escoillee* and others where women are subjected to excessive violence.[94] Collingwood notes

---

Nottingham MS 19152, includes the 24-line prologue that is essentially a diatribe against women, and analyses the narrative content disregarding the authorial intrusions of this manuscript. 'Sagesse and Misogyny in the Fabliau *La dame escoillee*', *Florilegium* 18.1 (2001): 51–63.

[91] Lacy, *Reading Fabliaux*, p. 62. Lacy also notes that until recently the 'fundamental misogyny' of the fabliaux was taken for granted, but that a 'revisionist spirit has led several recent scholars to challenge this traditional assumption, either denying the misogynistic intent of authors altogether or, [...] contending that the fabliaux, while perhaps antifeminist, [are] no more so than other medieval genres'. *Reading Fabliaux*, p. 68. Mary Leech argues that these tales are humorous because of the discomfort of these castration scenes, that the excessive brutality forces humour. Mary Leech, 'That's Not Funny: Comic Forms, Didactic Purpose, and Physical Injury in Medieval Tales', *The Journal for the Study of the Literary Artifact in Theory, Culture, or History* 1 (2008): 105–27.

[92] Collingwood, 'Sagesse and Misogyny', pp. 55, 58.

[93] Collingwood, 'Sagesse and Misogyny', p. 62.

[94] *Trubert*, an Old French text that is debatably a fabliau, is one such tale where brutality against people, men and women, seems to be part of the narrative delight. There is a particularly vicious scene where Trubert kills a woman and mutilates her, presenting her genitalia to his victim, the Duke, as 'proof' of his victory over the Duke's enemy. Norris Lacy gives the best and fullest account of this 3000-line tale in 'Trickery, Trubertage, and the Limits of Laughter', in *The Old French Fabliaux: Essays on Comedy and Context*, ed. Kristin L. Burr, John F. Moran, and Norris J. Lacy (Jefferson NC: McFarland and Co., 2007) 82–92. The text of *Trubert* appears in *Nouveau Recueil Complet des Fabliaux*, ed. Noomen and van den Boogaard: X, 143–262. *Trubert* is not part of this discussion because, despite its apparent brutality, there is little description or graphic detail of episodes like the mutilation of the woman, whose deception, death and mutilation are all recounted in eight lines (Lacy, 'Trickery, Trubertage', p. 89). Despite the proliferation of gratuitous violence and brutality, and repeated scenes where the Duke is tied to a tree and beaten, nothing in the text gives the impression of pain or actual

the implicit irony of the mother's advice to her daughter that also applies to the entire tale: 'those who wield power for its own sake run the risk of being controlled by others'.[95] The son-in-law attempts to exercise power over everyone in the tale, and there is a sense that after the narrative action concludes, he will have earned nothing but fear and the other characters will have learned only how to work around him and his capricious displays of violence. If the poet is a misogynist, then obviously the son-in-law is justified because he is more sympathetic, but if the poem condemns his over-arching desire for power and paints this punishment as excessive, the sympathy of the audience shifts to the women. Some scholars suggest the brutality is justified in the eyes of the poet, and perhaps of the audience, because she is a woman who has stepped out of place.[96] However, the mother-in-law is not tortured because she is a woman but for challenging accepted social authority. The fabliaux resist the notion that this brutality is part of acceptable gender regulation because the torture of women, even if they 'deserve it', is no more commendable in the corpus of the fabliaux than the torture of men. The characters, male and female, in these three fabliaux become victims of tyranny within their own societal contructs. Fabliaux justice whereby the cunning wife and her lover are the victors is replaced with vigilantism that contradicts all forms of law, real or farcical, and questions the stability of social structures where this kind of brutality is permitted or sanctioned, and goes unpunished.

In *The Scandal of the Fabliaux*, Bloch describes this fabliau as a parable of reintegration of law in which the actions of the count are 'a series of symbolic dismemberments', the most significant of which is the mock-castration of his mother-in-law, the ultimate outcome being the submission of the audience to the tale despite its status as fiction.[97] Collingwood writes that these episodes do affirm the status quo, and that there is a definitively conservative message at the heart of this fabliau that rests on the principle of male authority, but that they are also filled with details that tend to undermine this message and allow alternative interpretations.[98] The violence in this tale is more than symbolic;

---

injury. Like many of the fabliau, the violence in *Trubert* is formulaic; even though it exceeds the traditional formulae in many ways it does not amount to torture. Even the 'castration' of the woman's corpse, as grotesque as it is, is not torture because it is mutilation done *post mortem*. However, *Trubert* is certainly a tale worth further study and consideration, though it falls outside the parameters here.

[95] Collingwood, 'Sagesse and Misogyny', p. 53.

[96] For more on the discussion of misogyny in medieval texts and the fabliaux, see: R. Howard Bloch, *Medieval Misogyny and the Invention of Western Romantic Love* (Chicago: University of Chicago Press, 1991); R. Howard Bloch and Frances Ferguson, *Misogyny, Misandry, and Misanthropy* (Berkeley CA: University of California Press, 1989); Marie-Thérèse Lorcin, *Façons de sentir et de penser: les fabliaux français* (Paris: Champion, 1979); and Muscatine, *The Old French Fabliaux*, p. 122.

[97] Bloch, *The Scandal of the Fabliaux*, pp. 122–3.

[98] Collingwood, 'Sagesse and Misogyny', p. 54.

it represents a real fear of transgression and punishment and a genuine need to submit to authority despite the injustice of that submission. The humour of the tale exists in the invention of castration, the metaphoric condition, but the poem crosses the boundary into discomfort and distaste because it involves actual violence and bloodshed. The poet does not advocate a 'reintegration of the law',[99] but condemns the brutal abuse of power exercised by the son-in-law who oversteps his social boundaries by punishing another man's wife, even though technically he is of a higher status than his father-in-law and could invoke his feudal rights. Perhaps this is the heart of the poet's condemnation. If the son-in-law is nobler than his in-laws, then he should behave nobly and use the law properly, abiding by its processes and maintaining its order. There is no reintegration of law because the law has been abused and the son-in-law becomes a tyrant who rules through fear and violence rather than benevolence and justice.

As is the case with *Du prestre crucefié* and *De Connebert*, the poet of *La Dame escoillee* adopts a tone of sympathy in the recitation of torture. The count exercises power through tyranny without mercy, explaining that '"Por seul itant / Que trespasserent mon conmant"' ['For only then / did they transgress my command'] (lines 275–6). Even after the wife admits that she challenged his authority by countermanding his orders to the cook and repents her behaviour, he beats her within an inch of her life:

> '– Bele, ce dit li quens, par Dé,
> Ja ne vos sera pardoné
> Sanz le vostre chastiement!'
> Il saut, par les cheveus la prant,
> A la terre la met encline,
> Tant la bat d'un baston d'espine
> Qu'il l'a laissiee presque morte.
> Tote pasmee el lit la porte.
> Iluec jut ele bien trois mois,
> Qu'ele ne pot seoir as dois.   (lines 363–72)

> ['Dear Lady,' thus said the count, 'by God,/ you will not be pardoned / without your punishment!'/ He bounds, by the hair he takes her,/ to the ground he takes her down,/ so much he beats her with a thorn club / that he has left her almost dead;/ to the bed he takes her all fainted away./ There she lay a good three months/ before she could sit on the dais.]

While the husband may be exercising his marital rights, this brutal punishment for such a minor infraction is excessive, and while the fabliau genre is never absolutely homogenous, expectations have been established that lead an audience to believe that no real harm will come to anyone, except in a rare instance like the beatings in *Estormi* and *Aloul*. The count mutilates the cook for obeying the young wife in an act of substitution. The wife is punished and beaten for

---

[99] Bloch, *The Scandal of the Fabliaux*, pp. 122–3.

exercising power in what traditionally should be her domain,[100] and the cook's permanent dismemberment represents the knight's capacity for brutality that he cannot inflict on his wife. In the same way, killing the horse and the greyhounds is an 'instructive' demonstration of his power. He makes examples of them and the cook to control his wife; she is his audience, just as her father will be the audience for his cruelty later. All of these actions are then presented to the jongleur's audience as he recites the tale. These demonstrations and substitutions are representations of power and domination inherent in the practice of torture and are precursors to the final cruel scene. The array of brutal acts, while perhaps designed to prepare the audience for the narrative's ultimate violence, also adds up to a litany of abuse that cannot be justified by simple audience assent.

The punishment inflicted by the count on his mother-in-law is also a substitute for the punishment he believes should have been meted out by her husband; he subverts his role as son by taking that of husband and 'master'. The son-in-law oversteps the line by trying to reassert patriarchal control over a household he does not have the right to order, thus displacing the father who has worked out a scheme of control on his own. In a graphic display, the count 'removes' the testicles:

> Uns des serjanz le rasoir prant,
> Demi pié la nache li fent;
> Son poig i met enz et tot clos:
> Un des coillons au tor mout gros
> Ça et la tire, et ele brait.   (lines 481–5)
>
> [One of the servants took the razor,/ he split the buttock by half a foot;/ his fist he put in and all enclosed within,/ one of the big bull's balls / here and there he pulls, and she brayed.]

After the act is performed, the count shows the evidence to his father-in-law when he returns from hunting and convinces both of them that the mother-in-law has been castrated. At least *publicly* they seem convinced. The count manipulates both his in-laws by his performance and oversteps the line by forcing them into submission. Bloch asserts that the wife's belief in her own dismemberment brings her under the patriarchal law and the mimetic repetition of the scene of mutilation has the same effect on her daughter, and so the paternal order is re-established and the patriarchy restored.[101] One may ask if the mother-in-law actually believes that she possessed testicles, or if she is just wise enough not to contradict the man who has shown himself capable of such cruelty on a number of occasions. Whether the mother-in-law truly believes it or not, her scars remind her of the possibility of further punishment if she transgresses again. The poet attempts to make the audience aware of the cruelty of this

---

[100] Collingwood, '*Sagesse* and Misogyny', p. 56.
[101] Bloch, *The Scandal of the Fabliaux*, p. 123.

deception and the reality of this abuse of power to which they have become witnesses. The mother-in-law's behaviour is contrary and disagreeable, but the count undermines his own position by the violent manner in which he teaches her and his wife a lesson; he is othered by his actions. His brutality mars the assumption of nobility and chivalry and subverts the entire feudal order upon which society was based.

At the end of the tale, the audience is left with an instructive moral that has produced readings of the text as a misogynist treatise on controlling women:

> Honi soient, et il si ierent,
> Cil qui lor feme tel dangierent.
> Les bones devez mout amer,
> Et chier tenir et hennorer,
> Et il otroit mal et contraire
> A ramposneuse de put aire.
> Teus est de cest flabel la some:
> Dahet feme qui despit home!   (lines 567–74)[102]

> [May they be shamed, and thus they will be,/ those whom their wives dominate! / The good ones you should love much / and dearly hold and honour,/ And award those bad and contrary / With insults of nasty air / Those of whom this fable is the sum./ Damn women who despise men!]

Lacy argues that, based on the first twenty-four lines, there is no reason to assume that the poet is not serious in the rest of the tale or in the moral.[103] Perhaps he means to be taken seriously, just not literally. Perhaps his condemnation of this behaviour rests in the audience's reaction to it; he condemns the brutality by giving an exaggerated exhibition of it much as Chaucer does in the *Prioress's Tale*. The moral opens a way for some people to find this tale funny, 'covering' for the brutality by treating this excess as justifiable punishment. But the moral is contrary to the violence of the tale itself. Whatever the interpretation of the fabliau, the presence and purpose of torture is the same. It is used as a means of control, a public display of power demonstrated through cruelty employed, not by the alien Other outside the cultural boundaries, but by transgressive figures within them that threaten the social fabric. In reference to dramatic productions of violence, Enders writes, 'The banished, vanished criminal's public performance of iniquity has become a private but no less fearful performance of public fears about authoritarianism, public and private.'[104] In *La Dame escoillee*, the misuse of

---

[102] The verb *dangierent* is the third person plural form and can also mean 'to fear', 'to revere', 'to take care of' and may have been given this double meaning by the poet in an attempt to lessen the misogynist moral, or to play on the different interpretations of individual audiences who would hear what they wanted. My thanks to Ellen Friedrich for bringing this to my attention.
[103] Lacy, *Reading Fabliaux*, p. 61. Lacy is referring to the prologue of Nottingham MS 19152.
[104] Enders, *The Medieval Theater of Cruelty*, p. 217.

power by the count similarly represents authoritarianism and may be a reaction against extreme abuse of power, especially if examined in relation to the castration episodes in *Du prestre crucefié* and *De Connebert*.

In the Old French fabliaux, castration is the most prevalent fear, both figurative and literal. Bloch, in *The Scandal of the Fabliaux*, thoroughly analyses metaphors of castration from the perspective of Freudian psychoanalytic theory: for him the body and the humour of the fabliaux are inextricably linked. He also presents castration as a religious allegory and an expectation of the fabliaux humour where 'the priest is almost always dismembered – castrated, beaten, or killed – for his concupiscence'.[105] However, this castration is often only metaphorical; moreover, there are instances where castration is threatened but not enacted or else it is performed on a corpse. Bloch observes that 'We have seen how closely the representation of the body in the fabliaux is linked to the theme of fragmentation – to detached members, both male and female; to actual and metaphoric castrations; but most of all, to metaphor as castration'.[106] In these instances, severed body parts seem to exist independently of the act that severed them and the inherent societal fear is not presented in gruesome form, but as farce. The act of castration is never described and the penis just appears as if it were never part of a living body. The discussion of previously-cut-off penises does not involve pain, and while the implication of violent castration exists, it is not graphically presented to the audience in a display of power.

There are many figurative episodes of castration in the fabliaux, intricately and ingeniously wrought by the poets to substitute literal, physical castration with shame and disgrace. These are scenes of mock-castration, and the unwitting victim becomes the butt of the joke. Ultimately, the greatest injury is to the victim's pride and perhaps his marriage – there are no physical scars or reminders that cannot be shed like another man's pants. However, actual castrations in the fabliaux exceed figurative acts of punishment, focusing on pain and suffering instead of humiliation and potential humour, tapping into social anxieties about emasculation represented by historical figures like Abelard who attempts to refocus the implications of his punishment but who also contributes to the sense of injustice in reciting it. Bahktin associates the fabliaux with the humour of 'the lower part [...] the genital organs, the belly, and the buttocks',[107] but the palpable fear, threat, or act of castration in these three fabliaux turns celebration into a renunciation and a denial of sexuality, and becomes a demonstration of power. The power is corrupt and may mirror cultural anxieties about the depth and breadth of authoritative corruption and the instability of social structures in their own world. Bloch argues that the humour of the fabliaux, in fact all humour, is derived from something that has been dismembered or castrated:

---

[105] Bloch, *The Scandal of the Fabliaux*, p. 63.
[106] Bloch, *The Scandal of the Fabliaux*, p. 101.
[107] Bakhtin, *Rabelais and His World*, p. 21.

'that which provokes laughter always involves a cutting short, a foreshortening'.[108] In these tales the castration can be seen as a 'cutting short' of the proclivities, the adultery, the lascivious behaviour, and thus of the humour itself. Or it can be seen as enacting a horrific punishment condemned by practically all strata of society. Muscatine argues that the sexual sadism in each of these tales is made indirect by more powerful motives that it seems to be serving: 'In *Connebert* it is hatred (and envy?) of the clergy. The issue of *La Dame escoillee* [...] is domination.'[109] Both Bloch and Muscatine address the apparent purpose of castration in the fabliaux, but it is not sexual cruelty even though sex or the sex organs seem to be inextricably linked to it; it is brutality performed for power and fed by the various motivations in each tale.

Metaphoric castration pervades the fabliaux – exchanges of power predicated upon the exchange or absence of sexual desire signified by genitalia – but the plain, literal act of castration and its implications are often overlooked. The fear of castration was certainly real enough, as was the fear of torture after the institution of the inquisitorial process in the twelfth century. The realistic representations of bodily harm illuminate a medieval awareness and possible rejection of torture as a means of control or even as a means of extracting a confession in a regulated judicial process. Castration resists torture's exercise of power because it subverts accepted social ideas against genital mutilation, exemplified by its absence in the most brutal torture narratives and in the customary laws of the period and its presence in Abelard's construction of sympathy. Torture was an acceptable motif in female hagiography; saints like Christina and Agatha defy their pagan judges by withstanding their brutal attempts to force either confession of Christianity or conversion. Yet despite the proliferation of torture in medieval hagiography, genitalia remain untouched except in rare instances, because castration or vaginal mutilation violates the purity of the saint and contaminates the perception of virginity. It is a boundary rarely crossed by even the most salaciously brutal of pagan judges depicted in medieval hagiography, nor is it a punishment meted out to even the most deserving of traitors in epics and sagas.[110] As noted in

---

[108] Bloch, *The Scandal of the Fabliaux*, p. 111.

[109] Muscatine, *The Old French Fabliaux*, p. 128.

[110] According to Jean Froissart in his *Chronicles*, though not in other sources, public castration is exactly the punishment visited upon Hugh Despenser, Edward II's favourite. Jean Froissart, *Chronicles*, Paris, Bibliothèque Nationale, MS fr. 2643, fol. 11. The graphic illumination of Hugh Despenser being publicly disembowelled and castrated takes up a quarter of the left-hand column. The following transcription is mine: 'Quant it fut / ainsi loye on lui coupa tout / prennerement le vit [et] les / couillons pour tant quil / estoit heretique [et] sodomite/ [...] Et pour ce auoit/ le roy dechassee la royne de / lui [et] par son ennorteniet / Quant le vit [et] les couil/lons furent de lui coupez on / les getta ou feu pour adroit / Et après lui fut le aieur / coupe hor[es] du ventres et gette/ ou feu pour tant q'[i]l estoit / [fol. 11v] faubo [et] traytre de cuer et que/ par traytre conseil [et] enortement le roy' [When he had been tied up, his member and his testicles were first cut off, because he was a heretic and a sodomite,

Chapters 2, 3 and 4, evisceration, flaying, boiling, dismemberment and mutilation figure prominently in religious narratives but only occasionally in secular ones, and then only as a deterrent or a mark of dishonour and often only as a literary motif rather than actual practice. In secular literature like the fabliaux, where episodes of violence rarely approach the brutality of hagiography, incidents of castration are even more shocking and taboo because torture is not an accepted motif of the genre.

To manipulate this taboo, the poet must first establish a sympathetic characterization for its victim, contradicting the institution of torture and subverting the judicial process. The audience must care if the priest is castrated; if they do not, their fear and revulsion of castration transforms into approbation of a justified punishment enacted by a legitimate authority. The physical castration of the adulterous priest may be considered vengeance for the figurative and symbolic castration of the cuckolded husband. However, sympathy does not lie necessarily with the husband despite the fact that the priest is actually guilty, and his punishment could be considered justified in fabliaux representing calculated, staged, literal castration.[111] But is the brutal castration carried out in these tales proper justice? Bloch argues that behind every beating there is a lesson to be learned, that behind every castration there is a reimposition of the law, and that both *Du prestre crucefié* and *De Connebert* are exemplary tales of castrated priests.[112] This applies if the moral of the tales is taken literally, rather than as parody or satire. If the primary humour of the fabliau is a product of successful schemes with minimal consequences, then the re-establishment of the law and the status quo cannot be comic, especially if it is re-established through unwarranted brutality that actually contradicts accepted legal practice. Episodes of castration cannot be 'exemplary tales' if castration was forbidden and generally taboo. The very blood drawn in these scenes defies French customary law, which states that any party who causes the loss of blood or visible bruising, and is proven guilty by witnesses, is culpable for sixty *sous* in damages to the judge and fifteen *sous* to the plaintiff, and is responsible for the cost of the plaintiff's lost days of work and having the wound healed.[113] Castration is outside the law,

---

even, it was said, with the King, and this is why the King had driven away the Queen on his suggestion. When his private parts had been cut off they were thrown into the fire to burn, and afterwards his heart was torn from his body and thrown into the fire because he was a false-hearted traitor, who by his treasonable advice and promptings had led the King to bring shame and misfortune upon his kingdom ...]. Froissart, *Chronicles*, trans. Geoffrey Brereton (London: Penguin Books, 1978), p. 44. Its insidiousness is one of the reasons that castration is reserved for the worst offenders, though often performed *post mortem* as with Simon de Montfort after the Battle of Evesham (1265).

[111] Bloch, *The Scandal of the Fabliaux*, p. 112.
[112] Bloch, *The Scandal of the Fabliaux*, p. 120.
[113] *Customs of the Orléans District* 2:24, in *The Etablissements de Saint Louis*, p. 144. This particular statute gives townsmen and commoners equal status in paying remuneration for serious, but not life-threatening, wounds unless amputation is involved: 'But [the judge] must

and if the perpetrators succeed, then they invert judicial process and exercise illegitimate authority. These episodes parody the law and subvert it to such an extent that any humour is spoiled or destroyed in the bloody contravention of acceptable humour.

Chaucer: *The Miller's Tale*

Chaucer is unique among his contemporaries in adapting the fabliau form into English, while eliminating much of the comic violence and more consequential violence of that genre. Perhaps this is a product of a shift in sensibilities from the thirteenth to the fourteenth centuries – the debate about suffering and the body evolved, particularly as interrogatory torture in the pursuit of heterodox sects gathered steam on the Continent. Chaucer's audience, mixed as it may have been with merchants and nobility, may have wearied of violence from their own experiences in the midst of the Hundred Years War. Robert Yeager asserts that Chaucer was critical of warfare and chivalric militarism, criticism that essentially amounted to pacificism,[114] evident in his juxtaposition of the *Knight's Tale* with the ribald *Miller's Tale* that mocks chivalric conventions and lays bare the potential for real injury in seeking vengeance. Like the Old French fabliaux which dissent against excessive cruelty and brutality, and corrupt authorities who circumvent the law, both the *Miller's Tale* and the *Knight's Tale* participate in a very English discourse against personal vengeance and the perceived rights of the aristocracy to engage in such violence by prerogative under the guise of comedy and estates satire.[115] According to the *Laws and Customs of England*

---

look at where the blood came from, and if there is a serious wound [*plaie mortiex*], he must pay the fine mentioned above, according to the practice of the Orléans district; for townsmen and commoners pay no more than sixty sous as a fine, whatever offense they have committed, except larceny, or rape, or murder, or treachery [*traïson*]; or unless there is some loss of limb, such as foot or hand, nose or ear, or eye, according to the provisions of the charter, as it is stated above' (2:24). Even though castration is not mentioned, it must have fallen under the provisions for graver bodily crimes like amputation.

[114] R.F. Yeager, '*Pax Poetica*: On the Pacificism of Chaucer and Gower', SAC 9 (1987): 97–121.

[115] Several of Chaucer's works, such as the *Tale of Melibee*, have been situated in the context of the political turmoil of the late 1380s, and the upheaval in the Ricardian court as well as English military policy in France. See: V.J. Scattergood, 'Chaucer and the French War: *Sir Topas* and *Melibee*', in *Court and Poet: Selected Proceedings of the Third Congress of the International Courtly Literature Society*, ed. Glyn S. Burgess (Liverpool: Francis Cairns, 1981) 287–96; Lynn Staley Johnson, 'Inverse Counsel: Contexts for the *Melibee*', SP 87 (1990): 137–55; and Judith Ferster, *Fictons of Advice: The Literature and Politics of Counsel in Late Medieval England* (Philadelphia: University of Pennsylvania Press, 1996). Patricia DeMarco remarks that the 'benefit of such readings is that they account for those passages in the tale addressing the evils attendant upon all forms of warfare, and can speak to the reader's sense that the tale has a deep investment in peace. But with such a broad moral compass, critics

(c. 1220), 'all injuries, in principle, were considered injuries to the body politic, and hence it was up to the state, not private parties to pursue redress'.[116] This is contrary to thirteenth-century law codes from other regions that allowed feuds as long as they followed certain regulations. The *Customs of Beauvais* give specific right only to the nobility, 'an indication of how military aristocrats considered this right a privilege of their estate',[117] a tradition embodied by the count in *La Dame escoillee*. The violence of the *Knight's Tale* also proceeds on this assumption, adopting an attitude to personal justice that is answered and rejected by the *Miller's Tale*, which increases the stakes of the violence and ends without any recourse to law. Because the *Miller's Tale* and its companion the *Knight's Tale* engage in a humorous exchange between them and within their own narratives, these two tales fall into a different category of consideration than the *Prioress's Tale* and the *Man of Law's Tale*, discussed in Chapter 4. Here the violence is treated with the mock reverence of the fabliaux, and its implications regarding the 'Other within' are shrouded in the thin veil of humour.

In the *Canterbury Tales*, Chaucer models his tales on the sense of the fabliaux if not actual Old French sources, emphasizing sexual play and exchanges more than the farcical beatings so common in the French narratives.[118] Given to mostly secular pilgrims from the lower classes (the Miller, the Reeve, the Cook, the Merchant, the Shipman and the Summoner),[119] Chaucer's fabliaux are ribald texts concerned with deception, sexual gratification, duplicity, revenge and adultery. Despite the exchange of blows, the brawl that ensues and the legitimate suggestion of rape in the *Reeve's Tale*, violence plays a very small part in Chaucerian fabliaux. The most notable, and most controversial, brutality occurs in the

---

may overlook the tale's central intention: to discriminate between forms of violence, both legally and ethically' (p. 136 n. 31). 'Violence, Law, and Ciceronian Ethics in Chaucer's *Tale of Melibee*', *Studies in the Age of Chaucer* 30 (2008): 125–69. Chaucer's attitude towards sanctioned versus unsanctioned violence is relevant to any discussion of the farcical warfare in the *Knight's Tale* and Absolon's malicious branding of Nicholas in the *Miller's Tale*.

[116] Smail and Gibson, *Vengeance in Medieval Europe*, p. 317.

[117] Smail and Gibson, *Vengeance in Medieval Europe*, p. 317.

[118] Eichmann and DuVal note that all of Chaucer's fabliaux but the *Cook's Tale* have analogues among the French fabliaux, though it is difficult to pinpoint sources, and suggest that Chaucer may have learned some of these tales in school and then adapted them later. Eichmann and DuVal, 'Introduction', *The French Fabliau*, p. xxvii. Robert E. Lewis gives examples of possible English antecedents to Chaucer's fabliaux, most notably *Dame Sirith*, that may have provided a model in conjunction with French source material. He explains that the fabliau spirit was not lacking in England before Chaucer, just a body of fabliau in English. Robert E. Lewis, 'The English Fabliau Tradition and Chaucer's "Miller's Tale"', *Modern Philology* 79.3 (Feb. 1982): 241–55, p. 244.

[119] Eichmann and DuVal classify six and a half of the *Canterbury Tales* as fabliaux; those told by the Miller, the Reeve, the Cook (incomplete), the Merchant, the Summoner, the Shipman, and the Wife of Bath. 'Introduction', *The French Fabliau*, p. xxvii. However, there is some question as to whether the *Wife of Bath's Tale* is a fabliau and most critics categorize it as a romance considering its relationship to analogue texts.

Miller's Tale, when 'hende' Nicholas is branded with a hot coulter on his backside while engaging in a bit of rival humiliation. This event within the narrative has caused a certain amount of critical debate among scholars about the nature of this action and its consequences. Burger reads the tale in its answer to the Knight in terms of Sade and Masoch; quoting Bataille regarding Sade's paradoxical language, he writes: "'only the victim can describe torture; the torturer necessarily uses the hypocritical language of established order and power'".[120] Burger contends that 'while for some readers of the tale, both Theseus and the Knight might seem to fit the bill of "torturer", such an obfuscatory use of violence better describes the interventions of the Reeve in his tale'.[121] He suggests that symbolic violence and literal physical violence are split between the Knight and the Miller's tales.[122] The violence of the *Knight's Tale* takes a more real turn with the death of Arcite, and yet the expected reality of marital violence is absent. The physical violence of the *Miller's Tale* is mitigated by the absence of consequences at the end of the tale and the suggestions that legal recourse for Nicholas' injuries will not be forthcoming (as with the priest in *De Connebert*). Perhaps, like Abelard and the priests of the fabliaux, Nicholas left himself open to his punishment, but unlike Fulbert's servants, Absolon, acting equally outside the jurisdiction of his position, will not be punished in a like manner, if at all.

Some critics like Alvin W. Bowker argue that Nicholas is justly branded for his dark and sinister duplicity; others like Paul A. Olson contend that everyone in the tale is correctly punished according to his or her vices and sins, and that the tale's conclusion is one of 'poetic justice'.[123] W.A. Davenport sees a more sinister reflection of societal violence and tolerance for that kind of violence in what he considers an imbalanced conclusion, where there is a critical tendency to defend the tale as essentially 'wholesome and life-enhancing', and the unpunished Alisoun as 'some kind of free spirit allowed to giggle "Tehee!" with impunity'.[124] He writes that its pairing with the *Reeve's Tale* which engages in narrative vengeance 'is a reminder that *fabliau* tales are usually rather callous in their humour, and that most of the stories in the *Canterbury Tales* that are concerned with contemporary life have, in fact, some element of nastiness in them'.[125] Davenport sees this 'nastiness', not as Chaucer's reaction against the potential for human

---

[120] Burger, 'Erotic Discipline', p. 248.
[121] Burger, 'Erotic Discipline', p. 248.
[122] Burger, 'Erotic Discipline', p. 248.
[123] Alvin W. Bowker, 'Comic Illusion and Dark Reality in "The Miller's Tale"', *Modern Language Studies*, 4.2 (Autumn 1974): 27–34; Paul A. Olson, 'Poetic Justice in the *Miller's Tale*', *Modern Language Quarterly* 24 (1963): 227–36, p. 227.
[124] W.A. Davenport, '*Fabliau*, Confession, Satire', *Chaucer and His English Contemporaries: Prologue and Tale in 'The Canterbury Tales'* (Basingstoke: Macmillan, 1998), extracted in *Guides to Criticism: Chaucer*, ed. Corinne Saunders (Oxford: Blackwell, 2001): 250–69, p. 254.
[125] Davenport, '*Fabliau*, Confession, Satire', p. 254.

cruelty, but instead as 'Chaucer's view of the world in his own day as a violent, brutal one' and says it is not difficult to 'identify the aggressive quality even in the jokes'.[126] This suggests that Chaucer revels in the violence of the lower comedies and does nothing to mask the excesses of the genre. However, as evidenced in Chaucer's treatment of torture in his other tales, that kind of brutality is not his primary concern and he sets aside the conventions of the genre in his adaptations. In fact, Chaucer embraces the didactic resistance to brutality and injustice evident in texts like *De Connebert*. This resistance may be sparked by the very brutality Chaucer witnessed in his own world, and may reflect cultural anxieties about the persistence of violence and injustice in English society. This tale cannot be taken as simply comic; it has a lesson as well, one that preserves humour but paints a stark picture of the possibility of justice for those wronged by the clergy. Absolon, wielding his hot coulter, is symbolic of Church authorities who used violence and interrogatory torture as a tool of suppression and tyranny – particularly in their battles against heterodox sects – a particularly prominent issue in Chaucer's time on the Continent and in England. Absolon is the most transgressive figure, not for his unrequited lust, but for the brutal vengeance that marks him as the Other.

Central to the question of torture and comedy in the *Miller's Tale*, as with the Old French fabliaux, is the boundary between public and private justice, between legitimate and corrupted power, and the subversion of correct authority in the interests of personal vengeance. Patricia DeMarco explains that Chaucer was seriously concerned with the questions of public and private warfare.[127] Farrell writes that any attribution of justice must be done with caution: 'If the tale is as private as its emphasis on "pryvete" suggests, it cannot enact what Chaucer would have recognized as justice'.[128] And it does not – nothing about the conclusion of the tale suggests justice that would be recognizable to an English audience with expectations of jury trials, fair hearings, and fitting punishments. In fact, the question of justice is somewhat at odds with the genre of comedy. But considering the violent potential of fabliau subject matter, Chaucer's omission of more brutal scenes in his selection of tales suggests that for him scenes of torture and excessive brutality were not necessary for comedy. He manages to make several pointed social references without killing the joke, but the final scene of the *Miller's Tale* exhibits an uncharacteristic brutality lacking in Chaucer's other fabliau. While still comical, the image of Absolon inflamed with a Satanic desire for personal vengeance for a relatively small infraction has more sinister resonances with the escalation of clerical violence. He literally becomes the demonized Other, but one that resides and operates within this social structure.

---

[126] Davenport, '*Fabliau*, Confession, Satire', p. 254.
[127] DeMarco, 'Violence, Law, and Ciceronian Ethics in Chaucer's *Tale of Melibee*', pp. 136–7.
[128] Farrell, 'Privacy and the Boundaries', p. 778. However, Farrell acknowledges that the experience of reading the tale is less clear-cut.

Juxtaposed against the chivalric violence of the *Knight's Tale*, the *Miller's Tale* engages with the prominent anxieties of fourteenth-century England, embroiled not only in the intrigue and duplicity of the Ricardian court, but entangled in a wider struggle between rival popes and rival nations. Justice was often fleeting in times of war; knights who were meant to uphold law and operate by a higher code of honour often did not, as evidenced by the knight-rapist in the *Wife of Bath's Tale*. The Church, meant to be an institution of solace, sanctuary and salvation, was fraught with excess and corruption and, rather than regulating its own, split itself over a contested papacy. It is within this cultural context that the *Knight's Tale* and the *Miller's Tale* engage in a dialogue about the nature of medieval violence, its realities and fantasies, its boundaries and transgressions.

In the *Miller's Tale*, the branding of Nicholas centres the question of justice on Absolon who oversteps the parameters of his office, resorts to violence in an amorous affair inappropriate to his position as a clerk and claims vengeance to which he has no right, reinforcing Chaucer's criticism of corrupt authority, particularly religious authority in an echo of the fabliaux discussed earlier in this chapter. Situating this vengeful real-world violence against the formulaic martial violence of the *Knight's Tale* suggests that justice is not always done, and that even the most brutal acts can go unpunished in a world where individuals exact vigilante justice in contravention of accepted judicial procedures, or in illegitimate displays of retributive violence.

In the *Knight's Tale*, the desperate lovers meet in a grove once Palamon has escaped from prison. He overhears Arcite's confession of love sickness for Emelye and springs on him, calling his kinsman a 'false traytour wikke' (line 1580). They agree to meet the next day when Arcite can bring food, bedding and arms for Palamon and they can settle the matter in single combat. The Knight describes how 'Everich of hem heelp for to armen oother,/ As freendly as he were his owne brother' (lines 1651–2), but emphasizes their willingness to kill one another just as quickly. The duel is described in bloody language as they smite each other like wild boars, frothing at the mouth in anger 'up to the ancle foghte they in hir blood' (line 1660). But then the Knight leaves them fighting to speak of Theseus and his fortuitous sojourn into the woods. There is no real description of pain or injury to either Arcite or Palamon, despite the image of their flailing around in a pool of their own blood. Chaucer's audience would have been familiar with chronicles and accounts of warfare, particularly with the popular reception of contemporary Jean Froissart's *Chronicles*, which provides vivid and detailed accounts of the battles and bloodshed of the Hundred Years War (covering the years 1325–1401). This famous chronicle 'documents with care the culture and behavior of the military aristocracy of the age',[129] to which many of Chaucer's patrons and audience belonged. In it, Froissart describes not only the formal martial violence expected in war, but also the incidents of personal

---

[129] Smail and Gibson, *Vengeance in Medieval Europe*, p. 393.

vengeance that permeated the official combat – and resulted in duels not unlike that between Arcite and Palamon.[130] This battle, based on a chivalric notion of fair play, does not function as real violence but as a literary motif standard in a romance. Theseus rages at them to stop, and asks who they are to fight "'Withouten juge or oother officere,/ As it were in a lystes roially'" (lines 1712–13). His primary concern is not stopping the bloodshed, which would be perfectly acceptable considering the circumstances, but in placing that violence within the contained sphere of law and order. But the law here is subject to questions of legitimacy – neither lover has much regard for law or for any institutional structure, revealing anxieties about lawless knights cut loose in times of war. The *Calendar of Coroners Rolls* from London (c. 1324–1340) provides ample evidence of legal arbitration and attempts at finding justice for murder and other forms of bodily harm. Theseus' intervention and his attempts at arbitration are expected, and yet his solution fails to produce justice, just as the lack of legal process in the *Miller's Tale* allows for humour but no resolution. The tenets of just-war theory were clearly established by Augustine, and 'at the level of individual ethics, the just war was distinguished from simple violence through the examination of intent'.[131] In these terms neither of these 'wars' is just, nor do they end with the reinstitution of justice or order, a poignant stance given the world at war in which Chaucer lived.

When Palamon reveals himself and Arcite and explains their duplicity, he begs for death for them both, claiming that they deserve it, unlike Nicholas and Absolon, who neither admit guilt nor seem subject to it. Theseus agrees, "'Youre owne mouth, by youre confessioun,/ Hath dampned yow, and I wol it recorde;/ It nedeth noght to pyne yow with the corde'" (lines 1744–6). Since Palamon has offered both of them up, Theseus does not need to resort to torture in order to twist a confession from them with a cord about their heads. This brief reference to torture reveals a flaw in the magnanimous portrayal of Theseus much as it did with Alla in the *Man of Law's Tale*. While he does not resort to torture or interrogation, he is willing to put them to the question and wring a confession out of them, regardless of how much physical damage they have already inflicted on each other. It is only the intervention of the women that keeps Palamon and Arcite from being killed. They beg Theseus, weeping at the sight to their 'blody woundes' (line 1755) and pleading for mercy. Theseus is swayed by their pleas, and considers that every man would help himself in love if he could and break

---

[130] Smail and Gibson, *Vengeance in Medieval Europe*, p. 393. One of these examples is the duel between Sir John de Carogne and James le Gris over the rape by le Gris of Lord Carogne's wife while he is in the Holy Land. The complaint and accusation lead to a trial by combat with full sanction of the law, the parliament and the king. Ultimately, in what is seen as divine justice, James le Gris is killed and Carogne compensated for the injury done to his wife.

[131] DeMarco, 'Violence, Law, and Ciceronian Ethics in Chaucer's *Tale of Melibee*', p. 140.

out of prison. He forgives them for this trespass in every way, but says that since Emelye cannot marry them both they must fight to the death for her in an organized and orderly tournament. As Richard Firth Green points out, this willingness to resort to mortal combat reveals a flaw in the fabric of Theseus' justice. He writes, 'A legal system that is prepared to contemplate men fighting to the death on so slim a pretext as a disputed contract is one that provides but minimal protection against the incursions of anarchy – and anarchy [...] lurks darkly in the wings of the *Knight's Tale*'.[132] This observation applies equally to the context in which the *Knight's Tale* was written. Both Chaucer and his audience may have been aware of the anarchy 'lurk[ing] darkly in the wings' in England and the rest of Europe, and these transgressive figures reveal the potential for lawless brutality within their own community. Even though it is set in the distant classical past, told by a narrator with a dubious crusading history, the *Knight's Tale* may be an admonition to those knights who would continue to perpetuate such seemingly pointless brutality. Theseus later retracts his demand for mortal combat and considers "that it were destruccioun/ To gentil blood to fighten in the gyse/ Of mortal bataille now in this emprise'" (lines 2538–40), ordaining instead that they must fight in the lists without lethal weapons or force.

In attempting to contain the violence in the tale, the Knight focuses on the seemingly innocuous chivalric spectacle of the melee and lists. In reality, a jousting field or melee could be a very dangerous place; however, the Knight is concerned with the trappings of valour and the semblance of danger rather than the realities of battlefield violence with which he, and Chaucer, would have been familiar. He describes the shafts of spears shivering to pieces on thick shields, the 'helmes they tohewen and toshrede;/ Out brest the blood with stierne stremes rede;/ With myghty maces the bones they tobreste' (lines 2609–11). Yet, for all this bloodshed no one dies, and the only malice and hatred is between the two rivals who hunt each other down and with 'jelous strokes on hir helmes byte;/ Out rennet blood on bothe hir sydes rede' (lines 2634–5). Even in the final tally after Arcite's fall, 'Al were they soore yhurt, and namely oon, that with a spere was thirled his brest boon' (lines 2709–10); some have broken bones, some apply salves and medicines, and some drink sage to save their limbs. But even the one with the spear in his chest survives. Rather than emphasizing the realistic violence of battle with its deadly consequences, the Knight insists that there is no defeat or dishonour in being unhorsed in a joust or tournament, 'For fallyng nys nat but an aventure' (line 2722). Nor is there any dishonour in being led by force to the stake without having surrendered, or being taken by twenty knights and dragged by 'arme, foot, and too' (line 2726), or his steed driven with staves, 'It nas arretted hym no vileynye;/ Ther may no man clepen it cowardye' (lines

---

132 Richard Firth Green, 'Palamon's Appeal of Treason in the *Knight's Tale*', in *The Letter of the Law: Legal Practice and Literary Production in Medieval England*, ed. Emily Steiner and Candace Barrington (Ithaca NY: Cornell University Press, 2002) 105–14, p. 113.

2729–30). His tale is almost comical in its farcical displays of martial violence as ineffectual and fairly harmless. Perhaps the Knight suffered defeat in the lists or on the battlefield one too many times himself, and in trying to acquit the knights of his tale, he justifies his own failings, which reflect the failings of an entire chivalric class.

The absence of actual brutality despite the catalogue of injuries makes Arcite's death at the whim of Saturn even more pathetic and unfortunate. He survives single combat with Palamon, fights valiantly in the lists though bloodied by Palamon's blows, and wins the day only to be crushed by his horse. The Knight's description of his injuries is far more graphic than the scenes of battle. When Arcite falls he lies as if dead, 'His brest tobrosten with his sadel-bowe./ As blak he lay as any cole or crowe,/ So was the blood yronnen in his face' (lines 2691–3). It is a vivid image of a serious wound, but not one incurred during the course of the organized violence. His death is part of the chaos that Theseus attempts to explain unsuccessfully at the end. Arcite's condition worsens, his breast swells, increasing the pressure on his heart. The clotted blood, despite the efforts of leechcraft, decays and cannot be drained through any medical techniques, and the poison cannot be expelled: 'The pipes of his longes gonne to swelle,/ And every lacerte in his brest adoun/ Is shent with venym and corrupcioun' (lines 2752–4). It is a gruesome and painful death, fraught with lurid detail lacking in the earlier scenes of battle. The time it takes Arcite to die evokes sympathy and makes the final attempts of Theseus to explain it fall short, bringing to mind Palamon's earlier cry to the 'crueel goddes that governe' (line 1303): '"What is governance is in this prescience/ that giltelees tormenteth innocence?"' (lines 1313–14). What is justice when temporal authority cannot control the outcome of violence? As Green notes, whether 'we are being asked to focus on the ordering principles of social hierarchy, or courtly chivalry, or Ricardian polity, or medieval jurisprudence, a recognition of disruptive forces that are entailed by such structures is rarely far away'.[133] Arcite gains the victory but loses his life, and the Knight masks the reality of martial violence in the rhetoric of chivalry and honour. In a world at war, everyone loses – especially when the institutional authorities undermine their own legal traditions by implementing torture and brutality as weapons in that war.

It is this mask that the Miller penetrates in his exposition on justice and punishment in his tale. By situating the violence of the narrative as comedy, the Miller lowers the expectations of brutality and consequence; in a fabliau, no one is ever really supposed to be hurt. However, Nicholas's punishment at the hands of Absolon comes uncomfortably close. In mirroring the language of the Knight, the Miller not only mocks his pretensions and parodies his own base nature, but he also compares the stylized suffering of Arcite and Palamon and mocks the chivalric conventions that often ignore the realities of the violence they portray.

---

[133] Green, 'Palamon's Appeal of Treason', p. 113.

Absolon, who suffers from hot love as surely as Arcite, has his love quenched in the recesses of Alisoun's arse and plots vengeance. Arcite's love for Emelye never diminishes; even as he dies he utters her name. His is not real-world love; it is the *fin amour* of courtly convention, irrelevant to the reality of the Miller and the show of ordered violence in the lists. Instead of calling Alisoun out, or offering to duel Nicholas for her love, Absolon is bent on private revenge. He vows to 'quyte' her, in much the same way the Miller 'quits' the Knight, but he will do it with an appalling savagery and outside the boundaries of his authority or those of civil law: "'My soule bitake I unto Sathanas,/ But me were levere than al this toun," quod he,/ "Of this despit awroken for to be'" (lines 3750–2). He has completely discarded the façade of religious piety with which he shrouded himself in his endeavours to woo Alisoun, and as he borrows the coulter from the local smith he takes on the false persona of a righteous avenger, grasping the cold steel of the handle as he heads off to confront Alisoun. At the window, however, Absolon receives the sweet breath of Nicholas, not Alisoun, though he does not know that when he extracts his pound of flesh:

> And he was redy with his iren hoot,
> And Nicholas amydde the ers he smoot.
>   Of gooth the skyn an hande-brede aboute,
> The hoote kultour brende so his toute,
> And for the smert he wende for to dye.   (lines 3809–13)

Nicholas will not die and his cries will further the final action of the plot when John wakes thinking the flood has come, hacks at the ropes and comes tumbling to the floor, breaking his arm in the process. But Nicholas has been grievously wounded, branded in the buttocks in a brutal display of savagery by a member of the clergy whose responsibility is supposed to rest in the aid and comfort of his fellow man, not in exacting revenge against him. As the jilted and would-be lover, Absolon's desire for revenge is somewhat understandable, though neither it, nor the manner of it, is justified. The damage he planned to inflict on Alisoun would have branded her, literally and figuratively, as an adulteress, and she would have to explain those marks to her husband at the very least. Absolon's brutality transgresses both the social boundaries of marriage and the legal boundaries of vengeance. Nicholas' inadvertent substitution saves Alisoun from the potential consequences of Absolon's revenge, but leaves them all open to potential public censure and ridicule.

Despite Nicholas' cruelty in arranging his tryst with Alisoun by manipulating John's faith, Alisoun's willingness to cuckold her husband and the couple's glee at humiliating Absolon, nothing they do warrants the physical violence employed by Absolon in his rash quest for vengeance. In his lust to punish Alisoun and the subsequent injury to Nicholas, Absolon diminishes any sympathy the audience may have had for him. Rather than being laughable, he manifests the brutality lurking in priestly guise within the society. Burger argues that 'branding and kiss remain contiguous and mutually constitutive, however much the tale's ending attempts to hierarchize and substitute one for the other, just as the meaning of *The Knight's Tale* is (re)constructed by *its* forced encounters with the world of *The Miller's Tale*.[134] Farrell notes that 'privy' action is often recognizable as unjust,[135] and thus Absolon's vengeance, conducted as a secret act of personal revenge intended for another man's wife, is inherently unjust. It is not his place to punish either Alisoun, his intended target over whom he has no jurisdiction, or Nicholas, who has a valid grievance once he is branded; though Absolon, as a cleric, falls under Church jurisdiction rather than civil authority. Absolon goes from victim to persecutor, and in using a hot coulter against Nicholas merely for mocking him Absolon raises the spectre of judicial torture. Absolon has violated the principles of religious office in taking personal revenge in anger. The *Fasciculus Morum*, a treatise on the Seven Deadly Sins written by an unknown Franciscan in England in the early fourteenth century, clearly outlines the dangers of giving in to anger and cruelty:[136] wrath that is sinful is that born from an unbridled desire for vengeance, as expounded by Augustine.[137] The 'members' of wrath are hate and revenge, and one of the evil consequences of wrath is that it makes 'a person who suffers from it a member of the devil'.[138] Absolon embodies this kind of wrath, and Chaucer aligns him with this prohibited vengeance by having him as swear by Satan and by making the implement of his burning hatred a red-hot coulter. Absolon defies the very proscriptions of his vocation, and the admonitions of Augustine in the *City of God*, exacting a brutal revenge that is outside the boundaries of law, but manages to stay within the bounds of comedy because the full effect of his actions never materializes. It can still be funny because the consequences are mitigated; but it is not simply comic because of the lingering sense of brutality. As in the *Melibee*, this suggests that Chaucer was being 'more Augustinian – or rather more a Romanist – than Augustine himself at this moment, refusing to allow the doctrine that "war punishes sinners" to be conflated with a justification of warfare'.[139] There is no justification for Absolon's actions, though comedy suggests there need not be. Not only does he have no right to punish anyone; he transgresses his religious position by seeking Alisoun's favours in the first place. He embodies all of the cultural anxieties about corrupt clergy, a diseased Church and the excessive brutality of ecclesiastical justice in the application of canon law, from which English audiences may wish to distance themselves.

---

[134] Burger, 'Erotic Discipline', p. 251.
[135] Farrell, 'Privacy and the Boundaries', p. 776.
[136] Smail and Gibson, *Vengeance in Medieval Europe*, p. 363.
[137] *Fasciculus Morum* (2.1). *Fasciculus Morum: A Fourteenth-Century Preacher's Handbook*, trans. Siegfried Wenzel (University Park: Pennsylvania State University Press, 1989) 117–33; reproduced in Smail and Gibson, *Vengeance in Medieval Europe*, pp. 363–80.
[138] *Fasciculus Morum* (2.2); Smail and Gibson, *Vengeance in Medieval Europe*, p. 364.
[139] DeMarco, 'Violence, Law, and Ciceronian Ethics in Chaucer's *Tale of Melibee*', p. 144.

Bowker argues that Nicholas and Alisoun are the worst of these characters, that their antics are cruel and sinister, and yet he barely mentions Absolon's response or the violence with which he takes his revenge, except to say that as an audience, 'we have been allowed to laugh with Alisoun and Nicholas at his posturing and ridiculous pretences to courtly love; but nothing has prepared us for the depth of his anger and the cruelty of his reprisal'.[140] However, the Knight's tale and the Miller's skill at matching his story point for point have prepared the audience for a particularly violent response; the Miller essentially depicts what would happen in his real world if two men contested over the love of beautiful young woman, and if one of them was spurned and humiliated. That is not to say that thwarted lovers were brandishing hot coulters at every turn, but that violence is a part of life and human nature compels people to respond to insults brutally and often with dire consequences if legal structures and social institutions are unstable. The lack of justice for Nicholas (whether he really deserves it or not) highlights a disparity and instability in the judicial system. Nicholas will get no justice. Absolon's action is not a joke; he really intends to cause harm. The image of the prelate wielding a hot iron may have resonated with an audience familiar with inquisitorial interrogation procedures that often called for hot irons because members of the Church were prohibited from shedding blood.[141]

The Miller exposes the realities of retributive violence, but in mitigating the consequences of that violence he maintains the humour by covering up the horror.[142] As Angela Jane Weisl suggests, were this not a fabliau 'whoever was the "butt" of Absolon's joke would be in far too much pain to leap up and help humiliate John the Carpenter – if she or he were not dead'.[143] While the castration episodes of the Old French fabliaux cross the boundaries of humour, the *Miller's Tale* treads lightly, relaying realistic fears but refusing to dampen the comedy with realistic consequences. If the Miller had dwelt on the pain of Nicolas' scalding, it would have thrown off the comic timing in the cascade of events and made it even more difficult to laugh at the outcome. But a subversive social critique is masked by the comedy. Weisl writes that the humour in the *Miller's Tale* takes place against the backdrop of violence against women, which normalizes it by turning it into the punch line of a joke.[144] However, the violence is not actually inflicted on Alisoun; she escapes, unlike the daughter

---

[140] Bowker, 'Comic Illusion', pp. 31–2.
[141] Peters, *Torture*, p. 64. He writes that since secular courts had 'one power which church courts were for a long time denied, the power to shed blood, the Church consistently turned to lay defenders and rulers and courts in cases where clerical personnel were canonically prohibited from acting'.
[142] Angela Jane Weisl, '"Quiting" Eve: Violence against Women in the *Canterbury Tales*', in *Violence Against Women in Medieval Texts*, ed. Anna Roberts (Gainesville FL: University Press of Florida, 1998) 115–36, p. 119.
[143] Weisl, '"Quiting" Eve', p. 119.
[144] Weisl, '"Quiting" Eve', p. 120.

and mother-in-law of *La Dame escoillee*, and Nicholas is branded in her place. At the end of the tale the violence has not been completely normalized because there is an absence of literal justice even if there is a sense of poetic justice in the ensuing predicament. Nor is there justice in the *Knight's Tale*. The scales tip in Palamon's favour, but for Arcite there will be no retribution. No one is really at fault for his death, and all their mindless brutality against one another serves no purpose. In order for the fabliau formula to be completely realized, there must be a sense of triumph and victory enacted through the institution of justice, or the subversion of injustice – just punishments, just revenge, just outcomes – but this tale simply ends:

> Thus swyved was this carpenteris wyf,
> For al his kepyng and his jalousye,
> And Absolon hath kist hir nether ye,
> And Nicholas is scalded in the towte.
> This tale is doon, and God save al the rowte!   (lines 3850–4)

Farrell argues that this ending is the resolution that balances the *Knight's Tale*, revealing a natural path to justice: 'the apparent but deceptive chaos of his conclusion is the other side of the coin first presented in the Knight's overly sanguine depiction of meaning and order'.[145] He writes that in 'quitting' the Knight's tale, 'the grim and dubious battle against chaos [...] gives way to the cheerful surrender to justice in the *Miller's Tale*', suggesting the essentially Christian optimism underlying much of Chaucer's poetry.[146] But in either case, the sense of human justice is misplaced. In order for the Miller's cheerful surrender and humour to succeed, there cannot be any actual recourse to law or suggestion of lasting damage. And in order for the combat in the *Knight's Tale* to balance so each man's prayer is answered, one must *die*. Farrell aptly points out that this tale is 'life-affirming play or "game" in open rebellion against the rules and "ernest" of the *Knight's Tale*', play that was sanctioned by medieval society in order to 'reinvigorate acceptance of the need for rules. Even while it rebels, such play reinforces the order it mocks.'[147] But the tale reinforces the status quo only to an extent, because the rules that are lacking are the rules of civil governance and the suggestion of temporal authority. Each represents the 'Other within', subverting audience expectations of comedy. Theseus represents a figure of authority, but one that is willing to resort to torture if necessary in a rash moment of anger, and one that cannot justify the death of Arcite because it falls outside his realm of law and order. Absolon represents the authority of the Church,[148] but a corrup-

---

[145] Farrell, 'Privacy and the Boundaries', p. 790.
[146] Farrell, 'Privacy and the Boundaries', p. 790.
[147] Farrell, 'Privacy and the Boundaries', p. 790.
[148] Kathryn Walls makes a compelling argument about Absolon's dual professions, cleric and part-time barber-surgeon. She suggests that Absolon's vengeful strike might have reminded Chaucer's audience of surgical procedures that involve cauterization *in ano*, or the probing

tion of that authority in his willingness to resort to punishment reminiscent of torture in his rash anger.[149] In both cases, the resulting violence, whether stylized and highly valorized or mitigated by the exclusion of permanent consequences, seems unnecessary and excessive. The message for English and French audiences is that civilized society cannot exist in a legal vacuum; nations are defined by their application of law and justice, and those alien Others within a society threaten its stability as surely as any outside entity. Though Chaucer does not take his comedy or his violence as far as his earlier French models, the suggestion of excess is the same – those who use violence to wield power are in danger of being controlled by others, or in danger of being overthrown.

Chaucer includes a shadow of brutality and the implications of that brutality, but refocuses the audience response on the humour of the tale at the end, maintaining the sense of comedy. Because Nicholas does not really seem hurt, and his injury remains private even though the action has now become public with John's unfortunate fall and his own injury, the audience of all classes can laugh, both inside the tale and out:

> Whan folk hadde laughen at this nyce cas
> Of Absolon and hende Nicholas,
> Diverse folk diversely they seyde,
> But for the moore part they loughe and pleyde.
> Ne at this tale I saugh no man hym greve,
> But it were oonly Osewold the Reve.   (lines 3855–60)

Their laughter does not celebrate the violence nor necessarily condone it, but acknowledges how close the characters came to actual harm in a wave of comic relief. It is not an uneasy laughter, since no one is really grieved except the Reeve, but the brutality of Absolon's revenge plays on the anxieties of the audience about ecclesiastical abuses, particularly in the placement of the punishment, and suggests the transference of fear, or *schadenfreude*, at Nicholas' misfortune. Unlike the *Knight's Tale* which tries to explain the death of Arcite in plausible and acceptable terms, the *Miller's Tale* simply ends with a laugh, allowing the audience to ponder the significance and the possible unfulfilled consequences of exacting personal vengeance.

As opposed to the Old French castration episodes, the *Miller's Tale* does not cross the boundaries of comic violence. The violence of the *Miller's Tale* is, in

---

of the rectum with sharp instruments, and that when he wounds Nicholas instead of curing him, his action could be seen as morally curative. 'Absolon as Barber-Surgeon', *Chaucer Review* 35.4 (2001): 391–98, pp. 391–2.

[149] Walls notes that Absolon is inappropriately worldly for a parish clerk because of his unchecked worldliness and because of the conflict between his two professions, one which requires him to shed blood, and the other which prohibits it. Walls, 'Absolon as Barber-Surgeon', pp. 392–3. In many ways, Absolon represents a laxity in Church authority and regulations, which may also lead to his intemperate behaviour.

many ways, an extension of the violence in the *Knight's Tale*. The Host attempts to maintain social order by asking the Monk to "quite with the Knyghtes tale'" (line 3119); but instead it is the Miller who requites it, swearing "'By armes, and by blood and bones,/ I kan a noble tale for the nones,/ With which I wol now quite the Knyghtes tale'" (lines 3125–27). By arms, blood and bones, the Miller will requite the Knight, suggesting not only the parallel structure that follows, but also a recognition on the part of the Miller that violence is necessary to match the previous tale accurately. As Lee Patterson notes, the Miller's tale brilliantly enacts the very 'quiting' that it narrates; 'what happens to Absolon, Nicholas, and John *in* the Miller's Tale, in other words, happens to the Knight *by means of* the Miller's Tale'.[150] By potentially misreading the Host's meaning of 'quite' – 'reward' – as 'retaliate', 'he allows into the tale-telling game the linguistic subversion that characterizes his own tale', where seemingly innocuous words are 'all revealed to have meanings that subvert or 'quite' their conventional and intended meanings'.[151] The Miller's interruption is a deliberate contravention of the narrative social order, and though he is portrayed as drunk and ignorant his tale will match the Knight's in structure and form and turn a story of *courtois* into a fabliau. As Helen Cooper writes, the tales 'offer contrasting readings of human experience, of the world in which choices are made and actions are taken. [...] The Knight's Tale had opened up possibilities beyond the courtly, the moral, the providential; the Miller's Tale reads the world not for meaning but for fact.'[152] In his tale, violence is not merely a convention but a fact of physical retribution, and the Miller balances the prosaic and predictable martial violence of the previous tale with unexpected and potentially disastrous brutality. In all senses of the word, the Miller 'quites' the Knight, implying balance; the *Miller's Tale* 'poises equally but oppositely the strengths and weaknesses of its mate. In most respects, the *Miller's Tale* inverts or parodies whatever it finds in the Knight's: fabliau (of a sort) for romance (of a sort); the triangle of Alison, Nicholas, and Absolon for Emily, Palamon, and Arcite; carpenter John for master-builder Theseus and so on.'[153] Part of this inversion includes the juxtaposition of correct and acceptable martial violence against vengeful, rash and inappropriate violence and the institution of private vengeance in place of legal sanction. In order for the tale to end 'well' everyone must be requited, but Nicholas' burned flesh begs the question whether or not everyone receives justice. As Burger suggests, what makes the tale useful to Chaucer and his fourteenth-century audience is its attention to the politics of representation: 'that under the guise of generic and

---

[150] Lee Patterson, '"For the Wyves love of Bathe": Feminine Rhetoric and Poetic Resolution in the *Roman de la Rose* and the *Canterbury Tales*', *Speculum* 58.3 (July 1983): 656–95, p. 685.
[151] Patterson, '"For the Wyves love of Bathe"', p. 685. See also: Lee Patterson, *Chaucer and the Subject of History* (Madison: University of Wisconsin Press, 1991), p. 244.
[152] Cooper, *Oxford Guides to Chaucer*, p. 103.
[153] Farrell, 'Privacy and the Boundaries', p. 787.

social difference – a churl's tale in opposition to the nobility of the knight's – it can take into account the fluid and ambiguous status of gentility in the later Middle Ages as well as their own contradictory position as "new men" within nobility'.[154] But the knight is more a knight of the past than of the present; he has not taken part in any battles of the Hundred Years War unlike his son the Squire – unlike Chaucer himself who had seen service in France as a young squire, was captured and was ransomed from the French by Edward III.[155] His idealization of violence is markedly different from what Chaucer's audience and the poet himself would recognize. It is also markedly different from the reality of martial and chivalric violence of the fourteenth century.

Most critical discussions on the language of the *Miller's Tale*, in conjunction with rhetorical patterns of the Old French fabliaux, focus on the language of sex and the body rather than the rhetoric of violence. Audiences of Chaucer's works are very familiar with the sexual banter of the *Miller's Tale* and Nicolas's friendly groping of Alisoun's *queynte*; however, the conclusion of the tale disengages from the language of sex and turns the action of the narrative to violence and a sense of unmitigated brutality masked in the humour of the fabliaux. The Miller appropriates modes of fabliau violence in direct contradiction of the stylistic and organized bloodshed in the *Knight's Tale*, placing the potential for 'real' harm in the arena of the 'real' world. Farrell argues that the fabliau treats 'whatever kind of justice the tale contains as inessential, and emphasises instead gleeful savagery and insistent vengeance'.[156] But in order for the savagery to evoke glee, the violence must seem ineffectual and superficial, as Nicholas (despite his scalding) can participate in the jovial conclusion of the tale without any evidence of residual harm, unlike the priest in *De Connebert* seeking justice from an unsympathetic judge. This again calls to mind the castration of Abelard and the shockwave it sent though the minds of medieval audiences and poets who often recalled the singular brutality of the incident. Similarly, the murder of Edward II, according to legend sodomized with a hot poker in 1327, had a firm place in the popular imagination in Chaucer's time. Geoffrey le Baker's *Chronicon* (c. 1350), a Latin adaptation of a French chronicle by Thomas de la More, gives a full and graphic description of the King's murder at the hands of a hired assassin.[157] The image of a king deposed and then murdered through violent and suggestively homoerotic means parallels Absolon's vengeance (with far fewer consequences) against Nicholas. Considering that his noble audience was directly related to the unfortunate king, and Richard II, whose reign was

---

154 Burger, 'Erotic Discipline', p. 252.
155 Geoffrey Chaucer, *The Knight's Tale*, ed. A.C. Spearing (Cambridge: Cambridge University Press, 1995), pp. 7–8.
156 Farrell, 'Privacy and the Boundaries', p. 778.
157 The complete details and lasting impact of Edward II's assassination will be addressed more fully in Chapter Six in relation to Christopher Marlowe's sixteenth-century play *Edward II*.

unstable enough, was his great-grandson, Chaucer's comical depiction of this violent act would surely strike a nerve.

The Miller parodies the two-dimensional, blood-soaked violence of the *Knight's Tale*, though Muscatine aptly points out that this is no romantic fairy-castle world: 'the impressive, patterned edifice of the noble life, its dignity and richness, its regard for law and decorum, are all bulwark against the ever-threatening forces of chaos, and in constant collision with them'.[158] However, in the context of the following tale, the patterned edifice of the *Knight's Tale* is not a bulwark against chaos, but a façade to hide the reality of the warring class, where neither war, nor the pursuit of love in its midst, is noble. At a time when Edward III was determined to turn England into a nation at arms by decreeing that no one should play at any sport other than archery,[159] this is the darker side to the Knight's profession that he tries to hide in the trappings of glory, speeches and courtly convention, and the Miller picks up on its more sinister qualities, much like the fabliaux extract meaning from historical events and contemporary practice for its didactic intent. *The Canterbury Tales* as a whole was also composed in a period of uncertainty and instability as the English nobles warred among themselves over their right to the throne, and England and France waged a seemingly endless war over the right of inheritance. The big bloody battles of the Hundred Years War (Poitiers, Crécy) had been fought and chronicled, but the contest of chivalric violence still persisted. Richard II, born at Bordeaux (1367), was often seen as more French than English. Froissart writes that Richard's heart is 'so French that he cannot hide it, but a day will come to pay for all'.[160] Between the Miller and the Knight is not just a contest of class, but a contest of cultural identity, and much like Wat Tyler's short-lived rebellion in 1381, the Miller stands up to the Knight – subtly and through humour. But perhaps the didactic point of both tales, as with the castration narratives of the fabliaux, is that this kind of vengeful violence, perpetrated outside the boundaries of law and sense, really is not funny after all.[161]

The Miller's reversal and appropriation of sexual language are mirrored in the savagery of Absolon's revenge – where the Knight presents chivalric ideals, the

---

[158] Charles Muscatine, 'Form, Texture, and Meaning in Chaucer's *Knight's Tale*', PMLA 65:5 (Sep. 1950): 911–29, p. 929.

[159] Froissart, *Chronicles*, qtd. in West, *Chaucer 1340–1400*, p. 31.

[160] Froissart, *Chronicles*, qtd. in Desmond Seward, *The Hundred Years War: The English in France, 1337–1453* (New York: Atheneum, 1986), p. 127.

[161] Gregory M. Colón Semenza puts forward a compelling comparison between the Knight and Miller as successful athletes, specifically wrestlers, arguing that this distinction levels the playing field between the two, and explains their linguistic battle – as wrestling was more than a pleasant exercise, it was a 'battle in which contestants warred against each other in violent, bloody, and often deadly struggles.' 'Historicizing "Wrastlynge" in the *Miller's Tale*', *The Chaucer Review* 38.1 (2003): 66–82, p. 70.

Miller presents realistic scenarios that intertwine sex and violence.[162] The Miller ridicules the fighting man himself by dealing with real, potentially consequential violence at the end of the tale. The Knight's story is acknowledged as 'worthy for to drawen to memorie,/ And namely the gentils everichon' (lines 3112–13). The 'gentils' are delighted by this noble story, but the Miller even in his cups sees through the gilding of the classical, pagan tale, and reveals the sexuality and the violence in the Knight's narration and the hypocrisy of a knight who elevates himself in verse but is no better than his companions. As Timothy O'Brien writes, 'the typical pattern of romance in which the Knight rescues the injured, detained, or distressed female is reversed, becomes disenchanted, in [the *Knight's Tale*]: the knights' – and the narrating Knight's – attempt to rescue Emelye from the fulfillment and harmony she imagines, to force her into the men's world'.[163] This 'man's world' is one of battle and bloodshed, and the repeated duels over Emelye (unknown and unwilling to either contestant) diminishes the sacrifice of men on the battlefield. The Miller, resorting to a genre filled with inconsequential violence, treads carefully on the boundary of real bodily harm. Even if the tale is a conventional romance, as so many critics have argued, the Miller reverses the Knight's trope and instead creates a female character who is liberated by her own body, does not need to be rescued or fought for and who uses her body not only for her own pleasure – which Emelye seeks to deny herself in perpetual virginity – but to shame the bodies of the men who try to subject her. In attempting to requite her rebuff of his sexual advances through illegitimate violence, Absolon becomes a dangerous figure of unfettered personal vengeance unleashed on Nicholas in Alisoun's stead.

Alisoun draws the men into her world by acting on her sexuality and appropriating *queynte* for her own ends, as does Alisoun of Bath, but in the process leaves herself vulnerable to male retribution – from her husband if she's caught, from other male authorities in her society, and from other jealous suitors, even though they have no claim.[164] She happily lets Nicholas take her place at the window where he receives his (arguably) just punishment for deceiving John and presuming to attempt to manipulate Alisoun. She may be objectified, but she will transcend that inert position with her reaffirmation of agency at the end of the tale. West writes that with the blow of the hot coulter against Nicholas, 'the

---

[162] Patterson, '"For the Wyves love of Bathe"', p. 685. According to Patterson, Chaucer 'asserts that the dynamic of the *Canterbury Tales* will be self-generating rather than derivative, and that in its spontaneity and self-discovery it will resist mechanical and externally imposed structural dispositions, and especially those – such as estates satire – expressive of the established institutions of social authority'.

[163] Timothy D. O'Brien, 'Fire and Blood: "Queynte" Imaginings in Diana's Temple', *Chaucer Review* 33:2 (1998): 157–67, p. 164.

[164] Patterson fully examines the relationship between the Wife of Bath and the Miller, and argues that Alisoun of Bath is a 'force that both controls her own verbal world and the tale-telling game itself'. '"For the Wyves love of Bathe"', p. 687.

Miller has "quitted" the boring pomposity of the *Knight's Tale*.[165] But more than presenting a lively tale in response to a potentially boring one, Chaucer presents reflective views of sexuality and violence – both elements of the fabliau genre often inextricably linked – and interrogates the consequences of individual and excessive brutality in the context of humour. When the Miller's tale is finished and all the arms have been broken, the arses kissed, and the touts scalded, Alisoun alone controls the community response, and she comes out laughing with the crowd as 'every wight gan laughen at this stryf' (line 3849). The company of pilgrims also laugh, reinforcing the Miller's ribald tale but not necessarily the violence within it, though they could also laugh because they *know* that Nicholas can say nothing, and will *not* be able to 'quite' his injury. Perhaps they recognize the narrative elements of the Knight's 'noble storie' embedded in the fabliau of the Miller, his satire and its implications for the social fabric of their own society. Even the Knight seems able to laugh at himself and the witty criticism of his own tale, though it may be uneasy laughter at the revelation of his unintentional sexual humour. The only pilgrim who grieves is the Reeve, who feels he has been made the butt of the Miller's joke. He truly is base and misses the Miller's pointed criticism and sophisticated rhetorical parody. But by this time, the Host has lost all control of the contest, linguistic chaos ensues, and the social order has been left by the wayside as the Reeve ploughs on with his own fabliau of rape and retribution in an attempt to requite the Miller. As Patterson notes, the Reeve's 'jape of malice' (line 4338) indulges the fabliau's 'dark undercurrent of violence and victimization that the Miller's Tale managed to contain if not fully efface'.[166] Though malicious, the *Reeve's Tale* takes a much more conventional route in presenting inconsequential fabliau violence compared to the potential for real harm in Nicholas' scalding. The violence that ends the *Miller's Tale* is more excessive, more realistic than the pageantry and duels of the *Knight's Tale* and Arcite's death. The *Knight's Tale* and the *Miller's Tale* engage in a linguistic duel, juxtaposing sex and violence against a backdrop of two different worlds.

It is difficult to gauge how the fabliaux would have been received; as Muscatine observes, there is 'no simple formula by which we can describe fabliau social attitudes, and it is sometimes difficult to tell precisely what attitude is being evoked by a given poem'.[167] Perhaps these scenes were considered funny precisely because they crossed a boundary of violence and enacted secret retribution. Abelard's critics certainly took some delight in his misfortune, and Christine de Pizan mocks his predicament in her defence of Heloise. The truth of torture was in the eye of the beholder, 'so too was its cruelty and its theater', as Enders reminds

---

[165] West, *Chaucer 1340–1400*, p. 255.
[166] Patterson, '"For the Wyves love of Bathe"', p. 685.
[167] Muscatine, *The Old French Fabliaux*, p. 39.

us.[168] Torture was designed to elicit truth in a legitimate judicial process; but the truth extracted by torture in the fabliaux is that of fear, domination and power; of crime, arrogance and adultery; of transgression and social upheaval; and, for some, the truth of justice. The violence of torture, particularly castration, exceeds even the ubiquitous violence of the fabliaux and renders its presentation shocking and distasteful to some audiences. In the fabliaux, killings are rare, castration and torture even more so; and because of the rarity of torture in the fabliaux and other secular medieval texts, modern audiences and scholars are forced to challenge the preconceptions concerning the Middle Ages that have developed over time and realize that torture has a troubled place in all societies, but in the fabliaux under discussion the portrayal of torture is used to condemn its practice. In much the same way, Chaucer employs fabliaux as a means of subverting conventional norms and testing the boundaries of acceptable societal brutality.

The didactic condemnation of this kind of personal vengeance is evident in the tales of Chaucer, just as it is in *De Connebert*, *Du prestre crucefié* and *La Dame escoillee*. There are limits to the comedy evoked by vengeance and violence. These accounts may not deal directly with episodes of judicial torture within the context of medieval jurisprudence, but they contribute to the body of dissenting literature that places this kind of unmitigated violence outside civilized society and places it firmly within the realm of the Other but the 'Other within'. Embedded in the parody are the cultural anxieties of justice and the question of law. These tales reveal the instability at the very heart of two societies caught up in a literal war of self-definition. In the *Miller's Tale*, as in the three fabliaux, the perpetrator of vengeful brutality dressed in the rhetoric of legal justice is vilified for overstepping social boundaries regulating the application of punishment. Both poet and audience condemn their act as the sympathy is placed on the victims – and their lack of access to justice. Chaucer stops his tale before the implications of this vigilante action can be fully realized, but the injustice of this act resounds throughout *The Canterbury Tales*, masked only temporarily by the audience's laughter.

---

[168] Enders, *The Medieval Theater of Cruelty*, p. 179.

6

Medieval Torture and Early-Modern Identity[1]

> 'The movements grow, gathering simple people who have been aroused by other movements and who believe all have the same impulse of revolt and hope; and they are destroyed by the inquisitors, who attribute to one the errors of the other, and if the sectarians of one movement commit a crime, this crime will be attributed to each sectarian of each movement. The inquisitors are mistaken, rationally speaking, because they lump contradictory doctrines together.'
>
> Brother William of Baskerville, *The Name of the Rose*,
> Umberto Eco (p. 235)

The condemnation of excessive brutality and judicial torture prevalent in medieval literature is among the lasting legacies of the Middle Ages. As European society progressed through the tumultuous fifteenth century and into the early-modern period, the image of brutality as a signifier of medieval barbarity was reimagined in literature and on stage as torture gained a foothold in English jurisprudence. What many early-modern audiences perceived as a 'medieval' practice actually climaxed in the religious and political struggles of the sixteenth century. In the Preface to his *History of the World* (1614), Sir Walter Ralegh commented that 'whosoever in writing a modern History, shall follow truth too near the heels, it may happily strike out his teeth ... It is enough for me ... to write of the eldest times: wherein also why may it not be said, that in speaking of the past, I point at the present, and tax the vices of those that are yet living, in their persons that are long since dead'.[2] The past that early-modern poets and playwrights

---

[1] Much of this chapter was inspired by the National Endowment for the Humanities Teaching Institute 'Inquisitions and Persecutions in Early Modern Europe and the Americas' at the University of Maryland, hosted by the Center for Renaissance and Baroque Studies (13 June–15 July 2005), directed by Adell Seef. I am grateful to my colleagues at that institute for their ideas, suggestions and input.

[2] *Sir Walter Ralegh: Selected Writings*, ed. G. Hammond (Manchester: Carcanet, 1984), pp. 149–50; qtd. in Leah Scragg, 'Saxons Versus Danes: The Anonymous *Edmund Ironside*', in *Literary Appropriations of the Anglo-Saxons from the Thirteenth to the Twentieth Century*, ed. Donald Scragg and Carole Weinberg, Cambridge Studies in Anglo-Saxon England (Cambridge: Cambridge University Press, 2000) 93–106, p. 93.

often looked to for inspiration, and as a veil for commentary on their own time, was the medieval past. The vices and virtues of early-modern monarchs could be explored, critiqued and condemned in the figure of medieval monarchs long dead. The anxieties of national identity (invasion, autonomy, law, legitimacy and religion) and cultural inheritance integrated with questions of justice and correct rule persisted in a continuum from the Middle Ages to the early-modern period. Early-modern poets and playwrights could claim a medieval inheritance in their adaptation of earlier works and histories and situate royal injustice and brutality in the past while illuminating the same traits in their present.

Caught between conflicting notions of English identity grounded in medieval perceptions of the nation and foreign security threats of the sixteenth century, John Foxe creates a distinctly English hagiography from the narratives of his contemporary Protestant martyrs. This chapter situates Foxe's *Actes and Monuments* within the context of medieval hagiography discussed in Chapter 1, focusing on Foxe's negotiation of torture and religious crisis in the early-modern period. William Shakespeare's *Titus Andronicus* and Christopher Marlowe's *Edward II* look to classical and medieval subjects in their plays as a safe space in which to articulate their condemnation of torture in their own time. In his satirical text, *The Unfortunate Traveller*, Thomas Nashe elevates the 'civility' of England in opposition to continental enemies who use torture and brutality wantonly and with impunity.

Judicial torture as an intertextual motif comes to the fore in early-modern literature and plays as torture was used more widely in European jurisprudence – even in England, despite a once-enduring medieval prohibition. The inception of torture in England both licit and illicit created a crisis of identity for a nation that defined itself in opposition to its use throughout the thirteenth and fourteenth centuries. Now England could no longer say 'we do not torture' and the foundation of its national identity grounded in Anglo-Saxon notions of justice was rocked to the core. Early-modern authors followed their medieval predecessors in looking to an idyllic past of law and order, criticizing contemporary rulers through portrayals of medieval ones who either upheld the law (an ideal to be emulated) or subverted it. Ralegh's awareness of the usefulness of history in creating contemporary commentary 'bears witness to the readiness of his contemporaries both to read and deploy historical material as a species of coded comment on the present – a process of transhistorical exchange at work in the drama from as early as the 1530s'.[3] The anonymous *Edmund Ironside* directly engages in the discourse of racial difference and the foreign Other in its portrayal of the Saxons as 'Englishmen' while the Danes look to a 'foreigner' as their king,[4] echoing the anxieties of foreign invasion implied in *Havelok*. The anonymous *A Knack To Know A Knave* (1592) is set in the reign of the Anglo-Saxon

---

[3] Scragg, 'Saxons Versus Danes', p. 94
[4] Scragg, 'Saxons Versus Danes', p. 99.

king Edgar but deals exclusively with sixteenth-century abuses.[5] The English perception of itself was founded on these older traditions and the abuses of the sixteenth century; the religious wars and the introduction of torture in England vitiated that national identity.

From the twelfth century, English law forbade torture and its application in select instances was resisted by secular and religious authorities, except in the case of the Knights Templar (discussed in Chapter 4); but the use of both interrogative and punitive torture was on the rise at the close of the fifteenth century, and became a frequent threat during the reign of Henry VIII. Mutilation as a form of punishment largely ceased by the fourteenth century, and Bellamy notes that if there were no other 'penalties of the body' in the fifteenth century, they were common again under the Tudors.[6] Elizabeth Hanson notes that the use of torture in Elizabethan England was an aberration in English juridical practice, 'a brief departure from a legal tradition that abhorred and ridiculed the highly organized practice of judicial torture on the Continent'.[7] Its immediate purpose was political repression, like modern torture, a 'form of official terrorism, used to crush perceived dangers to the Elizabethan state, particularly, although by no means exclusively, the persistence and spread of Roman Catholicism'.[8] In such cases, an English audience might embrace torture as a weapon against foreign enemies, a means of protecting England from encroaching Continental influences. But the rejection of torture in early-modern literature and drama and its situation in the realm of the Other suggests an uncomfortable relationship between torture and security that destabilizes traditional notions of English justice and identity. Public authorities characterized the use of torture in the official warrants as the acquisition of knowledge, the same quest for truth that characterized its use in earlier periods.[9] However, the victims of this torture, and the most vocal opponents to its use, were Catholics who under Elizabethan rule were accused of treason rather than religious dissent. As Susannah Brietz Monta points out, since Catholics died under charges of treason and 'were targeted by polemicists imagining secretive, hidden traitors, their martyrologists focus insistently on questions of truth and distortion, inwardness and authenticity'.[10] As a consequence, torture becomes a didactic propaganda weapon in early-modern England, not only in the competing martyrologies of Protestants and Catholics, but also in literary texts and dramatic performances, taking centre stage in the

---

[5] Scragg, 'Saxons Versus Danes', p. 95.
[6] Bellamy, *Crime and Public Order*, p. 181.
[7] Elizabeth Hanson, 'Torture and Truth in Renaissance England', *Representations* 34 (Spring 1991): 53–84, p. 53.
[8] Hanson, 'Torture and Truth', p. 53.
[9] Hanson, 'Torture and Truth', p. 53.
[10] Susannah Brietz Monta, *Martyrdom and Literature in Early Modern England* (Cambridge: Cambridge University Press, 2005), p. 24.

early-modern imagination where it had lingered in the wings of the medieval mind.

As the examples of the preceding chapters have demonstrated, medieval literary works rarely embrace torture or judicial brutality as a motif except as a means of condemning corrupt authority, highlighting the brutality of certain characters as the barbarian Other or testing the boundaries of authority in a comic milieu. Literary and dramatic texts of the sixteenth century adopt a similar aversion to displays of torture or excessive brutality, not because they reject a supposed inheritance from earlier eras, but because the increased frequency of torture in the public sphere required public response. In the Tudor and Stuart periods, the English did 'experiment' with using torture to investigate crime, primarily treason, and there was a spike in known torture cases when the Reformation and the threat of Spanish invasion 'induced a sense of extreme national peril about domestic plots and foreign intrigue'.[11] Fears of invasion and religious corruption by an alien Other (in this case Spanish and French) led to the introduction of torture in English jurisprudence by Henry VIII – a policy that was embraced by his daughter Mary, and only diminished slightly during the reign of Elizabeth I.

There is evidence that torture may have been occasionally employed in England from the reign of Richard III, but it was during Elizabeth's reign that interrogatory torture became increasingly a 'recognized, although always unusual, part of the prosecution of important cases of felony'.[12] Bellamy points out that torture was essentially a Tudor development, with its formative years most likely in the 1520s and 1530s – though common lawyers claimed it was never practised under common law except on the fiat of the monarch.[13] In the early 1580s and early 1590s, the government's use of torture came under criticism, so the practice was briefly suspended, but 'it was thought too valuable to surrender entirely and so was soon reinstated'.[14] The rack was applied fairly frequently during the reign of Henry VIII, and in both the Yorkist and Tudor periods, torture was applied before trial, even before indictment or appeal.[15] As the seeds of the Reformation were planted throughout medieval Europe, and the Church struggled to maintain its hold on an increasingly fractious populace, the use and public spectacle of torture swelled, and its presence was felt in the popular imagination through literary and dramatic texts in a way somewhat foreign to most medieval texts.

---

[11] Langbein, *Torture and the Law of Proof*, pp. x-xi.

[12] Hanson, 'Torture and Truth', p. 57. Hanson's excellent study centres on the epistemological dualism 'as it manifests itself in the discursive practices that impinged on English torture' (p. 56). Stephen Greenblatt refers to the unrest and class hostility that afflicted England 'sporadically' throughout Elizabeth's reign that heightened tensions (pp. 14–15). 'Murdering Peasants: Status, Genre, and the Representations of Rebellion', *Representations* 1 (Feb. 1983): 1–29.

[13] John Bellamy, *Strange, Inhuman Deaths: Murder in Tudor England* (Stroud: Sutton, 2005), p. 186.

[14] Bellamy, *Strange, Inhuman Deaths*, p. 186.

[15] Bellamy, *Crime and Public Order*, p. 140.

In England, the use of torture suggests a conceptual alliance with the epistemology of discovery,[16] where it occurred within the context of developing criminal procedures and investigations and was defended by such notable philosophers and lawyers as Francis Bacon, who saw it as a means of discovery. But after the promulgation in 1570 of the papal bull *Regnans in excelsis* absolving Elizabeth's Catholic subjects of their loyalty to her, 'incidents of torture increased as the government struggled to detect the alleged treasonous activities of Catholic missionary priests'.[17] Margaret Owens argues that the Reformation figured as a traumatic rupture in sixteenth-century English culture, insofar as it 'ushered in a period of violent confrontations between government authorities and resistant individuals and movements'.[18] Where medieval literature often shies away from representations of torture, except in hagiography and the brutal depictions of the Passion, early-modern literature and drama tenuously embrace torture as a literary motif reflecting the increasing prevalence of torture in secular and religious prosecution and persecution, and as public spectacle. Torture was formally abolished in England in 1640 and in Scotland by Act of Parliament in 1708, suggesting a greater resistance to torture among early-modern cultures and the emergence of new attitudes toward the use of torture as punishment and discipline,[19] just as there was a significant aversion to torture within medieval culture, especially in societies that regularly employed it in judicial proceedings. According to Foucault, 'from the point of view of the law that imposes it, public torture and execution must be spectacular; it must be seen by all almost as its triumph. The very excess of the violence employed is one of the elements of its glory'.[20] But as the preceding chapters illustrate, the public spectacle of torture and brutality in medieval literary sources often backfires on those who employ it. Often the spectacle is what turns the audience from affirming power to resisting it and ultimately, as Scarry has pointed out, undermining the power structure that relies on these public spectacles. This potential for destabilization is a factor in the *Roland*, *Havelok*, Old Norse/Icelandic sagas, medieval hagiography and particularly in Chaucer's *Canterbury Tales*, where societal constraints are stretched and hierarchical structures parodied. Like their medieval predecessors,

---

[16] Hanson, 'Torture and Truth', pp. 54–55.
[17] Hanson, 'Torture and Truth', p. 57.
[18] Owens, *Stages of Dismemberment*, p. 22. Cynthia Marshall examines the erotics of violence, and the visual voyeurism of brutal acts as pornographic experiences in Foxes' *Actes and Monuments* and Shakespeare's *Titus Andronicus*. *The Shattering of the Self: Violence, Subjectivity and Early Modern Texts* (Baltimore: The Johns Hopkins University Press, 2002). Liz Oakley-Brown argues that *Titus* 'exhibits a nuanced fascination with the rituals and rhetoric of Elizabethan queenship' (p. 223). '"My lord, be ruled by me": Shakespeare's Tamora and the Failure of Queenship', in *The Rituals and Rhetoric of Queenship: Medieval to Early Modern*, ed. Liz Oakley-Brown and Louise J. Wilkinson (Dublin: Four Courts, 2009), 222–37.
[19] Molly Eso Smith, 'Spectacles of Torment in *Titus Andronicus*', *Studies in English Literature, 1500–1900* 36.2 Tudor and Stuart Drama (Spring 1996): 315–31, p. 318.
[20] Foucault, *Discipline and Punish*, p. 34.

many early-modern poets, playwrights, and authors resist the climate of violence and the resort to torture created by these events. While fully engaging in violent spectacle, they reject its necessity and generally condemn its use. Early-modern audiences were no more immune to depictions of brutality and torture than their medieval predecessors, but torture had a more visible and immediate presence in early-modern culture because of the Reformation and the religious and political upheaval that accompanied its inception. As medieval authors often distanced themselves from acts of cruelty and barbarism, so too did Henrician and Elizabethan poets and playwrights – even those engaged in perpetuating portrayals of torture in the exchange of martyrologies produced during the Reformation. Using medieval motifs of brutality, particularly in hagiography, early-modern English authors often situated torture and excessive violence outside their own society. These authors placed it in the classical and medieval past, imagining their world as more civilized than previous generations, while at the same time negotiating the prolific application of torture within their own judicial present.

Baraz identifies a momentous change in the cultural role of cruelty in the period between the middle of the fifteenth century and the sixteenth century, a change that cannot be seen only in terms of continuity with medieval developments.[21] He specifically examines 'the sheer quantity and range of cultural preoccupations with cruelty',[22] attributing much of this development to the atrocities committed on both sides in the wars of religion and the violence that accompanied the conquest of the New World. For Baraz, one of the most notable traits of this violent evolution is the widespread repercussion of early-modern cruelty where medieval brutality was often localized; and in certain respects he portrays early-modern texts as 'the outcome of an accelerated development of medieval tendencies'.[23] Early-modern texts use the same 'late-medieval building blocks' for representing cruelty in the form of massacres, sexual violence and cannibalism, as Baraz suggests,[24] but also for representing *torture* which carries significant cultural weight in early-modern discourses on power, corruption and abuse. Daryl W. Palmer suggests that what determines the severity of any given culture is how its members create and enforce limits on violence: 'More often than not, those limits will take shape in either judicial or religious terms. In the figure of the judge and the priest, a culture authorises interpretative practices that represent violence and make it productive. [...] According to their renderings, the death of a given victim may become a powerful triumph of secular and divine justice.'[25] But the deaths of these victims and the spectacle of the violence

---

[21] Baraz, *Medieval Cruelty*, p. 143.
[22] Baraz, *Medieval Cruelty*, p. 143.
[23] Baraz, *Medieval Cruelty*, p. 144.
[24] Baraz, *Medieval Cruelty*, p. 144.
[25] Daryl W. Palmer, 'Histories of Violence and the Writer's Hand: Foxe's *Actes and Monuments* and Shakespeare's *Titus Andronicus*', in *Reading and Writing in Shakespeare*, ed. David M. Bergeron (Newark NJ: University of Delaware Press, 1996) 82–115; p. 82.

inflicted upon them could also have reverse effects, inspiring resistance and disapproval rather than approbation, particularly in cases where judicial torture is applied excessively or in contravention of acceptable limits. Early-modern authors portrayed torture in the same way as medieval authors: as a delineation of the cultural Other, a mark of barbarism and tyranny, and an anathema to the progress of civilization and justice; and early-modern audiences responded in a similar vein to these spectacles. This rejection of torture takes on an additional dimension in the cultural anxieties of sixteenth-century England concerning the influence of Spain and Spanish judicial practice. A papal bull of 1478 authorized the Spanish monarchs Ferdinand and Isabella to appoint their own inquisitors, and the 'political needs of the state often affected Inquisitorial actions'.[26] This included the widespread use of interrogatory torture, which met with popular resistance, even in Spain. Patricia Manning writes, 'Almost immediately after its inception, writings against the Spanish Inquisition polemicized the institution on the Iberian peninsula and helped to launch a negative image of Spain that would culminate in the "leyenda negra" or Black Legend'.[27] Spain's power and influence threatened to subsume England by the mid-sixteenth century, especially with Mary's marriage to Philip II and his later claims to the English throne after her death, culminating in the defeat of the Spanish Armada in 1588. During Mary's reign torture was used on a wide variety of suspects: witches, robbers, horse thieves and rioters as well as traitors.[28] England's national identity, grounded in justice and a legal rejection of torture, was also threatened as England began to employ the same tactics as its enemies.

Torture is a symptom of instability in both the medieval and early modern periods. As regimes attempted to consolidate power or reaffirm a tenuous grasp on authority, they often resorted to drastic means of interrogation and control.[29] In a detailed analysis of legal records, Lisa Silverman provides an effective and graphic description of the evolution of torture in the Languedoc region from the tumultuous years of the thirteenth century through to the abolition of torture in French legal proceedings in the eighteenth century. Torture came into common usage 'as those who sought to govern turned to written codes of law to define the boundaries of their legal control, and it served to announce the independence of local political elites from seigneurial control as much as it served to curtail local

---

[26] Patricia W. Manning, *Voicing Dissent in Seventeeth-Century Spain: Inquisition, Social Criticism and Theology in the Case of* El Criticón, The Medieval and Early Modern Iberian World, Vol. 37 (Leiden: Koninklijke Brill, 2009), p. 1.

[27] Manning, *Voicing Dissent in Seventeeth-Century Spain*, p. 1.

[28] Bellamy, *Strange, Inhuman Deaths*, p. 186.

[29] Rebecca Lemon investigates the nearly hysterical paranoia of Elizabethan and Jacobean regimes in the context of treason and rebellion, and its influence in early-modern texts like *Richard II*, *Macbeth* and Donne's *Pseudo-Martyr*. She illuminates 'crises of sovereignty' where the government's reaction often undermines its legitimacy (p. 5). *Treason by Words: Literature, Law and Rebellion in Shakespeare's England* (Ithaca NY : Cornell University Press, 2006).

political conflict through coercion'.[30] Torture was an instrument of interrogation wielded in witch trials in the German principalities in the sixteenth century[31] and also in France, plagued by internal dissension and war that came to a head in the St Bartholomew's Day Massacre on 24 August 1572. Michel de Montaigne was so disgusted by what he saw as the corruption and disease of the French state that he compared the French monarchy and its inquisitors to cannibals, finding the cannibals to be more merciful and just. He writes,

> I consider it more barbarous to eat a man alive than to eat him dead; to tear by rack and torture a body still full of feeling, to roast it by degrees, and then give it to be trampled and eaten by dogs and swine – a practice which we have not only read about, but seen within recent memory, not between ancient enemies, but between neighbours and fellow-citizens and, what is worse, under the cloak of piety and religion – than to roast and eat a man after he is dead.[32]

The original logic behind the institution of interrogatory torture had long been lost and forgotten. Silverman contends that in the medieval context judicial torture possessed not only an institutional logic but a cultural logic, and that it made sense as a form of testimony, testifying both to the 'meaningfulness of human suffering and the corresponding valuelessness of human volition, and to the intimate connections among pain, truth, and the body'.[33] She acknowledges that the 'deliberate infliction of suffering in the cause of truth is a history that is peculiarly located in the south of France', but asserts that it has resonance for all of France,[34] and indeed for all of medieval Europe. The result is that 500 years after the introduction of torture in Toulouse and Languedoc, *parlementaires* and

---

[30] Lisa Silverman, *Tortured Subjects: Pain, Truth, and the Body in Early Modern France* (Chicago: University of Chicago Press, 2001), p. 7. Silverman's detailed study of judicial records between 1600 and 1780, when torture was banned from French legal procedure, indicates a decline in the deployment of torture during that period. She presents compelling evidence that interrogations reveal the gradual 'breakdown of the epistemology of torture' (p. 71). However, the extent to which this represents a continuation of medieval practice before 1600 is uncertain. There were waves of atrocities involving torture at the hands of inquisitorial authorities during the thirteenth-century persecution of the Albigensians and other heterodox sects, but whether the application of torture was consistent in this area throughout the medieval period is more difficult to ascertain.

[31] Arno Borst, *Medieval Worlds: Barbarians, Heretics, and Artists in the Middle Ages* (Chicago: The University of Chicago Press, 1996), p. 102.

[32] Michel de Montaigne, 'Of Cannibals', *Michel de Montaigne: Essays*, trans. J.M. Cohen (London: Penguin Classics, 1993) 105–19, p. 113.

[33] Silverman, *Tortured Subjects*, pp. 7–8.

[34] Silverman, *Tortured Subjects*, p. 8. Silverman also contrasts discussions about torture in modern society with those of the early-modern period. She correctly points out that while modern discussion envisions situations where pain is inflicted on a victim cruelly and arbitrarily by a governing regime 'for no other purpose than the physical and psychological destruction of its enemies', in early-modern France torture was not employed arbitrarily at the will of interrogators (p. 23). She also notes, 'we do not believe that torture produces reliable evidence, despite our acknowledgement that some truths are spoken under torture', whereas

philosophes came to debate the potential meaning of human suffering, a debate that would lead to the abolition of torture in the French system.[35] England was caught between the power of France and Spain and, feeling threatened, resorted to the same methods, undermining the very fabric of English national identity. English literary texts of the sixteenth century, like their medieval predecessors, interrogate the use of torture as a facet of national identity and likewise reject its use, relegating it to the realm of the barbarian Other.

One possible explanation for this shift in the polemics of torture may be that the political and religious anxieties of the early modern period were more deeply embedded – the rhetoric and language of persecution, torture and inquisition were more widely publicized than in the medieval period. John Lydgate (ca.1370– ca.1451) rejected the 'new emphasis on irrational cruelty and the increasingly explicit representation of sexual cruelty',[36] and the reluctance to adopt the new discourse is evident in the writings of William Cardinal Allen,[37] one of Elizabeth's most ardent critics, who 'used strictly legalistic medieval notions of cruelty to distinguish between Catholic persecution of Protestants and Protestant persecution of Catholics'.[38] This language entered the lexicon more widely and with it images and descriptions of torture appear to have become more popular in secular literature, without the stigma attached to episodes of torture in medieval texts. Torture seems to be more prevalent in early-modern secular literature because the discourse about torture (not necessarily the practice itself) was more open. From the Middle Ages to the early-modern period there appears to be an escalation in the presence of torture in literature; it enters the public discourse through secular literature as well as religious narratives and is not confined to hagiography or martyrology but appears in adventure novels, plays and poetry with a startling frequency in contrast to medieval antecedents.

The barrage of graphic images is not restricted to words and narratives alone. The woodcuts[39] that accompany many of these texts are exceptionally detailed, depicting the cruellest torments and the grimmest executions as part of a politico-religious propaganda blitz that washed through Europe throughout the sixteenth century. As literacy increased, book production developed with the advent of the printing press and these narratives became widely available to more diverse audiences. The development of theatres and play performance also meant that

---

truth was the primary goal of applying torture in both medieval and early-modern judicial proceedings (p. 23).

[35] Silverman, *Tortured Subjects*, p. 8.

[36] Baraz, *Medieval Cruelty*, p. 144.

[37] William Allen, *A True, Sincere, and Modest Defense of English Catholics*, ed. Robert M. Kingdon (Ithaca NY: Cornell University Press, 1965).

[38] Baraz, *Medieval Cruelty*, p. 144.

[39] Hanson notes that works such as Allen's *A briefe historie of the glorious martyrdom of the xij reverend priests* (1582), Robert Person's *An epistle of the persecution of Catholickes in England* (1582), and Richard Verstegan's *Theatrum Crudelitatum haereticorum nostri temporis* (1587) 'represented, both in text and picture, racking, disembowelling, and other cruelties' (p. 59).

texts and plays reached a far wider audience, both noble and common. Visual representations of brutality and torture circulated widely, and the artistic renderings accompanying martyr narratives reinforced the visual and visceral aspects of torture for reading audiences. Merback examines the work of Lucas Cranach the Elder, who produced a set of twelve woodcuts depicting the martyrdoms of the Twelve Apostles for his patron Frederick the Wise of Saxony (*ca.* 1512), and their reproduction and reception in the Protestant era.[40] In their original form, these woodcuts 'pack a visceral punch unmatched in the blood-spattered history of European religious art', but this imagery was reproduced and harnessed to successive editions of *Das Symbolum der Heiligen Aposteln* (*The Apostles' Creed*) with Martin Luther's catechetical gloss, and 'reactivated to uphold the cause of Lutheran religious indoctrination in a critical, later phase of the Reformation (roughly the 1530s and 1540s)'.[41]

In the early upheaval of the Reformation, Protestant reformers relied on the popular images of medieval saints to reinforce the doctrine of suffering and sacrifice necessary to produce actual reform, even if they considered the tradition that produced these earlier images and narratives corrupt, much like medieval heterodox sects may have used hagiography and the graphic accounts of torture as models of resistance against Church authorities. Merback notes that these images are a product of a time notorious for societal violence that manifests in artistic imagery and literary narratives. He writes,

> In the history of punishment the sixteenth century holds a special and, one could say, notorious place. Cranach's generation lived through a more rapid absorption of Roman law into European jurisprudence than in previous centuries and saw the criminal justice system expand to encompass a wider variety of punishable offenses – mostly those against property – and harsher penalties. The brutal and spectacular public punishments often ascribed to the Middle Ages *en bloc* actually reached their bloody zenith toward the middle of the century (execution rates for most European cities began to decline after 1600). Punishment functioned in large part as deterrent theater, a ritual of retribution staged by authorities, usually with the active cooperation of the community, whose interest in securing a good, Christian death (*bene moriendi*) for the penitent convict was paramount.[42]

Torture often takes centre stage in performances of this 'deterrent theater' as political opponents and religious dissenters were often subjected to torture in the interests of 'discovery' and truth. Both sides levied accusations of barbarity against the Other, and societies that had tried to distance themselves from the use of torture through literary protest in the thirteenth and fourteenth century

---

[40] Mitchell B. Merback, 'Torture and Teaching: The Reception of Lucas Cranach the Elder's Martyrdom of the Twelve Apostles in the Protestant Era', *Art Journal* 57:1 The Reception of Christian Devotional Art (Spring 1998): 14–23.
[41] Merback, 'Torture and Teaching', p. 14.
[42] Merback, 'Torture and Teaching', p. 20.

found themselves enmeshed in a crisis of national identity as the use of torture seemed to pervade Europe.

While the torture itself may not have been conducted in public, its effects were often visible later when capital sentences were carried out, or when the sufferings of these victims were publicized in written accounts. Medieval culture also included the 'spectacular juridical display of real punishment'[43] as well as dramatic episodes of figurative violence, but public displays of capital punishment took on a cultural urgency during the Reformation and the political unrest that accompanied shifting religious adherence. In prose texts like Nashe's *The Unfortunate Traveller* (1594), set during the not-so-distant-past of Henry VIII's reign, graphic accounts of torture are recited with a certain amount of approval and satisfaction, a rhetorical phenomenon unusual in, though not completely absent from, medieval secular literature. As the previous chapters have attempted to show, there is a taint of excess associated with torture, that, when applied, is wielded primarily by the dishonourable or as part of a dangerous mob response, such as the public approbation of the public executions in *The Unfortunate Traveller* that mirror medieval antecedents like the *Prioress's Tale*. Much like Voltaire's *Candide* which criticizes the judicial barbarities of the eighteenth century, Nashe's comic text parodies these events, farcically exaggerating them in pointed condemnation of institutional corruption. In early-modern secular literature torture appears to be more prevalent, but it is not always depicted with approbation, nor does its proliferation suggest that early-modern audiences were any more bloodthirsty than their medieval predecessors. Torture was clearly in the minds of early-modern audiences who understood its shadowy nature and who saw its brutal results enacted in the public sphere of political and religious dissent. Shakespeare, Marlowe and Nashe, among others, write torture into their plays and stories, in some cases as a part of the historical record, as in *Edward II*, in others as recognizable literary motifs that reflect the upheaval of their own age.

This literary progression of torture narratives contrasts sharply with images of the Middle Ages propagated by early-modern authors such as John Foxe in his *Actes and Monuments* (1563), and maintained by some early-modern scholars who see the medieval period as the progenitor of the barbarity and cruelty which the early-modern period merely inherited. According to Baraz, Foxe abandoned the path set by accounts of late-medieval Catholic martyrdom, rejecting the hagiographic traditions of the *Legenda aurea* in favour of compilations like Eusebius's *Historia ecclesiastica* 'in their factual, unsentimental tone and the detailed *acta*-like documentation they supply'.[44] In these martyrologies the emphasis is on the cruelty of the persecutors, not the graphic descriptions of torture and brutality, though Foxe does reproduce them. Baraz writes, 'cruelty ceases to be an absolute

---

[43] Enders, *Medieval Theater of Cruelty*, p. 209.
[44] Baraz, *Medieval Cruelty*, p. 145.

ethical entity as these works adopt a quantitative and comparative approach. Cruelty is measured and rated according to various criteria, such as the severity of the actions committed and the number of victims.'[45] However, a quantitative valuation does not completely apply to the discourse of torture, which still relies on the capacity of the victim – the individual – to endure heinous torments. Foxe found many reasons to be 'contemptuous' of the *LgA* and other medieval hagiography, but one of the most fundamental was that they distorted what he regarded as pure stories with miracles and fables.[46] His accounts of religious suffering and torture, grounded in eye-witness reports and in some instances credible first-person narratives, mark a distinct shift in the literary representation of torture from the Middle Ages to the early-modern period. The fantastic or purely literary motifs of torture and brutality in thirteenth- and fourteenth-century literature give way to *real*, recorded episodes of torture shaped into literary narratives. In such circumstances it is difficult to place the use of torture outside of English society in the realm of the Other because there are *witnesses*. In the early-modern period, the prevalence of persecution, torture and inquisition, and the pervasive anxiety about these procedures and their necessity, create a more visible discourse of torture in popular literature, both religious and secular. It informs and shapes the nature of early-modern narratives, undermining the cultural inheritance of English national identity because of its painful presence in the political process.

John Foxe: *Actes and Monuments*

The most obvious outlet for these complex and often contradictory anxieties is the martyrologies written on both sides of the religious divide. Monta's examination of competing discourses of persecution and execution during the sixteenth century provides compelling evidence of the pervasive influence these texts had on English literature and religious culture.[47] She notes that nine complete editions of John Foxe's *Book of Martyrs* were produced by 1684, and over fifty works concerning the persecution of English Catholics were published between 1566 and 1660.[48] In 1570 a copy of *Actes and Monuments* was placed in every English church; it was not only a religious text, but also a historical text that captured the development of English nationalism and identity, and 'writing, reading, and martyring had become fixtures in – even props of – English life.'[49] Like their antecedent medieval hagiographies, early-modern martyrologies used

---

[45] Baraz, *Medieval Cruelty*, p. 145.
[46] John R. Knott, 'John Foxe and the Joy of Suffering', *Sixteenth Century Journal* 27:3 (Autumn, 1996): 721–34, p. 725.
[47] Monta, *Martyrdom and Literature*, p. 1.
[48] Monta, *Martyrdom and Literature*, p. 1.
[49] Palmer, 'Histories of Violence', p. 86.

the discourse of torture as a political tool to further their religious aims and to reinforce the sanctity of their martyrs in a consistent display of propaganda. As Monta notes, 'martyrologies, texts seeking to draw firm boundaries between saint and sinner, often overlap uncomfortably with their polemical opposites in their rhetoric, conventions, and assumptions'.[50] As a consequence, each discourse must struggle to shape itself without the sense of similarity or shared inheritance. Even though Foxe rejected the early-Christian and medieval emphasis on the 'exceptional nature of martyrs and on the disjunction between vulnerable body and transported soul' and focused instead on the 'human qualities of his Protestant martyrs and the communal experience of the persecuted faithful',[51] he grounded his exposition on Christian suffering in the medieval hagiographic tradition with similar emphasis on the saint's ability to withstand torture without outward signs of pain. Foxe's work provided a 'bridge' for English Protestants, connecting themselves (via the Lollards, the Henrician and Marian martyrs) with the apostles and early Christian martyrs persecuted by Rome.[52] In early-modern religious literature, torture retains its sanctifying purpose in both Catholic and Protestant polemics; however, outside the earlier formulaic accounts included by Foxe, its presence is limited to factual accounts of actual torment.

After the establishment of the Spanish Inquisition in 1478 torture acquired a more sinister public presence in varying accounts of Catholic oppression and in Catholic responses to later Elizabethan repression.[53] Reformers who highlighted the corruption of the Church as an institution decried the application of torture as an interrogation method by the authorities in Spain, citing its barbarous traditions and calling for its dissolution.[54] Torture became a weapon of popular opinion by playing on cultural anxieties about national and religious identity; those who used it were demonized in the public sphere, but it was used with increasing frequency by secular authorities threatened by religious and political destabilization. In Spain, the establishment of the Inquisition shaped the popular discourse. In England and the Continent, the Reformation, with all its rhetoric of competing martyrologies, legitimized violence in the public sphere as a means of identifying and contextualizing the suffering of martyrs, both Protestant and Catholic. This competing discourse of torture contradicted earlier associations of torture as a means of discovering *truth*. As Hanson points

---

[50] Monta, *Martyrdom and Literature*, p. 1.
[51] Knott, 'John Foxe and the Joy of Suffering', p. 721.
[52] Thomas S. Freeman, 'Over their Dead Bodies: Concepts of Martyrdom in Late-Medieval and Early-Modern England', *Martyrs and Martyrdom in England, c. 1400–1700*, ed. Thomas S. Freeman and Thomas F. Mayer (Woodbridge: The Boydell Press, 2007) 1–34, p. 1.
[53] Arthur Williamson provides a comprehensive discussion of competing narratives of martyrdom, salvation and apocalypse in Spain and England during the early-modern period. *Apocalypse Then: Prophecy and the Making of the Modern World* (Westport CT: Praeger, 2008).
[54] Williamson, *Apocalypse Then*.

out, 'it would be a mistake to regard torture as yet another enactment (like the anatomy lesson) of the epistemology of discovery, or to regard the objectification of truth it entailed as morally equivalent to torture'.[55] She cites the assertions of Catholic opponents of Elizabethan rule, 'the most visible and vocal victims of English torture', that the claimed purpose of torture to discover the truth was fraudulent.[56] Along with these claims of fraud were allegations of abuse, not unlike those levied against medieval inquisitors, that suggested manufactured evidence or forced confessions to 'treasons the torturers had themselves invented'.[57] These merged with the spiritual debate of religious belief and led to the complaint 'that torturers were attempting to discover matters that had to do, not with the alleged treasonable activities of the victims, but with their spiritual experience – matters that were by nature not susceptible to discovery'.[58] Similar accusations were of course often raised against Catholics in this religio-political discourse on torture, and each side portrayed its enemies as barbarians, as the Other, for their use of torture. In the sixteenth century, this depiction played to the fears of English audiences already faced with the threat of foreign invasion, afraid of losing their identity under either French or Spanish control. The increasing use of torture in England signalled a shift in legal procedure which undermined English tradition.

English audiences could more easily relate to accounts of martyrs because they occur in a historical *past*. However, they also occur in a recognizable English context, subverting the power the use of torture was meant to reinforce in the first place and negating ideas of English justice. Both John Foxe and Catholic writers like Thomas Alfield and Cardinal Allen[59] report and glorify the deaths of religious dissidents persecuted under English monarchs. But unlike their medieval predecessors, these authors are largely limited by the actual events that were witnessed by many and widely reported. Unlike medieval audiences, early-modern readers often directly emulated these martyrs, embracing Protestantism

---

[55] Hanson, 'Torture and Truth', p. 55.
[56] Hanson, 'Torture and Truth', p. 55.
[57] Hanson, 'Torture and Truth', p. 55.
[58] Hanson, 'Torture and Truth', p. 55.
[59] Alfield published his work on Catholic martyrdom, titled *A True Report of the Death and Martyrdome of M. Campion Jesuite and prieste, [and] M. Sherwin, [and] M. Brian priests*, illegally at Smithfield in 1582 (Monta, *Martyrdom and Literature*, p. 24). Many of the Catholic responses to Foxe centred on the torture and execution of Edmund Campion and his companions. William Cardinal Allen's *A Briefe Historie of the Glorious Martyrdom of Twelve Reverend Priests, Father Campion [and] His Companions* was published in 1582 and seeks 'both to present transparent testifying subjects and to protect Catholic consciences from undue government scrutiny' (Monta, *Martyrdom and Literature*, p. 28). Freeman in the introduction to his collection of essays on martyrdom says the martyrological battles between the different confessions temporarily eased throughout the sixteenth century, only to be renewed later with 'increased vigour'. Freeman, 'Over their Dead Bodies', p. 26.

and embarking on a path to martyrdom,[60] citing as their models the same saints elevated in medieval Catholic hagiographies, and voicing a similar defiance in the face of torture. But instead of ancient Roman judges, these martyrs faced English monarchs and the effect was surely unsettling to English audiences and disastrous for royal attempts at control. The lessons to be derived from the stories of the saints seem to have been 'enacted in particularly remarkable behavior during the political and religious persecutions of the sixteenth and seventeenth centuries when thousands of men and women died in ways reminiscent of the earlier Christian saints and martyrs'.[61] Foxe's *Actes and Monuments* is the 'most outstanding witness to that, as well as to how an earlier hagiographic, if not historiographic, tradition is put to effective use in the service of religio-political convictions'.[62] The efficacy of the narrative relies on the credibility of the account, the patience and identifiable endurance of a martyr obviously suffering greatly. The proximity of disparate religious practitioners to one another in England made wholesale massacres and persecutions of these communities unrealistic; there was no geographic division between the two religions.[63] So the lines of identity were blurred, heightening cultural anxieties about the corrupting influence of the Other. Foxe's 'reserve in demonizing the persecutors of the English martyrs may have also been influenced to some degree by the Protestants' tendency to present themselves as loyal subjects and their reluctance to be seen as traitors, a tendency that may have tempered their criticism of authorities'.[64] Foxe was subversive enough in raising the spectre of tyranny. Thomas S. Freeman notes that the accusation of treachery levelled against many of these martyrs made many English people, otherwise sympathetic, 'reluctant to praise, much less venerate them'.[65] Far more than focusing on the use of judicial torture as a means of interrogation or political repression, these accounts emphasize the deaths of their martyrs chronicled by writers who abhorred the regimes that employed it. The criticism of torture is immediate and relevant as its use was a persistent and pressing concern for Foxe and his audience.

Foxe, perhaps in an attempt to distance himself and his society from the distinctly Catholic Middle Ages, catalogues the 'stripes and scourgings, drawings, tearings, stonings, plates of iron laid into them burning hot [...] gridirons, gibbets, and gallows' (1:109–10) recorded in the narratives of early Christian martyrs, but he celebrates the 'mild deaths of the [Protestant] saints' (1:521), describing them in minute detail and realistic ways, 'keeping the reader's gaze focused upon the actual scene of suffering and the disfiguring effects of the

---

[60] Freeman, 'Over their Dead Bodies', p. 2.
[61] Jankofsky, 'National Characteristics', p. 92.
[62] Jankofsky, 'National Characteristics', p. 92.
[63] Baraz, *Medieval Cruelty*, p. 162.
[64] Baraz, *Medieval Cruelty*, p. 162.
[65] Freeman, 'Over their Dead Bodies', p. 9.

flames'.[66] Foxe also emphasizes the triumphalism of these accounts, the victory of the saint over the pagan judge or Catholic persecutor, demonizing the persecutor and elevating the martyr, echoing the defiance of earlier heterodox (or proto-Protestant) sects who actively defied the Church and its use of torture. In that sense, he preserves the narrative of torture in the medieval hagiography, but while he accepts the seemingly miraculous tolerance of pain, he could not sanction the appearance of angels and 'other manifestations of the supernatural or the creation of a shrine' for the veneration of their bones.[67] Palmer notes that in Foxe's day people continued to debate the matter of saints' lives but no one questioned the practice of hagiography, and that Foxe addressed the need with his comprehensive collection of eye-witness accounts, official documents, letters, gossip, history and chronicles, and his own 'moral fictionalizing'.[68] Foxe negotiates the uncomfortable aspects of Catholic hagiography and appropriates the saint's endurance of torture as a sign of spiritual fortitude, a personal triumph, even though he reproduces many of the formulas of resistance 'that signal victory over pain and hence over the agency that inflicts it'.[69]

When English writers of the sixteenth century 'looked at Marian punishments of heretics, they reinvented the kind of judicial triumph [...] in the name of religious commitment'.[70] But the same cannot be said of medieval hagiography because there was no other side, there was no discourse available justifying the punishment of early Christian martyrs as criminals; the Roman judge is *always* the demonized Other. The persecution of thirteenth-century heretics could have given rise to conflicting narratives if the Church had not dealt swiftly with these movements, and despite its fairly complete elimination of heretical sects some dissent and tension lingered, gathering steam until 1517. As discussed in Chapter 1, the Church recorded its own frustration with the persistent defiance of heretics who may have also found their models of resistance in orthodox hagiography. However, in giving accounts of contemporary martyrs, Foxe has to reject the formulaic model of medieval hagiography and emphasize the reality, the humanity, the individuality of this suffering – the Protestant martyrs have to suffer, feel the pain, but endure it and accept it. Knott writes that Foxe thought he could 'contain the images of horror he captured within the frame of a narrative that celebrates the victories of the martyrs, neutralizing the terror such images might arouse by insisting upon the peacefulness and joy of the martyr in the flames. Yet the narrative frame can crack.'[71] The immediacy of these events for Foxe's audience, and the persistence of the collective memory, deny Foxe the opportunity to mitigate the horror of these executions as it also prohibits

---

[66] Knott, 'John Foxe and the Joy of Suffering', p. 722.
[67] Knott, 'John Foxe and the Joy of Suffering', p. 723.
[68] Palmer, 'Histories of Violence', p. 86.
[69] Knott, 'John Foxe and the Joy of Suffering', p. 723.
[70] Palmer, 'Histories of Violence', p. 84.
[71] Knott, 'John Foxe and the Joy of Suffering', p. 732.

him from embellishing these narrative accounts to include even more gruesome accounts of torture for further didactic emphasis. Unlike his medieval predecessors, Foxe had to contend with a need for reality and credibility and with a literary audience that may well have witnessed these or similar events firsthand. Palmer points to the narratives of Origen, who 'seems to have gone out of his way to ask his readers to think of themselves as audiences in audiences. In this way, the persecution that might seem a *mise abyme* to the participant becomes a triumphant theatrical event for the reader quietly contemplating the fate of religious victims after the fact.'[72] Palmer assumes a certain amount of pleasure at this violent spectacle, but also a distancing from the realities of the persecution that was more possible with medieval audiences of hagiography who were far removed from the immediacy of Roman tyranny, except in periods of resurgent religious rebellion during heresy persecutions. For early-modern audiences the persecution was far more immediate – the sense of triumphalism took on new dimensions for an audience who not only read accounts of these persecutions in their lifetime and the collective memory, but who also may have witnessed them. In these instances, the brutality of the persecution and the need to understand a purpose evokes a more emotive response. In some cases, the persecuted were people of the community, known to the neighbours who watched them burn, so the literary accounts take on a more detached view of torture and brutality, perhaps lessening the personal response in favour of a spiritual one. The detachment may also stem from a desire to mitigate collective culpability for these executions. The presence of an audience problematizes plausible deniability and vitiates a sense of English justice and identity that was founded on it. It is difficult to claim that a society does not torture when everyone watches it – and it was a claim important to medieval audiences. Early-modern audiences may have seen that identity slipping away, and so depersonalized the accounts of torture.

One of the most well known accounts in *Actes and Monuments* is the story of the Henrician martyr Anne Askew, who endured interrogation and torture before her execution by fire in 1546. Askew left a record of her trials in her own words which was smuggled out of England into Germany where John Bale printed it in his *Examinations*, and which was later incorporated into Foxe's *Book of Martyrs*. Palmer imagines Foxe's admiration for Askew and suggests that her account was a kind of template for the work he envisioned.[73] Unlike medieval female martyrs, Askew is not described in terms of her virginity nor is she of noble birth. She is a pious woman descended from a good merchant family, well educated, who eloquently answers each question of doctrine posed to her during her examinations. She is first examined in 1545 and enumerates her responses to that interrogation with a dispassionate succinctness despite the prospect of prison and torture.

---

[72] Palmer, 'Histories of Violence', p. 83.
[73] Palmer, 'Histories of Violence', p. 89.

Askew also records the gender bias of the inquisitors who reprimand her for uttering the scriptures, citing Saint Paul and his prohibition against women speaking or talking of the Word of God.[74] She answers adroitly that she knows Paul's meaning as well as he, 'which is, 1 Corinthians 14, that a woman ought not to speak in the congregation by way of teaching' (8:609). Like her medieval predecessors such as Saint Christina, Askew engages in a war of words and will with her persecutors, noting their flattery and their kind words, their patronizing tone and their insistence that she must be instructed in the correct beliefs. But unlike Christina, the emphasis in the narrative is not on the brutality of her torments but on her logical disputes and her convictions. When one of her questioners, an archdeacon, presumes to judge her book by its cover and proclaim it heretical material written by John Firth, Anne chastises him for his rash assumptions: 'Then I asked him if he were not ashamed for to judge of the book before he saw it within or yet knew the truth thereof. I said also that such unadvised and hasty judgment is token apparent of a very slender wit' (8:610). Her disdain is vindicated when she opens the book and he concedes that it was not the book he thought it was, and that he could find 'no fault therein' (8:610). Anne is a steadfast and eloquent advocate for her faith, but because these are her words and because the events of her examination and death could be corroborated, there is little room for hagiographical invention. Therefore the focus of her martyrdom is not on the gruesome scenes of her torture and her execution, but more on the substance of the interrogation and theological issues, particularly in her second examination in 1546: 'The Lord Chancellor asked what was her opinion of the sacrament. Her answer was, "I believe that so oft as I, in a Christian congregation, do receive the bread in remembrance of Christ's death and with thanksgiving according to His holy institution, I receive therewith the fruits also of his most glorious passion"' (8:611).[75] The narrative continues with the exhortations of the examiners for her to confess her error, which she refuses, and then a chronicle of the punishment they allot to her. But again, she merely describes these events as fact without any of the graphic details inherent in a large proportion of medieval hagiography. However, this does not lessen the impact of her words, nor of the torment that she suffers, not at the hands of pagan judges in a far distant past, but at the hands of inquisitors and secular judges in the employ of the English King Henry VIII. An uncomfortable fact for an audience reading this during the reign of his daughter, a discomfort only slightly mitigated by the fact that Elizabeth I was not prosecuting Protestants.

---

[74] All textual citations are from John Foxe, 'The first examination of Mrs. Anne Askew, before the Inquisitors, A.D. 1545', *Actes and Monuments*, ed. Rev. M. Hobart Seymour (New York: Worthington, 1850). I am grateful to Susan May for making this text available to me.
[75] John Foxe, 'The Second Apprehension and Examination of the worthy Martyr of God, Mistress Anne Askew, A.D. 1546', *Actes and Monuments*.

What Askew describes is systematic brutality where she is racked, then released, 'recovered' and then tortured again. Her fortitude in withstanding such torture is marked by her assertion that she did not cry out, though they took pains to rack her until she was 'nigh dead' (8:613). Foxe, however, interrupts her stoic account to supplement the description of her torture and to add details directly indicting the Lord Chancellor for enacting it, but ultimately exonerating the king – a shrewd political move considering Henry VIII's religious conversion and eventual dissolution of the English Catholic Church. Foxe writes:

> The manner of her racking in the Tower was thus; first she was led down into a dungeon, where the lieutenant commanded the jailor to pinch her with the rack. Which being done so much as he thought sufficient, he went to take her down, supposing that he had done enough. But Wriothesley the chancellor, not contented that she was loosed so soon, and having confessed nothing, commanded the lieutenant to strain her on the rack again. Which because he refused to do, pitying the weakness of the woman, he was threatened by Wriothesley, saying, that he would signify his disobedience to the king: and so he and Master Rich, throwing off their gowns, played the tormentors themselves, first asking her if she were with child. To whom she answered again, 'Ye shall not need to spare me for that, but do your will upon me;' and so quietly and patiently praying to the Lord, she bore their tyranny, till her bones and joints were almost pulled asunder, so that she was carried away in a chair. When the racking was over, Wriothesley and his fellow took their horses, and rode towards the court. (8:613)

The lieutenant who refuses to continue torturing Anne reports to King Henry, seeking absolution for disobeying the Chancellor, 'which when the king had understood, he seemed not very well to like their extreme handling of the woman, and also granted to the lieutenant his pardon, desiring him to return and see his charge' (8:613). Foxe treads very carefully among the pitfalls of English history and the difficulties of royal succession; he cannot criticize Henry as he might Queen Mary without potentially angering his other daughter Elizabeth, and whatever acts of tyranny Henry VIII may have perpetuated as defender of the Catholic faith, his conversion and dissolution of the monasteries places him on the side of later Protestants. But the rehearsal of Askew's torture opens a window on cultural anxieties about religious persecution and the continued use of interrogatory torture by the English monarchy. Foxe's attempts to exonerate Henry ring hollow and disingenuous. Even if, according to this narrative, King Henry did not sanction torture himself, he employed those who did, and if he did not authorize it, its use undermines his royal authority and destabilizes the monarchy. Foxe's audiences knew the reality was far different even though chronicle writers 'fail to mention the use of torture before the arrival of the Jesuits and seminary priests as part of the English mission around 1580'.[76] Bellamy writes that the practice of using torture on suspect traitors (as the Jesuits were regarded) became public knowledge for the first time and 'must have created

---

[76] Bellamy, *Strange, Inhuman Deaths*, p. 186.

alarm in some quarters, since a semi-official defence had to be drafted'.[77] Foxe's work may have been an implicit warning to Elizabeth not to follow the policies of her father too closely, and to maintain English justice rather than risk further instability to her reign. Askew's perseverance in the face of her torture and punishment serves as a model of English steadfastness and defiance – one that the reigning English monarchs would do well to keep in mind.

Askew attributes her perseverance to the grace of God, even in the face of her death sentence. Foxe adds a final note after her own testimony, recording her death and the condition in which she was brought to the stake:

> Wherefore the day of her execution was appointed, and she brought into Smithfield in a chair, because she could not go on her feet, by means of her great torments. When she was brought unto the stake she was tied by the middle with a chain that held up her body. [...] Thus she being troubled so many manner of ways, and having passed through so many torments, having now ended the long course of her agonies, being compassed in with flames of fire, as a blessed sacrifice unto God, she slept in the Lord, in anno 1546, leaving behind her a singular example of Christian constancy for all men to follow. (8:614)

Many of the accounts in Foxe's *Actes and Monuments* are far more brutal in their descriptions of the torments of the fire, but Askew's narrative combines many of the elements of earlier medieval female saints' lives and subtly demonizes the persecutors who would subject a mild-mannered and faithful woman to such horrors while not offending the lineage of the reigning monarch. As in *Christina* and *Agatha*, torture is the tool wielded by unstable regimes attempting to solidify their authority on the bodies of dissenters; Foxe marks that instability in the figure of Wriothesley, rather than Henry. This is problematic considering the persistence of torture after Henry's break with Rome. Foxe may have preferred to avoid direct resonance with the miraculous endurance of medieval saints, but in his accounts torture serves the same purpose that it did in medieval hagiography, a reaffirmation of the faith and sanctity of these martyrs persecuted by political institutions and a public testimony to that persecution. Both Foxe and his Catholic counterparts celebrate their religious martyrs, executed by governments, for a purpose as political as the executions. The presence of torture in religious literature is part of the formula of devotion and persecution, but its use also subverts orthodox structures and challenges the authority that employs it. The early-modern period was marked by persistent upheavals in political and religious structures, and torture and brutality were firmly placed in the minds of early-modern audiences. It functions as a literary motif that negotiates cultural anxieties about national identity, but it is also performative reality enacted not only on the scaffold but on the stages of Elizabethan England. Palmer writes that 'where the martyrologist seeks to define a single event, the playwright concentrates on the way the displaying of violence breeds more violence'; and where

---

[77] Bellamy, *Strange, Inhuman Deaths*, p. 186.

Foxe reiterates the triumph of every event, 'Shakespeare constantly interrupts the sense of a triumph'[78] in what is arguably his most gruesome play, *Titus Andronicus* (1593).

William Shakespeare: *Titus Andronicus*

Extant in three quarto versions and the First Folio, *Titus Andronicus* is one of Shakespeare's earliest tragedies, if not the earliest, and it has often been dismissed or overlooked by scholars because of its violent content. There has been a resurgence in scholarship about the play from a variety of theoretical perspectives,[79] and many critics have focused their discussions on the types of violence in the play and the consequences of brutality and revenge on the stability of the state. However, few have considered the specific acts of torture in the play, and none has done so in the context of interrogating an early-modern inheritance of what was perceived to be a medieval taste for torture or brutality. As Molly Eso Smith

---

[78] Palmer, 'Histories of Violence', p. 98. Palmer conducts an intriguing and compelling comparison of the violence in Foxe and *Titus Andronicus* and the various associations of martyrdom in both. Thomas P. Anderson draws similar connections, contributing to this comparison in terms of trauma, *Performing Early Modern Trauma from Shakespeare to Milton* (Burlington VT: Ashgate, 2006).

[79] Feminist scholars have been particularly prolific in producing analysis of the play, largely from the perspective of Lavinia's agency, lack of agency, rape and mutilation. Deborah Willis effectively addresses much of the feminist criticism about *Titus* in her article, '"The gnawing vulture": Revenge, Trauma Theory, and *Titus Andronicus*', *Shakespeare Quarterly* 53.1 (Spring 2002): 21–52. For further discussions of the play and Lavinia in terms of feminist theory, see: Karen Cunningham, '"Scars Can Witness": Trials By Ordeal and Lavinia's Body in *Titus Andronicus*', in *Women and Violence in Literature: An Essay Collection*, ed. Katherine Anne Ackley (New York and London: Garland, 1990) 139–62; Sara Eaton, 'A Woman of Letters: Lavinia in *Titus Andronicus*', in *Shakespearean Tragedy and Gender*, ed. Shirley Nelson Garner and Madelon Sprengnether (Bloomington IN: Indiana University Press, 1996) 54–74; Douglas E. Green, 'Interpreting "her martyr'd signs": Gender and Tragedy in *Titus Andronicus*', *Shakespeare Quarterly* 40 (1989): 317–26; Bernice Harris, 'Sexuality as a Signifier for Power Relations: Using Lavinia, of Shakespeare's *Titus Andronicus*', *Criticism* 38 (1996): 383–406; and Cynthia Marshall, '"I can interpret all her martyr'd signs": *Titus Andronicus*, Feminism, and the Limits of Interpretation', in *Sexuality and Politics in Renaissance Drama*, ed. Carole Levin and Karen Robertson (Lewiston, Queenston, Lampeter: Edwin Mellen Press, 1991) 193–213. On rape, see: Derek Cohen, *Shakespeare's Culture of Violence* (New York: St Martin's Press, 1993) 79–93; Lorraine Helms, '"The High Roman Fashion": Sacrifice, Suicide, and the Shakespearean Stage', *PMLA* 107 (1992): 554–65; and Catherine R. Stimpson, 'Shakespeare and the Soil of Rape', in *The Woman's Part: Feminist Criticism of Shakespeare*, ed. Carolyn Ruth Swift Lenz, Gayle Greene, and Carol Thomas Neely (Urbana IL: University of Illinois Press, 1980) 56–64. Coppélia Kahn's extended study of *Titus Andronicus* in her important book *Roman Shakespeare: Warriors, Wounds, and Women* (London and New York: Routledge, 1997) covers most of the above issues. Mary Laughlin Fawcett's 'Arms/Words/Tears: Language and the Body in *Titus Andronicus*', *ELH* 50 [1983]: 261–77, deals with similar issues.

suggests, in Shakespeare's clear association of villainy with sadistic pleasure in prolonged punishment there is a record of growing scepticism about the value of torture as punishment.[80] Like many of the medieval texts discussed in preceding chapters, *Titus* 'accentuates the value of dismemberment and mutilation even as it undermines the efficacy of physical public punishment'.[81] Though set in Rome and based in many ways on classical revenge narratives such as Ovid's *Metamorphoses*, which provides the template for Lavinia's rape and mutilation, *Titus Andronicus* also resonates with the Old Norse/Icelandic tradition of retributive violence in family sagas and the blood feud tradition found in early medieval texts like *Beowulf* and later medieval texts such as *Havelok the Dane*. But *Titus* goes beyond simple vengeance and the reliance on violence, and the resort to torture leads to the disintegration of the authoritarian structures that employ them.

Titus is a play about justice, injustice, the mutability of honour and law, and the abuse and corruption of power. There are few examples of explicit judicial torture; but the brutality of the play, even in Titus's vengeance, makes a similar point as many of the medieval texts where the use of torture is limited and often employed only by a barbarian Other, indicting those who trust a corrupt system and condemning authorities who either perpetuate atrocities or permit them. In *Titus* 'the carefully constructed polarities between Self and Other have been expertly displaced and rendered problematic. *Titus*, in short, epitomizes Renaissance conceptions of alterity as simultaneously horrific and fascinating, alien and similar'.[82] That similarity stretches not only to the classical models, but also to medieval ones. Titus' vengeance bears a striking resemblance not only to Ovid, but also to the calculated revenge of Vǫlundr in the *Vǫlundarkviða* which also includes the presentation of the children's heads to the offending parents, not as a feast but as vessels for the feast. Palmer traces the intersection of Foxe's *Actes and Monuments* and *Titus Andronicus* and irreconcilable versions of 'what can be made of violence, through the reading and writing of history, in sixteenth century England'.[83] He treats these two texts as common staples of English life, 'registers full of well-thumbed pages that reveal much about the way Tudor England represented its own violence to itself'.[84] Implicit in the torture and disintegration of law in *Titus* are the cultural anxieties inherent in losing the identity of

---

[80] Smith, 'Spectacles of Torment', p. 318. Smith's study is a comprehensive discussion of the spectacle of torment, dismemberment and violence in the plays, but she passes over the references to torture in the interests of the more vivid and active episodes of violence. However, the references to torture and the fact that these are the only scenes of brutality *not* carried out before either the audience of the actors on stage or the public audience directly reflect cultural apprehensions of 'legal' interrogation and judicial proceedings.

[81] Smith, 'Spectacles of Torment', p. 315.

[82] Smith, 'Spectacles of Torment', p. 316.

[83] Palmer, 'Histories of Violence', p. 84.

[84] Palmer, 'Histories of Violence', p. 85.

English justice. The image of the nation so carefully constructed in the thirteenth and fourteenth centuries as a fair and just realm relying on 'gode olde law' has been undermined and threatens to dissolve with the continued use of torture in Elizabeth's realm. Earlier nationalist resistance was grounded in opposition to the Catholic use of torture, but when it becomes a tool of both Reformation and Counter Reformation, this justification and identity of rebellion fails. Both texts build on an earlier medieval tradition, not of inherited violence or brutality, but of literary responses to state-sponsored violence and the potential corruption of both secular and religious authorities. In Shakespeare's hands, 'Roman inheritance is not a *thing* already passed on to England and possessed by its citizens. Instead, the inheritance resembles a promise still to be completed, one that can, therefore, go violently and unpredictably awry.'[85] Thomas Anderson suggests that the play itself is a martyr to history: 'with Lavinia's tortured body it bears witness to the continuing impact of the traumatic events depicted in Foxe, but the play is also a monument that memorializes the effects of the cultural desire for a Roman legacy.'[86] That Roman legacy is inextricably linked with images of torture and brutality, and *Titus* exhibits the full consequences of that legacy and the destabilizing effect it may have on English identity. *Titus* and Foxe enact the same obsession with dismembered bodies as signifiers of loss that cannot be forgotten no matter how great the desire to forget. Just as Foxe uses medieval hagiography as a model for his own collection and appropriates the material for a Protestant aesthetic, Shakespeare adapts the literary traditions of earlier texts, if not the texts themselves, and makes similar charges against abusive authority, questioning the viability of an institution that relies on the tactics of its enemies to prevail. For Shakespeare's audience, common and noble alike, this could be seen as an exhortation for England not to become too much like France or Spain in the adoption of their judicial practices.

In *Titus*, the title character is welcomed as a hero in Rome at which point he immediately orders the mutilation and sacrifice of a conquered foe, the oldest son of Tamora the Goth. She pleads for his life and the lives of her other sons, recalling their duty to their own people: 'must my sons be slaughtered in the streets/ For valiant doings in their country's cause?' (I.i.112–13).[87] Her pleas fall on deaf ears, and as Smith points out, every death or violent act in this play occurs as a by-product of public ceremony and celebration.[88] This unmerciful act of Titus will generate the series of revenge plots throughout the play. The public ritual of violence in *Titus* enacts a spectacle of brutality reminiscent of the public trials and executions in *Havelok the Dane*, and in each case as a legitimate

---

[85] Thomas P. Anderson, '"What Is Written Shall Be Executed": "Nude Contracts" and "Lively Warrants" in *Titus Andronicus*', *Criticism* 45.3 (Summer 2003): 301–21, p. 303.
[86] Anderson, *Performing Early Modern Trauma from Shakespeare to Milton*, p. 21.
[87] All textual citations for *Titus Andronicus* are taken from the Folger Shakespeare Library edition, ed. Barbara Mowat and Paul Werstine (New York: Washington Square Press, 2005).
[88] Smith, 'Spectacles of Torment', p. 318.

authority attempts to solidify its power by resorting to torture or brutal reparations, that power is tainted and potentially subverted.[89]

The series of brutal acts in the play have been thoroughly analysed by Smith in the context of defining the boundaries of the Other and Self; however, the brief episodes of torture inflicted according to judicial custom by the state authority are often overshadowed by the more gruesome spectacles of dismemberment and mutilation that populate Elizabethan drama.[90] While it can be argued that Chiron and Demetrius torture Lavinia, brutality is not enacted upon her as a means of judicial interrogation. In fact, the horrors inflicted upon her body produce no confession because she cannot speak, and though her accusation and testimony are written in her blood, this is not an act of judicial torture but savage personal vengeance fitting for these Goths – the unrepentant Other in this play. The state authorities orchestrate the two instances of judicial torture in the play. In each case, the power that resorts to torture as a means of eliciting a confession of guilt, reinforcing presumed guilt, or supplementing execution is tainted by its application of violence. The episodes of torture are particularly subversive because even in Roman law a citizen could not be tortured. So these acts are illegal and illegitimate in both the sixteenth-century context of the play and the Roman context of the subject. Saturnius orders Quintus and Martius to be tortured after the murder of Bassianus is discovered, telling Titus:

> Two of thy whelps, fell curs of bloody kind,
> Have here bereft my brother of his life. –
> Sirs, drag them from the pit unto the prison.
> There let them bide until we have devised
> Some never-heard-of torturing pain for them. (II.iii.282–6)

---

[89] Jack E. Reese argues that audiences are not 'terribly moved' by what happens on stage because the violence is formalized, and we do not believe in the humanity of the characters, they are classical echoes or 'types' (p. 79). 'The Formalization of Horror in *Titus Andronicus*', *Shakespeare Quarterly* 21.1 (Winter 1970): 77–84. Reese further suggests that the art of stagecraft mitigates any sense of violence for the audience and limits the impact of the gruesome scenes: 'Although the work is extraordinarily bloody, the blood which is shed is often clearly identifiable as red ink or whatever sixteenth-century stage managers used to simulate wounds. The elaborate system of balances and parallels, the repetition of motifs, the meticulously-arranged stage tableaux, the pictorial quality of many scenes all tend to de-emphasize the physical violence by stylizing it' (p. 84). But it would be counterproductive for the violence to be completely stylized, and it would be simplistic to imagine that stage violence desensitized all members of an early-modern audience to the brutality before them.

[90] Owens writes that acts of mutilation such as 'the amputation of hands, the lopping off of noses, and the gouging out of eyes are typically inflicted on characters of lesser importance to the plot', while the severed head stands out as a punishment for more important characters (p. 145). A number of other critics analyse the dismemberment in *Titus*, particularly in the imagery of disarticulated hands. See: Gillian Murray Kendall, '"Lend me thy hand": Metaphor and Mayhem in *Titus Andronicus*', *Shakespeare Quarterly* 40.3 (Autumn 1989): 299–316; Katherine A. Rowe, 'Dismembering and Forgetting in *Titus Andronicus*', *Shakespeare Quarterly* 45.3 (Autumn 1994): 279–303.

What torture they devise the audience never sees or hears. Despite the open acts of brutality throughout the play, the one that could be potentially justified as an instrument of law is obscured behind the scenes, and the pronouncement of their guilt before they have even been taken away suggests that any torture inflicted upon them is merely an act of revenge rather than an attempt at discovering truth. Torture, especially that enacted in secret, is illicit. Saturnius needs little encouragement to find them guilty once the forged letter has been produced, and refuses Titus their bail, remanding them into custody:

> Thou shall not bail them. See thou follow me. –
> Some bring the murdered body, some the murderers.
> Let them not speak a word. The guilt is plain.
> For, by my soul, were there worse end than death,
> That end upon them should be executed. (II.iii.300–4)

Neither Quintus nor Martius speaks again, and any protestation of innocence they may make is silenced.

Act Three opens upon the tail end of the judicial proceeding where the judges and senators have already ruled against Titus' sons and are leading them to their execution. The only voice heard at this point is the grieving father, who prostrates himself before these authorities and begs for their lives. They follow the law but do not enact justice. Like the barons in *Havelok*, the Roman senators become complicit in this subversion of law. Their collaboration with the illegitimate power undermines all sense of justice and culminates in the destabilization and the destruction at the end of the play. Lucius remarks on the stony nature of these men, 'Oh noble father, you lament in vain./ The Tribunes hear you not; no man is by,/ and you recount your sorrows to a stone' (III.i.27–9), and urges his father to stop his pleading. Titus expounds on the nature of this system populated by what he sees as heartless men:

> Why, 'tis no matter, man. If they did hear,
> They would not mark me; if they did mark,
> They would not pity me. Yet plead I must,
> And bootless unto them.
> Therefore I tell my sorrows to the stones,
> Who, though they cannot answer my distress,
> Yet in some sort they are better than the Tribunes,
> For that they will not intercept my tale.
> When I do weep, they humbly at my feet
> Receive my tears and seem to weep with me,
> And were they but attired in grave weeds,
> Rome could afford no tribunes like to these.
> A stone is soft as wax, tribunes more hard than stones;
> A stone is silent and offendeth not,
> And tribunes with their tongues doom men to death. (III.i.33–47)

Titus' lament echoes concerns for justice that proliferate in Elizabethan England as well as in Rome, and questions the efficacy of a legal system that relies on suspect accusations and evidence, and barbaric methods of extracting confessions. Torture is implicit in this exchange, as is the instability of Saturnius' regime because he has to resort to such measures to punish and to rule.

But Saturnius, clearly a villain in this play, is not the only authority that resorts to torture, nor is his regime the only one rendered illegitimate by excessive cruelty. At the end of the play, what Palmer calls an 'experiment in exhaustion',[91] Lucius appears to restore order and justice to Rome but in doing so he must punish Aaron the Moor, the author of so much of the violence and bloodshed. He is the ultimate alien Other, as Heng points out in her analysis of *RCL*,[92] yet because the Romans employ the same methods as he does they align themselves with that Other. The punishment Lucius selects is drawn from a desire for vengeance as much as from a sense of justice. He and Marcus supplicate the Romans, asking understanding for their actions, appealing to their sense of justice and rehearsing the crimes of others. Even though Lucius first receives Aaron's confession, it is Marcus who reveals it to the Romans:

> Now is my turn to speak. Behold the child.
> Of this was Tamora delivered,
> The issue of an irreligious Moor,
> Chief architect and plotter of these woes.
> The villain is alive in Titus' house,
> And as he is witness, this is true.
> Now judge was [cause] had Titus to revenge
> These wrongs unspeakable, past patience,
> Or more than any living man could bear.
> Now have you heard the truth. What say you Romans?
> Have we done aught amiss? Show us wherein,
> And from the place where you hold us pleading,
> The poor remainder of Andronici
> Will, hand in hand, all headlong hurl ourselves,
> And on the ragged stones beat forth our souls,
> And make a mutual closure of our house.
> Speak, Romans, speak, and if you say we shall,
> Lo, hand in hand, Lucius and I will fall.   (V.iii.120–38)

In the absence of any alternative, the tribunes now not only speak where they previously had ignored Titus' pleas for justices and audience, they receive the version of events of the Andronici as truth and proclaim Lucius the new emperor. But there is a residual air of injustice in the tribunes' sudden acknowledgment of the sufferings of the Andronici, for if the institution had functioned properly and carried out justice at any point during the play the tragedy need not have been as great. However, each character bears some of the responsibility for that

---

[91] Palmer, 'Histories of Violence', p. 107.
[92] Heng, 'The Romance of England', pp. 135–71.

instability, including Titus. Each character perpetuates the hatred and the cycle of revenge, actively seeking to mitigate his own part in the bloody drama, only to fulfil it in the end. Filled with images of brutality and dismemberment, this play finally ends with a public spectacle of torture that would have resonated with an Elizabethan audience familiar with public performances on the scaffold, though none necessarily as cruel as this one. Aaron's punishment, while deserved, is excessive, and rather than re-establishing a system of justice and correct rule, it furthers the violence of the society and threatens its stability. In this way, Shakespeare draws not only from the events of his own time, but from a medieval tradition that called for the public execution of traitors, as evidenced in the *Roland* and *Havelok the Dane*, but also recognized the limitations of audience approval of such measures.

In sentencing Aaron to a publicly torturous execution without an actual trial, as with the Jews in Chaucer's *Prioress's Tale*, both Marcus and Lucius participate in the same brutality orchestrated by the Moor and the Goths, potentially undermining their righteousness and aligning themselves with that brutality. After Lucius' appointment as emperor, Marcus charges that 'misbelieving Moor/ To be [adjudged] some direful slaught'ring death/ As punishment for his most wicked life' (V.iii.145–7). Shakespeare has Aaron sentenced to die spectacularly and brutally, but not silently. His death parodies the familiar scaffold speech and he 'promises the kind of confession and rehearsal of deeds that frequently informed the last minutes of the scaffold spectacle'.[93] As Palmer notes, Aaron's persistent dialogue and his refusal to be silenced during the course of his execution create a lasting impression of disorder and injustice, calling into question the legitimacy of Lucius' rule and the Roman system that validates it:

> **Roman:** You sad Andronici, have done with woes.
> Give sentence on this execrable wretch
> That hath been breeder of these dire events.
> **Lucius:** Set him breast-deep in earth and famish him.
> There let him stand and rave and cry for food.
> If anyone relieves or pities him,
> For the offense he dies. This is our doom.
> Some stay to see him fastened in the earth.

Lucius may well be proclaiming his doom as much as Aaron's because a state founded on judicial brutality and vengeance rather than law, order and justice can only hope to have a tenuous hold on power. By turning what would have been an abrupt execution into a spectacle, 'Aaron invests the mounting chaos with a sense of revelation and triumph, *a sense of the event*',[94] but his triumphalism subverts the intended triumph of the state, as the confession of Cutwolfe in *The Unfortunate Traveller* also subverts the intended discourse of authority.

[93] Palmer, 'Histories of Violence', p. 109.
[94] Palmer, 'Histories of Violence', p. 109.

As much as Lucius' action may seem justified, like the punishment of Godard and Godrich in *Havelok*, there is a sense that good governance should be tempered with justice and mercy, and that while Aaron should die, this spectacle undermines the legitimacy of his execution. Aaron's execution reflects cultural anxieties about justice and the maintenance of the English jury system – a facet of English identity – in the context of interrogatory torture and summary execution. There is no justice without trial, and the use of torture to extract a confession often removed the need for one. Aaron recognizes this opportunity to wreak further havoc on the authority of the Roman institution and vocalizes his resistance to tyranny as loudly as he had participated in it before:

> Ah, why should wrath be mute and fury dumb?
> I am no baby, I, that with base prayers
> I should repent the evils I have done.
> Ten thousand worse that ever yet I did
> Would I perform, if I might have my will.
> If one good deed in all my life I did,
> I do repent it from my very soul. (V.iii.186–92)

Aaron is led away by guards, but the image of his planned punishment and the potential forum that it will give him for further protestations diminishes the reestablishment of correct rule in Rome. Smith notes the incongruity of his punishment when juxtaposed against actual practice in the late sixteenth century, which would have been isolation. She writes, 'Aaron's punishment, which constitutes a form of public imprisonment and torture, presents an obverse rather than equivalent condition to that reserved for the worst criminals in Elizabethan England'.[95] Aaron suffers a 'very public humiliation and imprisonment, a sentence which, though intended as prolonged torture, instead provides him with yet another opportunity to use his considerable talent for persuasion'.[96] She also conjures up the image of Aaron's articulate head partially buried in the earth, 'a talking head left to torment Lucius and the Roman public in general by reminding them of his past victories over the Andronici', a spectacle that 'dominates our final impressions of the play'.[97]

But the play ends with Lucius' final pronouncements on the disposal of the dead, ordering the burial of Saturnius with his ancestors and consigning Tamora's corpse to the beasts and birds, rather than the continued protests of Aaron; and while the audience can imagine the severity of his torments the play does not give directions to stage them. Again, like the torture of Quintus and Martius designed to elicit a confession of guilt despite their innocence, the torture of Aaron that follows his confessions is performed off stage, removed from the sight of the audience that has already witnessed numerous horrors, suggesting

---

[95] Smith, 'Spectacles of Torment', p. 325.
[96] Smith, 'Spectacles of Torment', p. 325.
[97] Smith, 'Spectacles of Torment', p. 326.

the secret and insidious nature of such interrogations even when they appear justified. Smith argues that Lucius' injunction against anyone who gives Aaron aid during his final punishment hints at the emperor's misgivings in choosing torment over hanging, which was his original inclination when he captured him.[98] But Lucius is driven by revenge not necessarily common sense, and his desire to inflict the most horrible pain on Aaron, the last person upon whom he can vent his rage since Titus has dispatched everyone else, leaves him vulnerable to charges of excessive cruelty and provides a potential scenario where popular support may deviate from his authority. As Gillian Murray Kendall concludes, the play does not end simply with the ordering of the state, a common ending in Shakespeare's tragedies, 'but with a focus on Aaron that leaves him forever awaiting his punishment, forever speaking, the state forever fragmented'.[99] The fragmentation of the state and the instability of powers that rely on torture and brutality to maintain order are perhaps the greatest inheritance from medieval texts. As in the Old Norse/Icelandic texts such as *Njals saga* and *Hrafnkels saga*, there is no glory in this cycle of violence, no true approbation, but a warning to authorities and to individuals that the stability of a society cannot sustain such punishments. In *Titus*, the final restoration of stability is called into question when Lucius employs torture as a means of punishing Aaron. He resorts to the same tactics as Saturnius, contradicting his claim to just rule and suggesting that any regime that resorts to torture and brutality in attempting to stabilize or legitimize its power actually diminishes its authority. For the English, this means aligning themselves with France and Spain – negotiating the cultural and legal boundaries that had defined England as a just and law-based nation in the thirteenth and fourteenth centuries in opposition to Continental powers. By employing torture, the English government risks not only destabilizing its power structure, but also losing itself. There is no just resolution in *Titus Andronicus* because the audience is left with the potential for self-perpetuating violence, the cycle of retributive violence that marks earlier Anglo-Saxon and Norse societies that shaped England. As in *Havelok*, when the restoration of the royal couple comes with brutality there is a residual taint on the hand of justice; and while Aaron deserves punishment as Godard and Godrich do, the excessive brutality of these scenes tarnishes the justice that Lucius and Havelok are meant to represent. Not only does this play indict the classical era of Rome, it, like its medieval analogues, separates itself from the influence of the barbarian Other at an earlier time in English history, while warning Elizabethan authorities of sliding into tyranny.

[98] Smith, 'Spectacles of Torment', p. 326.
[99] Kendall, '"Lend me thy hand"', p. 316.

Christopher Marlowe: *Edward II*

Few historical accounts would have exemplified supposed medieval brutality to an early-modern audience more than the treacherous and gruesome murder of Edward II in 1327. The legend of his imprisonment, torture and murder circulated in chronicles beginning in 1350, though earlier records leave out specific details about the methods. Froissart does not even mention the cause of Edward's death, after giving a detailed account of Hugh Despenser's castration and decapitation.[100] In many ways, Edward II and his conniving, usurping barons could be held up to early-modern audiences as examples of medieval despotism, decadence and tyranny; rather than distancing his era from these earlier events, Christopher Marlowe draws striking and disturbing parallels with the upheavals, plots and repression of his own time. Written during the period of shifting loyalties, intricate plots and counter-plots against Elizabethan rule, Marlowe's play *Edward II* presents a particularly brutal episode of regicide on stage by enacting the sodomizing of Edward with a hot poker. Much has been said about the homoerotic preoccupations of this play[101] and about the brutality of this episode; however, the staged murder of Edward also opens the private actions of the murderers to the public and interrogates the boundaries of punishment in terms of misrule and usurpation. The England of the past is a mirror for the England of the Elizabethan present.

As many critics have noted, most of the play is concerned with the contest of wills between Edward and his barons over the exile or continued presence of his favourite, Piers Gaveston. While numerous threats are bandied back and forth between the warring factions, there is little actual violence on stage until the final acts. Thomas Cartelli notes that while the play derives its plots from Marlowe's 'dramatic compression' of his sources, 'it often seems to derive its shape and momentum from within, from the abrupt and seemingly unpatterned conflicts of rival passions and personalities.'[102] It is these conflicts, these passions and rivalries, that drive the play to its drastic and tragic conclusion; but throughout there is a shift of blame, a shift of sympathy as the arrogant and irresponsible king becomes an object of pity in his deposition and demise. When he is finally murdered there is no sense of approbation or triumph, no sense of justice. Like the final events of Chaucer's *Miller's Tale*, which has a physically similar consequence albeit with a comedic outcome, there is a sense that justice has not prevailed and that the brutality of reality underlies even the most outrageous events.

---

[100] Froissart, *Chronicles*, p. 44.
[101] Meredith Skura, 'Marlowe's *Edward II*; Penetrating Language in Shakespeare's *Richard II*', *Shakespeare Survey* (1998): 41–55.
[102] Thomas Cartelli, 'Edward II', in *The Cambridge Companion to Christopher Marlowe*, ed. Patrick Cheney (Cambridge: Cambridge University Press, 2004) 158–73, p. 159.

Revenge permeates the fabric of the play and like its medieval predecessors *Edward II* casts a questioning eye on the validity of vengeance in establishing and maintaining stable authority structures. Just as retributive violence precipitates the destruction of the Franks in the *Roland* and Godard and Godrich in *Havelok*, and sustains the cycles of violence in *Njals saga* and *Hrafnkels saga*, so does the revenge tragedy of *Edward II* lead to instability, fractured civil institutions, war and murder. Like these medieval texts, Marlowe's play raises questions of justice and negotiates cultural anxieties of identity in the resort to torture at the expense of law. While *Edward II* recalls the violence of an earlier age, it is a singular event in English history that, while rife with martial violence, wars, plots and counterplots, usurpations and restorations, rarely saw regicide in such a brutal and clinical fashion. Marlowe taps into an event with legendary status that indicts not only the wanton and irresponsible king, but also those who seek to supplant him for their own ends, who plot in the name of civil justice and national good, but in the end are only interested in serving their own agenda. James P. Bednarz suggests that Marlowe's play is part of a revenge dialogue on the Elizabethan stage where playwrights answered each other and their potentially subversive subjects.[103] A version of Shakespeare's *Henry VI, Part Three*, was initially printed as the *True Tragedie of Richard Duke of Yorke and the death of good king Henrie the Sixt...* (1595), a year after Marlowe's 'rejoinder' had appeared as *The troublesome raigne and lamentable death of Edward the second, King of England: with the tragicall fall of proud Mortimer*.[104] Bednarz writes that their titles' 'shared billing emphasises Shakespeare and Marlowe's mutual interest in conceiving of English history as revenge tragedy, forever doubled in the unremitting exchange of victor and victim'.[105] While the vengeful history of English royalty and the subsequent consequences for the English people may have their roots in the Middle Ages, the brutality of these early-modern works does not merely reflect an inheritance of violence from an earlier age. Like many of the medieval authors discussed in earlier chapters, both Shakespeare and Marlowe question the culture of brutality in their own time and interrogate the legitimacy of authorities that resort to torture to reaffirm or validate their rule. What seems to be inherited in these texts, and in the medieval subject matter of Marlowe's play, is a disaffection with corruption and abuse of power, and the perpetuation of tyranny evident in the cycle of usurpation.

Cartelli argues that *Edward II* emerges as Marlowe's most modern play, not just because it engages with the 'life and loves, and stages the brutal debasement, of a recognizably (if not exclusively) homosexual monarch, but also because it presents a decidedly direct and demystified portrayal of power politics at work,

---

[103] James P. Bednarz, 'Marlowe and the English Literary Scene', in *The Cambridge Companion to Christopher Marlowe*, ed. Patrick Cheney (Cambridge: Cambridge University Press, 2004) 90–105, p. 101.
[104] Bednarz, 'Marlowe and the English Literary Scene', p. 101.
[105] Bednarz, 'Marlowe and the English Literary Scene', p. 101.

showing political positions to be little more than transparent extensions of the personal desires and ambitions that motivate them'.[106] Marlowe presents the Edwardian court as corrupt and despotic, arbitrary and wanton, not simply because of Edward's misrule in his reliance on Gaveston and later on Hugh Despenser, but in the petty machinations of his nobles who are exceedingly willing to challenge his authority with plots of their own, just as corrupt despite their protestations of national benefit. In these circumstances, as in medieval texts like *Havelok*, the displacement of a corrupt authority may require drastic measures but if the supplanting power uses excessive means to establish itself there is no sense of restoration – things have not been set right, they merely promise to continue in a similar vein but by different means. In this way *Titus Andronicus* and *Edward II* both question the legitimacy of overthrowing tyranny only to replace it with the potential for more tyranny, but *Titus* removes that threat to the forum of ancient Rome, whereas *Edward II* haunts the halls of medieval English castles and courts. Ironically, the historical reality of Edward II's reign was one in which the rejection of torture became a defining feature of English identity. So, as with *Titus* which includes anachronistic episodes of Roman torture, *Edward II* employs methods more reminiscent of sixteenth-century England than its medieval past, despite the historical (or at least legendary) facts of Edward's murder.

It is not surprising that someone as ambitious and ruthless as Mortimer Junior, as portrayed by Marlowe, would resort to employing an assassin who will not only commit regicide, but will do so in an exceedingly brutal way. As Anderson explains, Marlowe has 'decentered any fixed notions of sympathy, as Edward wallows in misery and mud, and the noble Mortimer exalts in treachery and deceit'.[107] Marlowe is intent on demonstrating that both sides are 'equally unyielding, equally unmindful of anything that one would call the good of the kingdom'.[108] Mortimer proves an even less effective and more corrupt ruler than Edward; and Edward III, even though a child, will restore order swiftly and justly dispatches him at the end of the play. He sentences Mortimer, not just out of vengeance for his father's murder but also out of political necessity for murdering a king, executing him in the traditional fashion reserved for noble traitors – by beheading. As Owens argues, the symbolism of Mortimer's severed head on Edward II's hearse is a poignant image of royal authority: it 'encapsulates the transit of power over the course of the play, from Edward II to Mortimer and back to Edward's dynastic line'.[109] Mortimer dies as befits both a traitor and a usurper, and Edward III proves merciful in carrying out royal justice swiftly. Mortimer's severed head represents the reinstitution of correct order, but also a sense of royal brutality; this icon 'is encoded with specifically political meanings,

---

[106] Cartelli, 'Edward II', p. 158.
[107] Anderson, *Performing Early Modern Trauma*, p. 96.
[108] Cartelli, 'Edward II', p. 162.
[109] Owens, *Stages of Dismemberment*, p. 145.

readily identifiable to the Elizabethan audience'.[110] Like the heads of traitors on the gates of London, the display of Mortimer's head reinforces the visual of martial triumph, a ritual display that was as much 'militaristic as penal, resembling the collection of heads by warring factions on the battlefield, a practice that Elizabethan England typically disavowed and projected onto a host of cultural Others including Celts, New World Indians, and Turks'.[111] This kind of savagery is already marked as a practice of the Other; yet, in the play, Edward III provides an elevated model of English jurisprudence for his descendants on the throne regardless of the historical reality of his reign, punctuated as it was by war, plague and internal strife.

In the play, there are numerous references to violence, imprisonment and execution, but many are the empty threats of an unstable regime or the wilful whim of a petulant king. When Edward orders the spontaneous arrest of the Bishop of Coventry, he unleashes a maelstrom of violent reactions, and this rash act threatens the stability of Edward's rule almost immediately, placing him in the path of papal retaliation. In language similar to the warnings of *De Connebert*, the Earl of Kent urges his brother: 'lay not violent hands on him/ For he'll complain unto the See of Rome' (I.i.188–9).[112] But Gaveston, who will not be mollified, drives Edward and demands revenge for his exile; however, Edward does see the prudence in Kent's words and refuses to resort to murder:

> **Gaveston:** Let him complain unto the See of hell;
> I'll be revenged on him for my exile.
> **Edward:** No, spare his life, but seize upon his goods.
> Be thou Lord Bishop, and receive his rents,
> And make him serve thee as thy chaplain.
> I give him thee; here, use him as thou wilt.
> **Gaveston:** He shall to prison, and there die in bolts.
> **Edward:** Ay, to the Tower, the Fleet, or where thou wilt.
> **Coventry:** For this offense be thou accurst of God. (I.i.190–8)

Edward's willingness to ignore the possibility of papal censure or interdict to please the petty vindictiveness of his paramour undermines his authority as king, leaving him open to betrayal and revolt later in the play, much as the historical King John did in the early thirteenth century while England was in crisis and its nascent identity threatened. In many ways, Marlowe's Edward II is as capricious and petulant as the historical John – the subject of three plays; *Kynge Johan* (c. 1538) by John Bale, *The Troublesome Reign of King John* (c. 1589) and Shakespeare's *King John* (c. 1594/5). These plays are also marked by violence, and not surprisingly, 'this implicit hierarchization of theatrical violence corresponds to the social codes that governed the distribution of judicial penalties

---

[110] Owens, *Stages of Dismemberment*, p. 189.
[111] Owens, *Stages of Dismemberment*, p. 189.
[112] All references to Marlowe's play are taken from *Edward II*, in Christopher Marlowe, *The Complete Plays*, ed. Mark Thornton Burnett (London: Everyman, 1999) 148–240.

in early-modern England'.[113] However, nothing justifies the final actions of the power-hungry Mortimer, or the foul treatment of Edward before his murder and in that final act.

Act Five sets the stage for the dissolution of power and the disintegration of corrupt authority. At the beginning Edward vacillates, contemplating meeting the demands of his nobles and abdicating in favour of his son; he weighs his options and decides instead that his right to rule is stronger than their wishes. As the stage directions indicate, 'The King rageth: "I'll not resign, but, whilst I live be King!/ Traitors, begone, and join you with Mortimer./ Elect conspire, install, do what you will;/ their blood and yours shall seal these treacheries"' (V.i.86–9). Like the *Roland* and *Havelok*, the approbation of the barons is an important facet in the perception of justice – and like Charlemagne in the *Roland*, Edward plans to ignore them and do as he pleases, taking whatever vengeance he deems appropriate. His determination is foolhardy and his resistance somewhat futile but, as king, Edward has expectations of obedience. He still believes that he has not relinquished his birthright. His defiance, rather than being a manifestation of the tyranny he exhibited at the beginning of the play, is now a reaction against it. The tables have turned and Edward is no longer the tyrant but the supplicant, the dissenter, and the usurping force that sought to right the wrongs of his regime has instigated tyranny instead. The power struggle in this play reflects the pendulum of real world politics in recent Elizabethan memory where powers shifted according to popular support, martial force and assumption of right. Once the institutional authority adopts the practices of a former corrupt regime it is corrupted and must be replaced. The irony in this play is that Edward is never *that* corrupt, he does not resort to brutality or torture to maintain his tenuous control. He threatens cruelty like a child threatens to hold his breath, and swears that his barons will drive him to it and then see what real tyranny is:

> My swelling heart for very anger breaks!
> How oft have I been baited by these peers,
> And dare not be revenged, for their power is great?
> Yet shall the crowing of these cockerels
> Affright a lion? Edward, unfold thy paws
> And let their lives' blood slake thy fury's hunger.
> If I be cruel and grow tyrannous,
> Now let them thank themselves, and rue too late.   (II.ii.199–206)

His threats are idle and he will only take action after Gaveston has been murdered, an act, that while seemingly necessary for the stability of the realm actually galvanizes Edward to martial action.

Throughout the play it is abundantly clear that all Edward had to do was learn to rule his nobles and the realm better, as Lancaster tells him in Act One, Scene Four. But Edward will not be ruled by men; he will be ruled by his passion

---

[113] Owens, *Stages of Dismemberment*, p. 145.

and ultimately that will destroy him. Edward appears to engineer his own fall, which makes this a tragedy. As Katherine A. Sirluck explains,

> [...] this process by which the 'inside' of a man is somehow separated off from his social and political identity, which is shown to be a collaborative invention. The disencumbered residue of selfhood then redefines itself according to its capacity for rebellious passion or self-delusion, and plummets or is hurled into the abyss: while the sloughed skin of rule, the mask of rule-bound godhead, lies ready for the next incumbent to assume.[114]

Edward assumes that he must behave one way as king but is fundamentally incapable of behaving that way until it is too late. He equates rule with tyranny, not because he is necessarily a tyrant but because he cannot think of any other way to rule. Once he takes the field and defeats Mortimer and the barons he has the chance to redeem himself as a ruler, but fails in choosing to execute the least harmful of his opponents, inexplicably leaving Mortimer alive. Sirluck attributes this to a desire, on some level, to reserve 'one fatal enemy to be his executioner; and yet at this moment when he is conqueror, he would seem to have all the proof he needs of success and therefore of his right to rule'.[115] However much he seeks to validate and legitimize his rule through these actions and through his address to the conquered men, Edward finally gives rein to brutality himself, fundamentally undermining his right to rule. He should never have forced his barons into a position of opposition, and now that he has defeated them he has the power to grant mercy but orders instead 'Do speedy execution on them all' (III.ii.70). His command echoes that of Charlemagne in the *Roland*, but unlike Charlemagne, Edward will suffer the consequences of his brutality. His mercy for Mortimer is misplaced and fatal, and while Warwick and Lancaster accuse him of tyranny, the punishment of traitors (whatever their justification) is the one thing Edward gets right, tainted though it is by the air of personal vengeance rather than royal response to rebellion:

> **Edward:** Accursed wretches, was't in regard of us,
> When he had sent our messenger to request
> He might be spared to come speak with us,
> And Pembroke undertook for his return,
> That thou, proud Warwick, watched the prisoner,
> Poor Pierce, and headed him against law of arms?
> For which thy head shall overlook the rest
> As much as thou in rage outwent'st the rest.
> **Warwick:** Tyrant, I scorn thy threats and menaces;
> 'Tis but temporal that thou canst inflict.
> **Lancaster:** The worst is death, and better die to live
> Than live in infamy under such a king.

---

[114] Katherine A. Sirluck, 'Marlowe's "Edward II" and the Pleasure of Outrage', *Modern Language Studies* 22.2 (Spring 1992): 15–24, p. 19.
[115] Sirluck, 'Marlowe's "Edward II"', p. 21.

> Edward: Away with them, my Lord of Winchester.
> These lusty leaders, Warwick and Lancaster,
> I charge you roundly: off with both their heads. (III.ii.49–63)

Whatever claim Edward may have had on justice is diminished by his evocation of the poor prisoner Piers, reinforcing the personal nature of his vengeance and the corruption of his rule.

However, Edward's brief foray into the realm of judicial punishment does not match Mortimer's corruption and his willingness to subvert proper rule for his own authority, which becomes evident as he resorts to more and more arbitrary punishment, like the execution of Kent, in an attempt to maintain power. In his address to Isabella, Mortimer lays out the personal gains of his usurpation, deviating from his previous stance that all was done for the good of the country:

> Fair Isabel, now we have our desire,
> The proud corruptors of the light-brained King
> Have done their homage to the lofty gallows,
> And he himself lies in captivity.
> Be ruled by me, and we will rule the realm,
> In any case, take heed of childish fear,
> For now we hold an old wolf by the ears
> That, if he slip, will seize upon us both
> And grip the sorer, being gripped himself.
> Think therefore, madam, that imports us much
> To erect your son with all the speed we may,
> And that I be Protector over him,
> For our behoof will bear the greater sway
> Whenas a king's name shall be under writ. (V.ii.1–14)

Whatever Mortimer's original intentions in challenging Edward's retention of the throne, by the end of the play he has become worse than the despot he sought to remove. Now he has participated in murder and ordered executions without authority. He will continue to subvert the authority of the new king to be rid of political enemies and rivals, as well as orchestrating regicide through covert and brutal means. It is the murder of Edward II that has the most resounding impact on the play and elevates the action beyond a simple tragedy or history. The murder of the king, though certainly not uncommon in English history or in Elizabethan historical drama, touches on an uncomfortable taboo and illuminates the very tenuous hold that monarchs have on power and on life. In a time when numerous factions had threatened the queen's life, portraying the deposition of a king carried serious consequences, as it did for Shakespeare when *Richard II* was banned from the stage. But more than just depicting the overthrow of an ineffectual monarch, *Edward II* enacts his gruesome murder on stage, creating a public spectacle of a murder that was ostensibly private and secret. Marlowe throws a light on the dark past of regicide and interrogates the causes and effects of such action, ultimately condemning the illegitimate authority that resorts to torture as punishment but also warning princes to take care in their rule.

In arranging Edward's murder, Mortimer employs Lightborn, an expert assassin who has extensive experience in secretly dispatching his victims. He tells Mortimer that he does not need instructions because this is not the first time he has killed a man, and proceeds to catalogue his credentials:

> I learn'd in Naples how to poison flowers,
> To strangle with a lawn thrust down the throat,
> To pierce the wind pipe with a needle's point,
> Or, whilst one is asleep, to take a quill,
> And blow a little powder in his ears,
> Or open his mouth, and pour quick-silver down.
> But yet I have a braver way than these. (V.iiii.30–6)

Lightborn has no qualms about his occupation, and takes pride in his 'cruelly bureaucratic technologies of death',[116] but rather than sanitizing the impending act of murder, as Anderson suggests, it produces a chilling effect for the audience who can only imagine what a 'braver way than these' may be, or who, inured in the tradition of Edward's death know full well what is in store for him and shudder to think of its enactment on stage. Lightborn is the alien Other, trained on the Continent in the finer arts of torture and assassination – both of which require skill. He represents an insidious continental corruption that subverts English justice and threatens English identity. Anderson examines the nearly pathological precision with which the assassin commits the crime and suggests that his obsession with Edward's body during the murder mediates 'audience sympathies for the passive and suffering victim. The conflicted status of audience identification combined with the extreme violence of the crime suspends conventional separation between audience and the style.'[117] He argues for the 'inauthenticity' of the event that 'sustains the loss associated with the death of the deposed king'.[118] The perception of 'inauthenticity', however, depends on how both early-modern audiences and their medieval predecessors regarded the rumours surrounding Edward's death and their status as legendary history.

Marlowe relies on his sources (and their sources) for that final brutality. His three primary sources for *Edward II* are the contemporary accounts in the second edition of Holinshed's *Chronicles* (1587); the second edition of Stow's *Chronicles* (1580), appearing in 1592 with a new title, *The Annal of England*; and the fourth edition of *The Chronicle of Fabyan* (1559).[119] Anderson writes that Marlowe's reliance on Holinshed reflects an instability and ambivalence that 'precludes any moral fixity during the historical moment'.[120] Holinshed, who often talks with some relish about branding and punitive mutilation,[121] seems to show

---

[116] Anderson, *Performing Early Modern Trauma*, p. 94.
[117] Anderson, *Performing Early Modern Trauma*, p. 115.
[118] Anderson, *Performing Early Modern Trauma*, p. 116.
[119] Anderson, *Performing Early Modern Trauma*, p. 95.
[120] Anderson, *Performing Early Modern Trauma*, p. 95.
[121] Bellamy, *Crime and Public Order*, pp. 181–2.

sympathy for Edward and condemn his murderers, performing what Anderson calls a 'historiographic safety dance' that Marlowe echoes in the play, capturing the spirit of Holinshed's work as it challenges any notion of allegiance.[122] It is interesting to note that John Foxe's account of Edward's murder firmly sets him up as a villain and glosses over the methods employed against him, allaying any sympathy his audience may feel for the murdered monarch. Foxe writes that as Edward was

> personable in body and outward shape, so in conditions and evil dispositions he was much deformed, being unsteadfast in his word, and lightly disclosing secrets of great counsel; also refusing the company of his lords and men of honour, he associated with villains and vile personages, given moreover to drinking, and such vices as usually ensue on drunkenness. (4:199)

Foxe makes it very clear that Edward essentially got what he deserved for his inconstancy and carelessness without ever mentioning his sexual proclivities. His crimes were those of neglect and misrule, much like the arguments of the nobles in Marlowe's play; in fact, their dialogue reflects Foxe's disapproval of confiding in the two Spensers, 'following whose wanton counsel he gave himself to riot and debauchery; not ordering his government with gravity, discretion, or justice, which caused great variance between him and his nobles, so that he shortly became odious to them, and in the end was deprived of his kingdom' (4:199). For Foxe, writing a history of England as much as a history of Christian tradition and martyrdom, he must include these episodes but does so with a heavy editorial hand and judgement. His account of Edward's death is very brief: he recounts that the king was imprisoned after abdicating in favour of his son, 'where he is said to have felt great remorse' and then, 'it is thought by some writers, that the year following, by means of Sir Roger Mortimer, the king while in prison, was miserably slain: he was buried at Gloucester, after he had reigned nineteen years' (4:202). Foxe establishes the justice of Edward's abdication and makes virtually no comment on the appropriateness of regicide. For him, Edward was a king who, despite having the potential for just kingship, fell short and left himself vulnerable to overthrow; this is what happens when kings become tyrants and ignore the counsel of their barons.

But the shifting allegiances of Marlowe's play are also found in earlier sources for the murder of Edward II that circulated within a generation of the event. Geoffrey le Baker's *Chronicon* (c. 1350) is a Latin adaptation of a French chronicle by Thomas de la More, but Baker developed and expanded his text beyond More's account and incorporated complete phrases and entire sentences from Adam Murimuth's chronicle, which ends with the year 1341.[123] Neither Murimuth nor the anonymous *Annales Paulini*, both contemporary accounts of

---

[122] Anderson, *Performing Early Modern Trauma*, p. 96.
[123] G.P. Cuttino and Thomas W. Lyman, 'Where is Edward II?', *Speculum* 53.3 (July 1978): 522–44 p. 522.

Edward's death, explain the methods by which Edward was murdered, only that he was 'craftily killed'.[124] Baker's account is much more explicit and graphic:

> The brutes, seeing that death through stench could not prevail over such a strenuous man, at night on 22 September, having suddenly seized him lying in bed and having pressed him down and suffocated him with great pillows and a weight heavier than fifteen robust men, with a plumber's iron heated red hot, through a horn applied leading to the privy parts of the bowel, they burned out the respiratory organs past the intestines, fearing lest, a wound having been found on the royal body where wounds are usually required by any friend of justice, his tormentors would be bound to answer for an obvious offence and pay the penalty for it.[125]

Holinshed's account follows Baker's almost exactly, and it is possible that Baker's *Chronicon* is one of the works to which Holinshed alludes:

> they came suddenly one night into the chamber where he lay in bed fast asleep, and with heavy featherbeds or table (as some write) being cast upon him, they kept him down and withal put into his fundament an horn, and through the same they thrust up into his body a hot spit, or (as other have) through the pipe of a trumpet a plumber's instrument of iron made very hot, the which passing up into his entrails, and being rolled to and fro, burnt the same, but so as no appearance of any wound or hurt outwardly might be perceived. (2:587)[126]

The chronicles wielded considerable cultural authority in early-modern England.[127] In all of these sources, the primary emphasis is on the treacherous and secret nature of Edward's murder. Both medieval and early-modern audi-

---

[124] *Adae Murimuth continuatio chronicarum*, ed. Sir Edward M. Thompson, Rolls Series (London, 1889), qtd. in Cuttino and Lyman, 'Where is Edward II?', pp. 523–4.

[125] *Chronicon Galfridi le Baker de Swynebroke*, ed. Sir Edward M. Thompson (Oxford, 1889), pp. 33: 'Videntes tiranni quod viro strenuissimo non posset per fetorem mors prevalere, nocte, decima kalendas Octobris, in lecto cubantem subito preoccupatum, cum pulvinaribus magnis atque gravi mole amplius quam quindecim robustorum ipsum oppressum et subfocatum, cum ferro plumbarii incense ignito trans tubam ductilem ad egestionis partes secretas applicatam membra spiritalia post intestinas combusserunt, caventes ne, wlnere [sic] in regio corpore ubi solent wlnera [sic] requiri per aliquem iusticie amicum reperto, sui tortores de lesione manifesta respondere atque pro illa penam subire forent coacti.' Trans. and qtd. in Cuttino and Lyman, 'Where is Edward II?', p. 524.

[126] Holinshed's *Chronicle*, qtd. in Anderson, *Performing Early Modern Trauma*, p. 97. For further discussions on Holinshed's *Chronicle*, and variant readings on his rendering of Edward II's murder, see: Emily Bartels, *Spectacles of Strangeness* (Philadelphia: University of Pennsylvania Press, 1993); Annabel Patterson, *Reading Holinshed's* Chronicles (Chicago: University of Chicago Press, 1994). For a discussion of Marlowe's sources for *Edward II*, see: Vivien Thomas and William Tydeman, *Christopher Marlowe: The Plays and Their Sources* (New York: Routledge, 1994); and Josie Shumake, 'The Sources of Marlowe's Edward II' (University of South Carolina, 1984), PhD dissertation, unpublished. Joan Parks also reads *Edward II* against the chronicles as a coherent and influential projection of national identity and historical process. 'History, Tragedy, and Truth in Christopher Marlowe's *Edward II*', *Studies in English Literature, 1500–1900* 39.2 Tudor and Stuart Drama (Spring 1999): 275–90.

[127] Parks, 'History, Tragedy, and Truth', 278.

ences would have recognized the injustice in this episode much like that in the *Miller's Tale*. Edward's torture functions as a judicial punishment meted out by a corrupt authority that has no legal standing in this instance. It produces only an implicit confession of corruption; in these accounts the treachery of Mortimer is 'discovered' for successive generations to see, and Marlowe's play bears further witness to that crime. It is an indictment of actions that must be hidden, since medieval 'apert' justice is never private or secret,[128] and of regimes that resort to private brutality to maintain power in the public sphere.

Marlowe's depiction focuses on the semantics of Edward's murder and the significance of not shedding innocent blood, which Lightborn technically has never done because of the methods he employs. Lightborn's statement is an inversion of the medieval prohibition against clerics shedding blood and invokes images of inquisitors who employ hot irons as a means of extracting a confession without extracting blood (reminiscent of Chaucer's Absolon). As many critics have suggested, Lightborn is simply doing his job, going about his business with 'speed, specificity, and professional detachment'.[129] Lightborn is merely the technician, and an expendable one at that. Once he has performed his task he will also be murdered to contain the secret, which by its very nature can never be contained. It is a performative cycle of violence and the bodies pile up as the characters attempt to hide their crimes and silence their opposition to avoid the inevitable revelation. The scene of Edward's death enacts the ritual of the interrogation: imprisonment, sleep deprivation, foul conditions, foul food, and finally bodily injury, yet it achieves nothing because despite all of Mortimer's plots, his schemes will unravel. Like the bloody severed head at the end of *Arthur and Gorlagon*, the brutality of the tale and the corruption it masks must be revealed. As Chaunticleer says in the *Nun's Priest's Tale*, 'Mordre wol out!' (line 3052).

Edward exhibits the characteristics of a torture victim that would have been familiar to an Elizabethan audience. He tells Lightborn, whom he suspects as his murderer:

> And there in mire and puddle have I stood
> This ten days' space, and lest that I should sleep,
> One plays continually upon a drum.
> They give me bread and water, being a king,
> So that for want of sleep and sustenance
> My mind's distempered, and my body's numbed,
> And whether I have limbs or no I know not.
> O, would my blood dropped out from every vein
> As doth this water from my tattered robes.   (V.v.58–66)

Edward, soiled and exhausted, is still unbroken. He refuses to grovel and asks only that he may see his death blow before it is delivered, to 'see the stroke before

---

[128] Farrell, 'Privacy and the Boundaries', p. 775.
[129] Thomas Cartelli, *Marlowe, Shakespeare and the Economy of Theatrical Experience* (Philadelphia: University of Pennsylvania Press, 1991), p. 134.

it comes,/ That even then when I shall lose my life,/ My mind may be more steadfast on my God' (V.v.75–7). His language is that of the martyr, ironically reflective of Foxe's narratives; he remains steadfast in the face of persecution and tribulations and wishes to endure his death heroically. But he is taken in by Lightborn's assurances that 'These hands were never stained with/ innocent blood,/ Nor shall they now be tainted with a king's' (V.v.79–81), and the audience sees and hears the devastating effects of prolonged torture in the disjointed rambling that follows. Amidst these wandering thoughts, Lightborn seizes Edward, confirming his fears, but unlike the glorious martyrs of medieval hagiography or Foxe's *Actes and Monuments*, Edward will be denied a heroic death. It is all over in a frenetic moment and a flurry of action and stage direction:

> **Edward:** I am too weak and feeble to resist.
> Assist me, sweet God, and receive my soul.
> **Lightborn:** Run for the table.
> **Edward:** O spare me! Or dispatch me in a trice!
> [Matrevis *and* Gurney *bring in a table, a mattress and a red-hot spit.*]
> **Lightborn:** So, lay the table down and stamp on it,
> But not too hard, lest that you bruise his body.
> [Lightborn *murders* Edward *by penetrating him with the red-hot poker.*]
> **Matrevis:** I fear me that this cry will raise the town,
> And therefore let us take horse and away.
> **Lightborn:** Tell me, sirs, was it not bravely done?
> **Gurney:** Excellent well. Take this for thy reward.
>   [*Then* Gurney *stabs* Lightborn *who dies*]
> Come, let us cast the body in the moat,
> And bear the King's to Mortimer, our lord.

There is no sense of sympathy for Edward, at least not from his murderers as they dispose of their duties as though taking out the rubbish. Sirluck argues that Edward's murder is the product of passion and the pleasure of outrage, with which 'comes the punishment that both defines the world for him, with its ruthless codes of power, and annihilates the boundaries of his personhood, distinct from kingship. He is degraded, tortured and spitted through the anus in the ultimate diabolic parody of his role as pathic, sexually and politically.'[130] The scene is one of shocking violence, not only in the manner of its execution, but also in its secretive and covert nature. Marlowe captures not only the ambiguity of loyalties but also the pervasive fear of persecution, imprisonment and interrogation through judicial torture prevalent in the early modern period. As a medieval audience may have balked at the murder of a king and the insidious manner of his death, making its own correlations with the methods of inquisitorial authority, an early-modern audience may have felt the presence of such tyranny in their judicial process. Ultimately, at the end of Marlowe's play, there

---

130 Sirluck, 'Marlowe's "Edward II"', p. 18.

is no justice until correct rule has been restored, and those who govern well do not resort to torture and brutality to maintain power or reinforce their authority.

Thomas Nashe: *The Unfortunate Traveller*

The Unfortunate Traveller: or, the Life of Jack Wilton (1594) is arguably one of the most gratuitously violent literary texts of the early-modern period with grotesque scenes of rape and murder, massacre and execution, that 'exaggerate and reorganize patterns of violence that Nashe presents early in the narrative'.[131] Its apparent approbation of torture and brutality is also a comical satire of the corruption and disease in the world. The main character, Jack Wilton, seems to enjoy violence and manipulating others, but 'by entertaining us, Nashe focuses our attention on the pranks' humour, disguising violence',[132] much like the comic violence of the Old French fabliaux. The novel follows Jack's exploits and adventures on the Continent (primarily in France and Italy) as a page during the wars of religion. It is largely a chronicle of atrocities to which Jack is both witness and almost a victim:[133] he sees battles, plague and rape; he is nearly hanged and then nearly cut up as part of an anatomy dissection. The narrative culminates in the description of a vicious Italian vendetta, which gets him shot in the neck, before Jack can finally escape and return to England. David Kaula argues that the comedic exaggeration is the text's chief distinction, with its stylistic dexterity in its 'exuberant parodying of current literary modes'.[134] He further writes that even though it deals with near-contemporary personages and events, adopting a critical view of social convention similar in ways to that of the Spanish picaresque novel, it 'relies too heavily on extravagant and macabre effects to be credited with a consistent verisimilitude'.[135] Much of the violence is centred on large-scale events, such as the massacre of the Anabaptists in Munster, Westphalia (24 June 1535), events recognizable to Nashe's audience that speak to the cultural anxieties of foreign influence and invasion as well as imperial domination. As Andrew Fleck notes, 'this brutal episode exemplifies Nashe's often gruesome focus on the body, especially the body reduced to its parts, here and throughout *The Unfortunate Traveller*',[136] but also ties these spectacles to a 'nationalist complexion that evokes

---

[131] Susan Marie Harrington and Michal Nahor Bond, '"Good Sir, be Ruld by Me": Patterns of Domination and Manipulation in Thomas Nashe's *The Unfortunate Traveller*', *Studies in Short Fiction* (2000): 243–50, p. 244.

[132] Harrington and Bond, '"Good Sir, be Ruld by Me"', p. 245.

[133] The novel has several parallels to Voltaire's eighteenth-century *Candide*.

[134] David Kaula, 'The Low Style in Nashe's *The Unfortunate Traveller*', *Studies in English Literature, 1500–1900* 6.1: The English Renaissance (Winter, 1966): 43–57; p. 43.

[135] Kaula, 'The Low Style', p. 43.

[136] Andrew Fleck, 'Anatomizing the Body Politic: The Nation and the Renaissance Body in Thomas Nashe's *The Unfortunate Traveller*', *Modern Philology* 104.3 (2007): 295–328, p. 296.

the period's understanding of the political trope of the body politic'.[137] For all its violence – primarily set outside England – *The Unfortunate Traveller* rarely deals with judicial torture, but where it does it plays on xenophobia and public fears of interrogation and execution, highlighting the ridiculousness and unreliability of such measures in discovering 'truth' and revealing anxieties of national identity tied to the perpetuation of brutality.

Setting the violence outside England, as *The Prioress's Tale* does, mediates the potential for national culpability and fixes it firmly in the realm of the barbarian Other. What's more, because many of these reflect actual events, the English audience is reminded of the brutality of continental authorities embodied in the Roman Church and France. Wilton recounts the tale of an English captain who flees to the French, offering service against Henry VIII, tapping into cultural fears of betrayal, fears that were heightened during the period of religio-political upheaval after the Reformation. Betraying England to France is the ultimate treachery and it undermines any unified sense of English national identity. But even the French don't trust a traitor. Fearing treachery, the French king wants the captain examined 'but was askt *Quevela*' (p. 277).[138] He is questioned and suspects they will harm him: 'Then began he to smell on the villaine so rammishly, that none there but was ready to rent him in pieces' (p. 278). So he lies: 'Hereat the true king stept forth, and commaunded to lay hande on the Lozell, and that he should be tortured to confesse the truth, for he was a spie and nothing else' (p. 278). Faced with torture and the spectacle of the wheel, a punishment common on the Continent,[139] the prisoner implicates Wilton: 'He no sooner sawe the wheele and the torments set before him, but he cryde out like a Rascall, and said he was a poore Captaine in the English Campe, suborned by one Jack Wilton (a Noble mans Page) and no other, to come and kill the French King in a braverie and return, and that he had no other intention in the world' (p. 278). The instruments of torture are enough to provoke a confession, as often happened in judicial interrogations, but it is a false confession that potentially dooms an innocent man. Nashe places the torture in France, demonizing the French king as the barbarian Other willing to resort to such methods to secure his unstable and corrupt state, but Nashe also interrogates the efficacy of torture as a tool of discovery in England and reveals that the only 'truth' discovered in the process is a lie.

The novel is devoted to extolling the barbaric tendencies of foreign authorities in exaggerated, almost farcical, detail. Here the grim prospects of judicial

---

137 Fleck, 'Anatomizing the Body Politic', p. 297.
138 Thomas Nashe, *The Unfortunate Traveller or the life of Iacke Wilton*, in *Shorter Novels: Elizabethan and Jacobean* (London: J.M. Dent and Sons, 1929).
139 Froissart, who was Flemish, complains in his fourteenth-century *Chronicles* about the barbarism of the Hainaultian (modern Dutch) Germans: 'It would be better for a knight to be captured by infidels, out-and-out pagans or Saracens, than by Germans.' *Chronicles*, qtd. in West, *Chaucer 1340–1400*, p. 34.

torture are described almost gleefully without any sense of gravity, suggesting the wanton savagery of England's enemies but not without implying a certain complicity in Wilton, who recounts these events with barbaric delight. Nashe evokes the same gruesome carelessness with his description of the dismemberment of the Jews at the end, which may simply be symptomatic of anti-Judaic sentiments similar to those pronounced by Chaucer's Prioress, who, like Wilton, revels in the graphic and bloody details. Nashe's narrative reflects an awareness of judicial torture in early-modern society and seems to validate those procedures; but in locating these actions outside of England, Nashe distances himself and his audience from overt condemnation of his own government, masking his criticism in comedy. The French are not swayed by the supposed confession, but it 'moove them all to laughter' (p. 278) and they appear eager to employ torture even if it does not yield any more fruitful information: '[…] all this could not keepe his joynts from ransacking on the Wheele, for they vowed either to make him a Confessor or a Martyr with a trice: when still he sung all one song, they tolde the King he was a foole, and that some shrewd head had knavishly wrought on him, wherefore it should stand with his honour to whip him out of the Campe and send him home' (p. 278). The prisoner is tormented, broken on the wheel and finally whipped when the torture produces nothing but 'all one song'. It is ineffective and serves no purpose but to highlight Wilton's willingness to manipulate others and the willingness of French authorities to resort to prolonged torture, part of the conventional discourse of Englishness and a more embodied sense of the nation.[140] As in some medieval texts, continental figures, like the French, function as the barbarous Other against which England defines itself, but in the context of *The Unfortunate Traveller* this distinction is problematic because England has introduced similar measures into its own judicial process and is in danger of losing its historical identity as a nation governed by 'gode olde law'. According to Nashe, it is in other countries that Englishmen learn brutality and the art of murder, much like Marlowe's Lightborn in *Edward II*, but they should not participate in them: 'let others tell you strange accidents, treasons, poysonings, close packings in France, Spaine, and Italy: it is no harme for you to heare of them, but come not nere them' (p. 335). The spectre of inquisitorial torture and the Spanish Inquisition casts a dark shadow in the text, and Nashe argues that England is in danger of falling under that shadow through its own resort to torture.

Much of the novel is concerned with foreign taint, keeping Englishmen from the corruption of foreigners, particularly Jews. Fleck notes that this strain of anti-Judaism is not unusual, and Zadoch's offer to poison his adversary draws on a stock of cultural fears connecting the two,[141] fears that may have resonated with Nashe's audience as they saw their government succumb to foreign influence and

---

[140] Fleck, 'Anatomizing the Body Politic', p. 317.
[141] Fleck, 'Anatomizing the Body Politic', pp. 318–19.

felt their nation threatened. The Jews are the 'stock' figures of the alien Other in sixteenth-century plays like the *Jew of Malta* (c. 1589–90) and *The Merchant of Venice* (c. 1596–98), but here they function as agents of other continental influences – Spain and Italy – as convenient scapegoats for English fears of infiltration. Heng has noted that Muslims and Jews were often interchangeable for one another; Muslims were often depicted as the 'virtual Jew', representing medieval and later early-modern prejudices and fears of 'pollution'.[142] In an attempt to settle intra-European strife, 'the sixteenth century once again conjured up the medieval idea of the Crusades against barbaric nations'.[143]

Wilton falls afoul of Zadoch, who sells him to his colleague Dr Zacharie as a subject for anatomical dissection.[144] The plan is foiled by Juliana, the Marquis of Mantua's wife and the pope's concubine, who saves Wilton to keep him as a sex slave and plans to poison him when she has finished with him; she 'schemes for his release, then becomes the means for destroying his hated Jewish captors'.[145] The vivid description of Zadoch's execution surpasses the brutality of the *Prioress's Tale*. While this scene is set in the decadent See of Rome, Wilton (perhaps understandably) delights in recounting the executioner's methods, revealing a penchant for brutal vengeance in this stalwart Englishman that paints him with the same brush as his tormentors. Fleck argues that this episode suggests Foucault's understanding of the early-modern state's 'need symbolically to re-enact the crime against the body of the state on the body of the condemned',[146] but in re-enacting this crime against Zadoch, the Roman state is implicated in his brutality and its authority is called into question, undermining Catholic institutions. For an English Protestant audience this demonization of the Catholic See and other foreign and religious Others would have seemed logical and even laudatory, but since England participated in similar brutal spectacles and perpetuated similar atrocities, the audience's applause is hypocritical. Zadoch may deserve to die, but the measures taken against him are extreme, and while Jack Wilton may enjoy describing the torments inflicted upon his tormentor, the blood-thirsty imagery does him no credit. Zadoch's execution by impaling is enacted in the public square and the Roman audience is implicated in the spectacle by its approbation. He is brought to the place of execution

> where first and formost he was stript, then on a sharp yron stake fastened in the ground, he had his fundament pitcht, which stake ran up along into the bodie like a spit, under his arme-holes two of like sort, a great bon-fire they made round

---

[142] Heng, 'The Romance of England', p. 143.
[143] Borst, *Medieval Worlds*, p. 9.
[144] The subject of vivisection and the bodily obsessions of the novel are the primary concerns of Fleck's vivid and compelling article. He emphasizes the associations between the physical descriptions in *The Unfortunate Traveller* and a burgeoning interest in anatomy and medical texts circulating throughout the sixteenth century.
[145] Fleck, 'Anatomizing the Body Politic', p. 324.
[146] Fleck, 'Anatomizing the Body Politic', p. 324.

about him, wherewith his flesh roasted not burnd: and everas with the heate his skinne blistred, the fire was drawen aside, and they basted him with a mixture of Aqua fortis, allum water, and Mercury sublimatum, which smarted to the very soul of him, and searcht him to the marrowe. (p. 346)

The litany of torments continues: They scourge his back and buttocks with 'burning whips of red hot wier'; his head is anointed with pitch and tar and set on fire; they tie fireworks to his genitals; flay him with hot pincers; 'his breast and his belly with seale skins they grated ouer' and then they bathe the raw flesh with 'smiths syndry water [and] Aqua vitae'; they drive thorns under his fingernails, break all his fingers and toes (leaving them hanging by pieces of skin), until: 'In conclusion, they had a small oyle fire, such as men blow light bubbles of glasse with, and beginning at his feete, they let him lingringly burne vp lim by lim, till his heart was consumed, and then he died' (pp. 346–7). Zadoch is roasted like a pig and basted in flammable substances rather than drippings, in an ironic parody of his religious prohibition against eating pork. His penetration draws on similar homoerotic fears exhibited in Edward II's murder but instead of leaving his body unmarked this graphic mutilation inscribes tyranny and brutality on his flesh, much like the earlier medieval scene in *RCL* where the Saracen becomes a gruesome substitute for pork. Wilton apparently enjoys this spectacle, which partly reflects 'his relief at his own escape from Zacharie and the anatomy he had planned', and Fleck suggests that 'this displacement of fear of corporeal disintegration can be justified as a sort of retribution for Jack's experiences while in a shadowy Jew's captivity'.[147] But Wilton is a parody of those who support torture and brutality as long as it is employed against someone else. The image is shocking, and exceeds the punitive practices of sixteenth-century England, drawing distinctions between the perceived civility of the British Protestants and the apparent barbarism of the Italian Catholics. However, the scene also serves as a warning to the English monarchy about the destabilizing effects of employing torture and brutal punishments in the interests of state security. These methods undermine the very fabric of the English nation and may leave it open to invasion. Fleck finds the later descriptive dismemberment of the Italian Cutwolfe on the gallows much more troubling partly because Cutwolfe's crimes were vengeance,[148] but both episodes depict excessive authoritarian brutality and place it firmly outside the realm of the more 'civilized' England.

Cutwolfe's execution upon the wheel is meant to reinforce power structures and the authority of the state, but in his final speech Cutwolfe subverts these efforts like the final vocality of Aaron the Moor in *Titus Andronicus*. Both scenes twist the intentions of civil authority where the spectacles of violence against condemned men 'were meant to be instructive, to show that divine justice, coupled with the civil power's guarantee of maintaining order, would punish

---

[147] Fleck, 'Anatomizing the Body Politic', p. 325.
[148] Fleck, 'Anatomizing the Body Politic', p. 325.

those whose crimes impede the proper functioning of the system.'[149] But the defiance of the prisoners subverts the intentions of law, and their speeches question the validity of institutional punishment. As Fleck notes, the spectacle and accompanying confession 'should conform to the conventions of testifying to the civil authorities' justice, but Cutwolfe goes to his end without repentance.'[150] Not only does he not repent, but also he takes the opportunity to sway public opinion and tell his story of revenge, with which many may sympathize.

His scaffold speech gives him the opportunity to indict the authority that punishes brutality (which he can justify) with further, more gruesome brutality. Fleck argues that repentance is not strictly required, citing Foucault and suggesting that the 'lurid dissolution of Cutwolfe's body, rendered in compelling detail by Jack's eye-witness account, serves to inscribe the intended lesson, despite the revenger's efforts to derail the spectacle'.[151] But the validity of that lesson is also inscribed, and the refusal of the victim to relent suggests the instability of the civil authority. The intention may be to reaffirm power, but the excessive brutality of Cutwolfe's execution for justifiable crimes that begins by breaking his bones, challenges the justice that is meant to be 'published' on his body:

> Brauely did he drum on this *Cutwolfes* bones, not breaking them outright, but like a sadler knocking in of tackes, iarring on them quaueringly with his hammer a great while together. No ioint about him but with a hatchet he had for the nones he disioynted halfe, and then with boyling lead souldered vp the wounds from bleeding: his tongue he puld out, least he should blaspheme in his torment; venimous stinging wormes hee thrust into his eares, to keep his head rauingly occupied: with cankers scruzed to peeces he rubd his mouth and his gums: no lim of his but was lingeringly splinterd in shiuers. In this horror left they him on the wheele as in hell; where, yet liuing, he might beholde his flesh legacied amongst the foules of the aire. (p. 355)

The imagery of Cutwolfe's mutilated body, the cauterized wounds and the removal of his tongue recalls many of the torments suffered by saints in medieval hagiography, particularly Christina. He is not being elevated in his torment, but his tormenters, despite Wilton's apparent approval, are demonized in this spectacle; they are associated with the history of Roman persecution through this language and Cutwolfe's defiant speech. Wilton is also complicit in this brutality because of his approval, suggesting that the line between English civility and continental barbarism has grown very thin indeed. And despite the apparent

---

[149] Fleck, 'Anatomizing the Body Politic', p. 325. Fleck points to the arguments of Cynthia Marshall and Bruce Smith who both attribute these scenes to sadomasochism, and posits that Zadoch's execution certainly seems sadistic 'in its grisly and excessive narration, but this sadism comes from having turned the tables on the man who sold him as a living corpse for an anatomy, coupled with anti-Semitic xenophobia' (p. 325 n. 55). Marshall, *The Shattering of the Self*; Bruce R. Smith, 'Rape, Rap, Rupture, Rapture: R-Rated Futures on the Global Market', *Textual Practice* 9 (1995): 421–44.

[150] Fleck, 'Anatomizing the Body Politic', p. 326.

[151] Fleck, 'Anatomizing the Body Politic', p. 326.

comedy of the narrative, it is an uncomfortable association. Cutwolfe does not expound the virtues of Christian faith but recites the discourse of vengeance, a language embedded in many early-modern societies, scrutinizing the culture of revenge and its perpetuation in gruesome civil punishments.

Far more important than Wilton's recitation of these events is the fact that the spectacle of this torment compels him to mend his ways, marry his courtesan and rejoin the king's service in England. The episodes of torture may have served their purpose as a deterrent, rehabilitating Wilton, but they are also emblematic of the foreign tyranny and oppression that threaten to infiltrate England by example. Fleck links the new studies of the body to these discourses on violence and the evolution of national identity:

> As this revolution in anatomy swept across sixteenth-century Europe, the earliest stirrings of nationalist thought, often couched in terms of a body politic, received a new charge. The xenophobic representations of national difference that Nashe projects onto disciplined foreign bodies in *The Unfortunate Traveller* allow him to celebrate the bodily integrity of his English narrator and his escape both from the perils of his 'out-landish' experience generally and from a literal anatomy specifically.[152]

However, in demonizing foreign authorities, Nashe comes perilously close to indicting English authorities who also relied on spectacles of torture and punishment as deterrents against treachery or dissent. He satirizes the excesses of foreign powers while adroitly drawing conclusions about his own society. While he seems to advocate these methods as just punishment through his manipulative narrator, Nashe also illuminates their barbarity just as other early-modern authors appropriated supposedly 'medieval' methods of torture and brutality for their own ends, highlighting the barbarism of their own era.

The early-modern period was fraught with crises of identity: from religious division and schism to competing powers within the colonial discourse and the expansion of the known world. At the same time, authors recognized the brutality that had proliferated in their own societies, and often spoke vehemently against it, comparing themselves to those people who had been othered by popular perception and questioning the civility in their own judicial systems. The Spanish Dominican priest Bartolomé de las Casas (1484–1566) argued against the introduction of torture into the New World, indicting the Spanish monarchy for its brutality. He wrote that the 'Indians had good reasons to call their new Spanish masters barbarians, for it was the Spaniards who had ruined life there with their ill-considered intrusion.'[153] Michel de Montaigne urged the French populace and France's religious and political leaders to re-evaluate their resort to torture, arguing that the practice made them worse than New World

---

[152] Fleck, 'Anatomizing the Body Politic', p. 299.
[153] Borst, *Medieval Worlds*, p. 10.

cannibals whose original naiveté was 'becoming corrupted by European vices'.[154] In England, the debate over torture gained momentum as the practice, previously prohibited by English common law, was used against religio-political enemies of the English crown (real or imagined). In this climate, early-modern authors and playwrights often looked to the past as a means of contextualizing their present, looking for a sense of stability in an unstable world or attempting to situate excessive brutality outside the realm of their own consciousness as something archaic or 'medieval'. John Foxe appropriates the form of medieval hagiography for his veneration of contemporary Protestant martyrs, negotiating the hypocrisy of torture employed in his own time by English authorities. William Shakespeare and Christopher Marlowe firmly locate torture and judicial brutality in narratives of the classical and medieval past, while Thomas Nashe reinforces the medieval association of such practices with the continental Other through comic exaggeration. But rather than pushing torture back into the past, where it had a troubled history from the start, early-modern authors bring it forward and display its cruelty, its abuses and its contradictions in their own time. By rejecting the historical use of torture in literature and in plays, and demonizing its practitioners, early-modern authors also reject the resort to torture in sixteenth-century jurisprudence and question the stability of their world.

---

[154] Borst, *Medieval Worlds*, p. 10.

Conclusion

In the modern mind, torture has become inextricably linked to the medieval world. As modern civilization grapples with reports of abuses that include interrogatory torture from powers great and small, the concerns of medieval authors regarding judicial practices in their own time become particularly relevant. We look back on the medieval world armed with assumptions of alterity and Otherness, qualifying and defining a world of which we have only glimpses. In these circumstances, the wide range of medieval literary sources become invaluable tools for evaluating cultural responses to societal and judicial practice. Torture is notorious now, but it was also notorious then; its application coupled with scenes of excessive brutality often colours narratives against those who resort to such drastic and extreme measures and question the definitions of national identity. Even in literary texts that espouse orthodox ideologies, such as the extensive corpus of medieval hagiography, torture is an anathema; it is the weapon of pagan persecutors wielded against the faithful who stand steadfast and endure. Similarly, these narratives have the potential to turn on the propagators of violence, potentially providing tools for resisting Church authority in the struggle over heterodoxy. Religious literature and iconography are rife with images of broken and tortured bodies, bodies that cry out against the torment inflicted by illegitimate authorities and challenge the justice in applying torture as a means of 'discovery'.

From sparse twelfth-century roots, torture was introduced into European jurisprudence in the thirteenth century with the 'rediscovery' of Roman law. Its presence increased in legal proceedings as the Middle Ages progressed into the early-modern era, a process borne out in tracts like the German *Constitutio Criminalis Carolina* of 1532. Torture, as a legal procedure designed to enhance the reliability of the accused's confession in conjunction with other half-proofs,[1] rarely figures in the narrative framework of secular literature even if its historical practice is undisputed. Even in cultures that frequently employed torture as a method of interrogation, as in France, secular literature is ominously silent on the matter, avoiding its use as a prominent literary motif. The texts in this study exemplify a literary resistance to using or celebrating torture as part of the narrative fabric, and signify an aversion to the employment of torture or brutal punishments in the course of justice, even against the worst traitors and apostates. As European nations evolved, many societies attempted to define themselves in opposition to the use of judicial torture. For many medieval communities

---

[1] Langbein, *Torture and the Law of Proof*, p. 5.

CONCLUSION

this was manifested in a resistance to the legal and literary influence of France – a nation also grappling with its own identity for which the introduction of torture in canon law with secular application had a destabilizing effect. Rather than being a mimetic response to societal violence, these texts place torture and excessive brutality outside the boundaries of accepted practice, attributing its use to outsiders or condemning its abuse by authorities within their own past, and perhaps urging restraint in their present. Stable societies cannot be founded on a system of law that relies on torture or on brutality to reinforce power. In the *Chanson de Roland*, torture is employed in the punishment of the traitor Ganelon, whose crime in betraying Charlemagne's nephew and 20,000 of his men would seem to warrant such drastic measures. But taken in the context of legal punishments for treachery, the historical realities of Charlemagne's rule, and the sympathetic possibilities that may have justified Ganelon's actions against Roland, the brutality of his execution in the poem and its seemingly arbitrary suspension of justice indict tyranny and urge a poetic audience to exercise justice rather than vengeance. In an arguably nationalistic poem, this resort to excessive brutality reflects poorly on the society that still uses torture as a means of judicial control and questions legal systems where torture was regularly applied.

The *Roman van Walewein* places torture outside the realm of civilized Flemish society, perhaps reflecting reluctance on the part of civil authorities to use torture in the face of public opposition. Only in far away countries like Endi do kings and princesses use torture to bend people to their will or threaten them into submission. The courtly society of Europe, particularly that which aspires to live up to the ideals of the Arthurian tradition, cannot participate in a corrupt system that allows torture to become an arbitrary weapon of despotic rule, so Penninc and Pieter Vostaert place torture on the margins of their world and never allow it to be applied in their poem. Appropriating the French Arthurian tradition, but exercising poetic innovation by including episodes of torture absent from French romances, the *Roman van Walewein* distinguishes itself from French literary and legal traditions, indicting the legal practice so common in medieval jurisprudence. It is a threat that is never realized in the *Roman van Walewein* and that cannot persist in a world where justice and order prevail.

In Icelandic society, where torture had no place in traditional legal practice, and excessive punishment warranted swift and severe reprisals, rare instances of torture stand out against a backdrop of acceptable violence and indicate not historical reality, but perhaps literary exaggeration. Struggling to maintain its own traditions against the infusion of continental trends and against the colonial endeavours of Norway, Icelandic family sagas emphasize correct legal practice and condemn excesses and breaches of law. Hamstringing, a popular motif in Eddic poetry elevating the suffering of the supernatural hero in opposition to the evil machinations of a tyrant, also delineates the acceptable boundaries of blood feud and retributive violence in *Hrafnkels saga*, where killing is permitted but mutilation designed as a public form of humiliation is not. Punishments like that of Broðir take on a religious dimension when compared with the evisceration of saints and the potentially analogous martyrdom of Brian Boru. Rather than being indicative of a Norse delight in brutality, the evisceration of Broðir sets the evil apostate up against the saintly heroes of the hagiographic tradition, and suggests a desire to distance later medieval society from a more barbarous pagan past. Rejecting torture as a literary motif, these texts reflect a relatively unified dissent against a common legal practice of the thirteenth and fourteenth centuries and emphasize the alterity of torture in truly civilized societies.

Medieval torture did exist, particularly on the European continent, but its use was not wholly accepted by society, and abuses of the judicial system were subject to the condemnation of ordinary people and poets. According to Langbein, 'European criminal procedure in the Middle Ages developed a demanding law of proof, meant as a safeguard against judicial error or corruption, which caused the national legal systems then forming to become dependent upon extracting tortured confessions in cases of serious crime.'[2] Torture was not developed because of a monstrous delight in violence, nor as a need for gruesome punitive measures; its purpose was interrogative, based on evidence and an assumption of guilt. That is not to excuse torture in medieval jurisprudence, only to contextualize its evolution and recognize that by reinstituting physical coercion – torture – as a means of extracting confessions, modern society rejects the medieval interest in pursuing justice by the fairest means possible and is guilty of its own attempts to distance itself from a supposedly more barbarous past. Literature was often a vehicle for social critique and these narratives apply that critical eye to the presence of torture in their world, condemning its use, its abuse, its potential for destabilizing society, and relegate it to the world of the Other. Ultimately, European 'criminal procedure failed at its centuries-long effort to devise rules and procedures that would make tortured confessions reliable'[3] and abandoned it. In some countries, like medieval England, 'tortured confession never became part of the ordinary criminal procedure.'[4] Later governments would resort to torture, but medieval doctors of law flirted with the process and found that it never really yielded the truth. This is evident in the stigma attached to torture in medieval secular literature like the *Roman van Walewein*, where torture is relegated to the realm of the Other, the monstrous and the barbarous. In Old Norse/Icelandic literature torture is symptomatic of corrupt societies, perhaps responding to pervasive continental pressures that influenced literary traditions throughout Europe. As Iceland struggled to maintain its own cultural identity under Norwegian colonial endeavours, Icelandic authors portrayed their historic society as violent and harsh, but just.

England's uneasy relationship with judicial torture, illegal through most of the medieval period, produces some of the most shockingly brutal literary narratives as English authors attempt to define themselves in opposition to other, more

---

[2] Langbein, *Torture and the Law of Proof*, p. x.
[3] Langbein, *Torture and the Law of Proof*, p. x.
[4] Langbein, *Torture and the Law of Proof*, p. x.

brutal societies. *Havelok the Dane* attempts to negotiate not only the question of inherited violence but of cultural identity embedded in the application of judicial torture – the 'Other within'. Written in England for an audience of Anglo-Danish descent, *Havelok* interrogates assumptions of cultural assimilation and the progress of society by situating the practices of brutality outside of England and firmly in the Danish past.

Werewolf narratives like *Bisclavret* and *Arthur and Gorlagon* investigate shifting boundaries of humanity and violence, where torture is employed as a judicial necessity to uncover deception and crime but is employed without any sense of delight or pleasure. In these texts, the authors delicately balance the brutality of torture against the cruel actions and deceit of the antagonists, not revelling in its application but treating it as a grim reality, and challenging its place in civilized societies. In much the same way, Chaucer inserts sparse references to torture in a few of his *Canterbury Tales*, dwelling not on the gruesome details of the judicial process but on the duplicity that forces legitimate authorities to resort to such measures. In the *Prioress's Tale* Chaucer criticizes the ignorance of clergy and the mob violence provoked by anti-Judaic propaganda and questions the stability of societies where citizens are punished without trial and where an entire community is forced to answer for the actions of a few. But in each of these cases, the brutality of torture is exercised outside of England, in a foreign world, a geographical and cultural Other.

As with much modern comedy, medieval comic literature often makes fun of horribly uncomfortable situations, crossing boundaries of propriety and justice. The Old French fabliaux, and Chaucer's Middle English contributions to the genre, often mock authority that oversteps its bounds by making light of excessive brutality. Rarely do these tales employ torture in their social critique, but some fabliaux skirt the edges of comedy by presenting narratives of unmitigated brutality involving castration. *Du prestre crucefié*, *De Connebert* (*Li prestre ki perdi les colles*), and *La Dame escoillee* all offer scenes of castration that seem to applaud the comic use of brutality, but embedded in each of these narratives is a condemnation of the abuse of power and of the failures of the judicial system. Chaucer's *Miller's Tale*, in response to the innocuous violence of the *Knight's Tale*, critiques similar systems of authority and questions the validity of a judicial system that does not seem to apply evenly to everyone. Implicit in the humour of these tales is a stark condemnation of judicial torture and societal brutality that is often enacted within the framework of civil and religious authority.

As the Middle Ages drew to a close with the Wars of the Roses and the accession of Henry VIII to the English throne, early-modern society was faced with crises of conscience as the Reformation split European Christendom and religious and secular authorities engaged in a war of words and martyrdom, where judicial torture was employed with increasing and alarming frequency. Torture, which had been illegal in England, was now sanctioned in this war of faith as kings, courts, priests and popes fought for the souls of the Christian populace. Martyrologies like John Foxe's *Actes and Monuments* integrated the violence of medieval hagiography with the first-hand narratives of Protestant martyrs, creating within the discourse of judicial torture a resistance to illegitimate authority resonant of its predecessors, but unique in its immediacy and its reality. Looking back at the classical and medieval worlds, authors like William Shakespeare and Christopher Marlowe interrogated early-modern assumptions of civility and cultural progress by employing violent imagery on the Elizabethan stage often as a condemnation of excessive brutality. *Edward II* and *Titus Andronicus* question the viability of governments that employ torture, and illuminate the instability of such regimes. In these plays, and in the satire of Thomas Nashe, torture is the mark of a diseased society desperately trying to cling to its power and its legitimacy through any means necessary, undermining its own social fabric in the process.

There is a modern disconnect from medieval reactions to violence. Enders writes, 'Modern responses to the medieval aesthetics of violence sometimes disclose a pitched sense of alienation from the Middle Ages that is as intriguing for what it reveals as for what it denies.'[5] This alienation is often associated with modern ideas of 'progress'. Mickel argues that scholars often perceive records of the past through the post-eighteenth-century lens of progressive ideas, frequently assuming that

> crueler, less enlightened forms of conduct would naturally be present in older institutions and forms of law. It is expected that later societies have modified this primitive behavior. Such assumptions often lead to misreadings and 'silent glosses' which add to the text what one assumes to be true. That torture might be a formal part of a more primitive criminal procedure, given the harsh nature of corporal punishment for relatively (by today's standards) minor crimes, would not seem implausible to many.[6]

There is a sense that the presence of torture in medieval literature further separates the modern reader or critic from this distant past, and that the persistence of violence in these works is symptomatic of a corrupted and cankerous society. Literary episodes of torture do not 'own' it; they repel it and disown it – firmly placing these practices outside their native sphere of cultural and social practice by writing these scenes as counterproductive at best and barbaric at worst. Enders aptly points out, 'The very idea that a violent or tortured inventional scene could engender the useful or beautiful discourses of law, drama, or poetry suggests that – troubling though the linkage of torture, truth, inventional discovery, and creativity may be – the innumerable medieval scenes of torture that have so revolted the modern reader actually enact that scenario.'[7] Classifying scenes of torture as 'innumerable' limits the scope of investigation and denies the nuanced

---

[5] Enders, *The Medieval Theater of Cruelty*, p. 21.
[6] Mickel, *Ganelon, Treason*, p. 40.
[7] Enders, *The Medieval Theater of Cruelty*, p. 26.

use of torture in specific genres, but it also feeds into the modern assumption that torture and brutality were accepted motifs of medieval culture and society.

As modern popular culture often teaches society about the extremes, the taboos and the fantasy rather than the reality of life, so too does most medieval and early-modern literature. Rather than painting a picture of an irrevocably violent age fraught with sadism, corruption and abuse in the application of torture and capital punishment, literary texts of the Middle Ages and the Reformation record the wishes, the desires and the yearning for justice of a populace confronted with an often-brutal reality. But that brutal reality is not an alien past from which humanity has progressed, nor is it the only reality of medieval life. Modern culture, like its early-modern predecessors, makes assumptions about the Middle Ages based on a desire to be different, to have evolved from that which we consider barbaric and indeed 'medieval'. Medieval authors and poets had the same desire – casting barbarians and tyrants as figures outside their own boundaries, placing torture in the hands of unjust persecutors rather than the agents of law.

Select Bibliography

Unpublished Primary Sources

De Connebert. Ed. and trans. Nathaniel Dubin, 1994.
La Dame escoillee. Ed. and trans. Nathaniel Dubin, 1994.
Froissart, Jean. *Chronicles*. Paris, Bibliothèque Nationale, MS fr. 2643, fol. 11. Flanders, Bruges. Fifteenth century.
The Gilte Legende. London, British Library, MS Harley 630. Mid-fifteenth century.
Du prestre crucefié. Ed. and Trans. by Nathaniel Dubin, 1994.

Printed Primary Sources

Allen, Cardinal William. *A True, Sincere, and Modest Defense of English Catholics*. Ed. Robert M. Kingdon. Ithaca NY: Cornell University Press, 1965.
Aristotle. *On Rhetoric: A Theory of Civic Discourse*. Ed. George A. Kennedy. New York and Oxford: Oxford University Press, 1991: 109–18.
Arthur and Gorlagon. Trans. Frank A. Milne. *Folk-Lore* 15 (1904): 40–67.
'Arthur and Gorlagon'. Ed. and trans. George Lyman Kittredge. In *Harvard Studies and Notes in Philology and Literature* 8 (1903): 149–273. Reprinted as an individual text New York: Haskell House, 1966.
Bisclavret. In *The Lais of Marie de France*. Trans. Robert Hanning and Joan Ferrante. Grand Rapids MI: Baker Books, 1978, seventh printing, 2002.
Brennu-Njáls saga. Ed. Einar Ól. Sveinsson. Íslenzk Fornrit 12, Reykjavik: Hið islenzka fornritafélag, 1954.
Caesarius of Heisterbach. *Dialogue on Miracles: At the Stake*. In *Heresy and Authority in Medieval Europe: Documents in Translation*. Ed. Edward Peters. Philadelphia: University of Pennsylvania Press, 1980: 193–4.
La Chanson de Roland. Ed. Léon Gautier. Tours: Mame et fils, 1872.
Charlemagne. 'Sanctuary and enforcing the payment of *wergeld*'. Doc. 15a. Trans. Kelly Gibson. In *Vengeance in Medieval Europe: A Reader*. Ed. Daniel Lord Smail and Kelly Gibson. Readings in Medieval Civilizations and Cultures: XIII. Toronto: University of Toronto Press, 2009.
Chaucer, Geoffrey. *The General Prologue. The Riverside Chaucer*. Ed. Larry D. Benson. Boston MA: Houghton Mifflin Company, 1987.
——. *The Knight's Tale. The Riverside Chaucer*. Ed. Larry D. Benson. Boston MA: Houghton Mifflin Company, 1987.
——. *The Miller's Prologue and Tale. The Riverside Chaucer*. Ed. Larry D. Benson. Boston MA: Houghton Mifflin Company, 1987.

———. *The Prioress's Tale. The Riverside Chaucer.* Ed. Larry D. Benson. Boston MA: Houghton Mifflin Company, 1987.

———. *The Reeve's Prologue and Tale. The Riverside Chaucer.* Ed. Larry D. Benson. Boston MA: Houghton Mifflin Company, 1987.

———. *The Second Nun's Prologue and Tale. The Riverside Chaucer.* Ed. Larry D. Benson. Boston MA: Houghton Mifflin Company, 1987.

Chrétien de Troyes. *Cligès.* In *Arthurian Romances.* Trans. William W. Kibler. London: Penguin Books, 1991.

Christine de Pizan. *The Book of the City of Ladies.* Trans. Earl Jeffrey Richards. New York: Persea Books, 1998.

De Connebert. In *Nouveau Recueil Complet des Fabliaux.* Ed. Willem Noomen and Nico van den Boogaard. 10 vols. Assen: Van Gorcum, 1983–1998. Vol. 7, 1993.

Contes à rire du nord de la France: Fabliaux abbevillois, amiénois, artésiens, douaisiens, flamands, hennuyers... La vie D'Eustache le Moine. Trans. R. Berger and Aimé Petit. Troesnes, La Ferté-Milon: Corps 9 Éditions, 1987.

Costuma d'Agen. Agen, France, Archives départementales de Lot-et-Garonne, MS 42, fol. 42v. Trans. F.R.P. Akehurst, 'Name, Reputation, and Notoriety in French Customary Law.' In *Fama: The Politics of Talk and Reputation in Medieval Europe.* Ed. Thelma Fenster and Daniel Lord Smail. Ithaca NY: Cornell University Press, 2003.

Councils and Synods with Other Documents Relating to the English Church, 11, A.D. 1205–1313, pt. 2, 1265–1313. ed. F.M. Powicke and C.R. Cheney. Oxford: Oxford University Press, 1964: 1267–9.

La Dame escoillee. In *Nouveau Recueil Complet des Fabliaux.* Ed. Willem Noomen and Nico van den Boogaard. 10 vols. Assen: Van Gorcum, 1983–1998. Vol. 8, 1994.

The Early South-English Legendary or Lives of Saints, MS Laud 108 in the Bodleian Library. Ed. Carl Horstmann. EETS, os 87. Oxford: Oxford University Press, 1887; reprinted 2000.

Eco, Umberto. *The Name of the Rose.* Trans. William Weaver. New York: Warner Books/Harcourt Brace Jovanovich, 1983.

Einhard. *The Life of Charlemagne.* In *Einhard and Notker the Stammerer: Two Lives of Charlemagne.* Ed. David Ganz. London: Penguin Books, 2008: 17–44.

The Etablissements de Saint Louis: Thirteenth-Century Law Texts from Tours, Orléans, and Paris. Trans. F.R.P. Akehurst. Philadelphia: University of Pennsylvania Press, 1996.

Fabliaux. Ed. R.C. Johnston and D.D.R. Owen. Oxford: Basil Blackwell, 1957.

Fabliaux, Fair and Foul. Trans. John DuVal. Binghamton NY: Medieval and Renaissance Texts and Studies, 1992.

Fabliaux français du Moyen Age. Ed. Philippe Ménard. Geneva: Libraire Droz S.A., 1979.

Fasciculus Morum: A Fourteenth-Century Preacher's Handbook. Trans. Siegfried Wenzel. University Park PA: Pennsylvania State University Press, 1989.

Faulkes, Anthony, ed. *Two Icelandic Stories: Hreiðrs þáttr, Orms þáttr.* London: Viking Society for Northern Research Text Series 4, 1968: 100–1.

Foxe, John. 'The First Examination of Mrs. Anne Askew, before the Inquisitors,

A.D. 1545.' In *Actes and Monuments*. Ed. Rev. M. Hobart Seymour. New York: Worthington, 1850.

———. 'The Second Apprehension and Examination of the Worthy Martyr of God, Mistress Anne Askew, A.D. 1546.' In *Actes and Monuments*. Ed. Rev. M. Hobart Seymour. New York: Worthington, 1850.

The French Fabliau: B.N. Ms. 837. Ed. and trans. Raymond Eichmann and John DuVal. Vol.1 and 2. New York: Garland, 1984.

Gilte Legende, Vol. 1. Ed. Richard Hamer with the assistance of Vida Russell. EETS, os 327. Oxford: Oxford University Press, 2006.

Gilte Legende, Vol. 2. Ed. Richard Hamer with the assistance of Vida Russell. EETS, os 328. Oxford: Oxford University Press, 2007.

Gisli Sursson's Saga and The Saga of the People of Eyri. Ed. and trans. Martin S. Regal and Judy Quinn. Introduction by Vésteinn Ólason. London: Penguin Books, 2003.

Gregory of Tours. *The History of the Franks*. Ed. and trans. Lewis Thorpe. London: Penguin Books, 1974.

Gui, Bernard. *The Inquisitor's Guide: A Medieval Manual on Heretics*. Ed. and trans. by Janet Shirley. Welwyn Garden City, UK: Ravenhall Books, 2006.

Havelok the Dane. In *Middle English Romances*. Ed. Stephen H.A. Shepherd. New York: W.W. Norton and Company, 1995: 3–74.

Hrafnkels saga freysgoða. From Jón Jóhannesson, *Hrafnkels saga freysgoða*, Íslenzk Fornrit 11, Reykjavik: Hið islenzka fornritafélag, 1950. In *An Introduction to Old Norse*. Ed. E.V. Gordon. Oxford: Oxford Clarendon Press, second edition, 1956.

Hrafnkel's Saga and Other Icelandic Stories. Ed. and trans. Hermann Pálsson. London: Penguin Books, 1971.

Jacobus de Voragine. *The Golden Legend: Readings on the Saints*. Ed. and trans. William Granger Ryan, 2 vols. Princeton NJ: Princeton University Press, 1993.

———. *The Golden Legend*. Ed. and trans. Christopher Stace. Introduction by Richard Hamer. London: Penguin Books, 1998.

Jean de Meun. *Roman de la Rose*. In *The Romance of the Rose*. Trans. Charles Dahlberg. Princeton NJ: Princeton University Press, 1971.

Le Jongleur par lui-meme: Choix de dits et se fabliaux. Ed. Willem Noomen. Louvain: Peeters, 2003.

Latin Arthurian Literature. Trans. and ed. Mildred Leake Day. Cambridge: D.S. Brewer, 2005.

The Legend of Good Women. Ed. Ann McMillan. Houston TX: Rice University Press, 1987.

The Letters of Abelard and Heloise. Ed. Betty Radice. London: Penguin Books, 1974.

Libro de los fueros de Castiella. Ed. G. Sanchez. Barcelona, 1981 [1924], 58–59, titulo 116.

The Life of Saint Agatha. In *The Gilte Legende*. Ed. Richard Hamer with the assistance of Vida Russell. Vol. 1, EETS, os 327. Oxford: Oxford University Press, 2006: 175–9.

The Life of Saint Agatha. In *The South English Legendary: Corpus Christi College Cambridge MS 145 and British Museum MS Harley 2277*. Ed. Charlotte D'Evelyn and Anna J. Mill. Vol. 1, EETS, os 235. Oxford: Oxford University Press, 1956, reprinted 1967: 54–9.

The Life of Saint Christina. In *The Gilte Legende*. Ed. Richard Hamer with the assistance of Vida Russell. Vol. 1, EETS, os 327. Oxford: Oxford University Press, 2006: 483–6.

The Life of Saint Christina. In *The South English Legendary: Corpus Christi College Cambridge MS 145 and British Museum MS Harley 2277*. Ed. Charlotte D'Evelyn and Anna J. Mill. Vol. 2, EETS, os 235. Oxford: Oxford University Press, 1956, reprinted 1967: 315–27.

The Life of Saint Edmund, King. In *The Early South-English Legendary or Lives of Saints, MS Laud 108 in the Bodleian Library*. Ed. Carl Horstmann. EETS, os 87. Oxford: Oxford University Press, 1887; reprinted 2000: 296–9.

The Life of Saint Laurence. In *The Early South-English Legendary or Lives of Saint: MS Laud 108 in the Bodleian Library*. Ed. Carl Horstmann. EETS, os 87. Oxford: Oxford University Press, 1887; reprinted 2000: 340–5.

The Life of Saint Lawrence. In *Gilte Legende*. Ed. Richard Hamer with the assistance of Vida Russell. Vol. 2, EETS, os 328. Oxford: Oxford University Press, 2007: 552–60.

The Life of Saint Wulfstan. In *The Early South-English Legendary or Lives of Saints, MS Laud 108 in the Bodleian Library*. Ed. Carl Horstmann. EETS, os 87. Oxford: Oxford University Press, 1887; reprinted 2000: 70–7.

Marlowe, Christopher. *Edward II. The Complete Plays*. Ed. Mark Thornton Burnett. London: Everyman, 1999: 148–240.

Narratio de Arthuro rege Britanniae et rege Gorlagon lycanthropo. In *Latin Arthurian Literature*. Ed. and trans. Mildred Leake Day. Cambridge: D.S. Brewer, 2005: 208–35.

Nashe, Thomas. *The Unfortunate Traveller or the life of Iacke Wilton*. In *Shorter Novels: Elizabethan and Jacobean*. London: J.M. Dent and Sons, 1929.

Njal's Saga. Ed. and trans. Robert Cook. London: Penguin Books, 2001.

Notker Balbulus. *The Second Book of the Deeds of Charles*. In *Einhard and Notker the Stammerer: Two Lives of Charlemagne*. Ed. David Ganz. London: Penguin Books, 2008: 86–116.

Nouveau Recueil Complet des Fabliaux. Ed. Willem Noomen and Nico van den Boogaard. 10 vols. Assen: Van Gorcum, 1983–1998.

Otten, Charlotte F., ed. *A Lycanthropy Reader: Werewolves in Western Culture*. Syracuse NY: Syracuse University Press, 1986.

Penninc and Pieter Vostaert. *Roman van Walewein*. Ed. and trans. David F. Johnson. New York: Garland, 1992.

Peter Abelard, *Historia calamitatum*. Ed. Jacques Monfrin. Paris: Vrin, 1962. English translation: *The Story of Abelard's Adversities*. Trans. J.T. Muckle. Toronto: Pontifical Institute of Mediaeval Studies, 1964.

Du prestre crucefié. In *The French Fabliau: B.N. Ms. 837*. Trans. and ed. by Raymond Eichmann and John DuVal. Vol. 1 and 2. New York: Garland, 1984.

Du prestre crucefié. In *Nouveau Recueil Complet des Fabliaux*. Ed. Willem Noomen and Nico van den Boogaard. 10 vols. Assen: Van Gorcum, 1983–1998. Vol. 4, 1988.

Saga of the Volsungs: The Norse Epic of Sigurd the Dragon Slayer. Trans. Jesse Byock. Berkeley CA: University of California Press, 1990.

Selected Fabliaux: Edited from B.N. Fonds Français 837, Fonds Français 19152, and Berlin Hamilton 257. Ed. by B.J. Levy. Hull, UK: University of Hull Press, 1978.
Shakespeare, William. *Titus Andronicus.* Folger Shakespeare Library edition. Ed. Barbara Mowat and Paul Werstine. New York: Washington Square Press, 2005.
The Song of Roland. Ed. and trans. Glyn Burgess. London: Penguin Books, 1990.
The South English Legendary: Corpus Christi College Cambridge MS 145 and British Museum MS Harley 2277, Vol. 1. Ed. Charlotte D'Evelyn and Anna J. Mill. EETS, os 235. Oxford: Oxford University Press, 1956, reprinted 1967.
Supplementary Lives in Some Manuscripts of the Gilte Legende. Ed. Richard Hamer and Vida Russell. EETS, os 315. Oxford: Oxford University Press, 2000.
Three Lives from the Gilte Legende Edited from MS BL Egerton 876. Ed. Richard Hamer. Heidelberg: Universitätsverlag Carl Winter, 1978.
Trubert. In *Nouveau Recueil Complet des Fabliaux.* Ed. Willem Noomen and Nico van den Boogaard. 10 vols. Assen: Van Gorcum, 1983–1998. Vol. X: 143–262.
Woman Defamed and Woman Defended: An Anthology of Medieval Texts. Ed. Alcuin Blamires. Oxford: Clarendon Press, 1992.
Women Saints' Lives in Old English Prose. Ed. and trans. Leslie Donovan. Cambridge: D.S. Brewer, 1999.
Vǫlundarkviða (Lay of Volund). Poems of the Elder Edda: Revised Edition. Ed. and trans. Patricia Terry. Philadelphia: University of Pennsylvania Press, 1969, revised edition 1990.

Secondary Sources

Adams, Tracy. *Violent Passions: Managing Love in the Old French Verse Romance.* New York: Palgrave MacMillan, 2005.
Akehurst, F. R. P. 'Customary Law in Old French Fabliaux.' In *The Old French Fabliaux: Essays on Comedy and Context.* Ed. Kristen L. Burr, John F. Moran, and Norris J. Lacy Jefferson NC: McFarland and Co., 2007.
——. 'Name, Reputation, and Notoriety in French Customary Law.' In *Fama: The Politics of Talk and Reputation in Medieval Europe.* Ed. Thelma Fenster and Daniel Lord Smail. Ithaca NY: Cornell University Press, 2003.
Alexandre, Monique. 'Early Christian Women.' In *A History of Women in the West, vol. I: From Ancient Goddesses to Christian Saints.* Ed. Pauline Schmitt Pantel. Cambridge MA: Harvard University Press, 1992: 409–44.
Alford, John A. 'The Wife of Bath versus the Clerk of Oxford: What Their Rivalry Means.' *The Chaucer Review: A Journal of Medieval Studies and Literary Criticism* 21.2 (1986): 108–32.
Anderson, Thomas P. '"What Is Written Shall Be Executed": "Nude Contracts" and "Lively Warrants" in *Titus Andronicus.*' *Criticism: A Quarterly for Literature and the Arts* 45.3 (2003): 301–21.
——. *Performing Early Modern Trauma from Shakespeare to Milton.* Burlington VT: Ashgate, 2006.
Andersson, Theodore, and William Ian Miller. *Law and Literature in Medieval Iceland: Ljósvetninga saga and Valla-Ljóts saga.* Stanford CA: Stanford University Press, 1989: 44–5.

Ashton, Gail. *The Generation of Identity in Late Medieval Hagiography: Speaking the Saint*. London: Routledge, 2000.

Bahktin, Mikhail. *Rabelais and His World*. Trans. Hélène Iswolsky. Bloomington, IN: Indiana University Press, 1984.

Baraz, Daniel. *Medieval Cruelty: Changing Perceptions, Late Antiquity to the Early Modern Period*. Ithaca NY: Cornell University Press, 2003.

Barber, Malcolm. *The Trial of the Templars*. Cambridge: Cambridge University Press, 1978, reprinted Canto Edition, 1993.

Barron, W. R. J. 'The Penalties for Treason in Medieval Life and Literature.' *Journal of Medieval History* 7 (1981): 187–202.

Bartels, Emily. *Spectacles of Strangeness: Imperialism, Alienation, and Marlowe*. Philadelphia: University of Pennsylvania Press, 1993.

Bartlett, Anne Clark. *Male Authors, Female Readers: Representations and Subjectivity in Middle English Devotional Literature*. Ithaca NY: Cornell University Press, 1995.

Bartlett, Robert. *Trial by Fire and Water: The Medieval Judicial Ordeal*. Oxford: Clarendon Press, 1986.

Baum, Paull F. *Chaucer: A Critical Appreciation*. Durham NC: Duke University Press, 1958.

——. 'Characterization in the "Knight's Tale".' *Modern Language Notes* 46.5 (May, 1931): 302–4.

Bédier, Joseph. *Les Fabliaux: Études de littérature populaire et d'histoire littéraire du moyen age*. Sixth edition. Paris: Champion, 1964.

Bednarz, James P. 'Marlowe and the English Literary Scene.' In *The Cambridge Companion to Christopher Marlowe*. Ed. Patrick Cheney. Cambridge: Cambridge University Press, 2004: 90–105.

Beidler, Peter C. '*The Gelded Lady*, an Old French Fabliau: New Views and a New Translation.' *ANQ: A Quarterly Journal of Short Articles, Notes and Reviews* 17.4 (Fall 2004): 3–37.

Bell, Kimberley K. 'Resituating Romance: The Dialectics of Sanctity in MS Laud Misc. 108's *Havelok the Dane* and Royal *Vitae*.' *Parergon* 25.1 (2008): 27–51.

Bellamy, John. *Crime and Public Order in England in the Later Middle Ages*. London: Routledge and Kegan Paul, 1973.

——. *The Law of Treason in England in the Later Middle Ages*. Cambridge: Cambridge University Press, 1970.

Benson, C. David. *Chaucer's Drama of Style: Poetic Variety and Contrast in the Canterbury Tales*. Chapel Hill NC: University of North Carolina Press, 1986.

Bernstein, Alan E. *The Formation of Hell: Death and Retribution in the Ancient and Early Christian Worlds*. Ithaca NY: Cornell University Press, 1993.

Bestul, Thomas. *Texts of the Passion: Latin Devotional Literature and Medieval Society*. Philadelphia: University of Pennsylvania Press, 1996.

Bloch, R. Howard. *The Anonymous Marie de France*. Chicago: The University of Chicago Press: 2003.

——. *Medieval Misogyny and the Invention of Western Romantic Love*. Chicago: University of Chicago Press, 1991.

——. *Medieval French Literature and Law*. Berkeley CA: University of California Press, 1977.

Bloch, R. Howard, and Frances Ferguson. *Misogyny, Misandry, and Misanthropy.* Berkeley CA: University of California Press, 1989.

——. *The Scandal of the Fabliaux.* Chicago: University of Chicago Press, 1986.

Bolton, W.F. 'The Topic of the *Knight's Tale*.' *The Chaucer Review: A Journal of Medieval Studies and Literary Criticism* (1967): 217–27.

Bowden, Muriel. *A Commentary on the General Prologue to the Canterbury Tales.* London: Macmillan, 1967.

Bowker, Alvin W. 'Comic Illusion and Dark Reality in "The Miller's Tale".' *Modern Language Studies* 4.2 (Autumn 1974): 27–34.

Boyarin, Daniel. *Dying for God: Martyrdom and the Making of Christianity and Judaism.* Stanford CA: Stanford University Press, 1999.

Brewer, Derek. *Chaucer in His Time.* Camden NJ: Nelson, 1963.

——. 'Chivalry.' In *A Companion to Chaucer.* Ed. Peter Brown. Malden MA: Blackwell, 2000.

——. 'Escape from the Mimetic Fallacy.' In *Studies in Medieval English Romances.* Ed. Derek Brewer. Cambridge: D.S. Brewer, 1988, reprinted 1991.

Brownlee, Kevin. 'Martyrdom and the Female Voice: Saint Christine in the *Cité des Dames*.' In *Images of Sainthood in Medieval Europe.* Ed. Renate Blumenfeld-Kosinski and Timea K. Szell. Ithaca NY: Cornell University Press, 1991: 115–35.

Brundage, James A. *Law, Sex, and Christian Society in Medieval Europe.* Chicago: University Chicago Press, 1987.

Bryan, W.F. and Germaine Dempster, ed. et al. *Sources and Analogues of Chaucer's Canterbury Tales.* Chicago: University of Chicago Press, 1939.

Bynum, Caroline Walker. *Fragmentation and Redemption: Essays on Gender and the Human Body in Medieval Religion.* New York: Zone Books, 1992.

——. *Holy Feast and Holy Fast: The Religious Significance of Food to Medieval Women.* Berkeley CA: University of California Press, 1987.

——. *The Resurrection of the Body in Western Christianity, 200–1336.* New York: Columbia University Press, 1995.

Bynum, Caroline Walker, and Paul Freedman, eds. *Last Things: Death and the Apocalypse in the Middle Ages.* Philadelphia: University of Pennsylvania Press, 2000.

Byock, Jesse. *Feud in the Icelandic Saga.* Berkeley CA: University of California Press, 1982; rpt. in paperback, 1993.

——. *Viking Age Iceland.* London: Penguin Books, 2001.

Calabrese, Michael. 'Performing the Prioress: "Conscience" and Responsibility in Studies of Chaucer's *Prioress's Tale*.' *Texas Studies in Literature and Language* 44:1 (Spring 2002): 66–91.

Cantor, Norman F. *The Civilization of the Middle Ages.* New York: Harper Collins, 1963; reprinted 1993.

Carey, John. 'Werewolves in Medieval Ireland.' *Cambrian Medieval Celtic Studies* 44 (Winter 2002): 37–72.

Carruthers, Mary J. 'The Lady, the Swineherd, and Chaucer's Clerk.' *The Chaucer Review: A Journal of Medieval Studies and Literary Criticism* 17.3 (1983): 221–34.

Cartelli, Thomas. *Marlowe, Shakespeare and the Economy of Theatrical Experience.* Philadelphia: University of Pennsylvania Press, 1991.

——. 'Edward II.' In *The Cambridge Companion to Christopher Marlowe.* Ed. Patrick Cheney. Cambridge: Cambridge University Press, 2004: 158–73.

Chute, Marchette. 'Sketches of the Characters in *The Canterbury Tales*.' In *Readings on the Canterbury Tales*. Ed. Don Nardo. San Diego CA: Greenhaven Press, 1997. Excerpted from *Geoffrey Chaucer of England*, copyright 1946 by E.P. Dutton.

Classen, Albrecht, ed. *Violence in Medieval Courtly Literature: A Casebook*. New York: Routledge, 2004.

Cobby, Anne Elizabeth. *Ambivalent Conventions: Formula and Parody in Old French*. Amsterdam and Atlanta GA: Rodopi B.V., 1995.

Cohen, Derek. *Shakespeare's Culture of Violence*. New York: St. Martin's Press, 1993: 79–93.

Cohen, Jeffrey Jerome. 'Decapitation and Coming of Age: Constructing Masculinity and the Monstrous.' In *The Arthurian Yearbook III*. Ed. Keith Busby. New York: Garland, 1993: 173–92.

Coletti, Theresa. 'Paupertas est donum Dei: Hagiography, Lay Religion, and the Economics of Salvation in the Digby *Mary Magdalene*.' *Speculum* 76.2 (2001): 337–78.

Collingwood, Sharon. '*Sagesse* and Misogyny in the Fabliau *La Dame escoilleé*.' *Florilegium* 18.1 (2001): 51–63.

Collis, Louise. *Memoirs of a Medieval Woman: The Life and Times of Margery Kempe*. New York: Harper and Row, 1964.

Cook, Robert Francis. *The Sense of the Song of Roland*. Ithaca NY: Cornell University Press, 1987.

Cooke, Thomas D. *The Old French and Chaucerian Fabliaux: A Study of Their Comic Climax*. Columbia MO: University of Missouri Press, 1978.

——. 'Pornography and the Comic Spirit.' In *Humor of the Fabliaux: A Collection of Critical Essays*. Ed. Thomas D. Cooke and Benjamin L. Honeycutt. Columbia MO: University of Missouri Press, 1974: 137–62.

Cooke, Thomas D., and Benjamin L. Honeycutt, eds. *The Humor of the Fabliaux: A Collection of Critical Essays*. Columbia MO: University of Missouri Press, 1974.

Cooper, Helen. *Oxford Guides to Chaucer: The Canterbury Tales*, second edition, Oxford: Oxford University Press, 1996.

Copeland, Rita. 'The Pardoner's Body and the Disciplining of Rhetoric.' In *Framing Medieval Bodies*. Ed. Sarah Kay and Miri Rubin. Manchester and New York: Manchester University Press, 1994: 138–59.

Cormack, Margaret. 'Barbarian Atrocities and Hagiographic Motifs: A Postscript to Some Recent Articles.' *Saga-Book* 25.3 (2000): 316–17.

Cormier, Raymond J. 'Brutality and Violence in Medieval French Romance and Its Consequences.' In *Violence in Medieval Courtly Literature: A Casebook*. Ed. Albrecht Classen. New York and London: Routledge, 2004.

Couch, Julie Nelson. 'The Vulnerable Hero: *Havelok* and the Revision of Romance.' *The Chaucer Review: A Journal of Medieval Studies and Literary Criticism* 42.3 (2008): 330–52.

Cox, Catherine S. *Gender and Language in Chaucer*. Gainesville FL: University Press of Florida, 1997.

Crachiolo, Beth. 'Female and Male Martyrs in the *South English Legendary*.' In *'A Great Effusion of Blood'?: Interpreting Medieval Violence*. Ed. Mark D. Meyerson, Daniel Thiery and Oren Falk. Toronto: University of Toronto Press, 2004: 147–63.

Cunningham, Karen. '"Scars Can Witness": Trials By Ordeal and Lavinia's Body in *Titus Andronicus*.' In *Women and Violence in Literature: An Essay Collection*. Ed. Katherine Anne Ackley. New York and London: Garland, 1990: 139–62.

Cuttino, G.P., and Thomas W. Lyman. 'Where is Edward II?' *Speculum* 53.3 (1978): 522–44.

Dahood, Roger. 'The Punishment of the Jews, Hugh of Lincoln, and the Question of Satire in Chaucer's *Prioress's Tale*.' *Viator* 36 (2005): 465–91.

Davidson, Clifford, and Thomas H. Seiler, eds. *The Iconography of Hell*. Kalamazoo MI: Medieval Institute Publications, 1992.

Dean, James. 'Dismantling the Canterbury Book.' *PMLA: Journal of Modern Language Association of America*, 100.5 (1985): 746–62.

Dean, James, and Christian K. Zacher, eds. *The Idea of Medieval Literature*. Newark NJ: University of Delaware Press, 1992.

Dean, Trevor. *Crime in Medieval Europe*. London: Pearson Education, 2001.

Delany, Sheila. 'Asia in the *Prioress's Tale*.' In *Chaucer and the Jews: Sources, Contexts, Meanings*. Ed. Sheila Delany. London: Routledge, 2002: 43–68.

——. 'Chaucer's Prioress, the Jews, and the Muslims.' *Medieval Encounters* 5.2. (1999): 198–213.

Delasanta, Rodney. 'Penance and Poetry in the Canterbury Tales.' *PMLA: Journal of Modern Language Association of America* 93.2 (1978): 240–7.

Di Gangi, John J. 'Chaucer's "Hende Nicholas": A Possible Identification.' *American Notes and Queries*. 13 (1974): 50–1.

Dinshaw, Carolyn. *Getting Medieval: Sexualities and Communities, Pre- and Postmodern*. Durham NC: Duke University Press, 1999.

Donaldson, E.T. *Chaucer's Poetry*. New York: John Wiley and Sons, 1958, reprinted 1975.

Duffy, Eamon. *The Stripping of the Altars: Traditional Religion in England 1400–1580*. New Haven CT: Yale University Press, 1992.

Dunbabin, Jean. *Captivity and Imprisonment in Medieval Europe 1000–1300*. Medieval Culture and Society Series. New York: Palgrave MacMillan, 2002.

Easton, Martha, 'Pain, Torture and Death in the Huntington Library *Legenda aurea*.' In *Gender and Holiness: Men, Women and Saints in Late Medieval Europe*. Ed. Samantha J.E. Riches and Sarah Salih. Routledge Studies in Medieval Religion and Culture. London and New York: Routledge, 2002: 49–64.

Eaton, Sara. 'A Woman of Letters: Lavinia in *Titus Andronicus*.' In *Shakespearean Tragedy and Gender*. Ed. Shirley Nelson Garner and Madelon Sprengnether. Bloomington IN: Indiana University Press, 1996: 54–74.

Echard, Siân. *Arthurian Narrative in the Latin Tradition*. Cambridge: Cambridge University Press, 1998.

——. 'Latin Arthurian Literature.' In *A History of Arthurian Scholarship*. Ed. Norris J. Lacy. Cambridge: D.S. Brewer, 2006: 62–76.

Einarsson, Bjarni. 'The Blood-Eagle Once More: Two Notes.' *Saga-Book* 23.2 (1990): 80–1.

——. '*De Normannorum Atrocitate*, or on the Execution of Royalty by the Aquiline Method.' *Saga-Book* 22.1 (1986): 79–82.

Elliott, Dyan. *Fallen Bodies: Pollution, Sexuality, and Demonology in the Middle Ages*. Philadelphia: University of Pennsylvania Press, 1999.

Ellis, Roger. *Patterns of Religious Narrative in the Canterbury Tales*. London: Croom Helm, 1986.

Enders, Jody. *The Medieval Theater of Cruelty: Rhetoric, Memory, Violence*. Ithaca NY: Cornell University Press, 1999.

——. *Death by Drama and Other Medieval Urban Legends*. Chicago: University of Chicago Press, 2002.

Evans, Ruth. 'Chaucer's Legendary Good Women.' *Medium Aevum* 69.2 (2000): 303–5.

Farrell, Thomas. 'Privacy and the Boundaries of Fabliau in *The Miller's Tale*.' *English Literary History (ELH)* 56.4 (1989): 773–95.

Fawcett, Mary Laughlin. 'Arms/Words/Tears: Language and the Body in *Titus Andronicus*.' *English Literary History (ELH)* 50 (1983): 261–77.

Ferrante, Joan. *To the Glory of Her Sex: Women's Roles in the Composition of Medieval Texts*. Indianapolis: Indiana University Press, 1997.

Fleck, Andrew. 'Anatomizing the Body Politic: The Nation and the Renaissance Body in Thomas Nashe's *The Unfortunate Traveller*.' *Modern Philology* 104.3 (2007): 295–328.

Fleming, John V. *Classical Imitation and Interpretation in Chaucer's Troilus*. Lincoln NE: University of Nebraska Press, 1990.

Foucault, Michel. *Discipline and Punish: The Birth of the Prison*. Trans. Alan Sheridan. New York: Random House (Vintage), 1977/79.

Fouracre, Paul. 'Attitudes towards Violence in Seventh- and Eighth-Century Francia.' In *Violence and Society in the Early Medieval West*. Ed. Guy Halsall. Woodbridge: The Boydell Press, 1998: 60–75.

Fradenburg, Louise O. 'Criticism, Anti-Semitism, and the *Prioress's Tale*.' *Exemplaria* 1 (1989): 69–115.

Frank, Roberta. 'The Blood-Eagle Again.' *Saga-Book* 22.5 (1988): 288.

——. 'Ornithology and Interpretation of Skaldic Verse.' *Saga-Book* 23.2 (1990): 81–3.

——. 'Viking Atrocity and Skaldic Verse: The Rite of the Blood-Eagle.' *The English Historical Review (EHR)* 99 (1984): 341–3.

Frankis, John. 'From Saint's Life to Saga: The Fatal Walk of Alfred Ætheling, Saint Amphibalus and the Viking Broðir.' *Saga-Book* 25.2 (1999): 121–37.

Freedman, Paul, and Gabrielle M. Spiegel. 'Medievalisms Old and New: The Rediscovery of Alterity in North American Medieval Studies.' *The American Historical Review*, 103.3 (1998): 677–704.

Freeman, Thomas S. 'Over their Dead Bodies: Concepts of Martyrdom in Late-Medieval and Early Modern England.' In *Martyrs and Martyrdom in England, c. 1400–1700*. Ed. Thomas S. Freeman and Thomas F. Mayer. Woodbridge: The Boydell Press, 2007: 1–34.

Friedman, Albert F. '*The Prioress's Tale* and Chaucer's Anti-Semitism.' *The Chaucer Review: A Journal of Medieval Studies and Literary Criticism* 9 (1974–1975): 118–29.

Gallick, Susan. 'A Look at Chaucer and His Preachers.' *Speculum*, 50.3 (1975): 456–76.

Gaylord, Alan T. 'The Unconquered Tale of the Prioress.' *Papers of the Michigan Academy of Science, Arts and Letters* 47 (1962): 613–66.

Gillingham, John. *The English in the Twelfth Century: Imperialism National Identity and Political Values*. Woodbridge: The Boydell Press, 2000

——. 'Events and Opinions: Norman and English Views of Aquitaine, c.1152–c.1204.' In *The World of Eleanor of Aquitaine: Literature and Society in Southern France between the Eleventh and Thirteenth Centuries*. Ed. Marcus Bull and Catherine Léglu. Woodbridge: The Boydell Press, 2005: 57–81.

Givens, James B. *Inquisition and Medieval Society: Power, Discipline, and Resistance in Languedoc*. Ithaca NY: Cornell University Press, 1997: 53–4.

Gragnolati, Manuele. 'From Decay to Splendor: Body and Pain in Bonvesin da la Riva's *Book of the Three Scriptures*.' In *Last Things: Death and the Apocalypse in the Middle Ages*. Ed. Caroline Walker Bynum and Paul Freedman. Philadelphia: University of Pennsylvania Press, 2000: 83–97.

Green, Douglas E. 'Interpreting "her martyr'd signs": Gender and Tragedy in *Titus Andronicus*.' *Shakespeare Quarterly* 40 (1989): 317–26.

Green, Richard Firth. 'Palamon's Appeal of Treason in the *Knight's Tale*.' In *The Letter of the Law: Legal Practice and Literary Production in Medieval England*. Ed. Emily Steiner and Candace Barrington. Ithaca NY: Cornell University Press, 2002: 105–14.

Greenblatt, Stephen. 'Murdering Peasants: Status, Genre, and the Representations of Rebellion.' *Representations* 1 (Feb. 1983): 1–29.

Haidu, Peter. *The Subject of Violence: The Song of Roland and the Birth of the State*. Bloomington IN: Indiana University Press, 1993.

Hallissy, Margaret. *A Companion to Chaucer's Canterbury Tales*. Westport CT: Greenwood Press, 1995.

Halsall, Guy. 'Violence and Society in the Early Medieval West: An Introductory Survey.' In *Violence and Society in the Early Medieval West*. Ed. Guy Halsall. Woodbridge: The Boydell Press, 1998: 1–45.

Ham, Edward B. 'Knight's Tale 38.' *English Literary History (ELH)* 17:4 (Dec. 1950): 252–61.

Hanson, Elizabeth. 'Torture and Truth in Renaissance England.' *Representations* 34 (Spring 1991): 53–84.

Hardin, Russell. *Trust and Trustworthiness*. New York: Russell Sage Foundation, 2002.

Harrington, Susan Marie, and Michal Nahor Bond. '"Good Sir, be Ruld by Me": Patterns of Domination and Manipulation in Thomas Nashe's *The Unfortunate Traveller*.' *Studies in Short Fiction* (2000): 243–50.

Harris, Bernice. 'Sexuality as a Signifier for Power Relations: Using Lavinia, of Shakespeare's *Titus Andronicus*.' *Criticism: A Quarterly for Literature and the Arts* 38 (1996): 383–406.

Helms, Lorriane. '"The High Roman Fashion": Sacrifice, Suicide, and the Shakespearean Stage.' *PMLA: Journal of the Modern Language Association of America* 107 (1992): 554–65.

Heng, Geraldine. 'The Romance of England: *Richard Coer de Lyon*, Saracens, Jews, and the Politics of Race and Nation.' In *The Post Colonial Middle Ages*. The New Middle Ages. Ed. Jeffrey Jerome Cohen. New York: Palgrave, 2001: 135–71.

Hill, Thomas. 'The Evisceration of Broðir in *Brennu-Njals Saga*.' *Traditio* 37 (1981): 437–44.

Hostia, Sister Mary. 'The Prioress and Her Companion.' *College English* 14.6 (March 1953): 351–2.

Huizinga, Johan. *The Waning of the Middle Ages*. Trans. F. Hopman. London: Penguin Books, 1924; reprinted 1990.

Hyams, Paul R. *Rancor and Reconciliation in Medieval England*. Ithaca NY: Cornell University Press, 2003.

Jacobs, Kathryn. *Marriage Contracts from Chaucer to the Renaissance Stage*. Miami FL: University Press of Florida, 2001.

Janssens, J.D. *Koning Artur in de Nederlanden*. Utrecht: HES Uitgevers, 1985. Qtd in Penninc and Pieter Vostaert. *Roman van Walewein*. Ed. and trans. David F. Johnson. New York: Garland, 1992.

——. 'The "Roman van Walewein," An Episodic Arthurian Romance.' In *Medieval Dutch Literature and its European Context*. Ed. Erik Kooper. Cambridge: Cambridge University Press, 1994: 113–28.

Jones, H.S.V. 'The Clerk of Oxenford.' *Publications of the Modern Language Association of America*. 27.1 (1912): 106–15.

Jones, Terry. *Chaucer's Knight: The Portrait of a Medieval Mercenary*. New York: Methuen, 1985.

Jost, Jean. 'Why is Middle English Romance So Violent? The Literary and Aesthetic Purposes of Violence.' In *Violence in Medieval Courtly Literature: A Casebook*. Ed. Albrecht Classen. New York: Routledge, 2004: 241–67.

——. Introduction. *Chaucer's Humor: Critical Essays*. New York: Garland, 1994.

Kaeuper, Richard W. *Chivalry and Violence in Medieval Europe*. Oxford: Oxford University Press, 1999.

——. 'The Societal Role of Chivalry in Romance: Northwestern Europe.' In *The Cambridge Companion to Medieval Romance*. Ed. Roberta L. Krueger. Cambridge: Cambridge University Press, 2000.

Kahn, Coppélia. *Roman Shakespeare: Warriors, Wounds, and Women*. London and New York: Routledge, 1997.

Kaske, R.E. 'Chaucer's Marriage Group.' In *Chaucer the Love Poet*. Ed. Jerome Mitchell and William Provost. Athens GA: University of Georgia Press, 1973: 45–65.

Kaula, David. 'The Low Style in Nashe's *The Unfortunate Traveller*.' *Studies in English Literature, 1500–1900*, 6.1: *The English Renaissance* (Winter, 1966): 43–57.

Kelly, Henry Ansgar. 'Inquisition and the Prosecution of Heresy: Misconceptions and Abuses.' *Church History* 58:4 (1989): 439–51.

Kelly, Kathleen Coyne. *Performing Virginity and Testing Chastity in the Middle Ages*. London: Routledge, 2000.

——. 'Useful Virgins in Medieval Hagiography.' In *Constructions of Widowhood and Virginity in the Middle Ages*. Ed. Cindy Carlson and Angela Jane Weisl. New York: St. Martin's Press, 1999: 135–64.

Kendall, Gillian Murray. '"Lend me thy Hand": Metaphor and Mayhem in *Titus Andronicus*.' *Shakespeare Quarterly* 40.3 (1989): 299–316.

Kirby, Thomas A. *Chaucer's Troilus: A Study in Courtly Love*. Baton Rouge LA: Louisiana State University Press, 1940.

Kirkpatrick, Robin. 'Dante and the Body.' In *Framing Medieval Bodies*. Ed. Sarah Kay and Miri Rubin. Manchester: Manchester University Press, 1994.

Kittredge, George Lyman. *Chaucer and his Poetry*. Cambridge MA: Harvard University Press, 1920.

Knapp, Peggy A. 'Knowing the Tropes: Literary Exegesis and Chaucer's Clerk.' *Criticism: A Quarterly for Literature and the Arts* 27.4 (1985): 331–45.

—— . *Chaucer and the Social Contest*. New York: Routledge, 1990.

Knott, John R. 'John Foxe and the Joy of Suffering.' *Sixteenth Century Journal* 27:3 (1996): 721–34.

Lacy, Norris J. *Reading Fabliaux*. New York: Garland, 1993.

——. 'Convention and Innovation in the Middle Dutch *Roman van Walewein*.' In *Arthurian Literature XVII: Originality and Tradition in the Middle Dutch Roman van Walewein*. Ed. Bart Besamusca and Erik Kooper. Cambridge: D.S. Brewer, 1999.

——. 'Trickery, Trubertage, and the Limits of Laughter.' In *The Old French Fabliaux: Essays on Comedy and Context*. Ed. Kristin L. Burr, John F. Moran, and Norris J. Lacy. Jefferson NC: McFarland, 2007.

Langbein, John H. *Torture and the Law of Proof: Europe and England in the Ancien Régime*. Chicago: The University of Chicago Press, 1976, revised 2006.

Langmuir, Gavin I. 'The Knight's Tale of Young Hugh of Lincoln.' *Speculum* 47:3 (1972): 459–82.

Larrington, Carolyne. *Women and Writing in Medieval Europe*. London: Routledge, 1995.

Lea, Henry C. *Superstition and Force: Torture, Ordeal, and Trial by Combat in Medieval Law*. New York: Barnes and Noble Books, 1996.

Lewis, Katherine J. '"Lete me suffer": Reading the Torture of St Margaret of Antioch in Late Medieval England.' In *Medieval Women: Texts and Contexts in Late Medieval Britain: Essays for Felicity Riddy*. Ed. Jocelyn Wogan-Browne et al. Turnhout, Belgium: Brepols, 2000: 69–82.

—— . 'Model Girls? Virgin Martyrs and the Training of Young Medieval Women in Late Medieval England.' In *Young Medieval Women*. Ed. Lewis, Noël James Menuge and Kim M. Phillips. Stroud: Sutton, 1999: 25–46.

Lewis, Robert E. 'The English Fabliau Tradition and Chaucer's "Miller's Tale".' *Modern Philology* 79.3 (1982): 241–55.

Leyser, Henrietta. *Medieval Women: A Social History of Women in England 450–1500*. London: Phoenix Grant, 1995.

Livingston, Charles H., ed. *Le Jongleur Gautier le Leu: Étude sur les fabliaux*. Cambridge, MA: Harvard University Press, 1951.

Lorcin, Marie-Thérèse. *Façons de sentir et de penser: les fabliaux français*. Paris: Champion, 1979.

Lumiansky, R.M. 'Chaucer's Parlement of Foules: A Philosophical Interpretation.' *The Review of English Studies*, 24.94 (1948): 81–9.

MacMullen, Ramsay. *Changes in the Roman Empire: Essays in the Ordinary*. Princeton NJ: Princeton University Press, 1990.

Maddern, Philippa C. *Violence and Social Order: East Anglia 1422–1442*. Oxford Historical Monograph Series. Oxford: Clarendon Press, 1992.

Martin, Priscilla. *Chaucer's Women: Nuns, Wives, and Amazons*. Iowa City: University of Iowa Press, 1990.

Marshall, Cynthia. *The Shattering of the Self: Violence, Subjectivity, and Early Modern Texts*. Baltimore MD: Johns Hopkins University Press, 2002.

——. '"I can interpret all her martyr'd signs": *Titus Andronicus*, Feminism, and the Limits of Interpretation.' In *Sexuality and Politics in Renaissance Drama*. Ed. Carole Levin and Karen Robertson. Lewiston NY: Edwin Mellen Press, 1991: 193–213.

Massey, Jeff. 'The Werewolf at the Head Table: Metatheatric "Subtlety" in *Arthur and Gorlagon*.' In *Heads Will Roll: Decapitation in the Medieval and Early Modern Imagination*. Ed. Larissa Tracy and Jeff Massey. Medieval and Renaissance Authors and Texts. Leiden: Koninklijke Brill, forthcoming.

Maxfield, Ezra Kempton. 'Chaucer and Religious Reform.' *PMLA: Journal of the Modern Language Association of America*, 39.1 (1924): 64–74.

McKinnell, John. 'The Context of Vǫlundarkviða.' In *The Poetic Edda: Essays on Old Norse Mythology*. Ed. Paul Acker and Carolyne Larrington. New York and London: Routledge, 2002: 195–212.

Merback, Mitchell B. *The Thief, the Cross and the Wheel: Pain and the Spectacle of Punishment in Medieval and Renaissance Europe*. London: Reaktion Books, 1999.

——. 'Torture and Teaching: The Reception of Lucas Cranach the Elder's Martyrdom of the Twelve Apostles in the Protestant Era.' *Art Journal* 57:1. The Reception of Christian Devotional Art (Spring 1998): 14–23.

Meyerson, Mark D., Daniel Thiery, and Oren Falk, eds. *'A Great Effusion of Blood'?: Interpreting Medieval Violence*. Toronto: University of Toronto Press, 2004.

Mickel, Emanuel J. *Ganelon, Treason, and the 'Chanson de Roland.'* University Park, PA: The Pennsylvania State University Press, 1989.

Middleton, Anne. 'The Clerk and His Tale: Some Literary Contexts.' *Studies in the Age of Chaucer* 2 (1980): 121–50.

Miller, William Ian. *Bloodtaking and Peacemaking: Feud, Law, and Society in Saga Iceland*. Chicago: University of Chicago Press, 1990.

Mills, Robert. *Suspended Animation: Pain, Pleasure, and Punishment in Medieval Culture*. London: Reaktion Books, 2005.

Monta, Susannah Brietz. *Martyrdom and Literature in Early Modern England*. Cambridge: Cambridge University Press, 2005: 24.

Mooney, Catherine M., ed. *Gendered Voices: Medieval Saints and Their Interpreters*. Philadelphia: University of Pennsylvania Press, 1999.

Morgan, Gerald. 'Moral and Social Identity and the Idea of Pilgrimage in the *General Prologue*.' *Chaucer Review* 37.4 (2003): 285–314.

——. 'Medieval Misogyny and Gawain's Outburst Against Women in "Sir Gawain and the Green Knight".' *The Modern Language Review* 97.2 (April 2002): 265–78.

Muscatine, Charles. *The Old French Fabliaux*. New Haven CT: Yale University Press, 1986.

——. *Medieval Literature, Style and Culture*. Columbia SC: University of South Carolina Press, 1999.

——. 'Form, Texture, and Meaning in Chaucer's *Knight's Tale*.' *PMLA: Journal of the Modern Language Association of America* 65.5 (Sep. 1950): 911–29.

Musson, Anthony. *Medieval Law in Context: The Growth of Legal Consciousness from Magna Carta to the Peasant's Revolt*. Manchester: Manchester University Press, 2001.

Nirenberg, David. *Communities of Violence: Persecution of Minorities in the Middle Ages*. Princeton NJ: Princeton University Press, 1996.

Nolan, Maura. '"Acquiteth yow now": Textual Contradiction and Legal Discourse in the Man of Law's Introduction.' In *The Letter of the Law: Legal Practice and Literary Production in Medieval England*. Ed. Emily Steiner and Candace Barrington. Ithaca NY: Cornell University Press, 2002: 136–53.

Nussbaum, Martha. 'Under Pressure: From the Laboratories of Stanford to the Cells of Abu Ghraib: How Imagination Can Halt Man's Cruelty to the Powerless.' *Times Literary Supplement* (19 October 2007): 3–5.

Nykrog, Per. *Les Fabliaux: Étude d'histoire littéraire et de stylistique médiévale*. Copenhagen: Ejnar Munksgaard, 1957.

O'Brien, Timothy D. 'Fire and blood: "Queynte" Imaginings in Diana's Temple.' *Chaucer Review* 33:2 (1998): 157–67.

Olson, Paul A. 'Poetic Justice in the *Miller's Tale*.' *Modern Language Quarterly* 24 (1963): 227–36.

Overing, Gillian. *Language, Sign, and Gender in 'Beowulf*. Carbondale and Edwardsville IL: Southern Illinois University Press, 1990: 102–3.

Owen, Charles A., Jr. 'Morality as a Comic Motif in the Canterbury Tales.' *College English*, 16.4 (1955): 226–32.

Owens, Margaret E. *Stages of Dismemberment: The Fragmented Body in Late Medieval and Early Modern Drama*. Newark NJ: University of Delaware Press, 2005.

Pagels, Elaine. *The Gnostic Gospels*. New York: Vintage Books, 1979.

Palmer, Daryl W. 'Histories of Violence and the Writer's Hand: Foxe's *Actes and Monuments* and Shakespeare's *Titus Andronicus*.' In *Reading and Writing in Shakespeare*. Ed. David M. Bergeron. Newark NJ: University of Delaware Press, 1996: 82–115.

Parks, Joan. 'History, Tragedy, and Truth in Christopher Marlowe's *Edward II*.' *Studies in English Literature, 1500–1900*. 39.2: *Tudor and Stuart Drama* (Spring 1999): 275–90.

Patterson, Annabel. *Reading Holinshed's* Chronicles. Chicago: University of Chicago Press, 1994.

Patterson, Lee. Introduction. 'Critical Historicism and Medieval Studies.' In *Literary Practice and Social Change in Britain, 1380–1530*. Ed. Lee Patterson. Berkeley CA: University of California Press, 1990.

——. 'The Living Witness of Our Redemption': Martyrdom and Imitation in Chaucer's Prioress's Tale.' *Journal of Medieval and Early Modern Studies* 31.3 (2001): 507–60.

——. *Chaucer and the Subject of History*. Madison WI: University of Wisconsin Press, 1991.

Payne, Robert O. *The Key of Remembraunce*. London: Yale University Press, 1963.

Pearcy, Roy J. *Logic and Humour in the Fabliaux: An Essay in Applied Narratology*. Gallica, Cambridge: D.S. Brewer, 2007.

Pearsall, Derek. *The Canterbury Tales*. Boston MA: George Allen and Unwin, 1985.

Percival, Florence. *Chaucer's Legendary Good Women*. New York: Cambridge University Press, 1998.

Peters, Edward. 'Destruction of the Flesh – Salvation of the Spirit: The Paradoxes of Torture in Medieval Christian Society.' In *The Devil, Heresy and Witchcraft in the Middle Ages: Essays in Honor of Jeffrey B. Russell.* Ed. Alberto Ferreiro. Leiden: Koninklijke Brill, 1998: 131–48.

Peters, Edward. *Inquisition.* Los Angeles: University of California Press, 1989.

——. *Torture.* Philadelphia: University of Pennsylvania Press, 1985.

——, ed. *Heresy and Authority in Medieval Europe. Documents in Translation.* Philadelphia: University of Pennsylvania Press, 1980.

Pfeffer, M. 'Die Formalitäten des gottesgerichtlichen Zweikampfs in der altfranzösischen Epik.' *Zeitschrift für Romanische Philologie* 9 (1885).

Pigg, Daniel F. 'The Semiotics of Comedy in Chaucer's Religious Tales.' In *Chaucer's Humor: Critical Essays.* Ed. Jean E. Jost. New York: Garland, 1994: 321–48.

Power, Eileen. 'Chaucer's Prioress in Real Life.' In *Readings on the Canterbury Tales.* Ed. Don Nardo. San Diego CA: Greenhaven Press, 1997: 136–47.

Preston, Raymond. 'Chaucer, His Prioress, the Jews, and Professor Robinson.' *Notes and Queries* 206 (January 1961): 7–8.

Quilligan, Maureen. *The Allegory of Female Authority: Christine de Pisan's* Cité de Dames. Ithaca NY: Cornell University Press, 1991.

Reese, Jack E. 'The Formalization of Horror in *Titus Andronicus.' Shakespeare Quarterly* 21.1 (Winter 1970): 77–84.

Régnier-Bohler, Danielle. 'Literary and Mystical Voices.' In *A History of Women in the West, vol. II: Silences of the Middle Ages.* Ed. Christiane Klapisch-Zuber. Trans. Arthur Goldhammer. Cambridge MA: Belknap Press of Harvard University Press, 1992: 427–82.

Riches, Samantha J. E., and Sarah Salih, eds. *Gender and Holiness: Men, Women and Saints in Late Medieval Europe.* Routledge Studies in Medieval Religion and Culture. London and New York: Routledge, 2002.

——. 'St George as a Male Virgin Martyr.' In *Gender and Holiness: Men, Women and Saints in Late Medieval Europe.* Ed. Samantha J.E. Riches and Sarah Salih. Routledge Studies in Medieval Religion and Culture. London and New York: Routledge, 2002.

Ridley, Florence H. 'A Tale Told Too Often.' *Western Folklore* 26:3 (1967): 153–6.

——. *The Prioress and the Critics.* Berkeley CA: University of California Press, 1965.

Rigby, S.H. *Chaucer in Context: Society, Allegory and Gender.* Manchester: Manchester University Press, 1996.

Robertson, D.W., Jr. *A Preface to Chaucer.* Princeton NJ: Princeton University Press, 1962.

Robinson, Ian. *Chaucer and the English Tradition.* Cambridge: Cambridge University Press, 1972.

Rouse, Robert Allen. 'English Identity and the Law in *Havelok the Dane, Horn Childe and Maiden Rimnild* and *Beues of Hamtoun.'* In *Cultural Encounters in the Romance of Medieval England.* Ed. Corinne Saunders. Cambridge: D.S. Brewer, 2005: 69–83.

Rowe, Katherine A. 'Dismembering and Forgetting in *Titus Andronicus.' Shakespeare Quarterly* 45.3 (1994): 279–303.

Rowland, Beryl, ed. et al. *Companion to Chaucer Studies.* London: Oxford University Press, 1979.

Rubin, Miri. 'The Person in the Form: Medieval Challenges to Bodily "Order".' In

Framing Medieval Bodies. Ed. Sarah Kay and Miri Rubin. Manchester: Manchester University Press, 1994: 100–22.

Ruggieri, Ruggero. *Il processo di Gano nella Chanson de Roland.* Florence: Sansini, 1936.

Ruggiers, Paul G. 'The Form of The Canterbury Tales: Respice Fines.' *College English,* 17.4 (1956): 439–44.

Russell, Jeffery Burton. *Dissent and Reform in the Early Middle Ages.* Berkeley CA: University of California Press, 1965.

——. *Dissent and Order in the Middle Ages: The Search for Legitimate Authority.* Twayne Studies in Intellectual and Cultural History. New York: Twayne, 1992.

Salih, Sarah. 'Performing Virginity: Sex and Violence in the Katherine Group.' In *Constructions of Widowhood and Virginity in the Middle Ages.* Ed. Cindy L. Carlson and Angela Jane Weisl. New York: St. Martin's Press, 1999: 95–112.

——. *Versions of Virginity in Late Medieval England.* Cambridge: D.S. Brewer, 2001.

Sanock, Catherine. *Her Life Historical: Exemplarity and Female Saints' Lives in Late Medieval England.* The Middle Ages Series. Philadelphia: University of Pennsylvania Press, 2007.

Scarry, Elaine. *The Body in Pain: The Making and Unmaking of the World.* Oxford: Oxford University Press, 1985.

Schenck, Mary Jane Stearns. *The Fabliaux: Tales of Wit and Deception.* Philadelphia: John Benjamins Publishing, 1987.

Schoeck, Richard J. 'Chaucer's Prioress: Mercy and a Tender Heart.' In *The Bridge: A Yearbook of Judaeo-Christian Studies II.* Ed. John M. Oesterreicher. New York: Pantheon Books, 1956: 239–55.

Schulenberg, Jane Tibbetts. 'Saints' Lives as a Source for the History of Women, 500–1100.' In *Medieval Women and the Sources of Medieval History.* Ed. Joel T. Rosenthal. Athens GA: University of Georgia Press, 1990: 285–320.

——. *Forgetful of Their Sex: Female Sanctity and Society ca. 500–1100.* Chicago: University of Chicago Press, 1998.

Scragg, Donald and Carole Weinberg, eds. *Literary Appropriations of the Anglo-Saxons from the Thirteenth to the Twentieth Century.* Cambridge Studies in Anglo-Saxon England. Cambridge: Cambridge University Press, 2000.

Silverman, Lisa. *Tortured Subjects: Pain, Truth, and the Body in Early Modern France.* Chicago: University of Chicago Press, 2001.

Simmonds, James D. '"Hende Nicholas" and the Clerk.' *Notes and Queries* 9 (1962): 446.

Sirluck, Katherine A. 'Marlowe's "Edward II" and the Pleasure of Outrage.' *Modern Language Studies* 22.2 (Spring 1992): 15–24.

Skura, Meredith. 'Marlowe's *Edward II*; Penetrating Language in Shakespeare's *Richard II.*' *Shakespeare Survey* (1998): 41–55.

Smith, Anthony D. 'National Identities: Modern and Medieval?' In *Concepts of National Identity in the Middle Ages.* Ed. Simon Forde, Lesley Johnson and Alan V. Murray. Leeds Texts and Monographs, New Series 14 (Leeds: Leeds Studies in English, 1995): 21–46.

Smith, Bruce R. 'Rape, Rap, Rupture, Rapture: R-Rated Futures on the Global Market.' *Textual Practice* 9 (1995): 421–44.

Smith, Molly Eso. 'Spectacles of Torment in *Titus Andronicus*.' *Studies in English Literature, 1500–1900* 36.2: Tudor and Stuart Drama (Spring 1996): 315–31.

Smyth, Alfred P. 'The Effect of Scandinavian Raiders on the English and Irish Churches: A Preliminary Reassessment.' In *Britain and Ireland 900–1300: Insular Responses to Medieval European Change*. Ed. Brendan Smith. Cambridge: Cambridge University Press, 1999: 1–38.

——— . 'The Emergence of English Identity, 700–1000.' In *Medieval Europeans: Studies in Ethnic Identity and National Perspectives in Medieval Europe*. Ed. Alfred. P. Smyth. New York: Palgrave 2002: 44.

———. *Scandinavian Kings in the British Isles 850–880*. Oxford: Oxford University Press, 1977.

Spector, Stephen. 'Empathy and Enmity in the *Prioress's Tale*.' In *Geoffrey Chaucer's The Canterbury Tales: A Casebook*. Ed. Lee Patterson. Oxford: Oxford University Press, 2007: 183–209. Reprinted from *The Olde Daunce: Love, Friendship, Sex, and Marriage in the Medieval World*. Ed. Robert R. Edwards and Stephen Spector. Albany NY: State University of New York Press, 1991: 211–28.

Speed, Diane. 'The Construction of the Nation in Medieval English Romance.' In *Readings in Medieval English Romance*. Ed. Carol M. Meale. Cambridge: D.S. Brewer, 1994: 135–57.

Staines, David. '*Havelok the Dane*: A Thirteenth-Century Handbook for Princes.' *Speculum* 51:4 (1976): 602–23.

Strohm, Paul. *Social Chaucer*. London: Harvard University Press, 1989.

Sturges, Robert S. '*The Canterbury Tales*' Women Narrators: Three Traditions of Female Authority.' *Modern Language Studies* 13.2 (1983): 41–51.

Taylor, Andrew. *Textual Situations: Three Medieval Manuscripts and Their Readers*. Philadelphia: University of Pennsylvania Press, 2002.

Taylor, Jerome, ed. *Chaucer Criticism I*. Notre Dame IN: Notre Dame University Press, 1960, rpt. 1965.

Thijssen, J.M.M.H. 'Master Amalric and the Amalricians: Inquisitorial Procedure and the Suppression of Heresy at the University of Paris.' *Speculum* 71.1 (1996): 43–65.

Thomas, Vivien, and William Tydeman. *Christopher Marlowe: The Plays and Their Sources*. New York: Routledge, 1994.

Thurston, Robert. *Witch, Wicce, Mother Goose: The Rise and Fall of the Witch Hunts in Europe and North America*. London: Pearson Education, 2001: 134.

Tracy, Larissa. 'Torture Narrative: The Imposition of Medieval Method on Early Christian Texts.' *Journal of the Early Book Society* 7 (2004): 33–50.

———. 'British Library MS Harley 630: John Lydgate and St. Albans.' *Journal of the Early Book Society* 3 (2000): 36–58.

———. 'The Uses of Torture and Violence in the Fabliaux: When Comedy Crosses the Line.' *Florilegium* 23.2 (2006): 143–68.

———. 'Introduction'. In *Women of the Gilte Legende: A Selection of Middle English Saints' Lives*. Cambridge: D.S. Brewer, 2003.

Traversi, Derek. *The Canterbury Tales: A Reading*. Newark NJ: University of Delaware Press, 1983.

Tuchman, Barbara. *A Distant Mirror: The Calamitous Fourteenth Century*. New York: Ballantine Books, 1978.

Turville-Petre, Thorlac. *England the Nation: Language, Literature, and National Identity, 1290–1340*. Oxford: Clarendon Press, 1996.
Ussery, Huling E. 'Fourteenth-Century English Logicians: Possible Models for Chaucer's Clerk.' *TSE: Tulane Studies in English* 18 (1970): 1–15.
——. 'How Old Is Chaucer's Clerk?' *TSE: Tulane Studies in English* 15 (1967): 1–18.
Vann, Theresa M. 'Private Murders and Public Retribution: Castilian Foral Law and the Blood Feud.' In *Proceedings of the Tenth International Congress of Medieval Canon Law*. Ed. Kenneth Pennington, Stanley Chodorow, and Keith H. Kendall. *Monumenta Iuris Canonici*, Vol. 11. Vatican City: Biblioteca Apostolica Vaticana, 2001.
Wagenknecht, Edward Charles. *The Personality of Chaucer*. Norman OK: University of Oklahoma Press, 1968.
Walls, Kathryn. 'Absolon as Barber-Surgeon.' *The Chaucer Review: A Journal of Medieval Studies and Literary Criticism* 35.4 (2001): 391–8.
Warner, Marina. *Alone of All Her Sex: The Myth and Cult of the Virgin Mary*. New York: Vintage Books, 1976.
Weisl, Angela Jane. '"Quiting" Eve: Violence against Women in the *Canterbury Tales*.' In *Violence Against Women in Medieval Texts*. Ed. Anna Roberts. Gainesville FL: University Press of Florida, 1998: 115–36.
Weiss, Judith. 'Structure and Characterisation in *Havelok the Dane*.' *Speculum* 44:2 (1969): 247–57.
Whitmore, Sister Mary Ernestine. *Medieval English Domestic Life and Amusements in the Works of Chaucer*. New York: Cooper Square Publishers, 1972.
Williams, David. *Deformed Discourse: The Function of the Monster in Medieval Thought and Literature*. Exeter: University of Exeter Press, 1996.
Williams, Deanne. *The French Fetish from Chaucer to Shakespeare*. Cambridge: Cambridge University Press, 2004.
Willem van Henten, Jan. 'The Maccabean Martyrs as Saviours of the Jewish People: A Study of 2 and 4 Maccabees.' In *Supplements to the Journal for the Study of Judaism*. Leiden: E.J. Brill, 1997.
Wilsbacher, Greg. 'Lumiansky's Paradox: Ethics, Aesthetics and Chaucer's *Prioress's Tale*.' *College Literature* 32.4 (2005): 1–28.
Winstead, Karen. *Virgin Martyrs: Legends of Sainthood in Late Medieval England*. Ithaca NY: Cornell University Press, 1997.
——. *Chaste Passions: Medieval English Virgin Martyr Legends*. Ithaca NY: Cornell University Press, 2000.
Wogan-Browne, Jocelyn, ed. *Language and Culture in Medieval Britain: The French of England c. 1100–c. 1500*. York: York Medieval Press, 2009.
——. *Saints' Lives and Women's Literary Culture c. 1150–1300: Virginity and its Authorisations*. Oxford: Oxford University Press, 2001.
——. 'Chaste Bodies: Frames and Experiences.' In *Framing Medieval Bodies*. Ed. Sarah Kay and Miri Rubin. Manchester: Manchester University Press, 1994.
Wogan-Browne, Jocelyn, and Glyn S. Burgess, trans. 'Introduction'. In *Virgin Lives and Holy Deaths: Two Exemplary Biographies for Anglo-Norman Women*. London: J.M. Dent, Everyman, 1996.
Youngs, Deborah and Simon Harris, 'Demonizing the Night in Medieval Europe:

A Temporal Monstrosity?' In *The Monstrous Middle Ages*. Ed. Bettina Bildhauer and Robert Mills. Toronto: University of Toronto Press, 2003: 134–54.

Unpublished Theses and Papers

Dubin, Nathaniel. '"Chevalerie" is Old French for "Horseplay".' Presented at the International Medieval Congress at Kalamazoo, 2002.

Massey, Jeff. '"There, Wolf ... There, Castle": Comedy, Romance, and the Self-Deconstructing Medieval Monster.' Presented at the International Medieval Congress, Kalamazoo, 2007.

Shumake, Josie. 'The Sources of Marlowe's *Edward II*.' University of South Carolina, 1984, PhD dissertation.

Websites and Other Media

Branigin, William. 'Across the U.S., Zarqawi's Death Hailed as Victory.' *The Washington Post*. 8 June 2006. Accessed via www.washingtonpost.com, 8 June 2006.

CNN.com. 'Video shows interrogation of teen at Guantanamo.' www.cnn.com/2008/POLITICS. Accessed 1 August 2008.

CNN.com. 'Ex-Pentagon official defends "harsh treatment".' www.cnn.com/2008/POLITICS. Accessed 1 August 2008.

CNN.com. 'Ashcroft defends waterboarding before House panel.' www.cnn.com/2008/POLITICS. Accessed 1 August 2008.

CNN.com. 'Previously secret torture memo released.' www.cnn.com/2008/POLITICS. Accessed 1 August 2008.

Colbert, Stephen. 'The Word.' *The Colbert Report*. Air date: Tuesday, 29 July 2008.

Gardiner, Nile, director of the Margaret Thatcher Center for Freedom at the Heritage Foundation. Interview. 'NATO Summit.' *Diane Rehm Show*. Hosted by Susan Page. 3 April 2008.

Index

Abbo of Fleury, 109
Abelard, Peter, x, 193, 195, 196, 198–9, 201, 205, 207–11, 214, 221–2, 226, 238, 241
Aberth, John, 160, 162, 181
Abu Ghraib, 14, 15
Æthelwold, king, 140–1, 146, 140
Akehurst, F.R.P, 200, 207, 212
Albigensian Crusade, see: crusades
Anderson, Benedict, 8
Anderson, Thomas P., 263, 265, 274, 279–80, 281
Andrew, John, 23
Anglo-Saxon England, 77–8, 123, 150, 168, 170, 271
  heritage, 4–5, 28, 72, 114, 121, 132–6, 140–55, 171, 244
  saints, 35, 65
anti-Semitism, 175 n. 172, 177, 181–5, 289
Aquinas, St Thomas, 5, 65
Aristotle, 20
Arthur and Gorlagon, 18, 26, 29, 134, 136, 145, 155–168, 175, 186, 190, 202, 214, 282, 295
Arthur, King, 29, 72, 96–106, 102, 155–168
  Arthurian Tradition, 25–27, 29, 71, 73, 74, 79, 96–106, 107, 111–14, 134, 157, 163, 293
Askew, Anne, 59, 259–262
Ambrose, Saint, 37
Augustine, Saint (of Hippo), 7 n. 34, 54, 229, 233
Augustine, Saint (of Kent), 35

Bakhtin, Mikhail, 191, 204, 221
Balbulus, Notker, 77, 84, 85, 94,
Baraz, Daniel, 17, 49, 248, 251, 253–4, 257
Barber, Malcolm, 7, 52, 138–9, 140
Barron, W.R.J., 92, 93, 147
Bartlett, Anne Clark, 56 n. 99

Bartlett, Robert, 3–5, 20 n. 89, 21, 103, 124, 136, 164
Bednarz, James P., 273
Bell, Kimberley, 143, 149, 150
Bellamy, John, 17, 137, 139, 147, 175 n. 173, 208 n. 59, 245, 246, 249, 261, 262, 279
Beowulf, 77 n. 29, 102, 114, 121, 264
Besamusca, Bart, 98, 99, 100
Bestul, Thomas H., 31, 32, 50 n. 73
Blamires, Alcuin, 52, 54
Bloch, R. Howard, vii, 81, 86, 89, 157, 195–7, 199, 217, 218–19, 221–2, 223
blood feud, 107, 117, 122, 123, 129, 207 n. 59, 264, 293
Boniface VIII, pope, *Liber Sextus*, 48
Borst, Arno, 5, 250, 287, 290, 291
Brennu-Njals saga, 28, 109, 114, 116, 123–9
Brewer, Derek, 26, 189
Brian Boruma (Boru), high king of Ireland, 124–8, 130, 294
Brown, Peter, 51
Brundage, James A., 207, 208
Burger, Glenn, 194, 196–7, 226, 232, 233, 237, 238
Busby, Keith, 156
Bush, George W., US president, 1, 14
Bynum, Caroline Walker, 31, 33, 38, 50, 51
Byock, Jesse, 112, 113, 114, 117, 118, 122, 163

Calabrese, Michael, 175
Cantor, Norman F., 13
Cartelli, Thomas, 272, 273, 274, 282
Cathars, 39, 48; see also: heresy
Caxton, William, 34
Celtic tradition, 5, 79 n. 42, 98, 156, 168 n. 147
chansons de gestes, 72, 82, 99, 143
Chanson de Roland, 4, 28, 75–96, 106, 150, 293

Charlemagne, 5, 75–96, 103, 107, 145, 186, 276–7, 293
Chaucer, Geoffrey, 29, 37, 90, 94, 96, 134, 150, 161, 169–90, 192–7, 224–41, 242, 247, 269, 272, 282, 285–6, 295
  Canterbury Tales, 35, 174, 182–3, 186, 190, 196, 225–6, 239, 242, 247, 295
  Knight's Tale, 29, 187, 192, 194, 197, 224–41, 282, 295
  Man of Law's Tale, 29, 134, 170–1, 175, 187–8, 225, 229
  Miller's Tale, 29, 187, 192, 194, 196–7, 224–41, 272
  Nun's Priest's Tale, 170, 172
  Prioress's Tale, 90, 94, 96, 150, 168, 169–89, 269, 285–6
  Second Nun's Tale, 134, 170, 174–5
  Wife of Bath's Tale, 161, 225, 228, 240
Chrétien de Troyes, 73, 79, 99 n. 132, 180 n. 190
Christine de Pizan, 53–4, 211, 241
Classen, Albrecht, 81
Clement IV, pope, 39
Clement V, pope, 39, 138, 140,
Clement VI, pope, 176 n. 176
Clermont, x, 15, 17, 81
Clontarf, Battle of, 124–6, 127–8, 130
Cobby, Anne Elizabeth, 203, 206
Cohen, Derek, 263 n. 79
Cohen, Jeffrey Jerome, 26, 74, 27
Coletti, Theresa, 65, 66
Collingwood, Sharon, 215, 216, 217, 219
Concordia discordantium canonum; see *Decretum*
Cook, Robert, 126, 128, 129, 130
Cook, Robert Francis, 91
Cooke, Thomas D., 192, 193, 194, 195
Cooper, Helen, 173, 174, 176, 177, 188, 237
Cormier, Raymond, 197, 199,
Costuma d'Agen, 207
Couch, Julie Nelson, 74, 143, 150
Crachiolo, Beth, 31, 38, 39, 44, 52, 55, 62, 63, 67
crusades, 72, 81
  Albigensian Crusade, 32, 67, 78, 80, 135, 150
  First Crusade, 15, 75, 81, 125, 287
  Third Crusade, 72
  Fourth Crusade, 72, 78, 80, 81, 110

cultural anxieties, 2–4, 8–9, 27–9, 32–3, 56, 67, 71, 78–9, 88, 97, 103, 108, 129, 131, 133–4, 149, 151, 153, 161, 174, 189, 192, 195, 202, 208, 215, 221, 227–8, 233, 242, 244, 249, 254–5, 257, 261–2, 264, 270, 273, 284–5

Dahood, Roger, 175, 179–80, 181, 186, 188, 189
Danish raiders, 28, 36, 151, 153
  descendants of, 29, 134, 136, 142–3, 145, 148, 152, 154, 190, 295
Dante, 7 n. 34, 8 n. 38, 26, 34 n. 7
Davenport, W.A., 226, 227
David of Augsburg, 48
Day, Mildred Leake, 155, 162, 166, 167–8
Dean, Trevor, 7, 8, 19, 23, 24
Decretum, 21, 212
Delany, Sheila, 69, 175, 176, 177, 183
DeMarco, Patricia, 224, 227, 229, 233
Dinshaw, Carolyn, 15
Diocletian, 20
Driscoll, Matthew James, 97, 111, 112, 113
Dunbabin, Jean, 21, 22, 47
DuVal, John, 193, 198, 205, 225

Easton, Martha, 40, 61
Eco, Umberto, *The Name of the Rose*, 1, 31, 70, 108, 132, 191, 243
Edmund, king and saint, 36, 109
Edmund Ironside, 243–4
Edward I, king of England, 135, 154, 177 n. 183
Edward II, king of England, 135, 138–40, 156, 190, 222 n. 110, 272–84, 288
Edward III, king of England, 102, 135, 136, 159, 181, 238–9
Edward IV, king of England, 39, 139
Edward, the black prince, 183
Eichmann, Raymond, 193, 198, 205, 225
Einhard, 77, 84, 94
Elder Edda, 121–2
Elizabeth I, queen of England, 245–9, 251, 255–6, 260–2, 265
Eymeric, Nicolaus, 49
Enders, Jody, 10–11, 17, 25, 73, 200, 201, 202, 204, 220, 241, 253, 296
Enlightenment, the, 8, 10
Etablissements de Saint Louis, 212–13, 223
ethnicity, 3, 4, 9, 79, 80, 152–3, 159, 164
Evesham, Battle of, 135, 223 n. 110

INDEX

fabliaux, 4, 18, 29, 73, 74, 185, 190, 191–242
  De Connebert, 29, 192, 198, 202, 211, 212–15, 218, 221–3, 226–7, 238, 242, 275, 295
  La Dame escoillee, 29, 192, 198, 200, 202, 211, 215–24, 225, 235, 242, 295
  Du Prestre crucefié, 29, 192, 198, 202, 205–12, 218, 221, 223, 242, 295
  Trubert, 216–17 n. 94
Falk, Oren, 1, 17
Farrell, Thomas J., 194, 201, 204, 205, 227, 233, 235, 237, 238, 282
Fasciculus Morum, 233
Ferroul, Yves, 209
Finnegan, Patrick, brigadier general, 2
Fjalldal, Magnús, 110, 114, 132
Fleck, Andrew, 284, 285, 286, 287, 288, 289, 290
Froissart, Jean, 222–3 n. 110, 228, 239, 272, 285 n. 139
Foucault, Michel, 10, 11, 18, 19, 52, 95, 247, 287, 289
Fouracre, Paul, 19
Fourth Lateran Council, 53
Foxe, John, 30, 244, 247, 253, 254–63, 264, 265, 280, 283, 291, 295
  Actes and Monuments, 244, 247, 248, 253, 254–63, 264, 283, 295
Frank, Roberta, 110
Frankis, John, 116, 125, 130, 170, 171
Freedman, Paul, 11, 29
Freeman, Thomas S., 255, 256, 257

Ganelon, trial of, 71, 75–96, 122, 145, 164, 173 n. 161, 175, 179, 180, 186, 293
Gesta Romanorum, 16 n. 72
Gibson, Kelly, 15, 18, 87, 125–6, 197, 225, 228, 229, 233
Gillingham, John, 5, 8, 79, 80, 133, 141, 159, 190
Gilte Legende, x, 27, 31–69, 127
Givens, James, 50
Golden Legend, 34, 35, 37, 58
Gore, Al, US vice president, 14
Görlach, Manfred, 35
Gratian, 21
The Great Schism (1378–1417), 9, 169, 174–5

Green, Richard Firth, 9, 230, 231
Gregory IX, pope, 70
Gregory of Tours, 93
Gui, Bernard, 1, 31, 40, 47, 48, 49, 50
  Manual for Inquisitors, 47, 49, 50,
Guantanamo Bay, 2, 14 n. 64, 15
Guibert of Nogent, *Gesta dei per Francos*, 8, 75, 76

hagiography; see: saints' lives
Haidu, Peter, 85, 92, 94, 95
Hákon Hákonarson, king of Norway, 111, 112
Hamer, Richard, 34, 37, 41, 46, 57
Hanson, Elizabeth, 245, 246, 247, 251, 255, 256
Hastings, battle of, 86
Havelok the Dane, 4, 18, 28–9, 36, 63, 74, 90, 93, 121, 134, 136, 137, 140–55, 156, 164–6, 170, 177, 190, 244, 247, 264–5, 267, 269, 270, 271, 273, 274, 276, 295
Heng, Geraldine, 5, 8, 9, 10, 72, 136, 154, 160, 161, 187, 190, 268, 287
Henry II, king of England, 79, 102, 136 n. 17, 157–8, 159
Henry III, king of England, 135, 180–1
Henry IV, king of England, 59
Henry, VI, king of England, 39, 59
Henry VIII, king of England, 245–6, 253, 260–1, 285, 295
heresy, 9, 11, 13, 21, 23–4, 30, 31–69, 70, 138 n. 31, 212, 259–262
  Albigensian heresy, 40, 72, 250
Hill, Thomas D., 124, 125, 127, 129
Holinshed, Raphael, *Chronicles*, 279, 280, 281
Hoofnagle, Wendy, 76, 77, 78, 87, 88
Hrafnkels saga freysgoða, 28, 72, 109, 114–15, 116, 117–23, 129, 271, 273, 293
Hugh of Lincoln, murder of, 175 n. 173, 179 n. 189, 180–2, 187
Hughes Gérard, bishop of Cahors, 16
Huizinga, Johan, 12, 16
Hundred Years War, 92, 102, 136, 160, 167, 169, 185, 224, 228, 238, 239
Hyams, Paul R., 77, 83, 84, 85, 86, 89, 91, 135

Innocent III, pope, 21, 40, 72, 81

Innocent IV, pope, 22
Inquisition, 5, 11, 13, 31–69, 70, 99 n. 131, 139, 179, 251
  Spanish Inquisition, 32, 249, 255, 286
intertexuality, 25–7, 106
Irvine, Martin, 195, 196, 198, 199, 201, 205, 208, 209–10, 211, 214

Jacobus de Voragine, 34, 37, 58, 173
  Legenda aurea, 27, 33–4, 39, 40, 173, 253
Jankofsky, Klaus, 35, 36, 37, 257
Jean de Meun, 208, 211
  Romance of the Rose, 208
Jerome, Saint, 37, 65
Jesch, Judith, 110
Jews, persecution of, 90 n. 86, 94, 169–89, 269, 286–7
John, king of England, 72, 85, 94, 135–6, 275
John of Joinville, 72
John XXII, pope, 16
Johnson, David F., 96, 97, 98, 104, 106
Jost, Jean, 12, 75, 196
Judgment of Cambyses, 16 n. 72
Judicial ordeals, 6 n. 27, 20–1, 43, 62

Kaeuper, Richard, 75, 135
Kalinke, Marianne E., 111, 112
Kelly, Henry Ansgar, 13, 23, 24
Kelly, Kathleen Coyne, 44, 63, 64
Kill Bill, 18
King Horn, 36, 141, 143 n. 58
Kittredge, George Lyman, 155, 182, 188
Kjær, Jonna, 79, 111
Knapp, Peggy, 178, 183
Knott, John R., 254, 255, 258

Lacy, Norris J., 26, 98, 193, 194, 199, 200, 203, 204, 215, 216, 220
Langbein, John H., 14, 15, 17, 22, 137, 246, 292, 294
Langland, William, 35
  Piers Plowman, 35
Lea, Henry Charles, 19, 20, 32, 538
Lehmann, Winifred P., 122, 129
Lewis, Katherine J., 19, 61
Loki, 26
Lydgate, John, 60, 124 n. 72, 125 n. 76, 251

Maddern, Philippa C., 23
Maddox, Donald, 26
Magna Carta, 95, 135
Marie de France, *Bisclavret*, 155, 157–9, 171
Marlowe, Christopher, 30, 238, 244, 272–84, 286, 291, 296
  Edward II, 244, 253, 272–84, 286, 296
martyrdom, 11, 20, 30, 31–69, 101, 109, 127, 173, 213, 244–5, 248, 251, 252–63, 265, 280, 283, 286, 291, 294, 295–6
  virgin martyrs, 19 n. 86, 31–69, 173–4
Massey, Jeff, 155, 160, 161, 168
McKinnell, John, 122–3
Merback, Mitchell B., 6, 17, 19, 104, 252
Meyerson, Mark D., 1, 17, 31
Michel de Montaigne, 250, 290
Mickel, Emanuel J., 76, 77, 80, 82–5, 87 n. 74, 89–95, 107, 135, 138, 147, 180 n. 190, 207, 296
Mills, Robert, 16, 17, 55, 56, 63, 67–9, 147
Miller, William Ian, 115, 118
Mitchell, Sarah, 134, 135, 136, 159
Monta, Susannah Brietz, 245, 254–5, 256
Mooney, Catherine, 56 n. 99, 61
Muscatine, Charles, 213, 214, 215, 217, 222, 239, 241
Muslims, 71, 81–2, 160, 176, 183, 199 n. 31, 263–71, 285 n. 139, 287–8
Musson, Anthony, 137, 146, 150, 151

Nashe, Thomas, 30, 244, 253, 284–90, 291, 296
  The Unfortunate Traveller, 253, 284–90
national identity, 2–11, 15, 17, 32, 51–2, 67, 71–2, 73–4, 88, 90, 92, 95, 103, 107, 116, 121, 123, 128–9, 131, 134–7, 142, 146, 149, 152, 156, 160, 170, 177 n. 183, 186, 244–9, 251, 253–5, 262, 265, 281 n. 126, 284, 290, 292
nationalism, 3, 5, 8–9, 24, 25–8, 35–6, 77–8, 133, 136, 140–5, 149, 161, 169, 171, 190, 293
Natural Born Killers, 18
Nirenberg, David, 183, 184
Norman Conquest (Invasion), 37, 80, 103, 110, 142, 149, 151, 154, 159

INDEX

Notker Balbulus (the Stammerer), 84–5, 94

Obama, Barack, US president, 1, 2, 14
O'Brien, Timothy D., 240
Origen, 211, 259
Owens, Margaret E., 202, 247, 266 n. 90, 274, 275, 276

Palmer, Daryl W., 248, 254, 258, 259, 262–4, 268, 269
Pálsson, Herman, 115, 117, 118, 119, 123–4
Paris, Matthew, 8, 132–3, 135, 190
Passau Anonymous, 44, 48
Passion narratives, 31 n. 3, 46 n. 50, 50 n. 73, 60, 184, 247
Patterson, Lee, 11, 174, 189, 237, 240, 241
Pearsall, Derek, 15, 16
Pencak, William, 116, 118, 119
Peters, Edward, 6, 7, 10, 12, 13, 17, 21–5, 33, 44, 45, 48, 52, 71, 74, 100, 102, 115, 158, 201, 203, 234
Philip IV, king of France, 7, 72, 138
Pickens, Rupert T., 5, 78, 79, 134
Prometheus, 26
Pulp Fiction, 15
punishment:
  beheading, 13, 19, 25, 27, 56 n. 101, 74, 92, 127, 160, 272, 274
  blood-eagling, 109, 110 n. 8
  burning, 41, 44, 50, 140, 148, 158 n. 114
  castration, 29, 56 n. 101, 192, 193–6, 197–224, 234, 236, 238, 239, 242, 295
  crucifixion, 11, 50, 58, 181
  defenestration, 73
  dismemberment, 32 n. 5, 45, 46 n. 50, 51 n. 76, 62 n. 117, 67, 180 n. 190, 195, 200, 202, 211, 217, 219, 223, 264, 266, 269, 274, 288
  dragging, by horses, 85, 93, 94, 147, 150, 175, 180
  equine quartering, 16, 25, 74, 78, 91, 93, 121, 164, 175 n. 173, 179, 180, 186
  evisceration, 15 n. 68, 116, 124, 125, 127–9, 223, 294
  execution, 6, 16, 31, 40, 44–6, 54, 63, 71, 76, 78, 81, 85, 87–9, 90–6, 101, 105, 110, 124–6, 127–30, 144–9, 150–4, 158, 164, 169, 175, 177, 180–2, 186, 247, 251–4, 256, 258–69, 270, 275, 277, 278, 283–9, 293
  flaying, 11, 12 n. 53, 16, 25, 56, 62–3, 74, 92, 121, 140, 144–50, 152, 160, 164, 175, 223, 288
  hamstringing, 108, 116, 120, 123, 129, 293
  hanging, 16, 19, 68, 84–5, 87, 89, 92, 149–50, 180 n. 190, 189, 271
  hanging on the gibbet, 10, 11, 257
  mutilation, 6 n. 27, 16, 32, 43, 51 n. 76, 55, 59, 77, 93, 110, 114–21, 123, 129, 137, 140, 198, 207 n. 59, 208, 213, 216–19, 222, 245, 263–6, 279, 288, 293
  of traitors, 12 n. 53, 16, 63, 84, 86, 89, 92–4, 124, 144, 146–7, 149, 150–1, 154, 164–5, 173 n. 161, 175 n. 173, 180 n. 190, 181, 207 n. 59, 212, 222–3, 245–7, 249, 256–7, 261, 269, 274, 275–7, 292

race, 3, 5, 15, 153; see also: ethnicity
rebellion, 39, 59, 60, 66, 67, 69, 93, 135, 138, 206, 235, 239, 249 n. 29, 259, 265, 277
Regio of Prum, 3
Reformation, the, 10, 30, 57, 59, 246–8, 252–63, 265, 285, 295
Richard I, king of England, 72, 80, 85, 136 n. 17, 160,
Richard II, king of England, 156, 161, 169, 238–9
Richard III, king of England, 246
Richard Coer de Lyon (RCL), 5, 160
Riches, Samantha, 62
Riddy, Felicity, 100, 102, 103
Robert of Gloucester, 134–6, 142, 154, 159
Robert the Monk, *Historia Hierosolymitana*, 15, 125
Robinson, Fred, 13
Roman Empire, 19, 20, 76
Roman van Walewein, 26, 28, 71, 96–107, 293–4
Rouse, Robert Allen, 134, 136, 141, 143, 145–9, 152, 164, 166, 168
Rubin, Miri, 20, 176

Rumsfeld, Donald, 13
Russell, Jeffrey Burton, 23, 40, 47–9, 51, 53
Russell, Vida, 34, 41, 46, 57

saints and saints' lives, 11–12, 27–8, 31–69, 101, 109, 124–5, 127, 130, 136, 142, 179, 222, 252, 255–8, 260–2, 289, 294; see also: martyrdom
  Agatha, 31–2, 42, 45, 56–60, 64, 222, 262
  Agnes, 43, 58, 64
  Alban, 36, 60, 124, 125, 127
  Amphibalus, 116, 125, 127, 128
  Bartholomew, 53, 62–3, 147
  Cecilia, 173; see also Chaucer, *Second Nun's Tale*
  Christina, 31–2, 41–5, 47, 53–4, 57, 59, 60, 63–4, 66–7, 222, 260, 262, 289
  Dorothy, 54 n. 89, 64 n. 123
  Elizabeth of Hungary, 37, 64 n. 123, 66
  George, 62
  Lawrence (Laurence), 32, 44, 45–53, 61–3
  Lucy, 43, 64
  Margaret, 55
  Oswald, 136 n. 17
  Theodora, 64 n. 123
  virgin martyrs, 19 n. 86, 31–69, 173–4, 262; see: martyrdom
  Wulfstan, 36, 136 n. 17
Saint Bartholomew's Day Massacre, 250
Salih, Sarah, 56, 61, 62
Sanock, Catherine, 9, 32, 37–9, 52, 61
Scarry, Elaine, 18, 52, 68–9, 201, 247
Schenck, Mary Jane, 77, 82, 83, 86, 87, 92, 93, 94, 214
Scragg, Leah, 243, 244, 245
Shakespeare, William, 30, 244, 253, 263–71, 273, 278, 296
  Henry VI, Part Three, 273
  King John, 275
  Richard II, 249, 278
  Titus Andronicus, 244, 247, 263–71, 274, 288, 296
Silverman, Lisa, 8, 249, 250, 251
Simon de Montfort, 80, 135; see also: Albigensian Crusade

Simon de Montfort, earl of Leicester, 135, 223
Sirluck, Katherine A., 277, 283
Sisiphus, 26
Smail, Daniel Lord, 15, 18, 87, 125, 197, 200, 225, 228, 229, 233
Smith, Anthony D., 9
Smith, Caroline, 70, 71, 72, 73, 76, 80
Smith, Molly Eso, 247, 263–4, 265–6, 270, 271
Smyth, Alfred P., 109, 110, 130
South English Legendary, 27, 31–69, 142, 143
Spector, Stephen, 178, 182, 183, 185, 189
Speed, Diane, 77, 78, 133, 137, 141, 143, 154
Spiegel, Gabrielle M., 11, 29
Staines, David, 141, 148, 154
Suzzara, Guido, *Tractatus de tormentis*, 49

Tantalus, 26
Tartarus, 26
Taylor, Andrew, 77, 78, 79, 80
Templars, order of, 7, 52 n. 84, 138–40, 190, 161, 166, 245
Thiery, Daniel, 1, 17, 31, 169
Thijssen, J.M.M.H, 7, 21
Tibbetts Schulenburg, Jane, 38
torture, 1–30
  Anglo-Saxon law, 6 n. 27, 9, 10, 16 n. 72, 35, 135, 142–55, 158–9, 171, 265
  Danelaw, 153
  Denmark, 93, 99, 143, 149, 152–3
  England, 80, 132–90, 243–91
    law, 3, 6, 8–10, 28–9, 32–5, 39, 67, 74, 80, 87–8, 94, 102, 114, 133–59, 161–4, 166, 170–1, 176–9, 181, 187, 224–5, 239, 244–9, 264, 271, 273, 291, 294
  Flanders, 4, 6, 8, 9, 26–8, 71, 96–107, 293–4
    law, 71, 74, 99 n. 131, 100, 101, 106, 293
  Florence, 24
  France, 4–8, 21, 23, 27, 34 n. 9, 70–96, 97, 102–3, 107, 108, 110–14, 124, 132, 136, 138–41, 147,

150, 159–61, 169, 170, 175 n. 173, 183, 186–7, 190, 191–242, 250, 265, 271, 284–6, 290, 292–3
   law, 4–9, 39, 75–96, 137, 138, 139–40, 159, 187, 191–242, 249, 286
gender, 32, 38, 39, 43, 53–69, 196, 206, 217, 260
Germanic law, 78 n. 36, 82, 114, 125
Germany, 3, 5, 6, 28, 72, 99, 103, 115, 259
   law, 3, 6, 8, 28, 71, 73, 86, 292
Iceland, 4, 8–9, 26, 28, 72, 86, 88 n. 80, 108–31, 142, 152, 162, 190, 247, 264, 271, 293–4
   law, 86, 109, 114–20, 123, 125–9, 130–1, 162, 271, 293–4
Islamic law, 177
Ireland, 8, 123–30
Italy, 5, 6, 21, 28, 41, 71 n. 6, 72, 103, 124, 184, 284, 286–7
Judaic law, 177
law,
   customary, 3, 6, 24, 87–8, 91, 93, 199 n. 31, 200, 207 n. 59, 210, 212–13, 222–5; see also *Costuma d'Agen*
   Romano-canonical (Roman or canon), 3, 6, 10, 19, 20–4, 28, 42, 47, 50, 52, 57, 71, 76, 81, 83, 102, 124, 133, 138, 158, 196, 209, 233, 252, 265–7, 269, 289, 292
methods; see also: punishment,
   boiling, 62 n. 117, 223
   branding, 68, 225–6, 228, 232–4, 235, 279
   eye gouging, 12 n. 53, 266 n. 90
   gridiron, 1, 45, 46, 61, 257
   iron hooks, 23, 42, 58, 68
   Iron maiden, 1
   mastectomies, 11, 41, 55, 56 n. 101, 57, 59
   rack, 1, 7, 11, 12 n. 53, 22, 58, 109, 139, 165, 246, 250–1 n. 39, 261
   rods, 23
   strappado, 1, 7, 12 n. 53, 23, 139, 166
   switches, 23
   thumbscrew, 22

   wheel, 1, 6, 10, 11, 12 n. 53, 19, 42, 104–5, 285–6, 288–9
   whips, 11, 23, 58, 286, 288
Norway, 4, 28, 73, 110–16, 142, 293
Spain, 6, 8, 45 n. 45, 71, 79, 83, 207, 249, 255, 251, 265, 271, 286–7
Tuchman, Barbara W., 11, 12, 16
Tulinius, Torfi H., 108, 111, 112
Turville-Petre, Thorlac, 8, 133, 137, 141–4, 149–54, 155
Twomey, Michael, 25, 26
Thurston, Robert, 22, 23
Tracy, Larissa, 20, 31, 43, 60, 64, 125, 160
Tyler, Wat, rebellion of, 239

Urban II, pope, 15, 81, 125

Valante, Mary A., 125, 127, 128
Varangian Guard, 80, 110
vengeance, 13, 18, 29, 72, 75, 79, 83, 8–9, 91–6, 105, 115, 119–23, 130, 150, 154, 161–5, 168, 172, 188, 194, 197, 201, 204–5, 210, 214–15, 223–4, 226–9, 232–3, 236–8, 240, 242, 264, 266, 268–9, 273–4, 276–8, 287–8, 290, 293
Vikings, 108–11, 114, 116, 124–6, 127–8, 130, 151–4
Villehardouin, Geoffrey, 72, 80
Vǫlundarkviða, 116–17, 121–3, 129, 264

Waldensians, 39, 44, 47, 48; see also: heresy
Walls, Kathryn, 235–6
Warner, Marina, 61
Washington, George, US president, 2
Weisl, Angela Jane, 61, 234
Weiss, Judith, 148, 149
wergeld, 87
West, Richard, 172, 176, 240, 241
Wheeler, Bonnie, 196, 209, 210, 214
White, Stephen D., 83–4, 85, 88, 89, 90, 91
William I, king of England, 36, 78, 87, 103, 110
William Rufus, king of England, 207 n. 59
William of Palerne, 36, 158 n. 114
Williams, Deanne, 185, 186, 187

Wilsbacher, Greg, 175, 176, 177, 183, 187
Winstead, Karen, 33, 35, 39, 46, 55, 56, 65, 173–4, 317

Wogan-Browne, Jocelyn, 9, 31, 45, 56, 133

Yggdrasil, world tree, 26